AutoCAD 2027 Tutorial

Second Level 3D Modeling

AF693968

Randy H. Shih

Oregon Institute of Technology

SDC PUBLICATIONS

SDC Publications
P.O. Box 1334
Mission, KS 66222
913-262-2664
www.SDCpublications.com
Publisher: Stephen Schroff

Examination Copies
Books received as examination copies are for review purposes only and may not be made available for student use. Resale of examination copies is prohibited.

Electronic Files
Any electronic files associated with this book are licensed to the original user only. These files may not be transferred to any other party.

Trademarks
The following are registered trademarks of Autodesk, Inc.: 3D Studio, ADI, Advanced Modeling Extension, AME, AutoCAD, AutoCAD Mechanical Desktop, AutoCAD Development System, AutoCAD LT, Autodesk, Autodesk Animator, AutoLISP, AutoShade, AutoVision, and Heidi.
The following are trademarks of Autodesk, Inc.: ACAD, Autodesk Device Interface, AutoCAD DesignCenter, AutoTrack, Heads-up Design, ObjectARX and Visual LISP.
Microsoft and Windows are either registered trademarks or trademarks of Microsoft Corporation.
All other trademarks are trademarks of their respective holders.

The author and publisher of this book have used their best efforts in preparing this book. These efforts include the development, research and testing of the material presented. The author and publisher shall not be liable in any event for incidental or consequential damages with, or arising out of, the furnishing, performance, or use of the material.

ISBN-13: 978-1-63057-827-5
ISBN-10: 1-63057-827-4

Printed and bound in the United States of America.

Preface

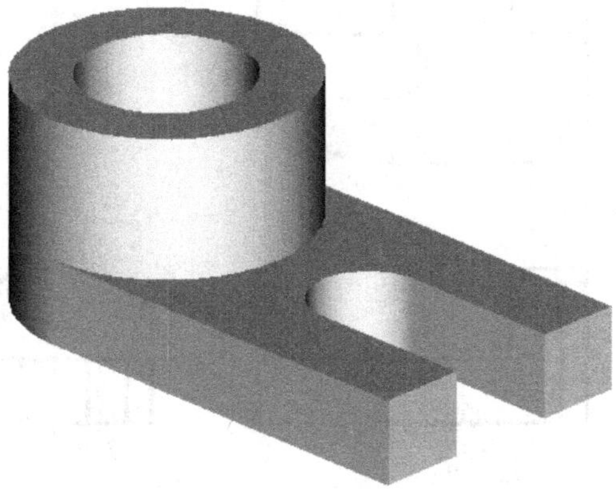

The primary goal of ***AutoCAD® 2027 Tutorial Second Level 3D Modeling*** is to introduce the aspects of **Computer Based Three-Dimensional Modeling**. This text is intended to be used as a training guide for students and professionals. This text covers *AutoCAD 2027* and the chapters proceed in a pedagogical fashion to guide you from constructing 3D wireframe models, 3D surface models and 3D solid models to making multiview drawings. This text takes a hands-on, exercise-intensive approach to all the important 3D modeling techniques and concepts. This textbook contains a series of twelve tutorial style chapters designed to introduce CAD users to 3D modeling with **AutoCAD 2027**. This text is also helpful to AutoCAD users upgrading from a previous release of the software. The new improvements and enhancements of the software are incorporated into the tutorials. The 3D modeling techniques and concepts discussed in this text are also designed to serve as the foundation to the more advanced feature-based CAD/CAE packages such as AutoCAD® Architecture Desktop and Autodesk Inventor®. The basic premise of this book is that the more 3D designs you create using AutoCAD 2027, the better you learn the software. With this in mind, each tutorial introduces a new set of commands and concepts, building on previous chapters. This book does not attempt to cover all of AutoCAD 2027's features, only to provide an introduction to the software. It is intended to help you establish a good basis for exploring and growing in the exciting field of Computer Aided Engineering.

Acknowledgments

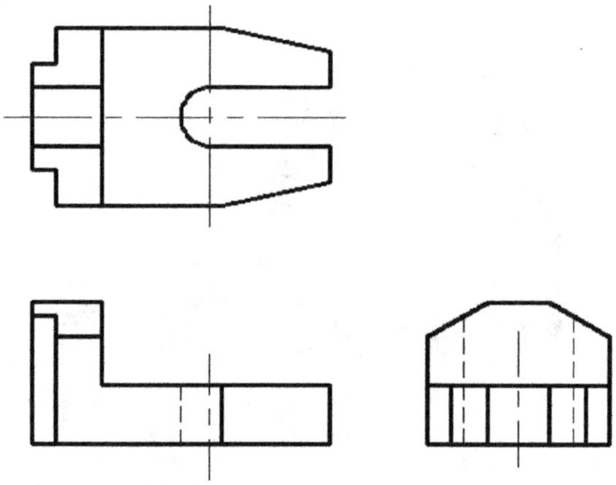

This book would not have been possible without a great deal of support. First, special thanks to two great teachers, Professor George R. Schade of University of Nebraska-Lincoln and Mr. Denwu Lee from Taiwan, who showed me the fundamentals, the intrigue, and the sheer fun of Computer Aided Design and Computer Aided Engineering.

The effort and support of the editorial and production staff of SDC Publications is gratefully acknowledged. I would especially like to thank Stephen Schroff for his support.

I am grateful that the Department of Mechanical and Manufacturing Engineering Technology at Oregon Institute of Technology has provided me with an excellent environment in which to pursue my passion in teaching and research. I would especially like to thank Emeritus Professor Charles Hermach for helpful comments and encouragement.

Finally, truly unbounded thanks are due to my wife Hsiu-Ling and our daughter Casandra for their understanding and encouragement throughout this project.

Randy H. Shih
Klamath Falls, Oregon
Spring, 2026

Table of Contents

Preface
Acknowledgments

Introduction
Getting Started

Introduction Intro-2
Development of Computer Geometric Modeling Intro-2
Why Use AutoCAD 2027? Intro-5
Getting Started with AutoCAD 2027 Intro-7
AutoCAD 2027 Screen Layout Intro-8
Application Menu Intro-9
Quick Access Toolbar Intro-9
AutoCAD Menu Bar Intro-9
Layout Tabs Intro-9
Drawing Area Intro-10
Graphics Cursor or Crosshairs Intro-10
Command Prompt Area Intro-10
Cursor Coordinates Intro-10
Status Toolbar Intro-10
Ribbon Tabs and Panels Intro-11
Draw and Modify Toolbar Panels Intro-11
Layers Control Toolbar Panel Intro-11
Viewport/View/Display Controls Intro-11
Mouse Buttons Intro-12
[Esc] - Canceling commands Intro-12
Online Help Intro-13
Leaving AutoCAD 2027 Intro-14
Creating a CAD File Folder Intro-14

Chapter 1
User Coordinate Systems and the Z-Axis

Introduction 1-2
The Floor Plan Design 1-2
Starting Up AutoCAD 2027 1-3
3D Basic Modeling WorkSpace 1-4
Drawing Units Setup 1-5
Drawing Area Setup 1-6
Grid and Snap Intervals Setup 1-7
Create Polylines 1-9
Create an Offset Polyline 1-10
Create Interior Walls 1-11

Complete the Doorway Using the Trim Command 1-14
User Coordinate System – It is an XY CRT, but an XYZ World 1-16
Viewing the 2D Design in 3D Space 1-17
Add the 3rd Dimension to the Floor Plan Design 1-18
View the Design Using the Hide Option 1-20
Add New Layers 1-21
Move Entities to a Different Layer 1-23
Reposition the UCS 1-23
Create the Roof 1-25
Rotating the UCS 1-27
Sketching on the Rotated UCS 1-28
View the Design Using the Hidden Option 1-29
Review Questions 1-30
Exercises 1-31

Chapter 2
3D Wireframe Modeling

Introduction 2-2
The Locator Design 2-3
Starting Up AutoCAD 2027 2-4
Activate the Startup Option 2-4
Create the Rectangular Base of the Design 2-6
Create a 3D Box 2-7
Object Snap Toolbar 2-10
Use the Snap Options to Locate the Top Corners 2-10
Use the Copy Option to Create Additional Edges 2-12
Use the Trim Command 2-14
Use the View Toolbar 2-16
Dynamic Rotation – Free Orbit 2-16
Use the Offset Command to Create Parallel Edges 2-17
Create a Circle above the UCS Sketch Plane 2-19
Complete the Wireframe Model 2-20
Review Questions 2-22
Exercises 2-23

Chapter 3
UCS, Viewports and Wireframe Modeling

Introduction 3-2
The V-Block Design 3-2
Starting Up AutoCAD 2027 3-3
3D Modeling Workspace 3-3
Layers Setup 3-4
Create the Rectangular Base of the Design 3-5
Create a Wireframe Box 3-6

Using the View and UCS Toolbars 3-7
Create Construction Lines in the Front View 3-8
Copy Objects in the Negative Z Direction 3-10
Create an Inclined Line at the Base of the Model 3-11
Create Object Lines 3-12
Multiple Viewports 3-14
Use the Mirror Command 3-15
Turn Off the Construction Lines 3-17
Create a New UCS 3-18
Create a New Named View 3-20
Create the V-Cut Feature on the Inclined Plane 3-22
Extend the Cut and GRIP Editing 3-23
Review Questions 3-25
Exercises 3-26

Chapter 4
Classical Faceted Surface Modeling

Introduction 4-2
Starting Up AutoCAD 2027 4-4
The UCS Toolbar and the Meshes Commands 4-5
Create a Mesh Surface Using the 2D Solid Command 4-5
Using the Visual Styles Toolbar 4-8
Create a Mesh Surface Using the 3D Face Command 4-10
The ViewCube 4-12
Create a Faceted Surface of Irregular Shape 4-14
Use the Invisible Edge Option 4-16
Repositioning with the Grip Editing Tools 4-17
The Locator Wireframe Model 4-18
Moving Objects to a Different Layer 4-18
Advanced Meshed Surface Modeling Commands 4-20
Use the Faceted Tabulated Surface Option 4-23
Use the Faceted Ruled Surface Option 4-24
Review Questions 4-27
Exercises 4-28

Chapter 5
Procedural and NURBS Surface Modeling

Introduction 5-2
Starting Up AutoCAD 2027 5-3
Turn on the UCS II Toolbar 5-3
Layers Setup 5-4
Create a Thin Surface Using the Extrude Command 5-5
Create another Profile 5-8
Complete the Profile Using Object Snap 5-9

Create another Thin Surface Using the Extrude Command 5-11
Create a Flat Planar Surface 5-13
Use the Trim option to adjust the Top Surface 5-14
Create another Planar Surface 5-16
Use the Trim option to adjust the New Surface 5-17
Combining two Overlapping Surfaces 5-19
Create a 3D Free Form NURBS Surface Model 5-21
AutoCAD Spline Curves 5-22
Start a New Drawing and Layers Setup 5-23
Create Two sets of Splines 5-24
Display the Control Vertices and Edit the Splines 5-28
Create a Network Surface 5-29
Convert the Network surface to a NURBS surface 5-31
Review Questions 5-32
Exercises 5-33

Chapter 6
Solid Modeling - Constructive Solid Geometry

Introduction 6-2
The Guide-Block Design 6-2
Constructive Solid Geometry Concept 6-3
Binary Tree 6-4
The Guide-Block CSG Binary Tree 6-5
Starting Up AutoCAD 2027 6-6
Layers Setup 6-7
Create the First 3D Object 6-7
Create the Second Solid Feature 6-9
Boolean Operation - Union 6-10
Create the Second Cylinder Feature 6-11
Boolean Operation - Subtract 6-12
Create another Solid Feature 6-13
Visual Styles Options 6-14
Create the Final Feature 6-15
Rotating the Rectangular Block 6-16
Reposition the Rectangular Block 6-17
The SteeringWheels 6-18
Review Questions 6-20
Exercises 6-21

Chapter 7
Regions, Extrude and Solid Modeling

Introduction 7-2
The V-Block-Solid Design 7-2
Starting Up AutoCAD 2027 7-3

Layers Setup 7-4
Setting Up a 2D Sketch 7-5
Defining the Front Edges of the Design 7-7
Create a Region 7-10
Extruding the Created Region 7-11
Create a 2D Sketch at the Base of the Model 7-13
Create a Mirrored Copy of the 2D Sketch 7-14
Create the Cutter Solids 7-15
Boolean Operation - Subtract 7-16
Mass Properties of the Solid Model 7-17
Align the UCS to the Inclined Face 7-18
Create the V-Cut 7-19
Review Questions 7-22
Exercises 7-23

Chapter 8
Symmetrical Features in Designs

Introduction 8-2
A Revolved Design: Pulley 8-2
Modeling Strategy - A Revolved Design 8-3
Starting Up AutoCAD 2027 8-4
Layers Setup 8-5
Set Up a 2D Sketch for the Revolved Feature 8-6
Perform 2D Boolean Operations 8-8
Create the Revolved Feature 8-12
Mirrored Image of the Part 8-13
Combine Two Parts into One 8-14
Use the 3D Array Command 8-15
Position and Perform the Cut 8-18
Review Questions 8-20
Exercises 8-21

Chapter 9
Multiview Drawings from 3D Models

Introduction 9-2
The V-Block Design 9-2
Starting Up AutoCAD 2027 9-3
AutoCAD Paper Space 9-4
Delete the Displayed Viewport 9-5
Add Borders and Title Block in the Layout 9-6
Setting Up the Standard Views 9-7
Determine the Necessary 2D Views 9-9
Establish an Auxiliary View 9-10

Complete the 2D Drawing 9-14
Open the Pulley Solid Model 9-15
AutoCAD Paper Space setup 9-16
Delete the Displayed Viewport 9-17
Add Borders and Title Block by Copy & Paste 9-17
Setting Up the Standard Views 9-19
Determine the Necessary 2D Views 9-21
Rotate the Base View 9-22
Establish a Section View 9-23
Adjust the Scale of the Base View 9-26
Add an Isometric View 9-27
Complete the 2D Drawing 9-28
Review Questions 9-29
Exercises 9-30

Chapter 10
Advanced Modeling Tools & Techniques

Introduction 10-2
A Thin-Walled Design: Oil Sink 10-2
Modeling Strategy 10-3
Starting Up AutoCAD 2027 10-4
Layers Setup 10-5
The First Extruded Feature 10-6
Create an Offset Geometry from an Extracted Surface 10-8
Extrude with Draft Angle 10-10
Align the Parts 10-11
Create another Extracted Surface 10-12
Combining Parts – Boolean Union 10-15
Create 3D Rounds and Fillets 10-16
Create a Shell Feature 10-18
Create a Rectangular Array Cut Feature 10-19
Create another Rectangular Array Cut Feature 10-21
Making a Design Change 10-23
Grip Editing Approach 10-23
Dynamic UCS Approach 10-24
Review Questions 10-27
Exercises 10-28

Chapter 11
Conceptual Design Tools & Techniques

Introduction 11-2
A Bird House Design 11-3
Starting Up AutoCAD 2027 11-4
Layers Setup 11-5

The Base Plate 11-6
Create the Compartments for the 1st Floor 11-7
Using the Press/Pull Command 11-8
Using the Press/Pull Command as an Editing Tool 11-10
Create another Cut Feature 11-11
Adjust the Compartments 11-13
Add Additional Compartments 11-14
Create the Doors 11-15
Create the 2nd Floor 11-16
Reposition the 2nd Floor 11-18
Modeling the Roof Section with the Press/Pull Command 11-19
Use the Imprint Command 11-21
Review Questions 11-24
Exercises 11-25

Chapter 12
Introduction to Photorealistic Rendering

Introduction 12-2
Start Up AutoCAD 2027 and Retrieve the Pulley Design 12-3
Environment Setup 12-4
Use the Render Command 12-7
Available Lighting Simulation Modes in AutoCAD 12-8
Use the Materials Options 12-9
Activate the Sun & Sky Background Option 12-11
Add Additional Walls 12-14
Create a Point Light 12-17
Changing the Applied Materials 12-19
Create a Spotlight 12-20
Removing a Light 12-22
Create a Distant Light 12-23
Create New Materials 12-26
Save the Rendered Images 12-29
Conclusion 12-30
Review Questions 12-31
Exercises 12-32

Index

Notes:

Introduction
Getting Started

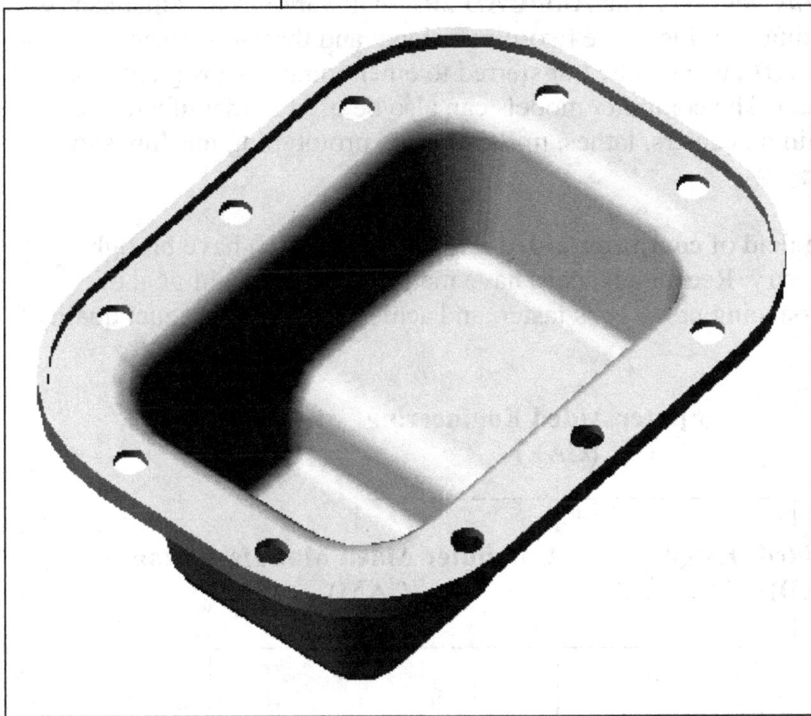

Learning Objectives

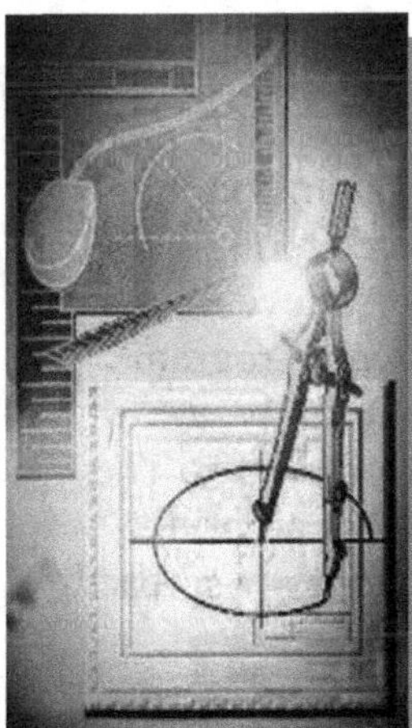

- **Development of Computer Aided Design**
- **Why use AutoCAD 2027?**
- **Getting started with AutoCAD 2027**
- **The AutoCAD Startup dialog box and Units setup**
- **AutoCAD 2027 screen layout**
- **Mouse buttons**

Introduction

Computer Aided Design (CAD) is the process of doing designs with the aid of computers. This includes the generation of computer models, analysis of design data, and the creation of the necessary drawings. **AutoCAD® 2027** is a computer-aided-design software developed by *Autodesk Inc.* The **AutoCAD 2027** software is a tool that can be used for design and drafting activities. The two-dimensional and three-dimensional models created in **AutoCAD 2027** can be transferred to other computer programs for further analysis and testing. The computer models can also be used in manufacturing equipment such as machining centers, lathes, mills, or rapid prototyping machines to manufacture the product.

The rapid changes in the field of **computer aided engineering** (CAE) have brought exciting advances in industry. Recent advances have made the long-sought goal of reducing design time, producing prototypes faster, and achieving higher product quality closer to a reality.

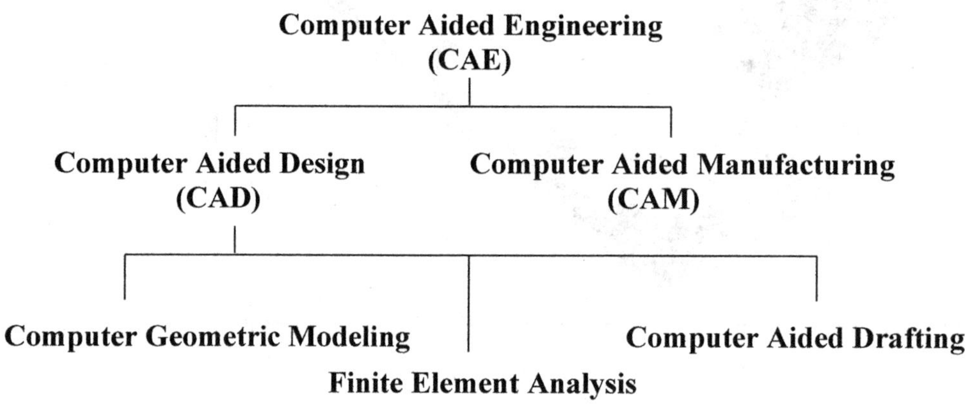

Development of Computer Geometric Modeling

Computer Aided Design is a relatively new technology and its rapid expansion in the last fifty years is truly amazing. Computer modeling technology advanced along with the development of computer hardware. The first-generation CAD programs, developed in the 1950s, were mostly non-interactive; CAD users were required to create program codes to generate the desired two-dimensional (2D) geometric shapes. Initially, the development of CAD technology occurred mostly in academic research facilities. The Massachusetts Institute of Technology, Carnegie-Mellon University, and Cambridge University were the lead pioneers at that time. The interest in CAD technology spread quickly and several major industry companies, such as General Motors, Lockheed, McDonnell, IBM, and Ford Motor Co., participated in the development of interactive CAD programs in the 1960s. Usage of CAD systems was primarily in the automotive industry, aerospace industry, and government agencies that developed their own programs for their specific needs. The 1960s also marked the beginning of the development of finite element analysis methods for computer stress analysis and computer aided manufacturing for generating machine toolpaths.

The 1970s are generally viewed as the years of the most significant progress in the development of computer hardware, namely the invention and development of **microprocessors**. With the improvement in computing power, new types of 3D CAD programs that were user-friendly and interactive became reality. CAD technology quickly expanded from very simple **computer aided drafting** to very complex **computer aided design**. The use of 2D and 3D wireframe modelers was accepted as the leading-edge technology that could increase productivity in industry. The developments of surface modeling and solid modeling technology were taking shape by the late 1970s, but the high cost of computer hardware and programming slowed the development of such technology. During this time period, the available CAD systems all required extremely expensive room-sized mainframe computers.

In the 1980s, improvements in computer hardware brought the power of mainframes to the desktop at less cost and with more accessibility to the general public. By the mid-1980s, CAD technology had become the main focus of a variety of manufacturing industries and was very competitive with traditional design/drafting methods. It was during this period of time that 3D solid modeling technology had major advancements, which boosted the usage of CAE technology in industry.

In the 1990s, CAD programs evolved into powerful design/manufacturing/management tools. CAD technology has come a long way, and during these years of development, modeling schemes progressed from two-dimensional (2D) wireframe to three-dimensional (3D) wireframe, to surface modeling, to solid modeling and, finally, to feature-based parametric solid modeling.

The first-generation CAD packages were simply 2D **Computer Aided Drafting** programs, basically the electronic equivalents of the drafting board. For typical models, the use of this type of program would require that several views of the objects be created individually as they would be on the drafting board. The 3D designs remained in the designer's mind, not in the computer database. The mental translation of 3D objects to 2D views is required throughout the use of the packages. Although such systems have some advantages over traditional board drafting, they are still tedious and labor intensive. The need for the development of 3D modelers came quite naturally, given the limitations of the 2D drafting packages.

The development of the 3D wireframe modeler was a major leap in the area of computer modeling. The computer database in the 3D wireframe modeler contains the locations of all the points in space coordinates and it is sufficient to create just one model rather than multiple models. This single 3D model can then be viewed from any direction as needed. The 3D wireframe modelers require the least computer power and achieve reasonably good representation of 3D models. But because surface definition is not part of a wireframe model, all wireframe images have the inherent problem of ambiguity.

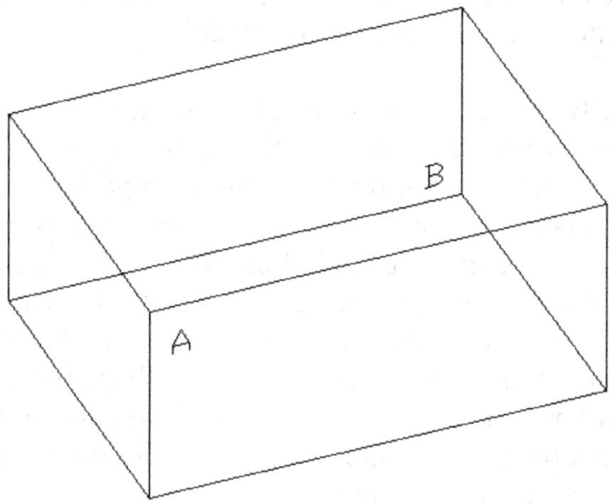

Wireframe Ambiguity: Which corner is in front, A or B?

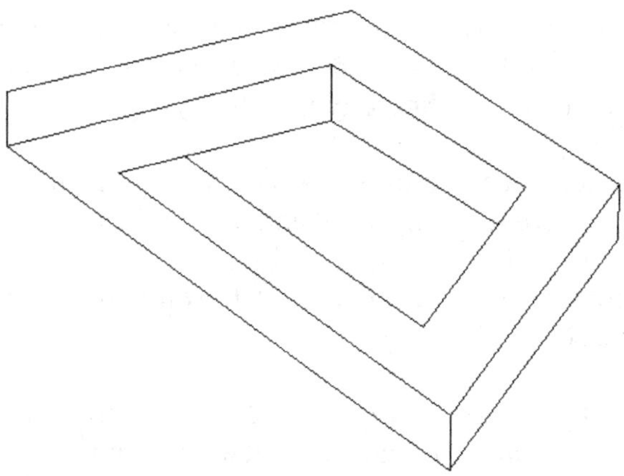

A non-realizable object: Wireframe models contain no surface definitions.

Surface modeling is the logical development in computer geometry modeling to follow the 3D wireframe modeling scheme by organizing and grouping edges that define polygonal surfaces. Surface modeling describes the part's surfaces but not its interiors. Designers are still required to interactively examine surface models to ensure that the various surfaces on a model are contiguous throughout. Many of the concepts used in 3D wireframe and surface modelers are incorporated in the solid modeling scheme, but it is solid modeling that offers the most advantages as a design tool.

In the solid modeling presentation scheme, the solid definitions include nodes, edges, and surfaces, and it is a complete and unambiguous mathematical representation of a precisely enclosed and filled volume. Unlike the surface modeling method, solid modelers start with a solid or use topology rules to guarantee that all of the surfaces are stitched together properly. Two predominant methods for representing solid models are

constructive solid geometry (CSG) representation and **boundary representation** (B-rep).

The CSG representation method can be defined as the combination of 3D solid primitives. What constitutes a "primitive" varies somewhat with the software but typically includes a rectangular prism, a cylinder, a cone, a wedge, and a sphere. Most solid modelers allow the user to define additional primitives, which can be very complex.

In the B-rep representation method, objects are represented in terms of their spatial boundaries. This method defines the points, edges, and surfaces of a volume, and/or issues commands that sweep or rotate a defined face into a third dimension to form a solid. The object is then made up of the unions of these surfaces that completely and precisely enclose a volume.

By the 1990s, a new paradigm called *concurrent engineering* had emerged. With concurrent engineering, designers, design engineers, analysts, manufacturing engineers, and management engineers all work closely right from the initial stages of the design. In this way, all aspects of the design can be evaluated, and any potential problems can be identified right from the start and throughout the design process. Using the principles of concurrent engineering, a new type of computer modeling technique appeared. The technique is known as the *feature-based parametric modeling technique*. The key advantage of the *feature-based parametric modeling technique* is its capability to produce very flexible designs. Changes can be made easily, and design alternatives can be evaluated with minimum effort. Various software packages offer different approaches to feature-based parametric modeling, yet the end result is a flexible design defined by its design variables and parametric features.

In this text, we will concentrate on creating designs using two-dimensional geometric construction techniques. The fundamental concepts and use of different **AutoCAD 2027** commands are presented using step-by-step tutorials. We will begin with creating simple geometric entities and then move toward creating detailed working drawings and assembly drawings. The techniques presented in this text will also serve as the foundation for entering the world of three-dimensional solid modeling using packages such as **AutoCAD Architectural Desktop** and **Autodesk Inventor**.

Why Use AutoCAD 2027?

AutoCAD was first introduced to the public in late 1982 and was one of the first CAD software products that were available for personal computers. Since 1984, **AutoCAD** has established a reputation for being the most widely used PC-based CAD software around the world. By 2020, it was estimated that there were over 6 million **AutoCAD** users in more than 150 countries worldwide. **AutoCAD 2027** is the forty-first release, with many added features and enhancements, of the original **AutoCAD** software produced by *Autodesk Inc.*

CAD provides us with a wide range of benefits; in most cases, the result of using CAD is increased accuracy and productivity. First of all, the computer offers much higher accuracy than the traditional methods of drafting and design. Traditionally, drafting and detailing are the most expensive cost elements in a project and the biggest bottleneck. With CAD systems, such as **AutoCAD 2027**, the tedious drafting and detailing tasks are simplified through the use of many of the CAD geometric construction tools, such as *grids*, *snap*, *trim*, and *auto-dimensioning*. Dimensions and notes are always legible in CAD drawings, and in most cases, CAD systems can produce higher quality prints compared to traditional hand drawings.

CAD also offers much-needed flexibility in design and drafting. A CAD model generated on a computer consists of numeric data that describe the geometry of the object. This allows the designers and clients to see something tangible and to interpret the ramifications of the design. In many cases, it is also possible to simulate operating conditions on the computer and observe the results. Any kind of geometric shape stored in the database can be easily duplicated. For large and complex designs and drawings, particularly those involving similar shapes and repetitive operations, CAD approaches are very efficient and effective. Because computer designs and models can be altered easily, a multitude of design options can be examined and presented to a client before any construction or manufacturing actually takes place. Making changes to a CAD model is generally much faster than making changes to a traditional hand drawing. Only the affected components of the design need to be modified, and the drawings can be plotted again. In addition, the greatest benefit is that, once the CAD model is created, it can be used over and over again. The CAD models can also be transferred into manufacturing equipment such as machining centers, lathes, mills, or rapid prototyping machines to manufacture the product directly.

CAD, however, does not replace every design activity. CAD may help, but it does not replace the designer's experience with geometry and graphical conventions and standards for the specific field. CAD is a powerful tool, but the use of this tool does not guarantee correct results; the designer is still responsible for using good design practice and applying good judgment. CAD will supplement these skills to ensure that the best design is obtained.

CAD designs and drawings are stored in binary form, usually as CAD files, to magnetic devices such as diskettes and hard disks. The information stored in CAD files usually requires much less physical space in comparison to traditional hand drawings. However, the information stored inside the computer is not indestructible. On the contrary, the electronic format of information is very fragile and sensitive to the environment. Heat or cold can damage the information stored on magnetic storage devices. A power failure while you are creating a design could wipe out the many hours you spent working in front of the computer monitor. It is a good habit to save your work periodically, just in case something might go wrong while you are working on your design. In general, one should save one's work onto a storage device at an interval of every 15 to 20 minutes. You should also save your work before you make any major modifications to the design. It is also a good habit to periodically make backup copies of your work and put them in a safe place.

Getting Started with AutoCAD 2027

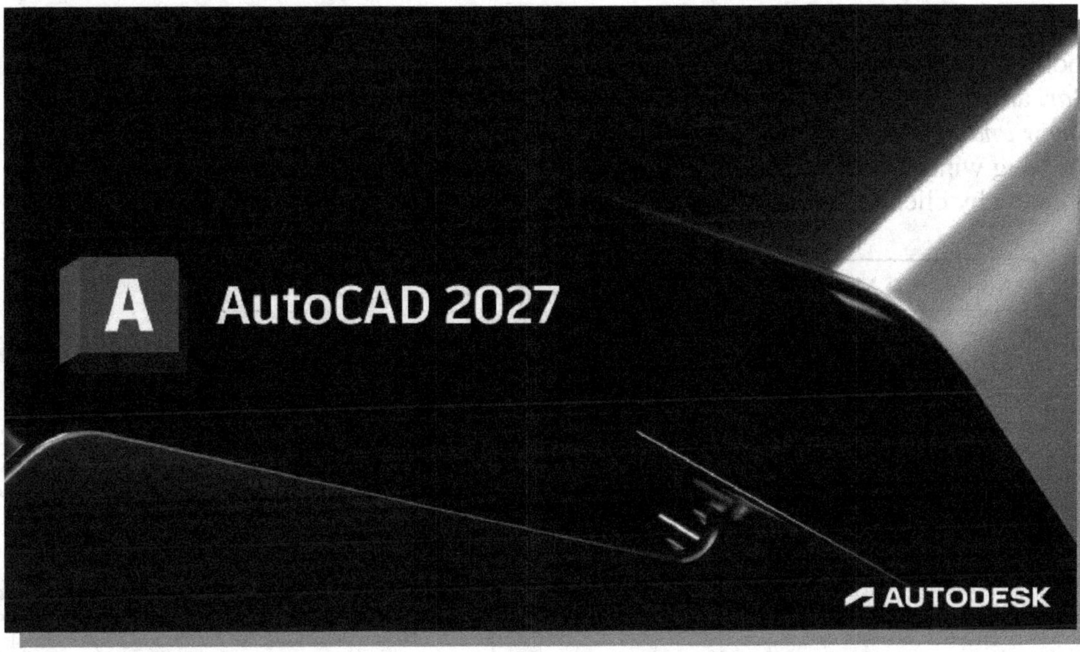

How to start **AutoCAD 2027** depends on the type of workstation and the particular software configuration you are using. With most *Windows* systems, you may select the **AutoCAD 2027** option on the *Start* menu or select the **AutoCAD 2027** icon on the *Desktop*. Consult with your instructor or technical support personnel if you have difficulty starting the software.

The program takes a while to load, so be patient. Eventually the **AutoCAD 2027** main *drawing screen* will appear on the screen. Click **Start Drawing** as shown in the below figure. The tutorials in this text are based on the assumption that you are using **AutoCAD 2027**'s default settings. If your system has been customized, some of the settings may not work with the step-by-step instructions in the tutorials. Contact your instructor and technical support to restore the default software configuration.

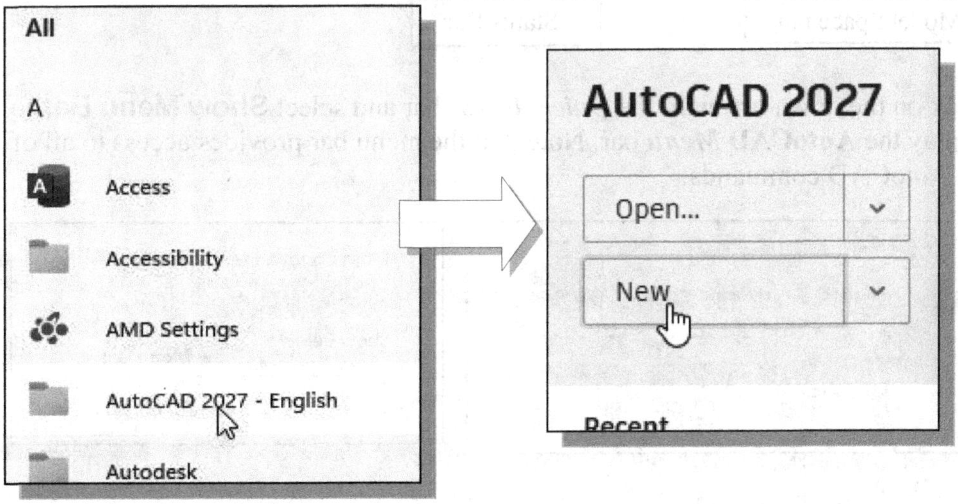

AutoCAD 2027 Screen Layout

The default **AutoCAD 2027** *drawing screen* contains the *pull-down* menus, the *Standard* toolbar, the *InfoCenter Help system,* the *scrollbars,* the *command prompt area*, the *Status Bar*, and the *Ribbon Tabs* and *Panels* that contain several *control panels* such as the *Draw and Modify* panel and the *Annotation* panel. You may resize the **AutoCAD 2027** drawing window by clicking and dragging at the edges of the window, or relocate the window by clicking and dragging at the window title area.

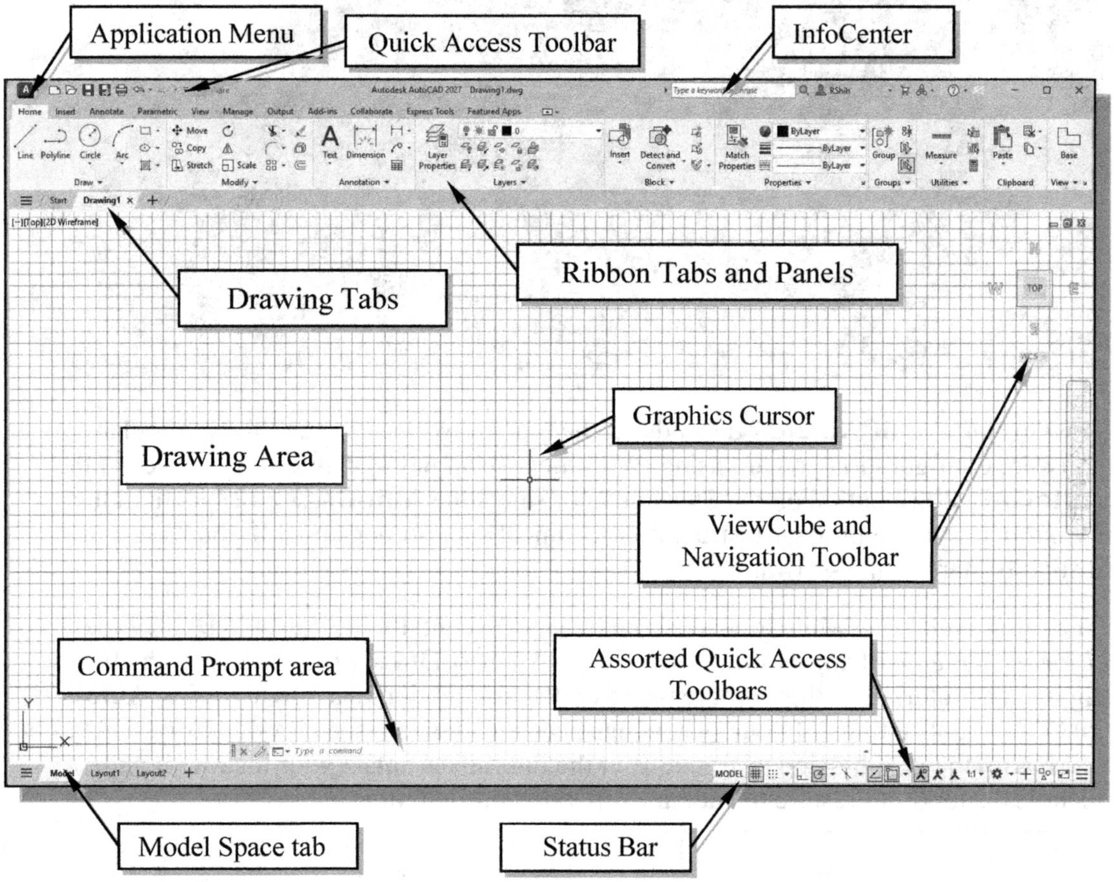

- Click on the down-arrow in the *Quick Access* bar and select **Show Menu Bar** to display the **AutoCAD *Menu*** bar. Note that the menu bar provides access to all of the AutoCAD commands.

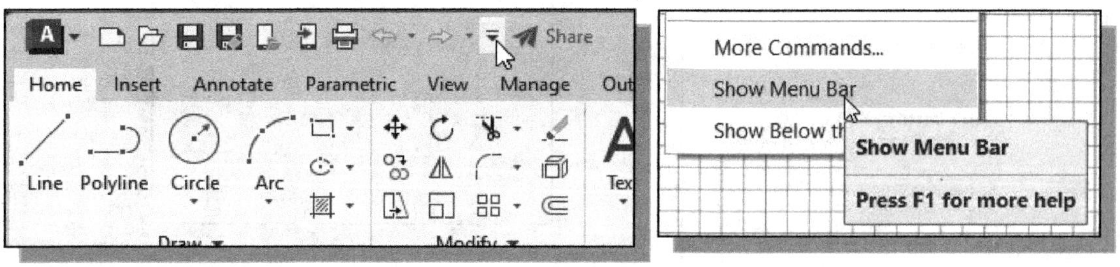

- **Application Menu**

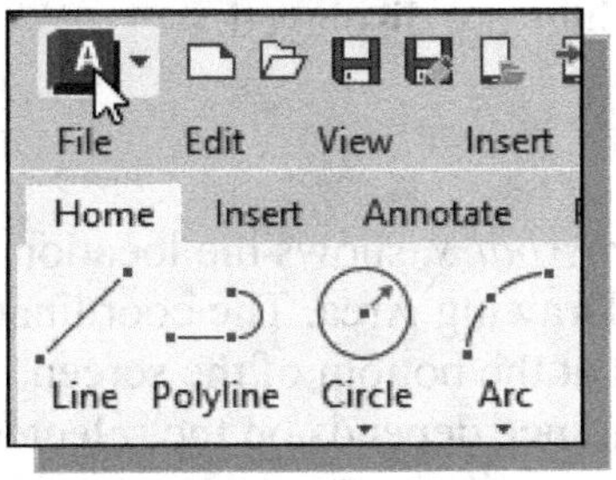

The *Application Menu* at the top of the main window contains commonly used file operations.

- **Quick Access Toolbar**

The *Quick Access* toolbar at the top of the *AutoCAD* window allows us quick access to frequently used commands, such as **Qnew**, **Open**, **Save** and also the **Undo** command. Note that we can customize the quick access toolbar by adding and removing sets of options or individual commands.

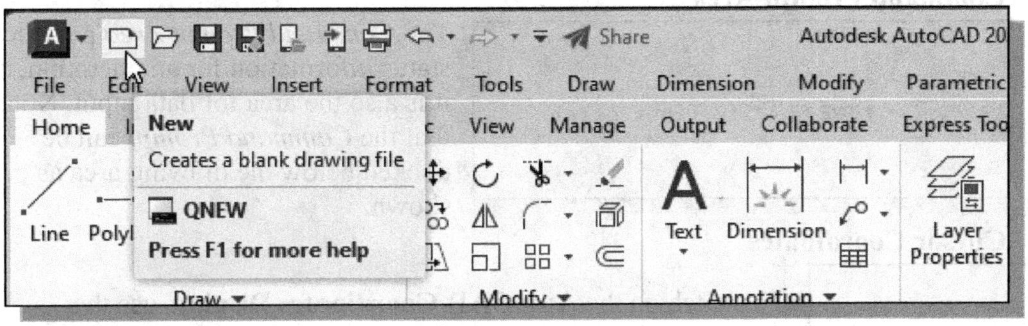

- **AutoCAD Menu Bar**

The *Menu* bar is the pull-down menu where all operations of AutoCAD can be accessed.

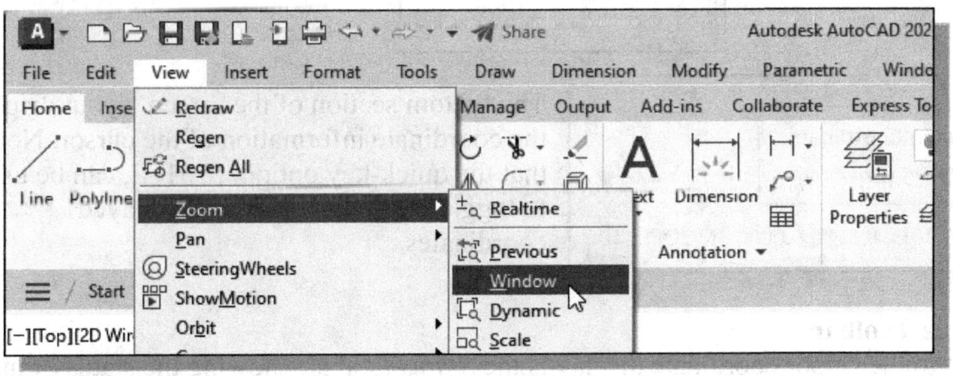

- **Layout Tabs**

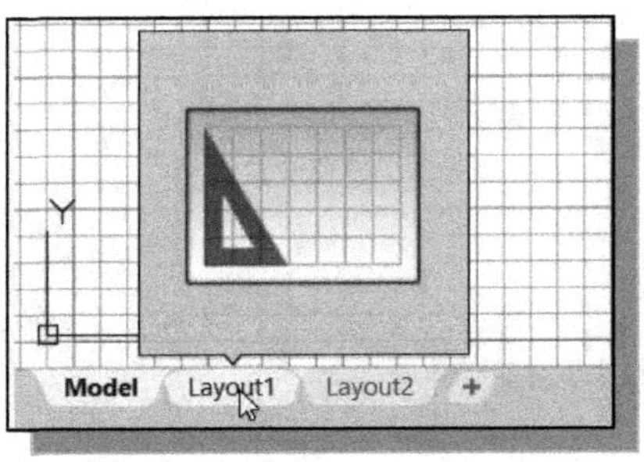

The Model/Layout tabs allow us to switch/create between different **model space** and **paper space**.

- **Drawing Area**
  The *Drawing Area* is the area where models and drawings are displayed.

- **Graphics Cursor or Crosshairs**

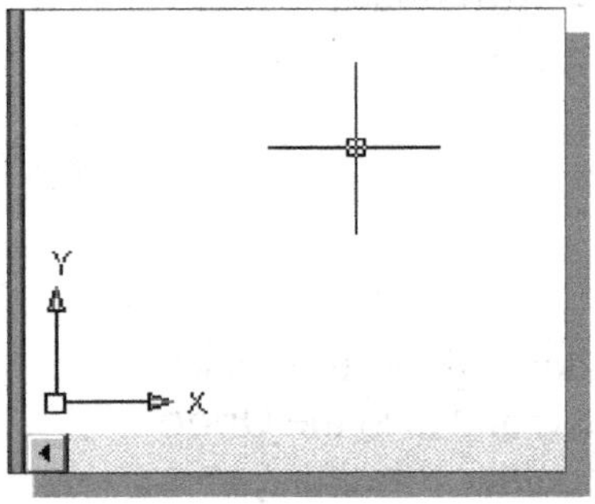

The *graphics cursor*, or *crosshairs*, shows the location of the pointing device in the Drawing Area. The coordinates of the cursor are displayed at the bottom of the screen layout. The cursor's appearance depends on the selected command or option.

- **Command Prompt Area**

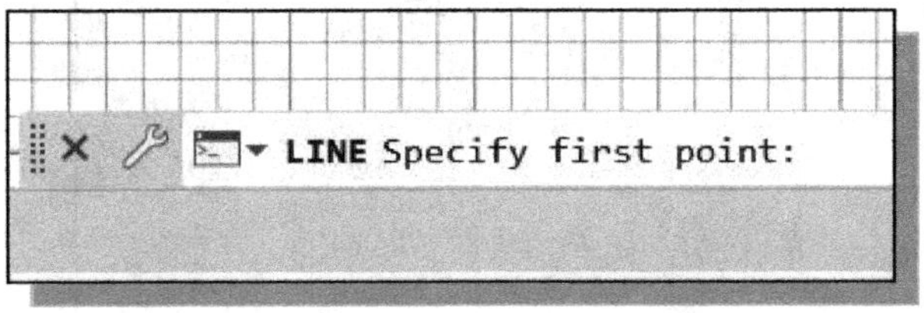

The *Command Prompt Area* provides status information for an operation, and it is also the area for data input. Note that the *Command Prompt* can be docked below the drawing area as shown.

- **Cursor Coordinates**

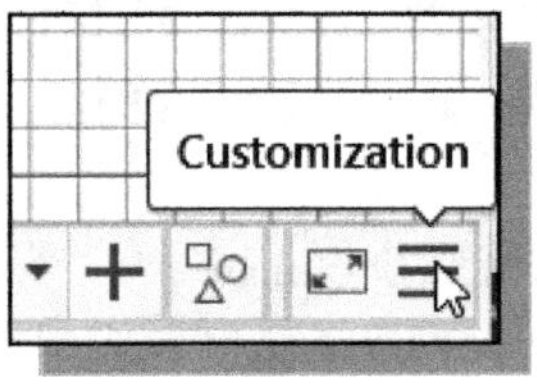

To switch on the **AutoCAD Coordinates Display**, use the *Customization option* at the bottom right corner.

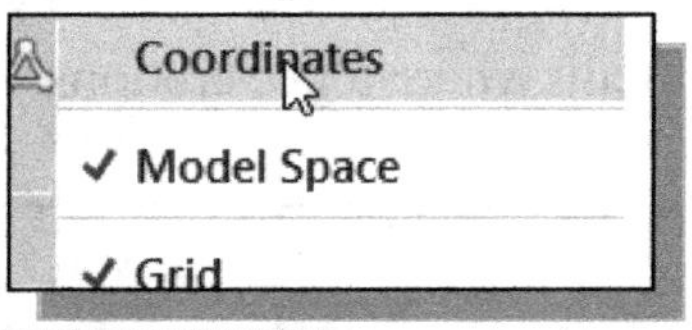

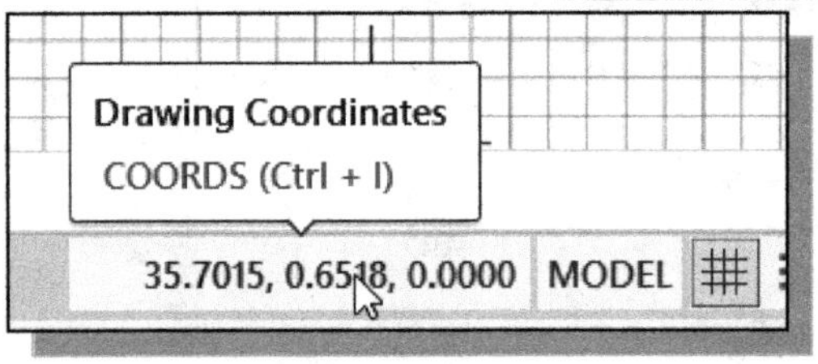

The bottom section of the screen layout displays the coordinate information of the cursor. Note that the quick-key option, [Ctrl+I], can be used to toggle the behavior of the displayed coordinates.

- **Status Toolbar**
  Next to the cursor coordinate display is the *Status* toolbar, showing the status of many commonly used display and construction options.

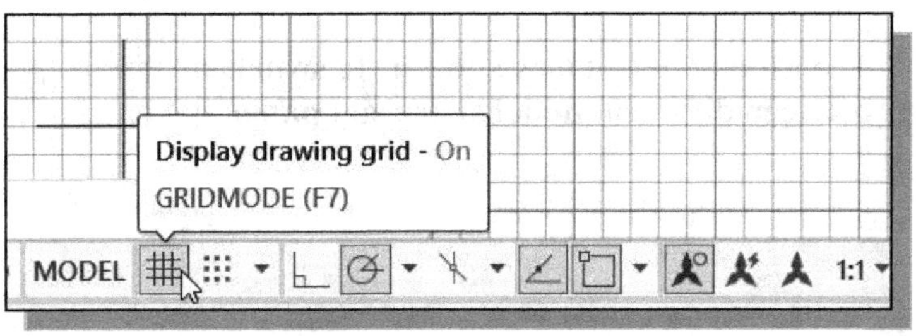

- **Ribbon Tabs and Panels**
  The top section of the screen layout contains customizable icon panels, which contain groups of buttons that allow us to pick commands quickly, without searching through a menu structure. These panels allow us to quickly access the commonly used commands available in AutoCAD.

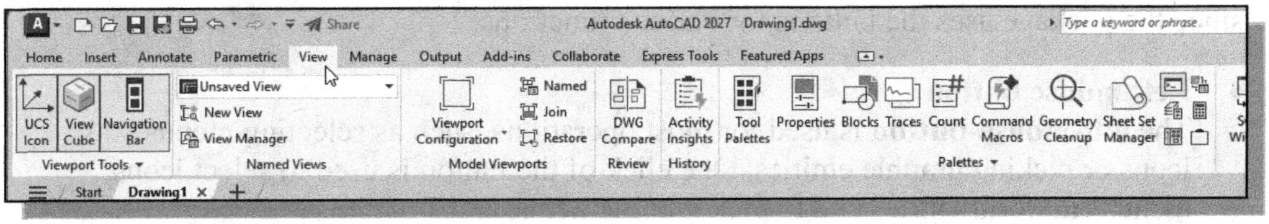

- **Draw and Modify Toolbar Panels**
  The *Draw* and *Modify* toolbar panels are the two main panels for creating drawings; the toolbars contain icons for basic draw and modify commands.

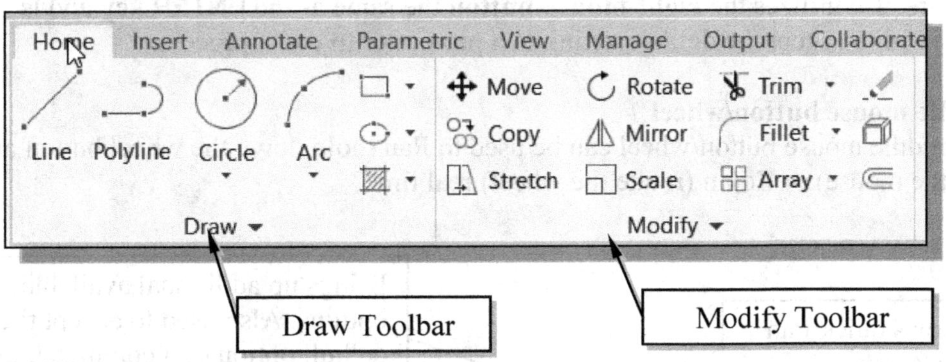

- **Layers Control Toolbar Panel**

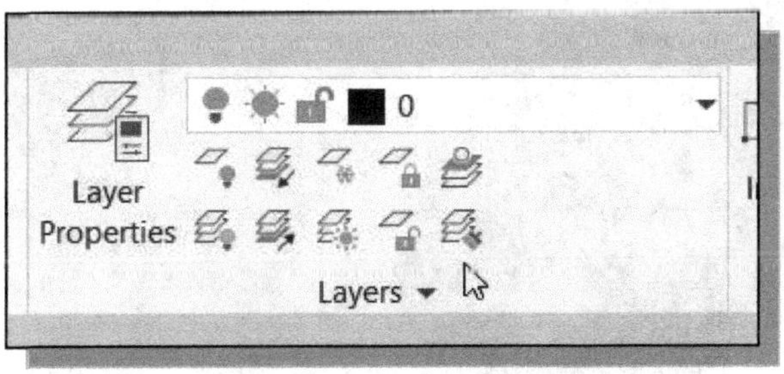

The *Layers Control* toolbar panel contains tools to help manipulate the properties of graphical objects.

- **Viewport/View/Display Controls**

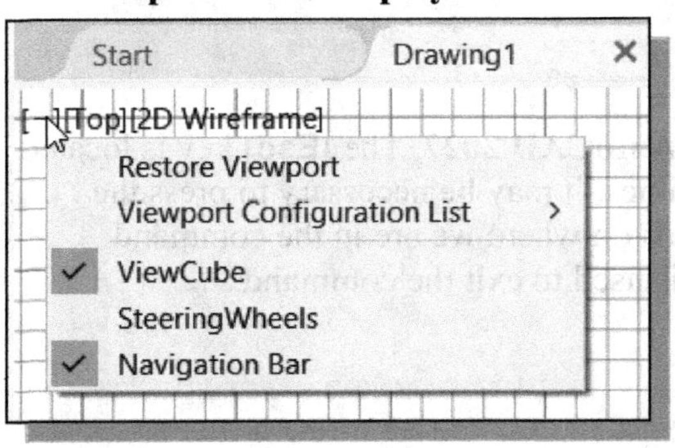

The *Viewport/View/Display controls panel* is located at the upper left corner of the graphics area, and it can be used to quickly access viewing related commands, such as Viewport and Display style.

Mouse Buttons

AutoCAD 2027 utilizes the mouse buttons extensively. In learning **AutoCAD 2027**'s interactive environment, it is important to understand the basic functions of the mouse buttons. It is highly recommended that you use a mouse or a tablet with **AutoCAD 2027** since the package uses the buttons for various functions.

- **Left mouse button**
  The **left-mouse-button** is used for most operations, such as selecting menus and icons or picking graphic entities. One click of the button is used to select icons, menus and form entries and to pick graphic items.

- **Right mouse button**
  The **right-mouse-button** is used to bring up additional available options. The software also utilizes the **right-mouse-button** the same as the **ENTER** key and is often used to accept the default setting to a prompt or to end a process.

- **Middle mouse button/wheel**
  The middle mouse button/wheel can be used to Pan (hold down the wheel button and drag the mouse) or Zoom (rotate the wheel) real time.

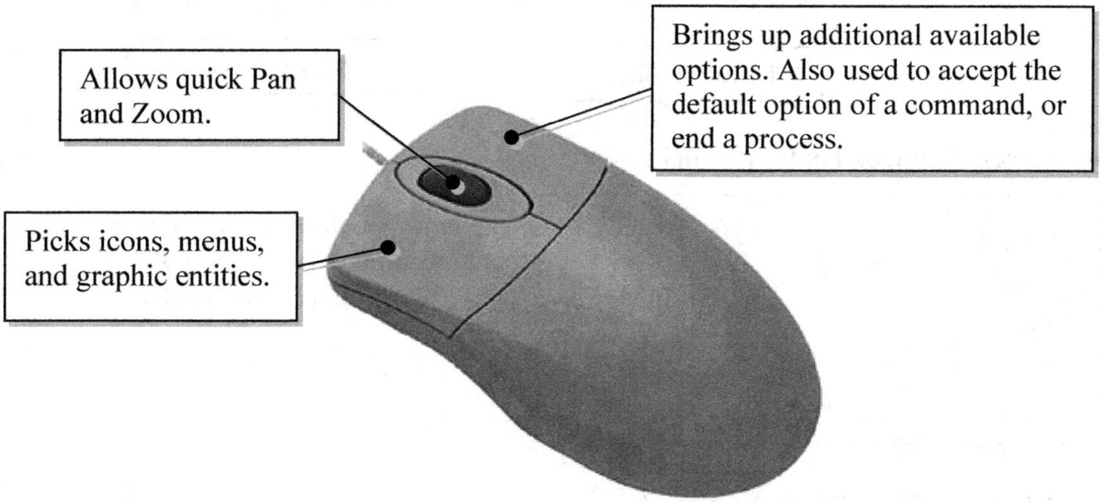

[Esc] – Canceling commands

The [**Esc**] key is used to cancel a command in **AutoCAD 2027**. The [**Esc**] key is located near the top-left corner of the keyboard. Sometimes, it may be necessary to press the [**Esc**] key twice to cancel a command; it depends on where we are in the command sequence. For some commands, the [**Esc**] key is used to exit the command.

Online Help

Several types of online help are available at any time during an **AutoCAD 2027** session. The **AutoCAD 2027** software provides many online help options:

- **Autodesk Exchange**:
  Autodesk Exchange is a central portal in AutoCAD 2027; AutoCAD Exchange provides a user interface for Help, learning aids, tips and tricks, videos, and downloadable apps. By default, *Autodesk Exchange* is displayed at **startup**. This allows access to a dynamic selection of tools from the *Autodesk community*; note that an internet connection is required to use this option.

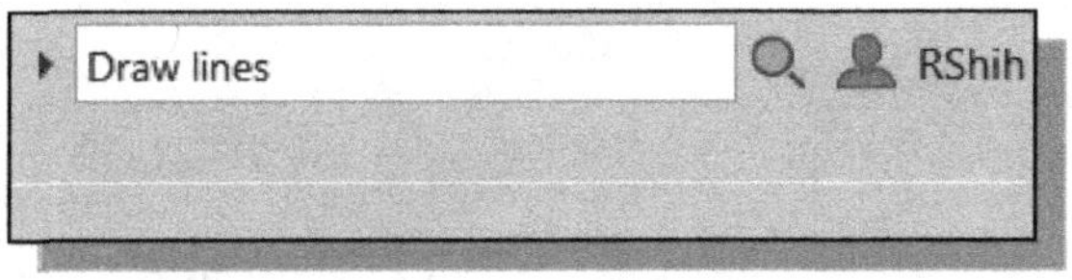

- To use *Autodesk Exchange*, simply type a question in the *input box* to search through the Autodesk's *Help* system as shown.

- A list of the search results appears in the *Autodesk Help* window, and we can also determine the level and type of searches of the associated information.

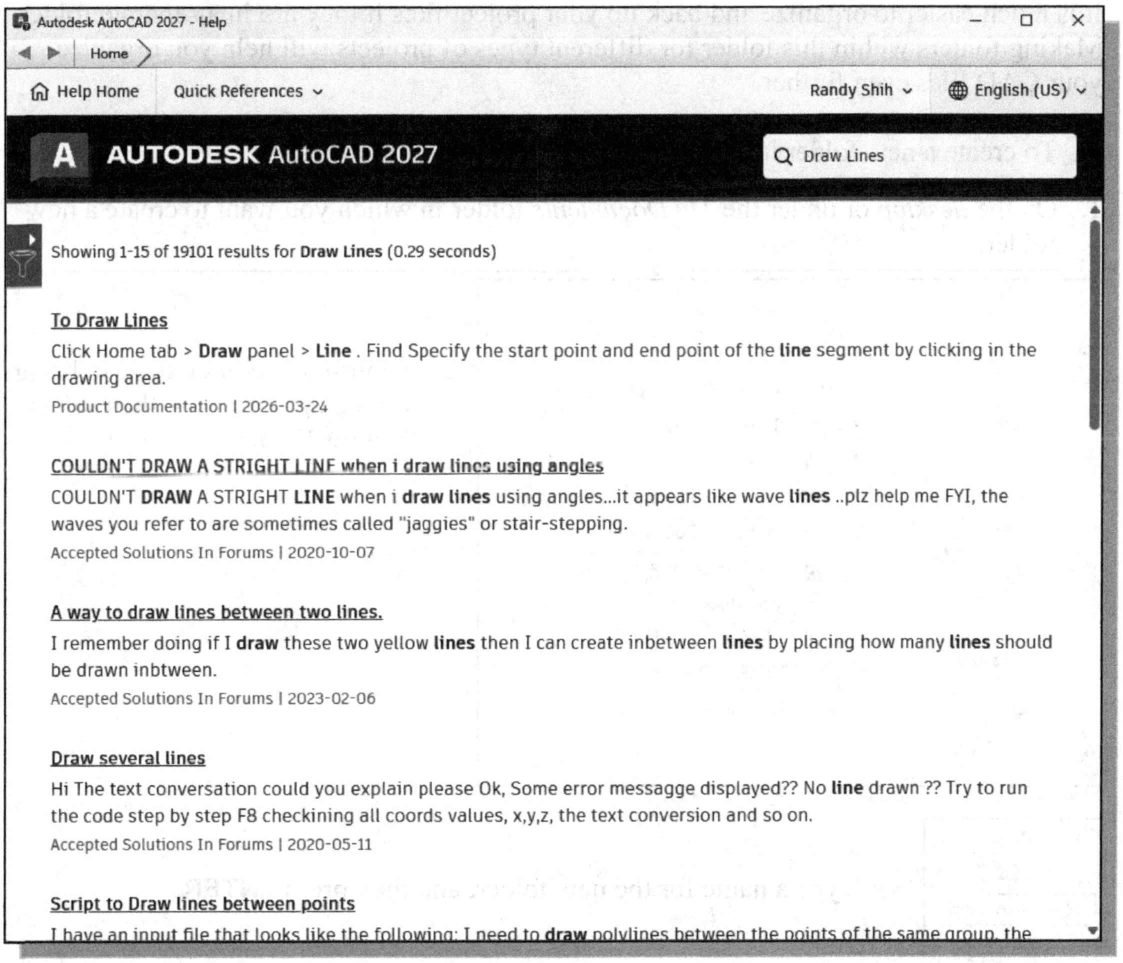

Leaving AutoCAD 2027

To leave **AutoCAD 2027**, use the left-mouse-button and click the **Application Menu** button at the top left corner of the **AutoCAD 2027** screen window, then choose **Exit AutoCAD** from the pull-down menu or type ***QUIT*** in the command prompt area.

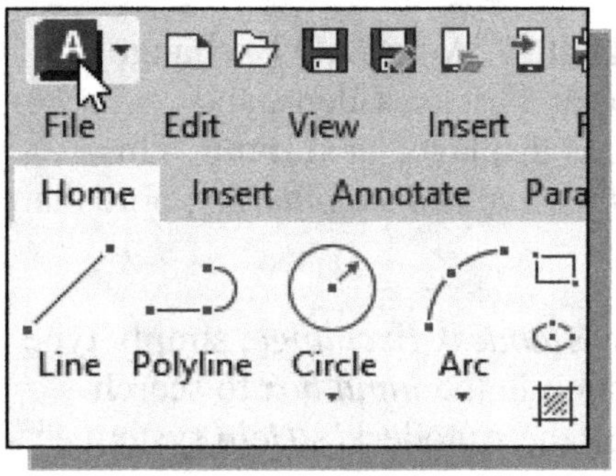

Creating a CAD File Folder

It is good practice to create a separate folder to store your CAD files. You should not save your CAD files in the same folder where the **AutoCAD 2027** application is located. It is much easier to organize and back up your project files if they are in a separate folder. Making folders within this folder for different types of projects will help you organize your CAD files even further.

➢ To create a new folder in the *Microsoft Windows* environment:

1. On the *desktop* or under the *My Documents* folder in which you want to create a new folder.

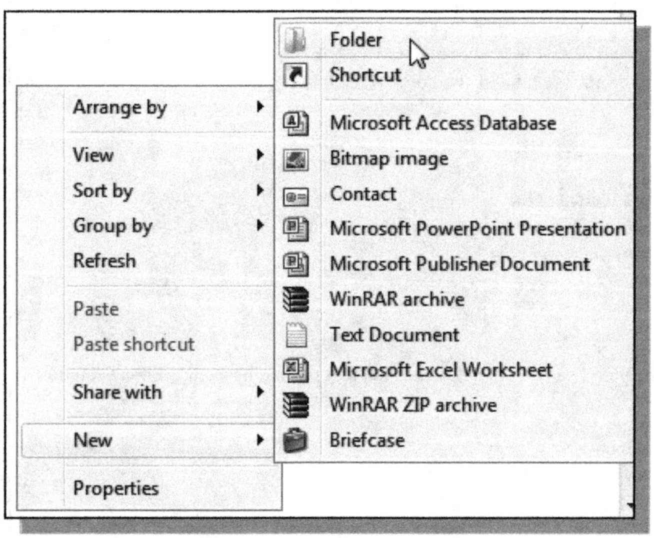

2. Right-mouse-click once to bring up the option menu, then select New→ Folder.

3. Type a name for the new folder, and then press **ENTER**.

Chapter 1
User Coordinate Systems and the Z-Axis

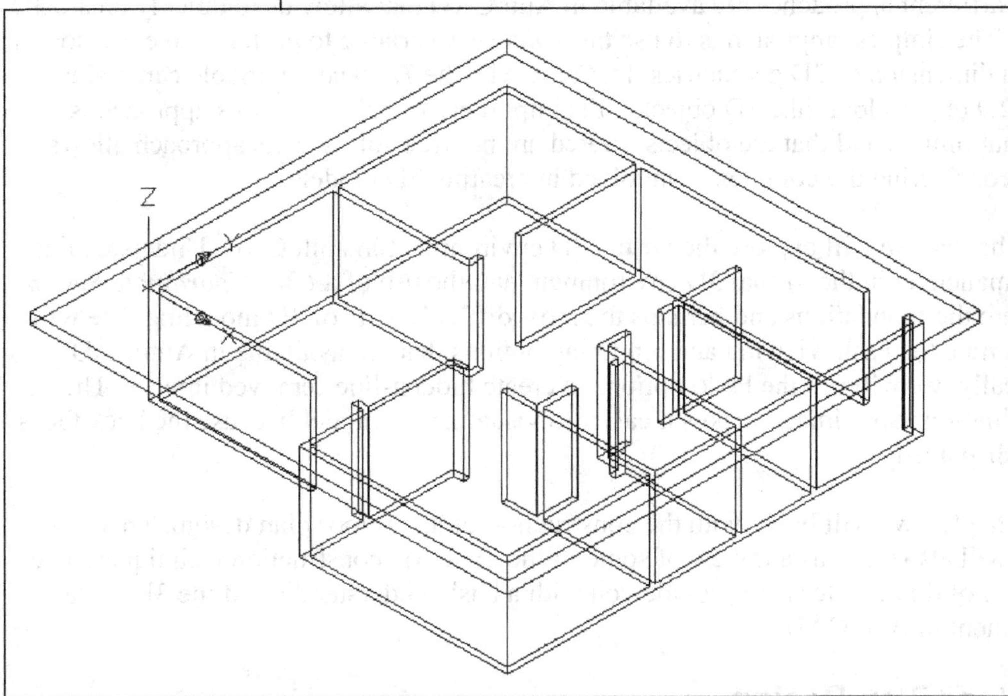

Learning Objectives

- Use the Drawing Units and Drawing Limits Commands
- Understand and Use the Thickness Option
- Understand the AutoCAD UCS
- Be able to Switch to Predefined Views
- Pre-selection of Objects
- Control Object Properties
- View with the Visual Styles Option

Introduction

Creating three-dimensional models on a CAD system provides us a means to check the integrity of a design. Creating realistic three-dimensional models helps us visualize our final design much more clearly than we can with 2D representations of the design. Several different approaches are available in AutoCAD that allow us to quickly create 3D models. The simplest approach is to use the *Thickness* variable to perform an extrusion in the third dimension of 2D geometries. In AutoCAD, the *Thickness* variable can make certain 2D objects look like 3D objects. It is important to realize that this approach is somewhat limited and that the objects created are not true solids. This approach allows us to start considering the complexity involved in creating 3D models.

In this chapter, we will explore the virtual 3D environment in AutoCAD. Understanding how to maneuver in the virtual 3D environment and the use of a *User Coordinate System* (UCS) are the foundations and perhaps the most difficult parts of 3D modeling. We will also examine the basic viewing and rendering options that are available in AutoCAD. Specifically, we will use the Hide options to create hidden-line-removed images. The hidden-line-removed image makes it easier to visualize the model because the back faces are not displayed.

In this chapter, we will begin with the construction of a 2D floor plan design. This tutorial will also serve as a review of some of the 2D CAD construction techniques. The main goal of this chapter is to provide you with a basic understanding of the 3D environment of AutoCAD.

The Floor Plan Design

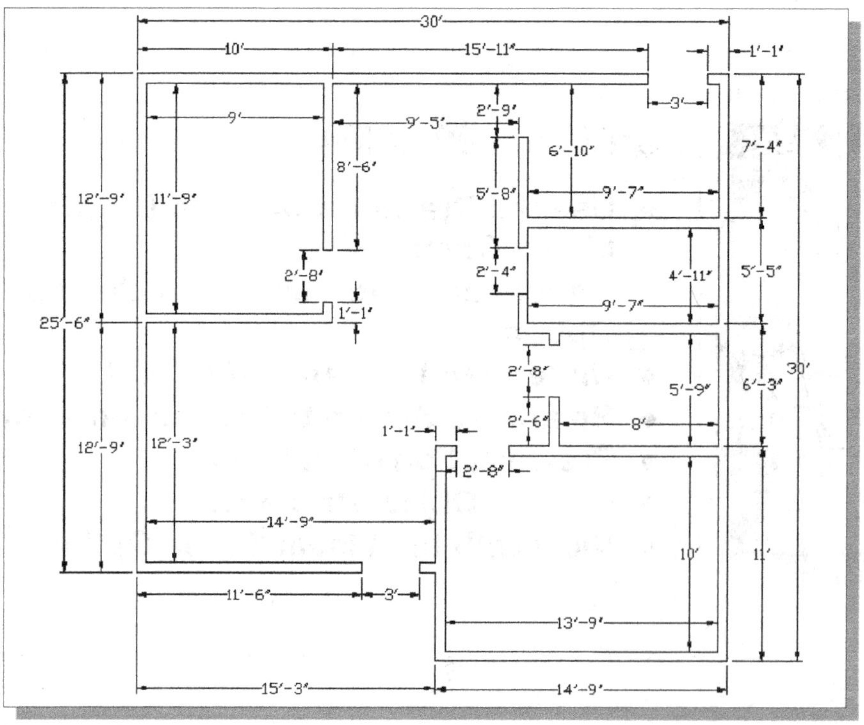

Starting Up AutoCAD 2027

1. Select the **AutoCAD 2027** option on the *Program* menu or select the **AutoCAD 2027** icon on the *Desktop*. Once the program is loaded into memory, the **AutoCAD 2027** drawing screen will appear on the screen.

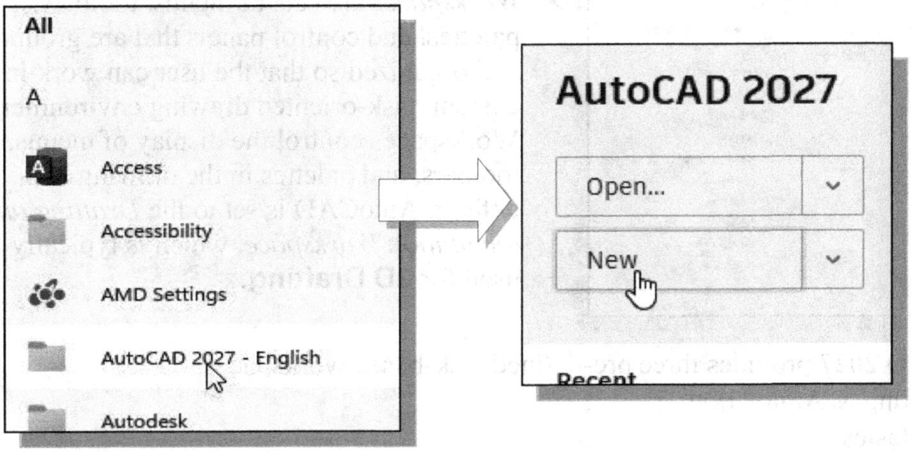

➢ Note that AutoCAD automatically assigns a generic name, *Drawing X*, as new drawings are created. In our example, AutoCAD opened the graphics window using the default system units and assigned the drawing name *Drawing1*.

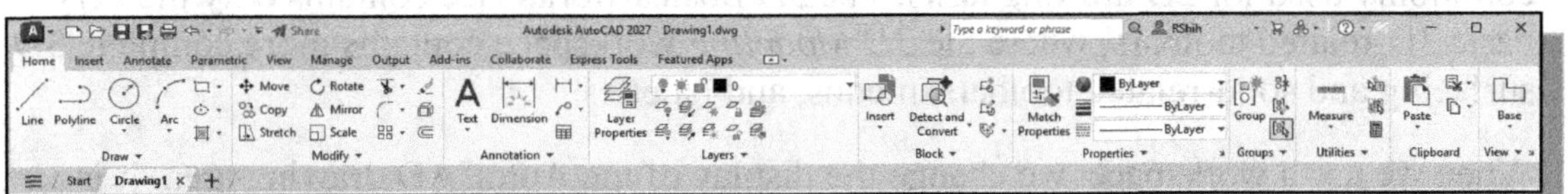

2. To display the **AutoCAD** ***Menu Bar*** at any time, click on the down-arrow in the *Quick Access Bar* and select **Show Menu Bar**. The *Menu Bar* provides access to almost all of the AutoCAD commands.

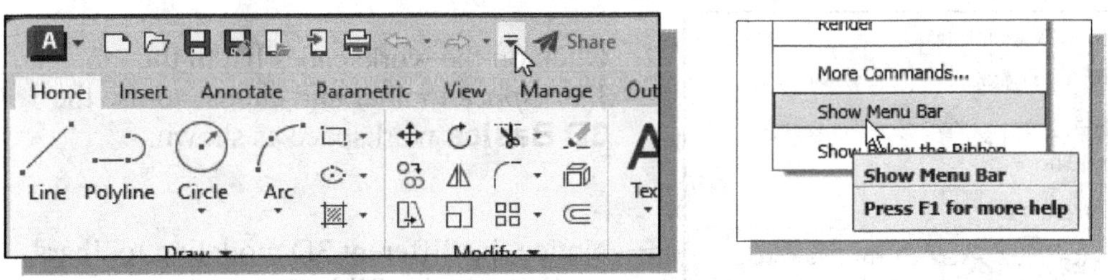

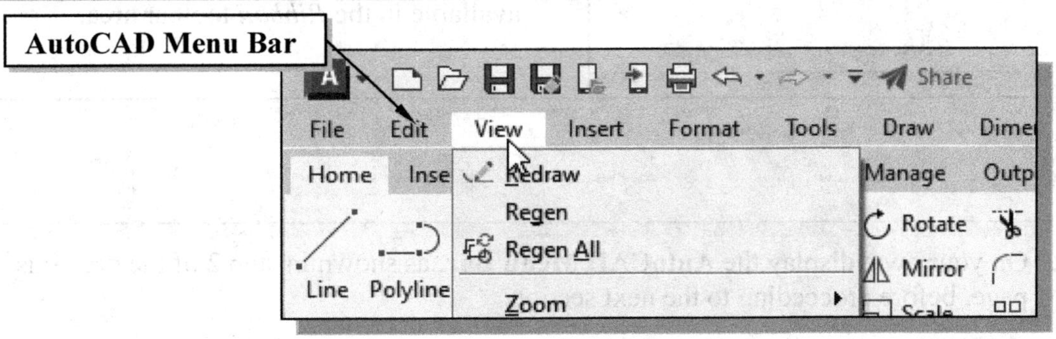

3D Basic Modeling WorkSpace

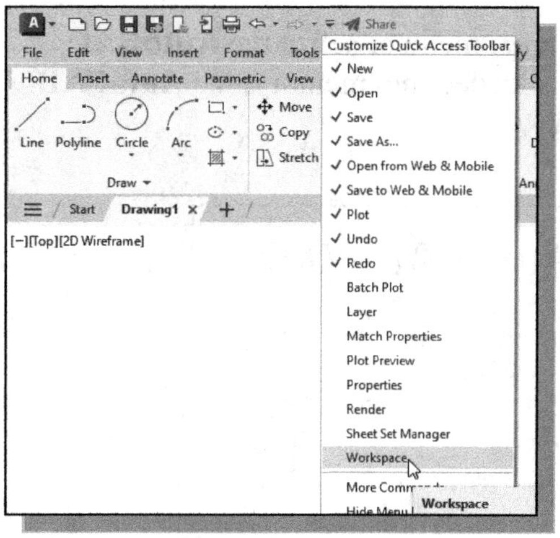

1. Turn on the **Workspace** option in the **Quick Access Toolbar** as shown.

➢ *Workspaces* are sets of menus, toolbars, palettes, and control panels that are grouped and organized so that the user can work in a custom, task-oriented drawing environment. Workspaces control the display of menus, toolbars, and palettes in the drawing area. By default, AutoCAD is set to the *Drafting and annotation Workspace*, which is typically used for **2D Drafting**.

➢ AutoCAD 2027 provides three pre-defined task-based workspaces:
- Drafting & Annotation
- 3D Basics
- 3D Modeling

The *Drafting & Annotation* workspace displays most of the toolbars and menus commonly used for 2D drafting tasks. The *3D Basics* workspace contains only the very basic 3D-related toolbars, where the *3D Modeling* workspace contains more complete 3D surfacing and solid-related toolbars, menus, and palettes.

When we use a workspace, we change the display of the AutoCAD drawing area. It is also important to note that we can still create 3D models using the *Drafting & Annotation* workspace. All of the AutoCAD commands are available regardless of which workspace we use. Using the workspaces is one of the many options available in AutoCAD 2027 that can help simplify our drafting/modeling tasks.

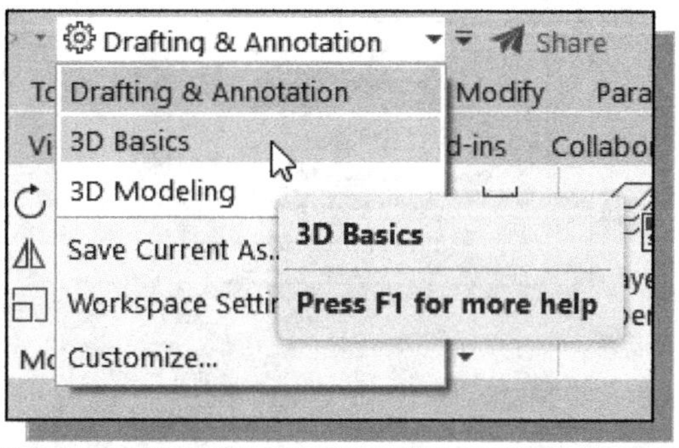

2. Click on the workspaces list in the *Workspace* toolbar and choose to use the **3D Basics** workspace as shown.

➢ Notice the different 3D modeling toolbars available in the *Ribbon* toolbar area.

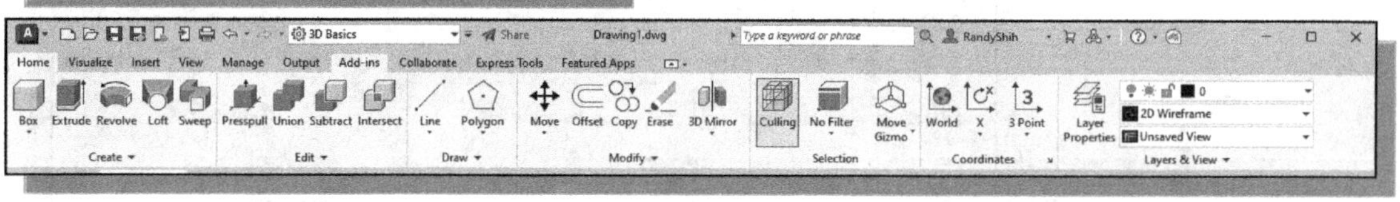

3. On your own, display the **AutoCAD Menu Bar**, as shown in step 2 of the previous page, before proceeding to the next section.

Drawing Units Setup

Every object we construct in a CAD system is measured in **units**. We should determine the value of the units within the CAD system before creating the first geometric entities.

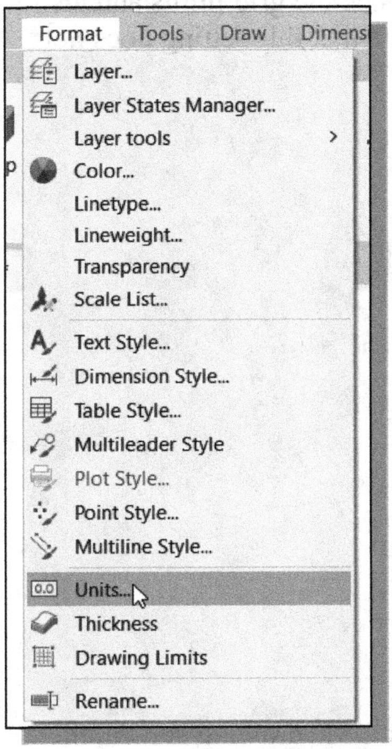

1. On your own, turn **on** the display of the **Menu Bar**, which was turned off when we switched to a different workspace.

2. In the *Menu Bar* area, select:

   [Format] → [Units]

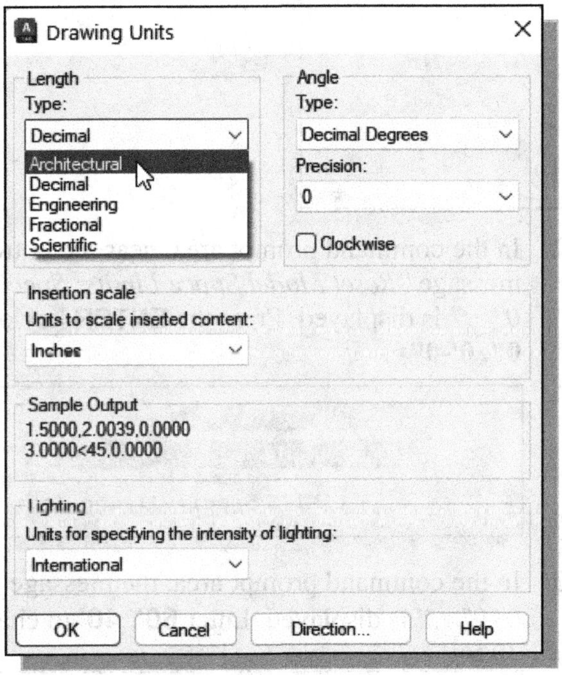

3. In the *Drawing Units* dialog box, set the *Length Type* to **Architectural**. This will set the measurement to the default **Architectural units, feet and inches**.

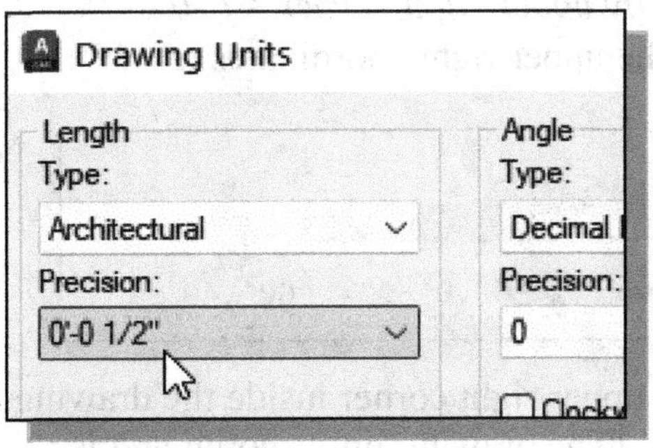

4. Set the *Precision* to **half-an-inch** as shown in the figure.

5. Click **OK** to exit the *Drawing Units* dialog box.

Drawing Area Setup

Next, we will set up the **Drawing Limits**; setting the Drawing Limits controls the extents of the display of the *grid.* It also serves as a visual reference that marks the working area. It can also be used to prevent construction outside the grid limits and also as a plot option that defines an area to be plotted/printed. Note that this setting does not limit the region for geometry construction.

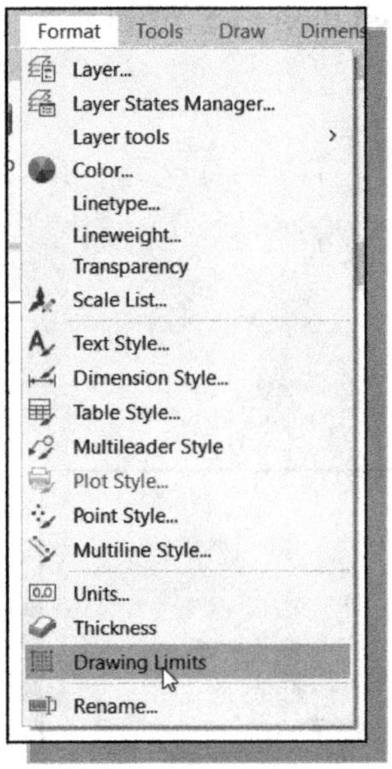

1. In the *Menu Bar* area, select:

   [Format] → [Drawing Limits]

2. In the command prompt area, near the bottom of the AutoCAD drawing screen, the message "*Reset Model Space Limits: Specify lower left corner or [On/Off] <0′-0″, 0′-0″>:*" is displayed. Press the **ENTER** key once to accept the default coordinates **<0′-0″, 0′-0″>**.

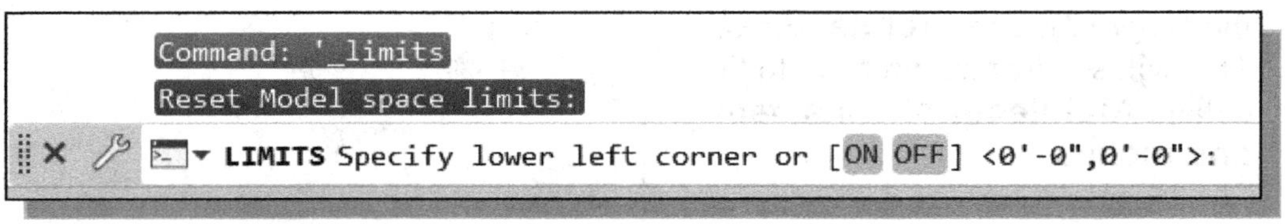

3. In the command prompt area, the message "*Specify upper right corner <1′-0″, 0′-9″>:*" is displayed. Enter **60′, 40′** to change the upper right coordinates to **<60′, 40′>**.

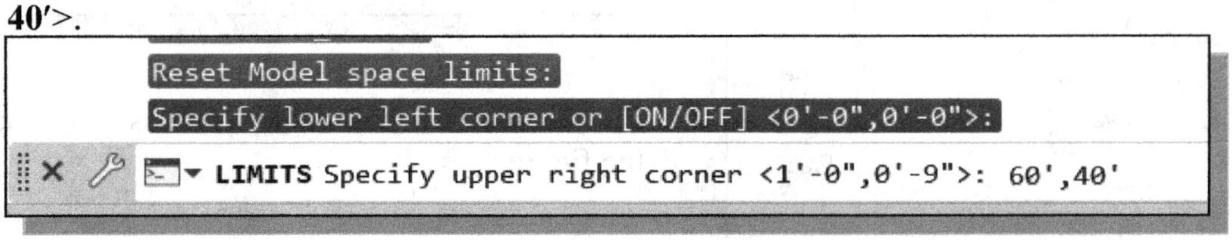

4. On your own, move the graphics cursor near the upper right corner inside the drawing area and note that the drawing area is unchanged. (The drawing limits command is used to set the drawing area, but the display will not be adjusted until a display related command is executed.)

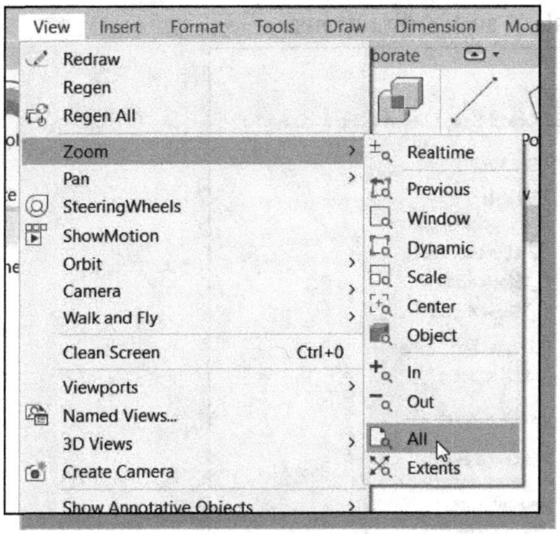

5. In the *Menu Bar* area, select:

   [View] → [Zoom] → [All]

❖ The **Zoom All** command can be used to adjust the display so that all objects in the drawing are displayed to be as large as possible. If no objects are constructed, the **Drawing Limits** are used to adjust the current viewport.

6. Move the graphics cursor near the upper right corner inside the drawing area and note that the display area is updated.

Grid and Snap Intervals Setup

1. In the *Menu Bar* area, select **[Tools] → [Drafting Settings]**.

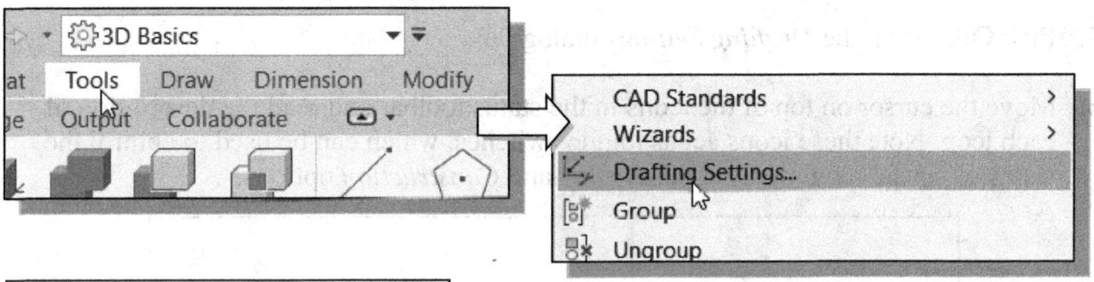

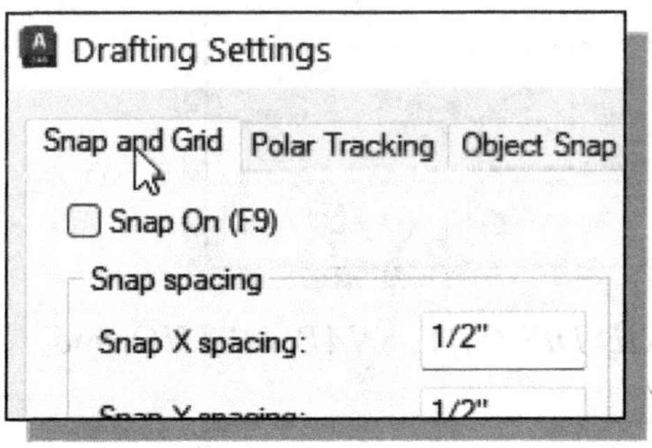

2. In the *Drafting Settings* dialog box, select the **Snap and Grid** tab if it is not the page on top.

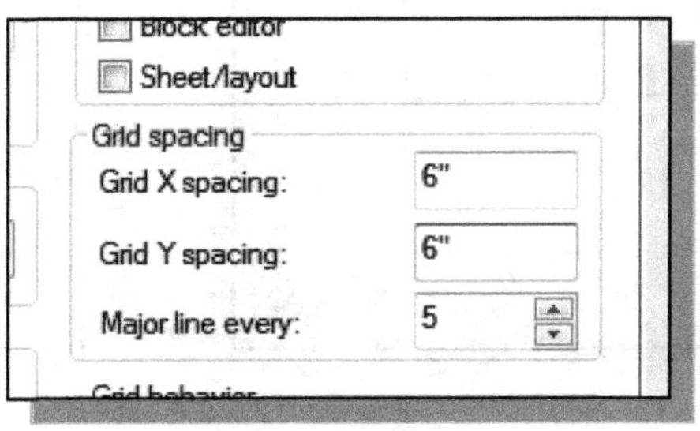

3. Change *Grid Spacing* to **6"** for both X and Y directions.

4. Also adjust the *Snap Spacing* to **6"** for both X and Y directions.

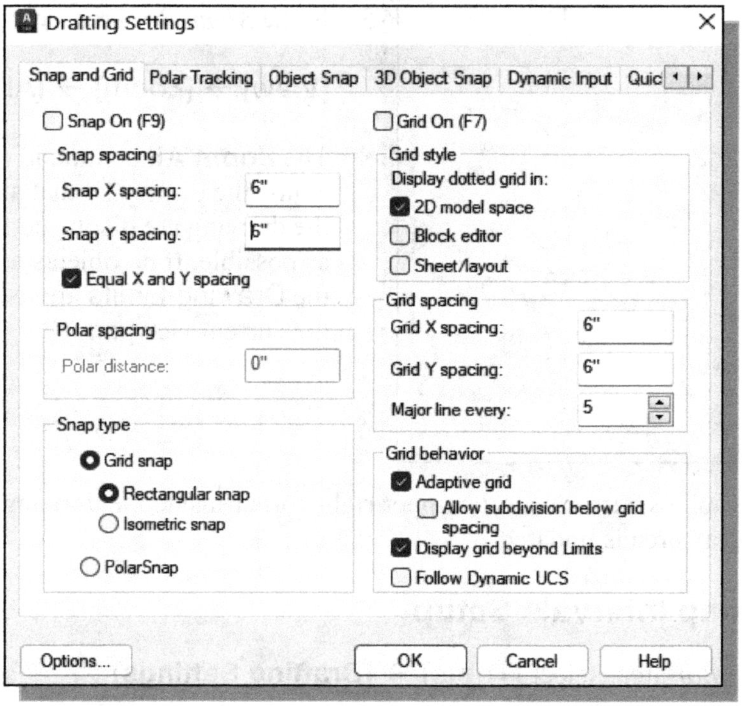

5. Pick **OK** to exit the *Drafting Settings* dialog box.

6. Move the cursor on top of the icons in the status toolbar and read the description of each icon. Note these icons act as toggle switches, which can be used to control the status of several commonly used *Display* and *Construction* options.

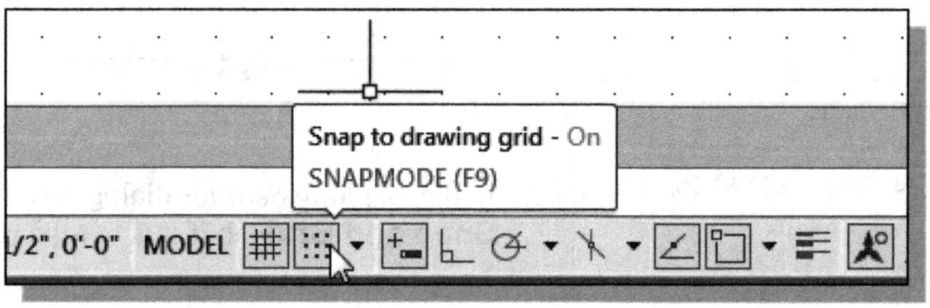

7. On your own, reset the option buttons so that *GRID DISPLAY*, *SNAP*, *ORTHO*, and *DYNAMIC INPUT* are switched ***ON***.

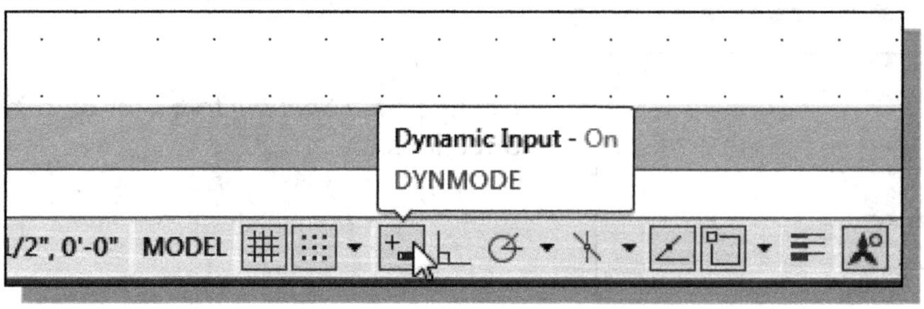

Create Polylines

In this tutorial, we will first create a 2D floor plan. The 2D floor plan will be converted into a 3D model with the **Thickness** command. In AutoCAD, a **polyline** is a connected sequence of line segments created as a single object. A polyline can contain straight line segments, arc segments, or a combination of the two.

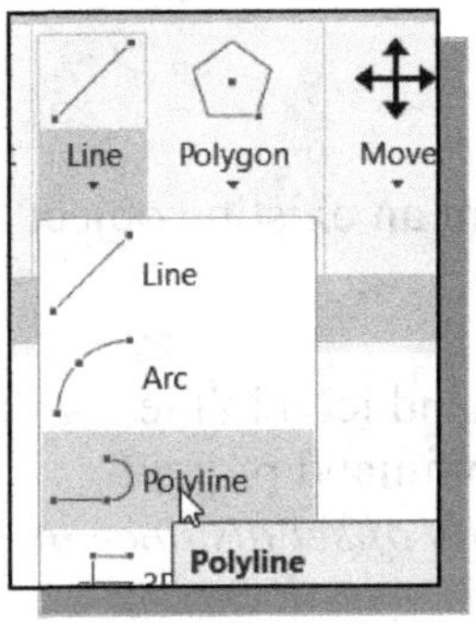

1. Select the **Polyline** command icon in the *Draw* toolbar.

2. In the *command prompt area*, the message "*Specify start point:*" is displayed. Select a location that is near the coordinates (**25′-0″, 10′-0″**) as the **starting point** of the *polyline*.

3. In the *command prompt area*, create a horizontal line by using the *relative rectangular coordinates entry method*, relative to the last point we specified. *Specify next point:* **@-11′6″, 0 [ENTER]**.

4. In the *command prompt area*, create a vertical line by using the *relative rectangular coordinates entry method*, relative to the last point we specified. *Specify next point:* **@0, 25′6″ [ENTER]**.

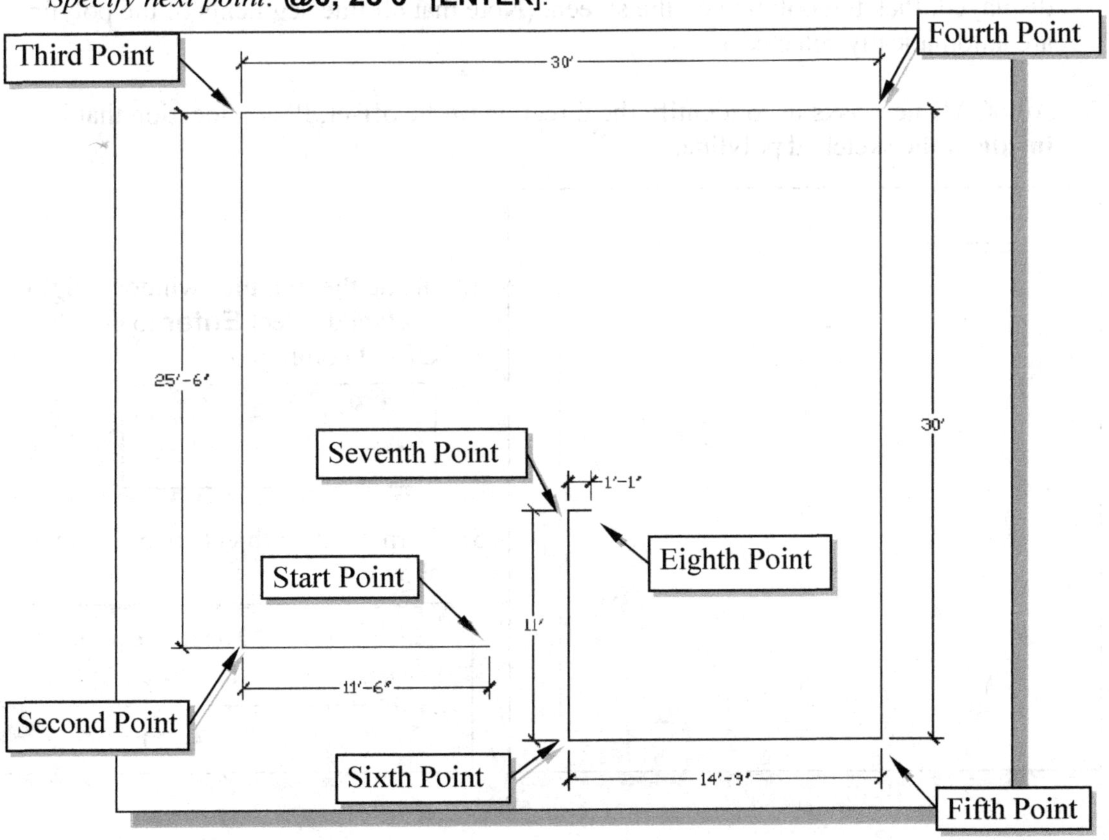

5. On your own, complete the polyline by specifying the rest of the points, *point four* through *point eight*.

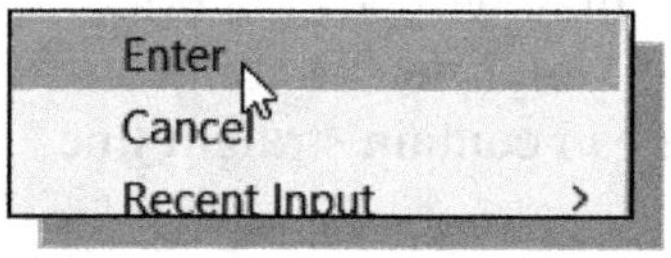

6. Inside the *graphics window*, **right-click** and select **Enter** to end the **Polyline** command.

Create an Offset Polyline

The **Offset** command creates a new object at a specified distance from an existing object or through a specified point.

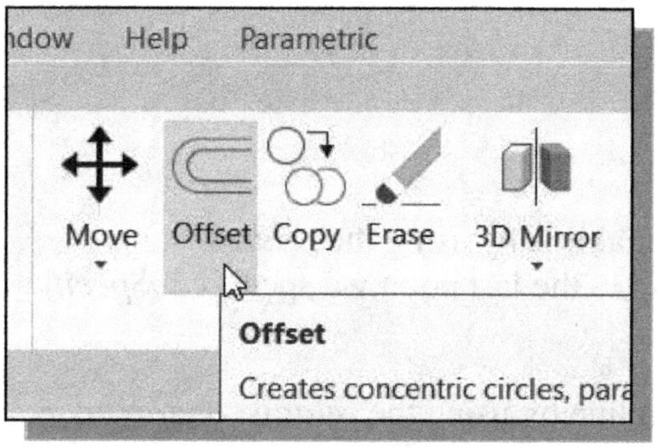

1. Select the **Offset** command icon in the *Modify* toolbar. In the command prompt area, the message *"Specify offset distance or [Through]:"* is displayed.

   Specify offset distance or [Through]]:
   6" [ENTER].

2. In the command prompt area, the message *"Select object to offset or <exit>:"* is displayed. Pick the polyline on the screen. (Note that all line segments of the polyline are automatically selected.)

3. AutoCAD next asks us to identify the direction of the offset. Pick a location that is **inside** of the sketched polyline.

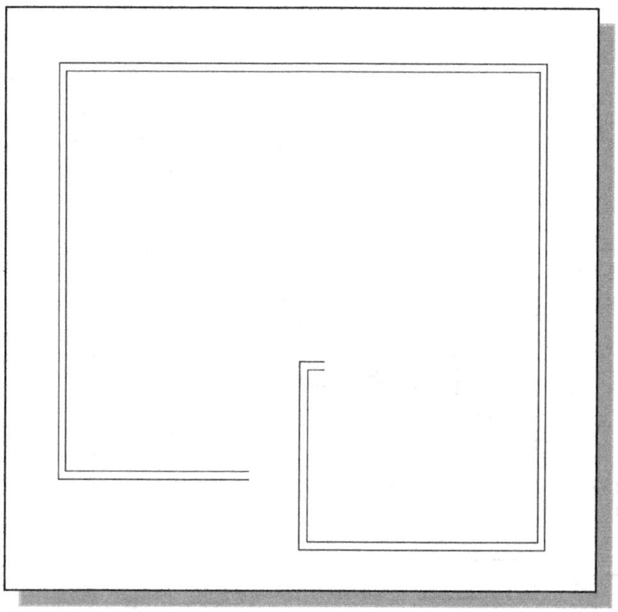

4. Inside the graphics window, **right-click** and select **Enter** to end the **Offset** command.

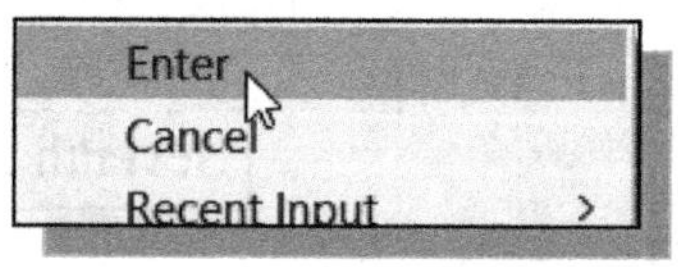

5. Turn off the Object snap option as shown.

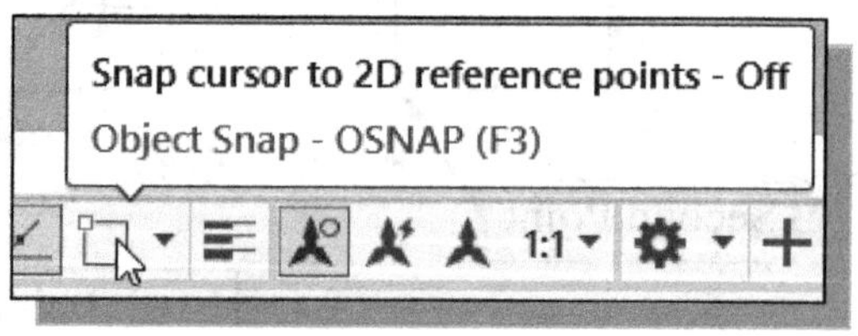

Create Interior Walls

1. In the *Menu Bar* area, choose **[Tools] → [Toolbars] → [AutoCAD]**.

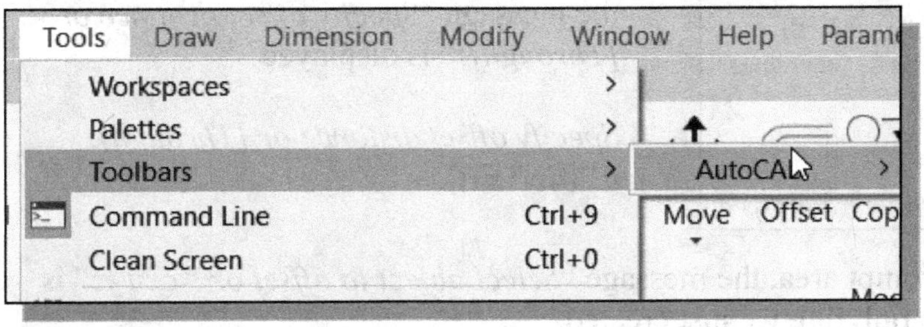

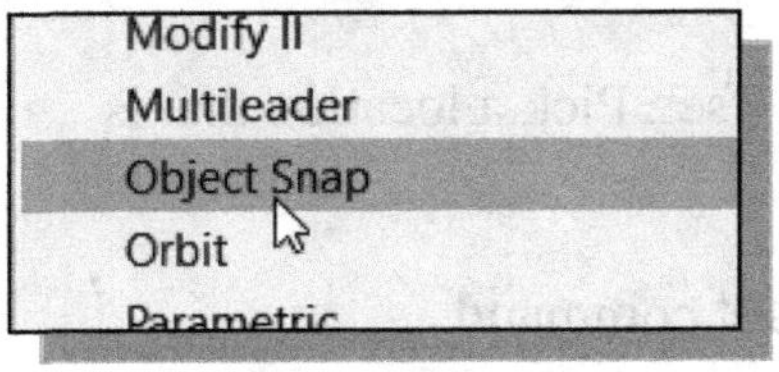

2. Select **Object Snap**, with the left-mouse-button, to display the *Object Snap* toolbar on the screen to assist the construction of the floor plan.

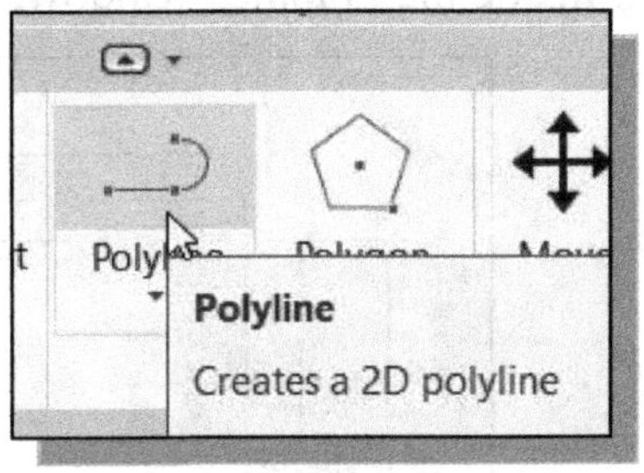

3. Select the **Polyline** command icon in the *Draw* toolbar. In the command prompt area, the message "*Specify start point or [Justification/ Scale/ Style]:*" is displayed.

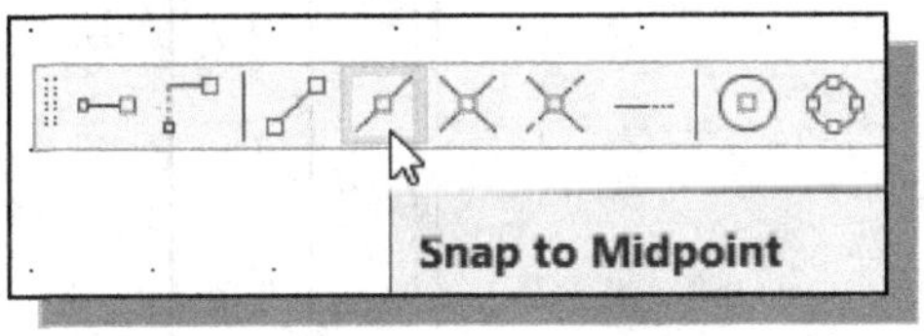

4. In the *Object Snap* toolbar, pick **Snap to Midpoint**. In the command prompt area, the message "*_mid of*" is displayed. AutoCAD now expects us to select a geometric entity on the screen.

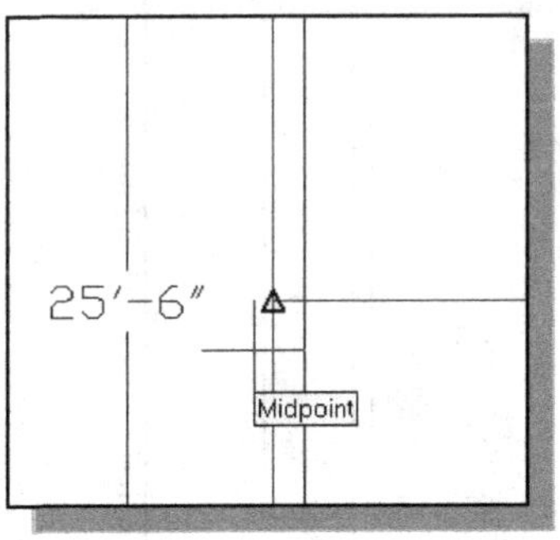

5. Select the vertical line on the left as shown.

6. At the *command prompt*, enter **@10', 0 [ENTER]**.

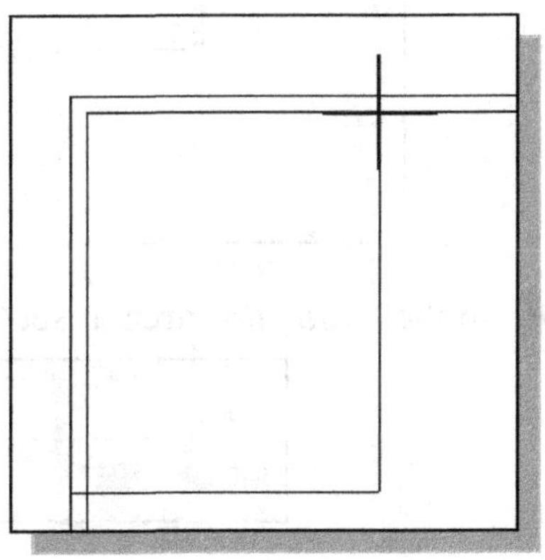

7. On your own, define a vertical line at the location as shown in the figure.

8. Inside the graphics window, **right-click** and select **Enter** to end the Polyline command.

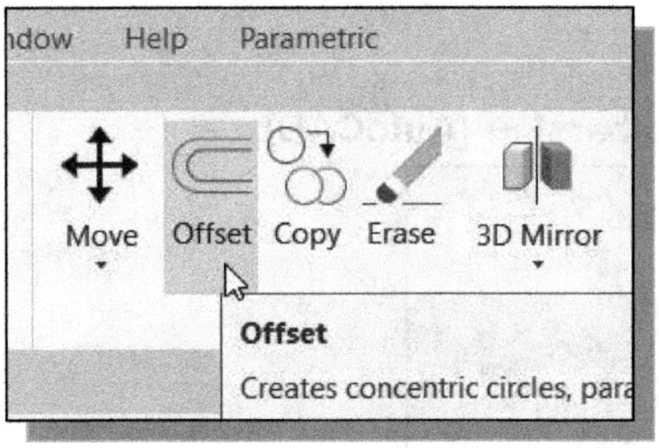

9. Select the **Offset** command icon in the *Modify* toolbar. In the command prompt area, the message "*Specify offset distance or [Through]:*" is displayed.

   Specify offset distance or [Through]:
   6" **[ENTER]**.

10. In the command prompt area, the message "*Select object to offset or <exit>:*" is displayed. Pick the **polyline** we just created.

11. AutoCAD next asks us to identify the direction of the offset. Pick a location that is toward the *upper left* corner of the design.

12. Inside the graphics window, **right-click** to end the Offset command.

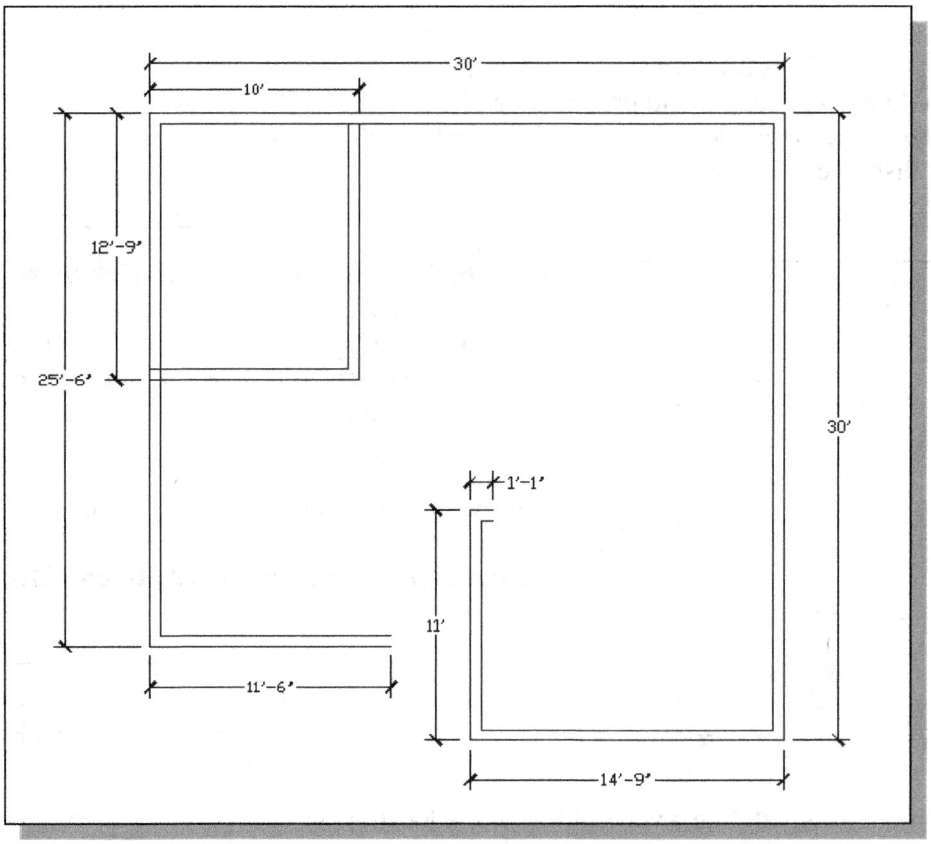

➢ In the *Status Bar* area, reset the option buttons and switch ***OFF*** all options.

- Next, we will create a 2′-8″ doorway using the Snap From option.

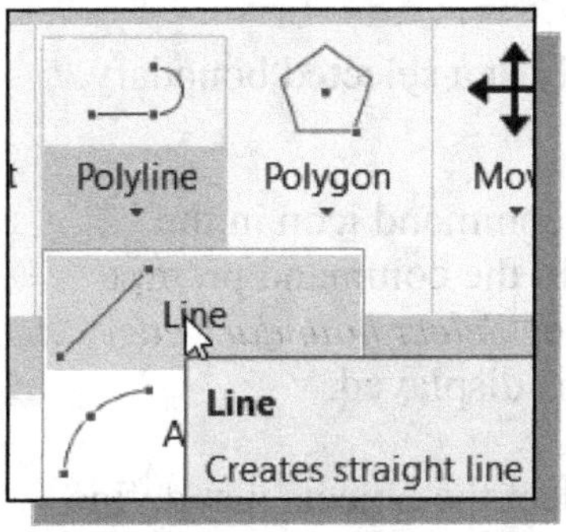

13. Select the **Line** command icon in the *Draw* toolbar. In the command prompt area, the message "*_line Specify first point:*" is displayed.

❖ We will demonstrate the use of the Snap From option, which allows us to snap to any measurements of an existing location.

14. In the *Object Snap* toolbar, pick **Snap From**. In the command prompt area, the message "*_from Base point*" is displayed. AutoCAD now expects us to select a geometric entity on the screen.

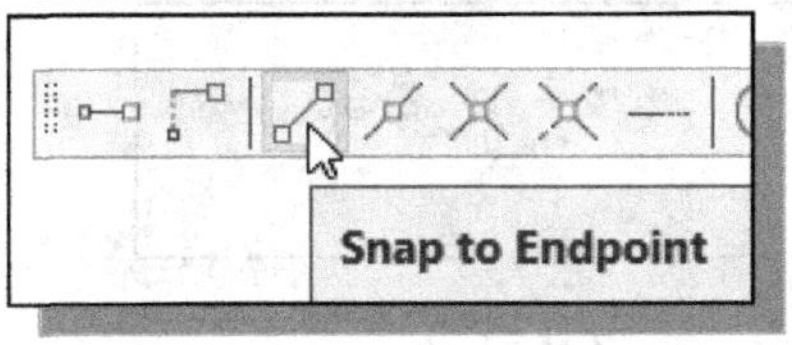

15. We will measure relative to the lower left corner of the interior wall. In the *Object Snap* toolbar, pick **Snap to Endpoint**.

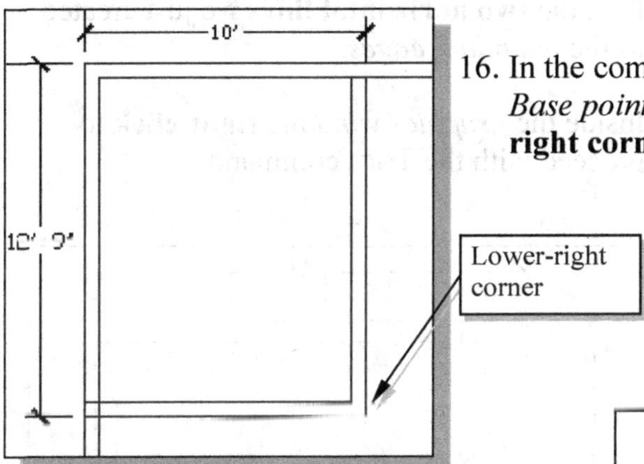

16. In the command prompt area, the message "*_from Base point: _endp of*" is displayed. Pick **the lower right corner** as shown.

17. At the command prompt, enter **@0,1′-1″ [ENTER]**.

18. At the command prompt, enter **@-6″, 0 [ENTER]**.

19. Inside the graphics window, right-click once and select **Enter** to end the Line command.

20. On your own, use the **Offset** command to create a parallel line that is **2′-8″** above the previous line.

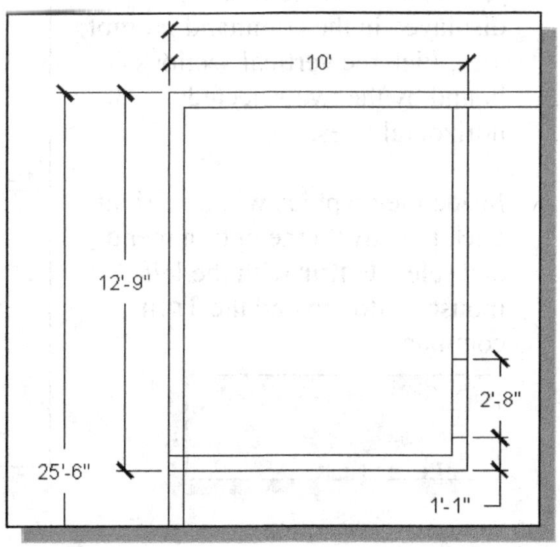

Complete the Doorway Using the Trim Command

The **Trim** command shortens an object so that it ends precisely at a selected boundary.

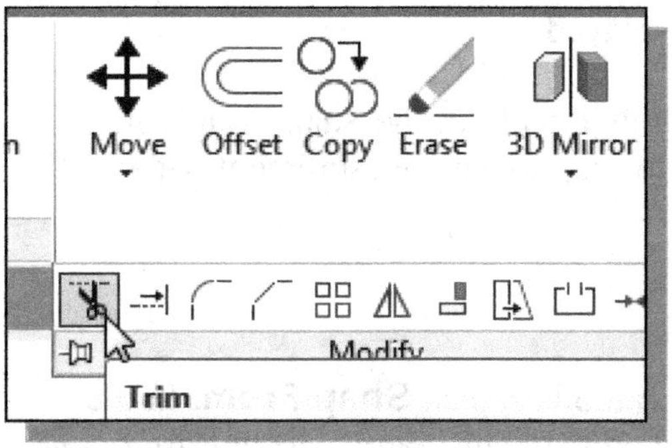

1. Select the **Trim** command icon in the *Modify* toolbar. In the command prompt area, the message "*Select boundary edges... Select objects:*" is displayed.

- First, we will select the objects that define the boundary edges to which we want to trim the object.

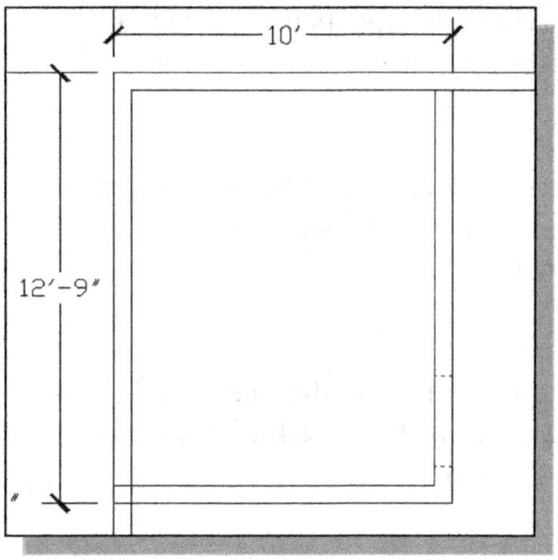

2. In the command prompt area, select **[cuTting edges]** as shown.

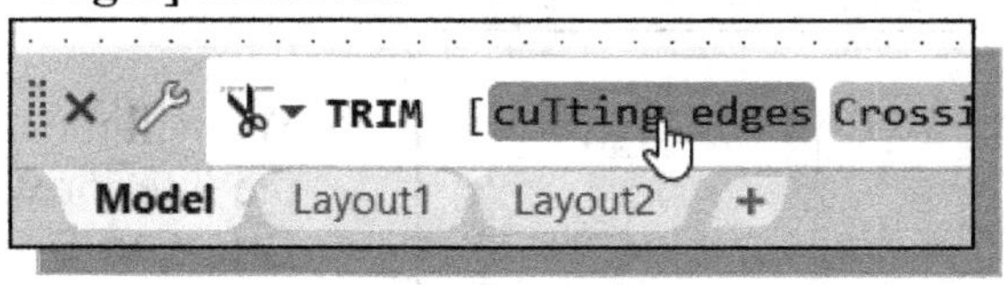

3. Pick the **two horizontal lines** we just created as the *boundary edges*.

4. Inside the *graphics window*, **right-click** to proceed with the Trim command.

5. The message "*Select object to trim or shift-select object to extend or [Project/ Edge/ Undo]:*" is displayed in the command prompt area. Pick the vertical sections bound by the two selected horizontal lines.

6. Inside the graphics window, right-click to activate the option menu and select **Enter** with the left-mouse-button to end the Trim command.

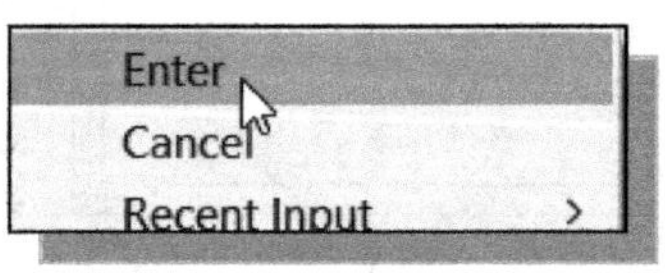

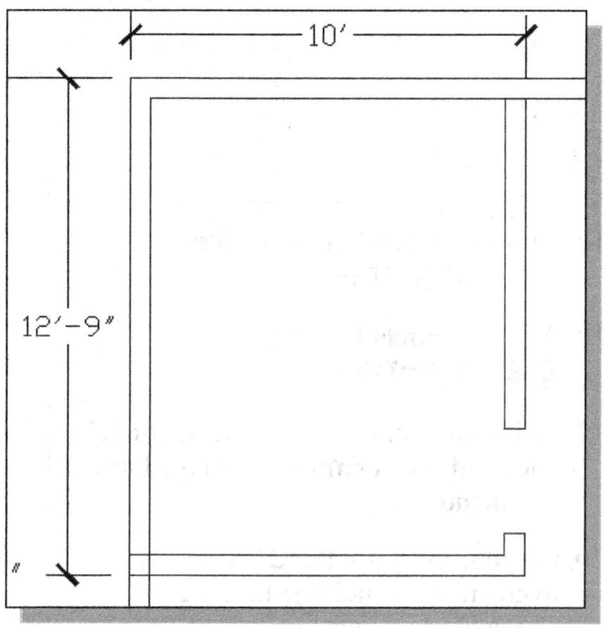

Using the **Polyline** and **Line** commands, create the additional walls and doorways as shown.

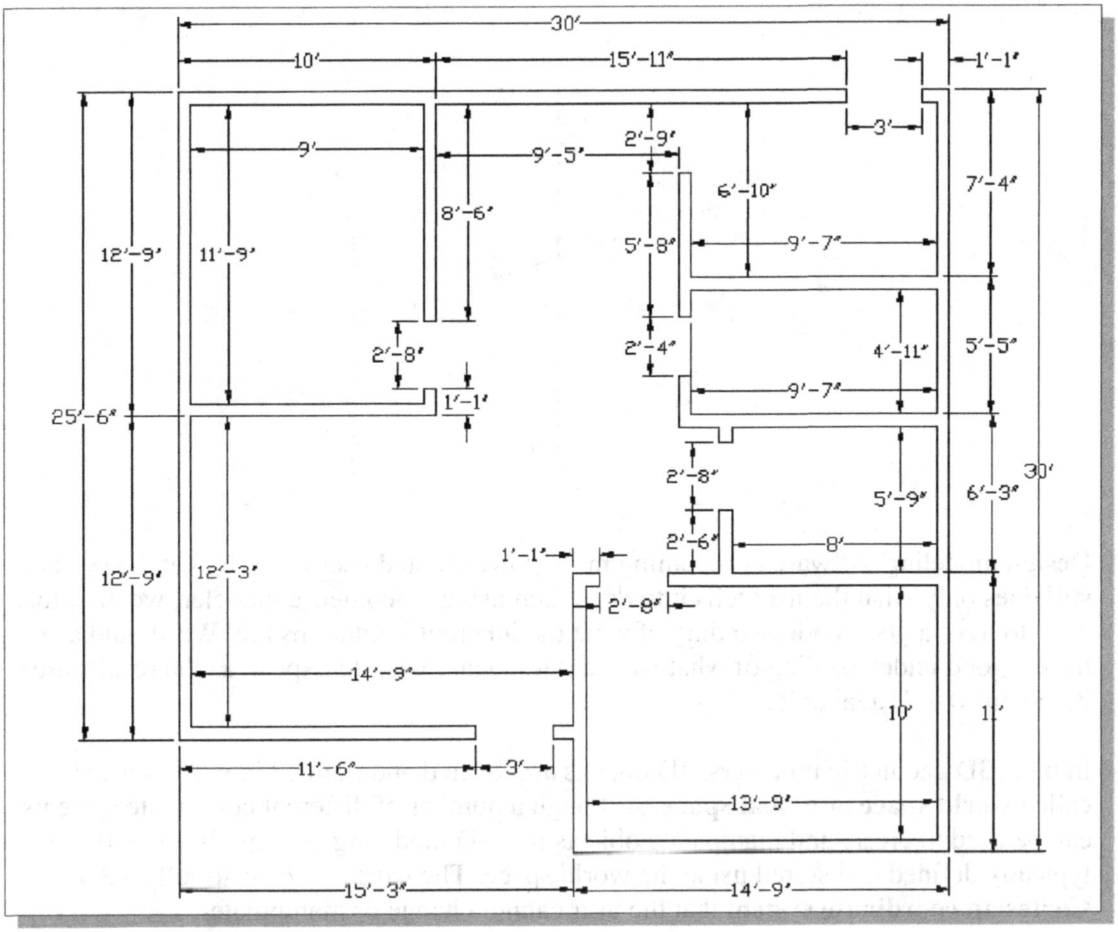

❖ Hints: Use the modify commands, such as **Trim/Extend** and **Erase** to assist the construction of the floor plan.

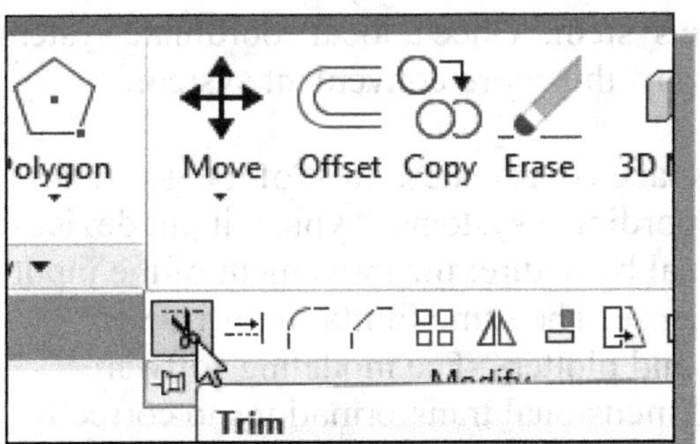

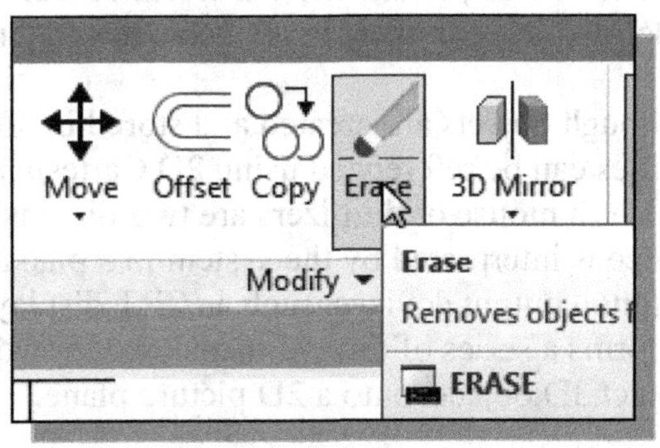

♦ Now is a good time to save the design. Select **[File] → [Save As]** in the pull-down menu and use ***FloorPlan*** as the *File name*.

User Coordinate System – It is an XY CRT, but an XYZ World

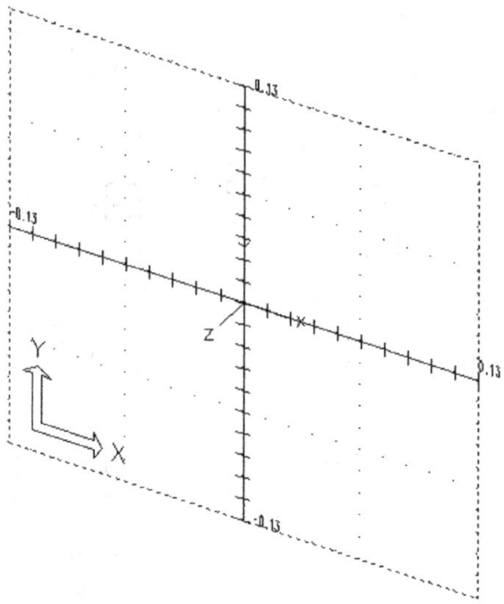

Design modeling software is becoming more powerful and user friendly, yet the system still does only what the user tells it to do. When using a geometric modeler, we therefore need to have a good understanding of what the inherent limitations are. We should also have a good understanding of what we want to do and what to expect, as the results are based on what is available.

In most 3D geometric modelers, 3D objects are located and defined in what is usually called **world space** or **global space**. Although a number of different coordinate systems can be used to create and manipulate objects in a 3D modeling system, the objects are typically defined and stored using the world space. The world space is usually a **3D Cartesian coordinate system** that the user cannot change or manipulate.

In most engineering designs, models can be very complex, and it would be tedious and confusing if only the world coordinate system were available. Practical 3D modeling systems allow the user to define **Local Coordinate Systems (LCS)** or **User Coordinate Systems (UCS)** relative to the world coordinate system. Once a local coordinate system is defined, we can then create geometry in terms of this more convenient system.

Although objects are created and stored in 3D space coordinates, most of the geometry entities can be referenced using 2D Cartesian coordinate systems. Typical input devices such as a mouse or digitizers are two-dimensional by nature; the movement of the input device is interpreted by the system in a planar sense. The same limitation is true of common output devices, such as CRT displays and plotters. The modeling software performs a series of three-dimensional to two-dimensional transformations to correctly project 3D objects onto a 2D picture plane.

AutoCAD's **User Coordinate System (UCS)** is a special construction tool that enables the planar nature of the 2D input devices to be directly mapped into the 3D coordinate system. The ***UCS*** is a local coordinate system that can be aligned to the world coordinate system, an existing face of a part, or a predefined plane. By default, the UCS is aligned to the XY plane of the world coordinate system.

Think of the UCS as the surface on which we can sketch the 2D profiles of designs. It is similar to a piece of paper, a whiteboard, or a chalkboard that can be attached to any planar surface. In the previous sections, we created the 2D design of a floor plan using the default settings where the UCS is aligned to the XY plane of the world coordinate system.

Viewing the 2D Design in 3D Space

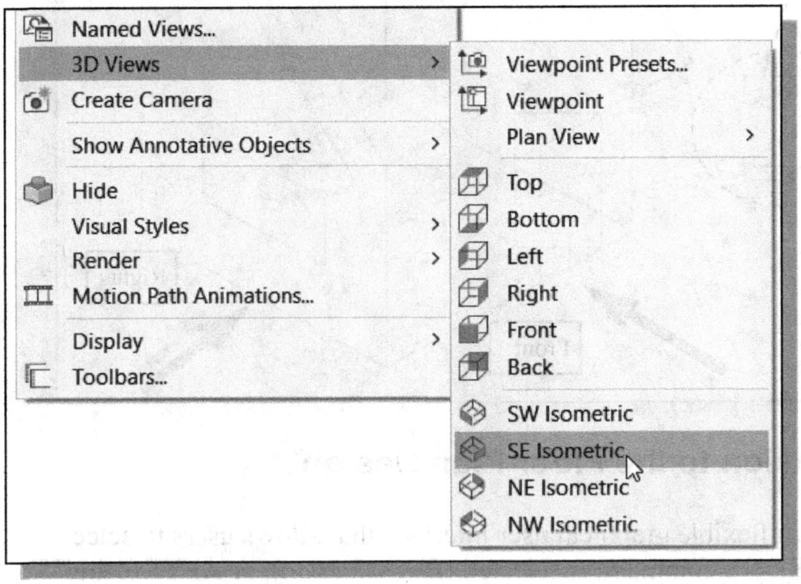

1. In the *Menu Bar* area, select:

   [View] → [3D Views] → [SE Isometric]

- AutoCAD provides a set of pre-defined views, which contain most of the standard 2D and 3D views as shown in the figure.

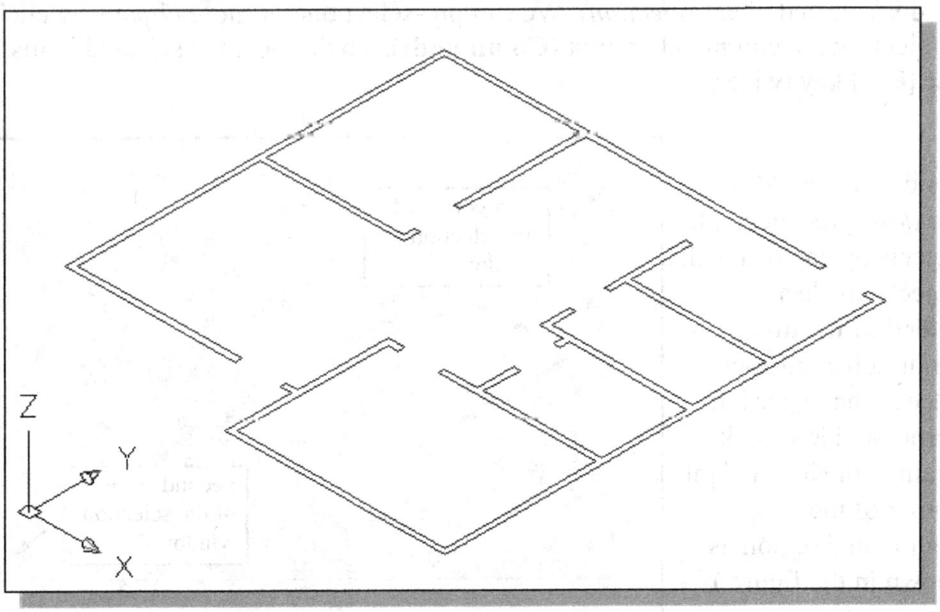

- The orientations of the preset 2D and 3D views are based on the world coordinate system as shown below. Note that the positive Y-axis direction is also identified as pointing toward **North** and the preset 3D views are oriented using the **North**, **East**, **South**, and **West** directions.

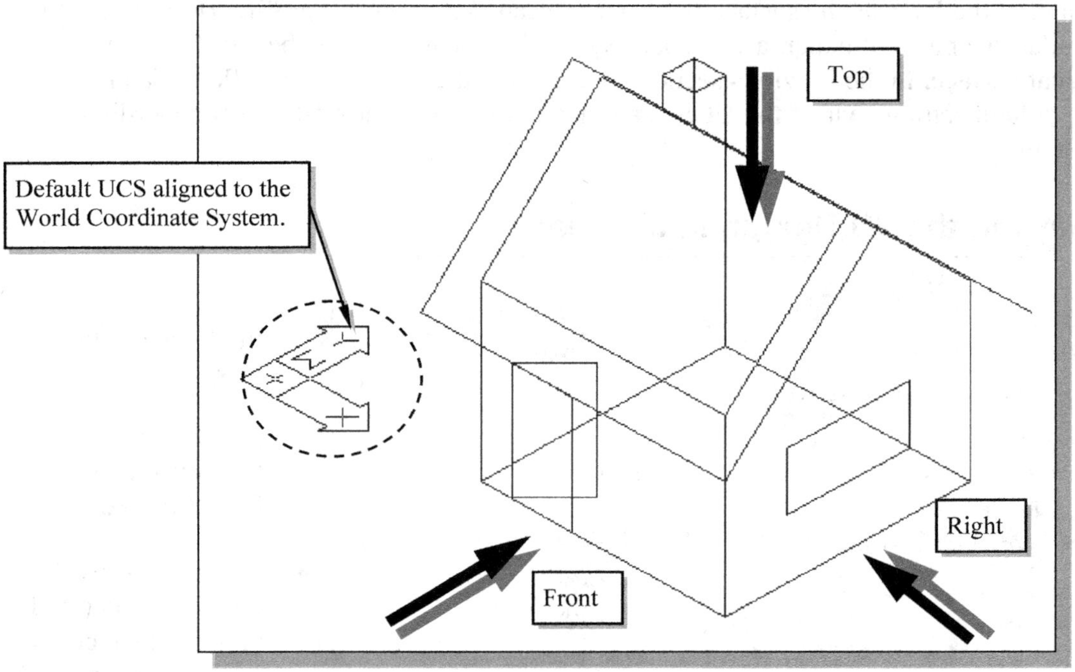

Add the 3rd Dimension to the Floor Plan Design

AutoCAD 2027 provides a flexible graphical user interface that allows users to select graphical entities **BEFORE** the command is selected (*Pre-selection*), or **AFTER** the command is selected (*Post-selection*). We can pre-select one or more objects by clicking on the objects at the command prompt (**Command:**). To deselect the selected items, press the **[Esc]** key twice.

1. Inside the *graphics window*, pre-select all objects by enclosing all objects inside a **selection window**. (Hint: left-mouse-click once at the upper left corner and left-click again at the lower right corner of the highlighted region as shown in the figure.)

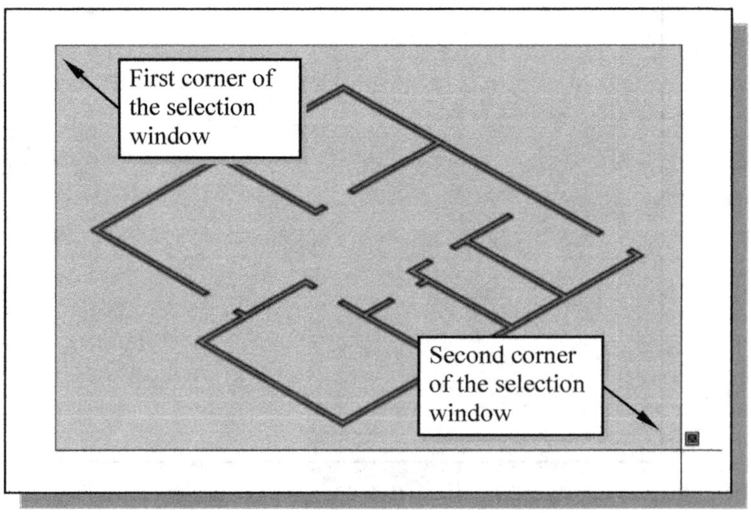

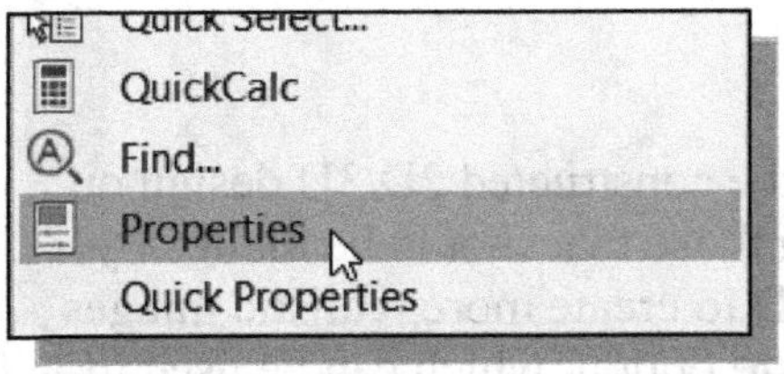

2. Inside the graphics window, **right-click** once to bring up the option list and select **Properties** as shown.

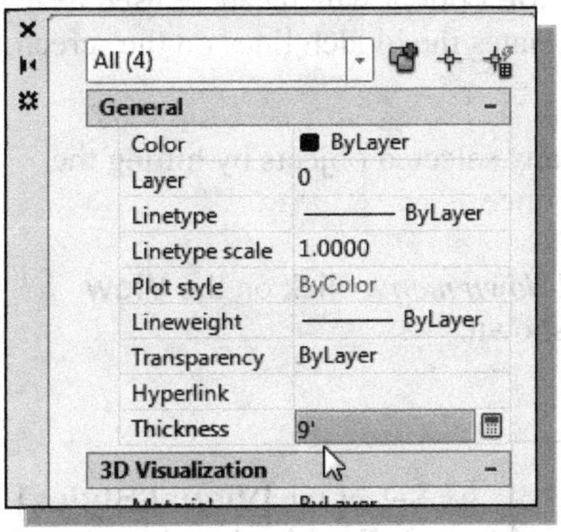

3. In the *Properties* dialog box, properties of the highlighted entities are displayed. Notice the current *Thickness* is set to 0″.

4. **Left-click** the *Thickness* box and enter a new value **9′ [ENTER]** as the new thickness value.

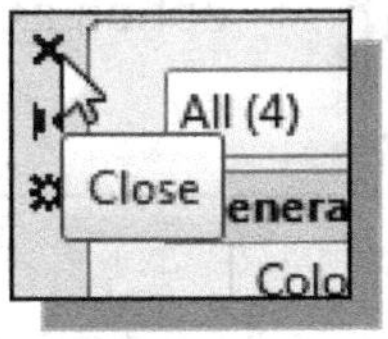

5. Click on the **[X]** button to exit the *Properties* dialog box.

In AutoCAD, the *thickness* of an object determines the distance that the object is extruded above or below its current Z-elevation. Positive thickness will extrude the objects upward (positive Z), negative thickness extrudes downward (negative Z), and zero thickness means no extrusion. The Z direction is determined by the orientation of the UCS at the time the object was created.

Changing the *thickness* of objects will change the appearance of certain geometric objects, such as circles, lines, polylines, arcs, 2D solids, and points. Note that the *Thickness* property is not available on certain geometric objects, such as *Splines* and *Multilines*. We can set the *thickness* of an object with the ***Thickness*** variable. AutoCAD applies the extrusion uniformly to an object. A single object cannot have different thickness for its various points.

Changing the thickness of objects simulates a simple Z extrusion of creating solid objects in AutoCAD. The main advantage of using the object thickness to create the Z-elevation instead of creating a true solid is that the operation is quick and easy. In AutoCAD, objects with thickness can be hidden, shaded, and rendered as if they are three-dimensional solids. Once an object's thickness is set, we can visualize the results in any view other than the plan view.

This method is also known as the **2½D solid modeling approach**. This modeling technique was first invented in the 1970s and was adopted by several of the first-generation solid-modeling packages. This approach requires no additional 3D construction tools and only minimum computing power is needed. Note that this modeling approach does not create true 3D solids and objects can only be extruded in one direction. This modeling approach is considered to be less flexible and its application is somewhat limited.

View the Design Using the Hide Option

By default, AutoCAD produces a wireframe image of the constructed 2D/3D design on the screen. All geometric entities are present, including those that should be hidden by other objects. Several options are available in AutoCAD to create more realistic images of 3D designs. In this section, we will introduce the **Hide** option, which can be used to adjust the display of the design; the **Hide** option eliminates the hidden lines on the screen.

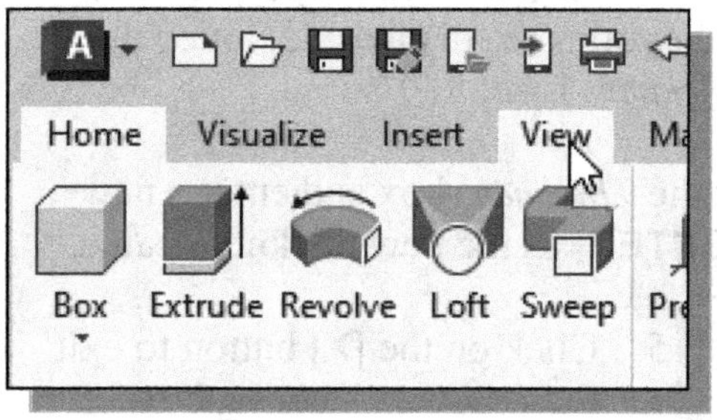

1. De-select any selected objects by hitting the **[Esc]** key once.

2. In the *pull-down menu*, click on the **View** option as shown.

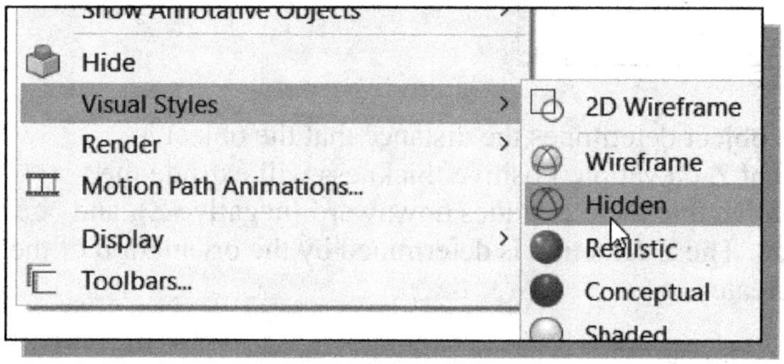

3. Select the **[Visual Styles] → [Hidden]** option, the 3rd option in the list, as shown.

4. To redisplay the wireframe image, select the 1st option: **[2D WireFrame]**.

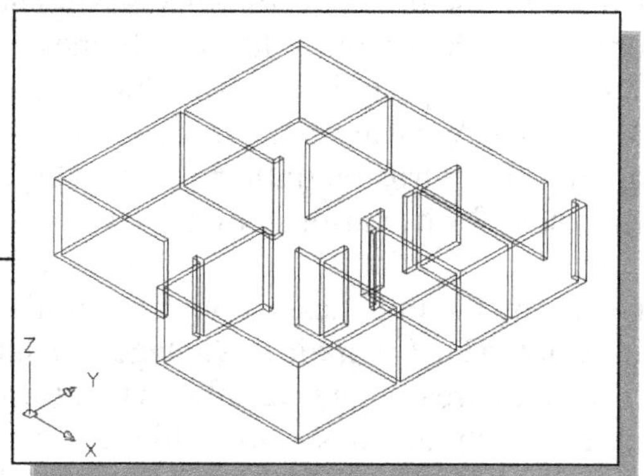

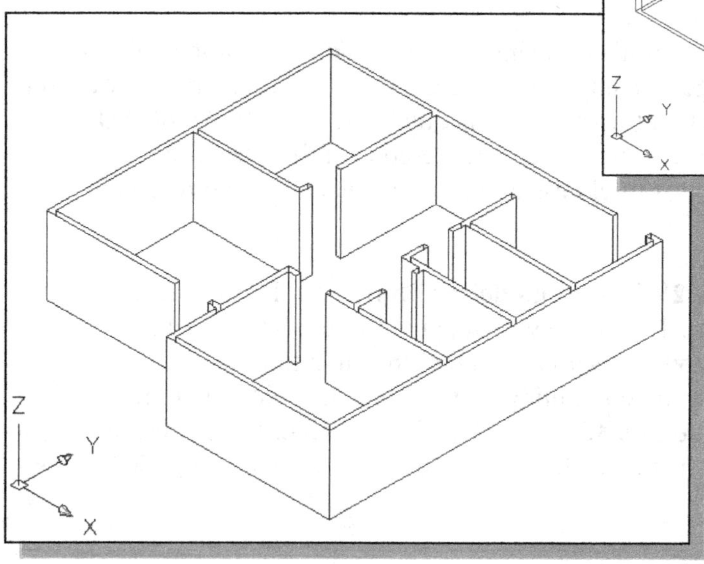

Add New Layers

1. In the *Menu Bar*, select **[Tools] → [Toolbars] → [AutoCAD] → [Layers]**.

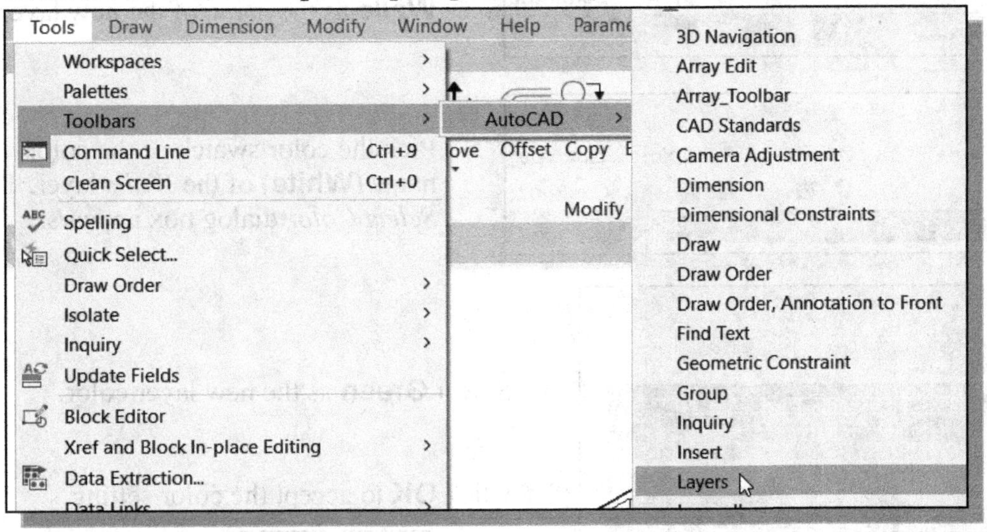

❖ The *Layer Properties Manager* dialog box appears. AutoCAD creates a default layer, *Layer 0*, which we cannot rename or delete. *Layer 0* has special properties used by the system.

2. Pick **Layers Properties Manager** in the *Layers* toolbar.

❖ In AutoCAD, we always construct entities on a layer. It may be the default layer or a layer that we create. Each layer has associated properties such as the visibility setting, color, linetype, lineweight, and plot style.

3. Click on the **New Layer** button. Notice a layer is automatically added to the list of layers.

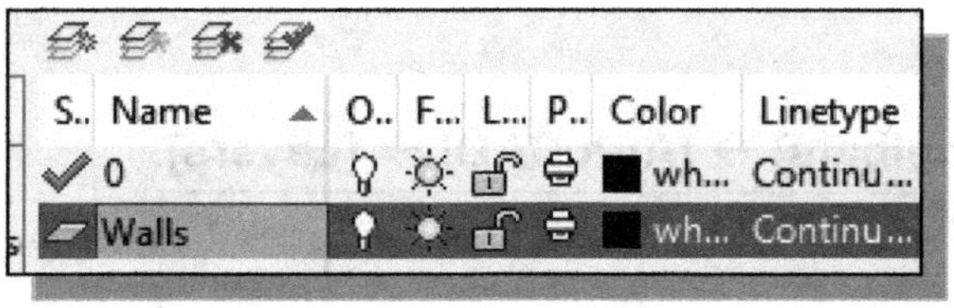

4. AutoCAD will assign a generic name to the new layer (*Layer1*). Enter **Walls** as the name of the new layer.

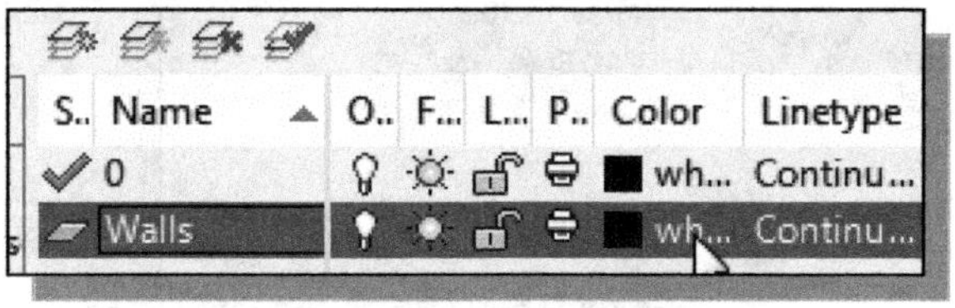

5. Pick the color swatch or the color name (**White**) of the *Walls* layer. The *Select Color* dialog box appears.

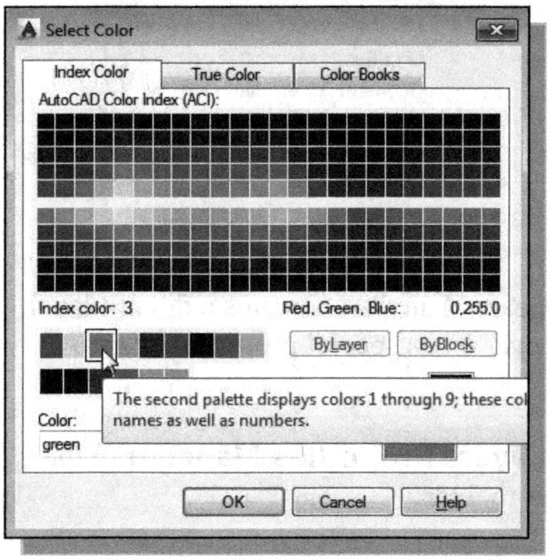

6. Select **Green** as the new layer color.

7. Click **OK** to accept the color setting.

8. On your own, create another layer (layer name: ***Roof***) and change the layer color to **Blue**.

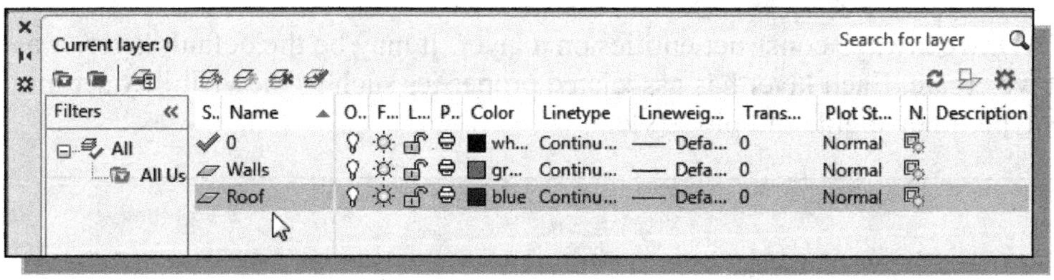

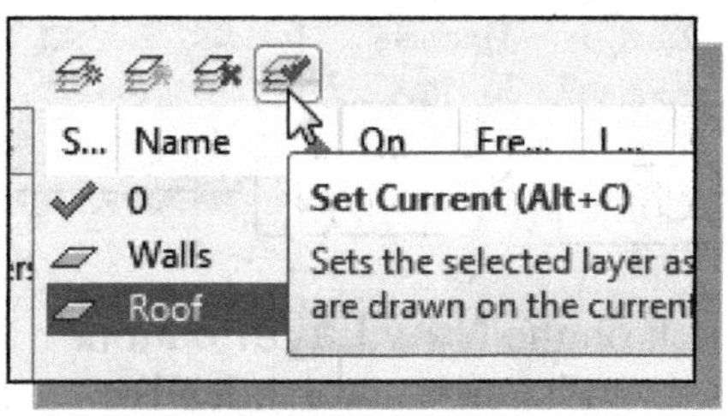

9. Click on the **Set Current** button and make **Roof** the *Current Layer*. There can only be one *Current Layer*, and new entities are automatically placed on the layer that is set to be the *Current Layer*.

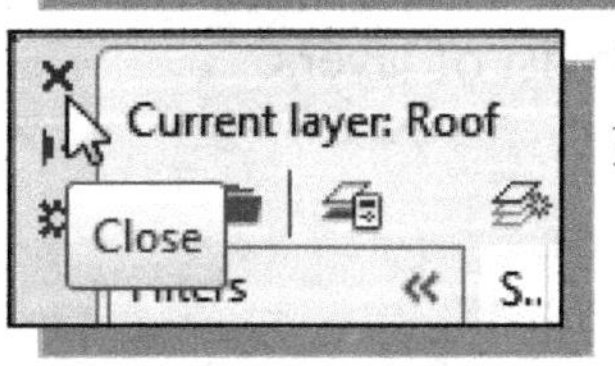

10. Click on the **Close** button to accept the settings.

Move Entities to a Different Layer

1. Inside the *graphics window*, pre-select **all objects** by enclosing all objects inside a **selection window.**

2. On the *Object Properties* toolbar, choose the ***Layer Control*** box with the left-mouse-button.

❖ Notice the layer name displayed in the *Layer Control* box is the selected object's assigned layer and layer properties.

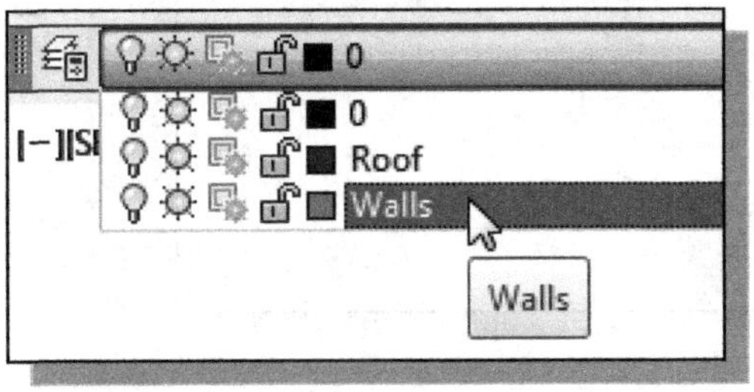

3. In the *Layer Control* box, click on the ***Walls*** layer name. The selected objects are now moved to the *Walls* layer.

4. Press the [**Esc**] key to deselect the pre-selected objects.

5. On your own, confirm the ***Roof*** layer is set as the ***Current Layer***.

Reposition the UCS

AutoCAD's **User Coordinate System (UCS)** is a special construction tool that enables the planar nature of the 2D input devices to be directly mapped into the 3D coordinate system. The **UCS** is a local coordinate system that can be repositioned and/or reoriented to an existing face of a part or a predefined plane. By default, the UCS is aligned to the XY plane of the world coordinate system. Several options are available to reposition and reorient the UCS in 3D space.

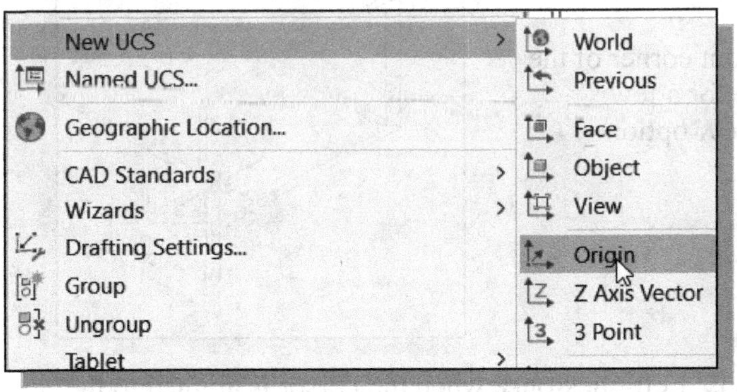

1. In the *Menu Bar* area, select:

   [Tools] → [New UCS] → [Origin]

2. We will use the *Object Snap* and *Object Tracking* options to aid the repositioning of the UCS.

3. In the *Status Bar* area, reset the option buttons so that the *Polar Tracking, Object Snap, Object Snap Tracking* options are switched ***ON***.

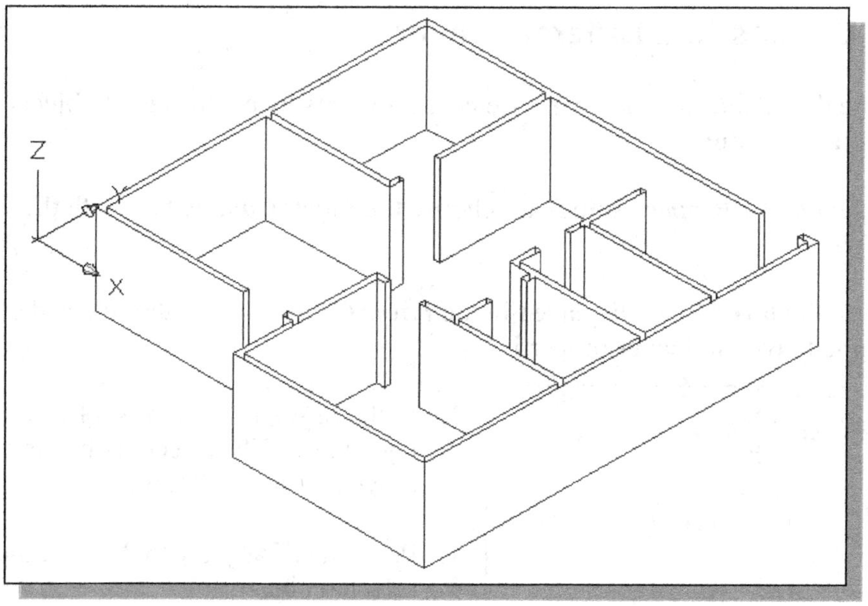

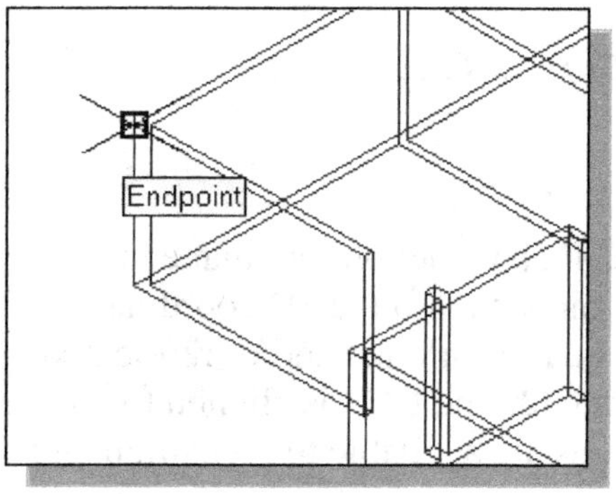

- We will reposition the UCS at the intersection of the left wall and the front wall; the intersection can be found by using the AutoCAD object tracking options.

4. Move the cursor on the top left corner of the external wall as shown; pause for a few seconds to activate the *OTRACK* option.

5. Move the cursor on the top front corner of the external wall as shown; pause for a few seconds to activate the *OTRACK* option.

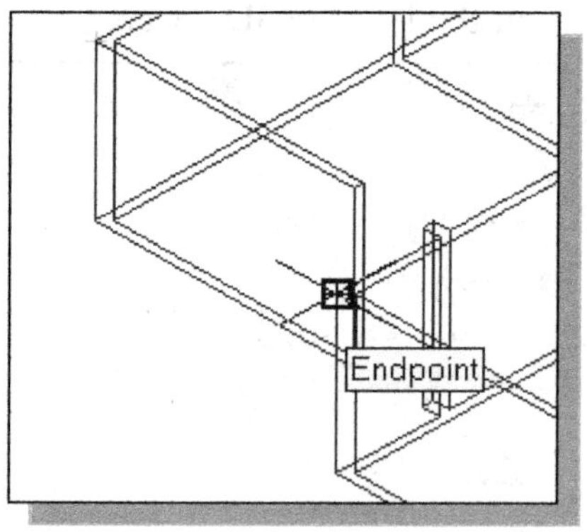

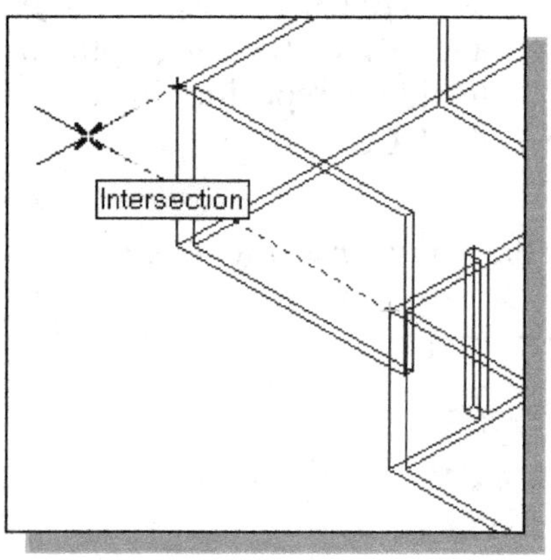

6. Left-click once when the cursor is aligned to the intersection of the left wall and the front wall as shown.

- The UCS is repositioned to the new location as shown. This location is the new origin for any geometric constructions.

Create the Roof

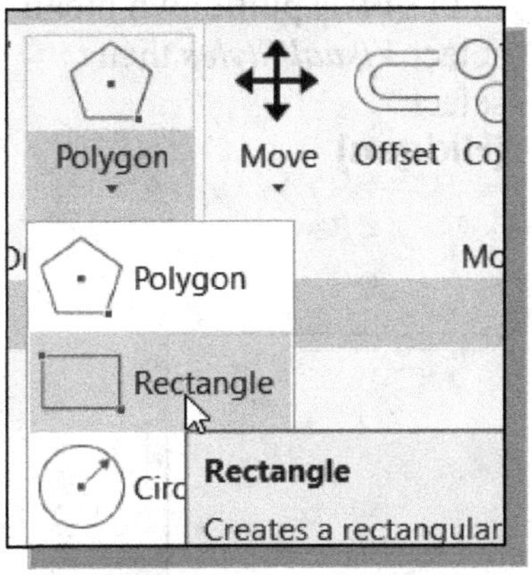

1. Select the **Rectangle** command icon in the *Draw* toolbar as shown.

2. In the command prompt area, the message "*Specify first corner point or [Chamfer/ Elevation/Fillet/ Thickness/Width]:*" is displayed. Move the cursor inside the graphics window and **right-click** to display the **option menu.**

- The thickness of certain geometry entities can be set as they are being created.

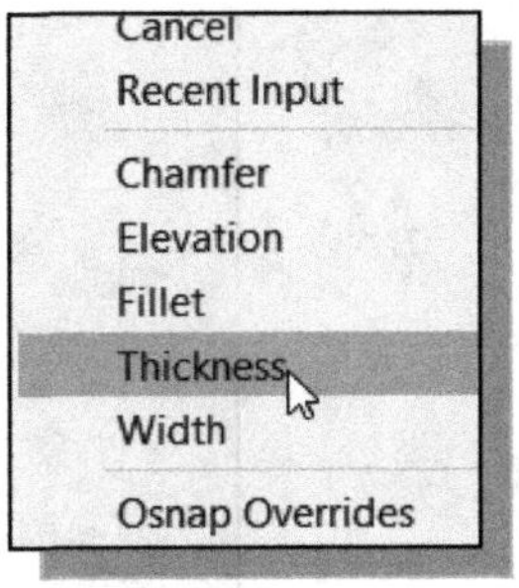

3. In the *option menu*, select **Thickness** by clicking once with the left-mouse-button.

4. In the command prompt area, the message "*Specify thickness for rectangles <0'-0">:*" is displayed. Enter **10" [ENTER]**.

5. At the command prompt, enter **-2',-2' [ENTER]**.

6. In the command prompt area, the message "*Specify other corner point or [Dimensions]:*" is displayed. Enter **@34',34' [ENTER]**.

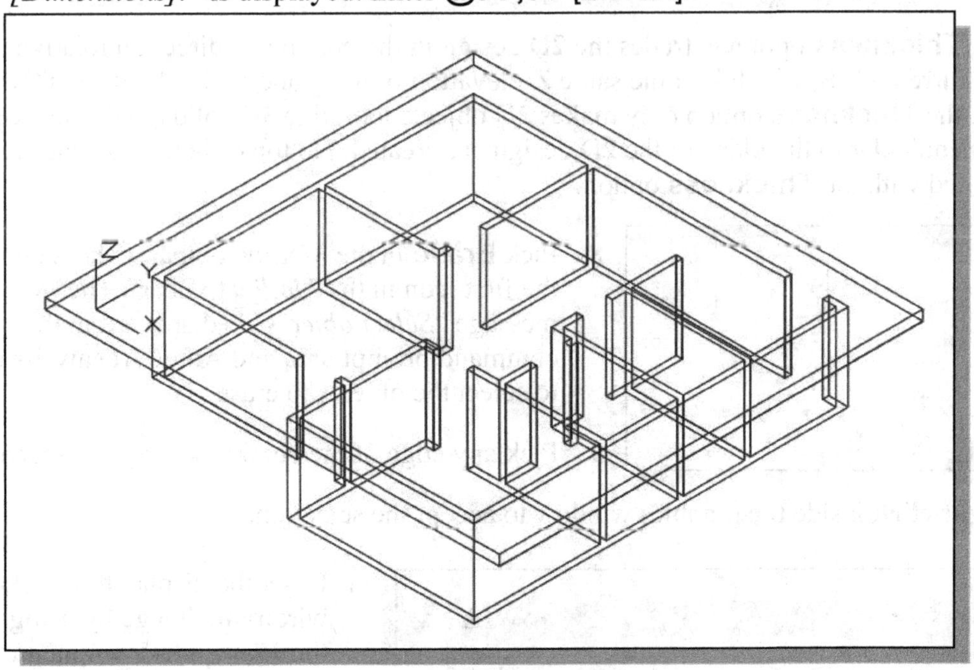

- Note that the coordinates entered are measured relative to the new UCS origin.

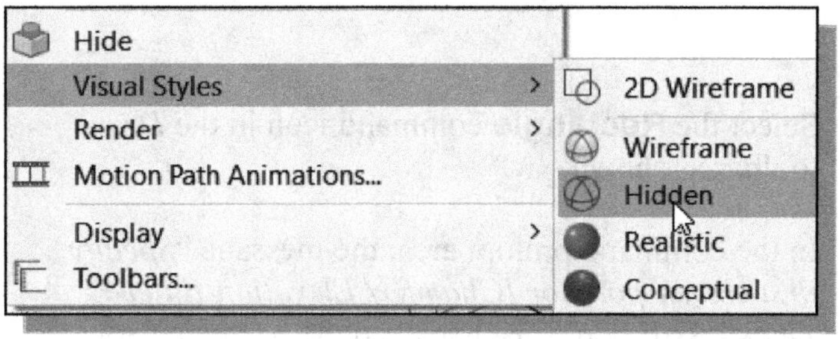

7. In the *View* pull-down menu, select *Visual Styles* then select **[Hidden]**

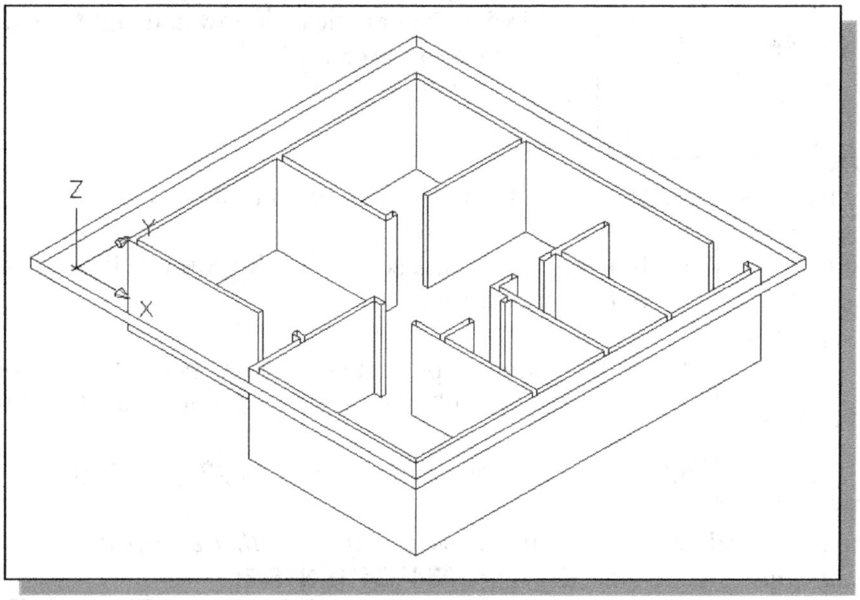

- The **Thickness** option extrudes the 2D design in the positive Z-direction relative to the current UCS, which is at the same Z-elevation of the plane of the 2D design. Note that the **Thickness** option only makes 2D objects look like 3D solids; only surfaces perpendicular to the plane of the 2D design are created. No top or bottom surfaces are created with the **Thickness** option.

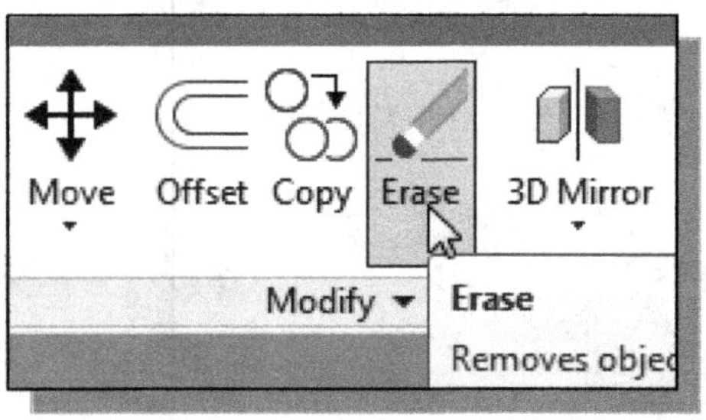

8. Pick **Erase** in the *Modify* toolbar. (The icon is the first icon in the *Modify* toolbar.) The message "*Select objects*" is displayed in the command prompt area and AutoCAD awaits us to select the objects to erase.

9. Pick any edge of the **rectangle** we just created.

10. **Right-click** inside the graphics window to accept the selection.

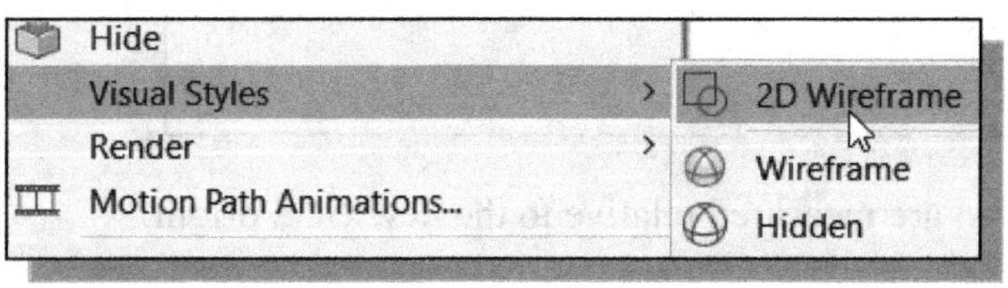

11. Reset the display to the 2D wireframe image by using the *View* pull-down menu: **[Visual Styles] → [2D wireframe]**

Rotating the UCS

AutoCAD's **User Coordinate System (UCS)** can be repositioned and reoriented in 3D space. All of the UCS options are organized and can be found in the *Standard* toolbar.

1. In the *Menu Bar* select **[Tools] → [Toolbars] → [AutoCAD]**.

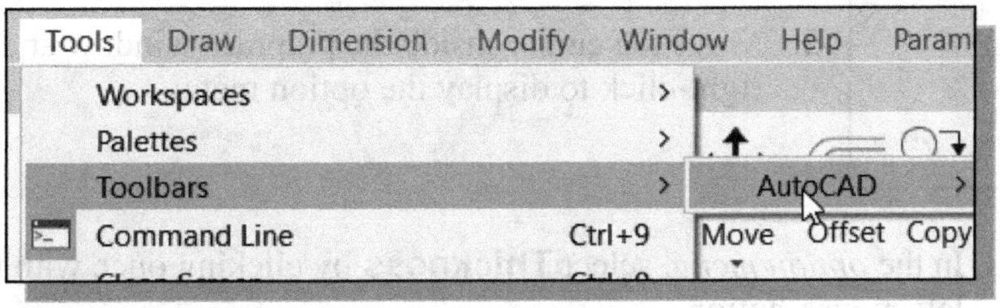

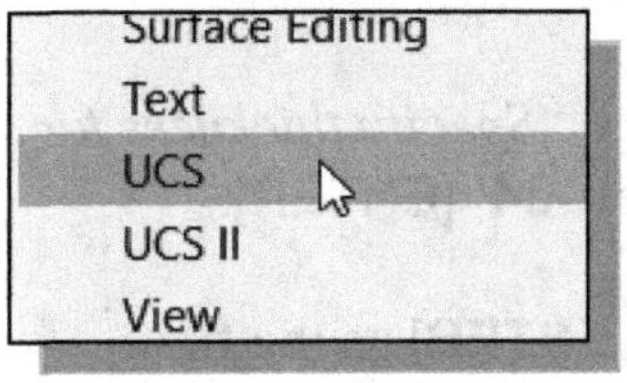

2. Select **UCS**, with the left-mouse-button, to display the *UCS* toolbar on the screen to assist the construction of the *Roof*.

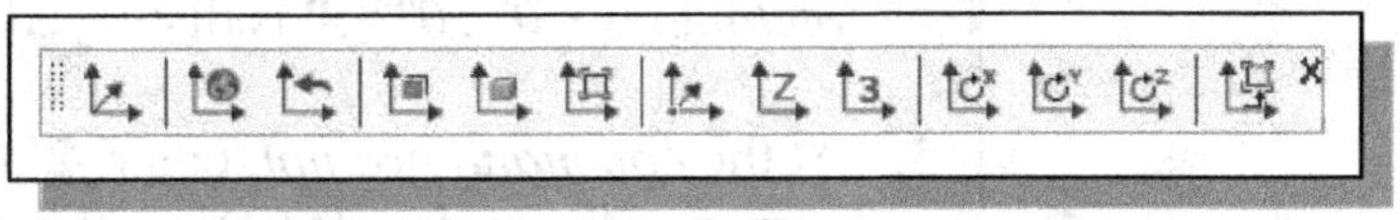

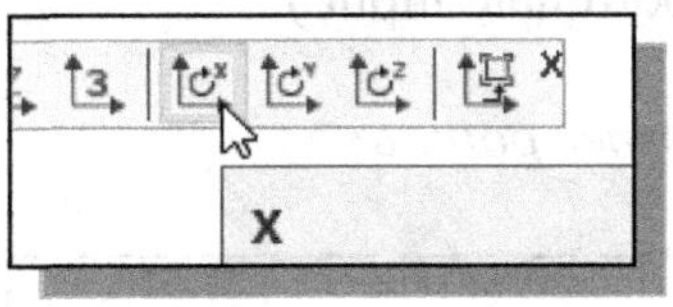

3. Select the **X Axis Rotate** option in the *UCS* toolbar as shown.

4. In the command prompt area, the message "*Specify rotation angle about X axis<90>:*" is displayed. Enter **90 [ENTER]**.

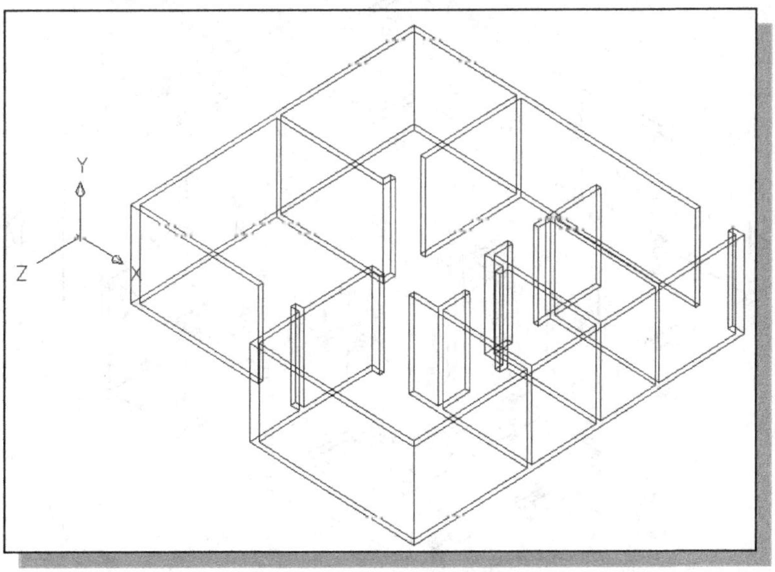

- The UCS rotation is done using the standard engineering convention, where positive values are treated as rotating counterclockwise. Also note that the *SNAP*, *GRID*, and *ORTHO* options all rotate in line with the UCS.

Sketching on the Rotated UCS

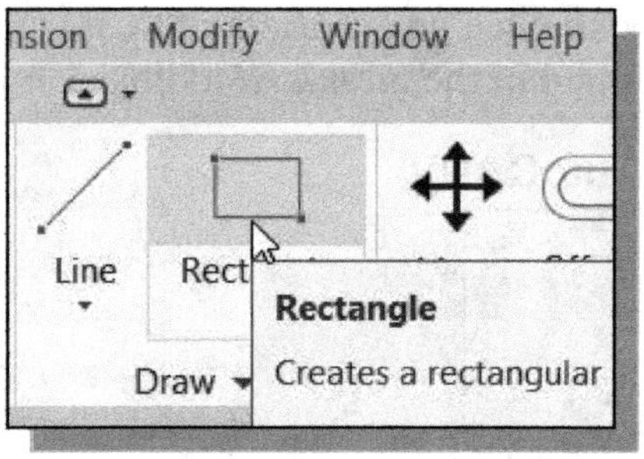

1. Select the **Rectangle** command icon in the *Draw* toolbar as shown.

2. Move the cursor inside the graphics window and right-click to display the option menu.

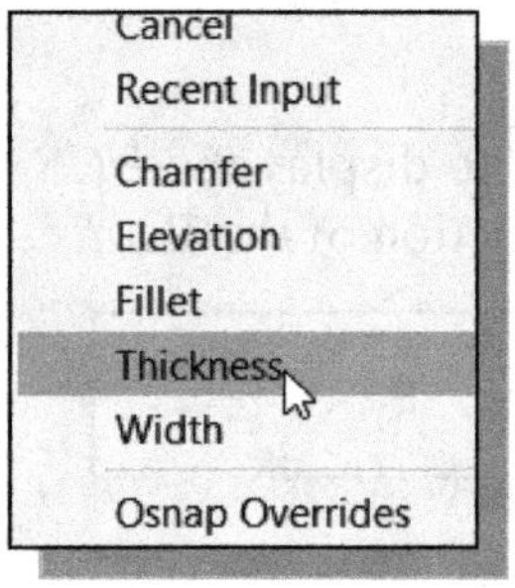

3. In the *option menu*, select **Thickness** by clicking once with the left-mouse-button.

4. In the *command prompt* area, the message "*Specify thickness for rectangles <0'-10">:*" is displayed. Enter **-34' [ENTER]**.

5. At the *command prompt*, enter **-2',0',2' [ENTER]** as the first corner of the rectangle. (Note the z-coordinate input.)

6. In the *command prompt* area, the message "*Specify other corner point or [Dimensions]:*" is displayed. Enter **@36',10" [ENTER]**.

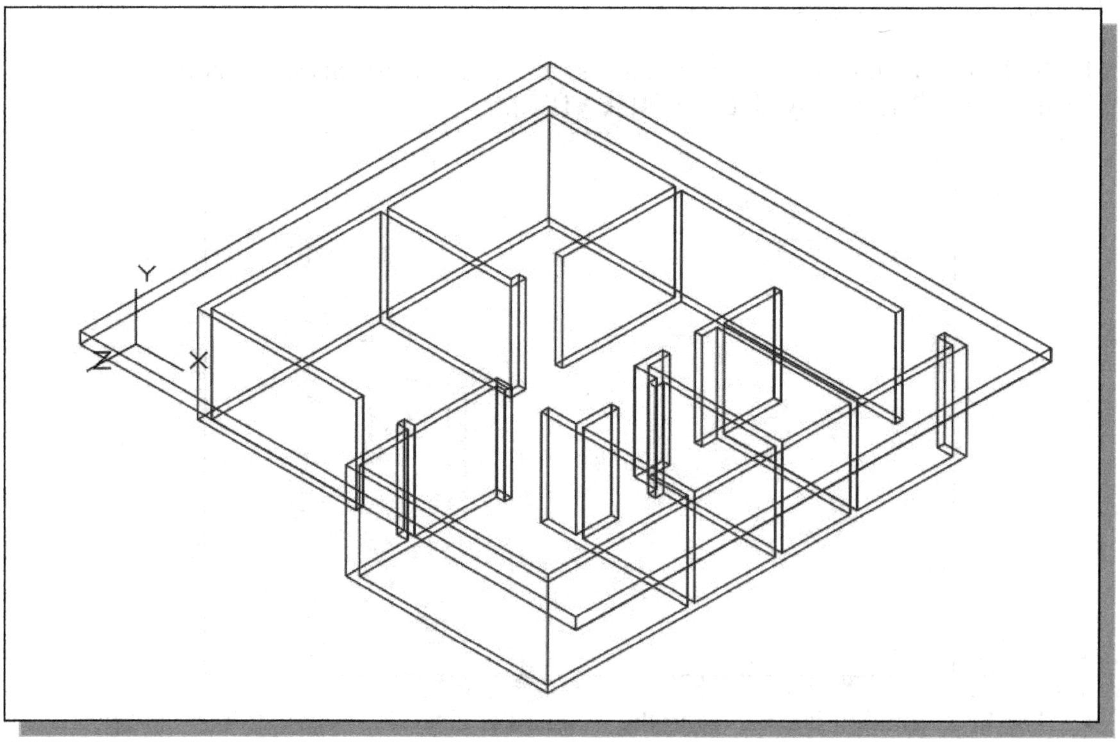

- The negative thickness extrudes the rectangle in the negative Z-direction of the current UCS.

View the Design Using the Hidden Option

Several options are available in AutoCAD to create more realistic images of 3D designs. The **Visual Styles - Hidden** option can also be used to eliminate the hidden lines on the screen. The **Visual Styles - Hidden** option performs a more complicated calculation of the display and usually produces a better image than the **Hide** option.

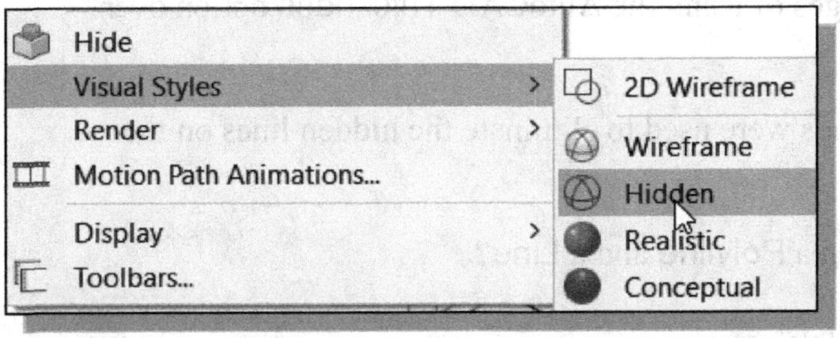

1. In the *View* toolbar panel, select:

   [Visual Styles] → [Hidden]

2. To display the 2D wireframe image, select:
   [Visual Styles] → [2D Wireframe]

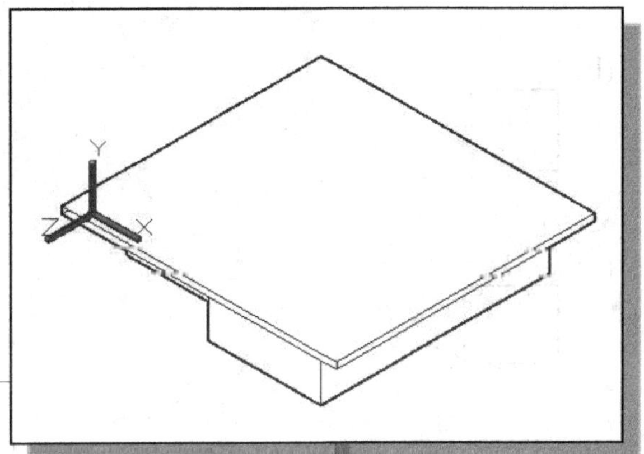

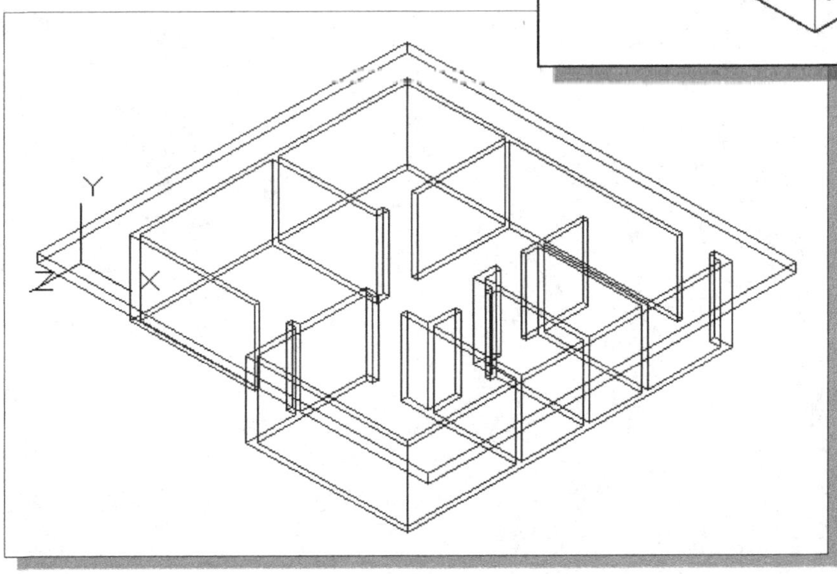

Review Questions:

1. What is the difference between *WCS* and *UCS*?

2. List and describe two available options to manipulate the UCS.

3. Describe some of the advantages of using the AutoCAD Thickness option over creating 2D or 3D models.

4. In the tutorial, which commands were used to eliminate the hidden lines on the screen?

5. What is the difference between a Polyline and a Line?

6. Identify the following commands:

(a)

(b)

(c)

(d)

Exercises:

1. Dimensions are in inches. Thickness: Base 0.25

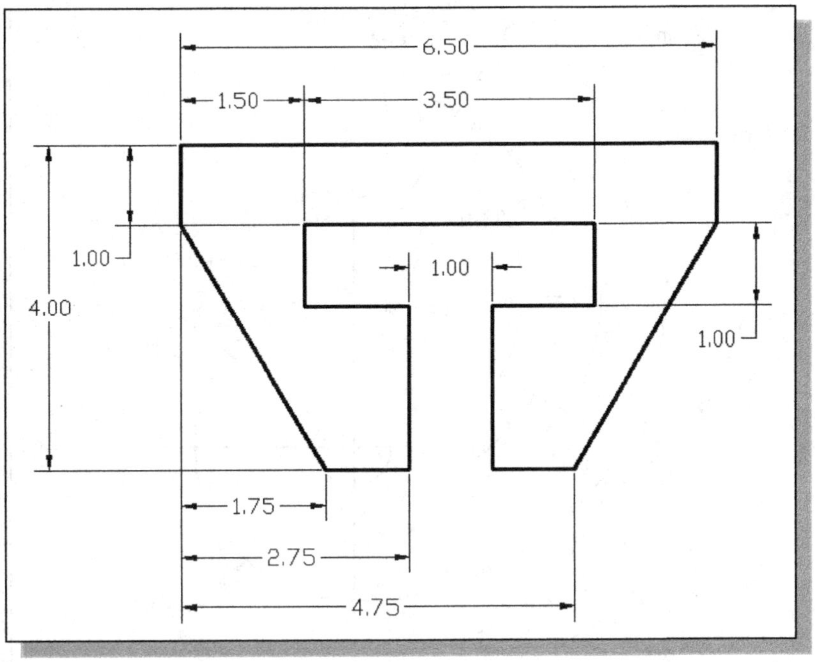

2. Wall thickness: 5 inches; height: 10 feet

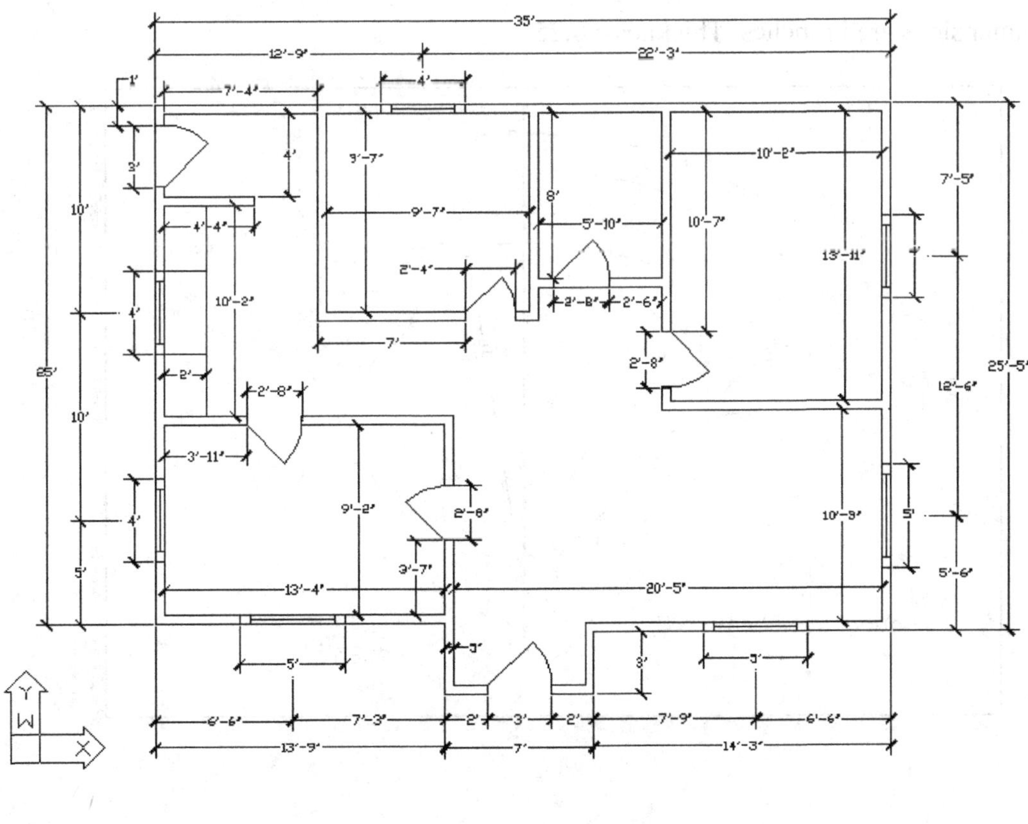

3. Dimensions are in inches. Thickness: 0.25

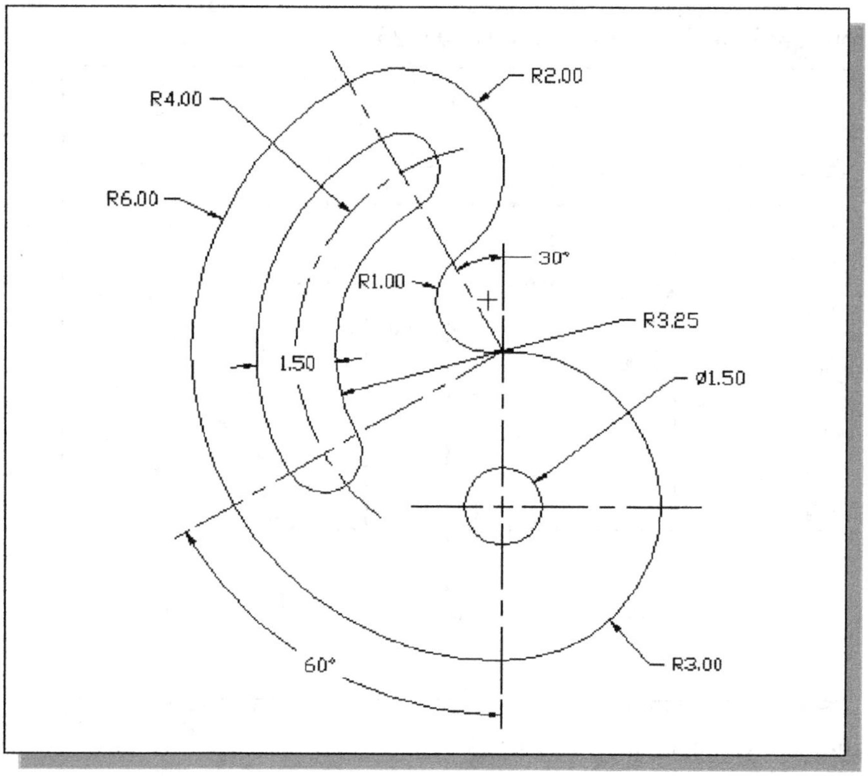

4. Dimensions are in inches. Thickness: 0.25

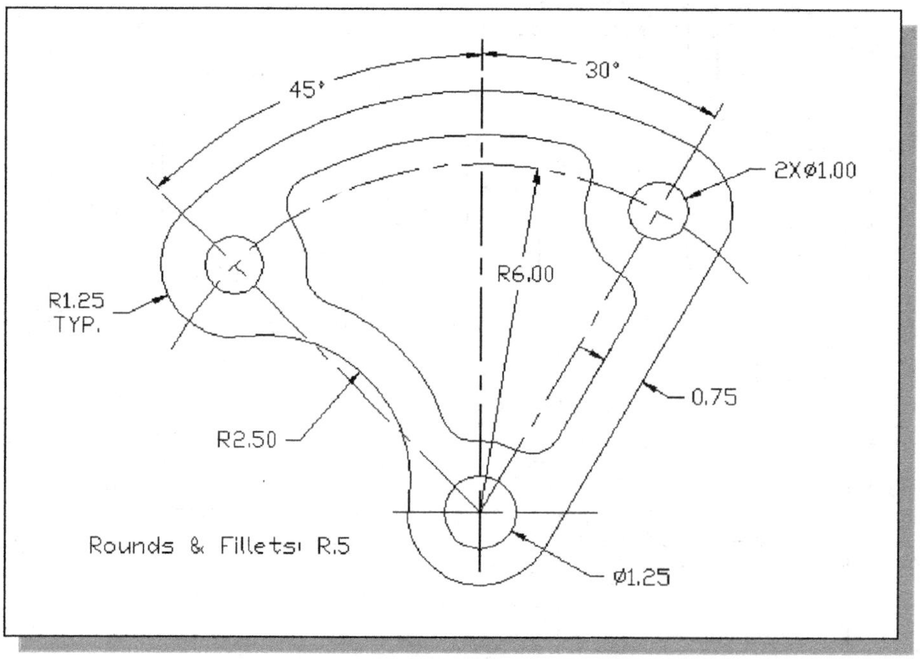

Chapter 2
3D Wireframe Modeling

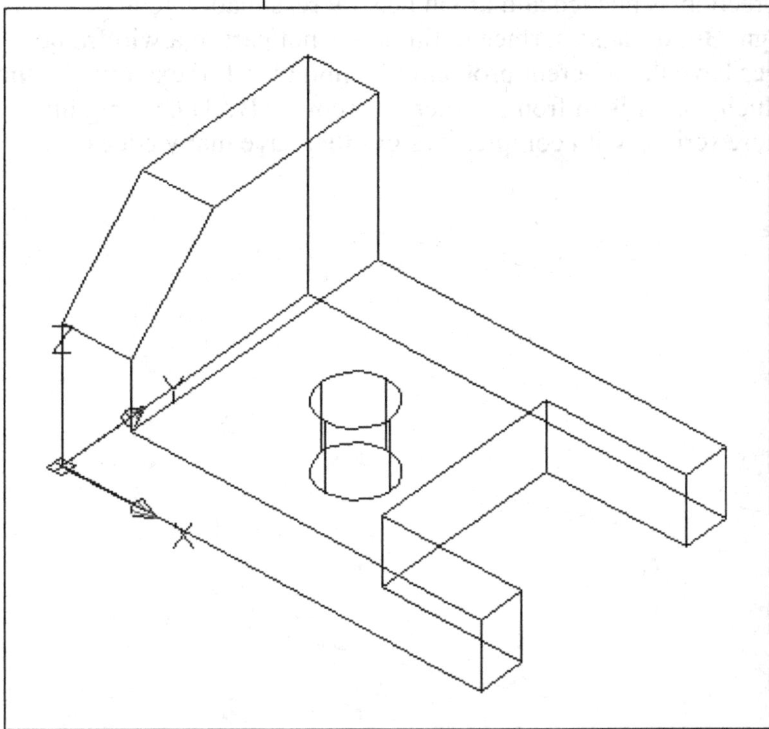

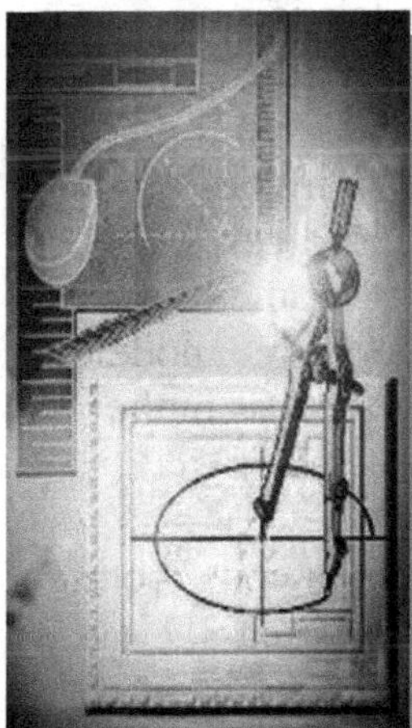

Learning Objectives

- Use the Setup Wizard
- Create Wireframe Models
- Apply the Box Method in Creating Models
- Construct with the Copy Command
- Understand the Available 3D Coordinates Input Options
- Use the View Toolbar
- Set up and Use the Trim options

Introduction

The first true 3D computer model created on CAD systems in the late 1970s was the 3D wireframe model. Computer generated 3D wireframe models contain information about the locations of all the corners and edges in space coordinates. The 3D wireframe models can be viewed from any direction as needed and are in general reasonably good representations of 3D design. But because surface definition is not part of a wireframe model, all wireframe images have the inherent problem of ambiguity. For example, in the figure displayed below, which corner is in front, corner A or corner B? The ambiguity problem becomes much more serious with complex designs that have many edges and corners.

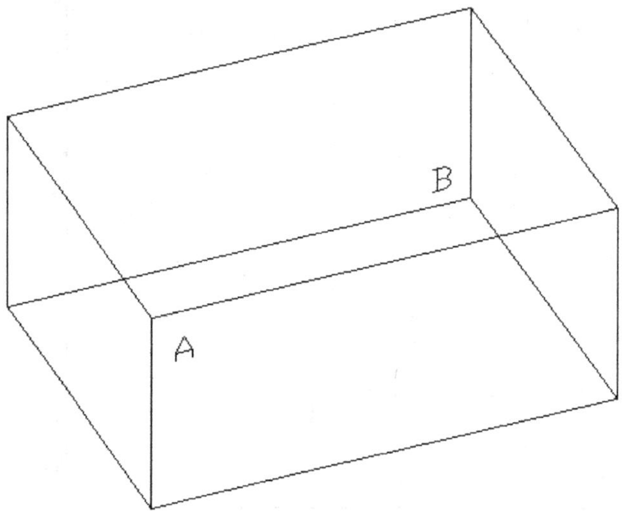

Wireframe Ambiguity: Which corner is in front, A or B?

The main advantage of using a 3D wireframe modeler to create 3D models is its simplicity. The computer hardware requirements for wireframe modelers are typically much lower than the requirements for surface and solid modelers. A 3D wireframe model, also known as a stick-figure model or a skeleton model, contains only information about the locations of all the corners and edges of the design in space coordinates. You should also realize that, in some cases, it could be quite difficult to locate some of the corner locations while creating a 3D wireframe model. Note that 3D wireframe modelers are usually used in conjunction with surfacing modelers, which we will discuss in the later chapters of this text, to eliminate the problem of ambiguity.

With most CAD systems, creating 3D wireframe models usually starts with constructing 2D entities in 3D space. Two of the most commonly used methods for creating 3D wireframe models are the **Box method** and the **2D Extrusion method**. As the name implies, the *Box method* involves the creation of a 3D box with the edges constructed from the overall height, width and depth dimensions of the design. The 3D wireframe model is typically completed by locating and connecting corners within the box.

The *2D Extrusion method* involves making copies of 2D geometries in specific directions. This method is similar to the 2½D extrusion approach illustrated in the previous chapter (Chapter 1) with several differences. First of all, we do not really extrude the wireframe entities; instead, we simply make copies of wireframe entities in the desired directions. Secondly, constructed wireframe entities have true 3D space coordinates, while the *thickness* approach creates entities with no true 3D coordinates. Finally, no surfaces are created in the 3D wireframe models.

In this chapter, we will illustrate the general procedure to construct a 3D wireframe model using both the box method and the 2D extrusion method. To illustrate the AutoCAD 3D construction environment, we will create the wireframe model using only the default UCS system, which is aligned to the world coordinate system. Repositioning and/or reorienting the User Coordinate System can be useful in creating 3D models. However, it is also feasible to create 3D models referencing only a single coordinate system. One important note about creating wireframe models is that the construction techniques mostly concentrate on locating the space coordinates of the individual corners of the design. The ability to visualize designs in the form of 3D wireframe models is extremely helpful to designers and CAD operators. It is hoped that the experience of thinking and working on 3D wireframe models, as outlined in this chapter, will enhance one's 3D visualization ability.

The Locator Design

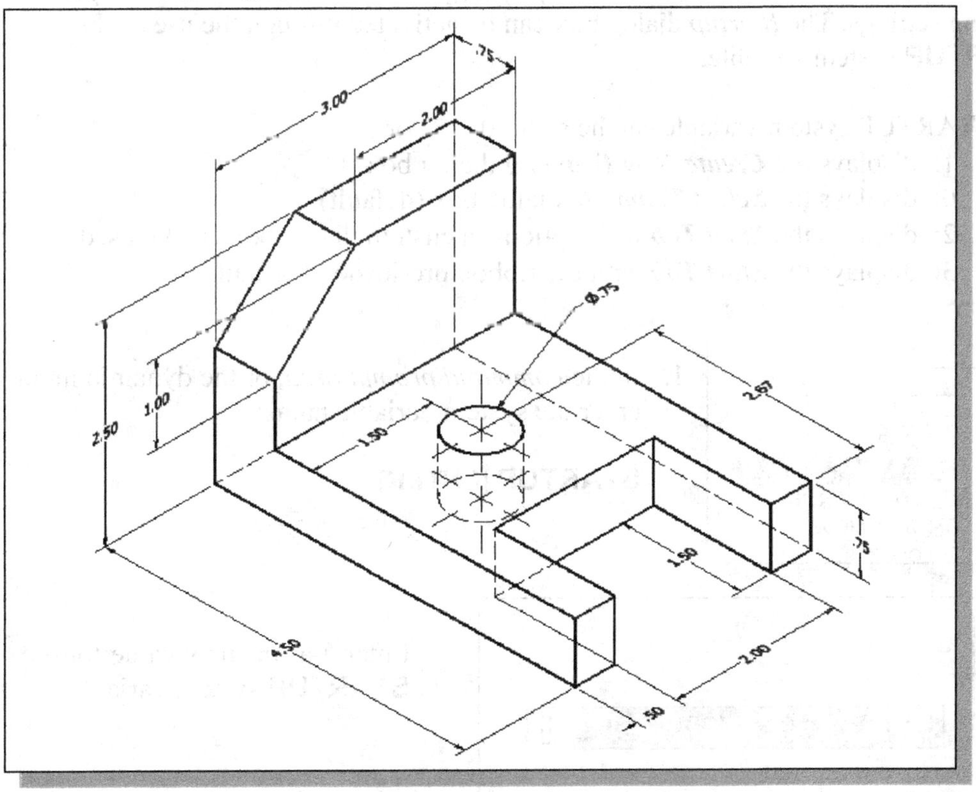

Starting Up AutoCAD 2027

1. Start **AutoCAD 2027** by selecting the *Autodesk* folder in the **Start** menu as shown. Once the program is loaded into the memory, click **Start Drawing** to start a new drawing.

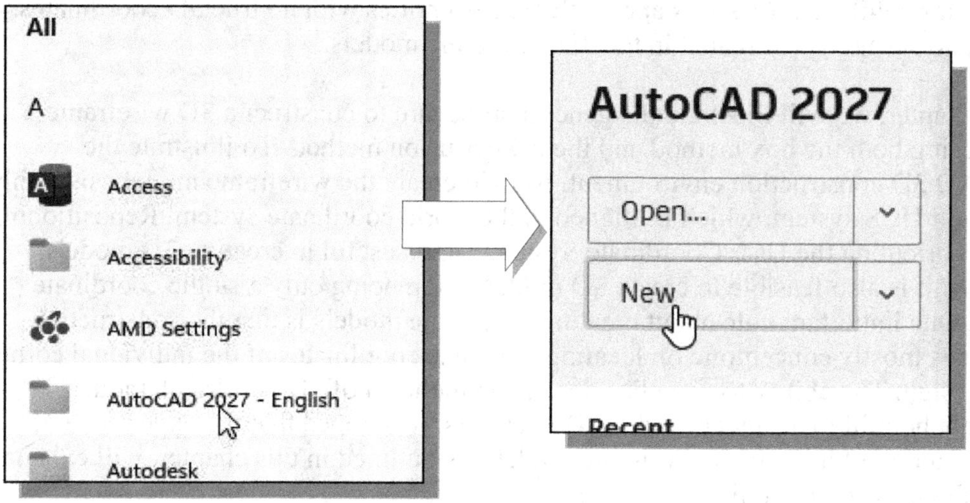

Activate the Startup Option

In **AutoCAD 2027**, we can use the *Startup* dialog box to establish different types of drawing settings. The *Startup* dialog box can be activated through the use of the **STARTUP** system variable.

The STARTUP system variable can be set to 0, 1, 2 or 3:

- 1: displays the ***Create New Drawing*** dialog box.
- 0: displays the ***Select Template*** dialog box (default).
- 2: displays the ***Start Tab*** with options; a custom dialog box can be used.
- 3: displays the ***Start Tab*** with the ribbon pre-loaded (default).

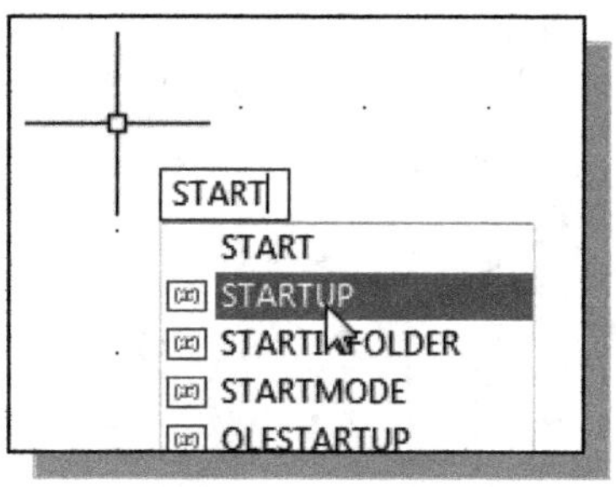

1. In the *command prompt area*, or the dynamic input box, enter the system variable name:

   STARTUP [ENTER]

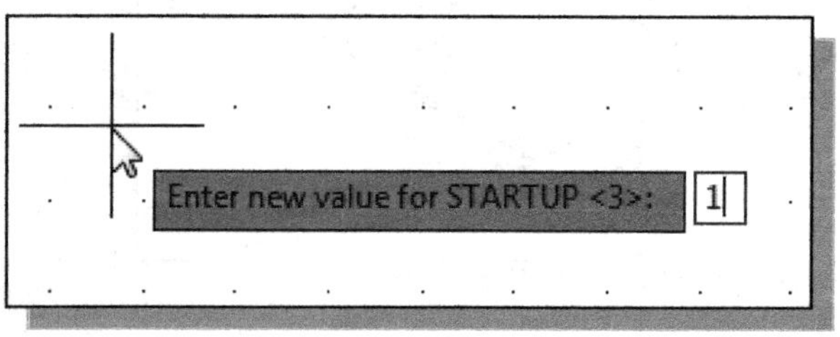

2. Enter **1** as the new value for the **STARTUP** system variable.

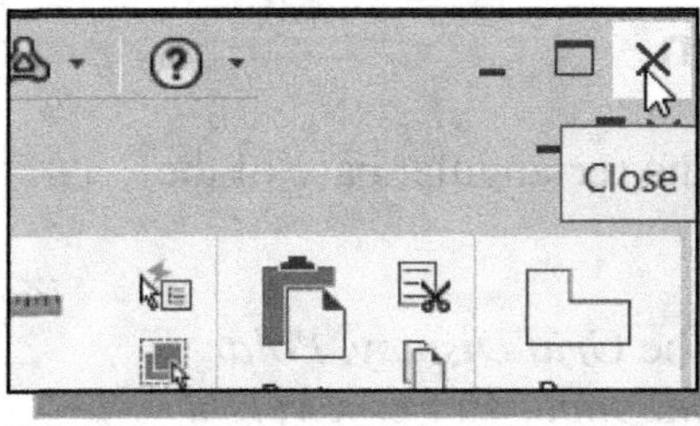

3. To show the effect of the *Startup* option, **exit** AutoCAD by clicking on the **Close** icon as shown.

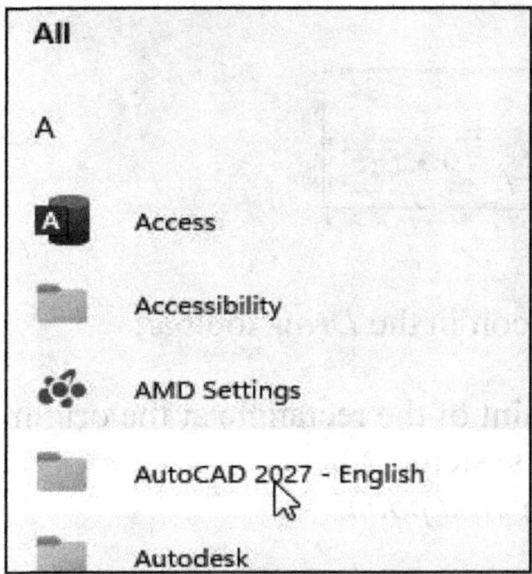

4. Restart AutoCAD by selecting the **AutoCAD 2027** option through the *Start* menu.

5. The *Startup* dialog box appears on the screen with different options to assist the creation of drawings. Move the cursor on top of the four icons and notice the four options available:
   (1) **Open a Drawing**
   (2) **Start from Scratch**
   (3) **Use a Template** and
   (4) **Use a Setup Wizard**.

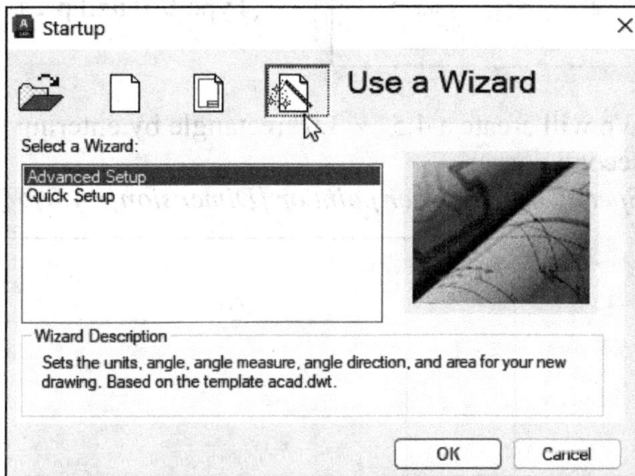

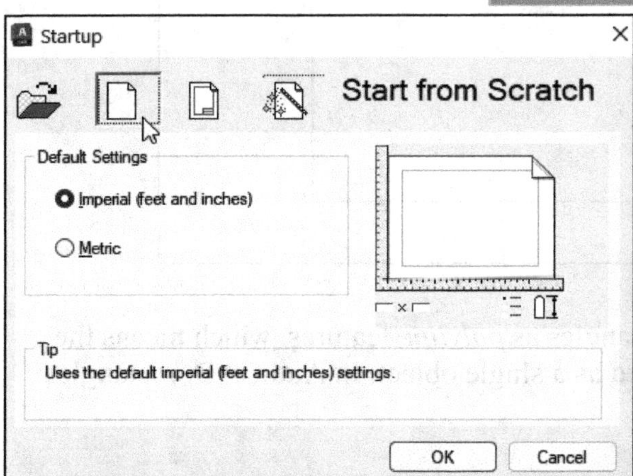

6. In the *Startup* dialog box, select the **Start from Scratch** option as shown in the figure.

7. Choose **Imperial** to use the *Standard English* units setting.

8. Click **OK** to accept the setting.

Create the Rectangular Base of the Design

We will first construct the wireframe geometry defining the rectangular base of the design.

1. In the *Status Bar* area, reset the options and turn ***ON*** the *Grid Display, Polar Tracking, Object Snap, Object Snap Tracking, Dynamic Input* and *Lineweight* options.

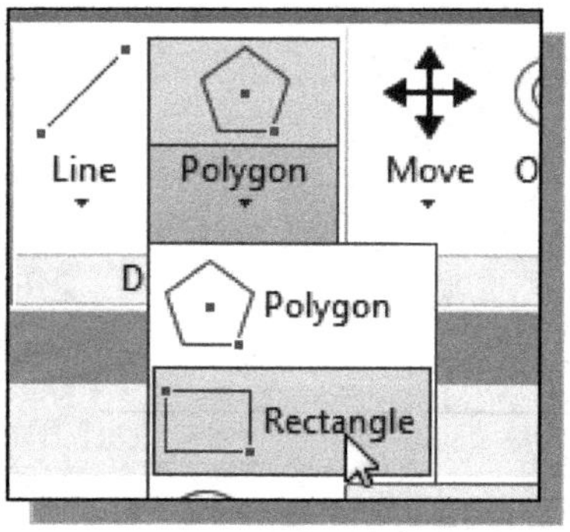

2. Select the **Rectangle** icon in the *Draw* toolbar.

3. Place the first corner-point of the rectangle at the origin of the world coordinate system.
Command: _line Specify first point:
0,0 [ENTER].
(Type ***0,0*** and press the **[ENTER]** key once.)

4. We will create a 4.5″ × 3.0″ rectangle by entering the absolute coordinates of the second corner.
Specify other corner point or [Dimension]: **4.5,3 [ENTER]**.

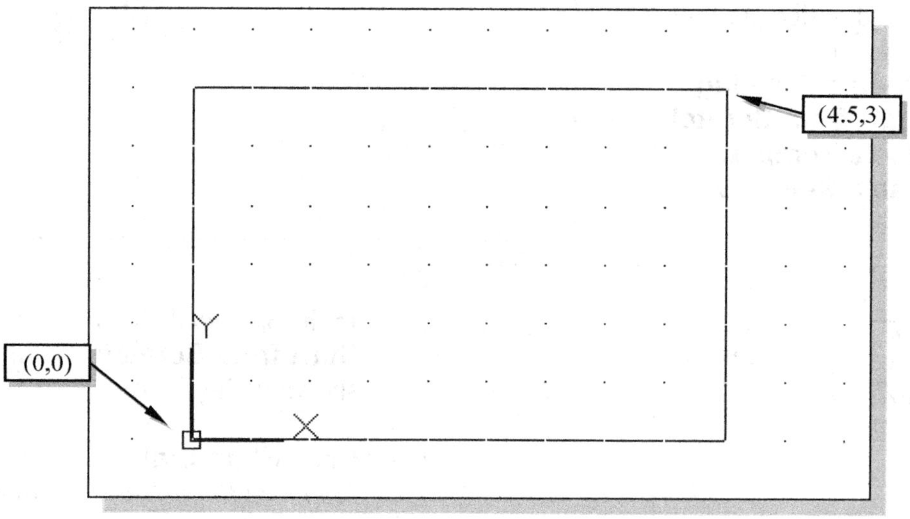

- The Rectangle command creates rectangles as *polyline* features, which means the four segments of a rectangle are created as a single object. In AutoCAD, rectangles are wireframe entities.

5. In the *Menu Bar*, select:
[View] → [3D Views] → [SE Isometric]

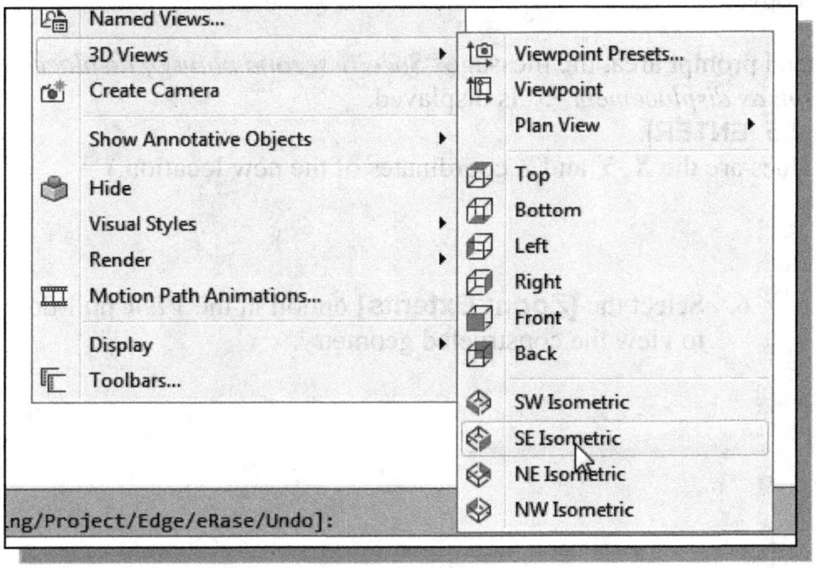

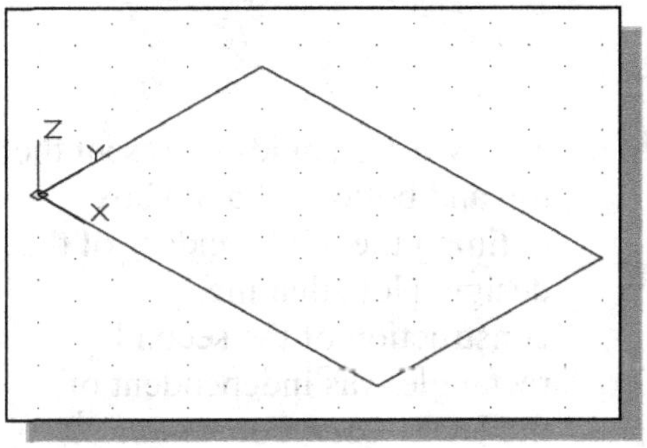

- Notice the orientation of the sketched 2D rectangle in relation to the displayed AutoCAD user coordinate system. By default, the 2D sketch-plane is aligned to the XY plane of the world coordinate system.

Create a 3D Box

We will create a 3D box to define the 3D boundary of the design. We will do so by placing a copy of the base rectangle at the corresponding height elevation of the design. The dimensions of the 3D box are therefore based on the height, width and depth dimensions of the design.

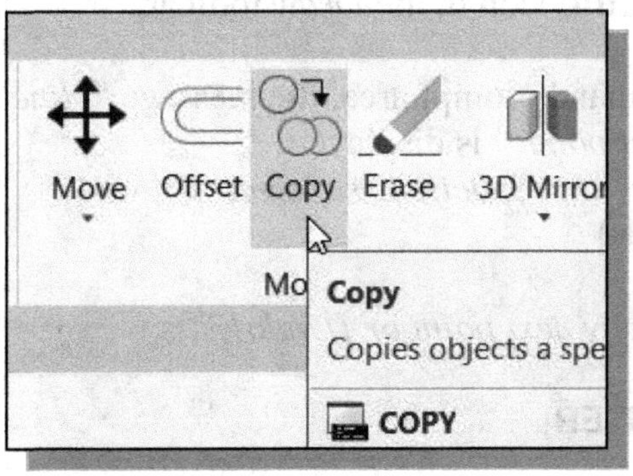

1. Click on the **Copy Object** icon in the *Modify* toolbar.

2. In the command prompt area, the message "*Select objects:*" is displayed. Pick any edge of the sketched rectangle.

3. Inside the graphics window, right-click once to accept the selection.

4. In the command prompt area, the message "*Specify base point or displacement, or [Multiple]:*" is displayed. Pick any **corner** of the sketched **rectangle** as a base point to create the copy.

5. In the command prompt area, the message "*Specify second point of displacement or <use first point as displacement>:*" is displayed.
   Enter **@0,0,2.5 [ENTER]**.
   (The three values are the X, Y and Z coordinates of the new location.)

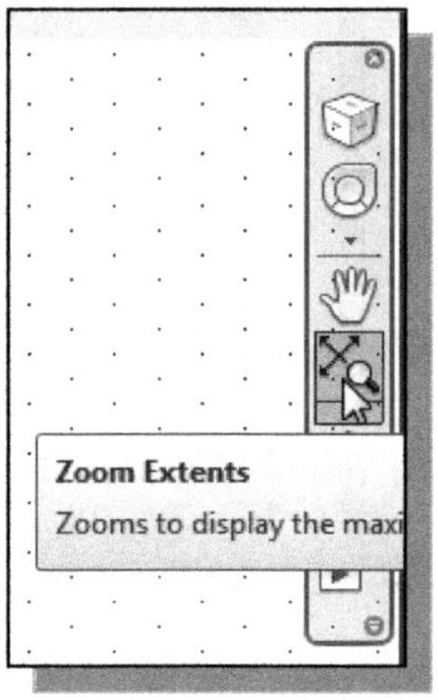

6. Select the **[Zoom Extents]** option in the ***View*** pull-down menu to view the constructed geometry.

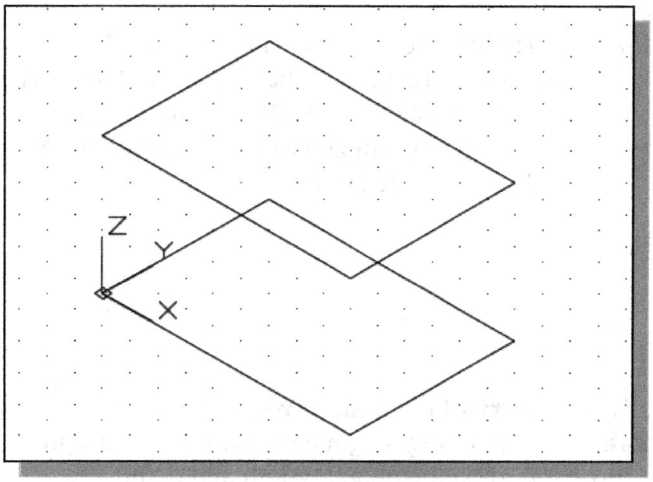

❖ The two rectangles represent the top and bottom of a 3D box defining the 3D boundary of the design. Note that the construction of the second rectangle was independent of the UCS, *User Coordinate System*; the UCS is still aligned to the *world coordinate system*.

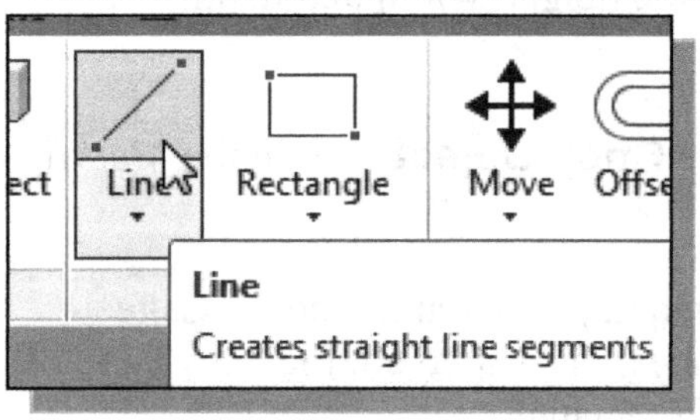

7. Select the **Line** icon in the *Draw* toolbar.

8. In the command prompt area, the message "*_line Specify first point:*" is displayed.
   Command: _line Specify first point:
   0,0 [ENTER]

9. In the command prompt area, the message "*Specify next point or [Undo]:*" is displayed.
   Command: _line Specify first point: **0,0,2.5 [ENTER]**.

❖ Notice the **Line** command correctly identified the entered 3D coordinates of the second point. The default Z-coordinate, which is set by the AutoCAD UCS, is applied automatically whenever the Z-coordinates are omitted.

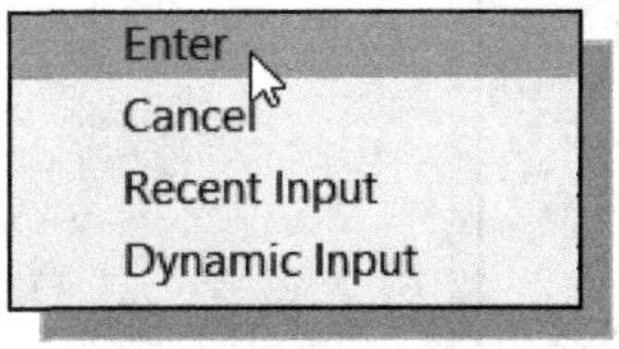

10. Inside the graphics window, right-click to activate the option menu and select **Enter** with the left-mouse-button to end the **Line** command.

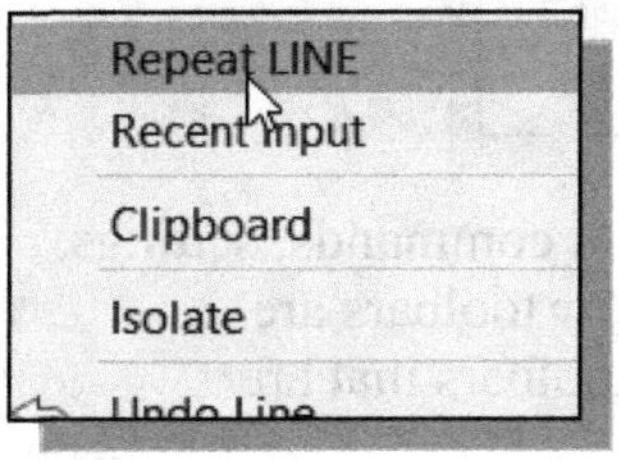

11. Inside the graphics window, **right-click** to bring up the pop-up option menu.

12. Pick **Repeat Line** with the left-mouse-button in the pop-up menu to repeat the last command.

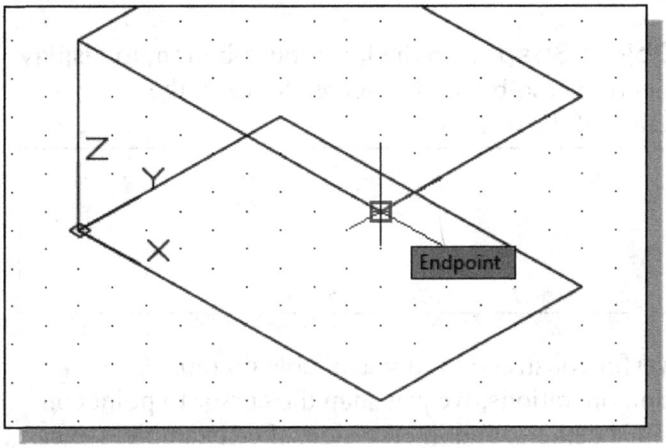

13. Move the cursor on top of the top front corner as shown. Note that AutoCAD's *Object Snap* and *Object Snap Tracking* features identify geometric features, such as endpoints, automatically.

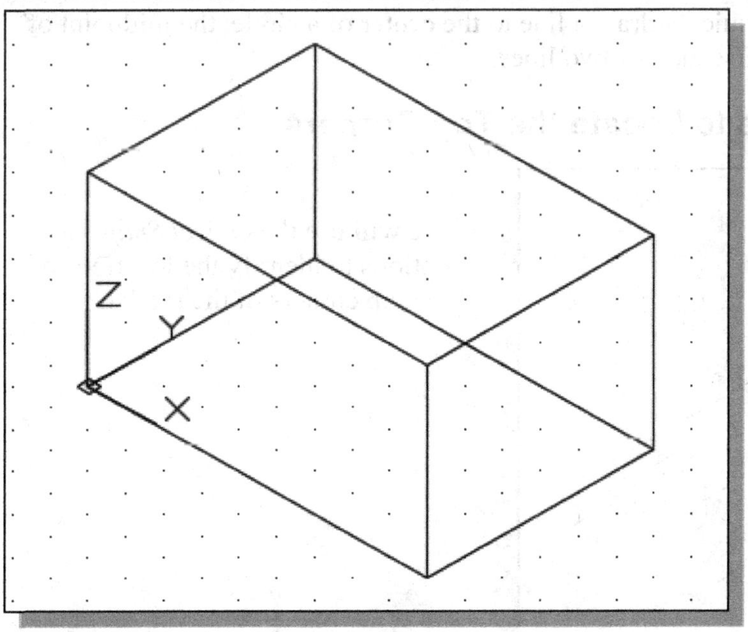

14. Left-click once to select the endpoint as shown in the above figure.

15. Create a line connecting to the endpoint directly below the previously selected point.

16. On your own, complete the 3D box by creating the two lines connecting the back corners of the 3D box as shown.

Object Snap Toolbar

1. In the *Menu Bar* select **[Tools] → [Toolbars] → [AutoCAD]**.

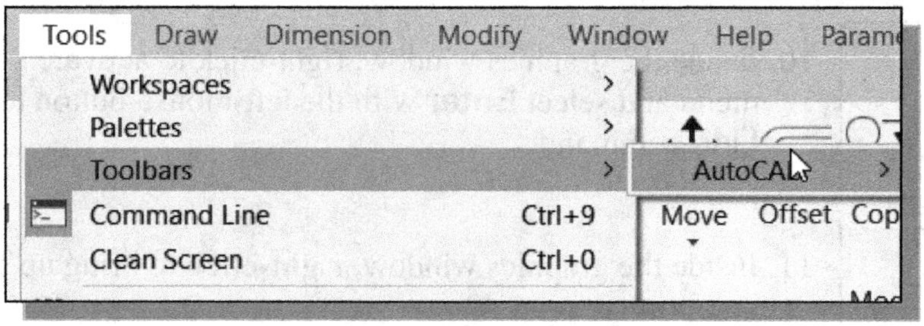

❖ AutoCAD provides many toolbars for access to frequently used commands, settings, and modes. The *Standard, Object Properties*, *Draw*, and *Modify* toolbars are displayed by default. The *check marks* in the list identify the toolbars that are currently displayed on the screen.

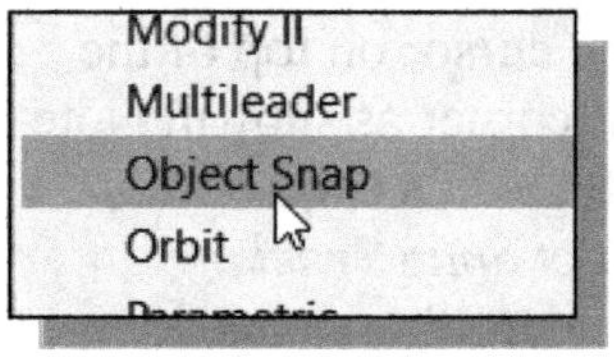

2. Select **Object Snap**, with the left-mouse-button, to display the *Object Snap* toolbar on the screen to assist the construction of the design.

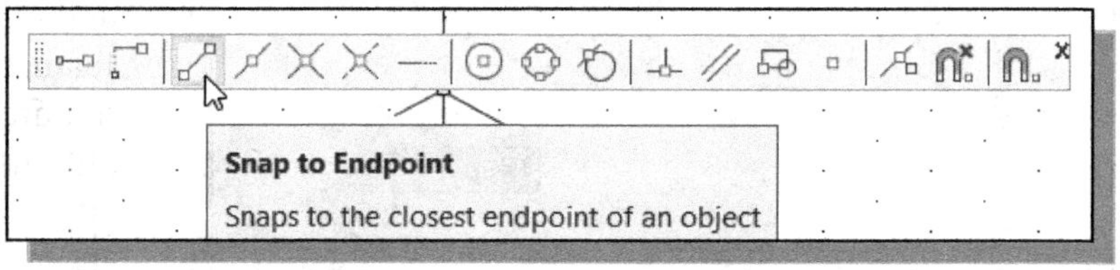

❖ ***Object Snap*** is an extremely powerful construction tool available on most CAD systems. During an entity's creation operations, we can snap the cursor to points on objects such as endpoints, midpoints, centers, and intersections. For example, we can turn on ***Object Snap*** and quickly draw a line to the center of a circle, the midpoint of a line segment, or the intersection of two lines.

Use the Snap Options to Locate the Top Corners

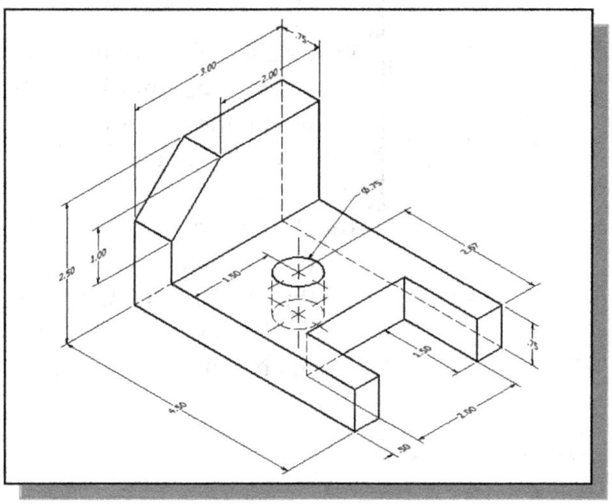

❖ We will use the *Object Snap* options to identify the locations of the top corners of the model.

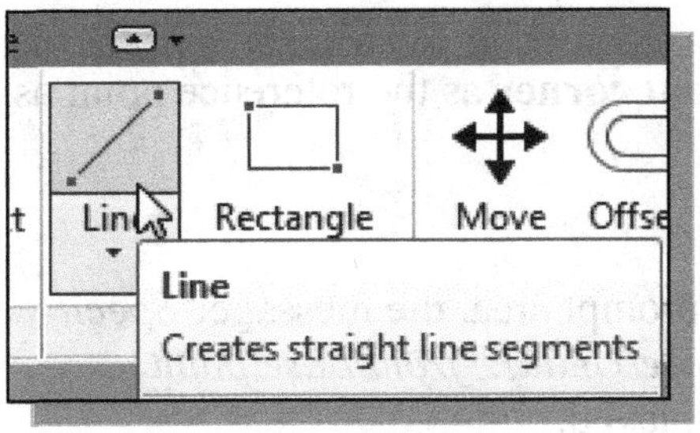

1. Select the **Line** icon in the *Draw* toolbar.

2. In the command prompt area, the message "*_line Specify first point:*" is displayed. Select **Snap From** in the *Object Snap* toolbar.

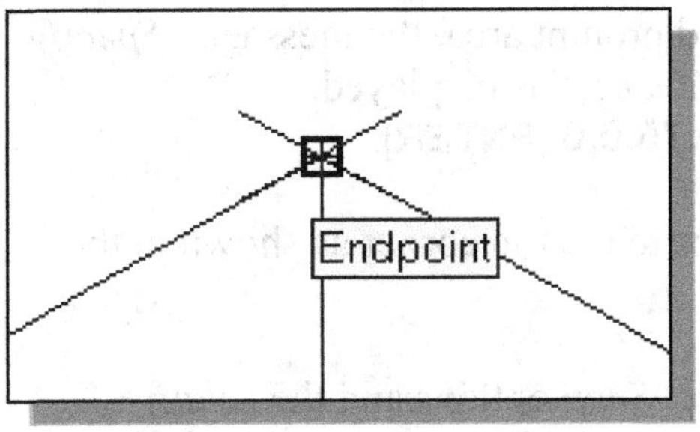

3. Select the **top back corner** as the reference point as shown.

4. In the command prompt area, the message "*_line Specify first point: from Base point:<Offset>:*" is displayed.

   Command: **@0.75,0,0 [ENTER]**.

❖ By using the relative coordinate input method, we can locate the position of any point in 3D space. Note that the entered coordinates are measured relative to the current UCS.

5. In the command prompt area, the message "*Specify next point or [Undo]:*" is displayed.
   Command: Specify next point or [Undo]: **@0,-2,0 [ENTER]**.

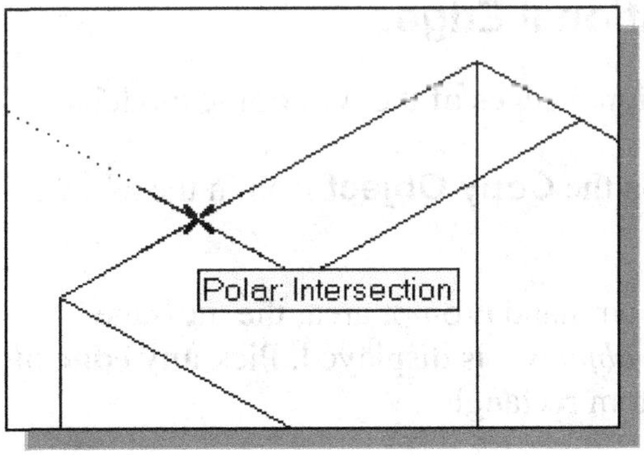

6. Move the cursor toward the left to create a perpendicular line. Select a location that is on the back line as shown; notice the displayed *Object Snap/Tracking* tips: **Polar: Intersection**.

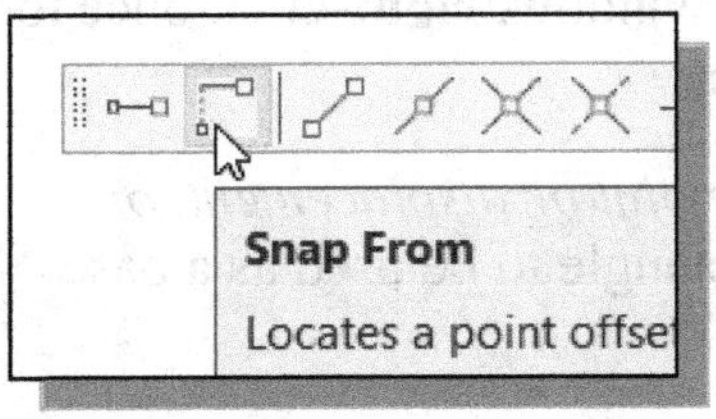

7. In the command prompt area, the message "*Specify next point or [Undo]:*" is displayed. Select **Snap From** in the *Object Snap* toolbar.

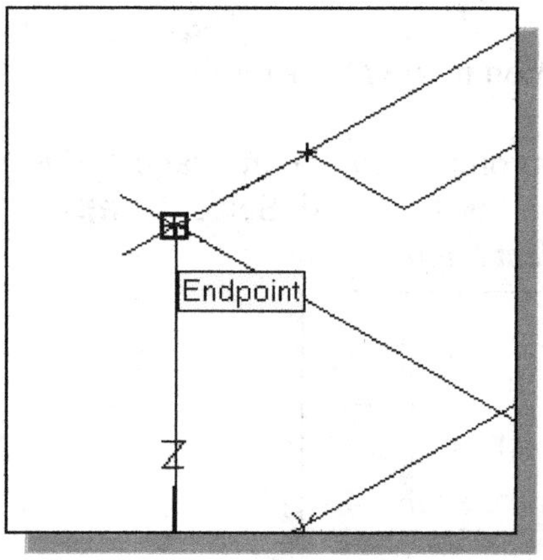

8. Select the **top front corner** as the reference point as shown.

9. In the command prompt area, the message "*Specify next point or [Close/Undo]: _from Base point <Offset>:*" is displayed.

   Command: **@0,0,-1 [ENTER]**.

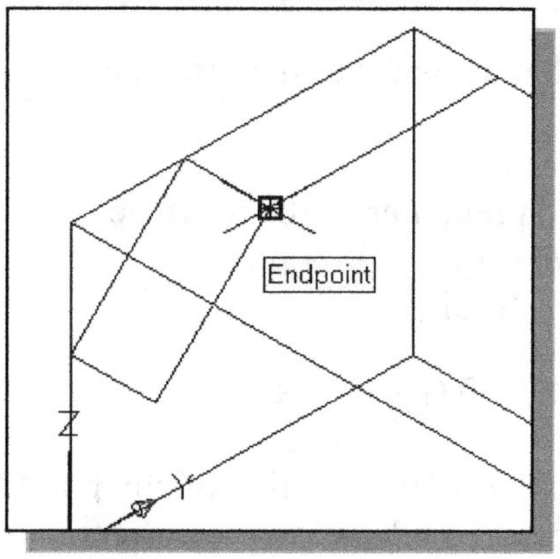

10. In the command prompt area, the message *"Specify next point or [Undo]:"* is displayed.
    Command: **@0.75,0,0 [ENTER]**.

11. Move the cursor to the top corner as shown in the figure.

❖ Using the *Object Snap* options and the *relative coordinate input method* allow us to quickly locate points in 3D space.

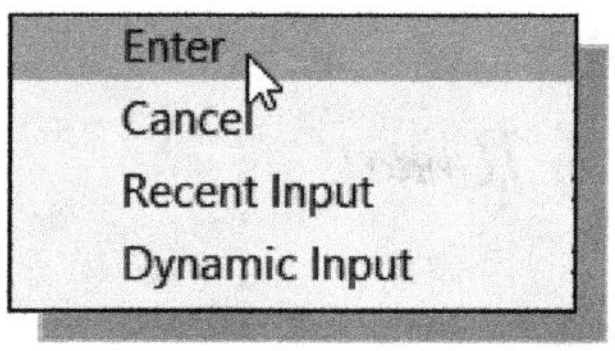

12. Inside the graphics window, right-click to activate the option menu and select **Enter** with the left-mouse-button to end the Line command.

Use the Copy Option to Create Additional Edges

The Copy option can also be used to create additional edges of the wireframe model.

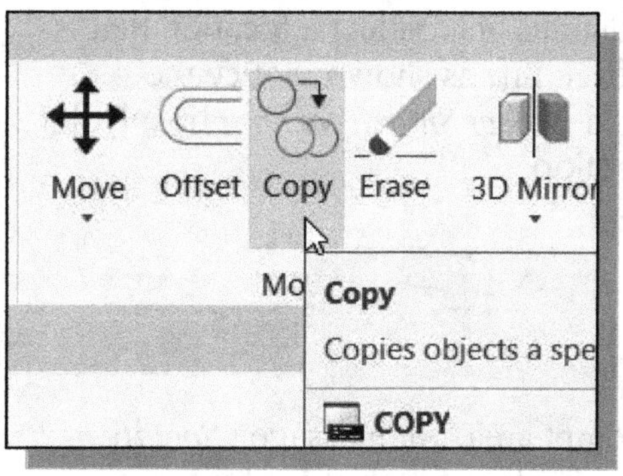

1. Click on the **Copy Object** icon in the *Modify* toolbar.

2. In the command prompt area, the message "*Select objects:*" is displayed. Pick **any edge** of the bottom rectangle.

3. Inside the graphics window, **right-click** once to accept the selection.

4. In the *command prompt area*, the message "*Specify base point or displacement, or [Multiple]:*" is displayed. Pick **any corner** of the base rectangle to be used as a base point to create the copy.

5. In the *command prompt area*, the message "*Specify second point of displacement or <use first point as displacement>:*" is displayed.
   Enter **@0,0,0.75 [ENTER]**.

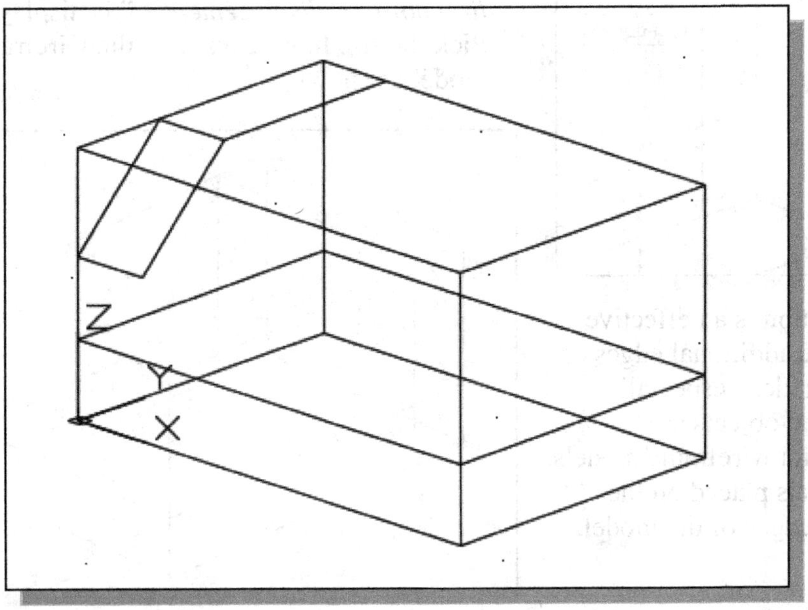

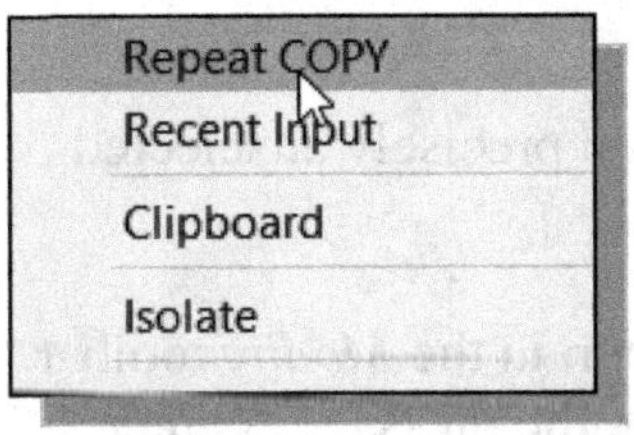

6. Inside the graphics window, right-click to bring up the pop-up option menu.

7. Pick **Repeat Copy Object** with the left-mouse-button in the pop-up menu to repeat the last command.

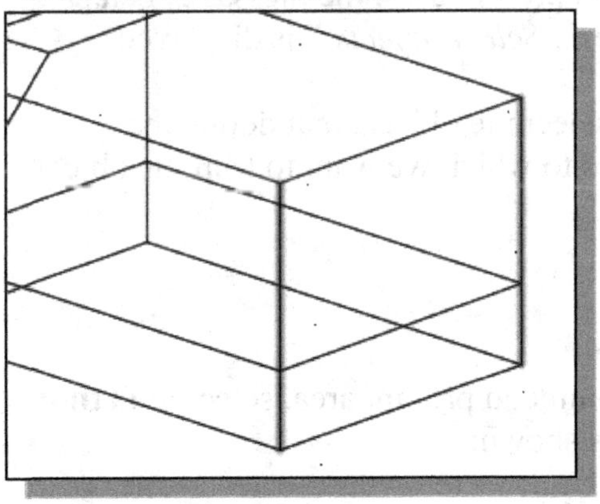

8. Pick the two **vertical lines** on the right side of the 3D box as shown.

9. Inside the graphics window, **right-click** once to accept the selection.

10. In the command prompt area, the message "*Specify base point or displacement, or [Multiple]:*" is displayed. Pick the **top back corner** of the wireframe as a base point to create the copy.

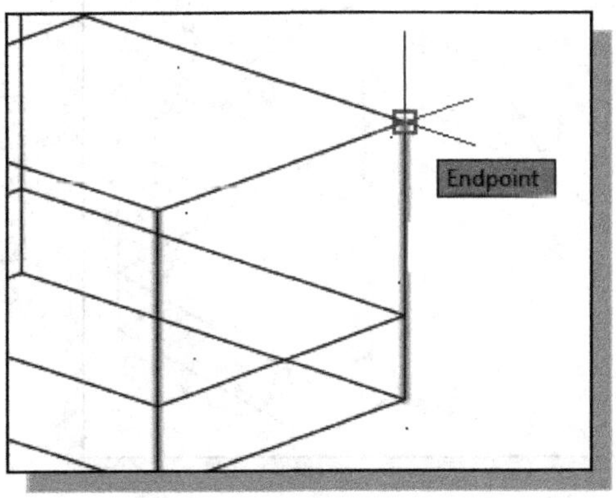

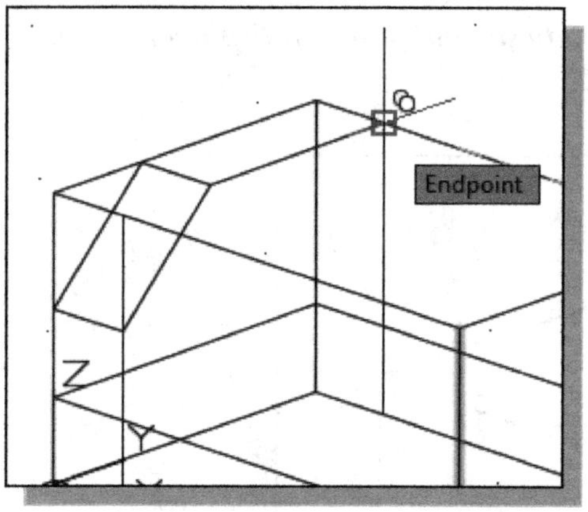

11. In the command prompt area, the message "*Specify second point of displacement or <use first point as displacement>:*" is displayed. Pick the **top back corner** of the wireframe model as shown.

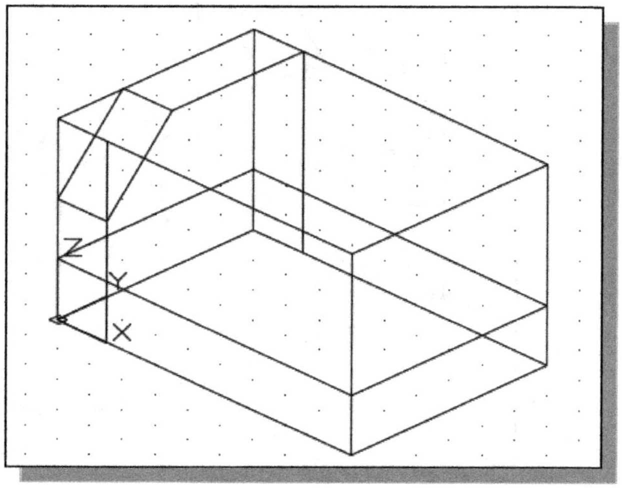

❖ The copy option is an effective way to create additional edges of wireframe models, especially when multiple objects are involved. With wireframe models, the emphasis is placed on the corners and edges of the model.

Use the Trim Command

The Trim command can be used to shorten objects so that they end precisely at selected boundaries.

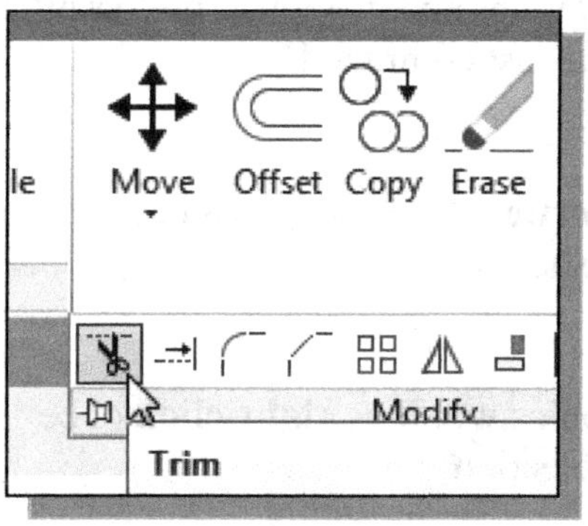

1. Select the **Trim** command icon in the *Modify* toolbar. In the command prompt area, the message "*Select boundary edges... Select objects:*" is displayed.

❖ First, we will select the objects that define the boundary edges to which we want to trim the object.

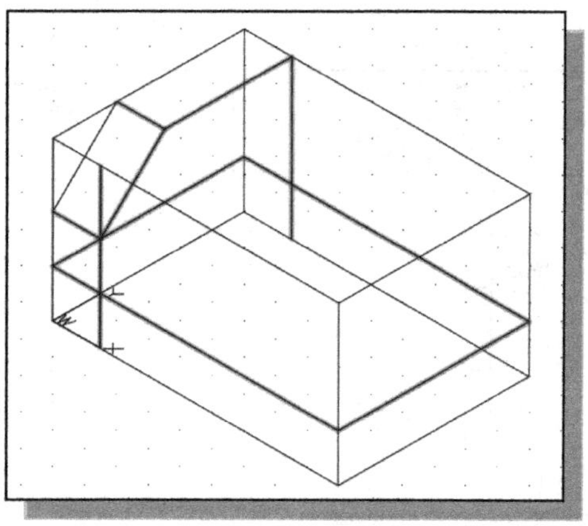

2. In the command prompt area, select [**cuTting edges**] as shown:

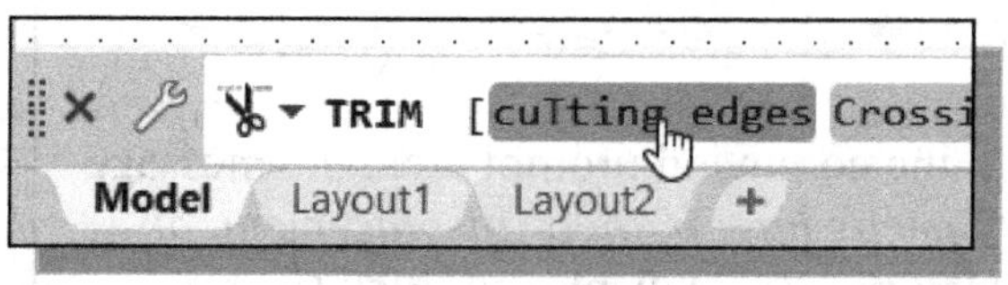

3. Pick the highlighted edges as shown in the figure; these edges are the *boundary edges*.

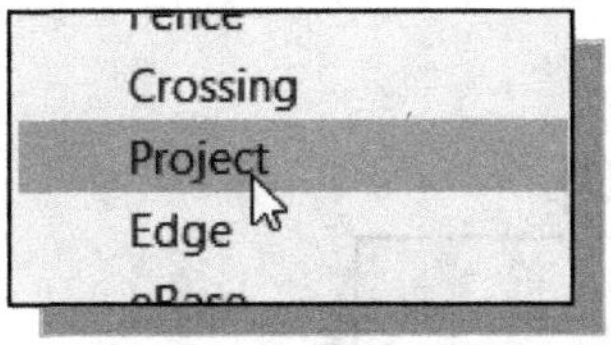

4. Inside the graphics area, right-click once to bring up the option menu and select **Project** as shown.

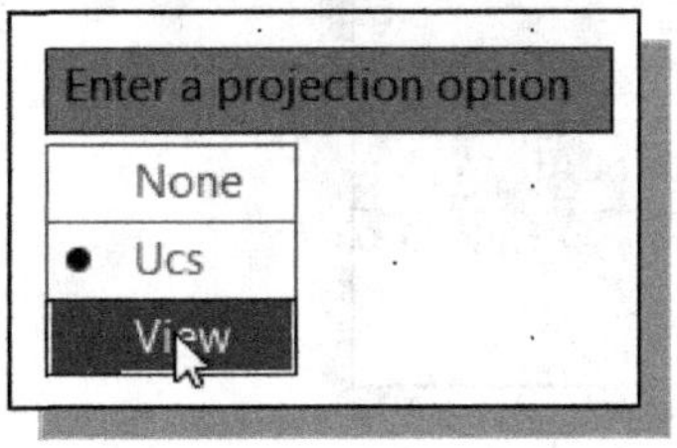

5. Inside the graphics area, right-click once to bring up the option menu and select **View** to allow trimming options based on the displayed view.

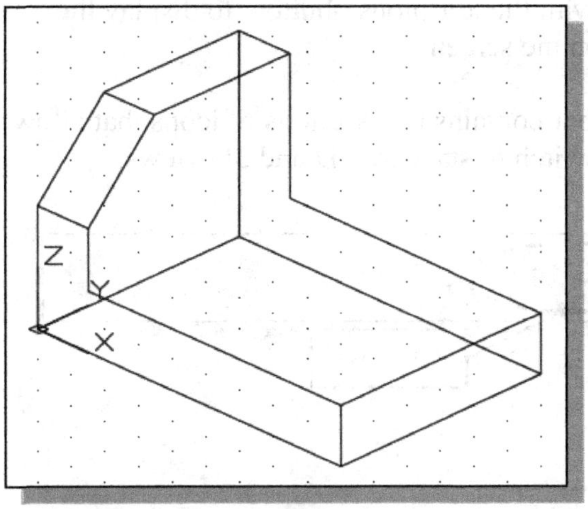

6. The message "*Select object to trim or shift-select object to extend or [Project/Edge/Undo]:*" is displayed in the command prompt area. Pick the portions of the entities to be trimmed so that the model appears as shown.

❖ Note that in AutoCAD 2027, the default AutoCAD trim projection setting is set to **UCS**, which allows us to trim objects that are perpendicular to the **UCS plane**.

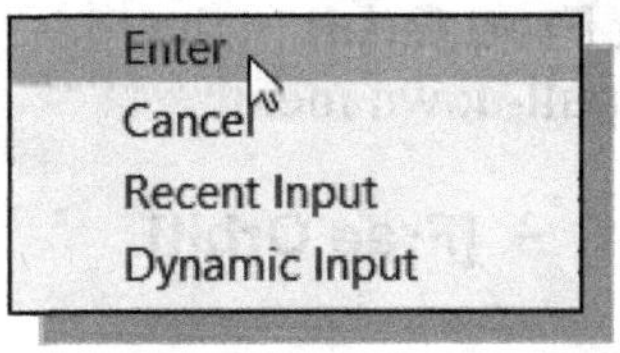

7. Inside the graphics window, right-click to bring up the option menu and select **Enter** to end the **Trim** command.

8. On your own, use the **Line** command to complete the inside corner of the wireframe model as shown.

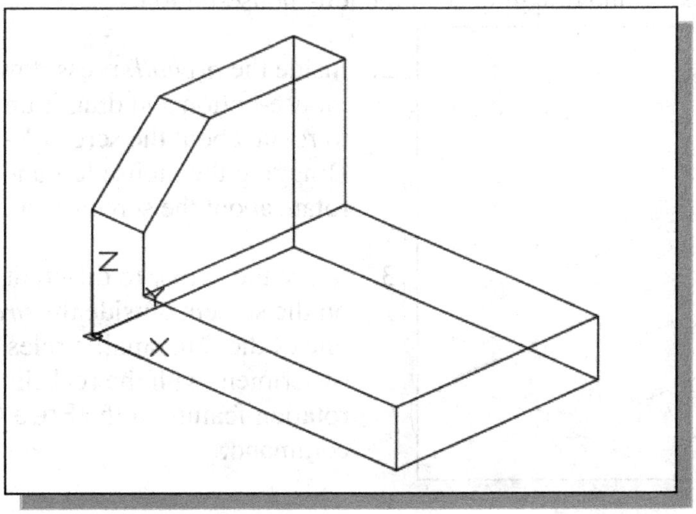

Use the View Toolbar

1. In the *Menu Bar* select **[Tools] → [Toolbars] → [AutoCAD]**.

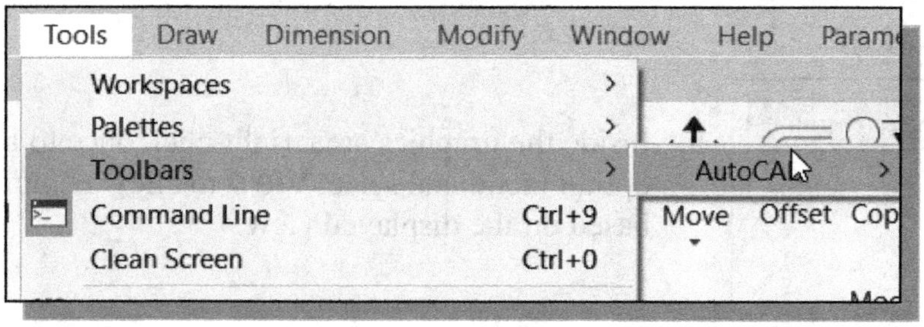

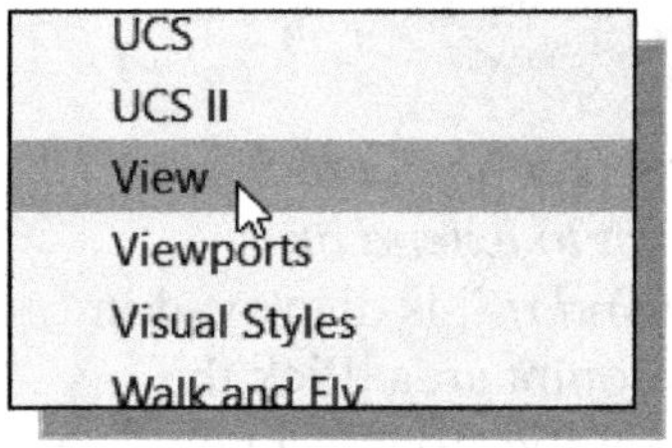

2. Select **View**, with the left-mouse-button, to display the *View* toolbar on the screen.

➢ The *View* toolbar contains two sections of icons that allow us to quickly switch to standard 2D and 3D views.

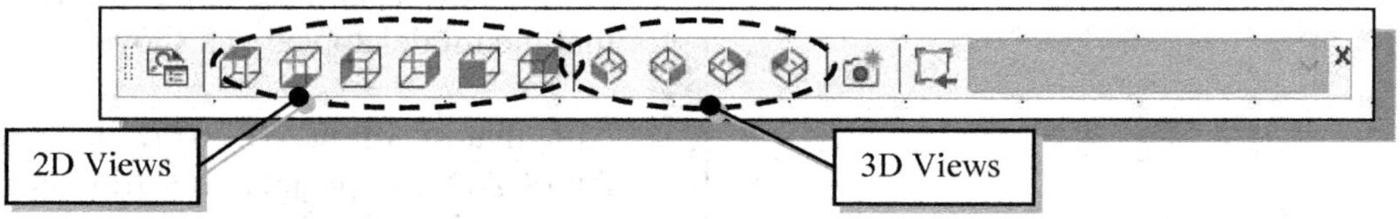

Dynamic Rotation – Free Orbit

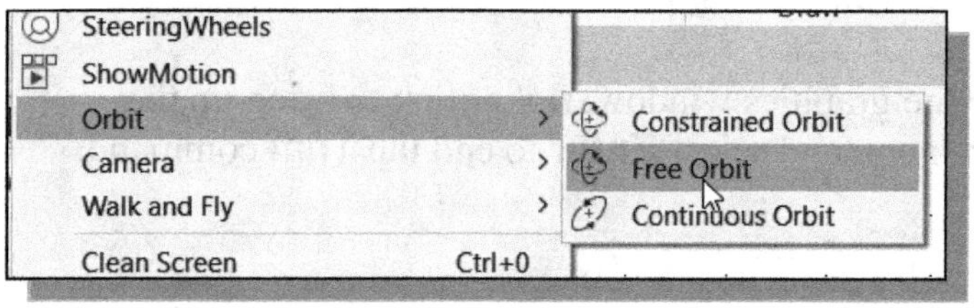

1. Select **Free Orbit** in the ***View*** pull-down menu:

   [Orbit] → [Free Orbit]

❖ The Free Orbit view displays an ***arcball***, which enables us to manipulate the view of 3D objects by clicking and dragging with the left-mouse-button.

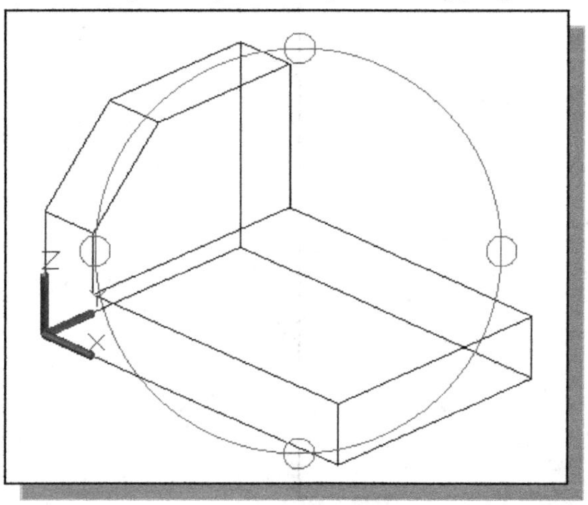

2. Inside the *arcball*, press down the left-mouse-button and drag it up and down to rotate about the screen X-axis. Dragging the mouse left and right will rotate about the screen Y-axis.

3. Move the cursor to different locations on the screen, outside the *arcball* or on one of the four small circles, and experiment with the real-time dynamic rotation feature of the Free Orbit command.

Use the Offset Command to Create Parallel Edges

The AutoCAD **Offset** option can also be used to create edges that are at specific distances to existing 3D wireframe edges. Prior to creating the parallel edges, we will first convert one of the polylines to individual line segments.

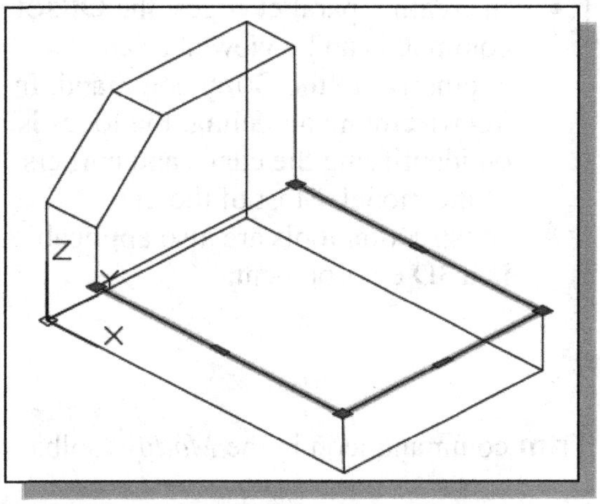

1. Pick the top right edge of the wireframe model.

- **AutoCAD 2027** provides a flexible graphical user interface that allows users to select graphical entities BEFORE the command is selected (*Pre-selection*), or AFTER the command is selected (*Post-selection*). The polyline we have pre-selected consists of three line-segments.

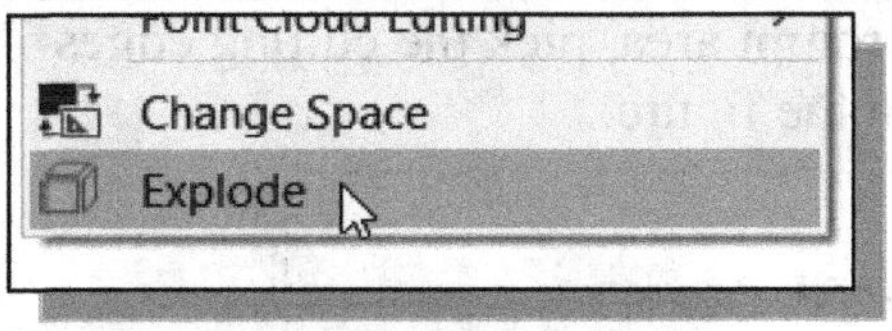

2. Select the **Explode** command in the ***Modify*** *pull-down menu* as shown.

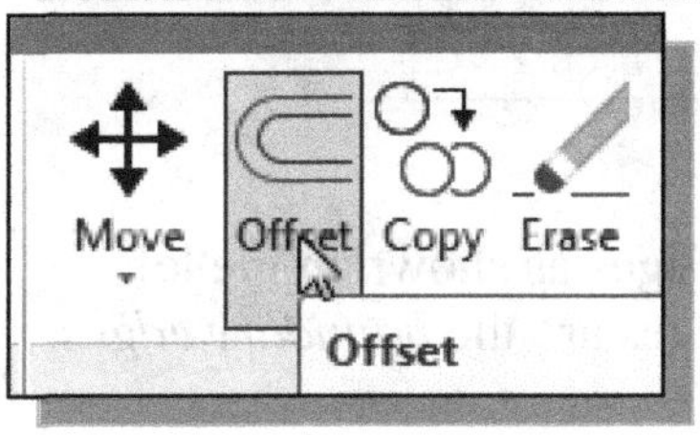

3. Pick **Offset** in the *Modify* toolbar as shown.

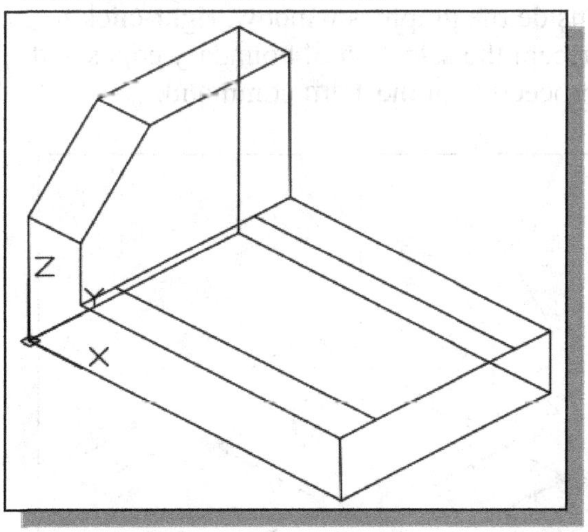

4. In the command prompt area, the message "*Specify offset distance or [Through] <Through>:*" is displayed. Enter **0.5** [**ENTER**].

5. Select the front line segment of the polyline we just exploded.

6. In the command prompt area, the message "*Specify point on side to offset:*" is displayed. Pick a location that is above the line to create the first parallel line.

7. Select the back line segment of the polyline we exploded and create another parallel line as shown.

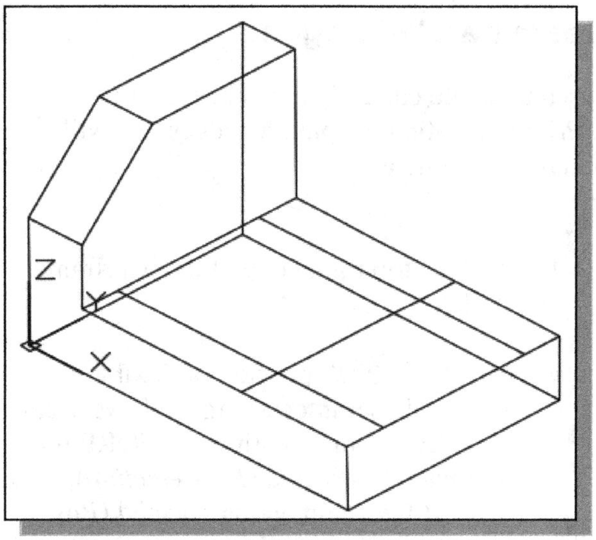

8. On your own, repeat the above steps and create another parallel line (distance: **1.5**) as shown.

- In creating parallel edges, the Offset command can be viewed as an alternative to the Copy command. In 3D wireframe modeling, the focus is on identifying the edges and corners of the model. Most of the 2D construction tools are also applicable in a 3D environment.

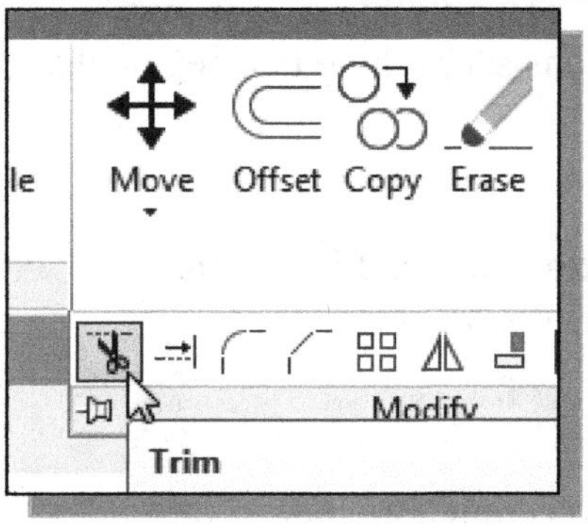

9. Select the **Trim** command icon in the *Modify* toolbar.

10. In the command prompt area, pick the cutting edges option as shown in the figure.

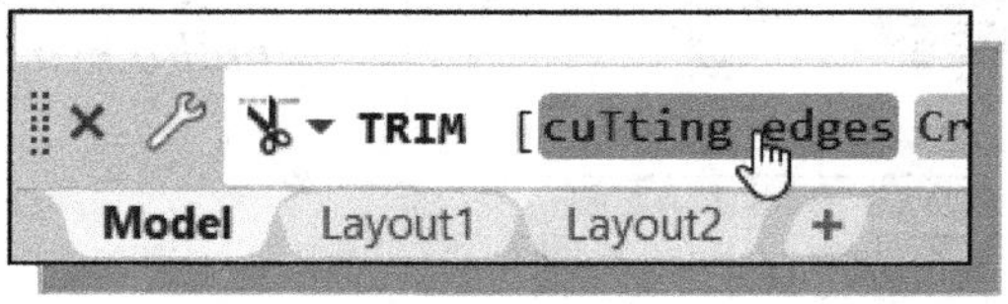

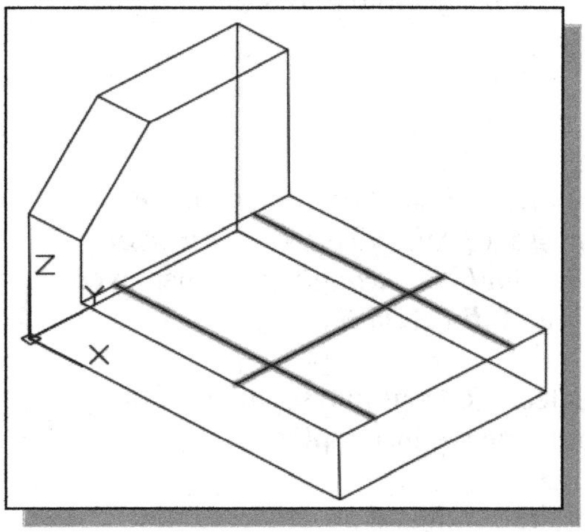

11. Pick the three edges as shown in the left figure; these edges are the *boundary edges*.

12. Inside the graphics window, right-click to accept the selection of boundary edges and proceed with the Trim command.

13. On your own, trim the line segments so that the wireframe model appears as shown.

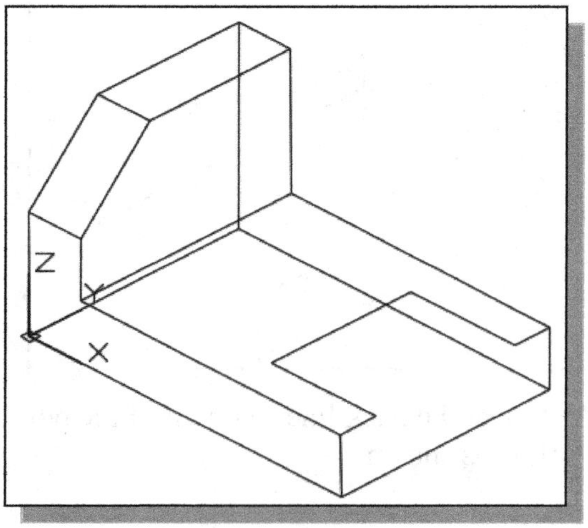

Create a Circle above the UCS Sketch Plane

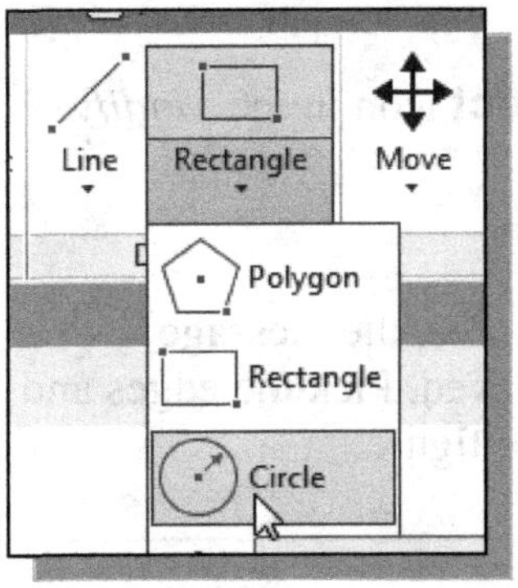

1. Select the **Circle** command icon in the *Draw* toolbar.

- By default, the XY plane of the UCS defines the sketching plane for constructing 2D geometric entities.

2. In the command prompt area, the message "*_circle Specify center point for circle or[3P/2P/Ttr (tan tan radius)]:*" is displayed. Select **Snap From** in the *Object Snap* toolbar.

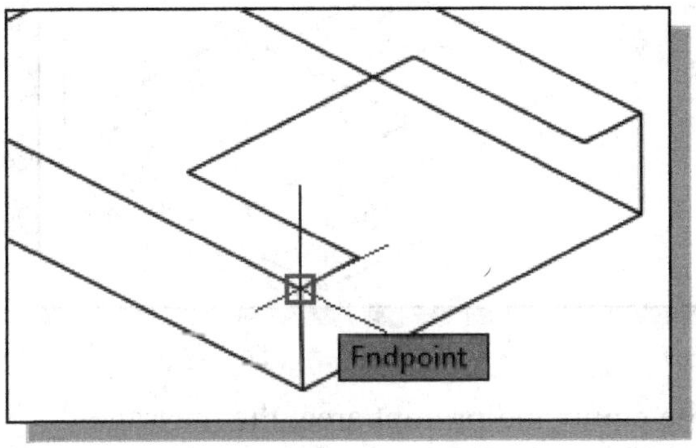

3. Select the **top right corner** as the reference point as shown.

4. In the command prompt area, the message "*Specify next point or [Close/Undo]:_from Base point <Offset>:*" is displayed.

   Command: **@-2.67,1.5 [ENTER]**.

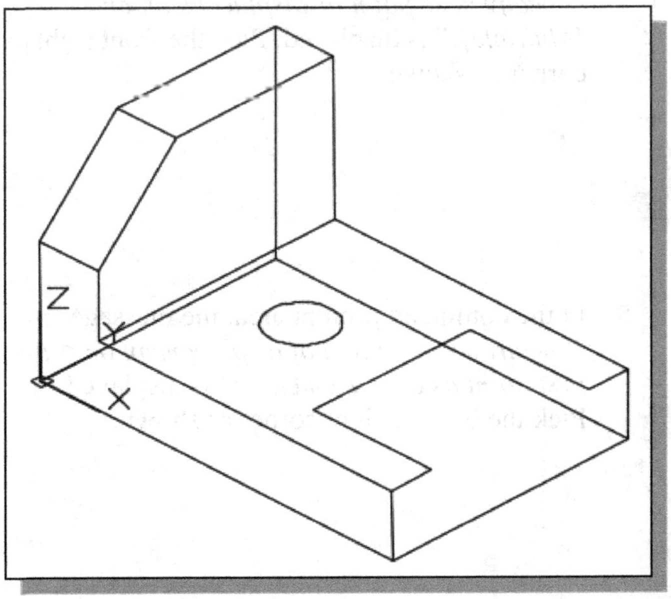

5. In the command prompt area, the message "*Specify radius of circle or [Diameter]:*" is displayed.

   Command: **0.375 [ENTER]**.

- The circle is created above the sketching plane with the **Snap From** option.

Complete the Wireframe Model

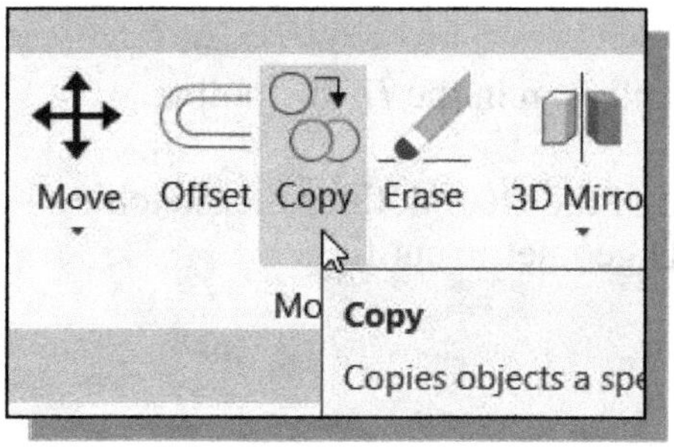

1. Click on the **Copy Object** icon in the *Modify* toolbar.

2. In the command prompt area, the message "*Select objects:*" is displayed. Pick the edges and the circle as shown in the figure.

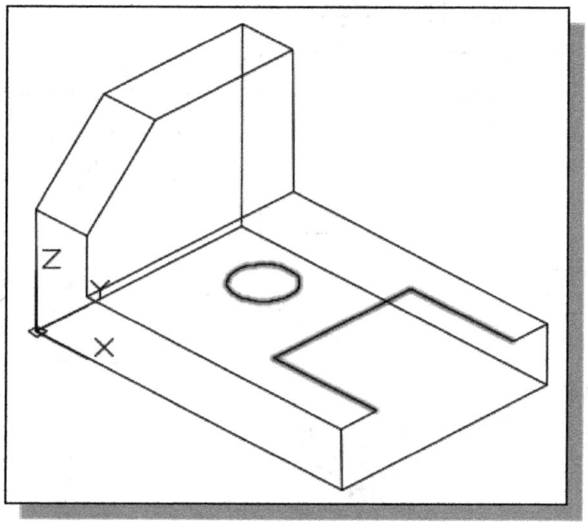

3. Inside the graphics window, right-click once to accept the selection.

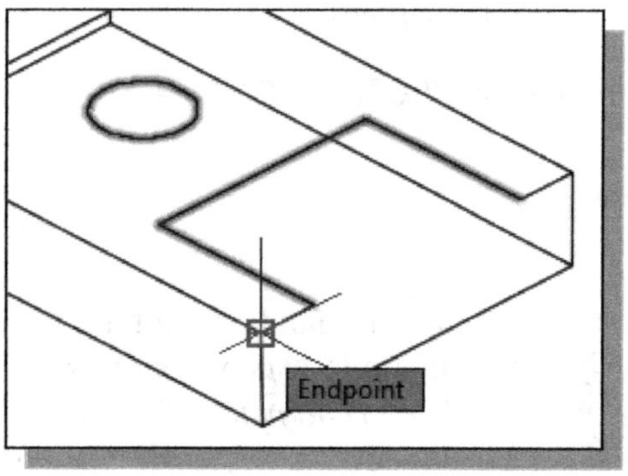

4. In the command prompt area, the message "*Specify base point or displacement, or [Multiple]:*" is displayed. Pick the front right corner as shown.

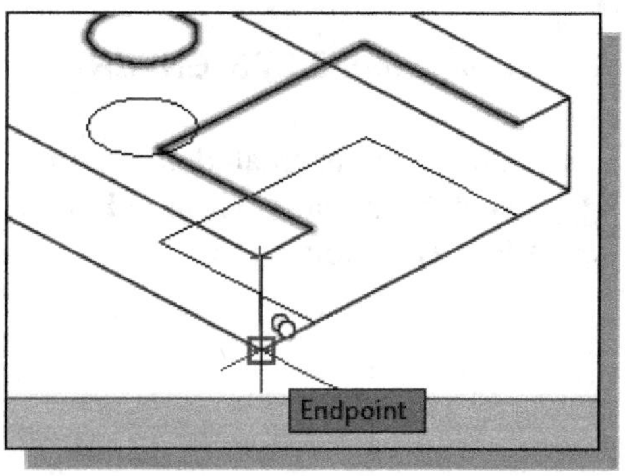

5. In the command prompt area, the message "*Specify second point of displacement or <use first point as displacement>:*" is displayed. Pick the bottom-right corner as shown.

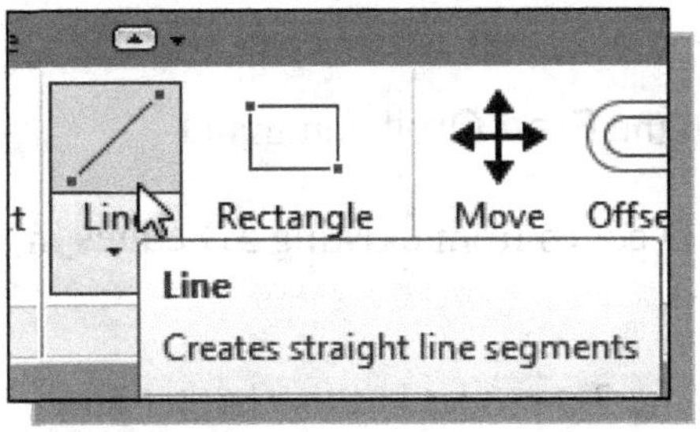

6. Select the **Line** icon in the *Draw* toolbar.

7. On your own, create the lines connecting the corners of the created edges as shown in the figure below.

8. Use the **Snap to Quadrant** option to create edges in between the two circles.

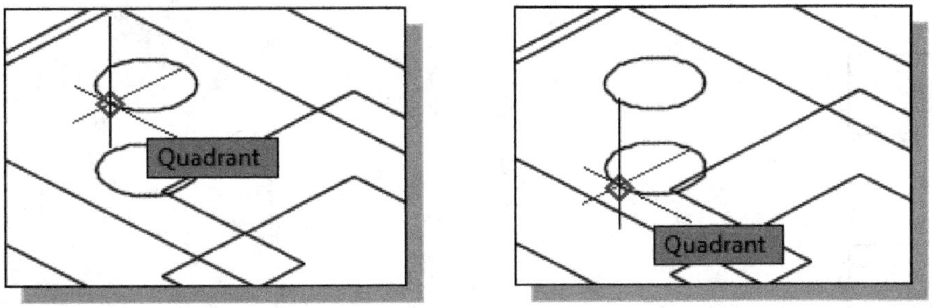

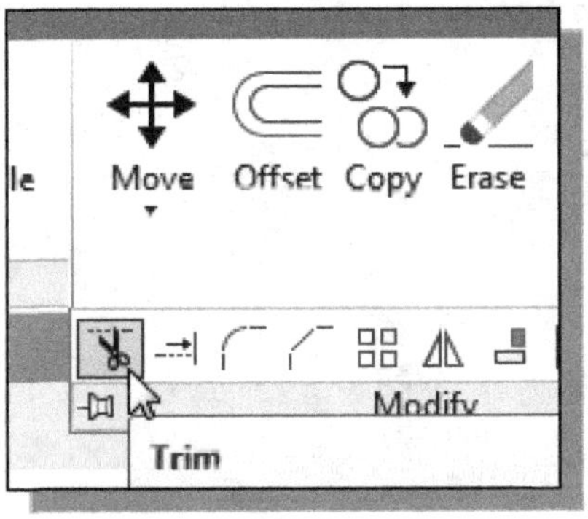

9. Select the **Trim** command icon in the *Modify* toolbar.

10. On your own, trim the center portion of the bottom right edge and complete the wireframe model as shown.

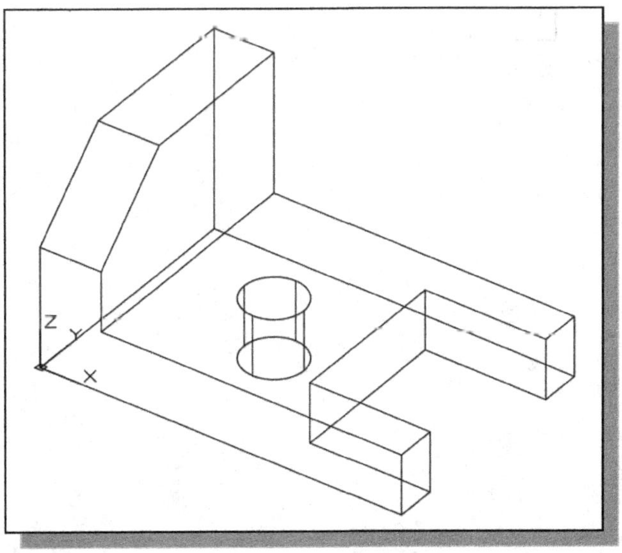

❖ On your own, save the ***Locator*** design (Locator.dwg); this model will be used again in the *Surface Modeling* chapter.

Review Questions:

1. Describe some of the control options available with the Free Orbit command.

2. List and describe two different methods to create 3D edges from existing 3D edges in **AutoCAD 2027**.

3. How many of the UCS options were used to create the 3D model in this chapter and how many were used to create the model in the previous chapter?

4. When and why would you use the Trim-Project-View option?

5. Identify the following commands:

(a)

(b)

(c)

(d)

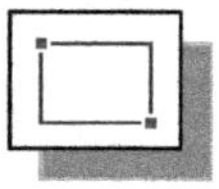

Exercises: All dimensions are in inches.

1. Thickness: Base **0.25** inches. Boss height **0.125** inches. The two diameter 1.00 holes are through holes.

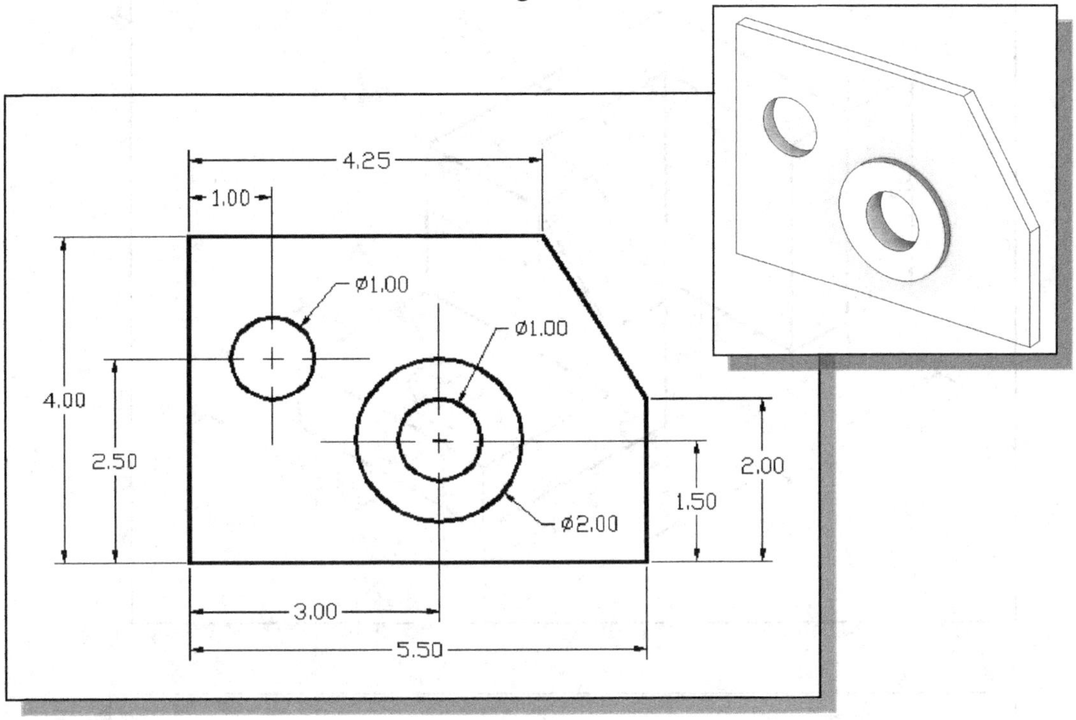

2.

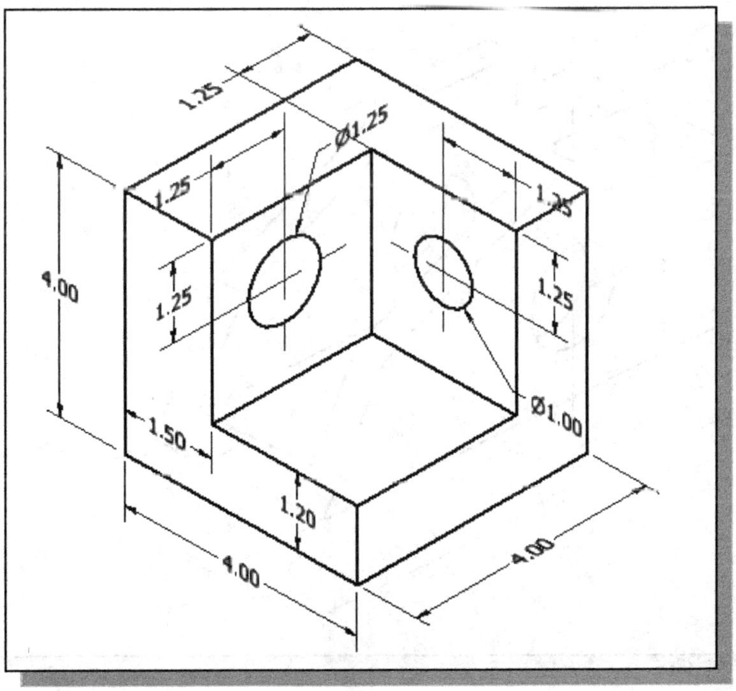

3.

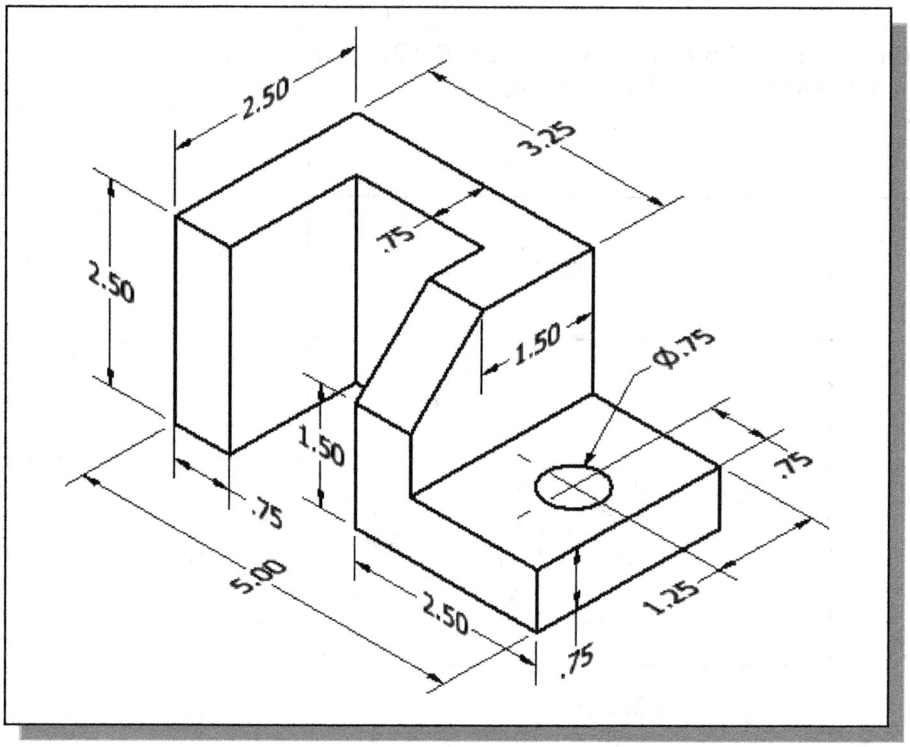
2.50
3.25
.75
2.50
1.50
Ø.75
1.50
.75
.75
5.00
2.50
1.25
.75

4.

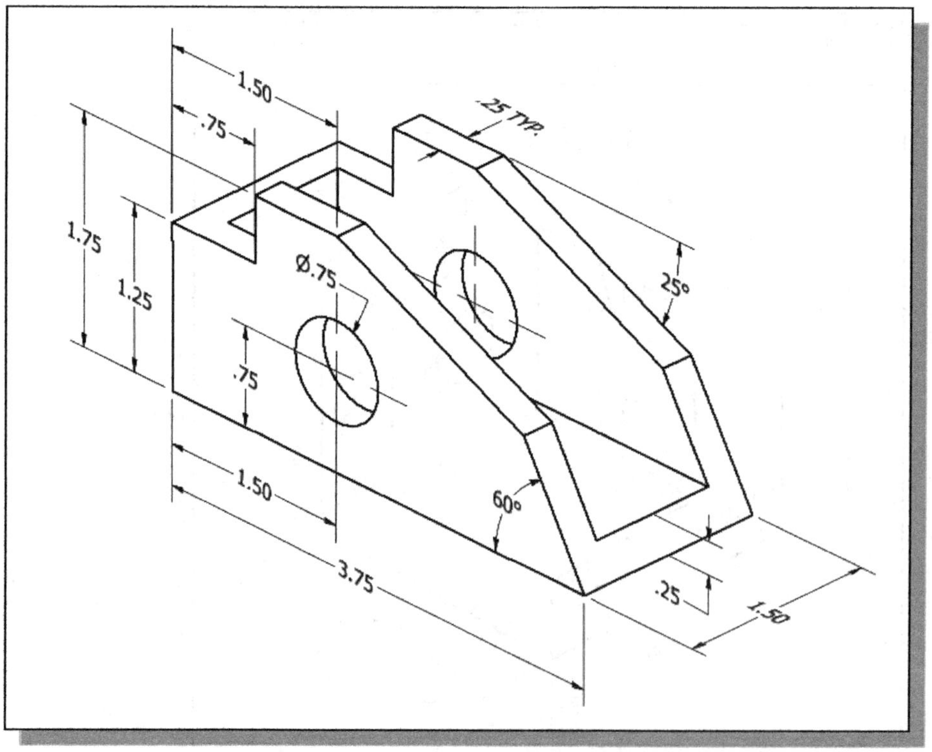
1.50
.75
.25 TYP.
1.75
1.25
Ø.75
25°
.75
1.50
60°
3.75
.25
1.50

5.

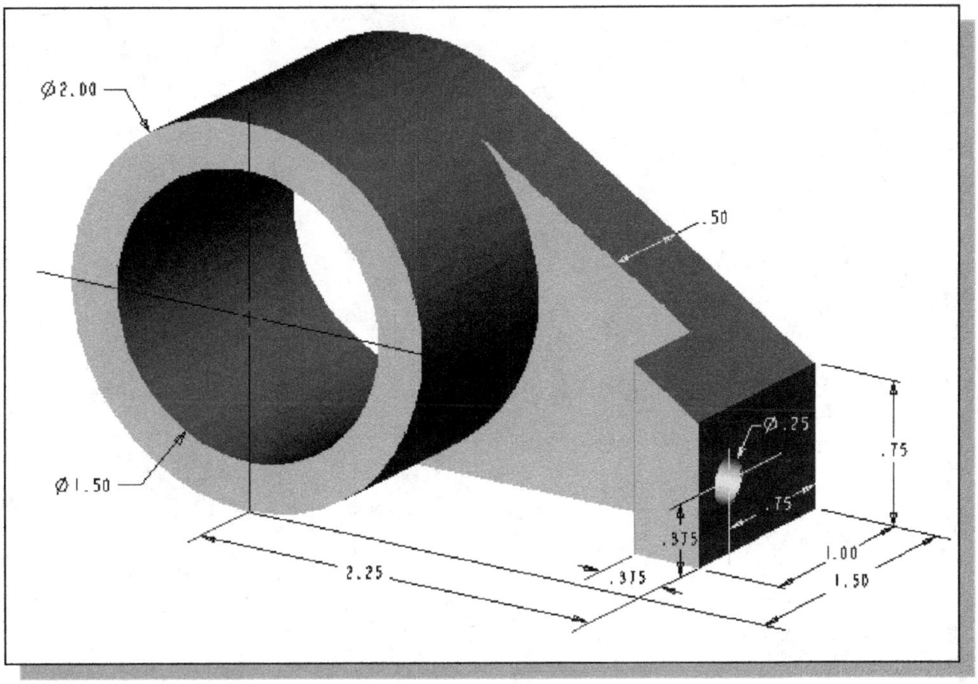
Ø2.00
.50
Ø.25
.75
Ø1.50
.75
.375
.375
2.25
1.00
1.50

6.

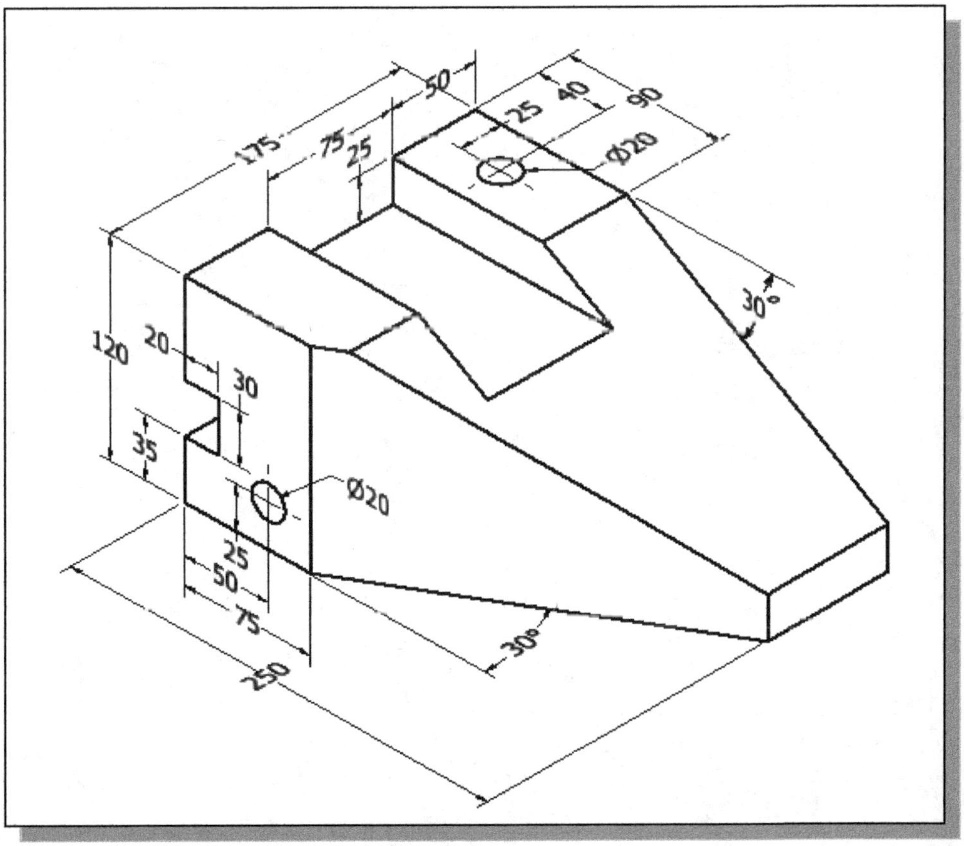
50
175
75
25
25
40
90
Ø20
30°
120
20
30
35
Ø20
25
50
75
250
30°

Notes:

Chapter 3
UCS, Viewports and Wireframe Modeling

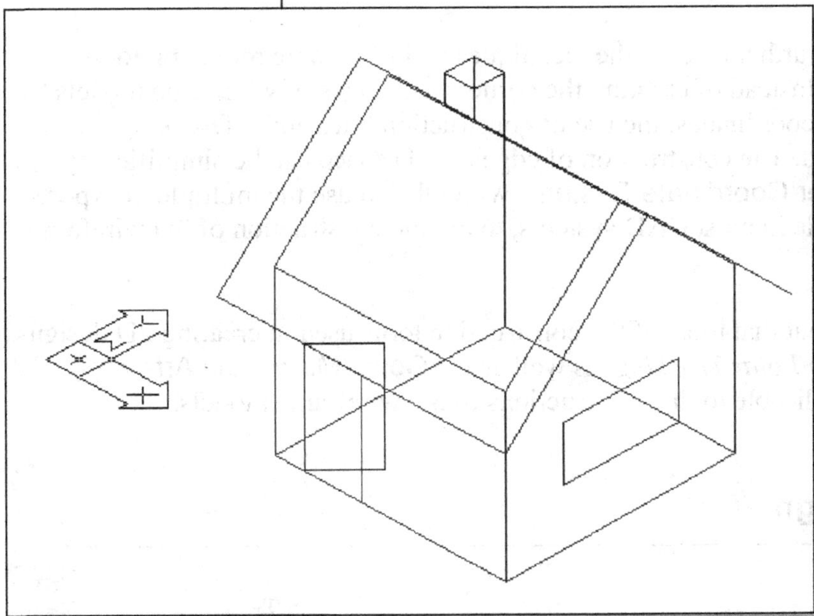

Learning Objectives

- ♦ **Understand the Use of UCS on More Complex Designs**
- ♦ **Display and Orient 3D Views**
- ♦ **Apply and Expand the Basic Wireframe Construction Techniques**
- ♦ **Use Additional Tools to Assist the Creation of 3D Wireframe Models**
- ♦ **Use the Named Views Option**

Introduction

In the previous chapter, we examined some of the basic techniques to create 3D wireframe models. Again, a wireframe model is a skeletal description of a 3D object. There are no surfaces in a wireframe model; it consists only of points, lines, and curves that describe the edges of the object.

In this chapter, we will further discuss the techniques and wireframe modeling tools available in AutoCAD. Instead of creating the corners and edges of wireframe models by entering the precise 3D coordinates, the use of construction lines and referencing techniques are illustrated. The construction of edges in 3D space can be simplified by using the *AutoCAD* User Coordinate System. We will also use the multiple viewports option, which is available in most CAD systems, to aid the construction of 3D wireframe models.

It is important to point out that most of the construction tools used in creating 2D designs, such as *Object Snap* and *Polar Tracking*, as well as the Copy, Mirror, and Array commands, are also applicable to the constructions of 3D wireframe models.

The V-Block Design

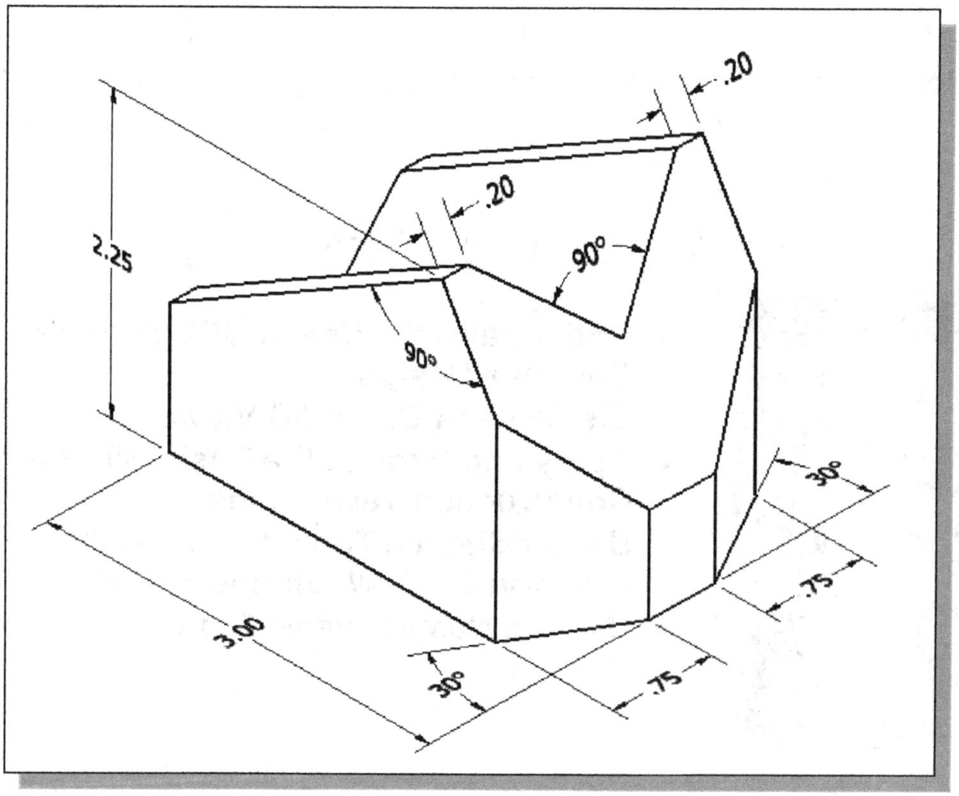

Starting Up AutoCAD 2027

1. Select the **AutoCAD 2027** option on the *Program* menu or select the **AutoCAD 2027** icon on the *Desktop*.

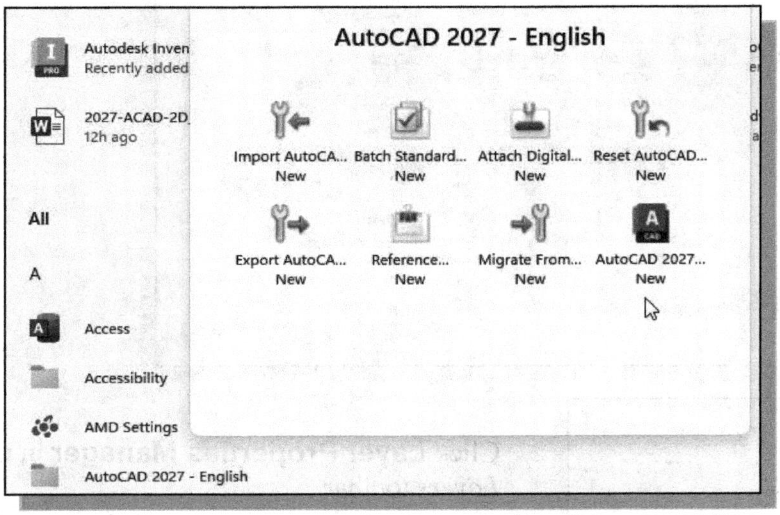

2. In the *Startup* window, select **Start from Scratch**.

3. In the *Default Settings* section, pick **Imperial (feet and inches)** as the drawing units.

4. Pick **OK** in the *Startup* dialog box to accept the selected settings.

3D Modeling Workspace

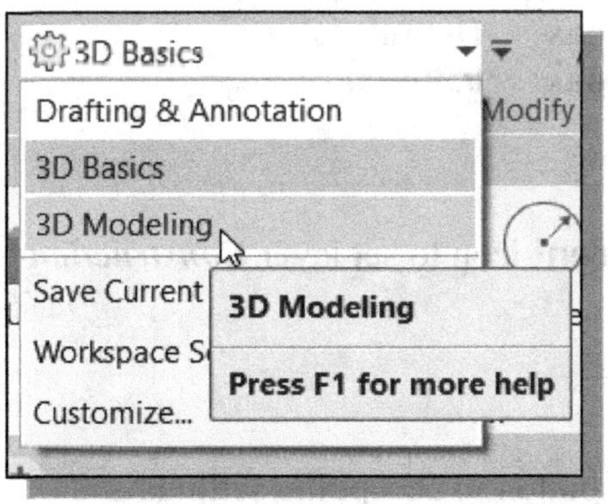

1. Click on the workspaces list in the *Quick Access* toolbar and choose to use the **3D Modeling** workspace as shown.

2. On your own, switch **on** the **Menu Bar**.

➢ Notice the different 3D modeling toolbars available in the *Ribbon* toolbar area as shown.

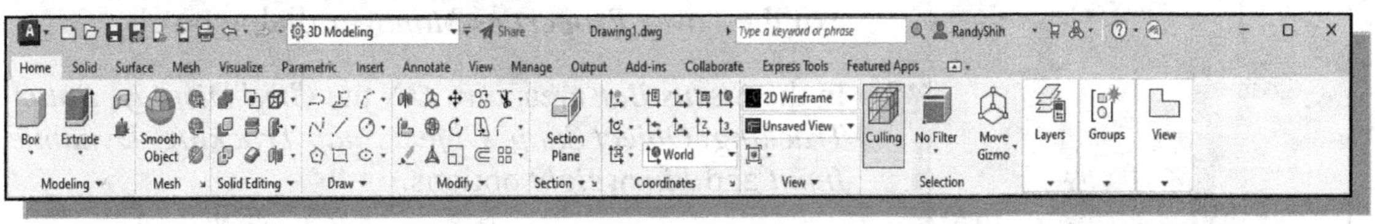

Layers Setup

1. In the *Menu Bar,* select **[Tools] → [Toolbars] → [AutoCAD] → [Layers]**.

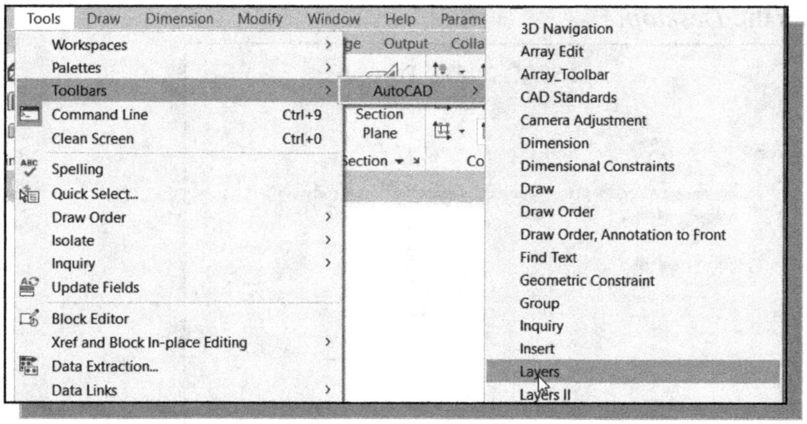

2. Click **Layer Properties Manager** in the *Layers* toolbar.

❖ In AutoCAD, we always construct entities on a layer. It may be the default layer or a layer that we create. Each layer has associated properties such as the visibility setting, color, linetype, lineweight, and plot style.

3. Click on the **New Layer** button. Notice a layer is automatically added to the list of layers.

4. Create **two new layers** with the following settings:

Layer	*Color*	*Linetype*	*Lineweight*
Construction	**Grey**	**Continuous**	**Default**
Object	**Cyan**	**Continuous**	**0.30mm**

5. Highlight the layer ***Construction*** in the list of layers.

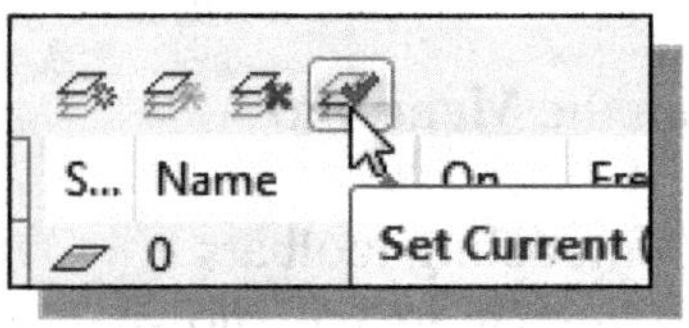

6. Click on the **Set Current** icon to set layer ***Construction*** as the *Current Layer.*

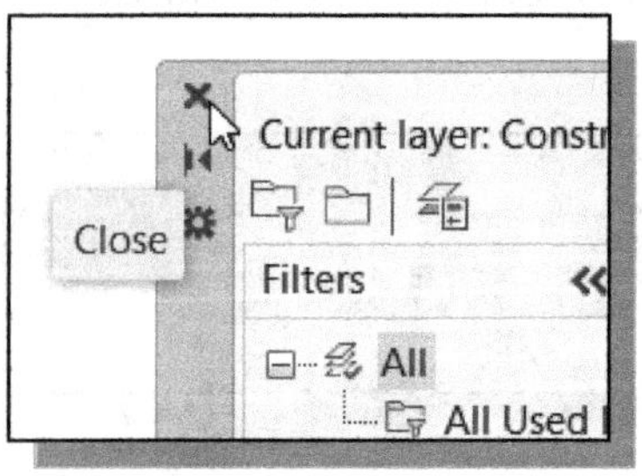

7. Click on the **Close** button to accept the settings and exit the *Layer Properties Manager* dialog box.

8. In the *Status Bar* area, turn ***ON*** the *Grid Display*, *Polar Tracking*, *Object Snap*, *Object Snap Tracking*, *Dynamic Input* and *Lineweight* options.

Create the Rectangular Base of the Design

We will first use construction geometry to define the outer edges of the design.

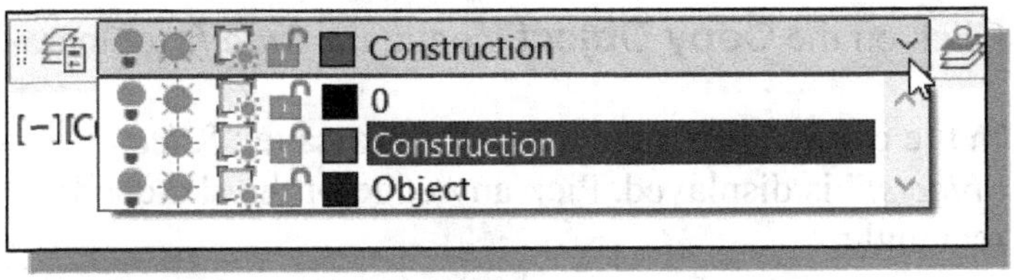

1. In the *Layer Control* box, confirm that layer *Construction* is set as the *Current Layer*.

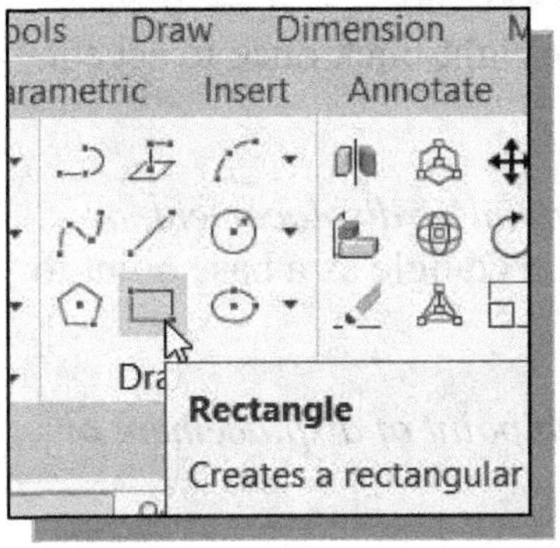

2. Select the **Rectangle** icon in the *Draw* toolbar. In the command prompt area, the message *"Specify first corner point or [Chamfer/Elevation/Fillet/ Thickness/ Width]:"* is displayed.

3. Place the first corner point of the rectangle near the lower left corner of the screen. Do not be overly concerned about the actual coordinates of the location; the drawing space is as big as you can imagine.

4. We will create a 3″ × 2″ rectangle by entering the coordinates of the second corner using the relative coordinates input method.
   Specify other corner point or [Dimension]: **@3,2 [ENTER]**.

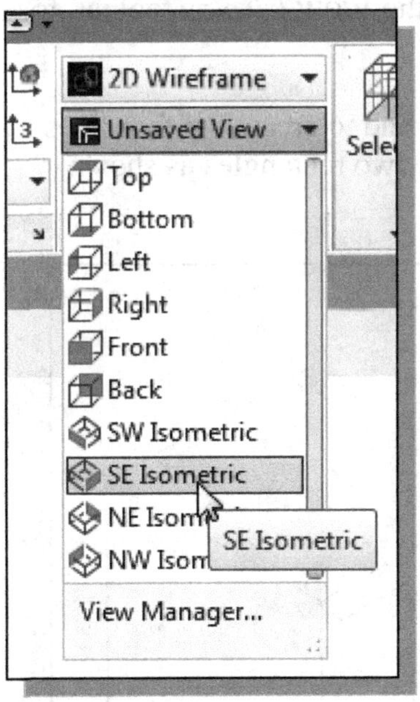

5. In the *View* panel, select:

   [Unsaved View] → [SE Isometric]

- Notice the orientation of the sketched 2D rectangle in relation to the displayed AutoCAD user coordinate system. By default, the 2D sketch plane is aligned to the XY plane of the world coordinate system.

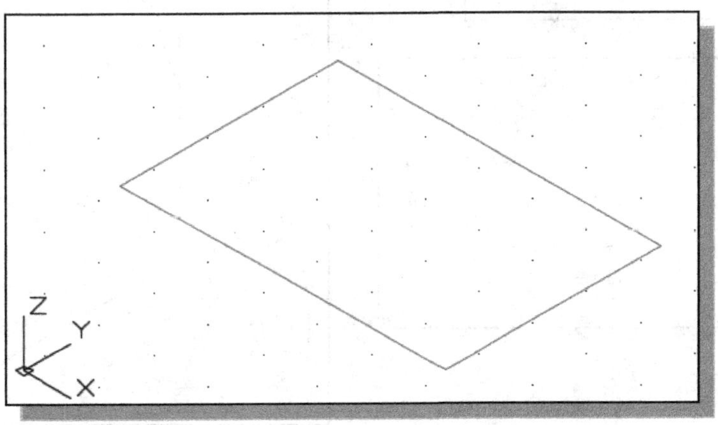

Create a Wireframe Box

Next, we will use the **Copy** command to define the 3D boundary of the design.

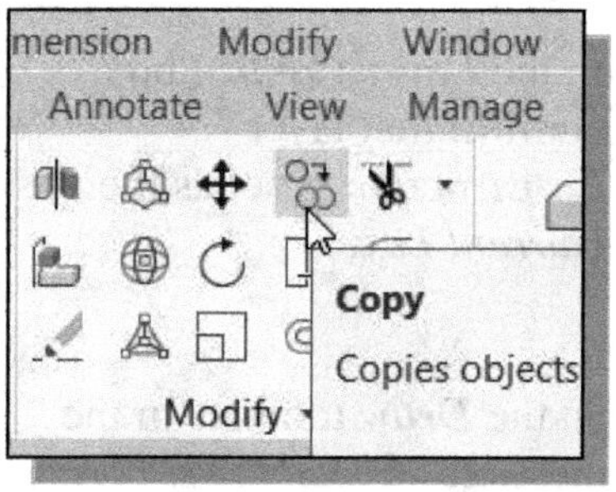

1. Click on the **Copy Object** icon in the *Modify* toolbar.

2. In the command prompt area, the message "*Select objects:*" is displayed. Pick any edge of the sketched rectangle.

3. Inside the graphics window, right-click once to accept the selection.

4. In the command prompt area, the message "*Specify base point or displacement, or [Multiple]:*" is displayed. Pick any corner of the sketched rectangle as a base point to create the copy.

5. In the command prompt area, the message "*Specify second point of displacement or <use first point as displacement>:*" is displayed.
   Enter **@0,0,2.25 [ENTER]**.

➢ Note that the three values represent the distance measured in the X, Y and Z directions relative to the current UCS.

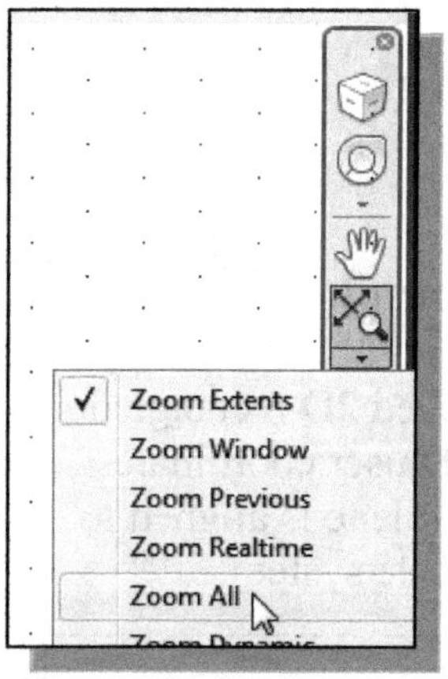

6. Use the **Zoom All** command, in the *View Display* toolbar, to adjust the display.

7. On your own, use the **Line** command to create the four lines connecting the four-corners of the two rectangles as shown.

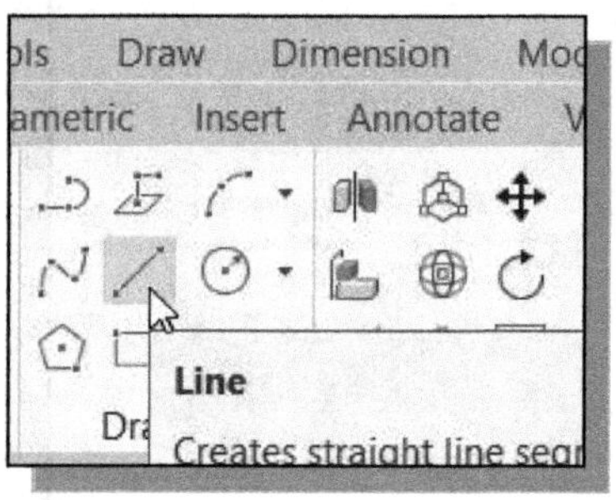

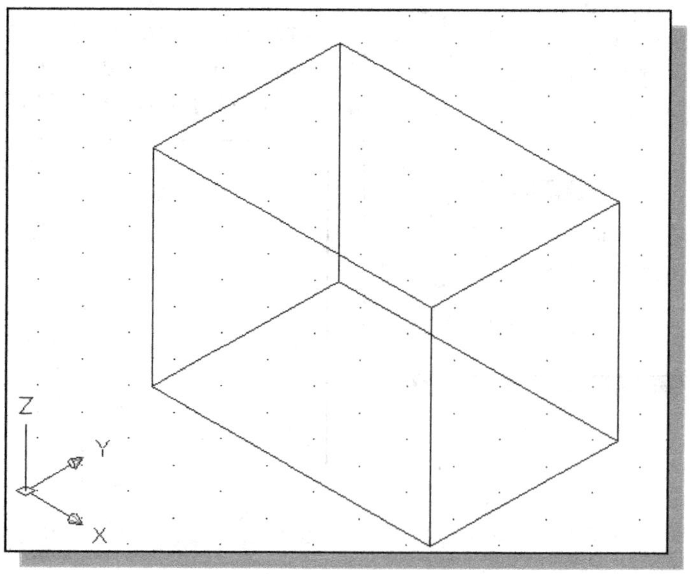

Using the View and UCS Toolbars

1. In the *Menu Bar,* select **[Tools] → [Toolbars] → [AutoCAD]**.

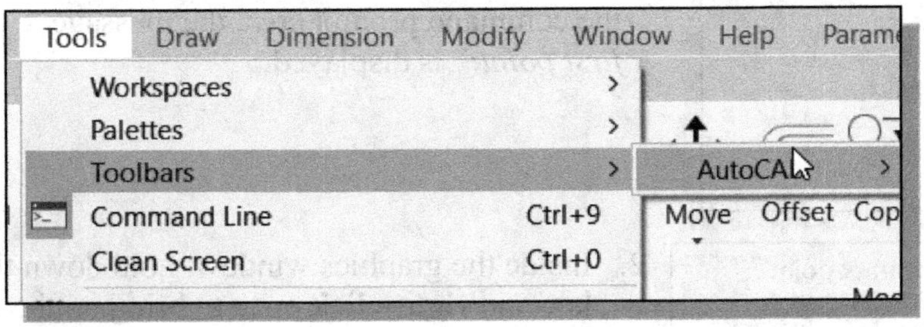

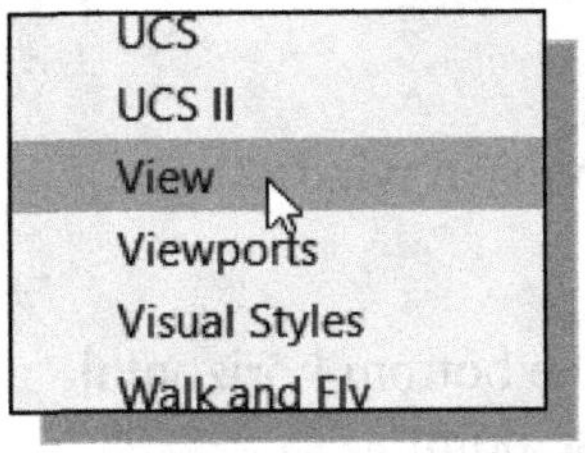

2. Select **View**, with the left-mouse-button, to display the *View* toolbar on the screen.

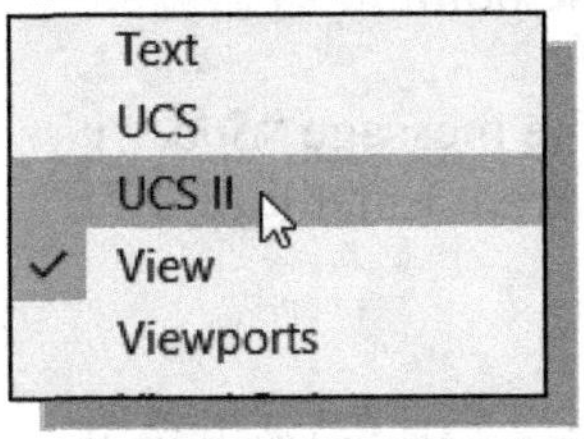

3. Move the cursor to the *Standard* toolbar area and **right-click** on any icon of the *Standard* toolbar to display a list of toolbar menu groups.

4. Select **UCS II**, with the left-mouse-button, to display the *UCSII* toolbar on the screen.

➢ The options available in *UCS II* toolbar allow us to quickly align the UCS to the preset standard 2D views.

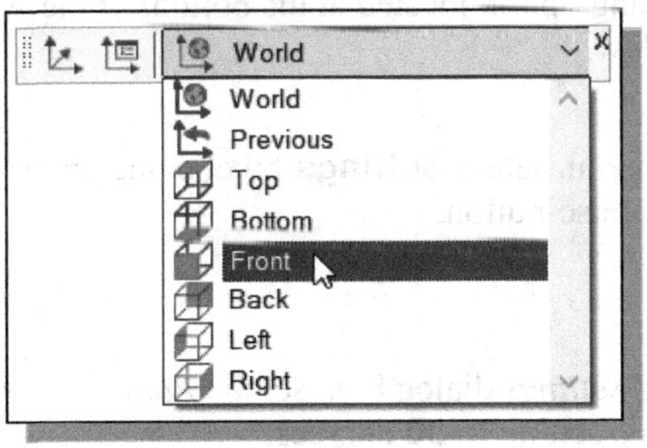

5. Note that the current *UCS* is aligned to the *World Coordinate System*. Select **Front** in the *UCS II* toolbar as shown.

➢ Note that the UCS has been adjusted and it is now aligned parallel to the front view of the wireframe box as shown in the figure.

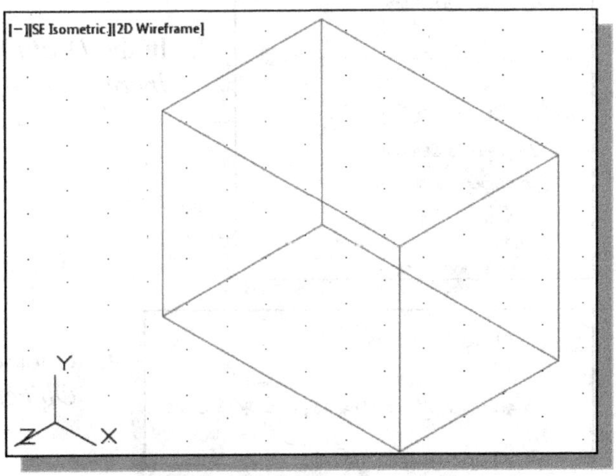

Create Construction Lines in the Front View

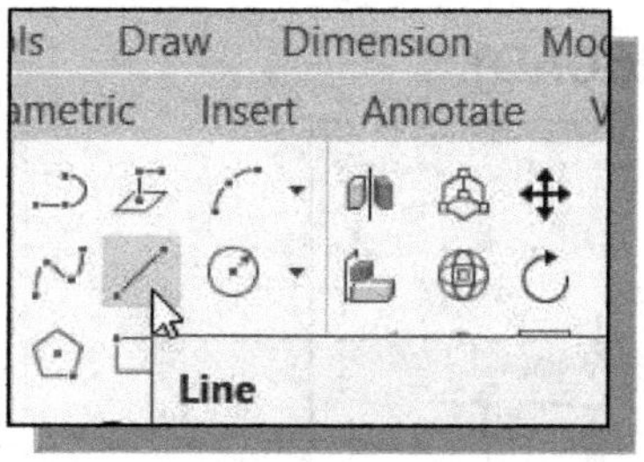

1. Select the **Line** command icon in the *Draw* toolbar. In the command prompt area, the message "*_line Specify first point:*" is displayed.

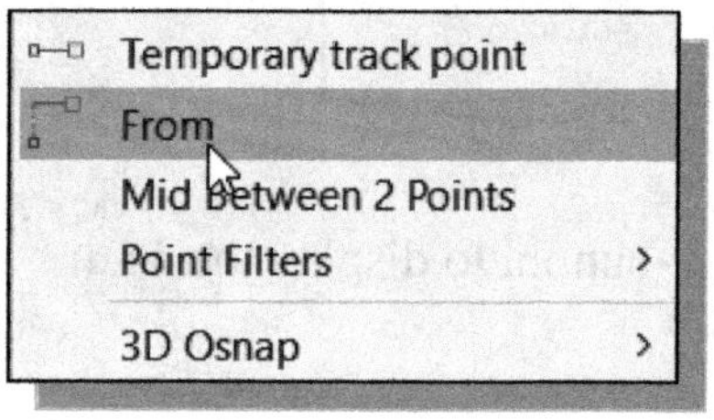

2. Inside the graphics window, hold down the **[SHIFT]** key and **right-click** once to bring up the *Object Snap* shortcut menu.

3. Select the **From** option in the pop-up window.

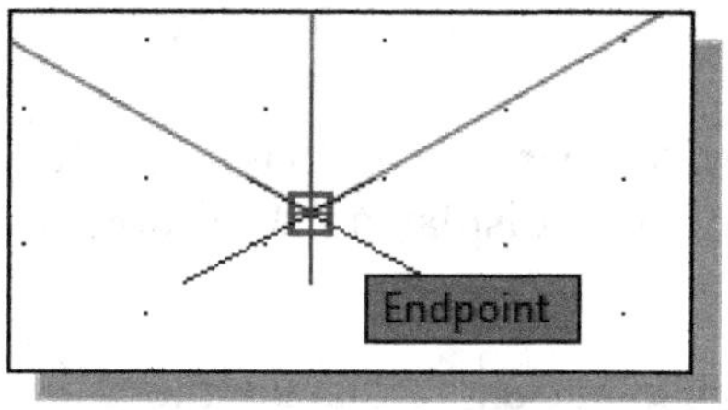

4. Pick the lower right corner of the bottom horizontal line in the front view as the base point.

5. In the command prompt area, the message "*Specify next point or [Undo]:*" is displayed. Enter **@0,0.75 [ENTER]**.

6. We will set up the *Polar Tracking* option to assist the creation of the next corner. **Right-click** once on the *POLAR* Tracking option located at the bottom of the graphics window.

7. In the option menu, select **Settings** by clicking once with the left-mouse-button.

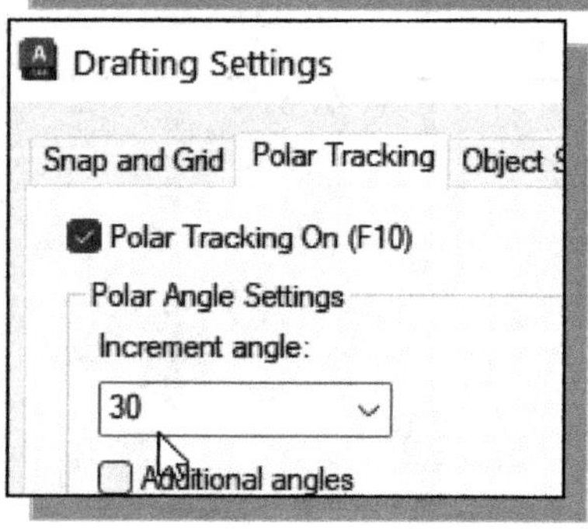

8. In the *Drafting Settings* dialog box, set the *Polar Increment Angle* setting to **30** degrees.

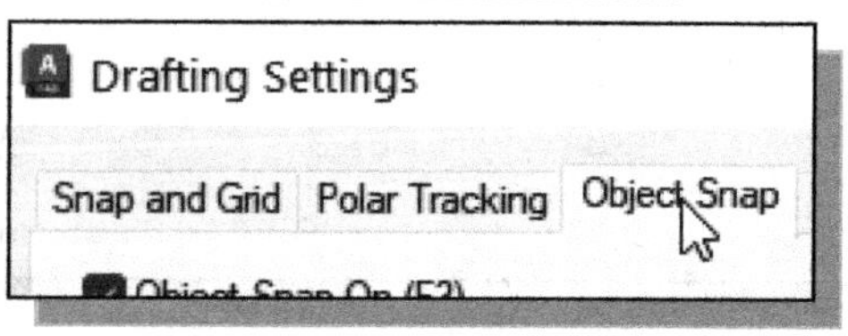

9. Click on the **Object Snap** tab to switch to the *Object Snap* option settings.

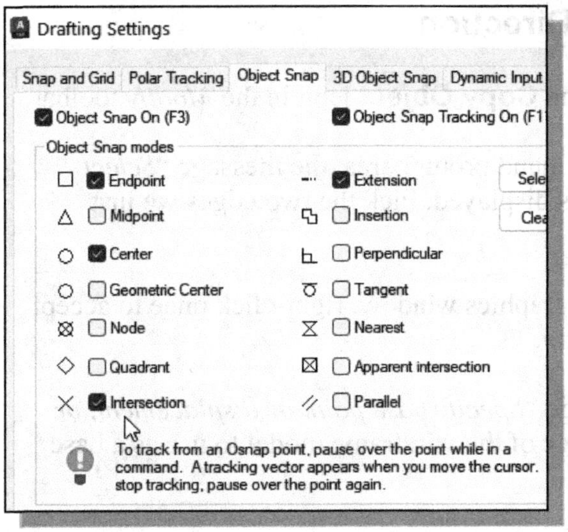

10. Confirm that the *Intersection* and *Extension* options are switched *ON* as shown.

11. Click on the **OK** button to accept the settings.

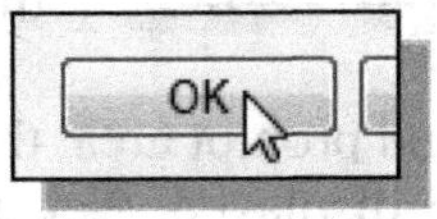

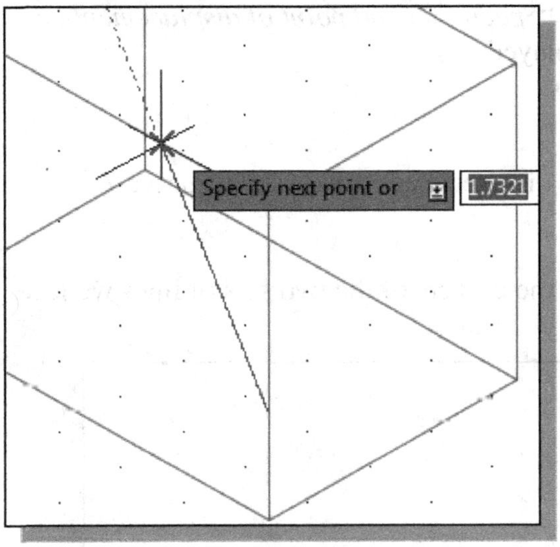

12. In the command prompt area, the message "*Specify next point or [Undo]:*" is displayed. Using the *Polar Tracking* option (30 degrees increment), create a line as shown in the figure.

13. Move the cursor near the left vertical edge of the front view and create the second line perpendicular to the last line we created.

14. Inside the graphics window, **right-click** to activate the option menu and select **Enter** with the left-mouse-button to end the **Line** command.

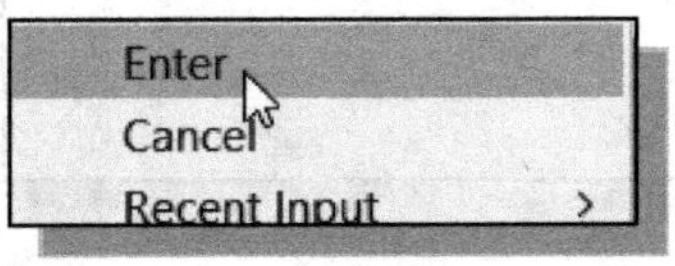

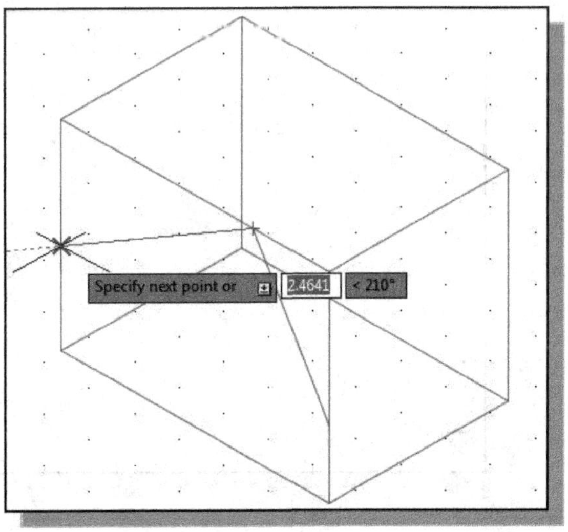

Copy Objects in the Negative Z Direction

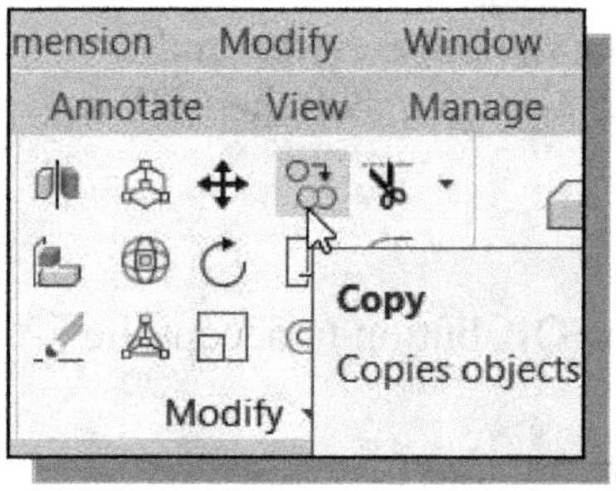

1. Click on the **Copy Object** icon in the *Modify* toolbar.

2. In the command prompt area, the message "*Select objects:*" is displayed. Pick the two edges we just created.

3. Inside the graphics window, right-click once to accept the selection.

4. In the command prompt area, the message "*Specify base point or displacement, or [Multiple]:*" is displayed. Pick any **corner** of the wireframe model to use as a base point to create the copy.

5. In the command prompt area, the message "*Specify second point of displacement or <use first point as displacement>:*" is displayed.

   Enter **@0,0,-2.0 [ENTER]**.

6. Note that the negative value represents the distance measured in the negative Z direction relative to the current UCS.

7. On your own, create three lines to connect the corners of the two sets of lines we just created, as shown below.

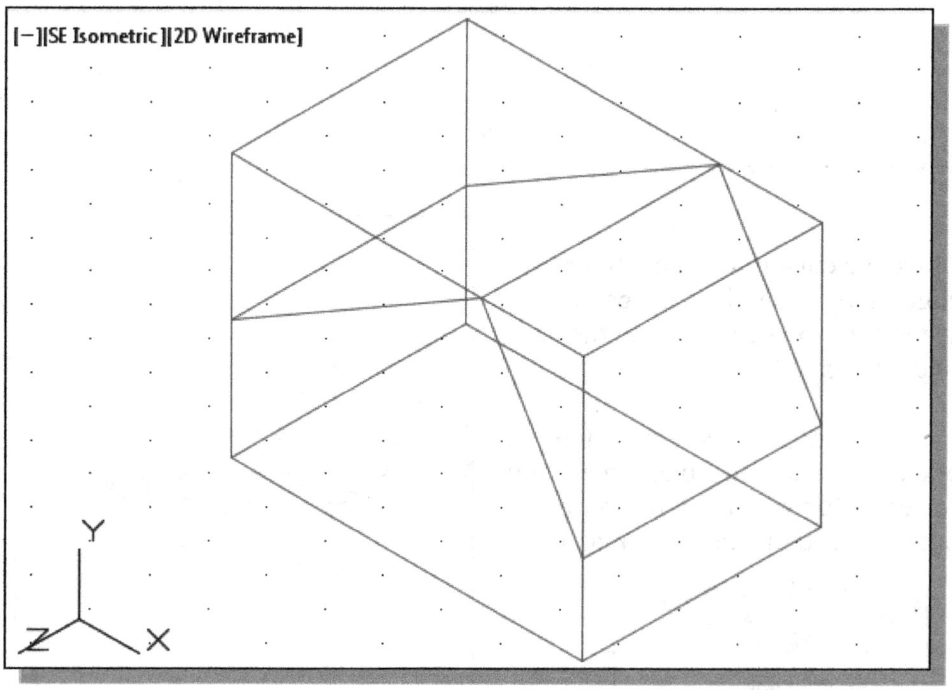

Create an Inclined Line at the Base of the Model

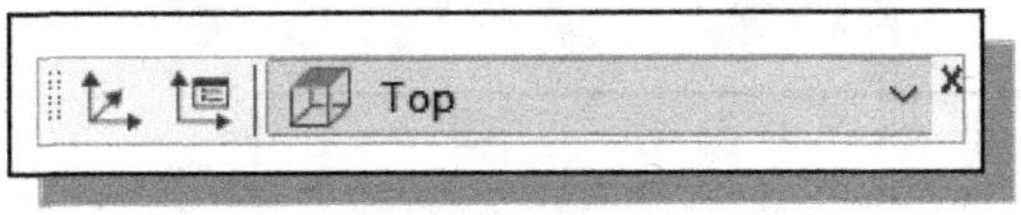

1. Select **Top** in the *UCS II* toolbar as shown.

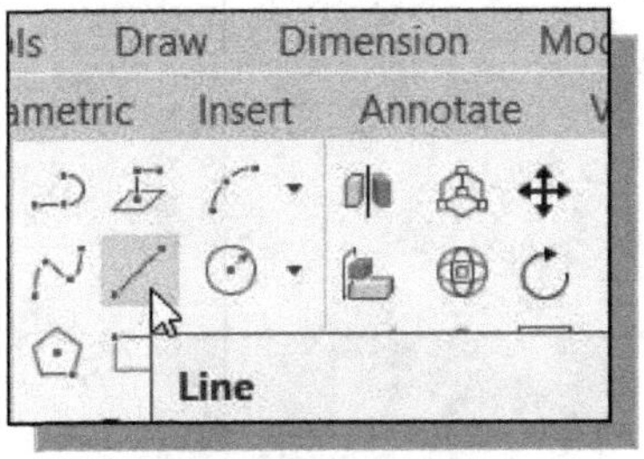

2. Select the **Line** command icon in the *Draw* toolbar. In the command prompt area, the message "*_line Specify first point:*" is displayed.

3. Inside the graphics window, hold down the **[SHIFT]** key and **right-click** once to bring up the *Object Snap* shortcut menu.

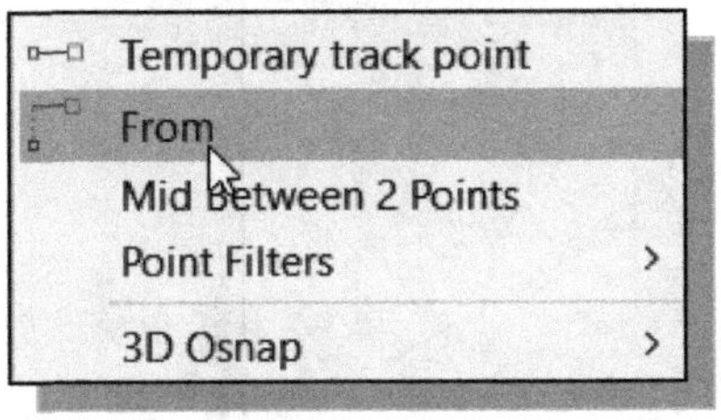

4. Select the **From** option in the pop-up window.

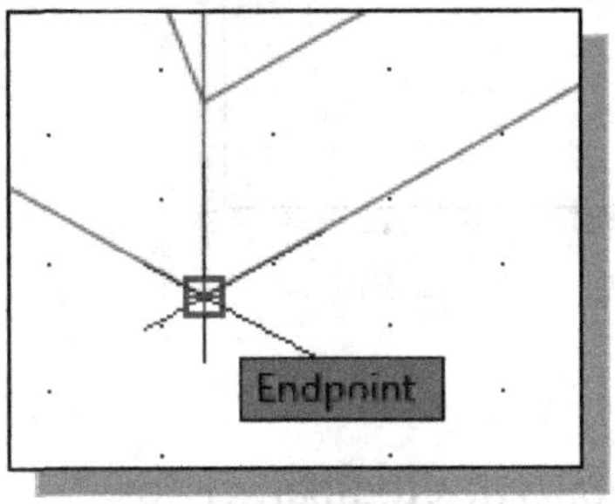

5. Pick the lower right corner of the bottom horizontal line as the base point as shown in the figure.

6. We will place the first point above the selected corner. Enter **@0,0.75 [ENTER]**.

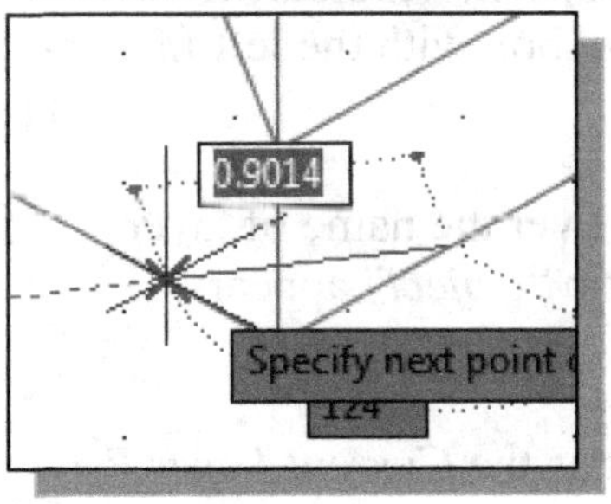

7. In the command prompt area, the message "*Specify next point or [Undo]:*" is displayed. Using the *Polar Tracking* option (30 degrees increment), create a line as shown in the figure.

8. Inside the *graphics window*, **right-click** to activate the option menu and select **Enter** with the left-mouse-button to end the Line command.

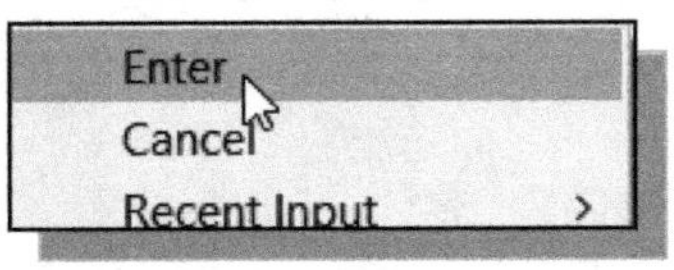

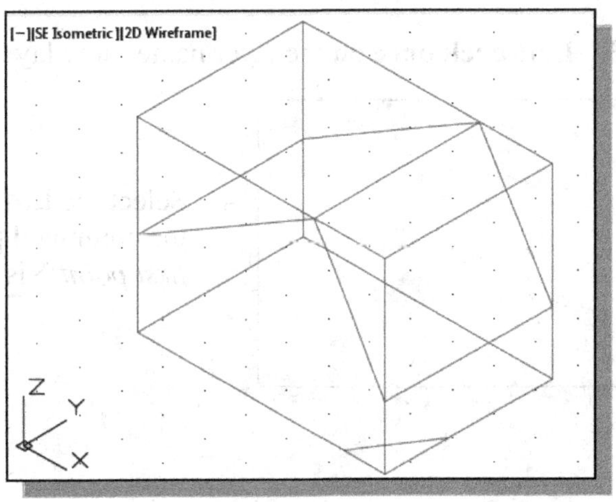

➢ On your own, use the **Copy** and **Line** commands to create additional edges so that the wireframe model appears as shown below.

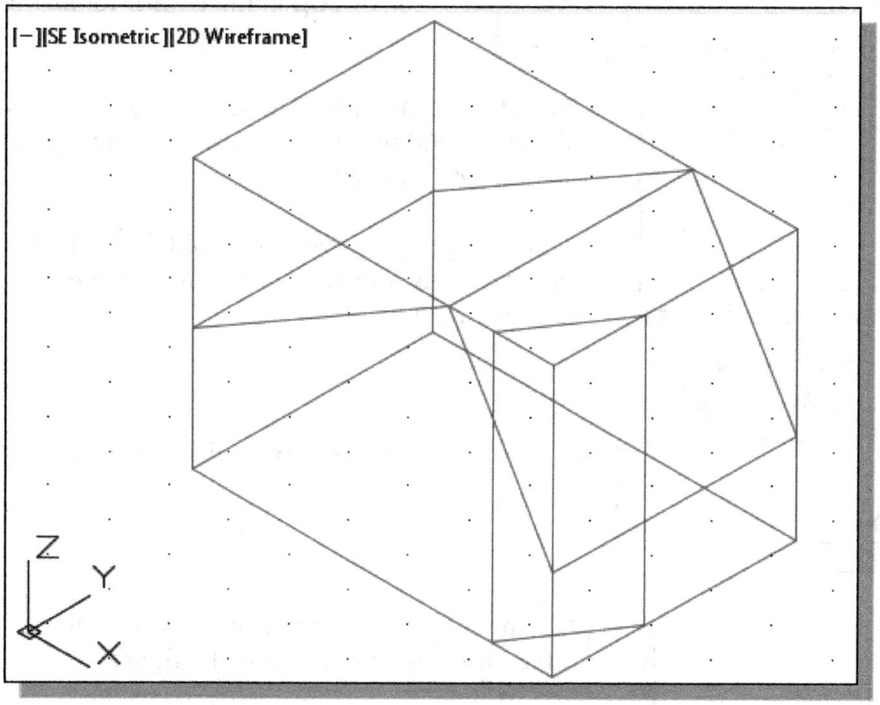

Create Object Lines

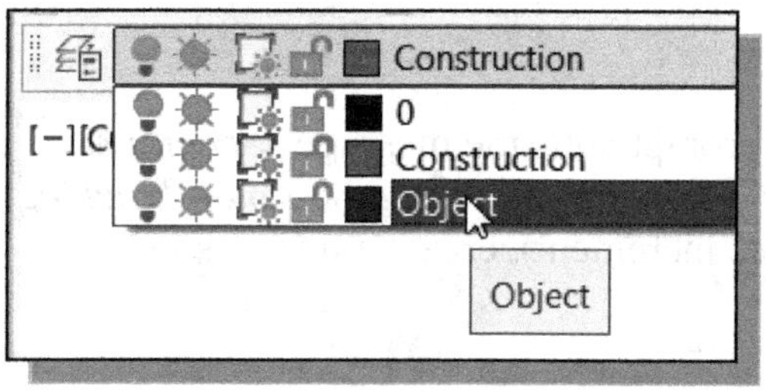

1. On the *Object Properties* toolbar, choose the ***Layer Control*** box with the left-mouse-button.

2. Move the cursor over the name of layer ***Object***; the tool tip "*Object*" appears.

3. **Left-click once** on the layer name; now layer *Object* is set as the *Current Layer*.

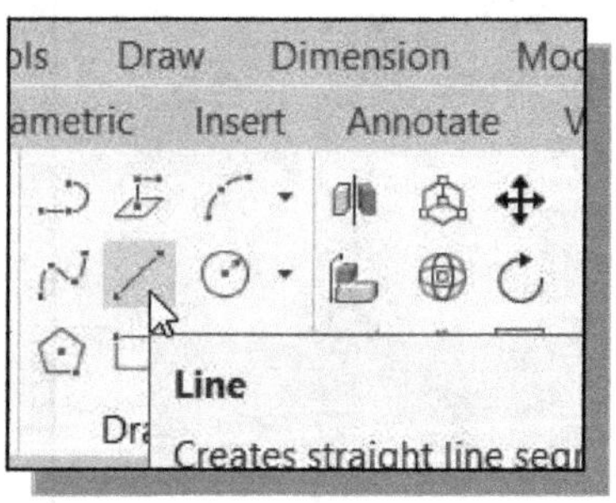

4. Select the **Line** command icon in the *Draw* toolbar. In the command prompt area, the message "*_line Specify first point:*" is displayed.

5. Pick the lower left corner of the bottom of the wireframe model as the starting point and create the four line segments as shown.

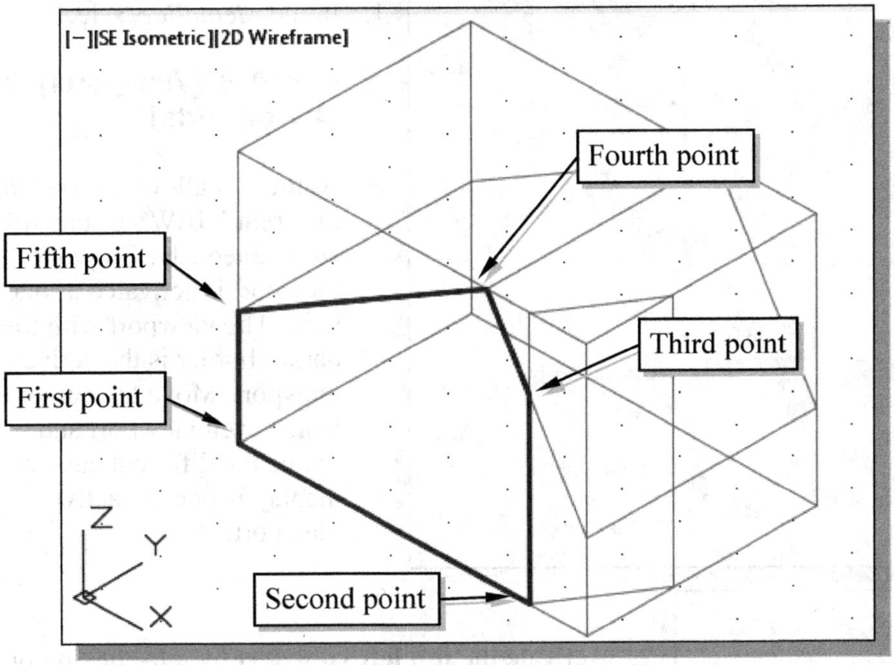

- Note that even though the UCS is aligned to the base plane of the model, the *Object Snap* option enables us to select points on the front plane of the model.

➤ On your own, create three additional lines representing the edges of the inclined face of the design as shown.

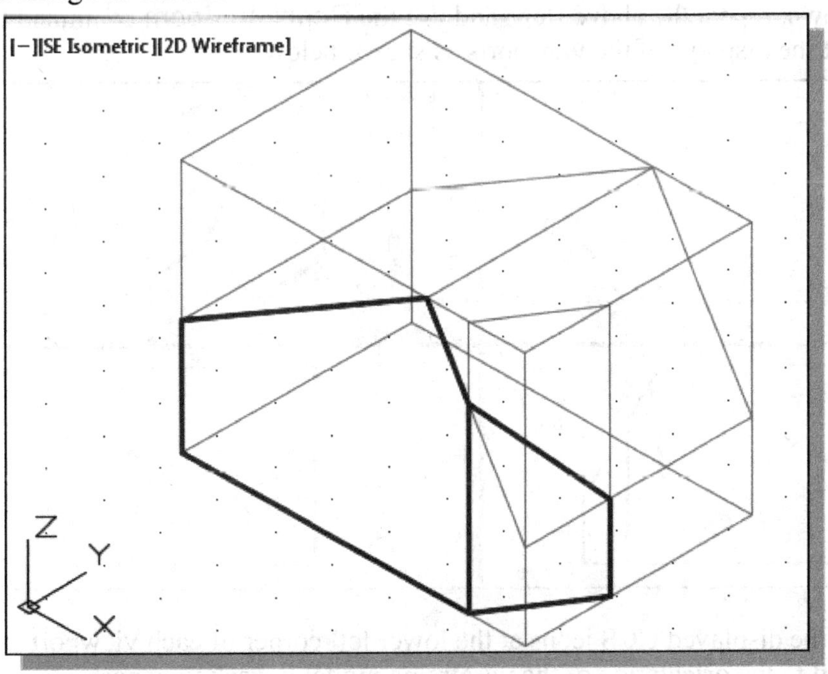

Multiple Viewports

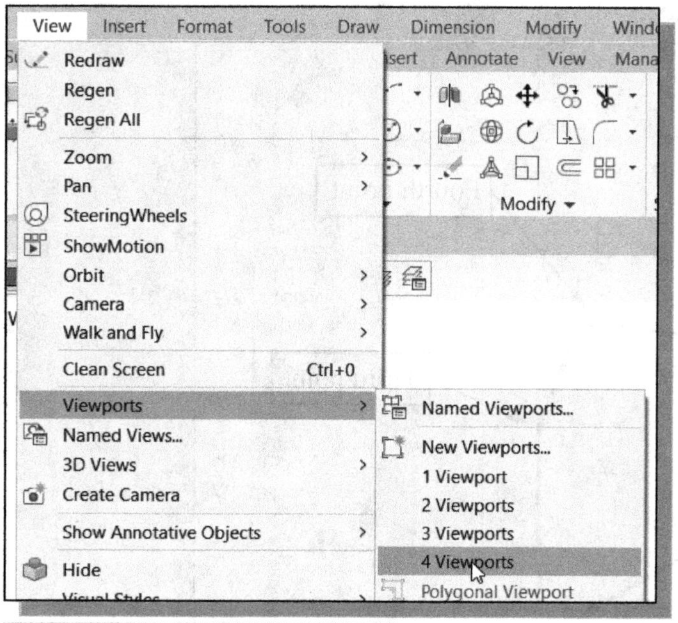

1. In the *Menu Bar*, select:

   [View] → [Viewports] → [4 Viewports]

➢ AutoCAD allows us to display different VIEWS of the model simultaneously. Only one viewport is activated at one time. The viewport with the darker border is the active viewport. Move the cursor inside each viewport and notice the different cursor-display inside the active viewport.

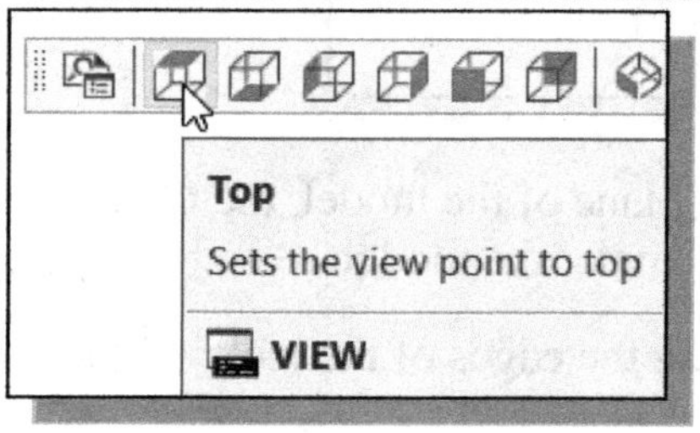

2. Activate the **top left viewport** by left-clicking once inside the viewport.

3. Select the **Top** view in the *View* toolbar to change the display of the viewport.

4. On your own, repeat the above steps and use the **Realtime Zoom** command to set and adjust the displays of the viewports as shown below.

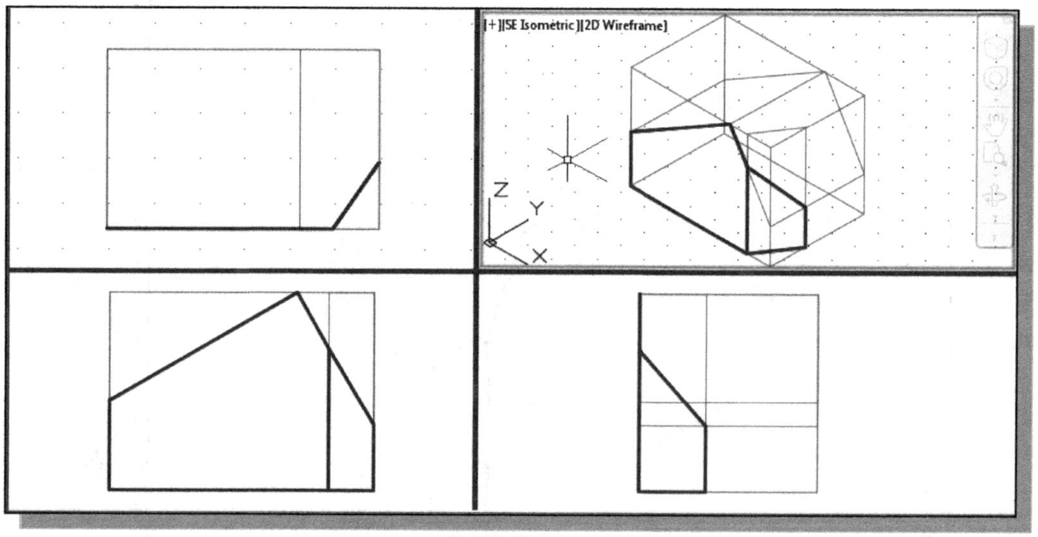

➢ Note that the displayed UCS icons at the lower left corner of each viewport correspond to the orientation of the wireframe model in each viewport.

Use the Mirror Command

1. Activate the top left viewport by left-clicking once inside the viewport.

2. ***Pre-select*** all the objects in the active viewport by using a selection window.

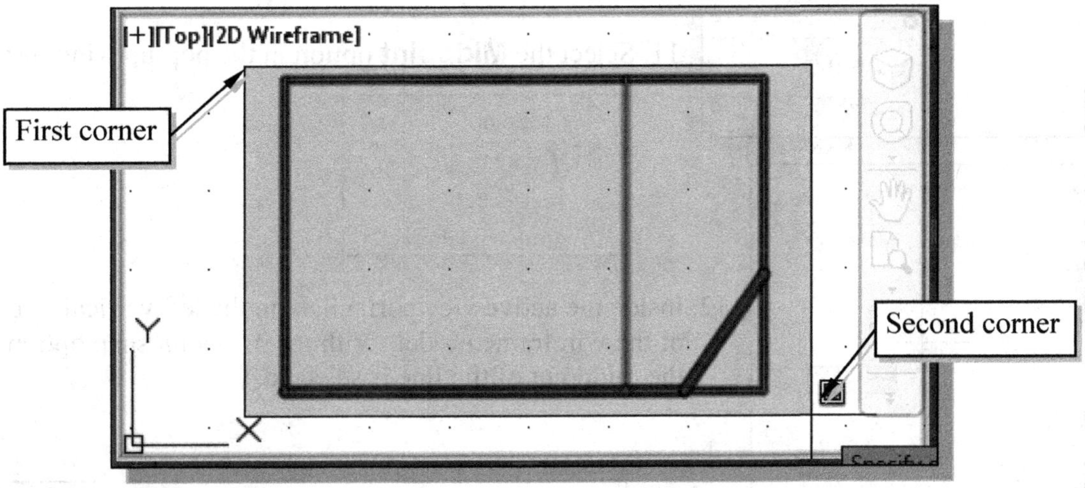

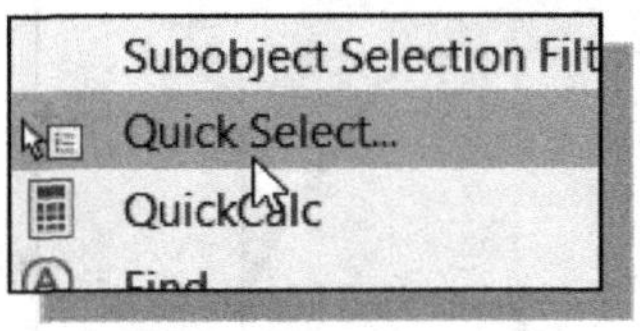

3. Inside the *active viewport*, **right-click** to bring up the pop-up option menu and select the **Quick Select** option.

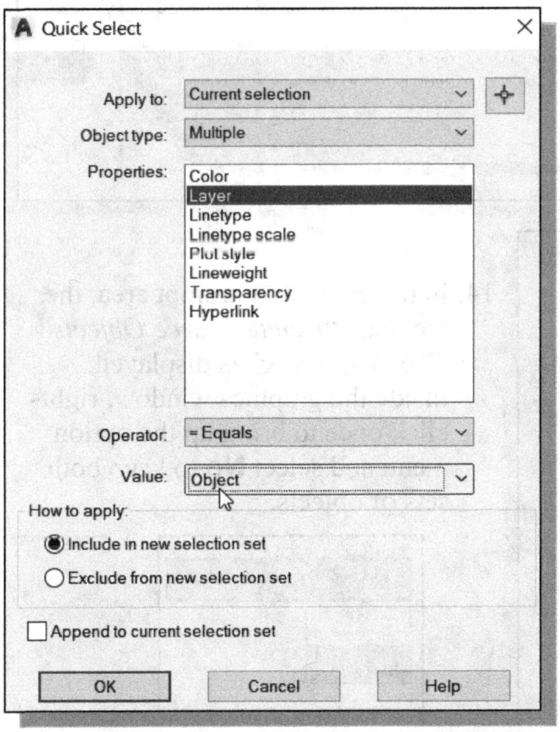

4. In the *Quick Select* dialog box, select **Layer** from the *Properties* list.

5. Set the *Value* box to **Object**.

6. In the *How to apply* section, confirm the **Include in new selection set** option is selected.

7. Switch *OFF* the **Append to current selection set**.

8. Click on the **OK** button to accept the settings.

- AutoCAD will now **filter out** objects that are not on layer *Object*.

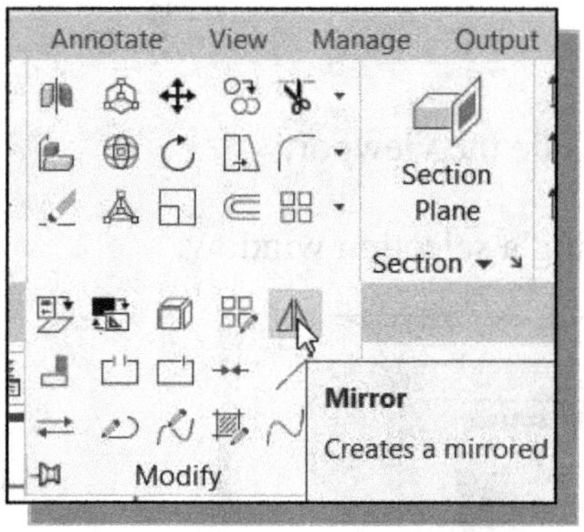

9. Click on the **Mirror** icon in the *Modify* toolbar.

10. Inside the graphics window, hold down the **[SHIFT]** key and **right-click** once to bring up the *Object Snap* shortcut menu.

11. Select the **Midpoint** option in the pop-up window.

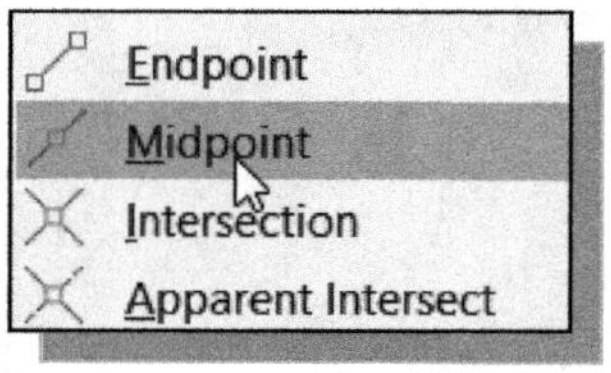

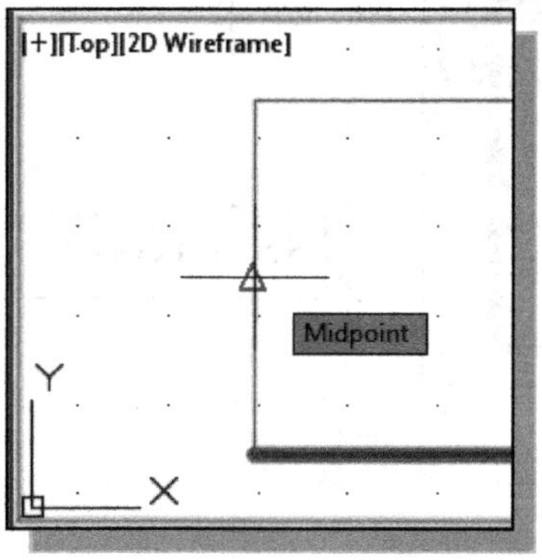

12. Inside the active viewport, click on the left vertical line of the wireframe model. With the *Midpoint* snap option, the midpoint of the line is selected.

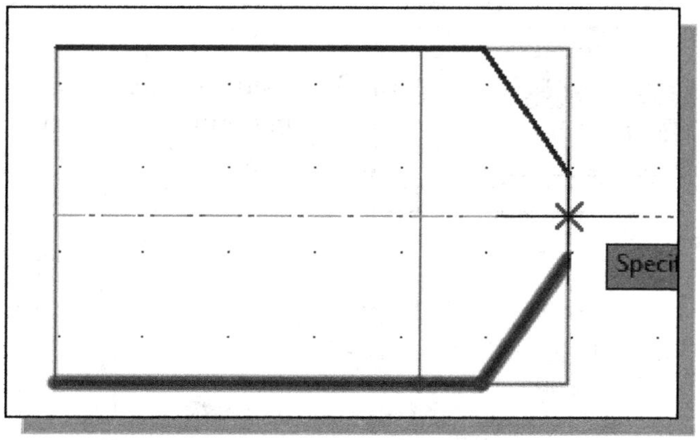

13. Move the cursor toward the right vertical line in the active viewport; left-click once when the **Intersection** symbol is displayed as shown.

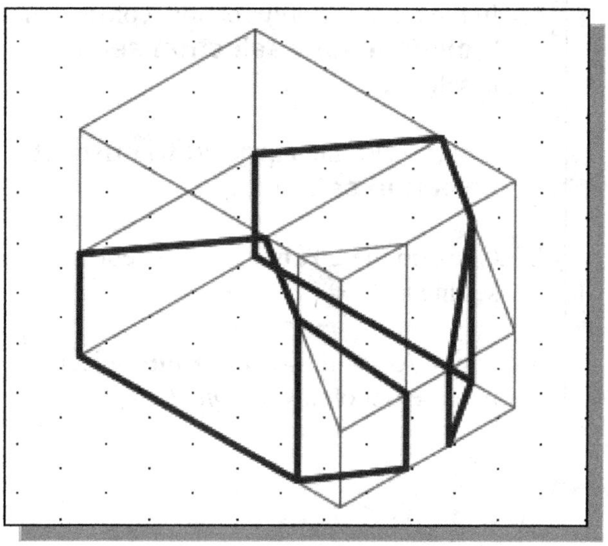

14. In the command prompt area, the message *"Delete Source Objects? [Yes/No] <N>:"* is displayed. Inside the graphics window, right-click once to bring up the option menu and select **No** to keep both sets of objects.

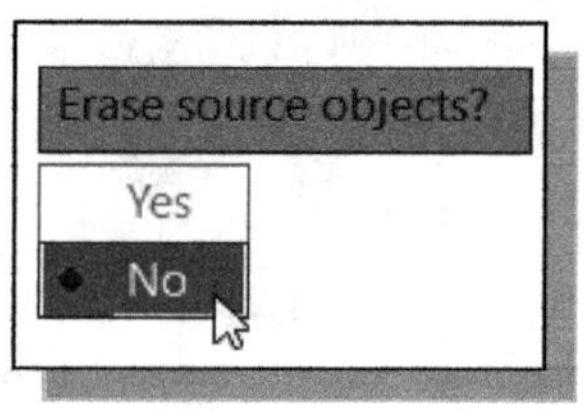

Turn Off the Construction Lines

1. On the *Object Properties* toolbar, choose the ***Layer Control*** box with the left-mouse-button.

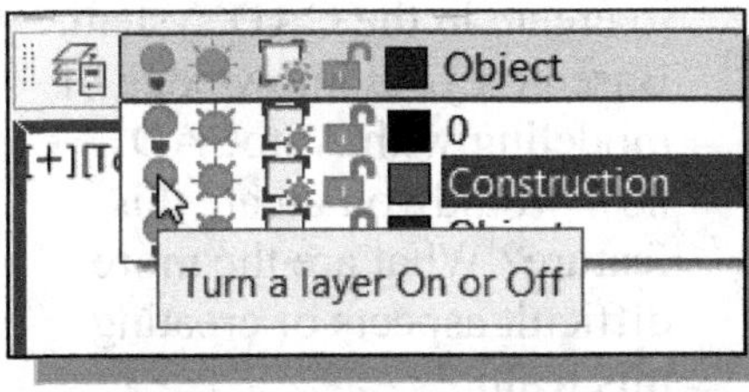

2. Move the cursor over the **light-bulb** icon for layer *Construction*, **left-click once**, and notice the icon color is changed to a gray tone color, representing the layer (layer *Construction*) is turned *OFF*.

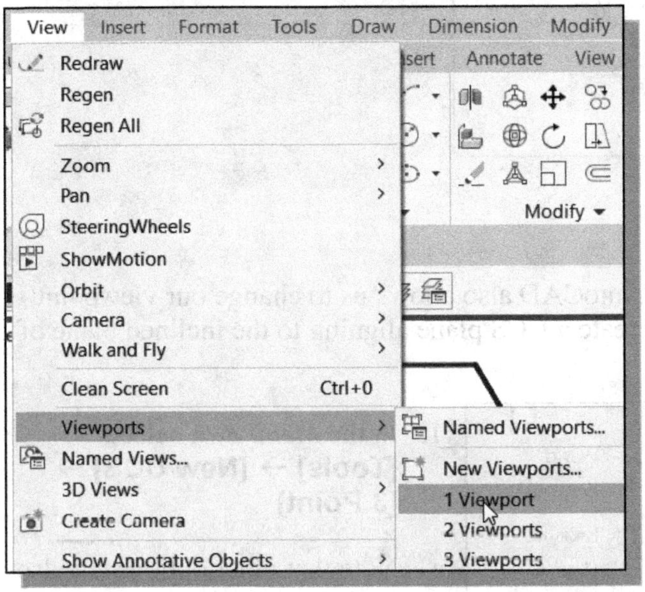

3. In the *Menu Bar*, select:

   [View] → [Viewports] → [1 Viewport]

- Viewports can also be used as a way of checking the integrity of the constructed 3D models. Feel free to switch to multiple viewports in the following sections of this tutorial.

4. On your own, create the additional **object lines** connecting the two sets of objects as shown below.

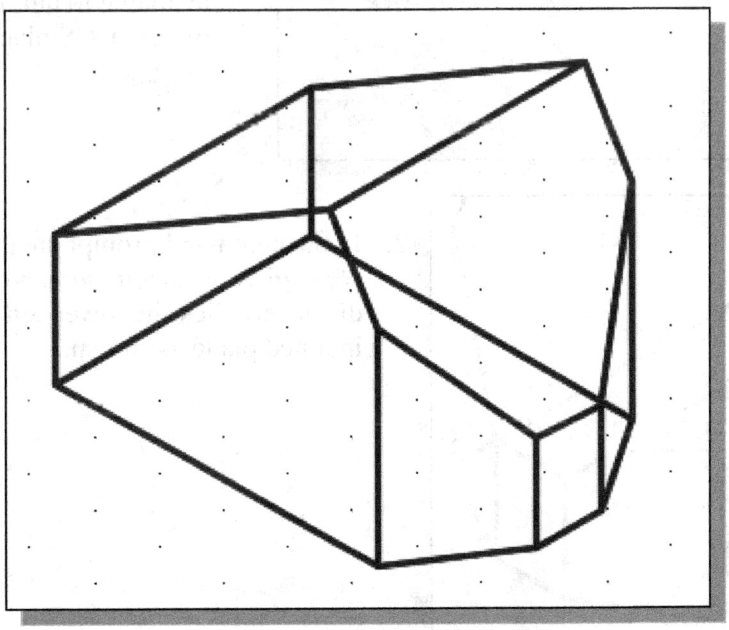

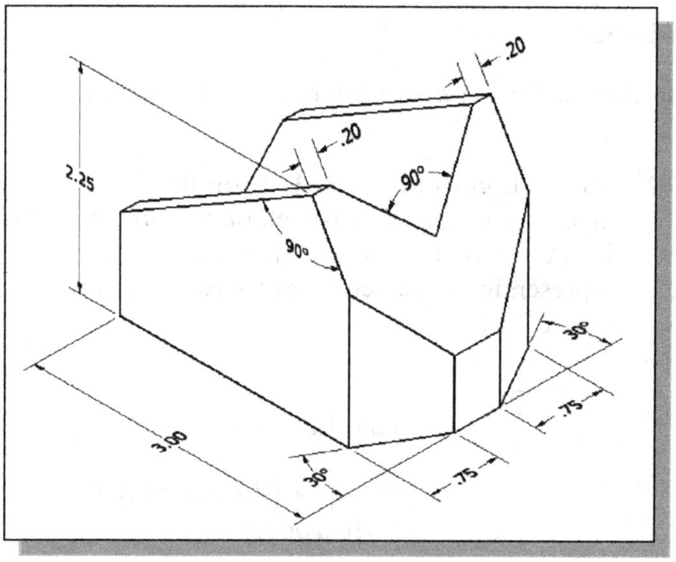

➢ The V-cut feature of the design is the last feature, and perhaps the most difficult one, to create in the CAD system. Based on your knowledge of modeling with AutoCAD, how would you create this feature? What are the more difficult aspects of creating this feature?

Create a New UCS

Besides using the preset UCS planes, AutoCAD also allows us to change our viewpoint and create new UCS planes. We will create a UCS plane aligning to the inclined plane of the design.

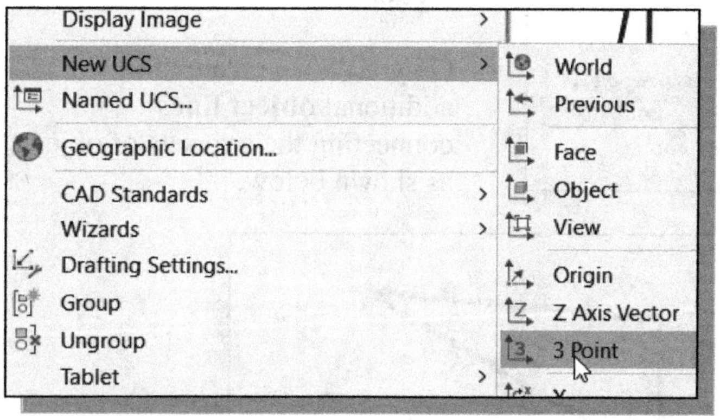

1. In the *Menu Bar*, select: **[Tools] → [New UCS] → [3 Point]**

- Note that other options are also available to aid in the creation of new UCS planes.

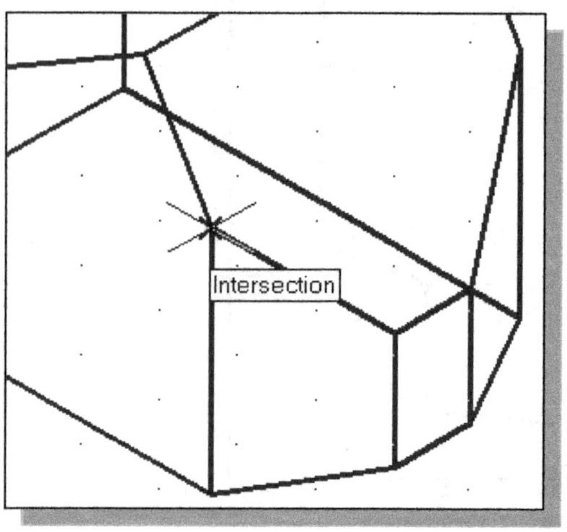

2. In the command prompt area, the message "*Specify New Origin point <0,0,0>:*" is displayed. Pick the lower-left corner of the inclined plane as shown.

3. In the command prompt area, the message "*Specify point on positive portion of X-axis:*" is displayed. Pick the lower right corner of the inclined plane as shown.

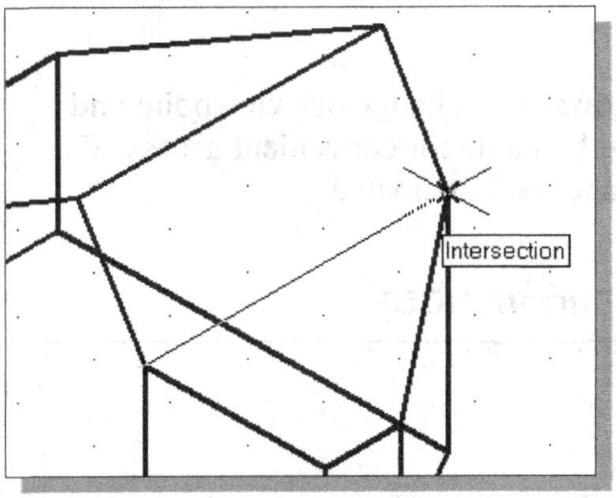

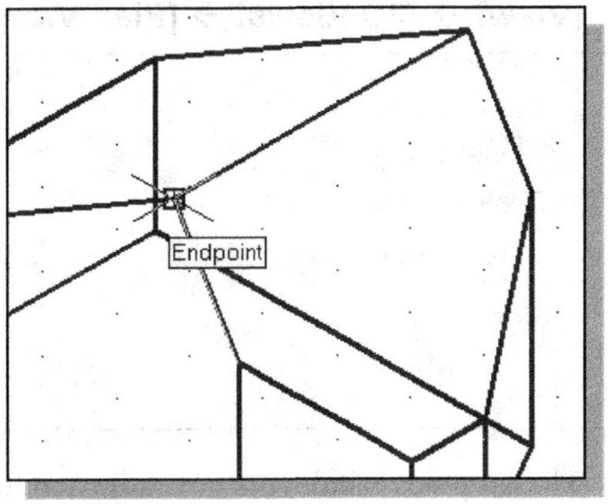

4. In the command prompt area, the message "*Specify point on positive portion of X-axis:*" is displayed. Pick the top left corner of the inclined plane as shown.

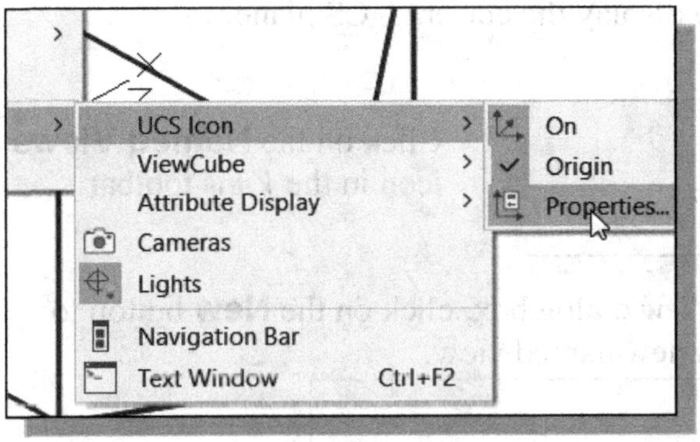

5. In the *Menu Bar*, select

   [View] → [Display] → [UCS Icon] → [Properties]

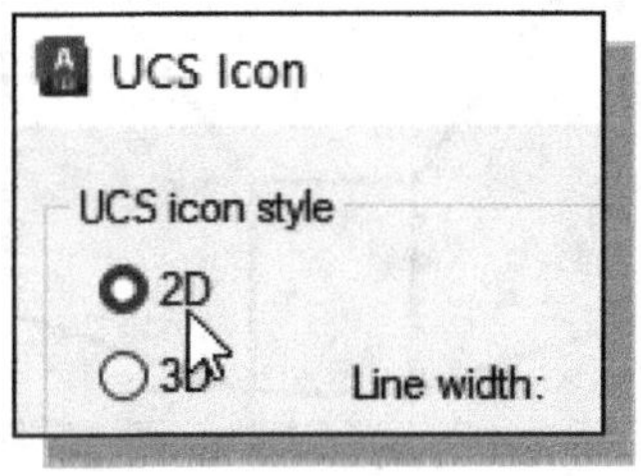

6. In the *UCS Icon* window, switch the *UCS icon style* to **2D** as shown.

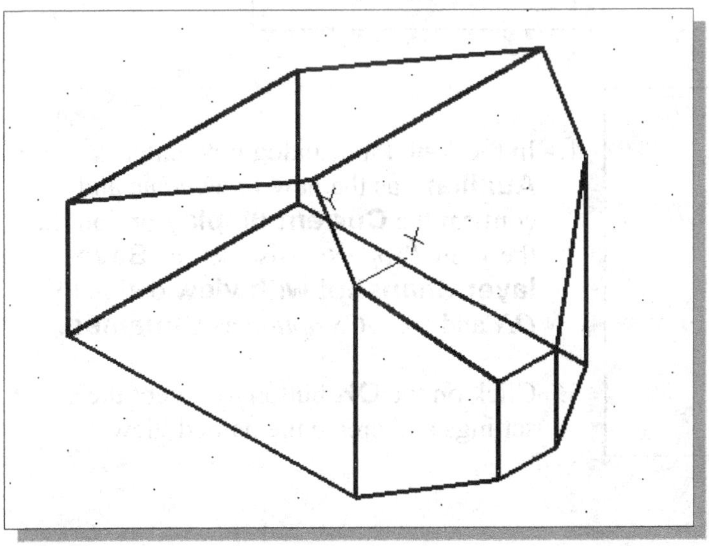

7. Click on the **OK** button to accept the settings.

Create a New Named View

Besides using the preset views, AutoCAD also allows us to change our viewpoint and create new views, which can be saved and restored by name for convenient access. We will create a new view aligned to the new UCS plane we just created.

1. In the *Menu Bar*, select
   [View] → [3D Views] → [Plan View] → [Current UCS].

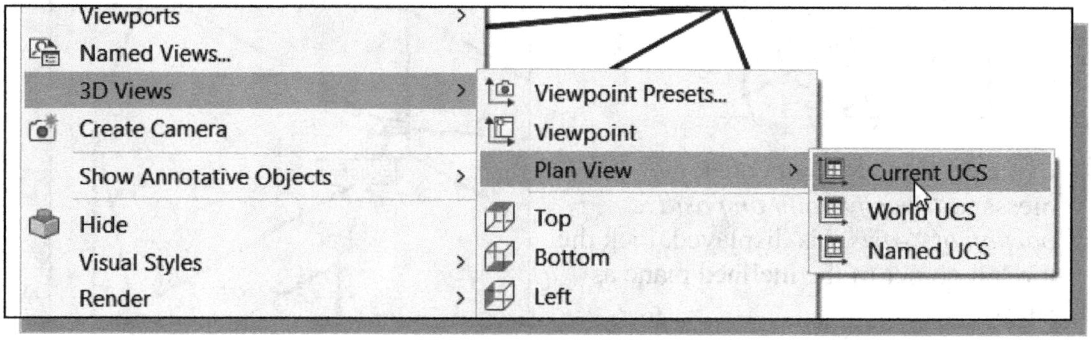

- The graphics window is now adjusted to display the current UCS plane.

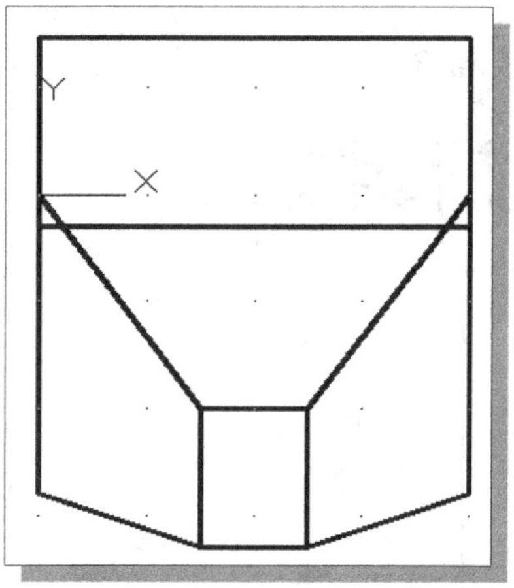

2. Click on the **Named Views** icon in the *View* toolbar.

3. In the *View* dialog box, click on the **New** button to create a new named view.

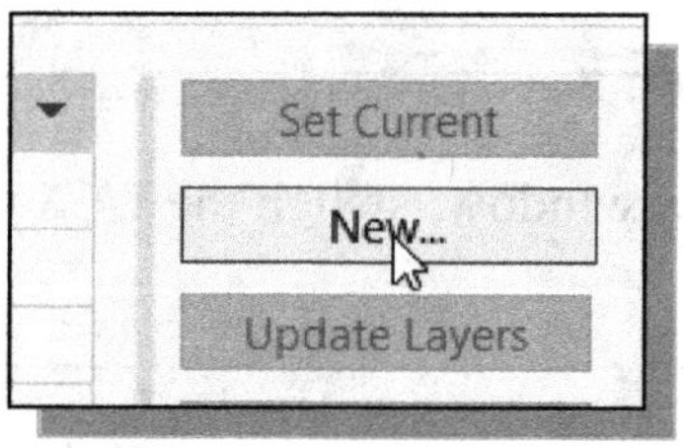

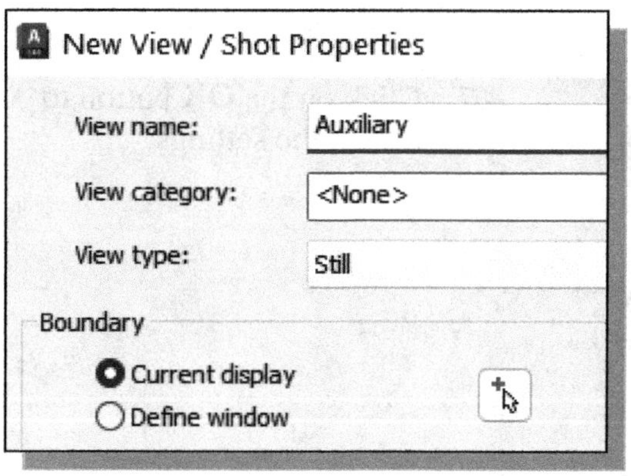

4. In the *New View* dialog box, enter **Auxiliary** as the new *View name* and confirm the **Current display** option. In the *View Properties* list, set the **Save layer Snapshot with view** option to ***ON*** and the *UCS option* as **Unnamed.**

5. Click on the **OK** button to accept the settings and create the named view.

6. In the *View* dialog box, the new named view (Auxiliary) is added to the *Named Views* list. Note that we can always switch to this view by using the **Set Current** option.

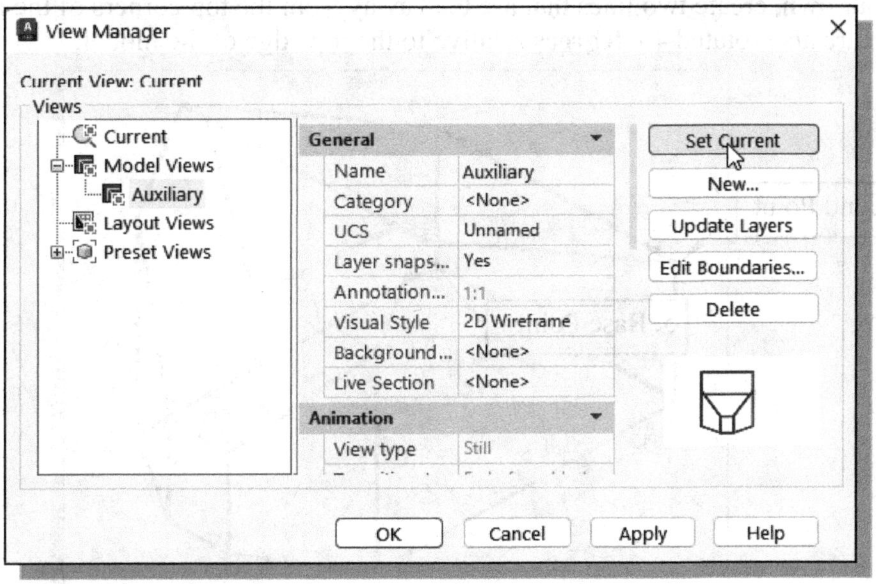

7. Click on the **OK** button to accept the settings.

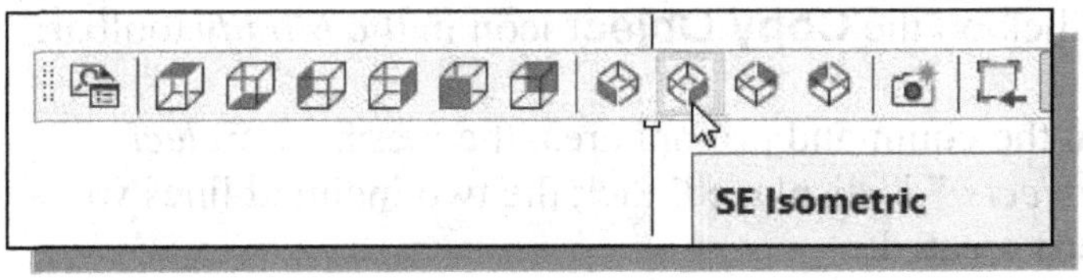

8. In the *View* toolbar, select **SE Isometric View**.

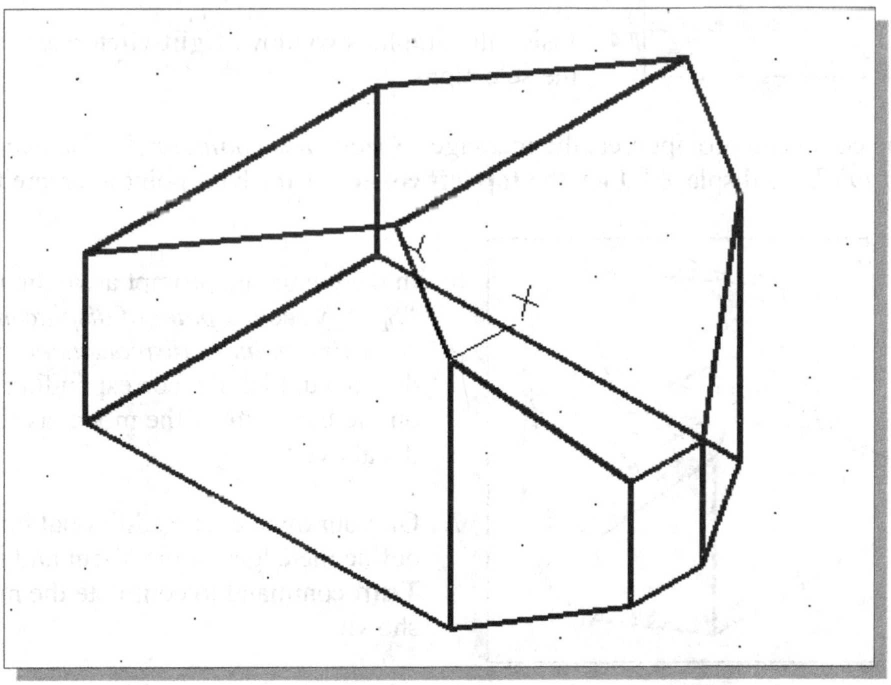

Create the V-Cut Feature on the Inclined Plane

1. On your own, create two lines that are **0.2″** away from the top corners of the model, which are also rotated **45 degrees** relative to the top edge of the model.

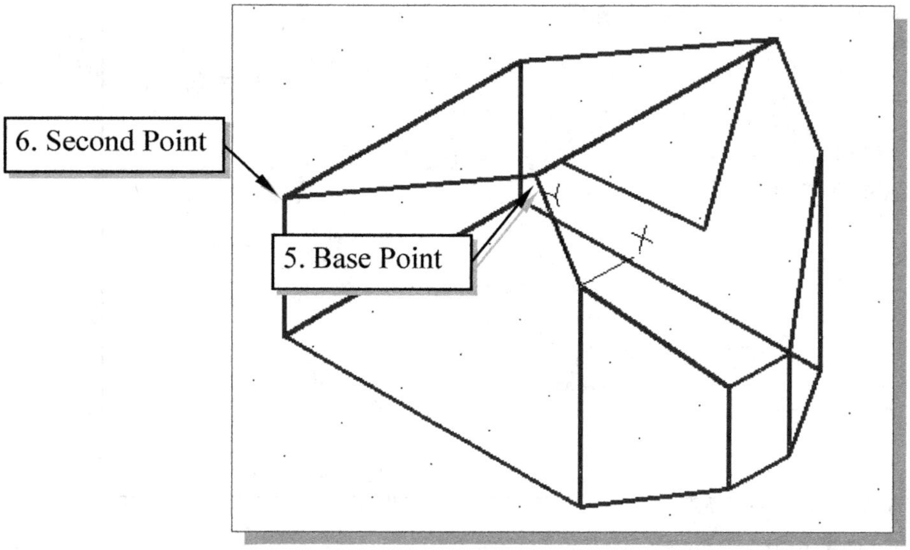

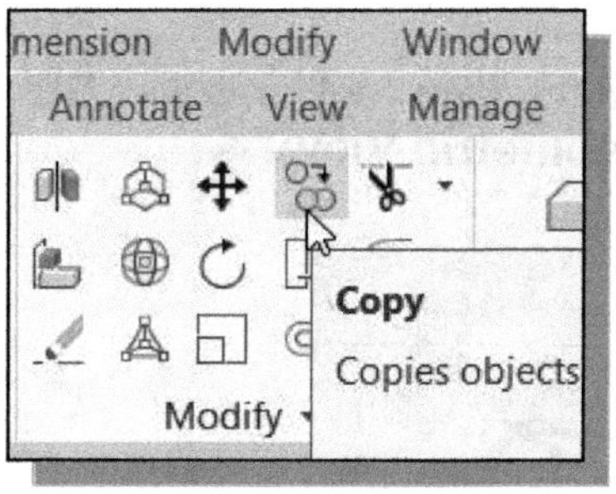

2. Click on the **Copy Object** icon in the *Modify* toolbar.

3. In the command prompt area, the message "*Select objects:*" is displayed. Pick the two inclined lines we just created.

4. Inside the graphics window, **right-click** once to accept the selections.

5. In the command prompt area, the message "*Specify base point or displacement, or [Multiple]:*" is displayed. Pick the **top left corner** as the base point to create the copy.

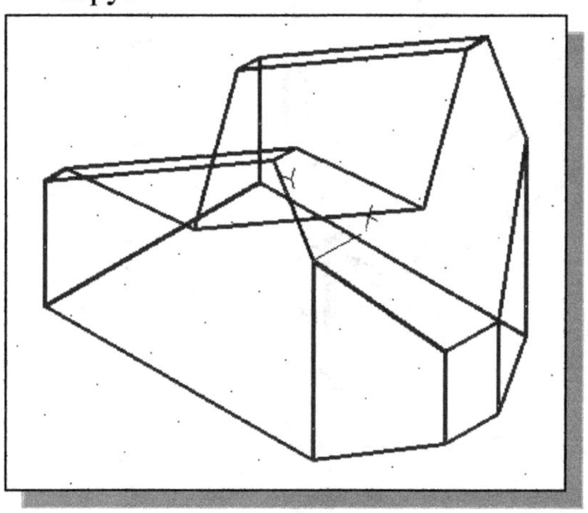

6. In the command prompt area, the message "*Specify second point of displacement or <use first point as displacement>:*" is displayed. Pick the corresponding corner on the **backside** of the model as shown in the above figure.

7. On your own, create additional lines to define the edges of the V-cut and use the **Trim** command to complete the model as shown.

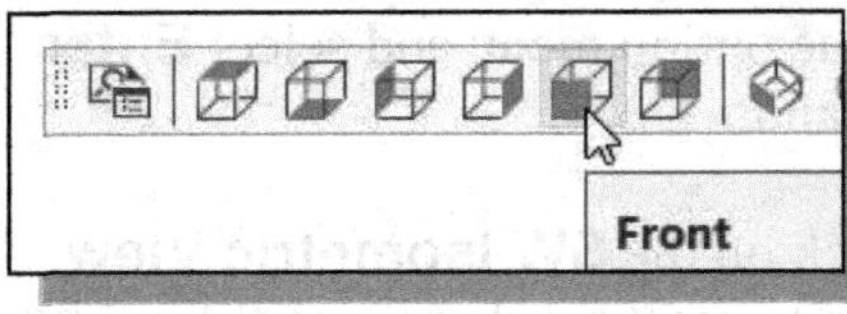

8. Click on the **Front View** icon in the *View* toolbar.

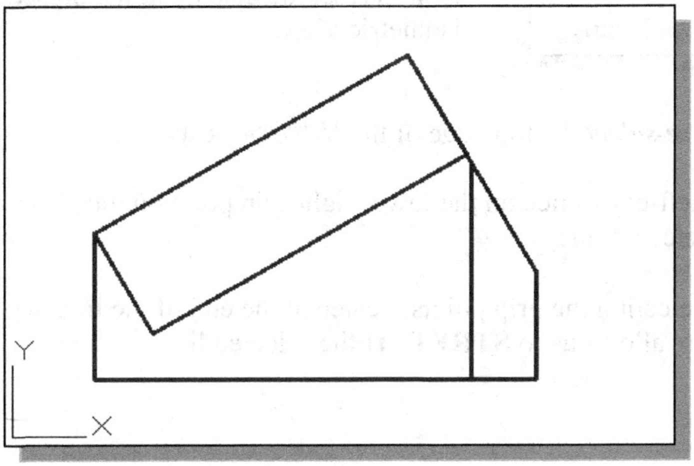

➢ Note that the V-cut we created, using the **Copy** command, does not represent a cut that passes through the entire block.

Extend the Cut and GRIP Editing

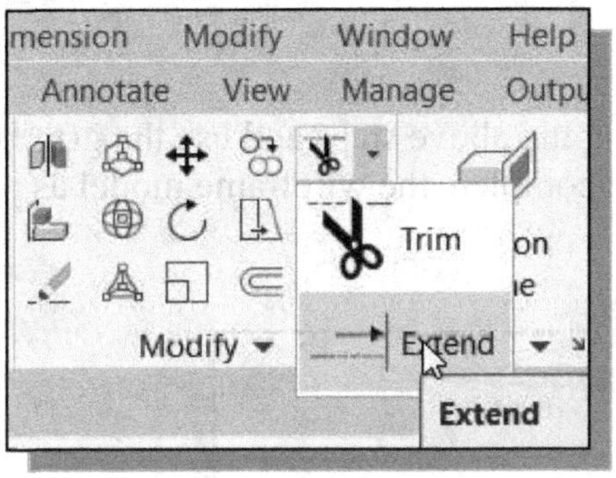

1. Select the **Extend** command icon in the *Modify* toolbar.

2. The message "*Select object to Extend or [Project/ Edge/ Undo]:*" is displayed in the command prompt area. Pick the bottom edge of the V-cut to extend.

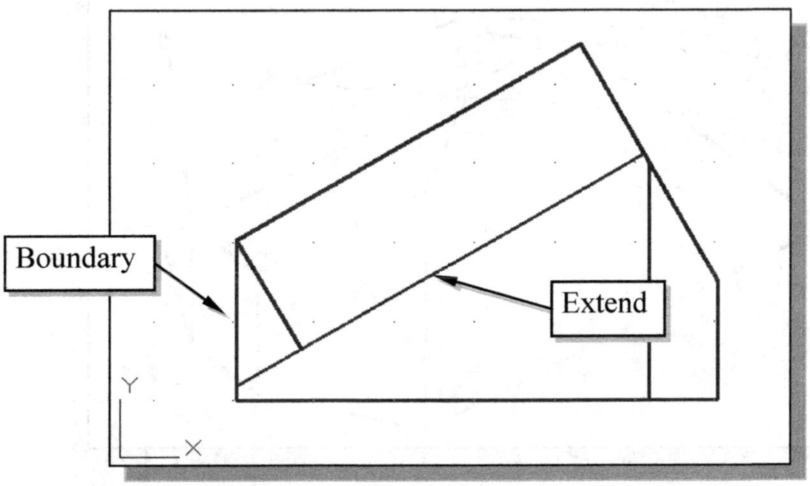

3. Inside the graphics window, **right-click** to activate the option menu and select **Enter** with the left-mouse-button to end the Extend command.

4. Click on the **SW Isometric View** icon to reset the display to the preset isometric view.

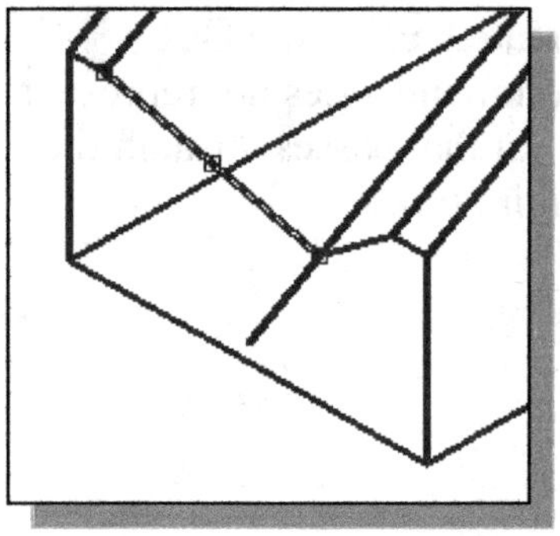

5. ***Pre-select*** the top edge of the *V-block* as shown.

6. Left-click once on the lower right grip point on the selected line.

- Selecting the grip points located at the end of the line or arc allows us to **STRETCH** the selected line.

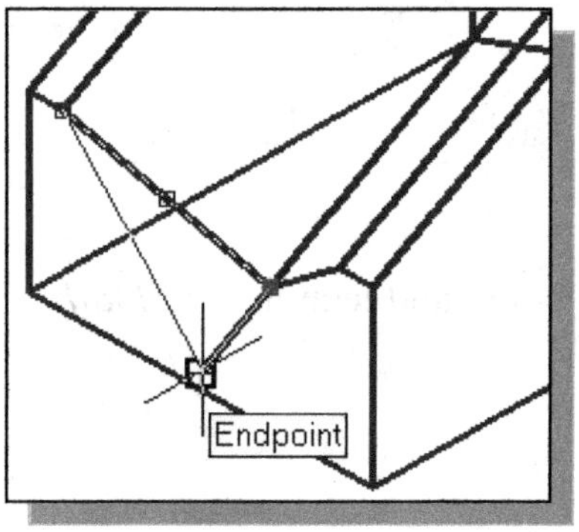

7. Move the cursor toward and select the lower corner of the V-cut as shown.

➢ On your own, repeat the above steps and use the grip editing options and complete the wireframe model as shown below.

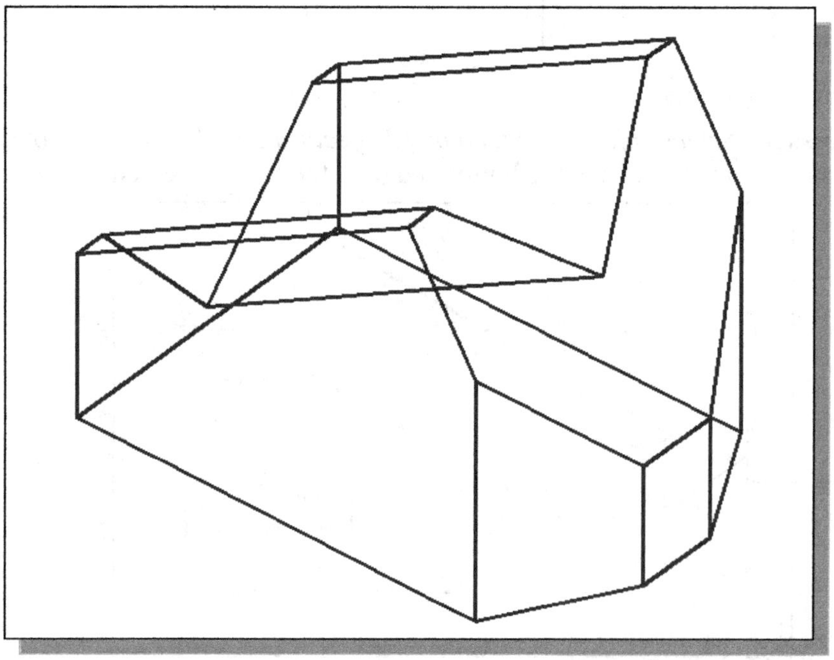

Review Questions:

1. List and describe three different types of 3D computer geometric modeling software available today.

2. What is a *Named View*?

3. What is the difference between Stretch and Extend?

4. List and describe the methods available in AutoCAD to create a new UCS plane.

5. What is the difference between Copy and Mirror in AutoCAD?

6. Identify and describe the following commands:

a)

b)

c)

d)

Exercises: (Unless otherwise specified, dimensions are in inches.)

1.

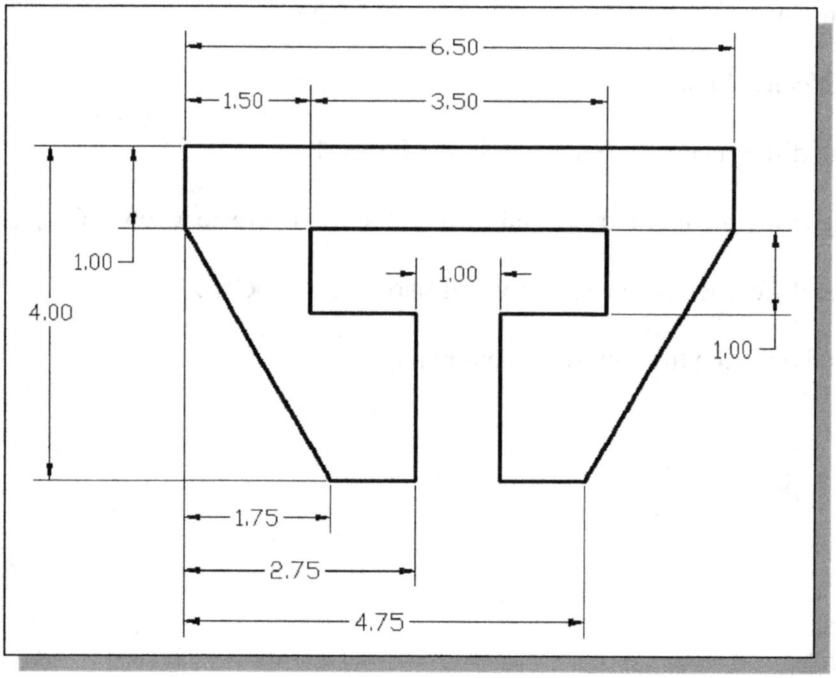

2.

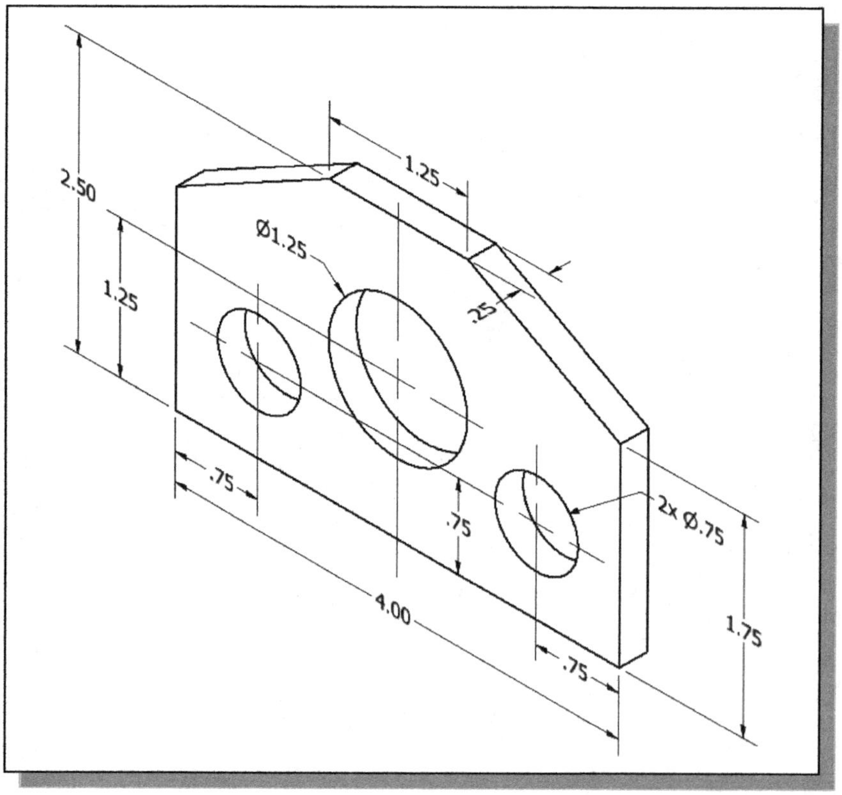

3.

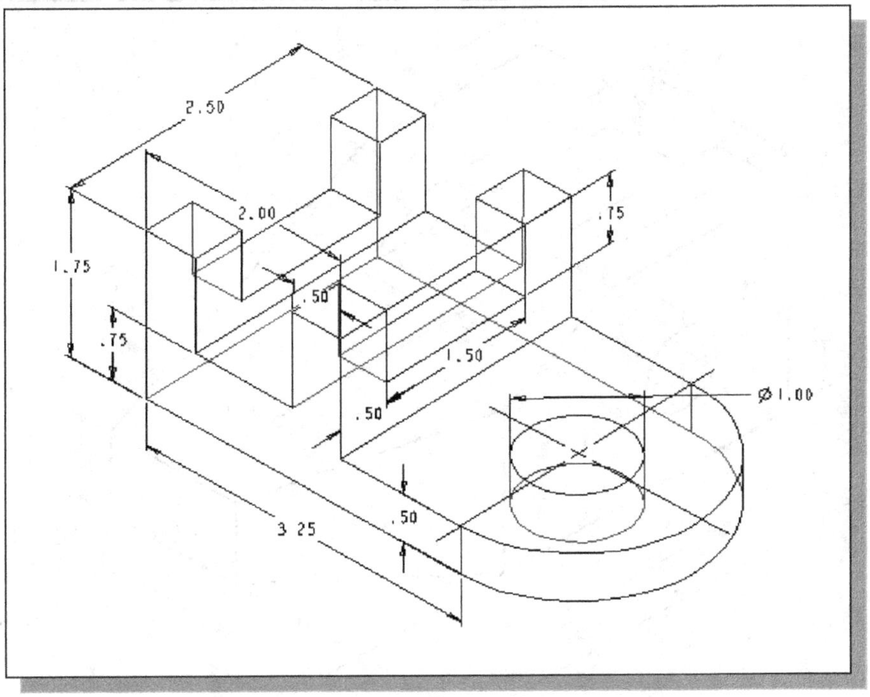
2.50
2.00
1.75
.75
.50
.75
1.50
.50
Ø1.00
.50
3.25

4.

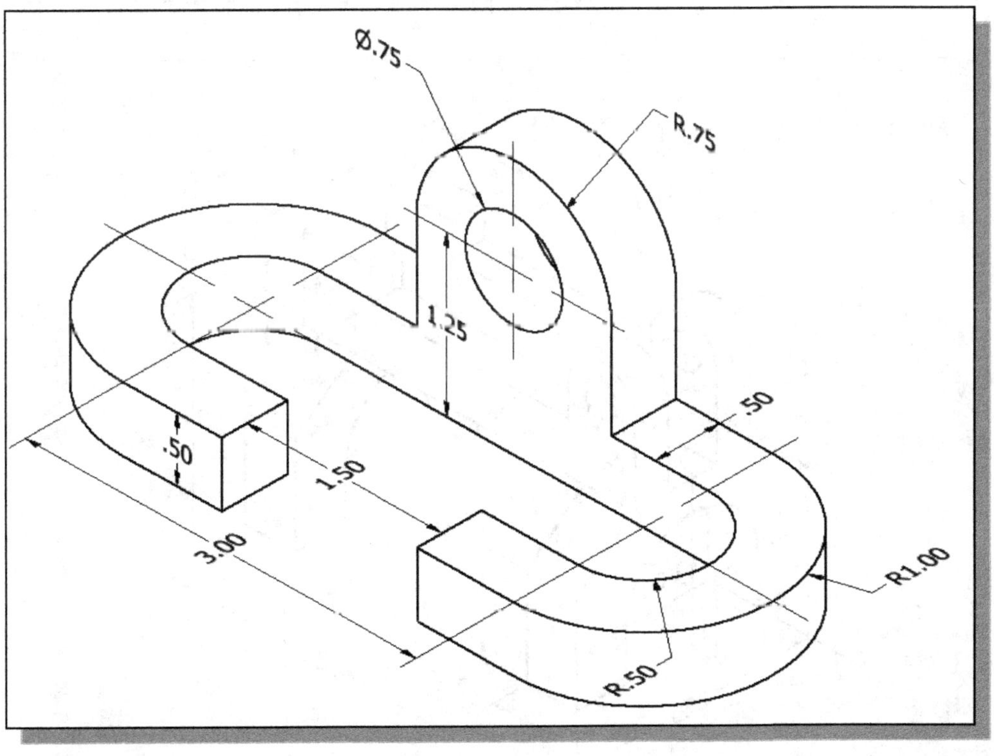
Ø.75
R.75
1.25
.50
.50
1.50
3.00
R1.00
R.50

5.

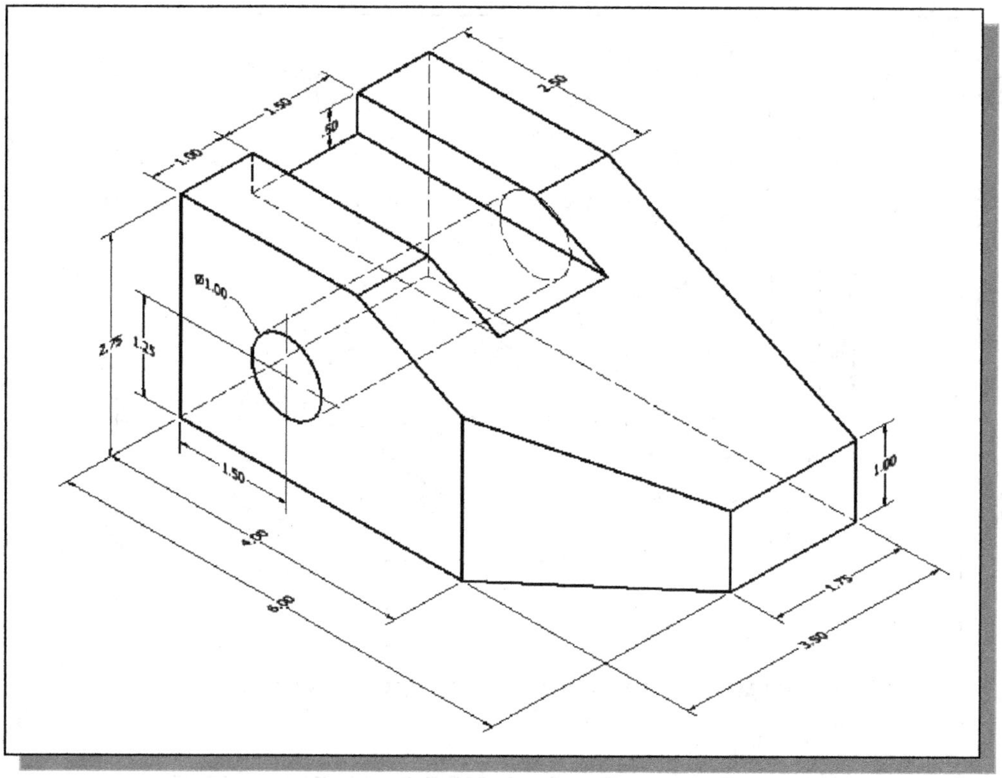
2.50
1.50
.50
1.00
Ø1.00
2.75
1.25
1.50
4.00
6.00
1.00
1.75
3.50

6.

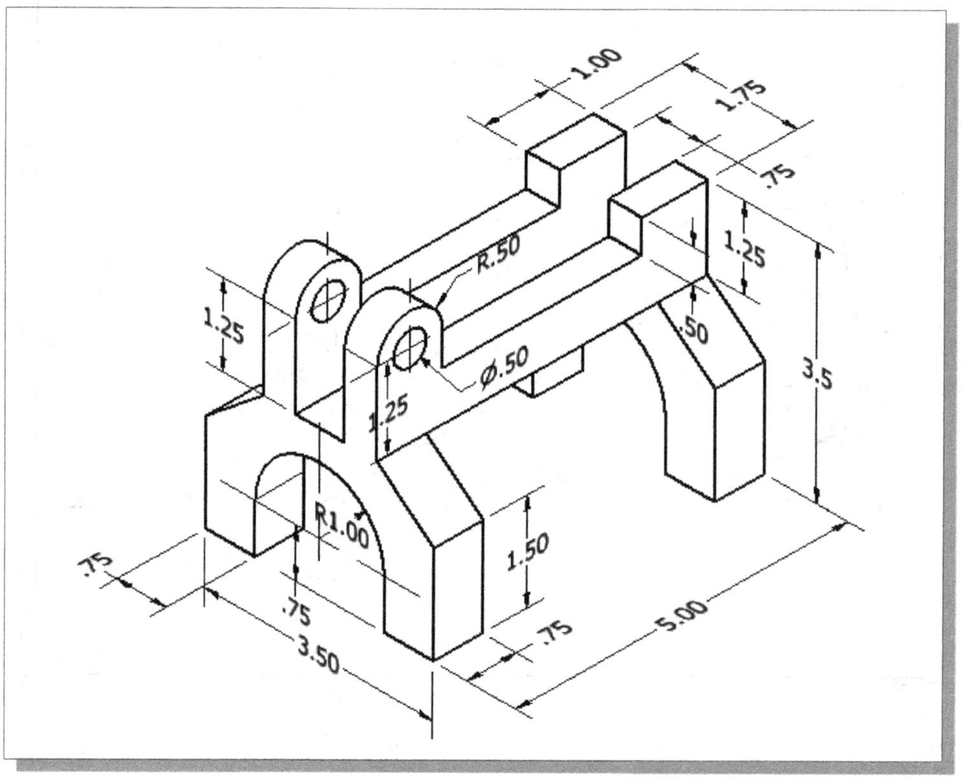
1.00
1.75
.75
R.50
1.25
1.25
.50
3.5
Ø.50
1.25
R1.00
1.50
.75
.75
3.50
.75
5.00

Chapter 4
Classical Faceted Surface Modeling

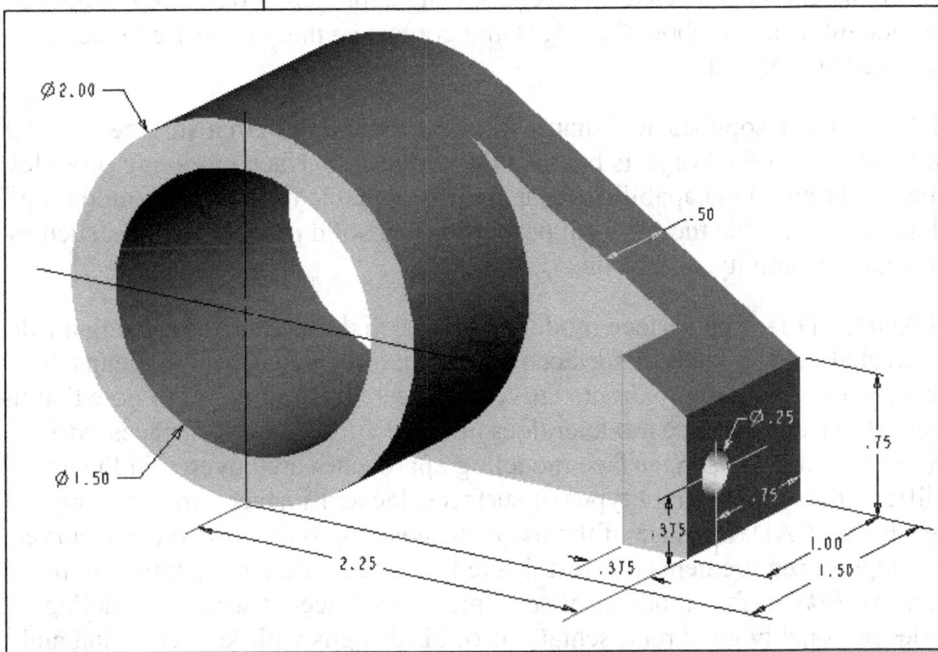

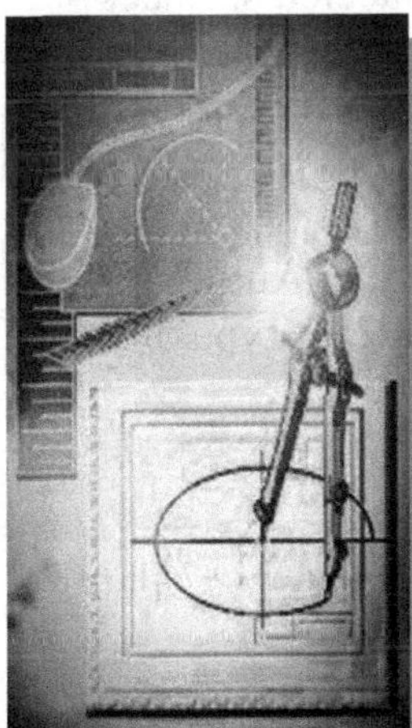

Learning Objectives

- ♦ **Create Faceted Surface Models**
- ♦ **Understand and Apply the Different Faceted Surface Modeling Techniques**
- ♦ **Understand the Use of the 2D Solid Command**
- ♦ **Understand the Use of 3D Face Command**
- ♦ **Use the Hidden Edge Option**

Introduction

As illustrated in the previous chapters, there are no surfaces in a wireframe model; it consists only of points, lines, and curves that describe the edges of the object. The first-generation surface modeling was developed to provide the surface information that is missing in wireframe modeling. Essentially, defining the skin of a design creates a surface model. In the classical faceted surface modeling approach, a wireframe model can be used to provide information about the edges and corners so that the desired faces can be easily positioned and placed.

Surface modeling is more sophisticated than wireframe modeling in that surface modelers define not only the edges of 3D objects but also the surfaces. Surface modeling provides hiding, shading, and rendering capabilities that are not available in wireframe modeling. Surface models do not provide the physical properties that solid models provide, such as mass, weight, center of gravity, and so on.

The classical AutoCAD faceted surface modeling approach defines surfaces using a filled polygon. The created faceted faces of surface models are only planar, which means the surface models can only have approximate curved surfaces. It is important to note that the classical AutoCAD faceted surface modeler does not create true curved surfaces. More advanced *Procedural* and *NURBS* surface modeling approaches are covered in the next chapter. To differentiate the different types of surfaces, faceted surfaces are generally called **meshes** in AutoCAD. Because of the use of faceted approximation on true curved surfaces, the computer requirements of most faceted surface modelers are typically much less than that of *NURBS* surface modeler or solid modelers. Faceted surface modeling usually provides reasonably good representations of 3D designs with fast rendering and shading capabilities. The more advanced NURBS surface models are also useful for creating geometry with unusual surface patterns, such as a 3D topographical model of mountainous terrain.

In **AutoCAD 2027,** three classical methods are available for creating faceted surfaces – the **2D Solid**, **3D Face** and **Region** commands. The three classical faceted surface commands were developed parallel to the historical development of the different types of computer modelers.

- **2D Solid**: The first-generation faceted surface command available in AutoCAD. Used mostly to fill an area in the sketch plane of the current UCS. This type of surface is not a true 3D surface.

- **3D Face**: Creates a true 3D planar faceted surface (allowing X, Y and Z coordinates) of three-sided or four-sided shapes. This is the type of surface developed primarily for creating faceted surface models.

- **Region**: Creates a 2D surface of arbitrary shape from existing 2D entities. This command creates the most flexible and the most complicated type of surface available in AutoCAD. This command was developed to allow manipulation of 2D surfaces using one of the solid modeling construction techniques, namely, the **Constructive Solid Geometry** method.

Although all three basic commands can be used to create planar faceted surfaces, the resulting surfaces are not equal. In fact, the three commands are developed with specific tasks in mind. The **2D Solid** command is mostly used in 2D drawings to create 2D filled area and the **Region** command is designed so that general 2D shapes can be easily transformed into solid models. The **3D Face** command is the only one that is designed specifically for faceted surface modeling and therefore it is the most suitable for such tasks. The use of the **2D Solid** and **Region** commands in 3D faceted surface modeling can be somewhat awkward and at times very difficult. Note that the use of the **Region** command will be focused on in the solid modeling chapters of this text.

As one can imagine, sketching each surface manually can be very time consuming and tedious. AutoCAD also provides additional tools for more advanced faceted surface modeling, such as **Tabulated surfaces**, **Ruled surfaces** and **Revolved surfaces**. These tools are basically automated procedures, which can be used to define and create multiple copies of faceted planar surfaces in specific directions. The principles and concepts used by these tools are also used in creating solid models, which are covered in chapter six through chapter eight of this text. You are encouraged to re-examine these commands after you have finished the solid modeling chapters.

In this chapter, the general procedures to create classical faceted surface models are illustrated. The use of the **2D Solid** and **3D Face** commands are illustrated and differences discussed. Two wireframe models, which were created in the previous chapters, will be converted into faceted surface models.

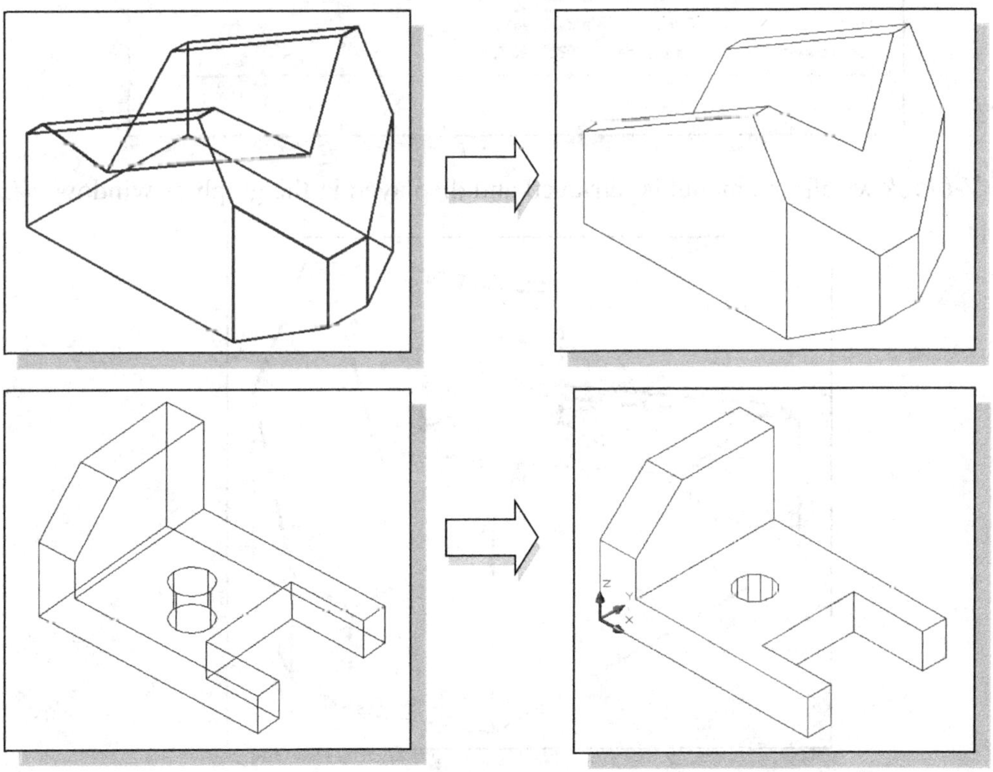

Starting Up AutoCAD 2027

1. Select the **AutoCAD 2027** option on the *Program* menu or select the **AutoCAD 2027** icon on the *Desktop*.

2. In the *AutoCAD Today Startup* dialog box, select the **Open a Drawing** icon with a single click of the left-mouse-button.

3. Click on the ***V-block.dwg*** filename to open the *V-block* wireframe model that was created in the previous chapter. (Use the **Browse** option to locate the file if it is not displayed.)

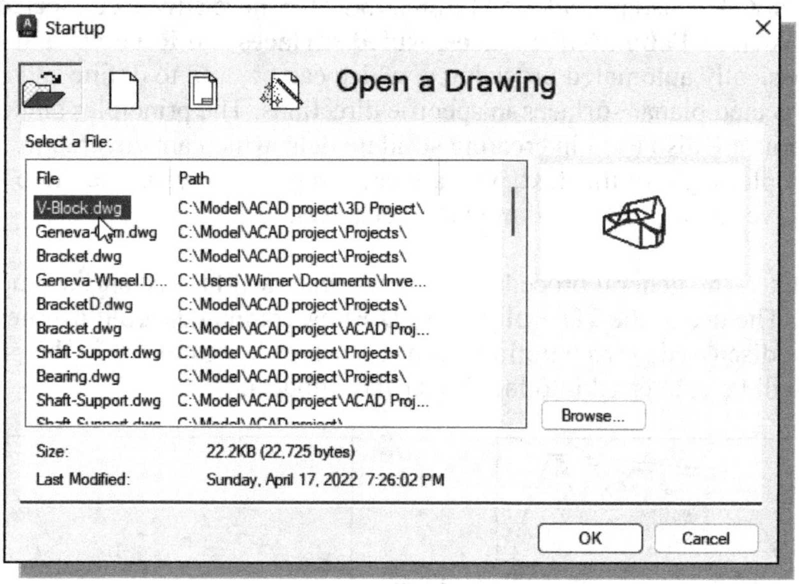

- The *V-block* wireframe model is retrieved and displayed in the graphics window.

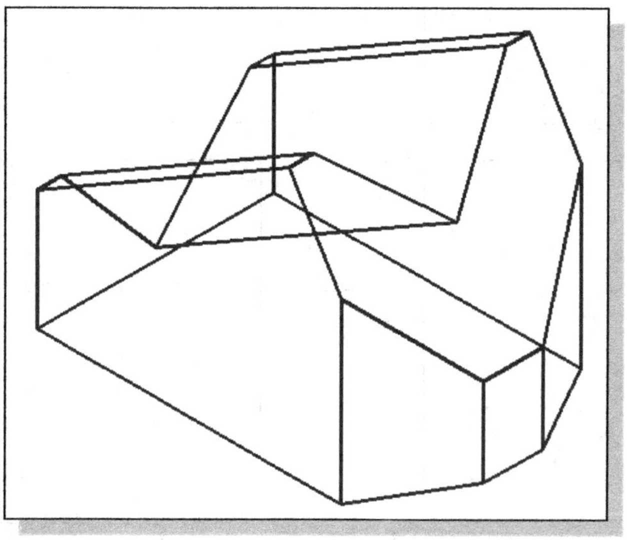

The UCS Toolbar and the Meshes Commands

1. In the *Menu Bar,* select **[Tools] → [Toolbars] → [AutoCAD]**.

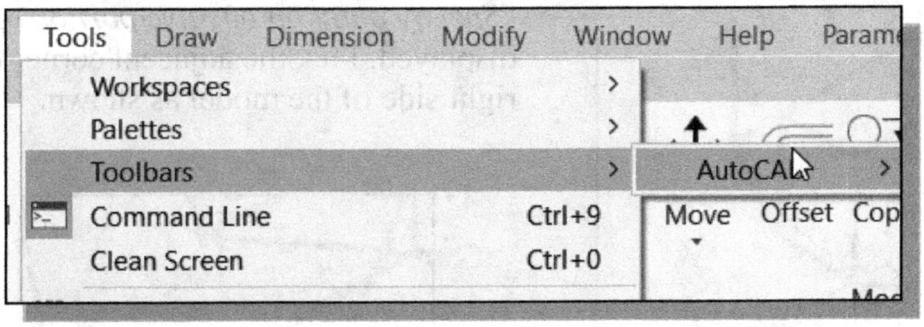

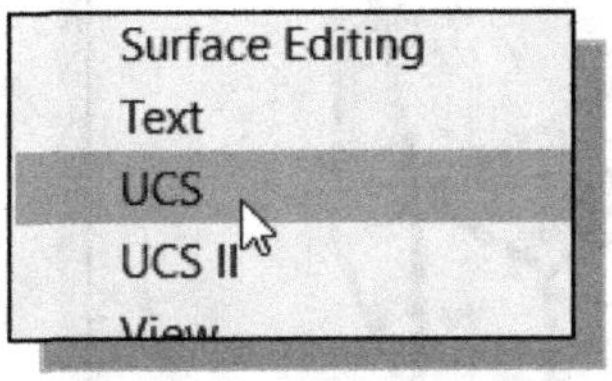

2. Select **UCS**, with the left-mouse-button, to display the *UCS* toolbar on the screen.

➢ The options available in the *UCS* toolbar allow us to quickly orient and align the UCS.

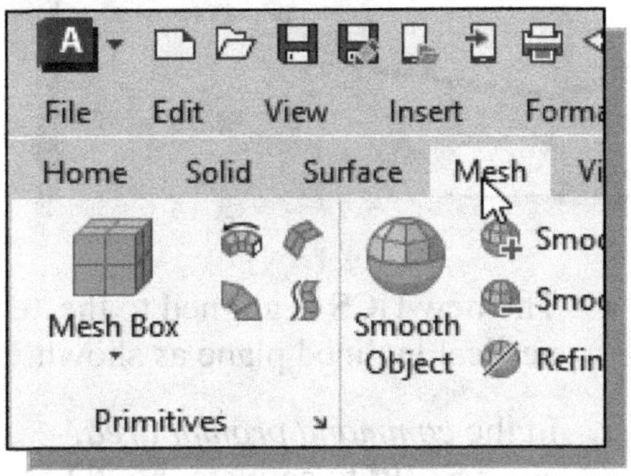

3. Click on the **Mesh** tab to show the mesh commands available in AutoCAD.

• Note that a variety of 2D-mesh modeling commands are available to create meshes. On your own, move the cursor on top of the different commands and read the brief description of the commands.

Create a Mesh Surface Using the 2D Solid Command

The first-generation faceted surface command available in AutoCAD was the **2D Solid** command. In AutoCAD 2027, this command can only be accessed through the command prompt area, which is an indication that this command is slowly being phased out. The **2D Solid** command is used to fill an area in the sketch plane of the current UCS. It is therefore necessary to properly orient the UCS prior to using the **2D Solid** command.

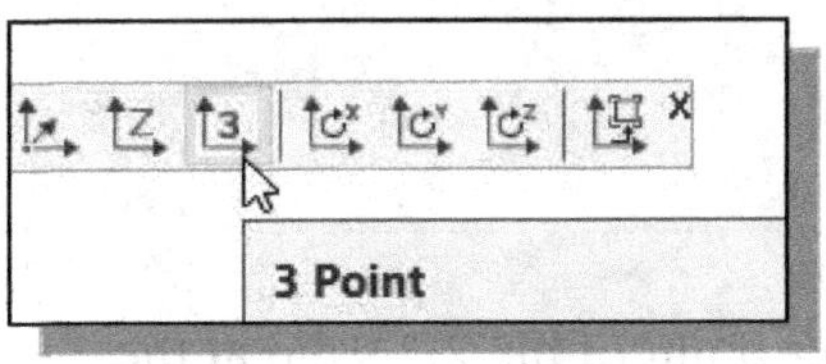

1. Select the **3 Point UCS** icon in the *UCS* toolbar.

• The **3 Point UCS** option allows us to specify the new X-axis and Y-axis directions to align the UCS.

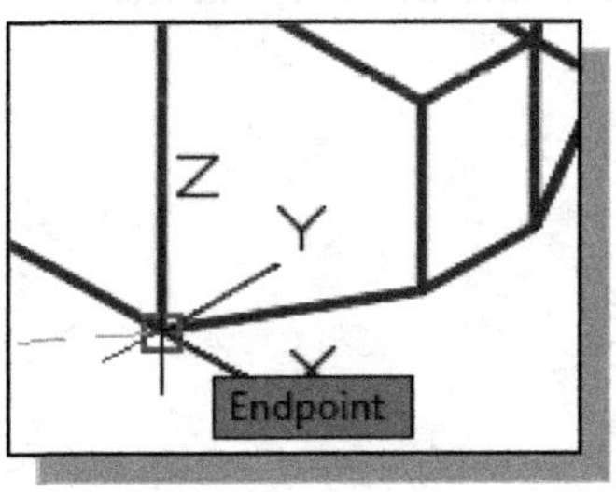

2. In the command prompt area, the message *"Specify new origin point<0,0,0>:"* is displayed. Pick the **lower right corner** of the front face of the wireframe model as shown.

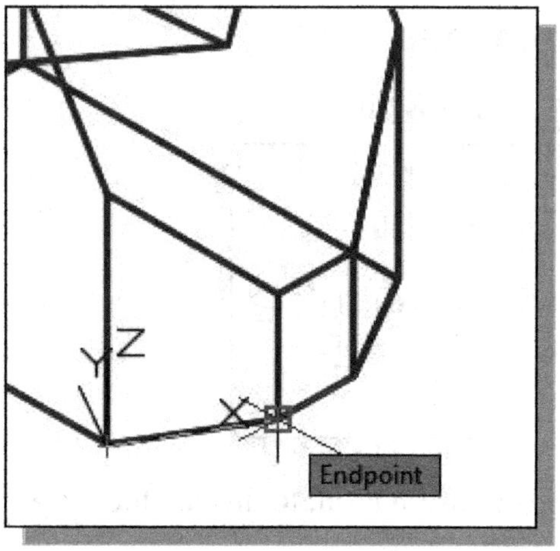

3. In the command prompt area, the message "*Specify point on positive portion of X-axis:*" is displayed. Pick the adjacent corner toward the right side of the model as shown.

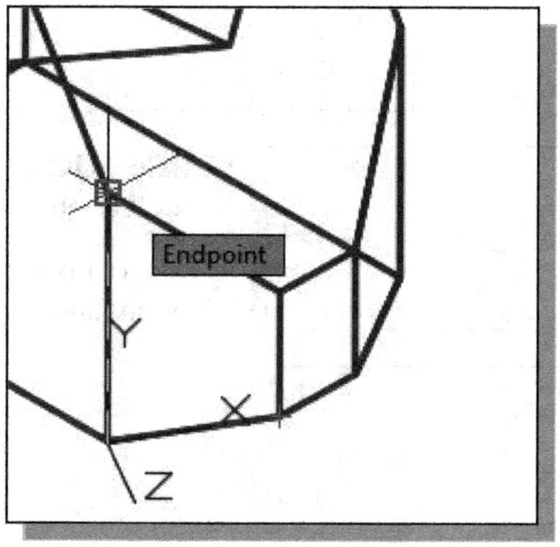

4. In the command prompt area, the message "*Specify point on positive portion of X-axis:*" is displayed. Pick the right corner of the inclined plane as shown.

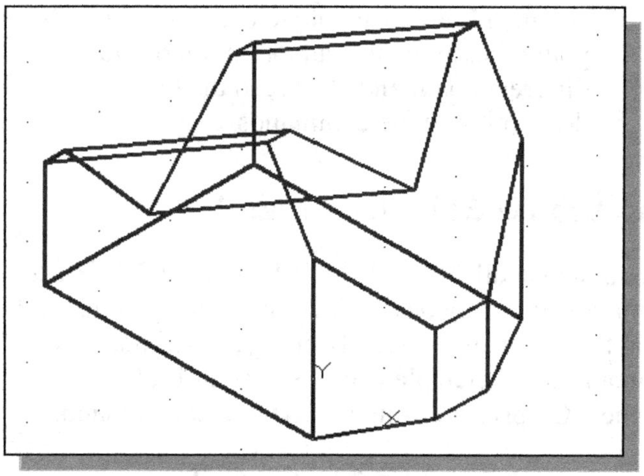

- The new UCS is aligned to the vertical inclined plane as shown.

5. In the *command prompt area*, enter **Solid** to activate the 2D Solid command.

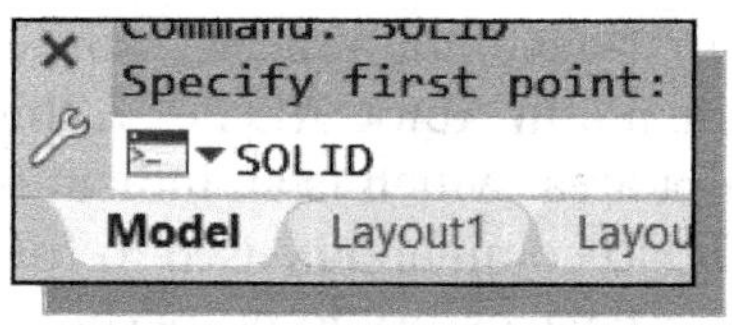

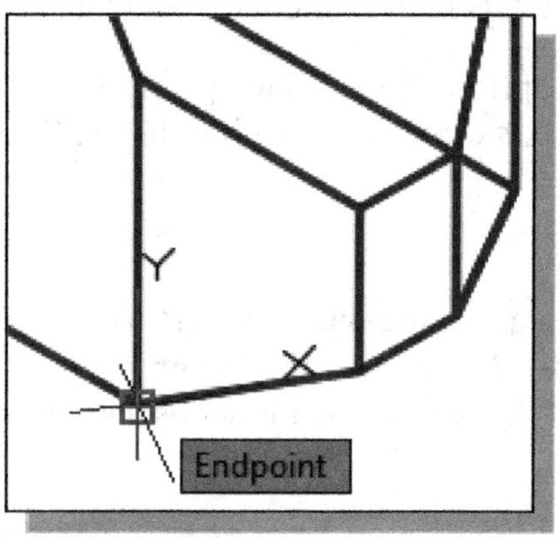

6. Place the first corner point of the 2D solid at the origin of the new UCS.

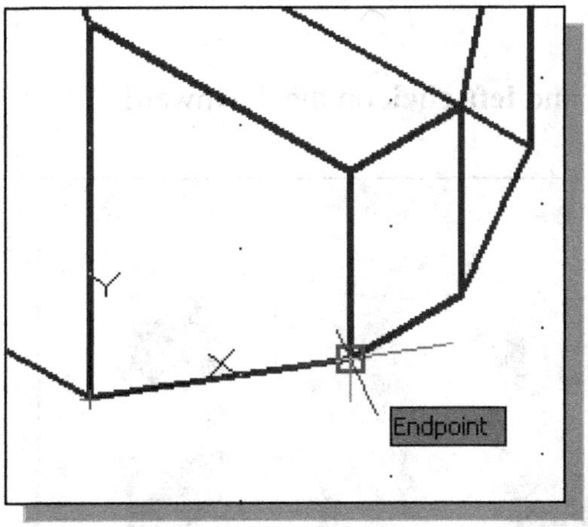

7. In the command prompt area, the message "*Specify second point:*" is displayed. Pick the bottom right corner of the inclined plane as shown.

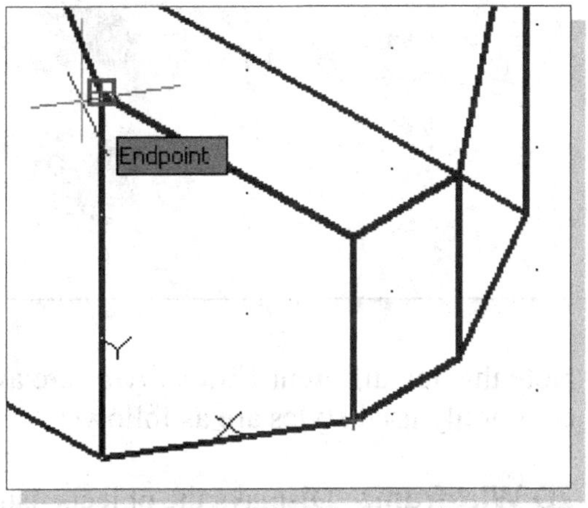

8. In the command prompt area, the message "*Specify third point:*" is displayed. Pick the corner directly above the origin of the UCS as shown.

- The **2D Solid** command requires the third point to be specified *diagonally opposite* to the second point. This seemingly strange way of specifying the third corner was established when the **2D Solid** command was first introduced back in the mid-1980s. Note that the **3D Face** command, the second-generation surface command in AutoCAD, does not follow this convention.

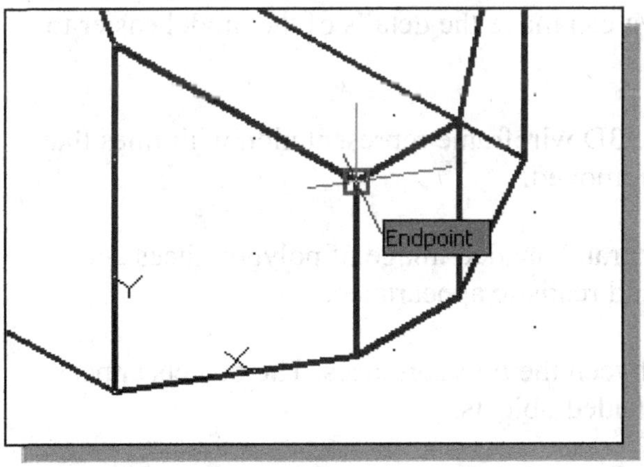

9. In the command prompt area, the message "*Specify fourth point or [Exit]:*" is displayed. Pick the corner directly above the second point we selected as shown in the figure.

10. Inside the graphics window, **right-click once** to end the **2D Solid** command.

- The **2D Solid** command allows the creation of *three-sided* or *four-sided* filled polygons, which can be used to represent faces of surface models. Note that in the above steps, we could accept the three-sided polygon after defining the third corner.

Using the Visual Styles Toolbar

1. Move the cursor to the *Visualize* toolbar panel and **left-click** on the downward triangle to display a list of available options.

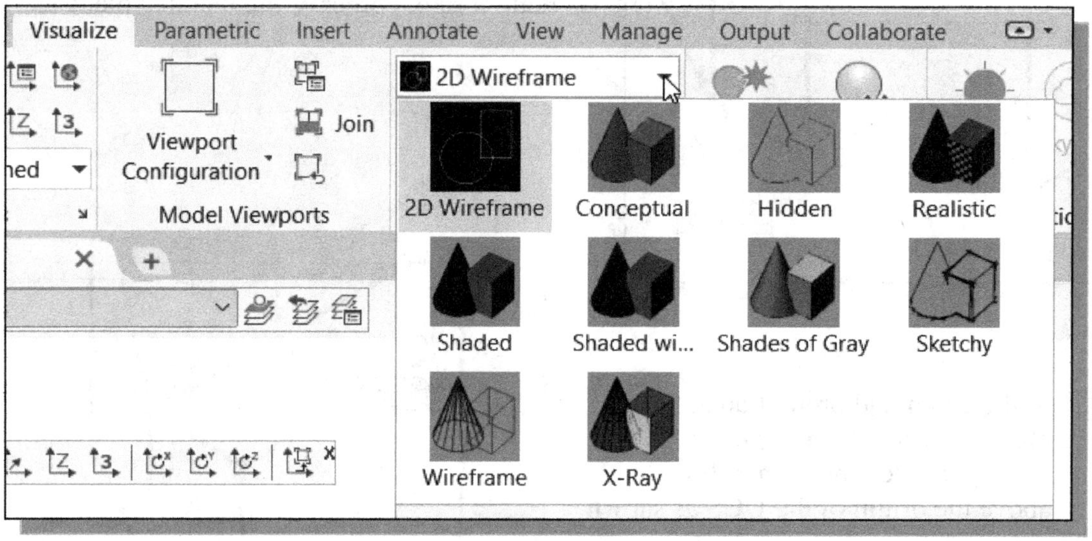

❖ Note that ten different *Visual Styles* are available; descriptions of the six more commonly used styles are as follows:

- **2D Wireframe**: Displays the objects using lines and curves to represent the boundaries of objects created. Linetypes and lineweights are visible with this option. Note that this is the default AutoCAD display mode.

- **Conceptual Visual Style**: Creates a shaded image of polygon faces and solids that uses the Gooch face style, a transition between cool and warm colors rather than dark to light. The effect is less realistic, but it can make the details of the model easier to see.

- **Hidden**: Displays the objects using the 3D wireframe representation with lines that are located behind surfaces and solids removed.

- **Realistic Visual Style**: Creates a Gouraud-shaded image of polygon faces and solids that gives the objects a smooth and realistic appearance.

- **Shaded Style**: Shades the objects between the polygon faces. The objects appear flatter and less smooth than Gouraud-shaded objects.

- **3D Wireframe**: Displays the objects using lines and curves to represent the boundaries of objects created. Displays a shaded 3D user coordinate system (UCS) icon. Note that linetypes and lineweights are not visible with this option.

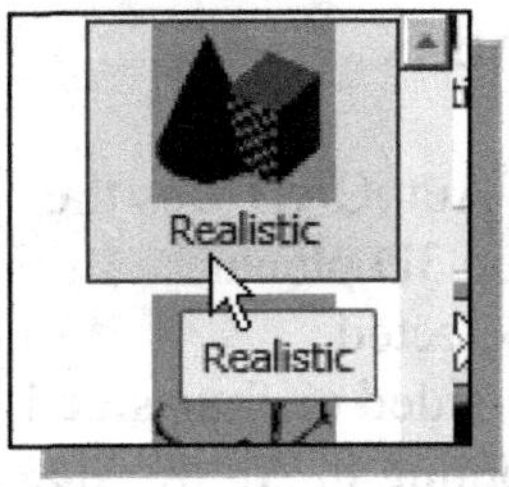

2. Click on the **Realistic Visual Style** icon to display the shaded image of the model.

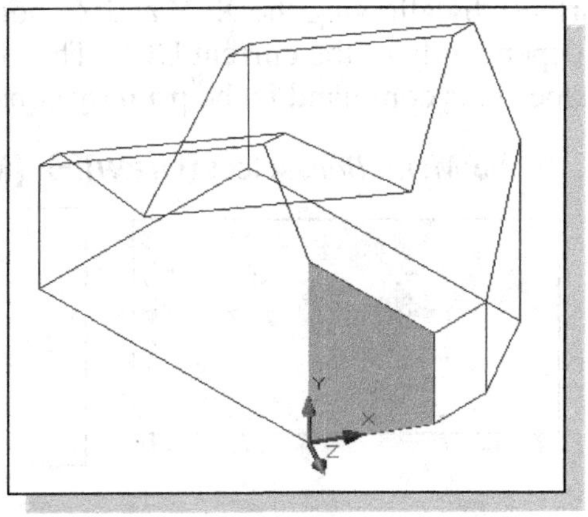

❖ Only one surface exists in our model. The surface was created with the 2D Solid command.

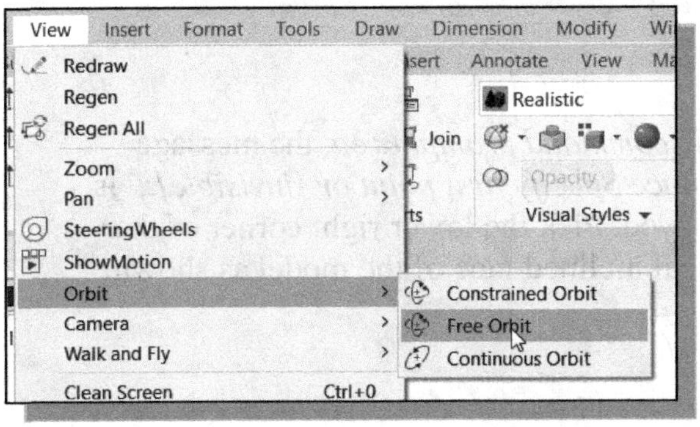

3. Select **Free Orbit** in the *View* pull-down menu as shown.

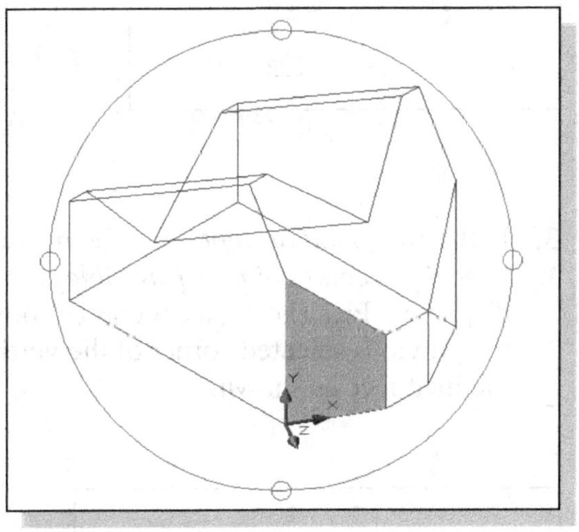

4. Inside the *arcball*, press down the left-mouse-button and drag it to rotate the model freely in 3D space. Observe the display of the shaded surface in contrast to the 3D wireframe edges that are located behind it.

5. In the *UCS* toolbar, select the **World UCS**. This option resets the UCS to align to the world coordinate system.

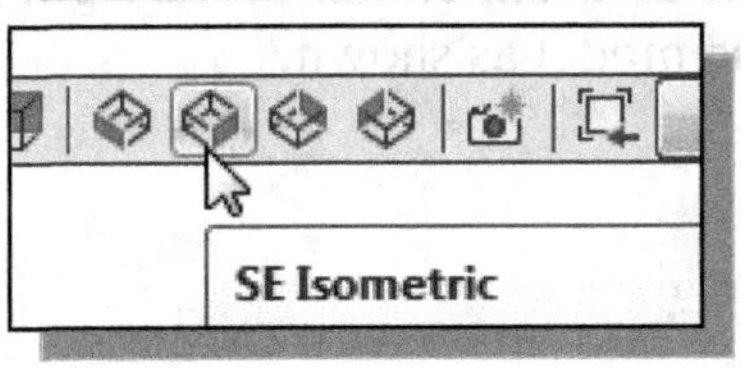

6. On your own, reset the display to the SE Isometric View before continuing to the next section.

Create a Mesh Surface Using the 3D Face Command

The second generation of faceted surface command made available in AutoCAD was the **3D Face** command. The 3D Face command can be used to create true 3D planar surfaces by allowing the X, Y and Z coordinates of the corners to be selected independently of the current UCS. The created polygon can be a three-sided or four-sided shape. This command is the primary construction tool for surface modeling in AutoCAD.

1. In the *Menu Bar*, select **[Draw] → [Modeling] → [Meshes] → [3D Face]**.

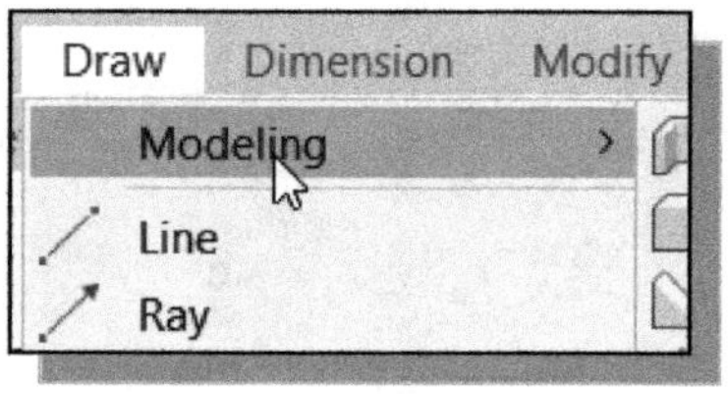

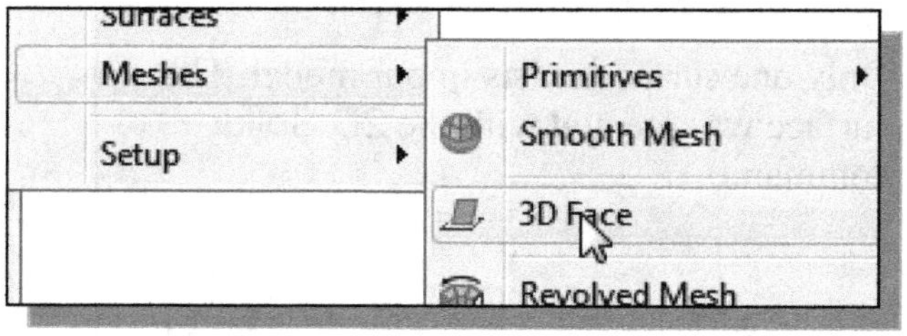

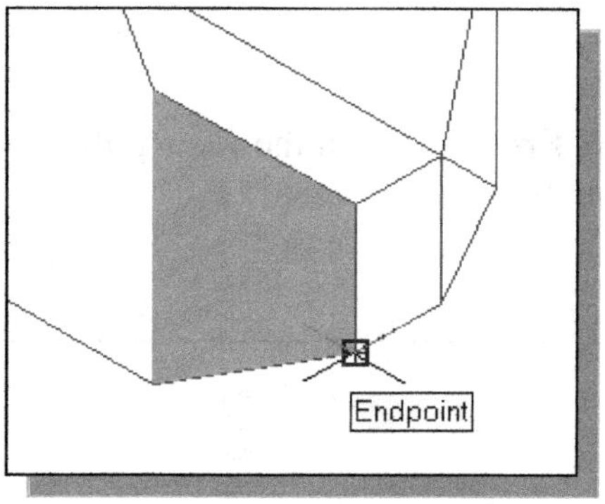

2. In the *command prompt area*, the message "*_3dface Specify first point or [invisible]:*" is displayed. Pick the lower right corner of the vertical inclined face of the model as shown.

3. In the *command prompt area*, the message "*Specify second point or [invisible]:*" is displayed. Pick the adjacent corner above the previous selected corner of the vertical inclined face as shown.

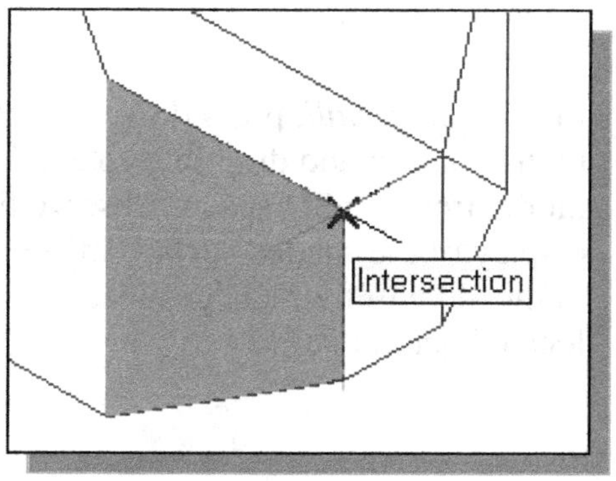

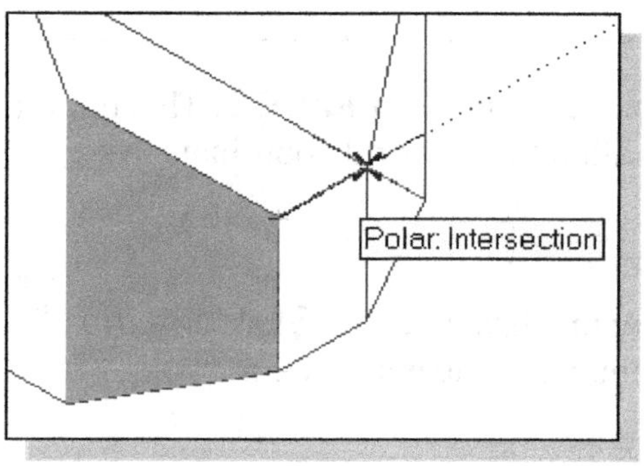

4. In the *command prompt area*, the message "*Specify third point or [invisible]:*" is displayed. Pick the adjacent corner of the right vertical face of the model as shown.

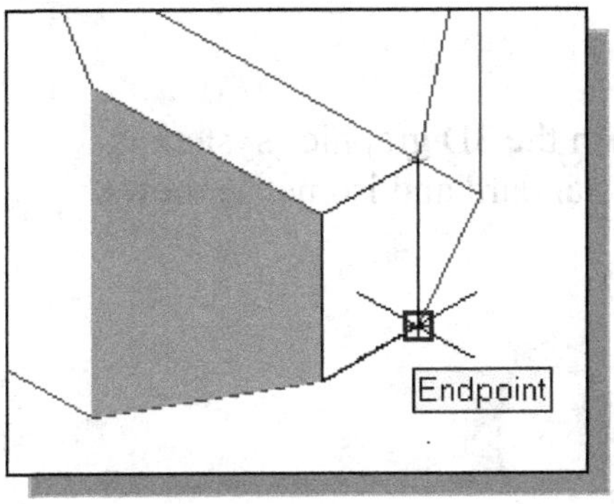

5. In the command prompt area, the message "*Specify fourth point or [invisible] <Create three-sided face>:*" is displayed. Pick the corner below the last selected corner as shown.

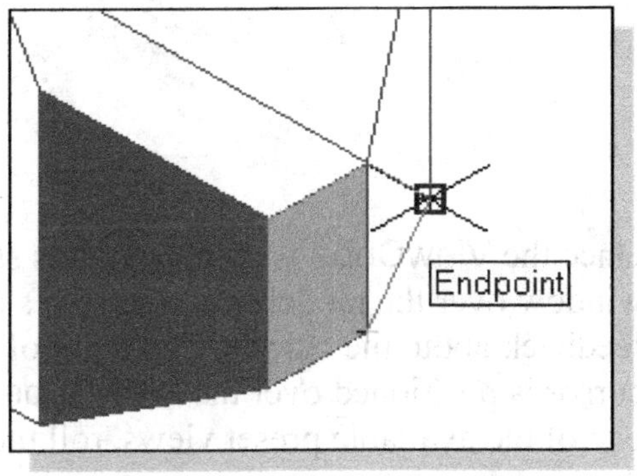

6. In the command prompt area, the message "*Specify third point or [invisible] <exit>:*" is displayed. Pick the back corner of the model as shown.

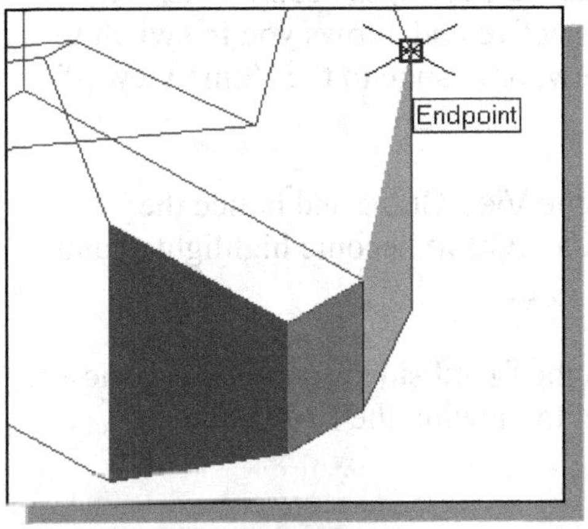

7. In the command prompt area, the message "*Specify fourth point or [invisible] <Create three-sided face>:*" is displayed. Pick the back corner of the model as shown.

- Note that this surface is created independent of the UCS, and two corners of the previous face were used to position this face.

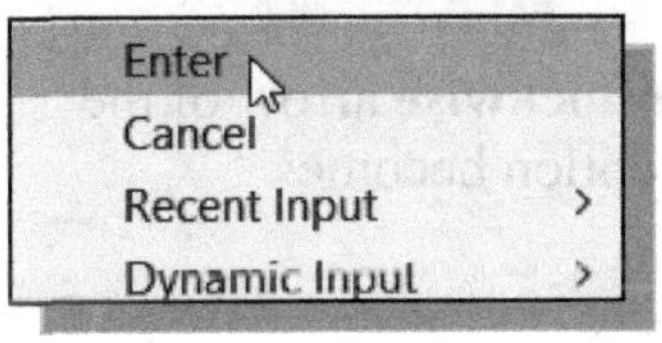

8. Inside the graphics window, right-click to activate the option menu and select **Enter** with the left-mouse-button to end the **3D Face** command.

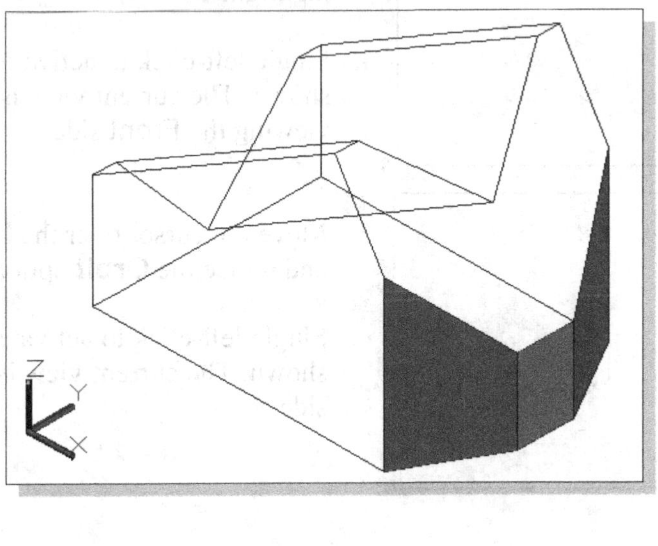

The ViewCube

The ViewCube is a 3D navigation tool that appears when the 3D graphics system is enabled. With the ViewCube, you can switch between standard and isometric views.

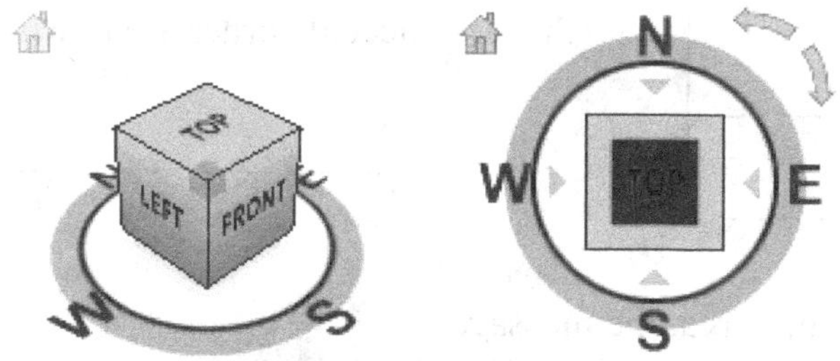

Once the ViewCube is displayed, it is shown in one of the corners of the graphics window over the model in an inactive state. The ViewCube also provides visual feedback about the current viewpoint of the model as view changes occur. When the cursor is positioned over the ViewCube, it becomes active and allows you to switch to one of the available preset views, roll the current view, or change to the Home view of the model.

1. Move the cursor over the ViewCube and notice the different sides of the ViewCube become highlighted and can be activated.

2. Single left-click when the Front side is activated as shown. The current view is set to viewing the Front side.

3. Move the cursor over the **counterclockwise** arrow of the ViewCube and notice the **Orbit** option becomes highlighted.

4. Single left-click to activate the **counterclockwise** option as shown. The current view is orbited 90 degrees; we are still viewing the Front side.

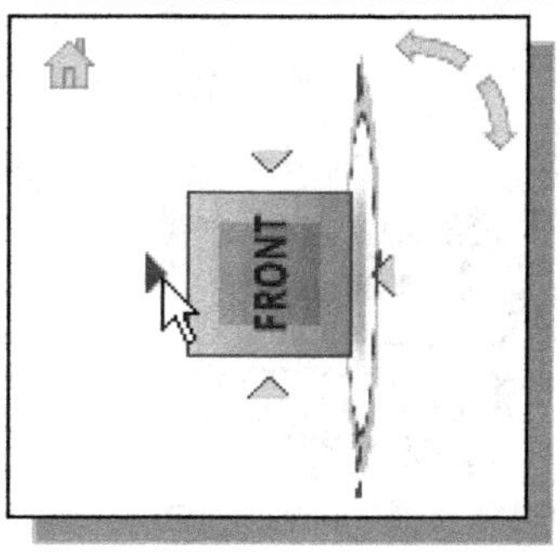

5. Move the cursor over the **Left** arrow of the ViewCube and notice the **Orbit** option becomes highlighted.

6. Single left-click to activate the **Left** arrow option as shown. The current view is now set to viewing the Top side.

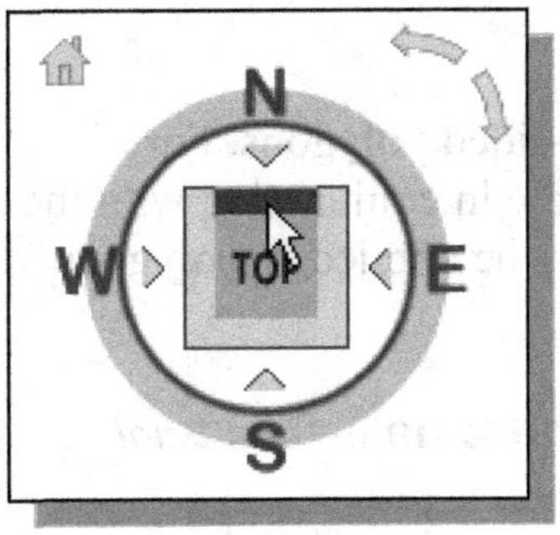

7. Move the cursor over the **top edge** of the ViewCube and notice the roll option becomes highlighted.

8. Single left-click to activate the **Roll** option as shown. The view will be adjusted to roll 45 degrees.

9. Move the cursor over the ViewCube and drag with the left-mouse-button to activate the **Free Rotation** option.

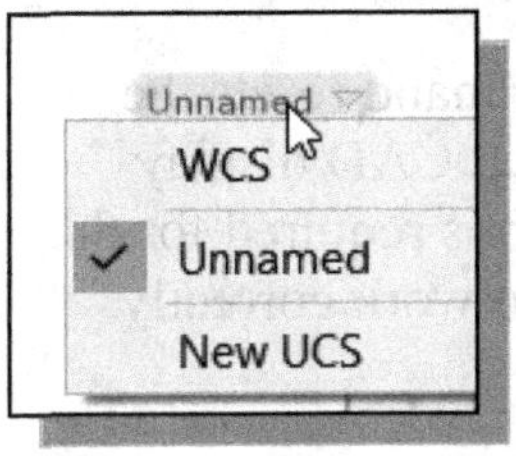

➢ The orientation of the model can also be changed to base on either the UCS or the WCS by clicking on the coordinate setting option below the ViewCube as shown.

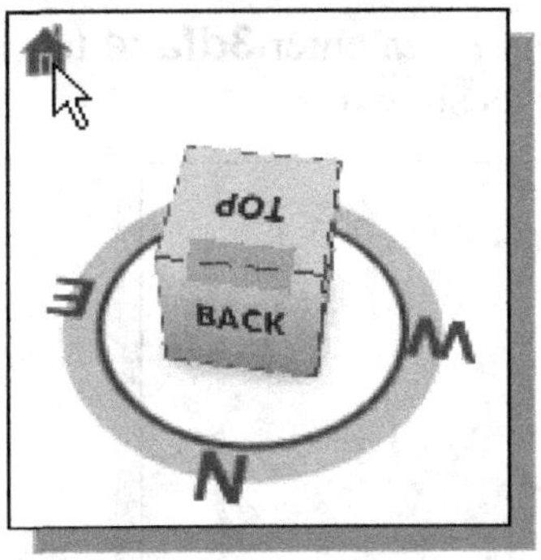

10. Move the cursor over the **Home** icon of the ViewCube and notice the **Home View** option becomes highlighted.

11. Single left-click to activate the **Home View** option as shown. The view will be adjusted back to the default **SW Isometric** view.

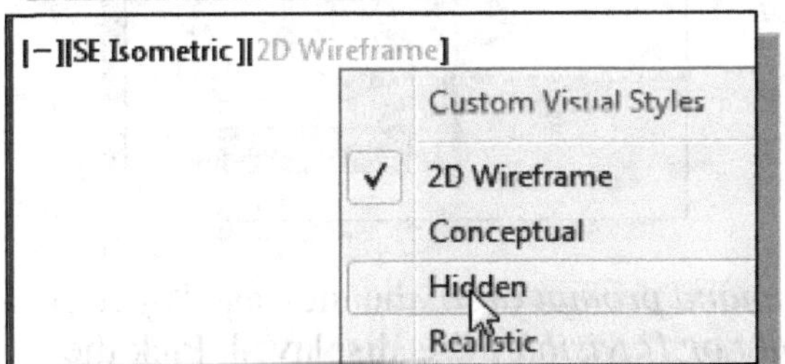

12. In the *Visual Style Controls* list, click on the **2D Wireframe → Hidden** icon to display the model with hidden lines removed.

- The *Quick Display* controls list, located near the upper left corner of the graphics area, provides quick access to many display-related commands.

13. On your own, use the **ViewCube** to rotate the model and examine the constructed surface model.

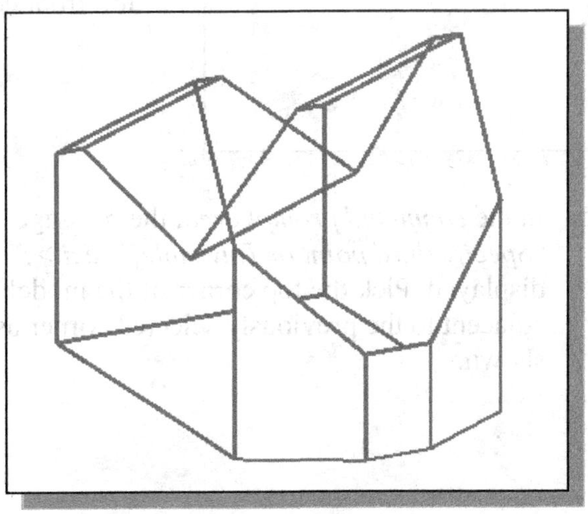

Create a Faceted Surface of Irregular Shape

The **3D Face** command allows us to create three-sided or four-sided polygons. For surfaces of irregular shape, the Invisible Edge option is available in conjunction with the 3D Face command. Note that the Invisible Edge option cannot be applied to polygons created by the 2D Solid command.

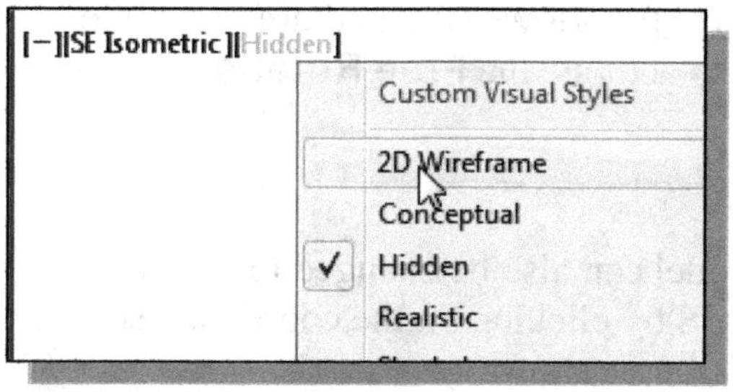

1. Select the **2D Wireframe** in the *Visual Styles* toolbar.

- The 2D Wireframe command resets the display to the default AutoCAD display mode. Note that this step is required for the Invisible Edge option to work correctly.

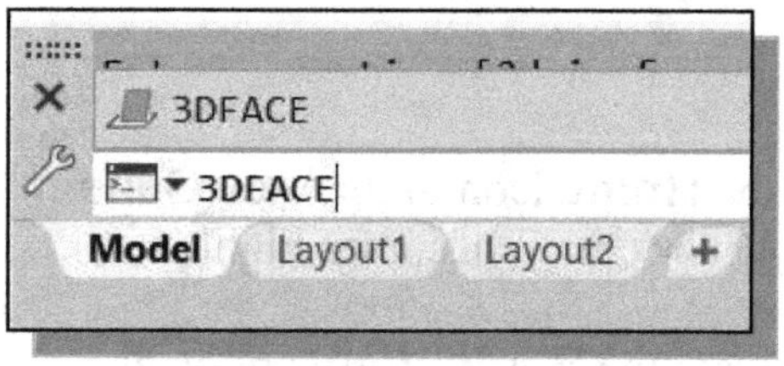

2. In the *command prompt area*, enter **3dface** to activate the command as shown.

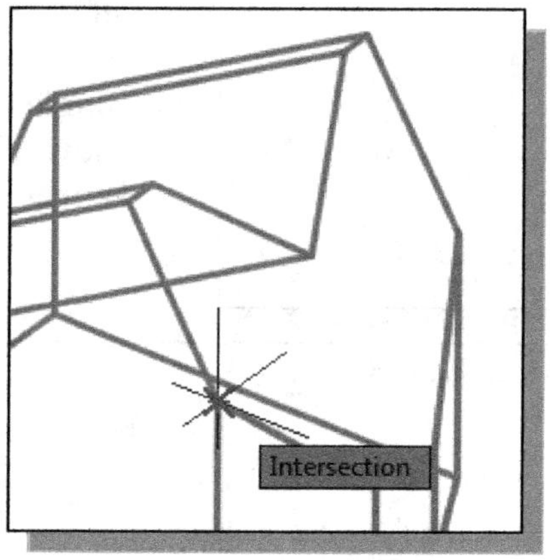

3. In the *command prompt area*, the message "*_3dface Specify first point or [invisible]:*" is displayed. Pick the right corner of the model as shown.

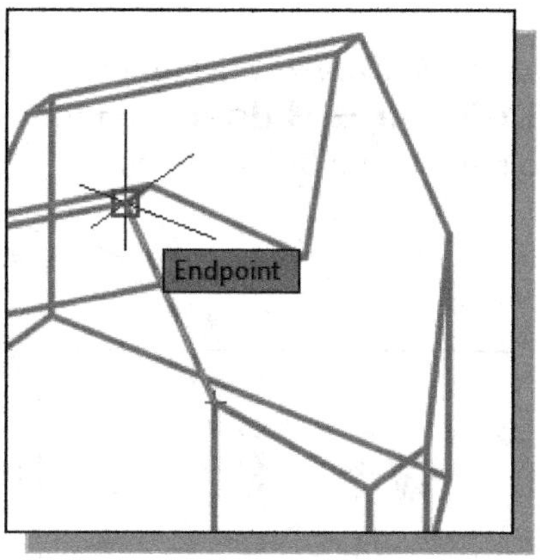

4. In the *command prompt area*, the message "*Specify second point or [invisible]:*" is displayed. Pick the top front corner of the model as shown.

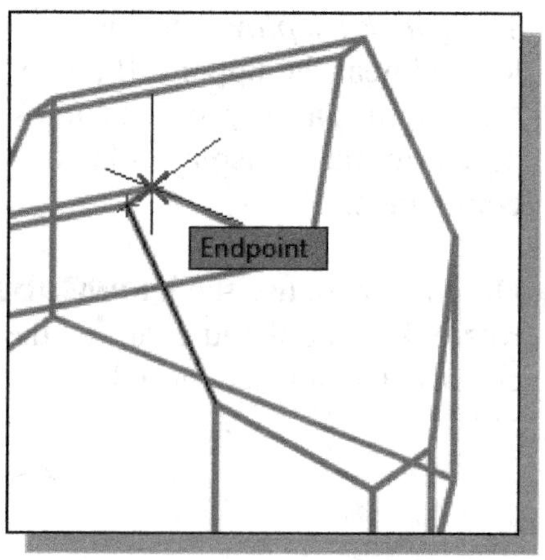

5. In the *command prompt area*, the message "*Specify third point or [invisible] <exit>:*" is displayed. Pick the top corner of the model adjacent to the previously selected corner as shown.

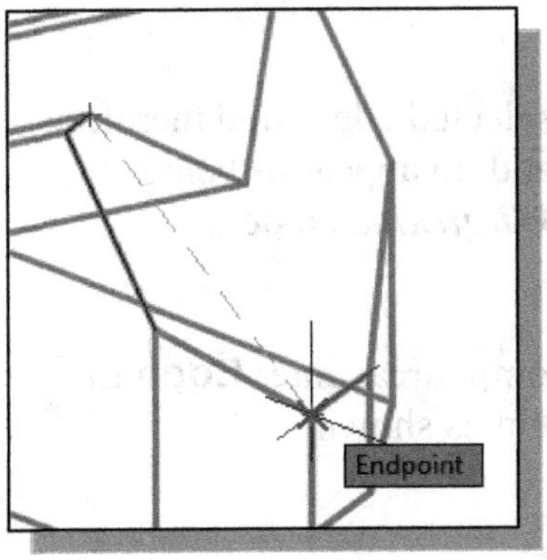

6. In the command prompt area, the message "*Specify fourth point or [invisible] <Create three-sided face>:*" is displayed. Pick the corner below the last selected corner as shown.

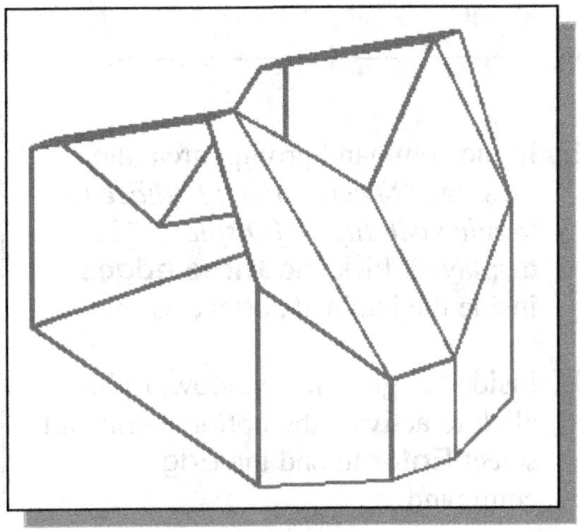

7. On your own, repeat the zigzagging pattern to define polygons until all corners of the inclined surface have been selected and additional polygons are created as shown in the figure. Note that the last polygon we created is a three-sided polygon.

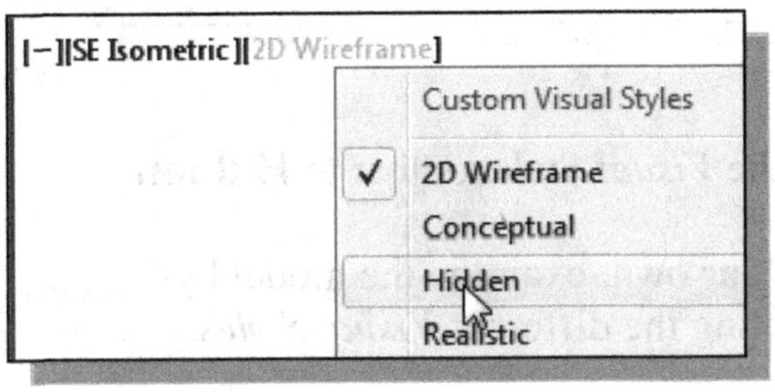

8. In the *Visual Styles* toolbar, click on the **Hidden** icon to display the model with hidden lines removed. Note that the edges of the polygons are displayed as shown.

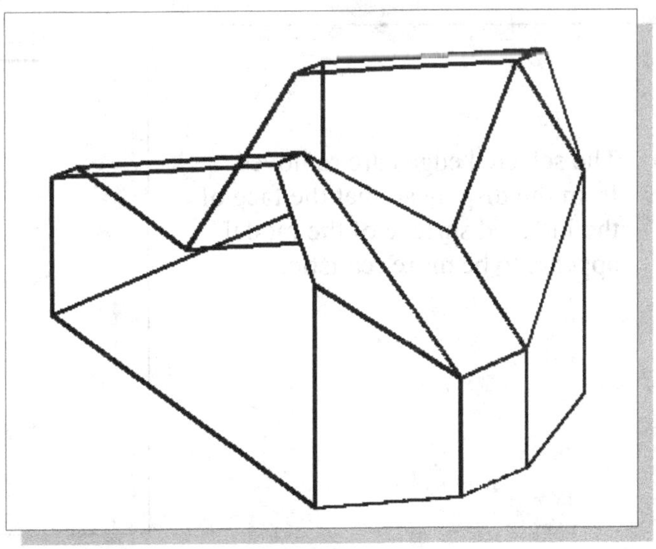

9. On your own, examine the model by selecting the different *Visual Styles*.

10. Reset the *Visual Styles* toolbar to **2D Wireframe**, the default AutoCAD display mode.

Use the Invisible Edge Option

The Invisible Edge option is used to turn off the display of selected edges and therefore allow the adjacent polygons, created by the 3D Face command, to appear as being joined together. (Note the operation must be done in the ***2D Wireframe*** mode.)

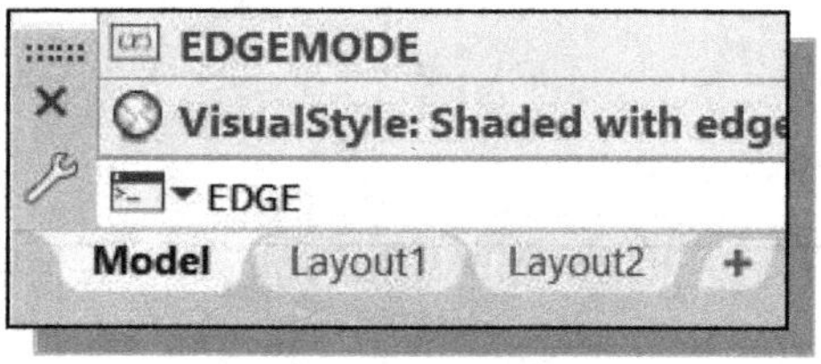

1. In the command prompt area, enter **Edge** to activate the command as shown.

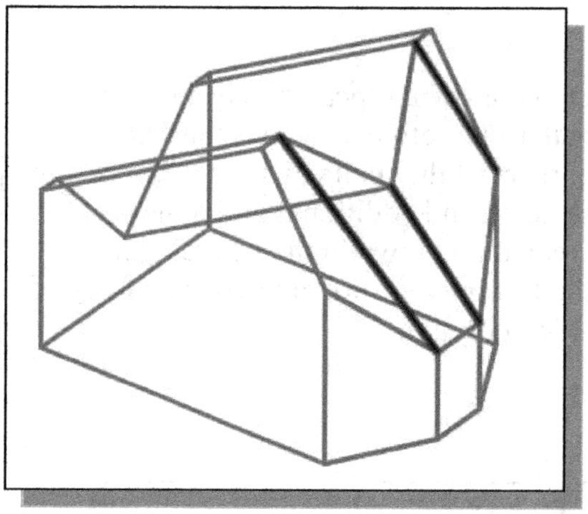

2. In the command prompt area, the message "*Specify edge of 3dface to toggle visibility or [Display]:*" is displayed. Pick **the three edges** inside the inclined surface as shown.

3. Inside the graphics window, right-click to activate the option menu and select **Enter** to end the Edge command.

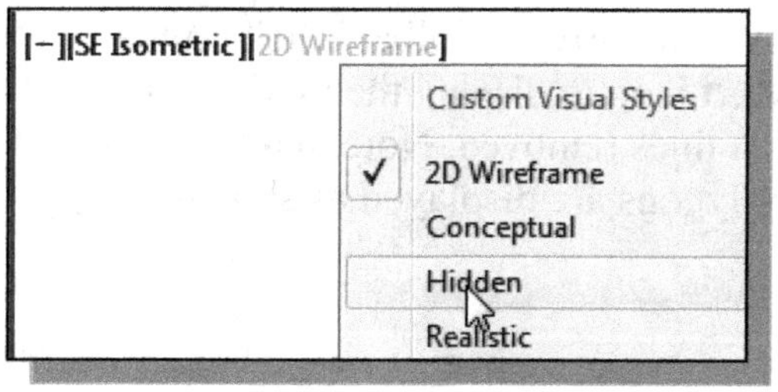

4. Set the *Visual Style* toolbar to **Hidden**.

5. On your own, examine the model by selecting the different *Visual Styles.*

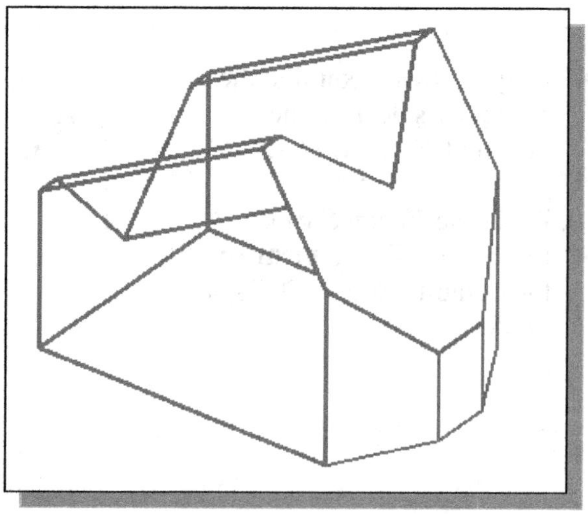

- The selected edges are removed from the display so that the face of the inclined surface of the model appears to be more realistic.

Repositioning with the Grip Editing Tools

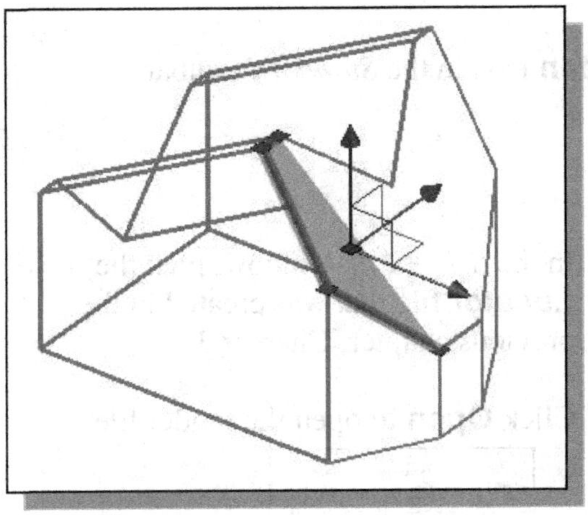

1. Select one of the 3D faces we created by clicking on the front edge of the inclined surface as shown.

- Four grip points, the small rectangles displayed at the corners of the highlighted polygon, can be used to adjust the size and shape of the highlighted polygon.

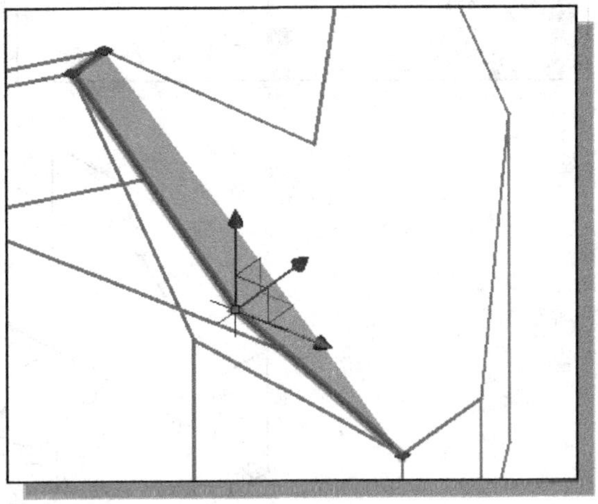

2. Move the cursor on one of the grip points. Notice the grip editing axes are automatically aligned to the grip point.

3. Click on one of the axes and drag with the left-mouse-button to move the grip point. (Clicking on the axis constrains the movement to the selected axis.)

4. Press the **[undo]** button to reset and deselect the highlighted entities.

➢ On your own, repeat the above steps and complete the surface model of the design.

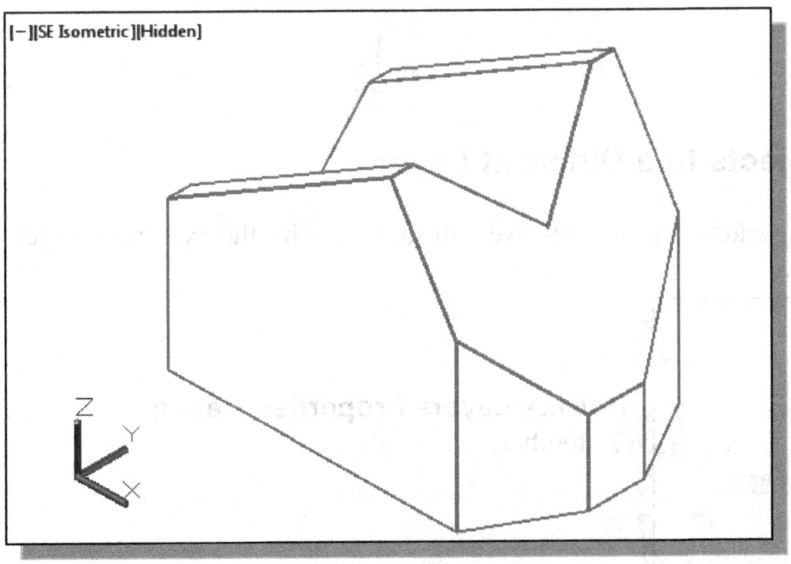

5. On your own, save the completed model as V-Block-Surf1.dwg.

The Locator Wireframe Model

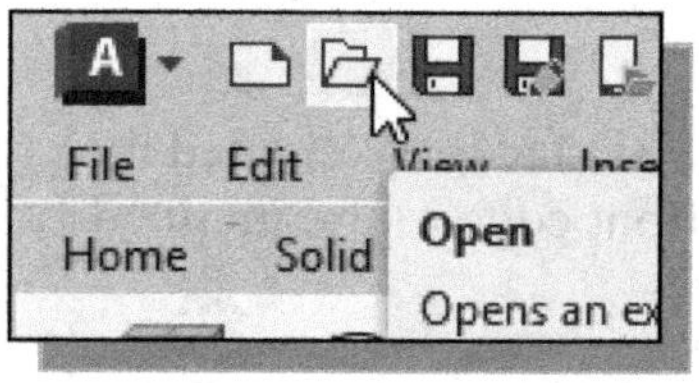

1. Click on the **Open** icon in the *Standard* toolbar.

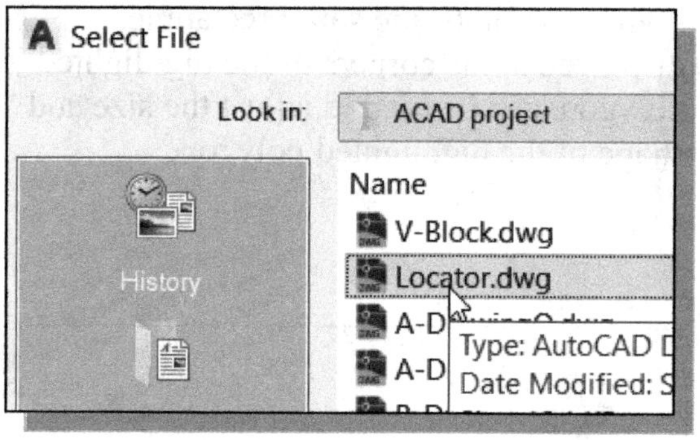

2. In the *Select File* window, pick the ***Locator*** file that was created in the previous chapter, Chapter 3.

3. Click **Open** to open the model file.

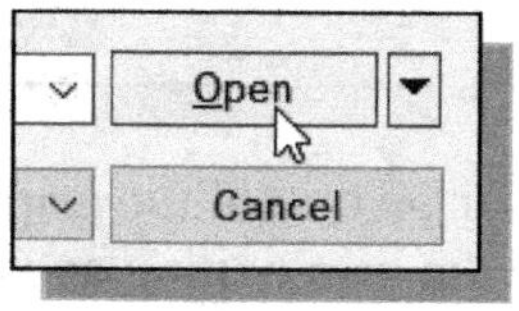

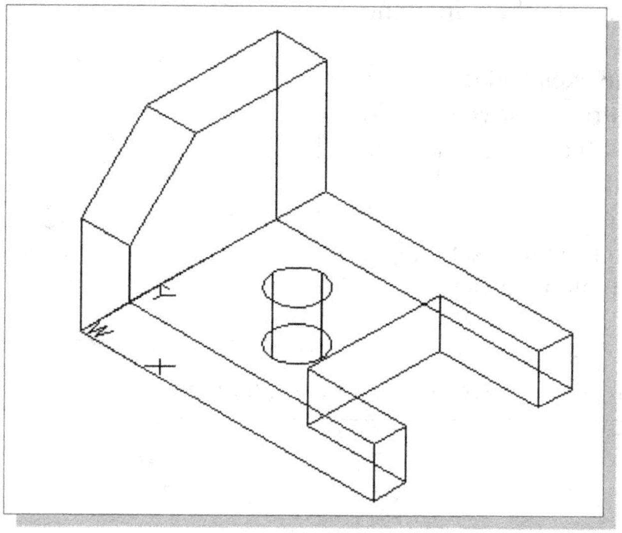

Moving Objects to a Different Layer

Prior to creating additional surfaces, we will first organize the existing geometry that has been constructed.

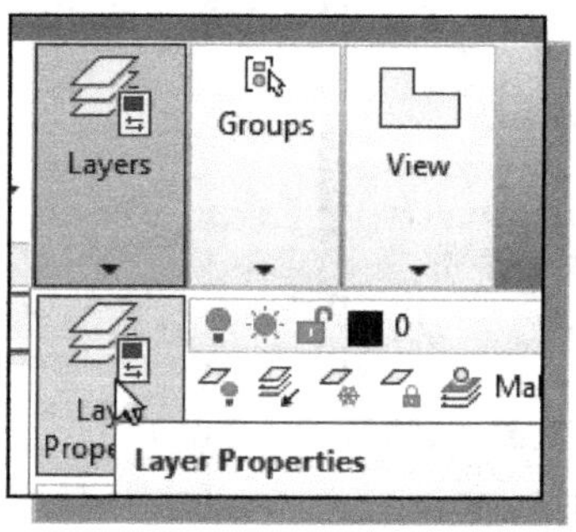

1. Click **Layers Properties Manager** in the *Layers* toolbar.

2. Click on the **New** button to create new layers.

3. Create **three new layers** with the following settings:

Layer	***Color***	***Linetype***	***Lineweight***
Construction	**White**	**Continuous**	**Default**
Surface	**Cyan**	**Continuous**	**Default**
Wireframe	**Blue**	**Continuous**	**0.30mm**

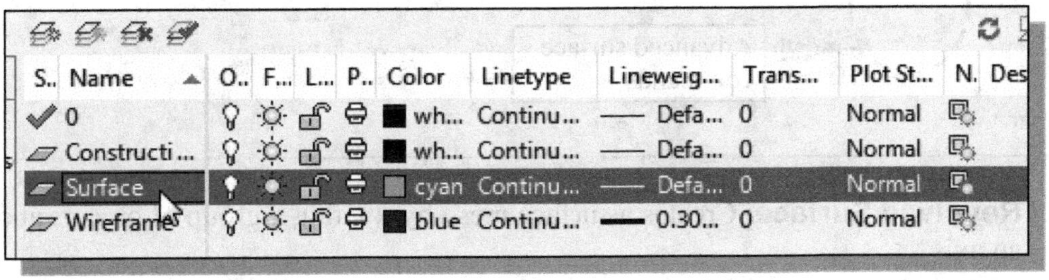

4. Click on the **Close** button to accept the settings and exit the *Layer Properties Manager* dialog box.

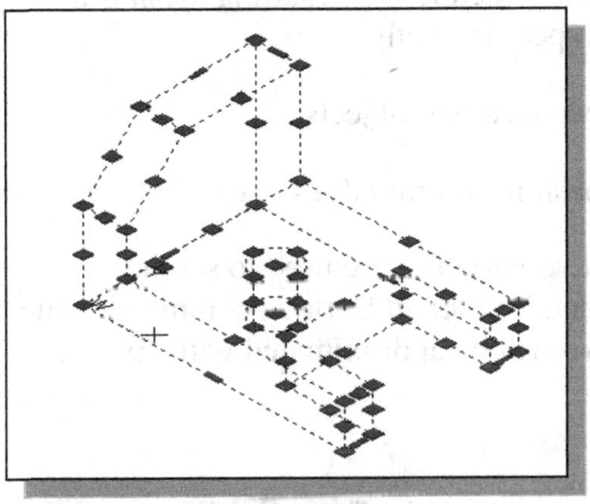

5. Inside the graphics window, pre-select all entities by using the left-mouse-button to create a *selection window* enclosing all entities.

• Note that all selected entities are highlighted.

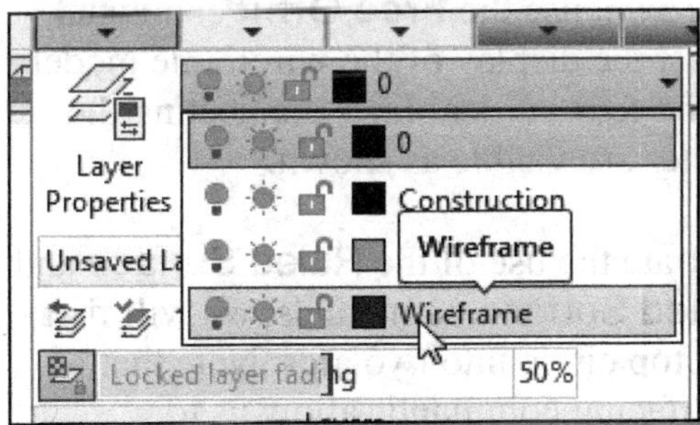

6. On the *Object Properties* toolbar, choose the ***Layer Control*** box with the left-mouse-button.

• Notice the layer name displayed in the *Layer Control* box is the selected object's assigned layer and layer properties.

7. In the *Layer Control* box, click on the ***Wireframe*** layer name as shown.

❖ All entities of the *Locator* model are moved to the *Wireframe* layer.

8. On your own, save the current model as *Locator-Layer*.dwg.

Advanced Meshed Surface Modeling Commands

Several of the advanced faceted surface-modeling commands are displayed in the *Meshed Surface Modeling* toolbar, which is placed under the **Mesh** tab in the *Ribbon*. These commands allow us to quickly create and duplicate faceted surfaces in specific manners.

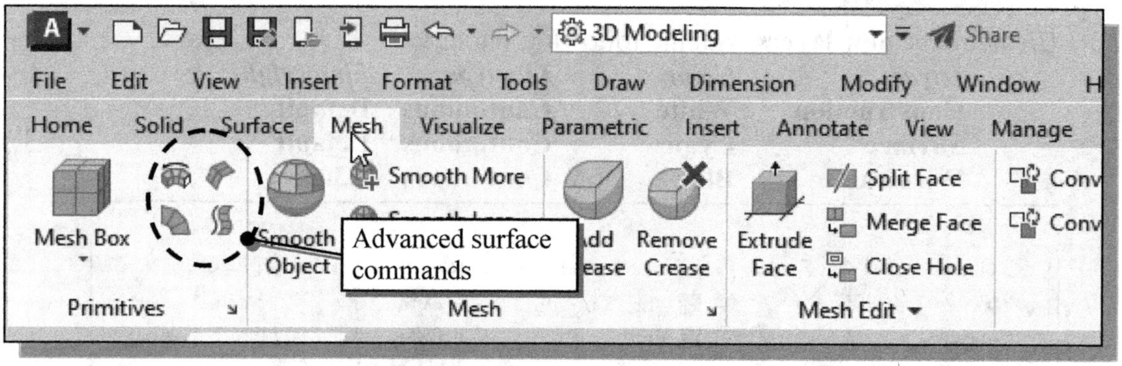

- **Revolved Surface**: Creates a surface mesh by rotating a group of objects about an axis.

- **Tabulated Surface**: Creates a surface mesh representing a general tabulated surface defined by a path curve and a direction vector. The resulting mesh is a series of parallel polygons running along a specified path.

- **Ruled Surface**: Creates a surface mesh between two objects.

- **Edge Surface**: Creates a surface patch mesh from four edges.

SurfTab1 & SurfTab2 system variables: These two variables are used to set the number of increments used by the Ruled Surface and Tabulated Surface commands. The default values are set to six, which means any curve will be approximated with six straight lines.

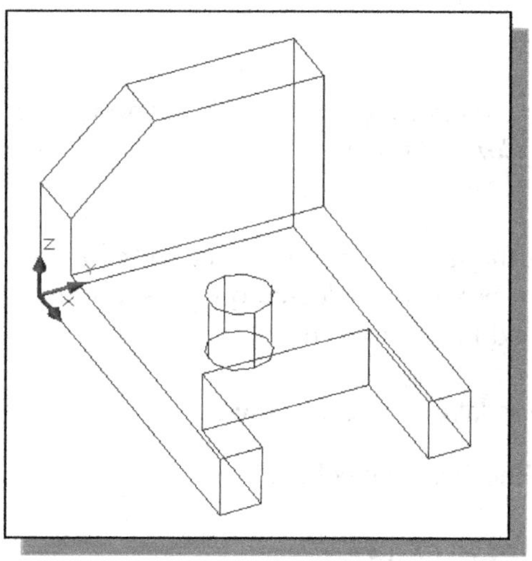

1. On your own, use the **Free Orbit** command and adjust the display of the wireframe model so that the four vertical lines connecting the two circles are visible as shown.

- To illustrate the use of the Ruled Surface and Tabulated Surface commands, we will first split the top circle into two arcs. Note that these surfacing commands allow us to construct a polygon mesh for different situations and regions. The split of the circle is necessary in creating a mapped surface on the top plane of the model.

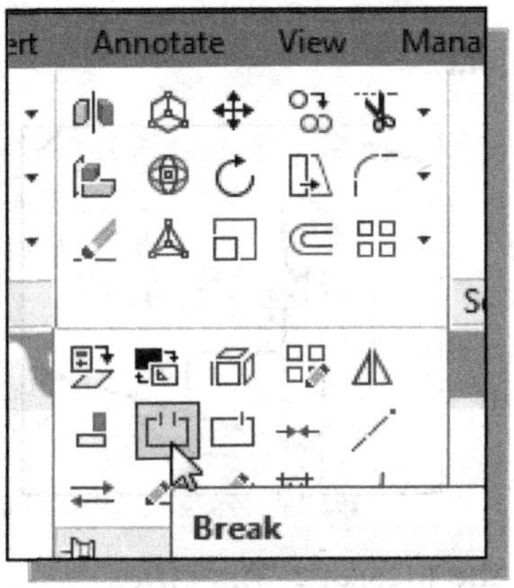

2. Select **Break** in the *Modify* toolbar under the **Home** tab.

- The **Break** command can be used to erase parts of objects or split an object in two. Note that we can only erase parts of a circle. We will therefore erase a portion of the circle and then split the circle into two arcs.

3. Select the top circle as shown. Note that the portion defined by two selected points will be erased.

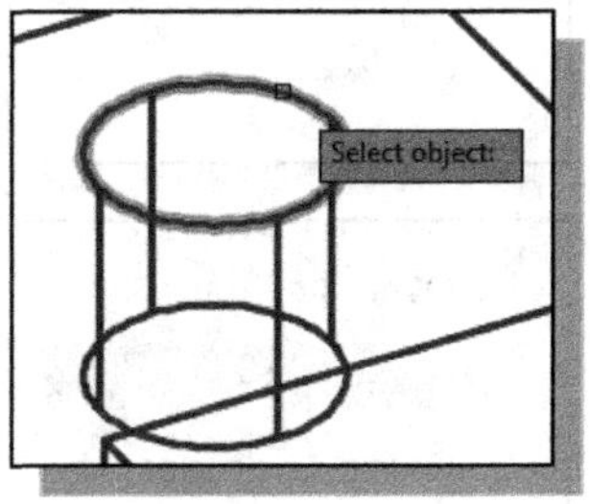

- By default, AutoCAD treats the selection point as the first break point. We can override the first point by choosing **First point** in the option menu.

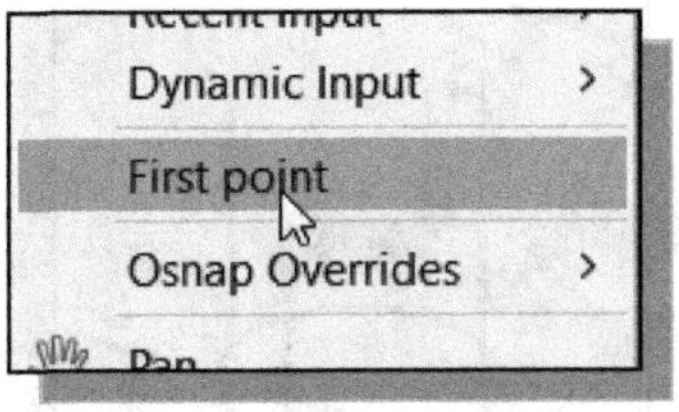

4. In the command prompt area, the message "*Specific second break point or [First point]:*" is displayed. Right-click once and select **First point** in the option menu.

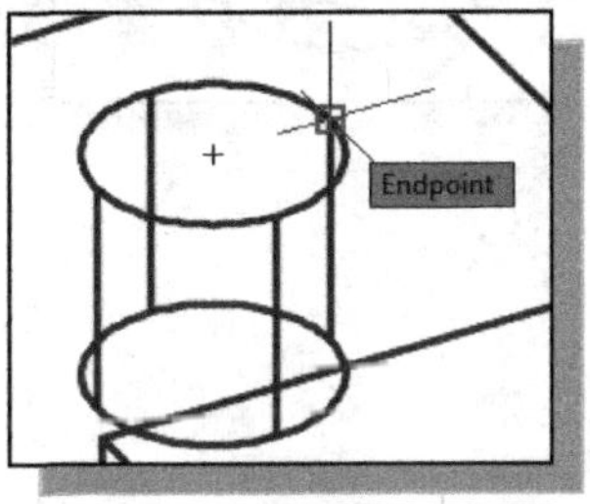

5. In the command prompt area, the message "*Specific first break point:*" is displayed. Choose the top endpoint of the vertical line on the right as shown.

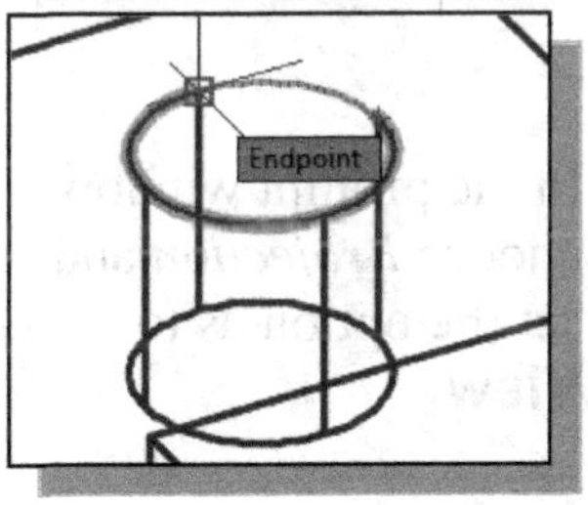

6. In the command prompt area, the message "*Specific second break point:*" is displayed. Choose the top endpoint of the vertical line as shown.

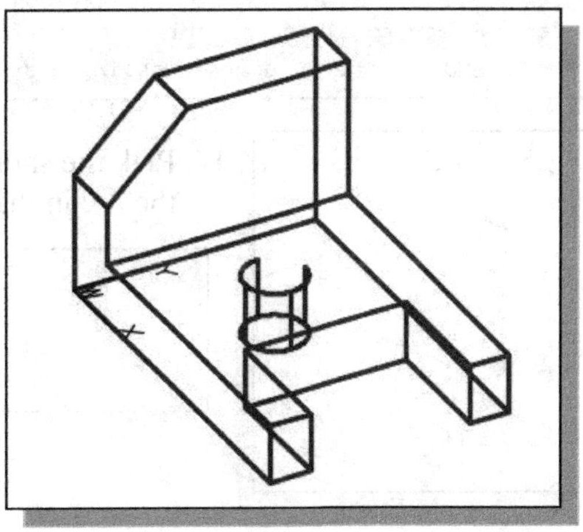

- One quarter of the circle has been erased. We will next split the arc into two arcs, again using the **Break** command.

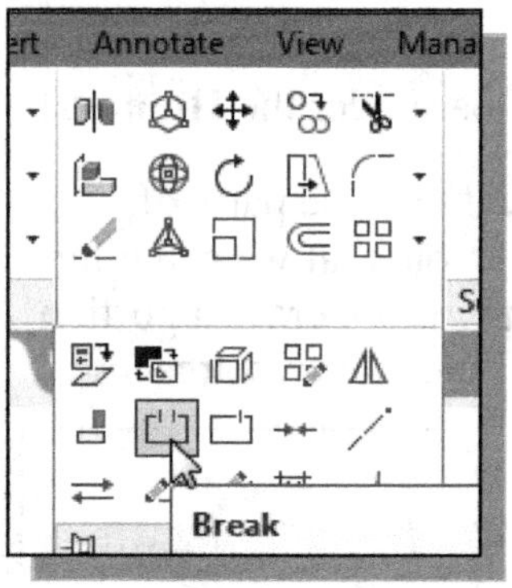

7. Select **Break** in the *Modify* toolbar.

8. Select the top arc as shown.

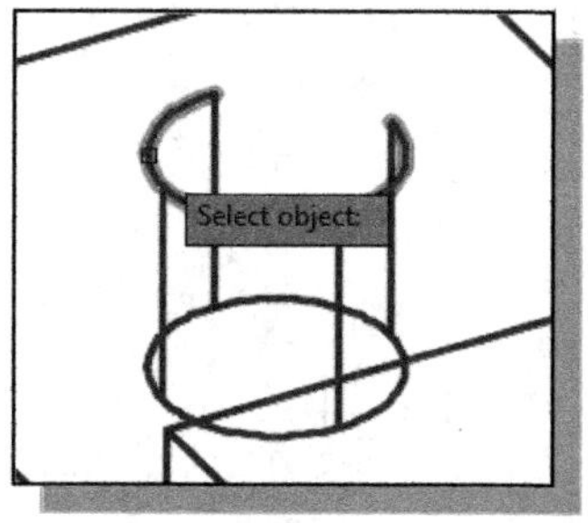

- By default, AutoCAD treats the selection point as the first break point. We can override the first point by choosing **First point** in the option menu.

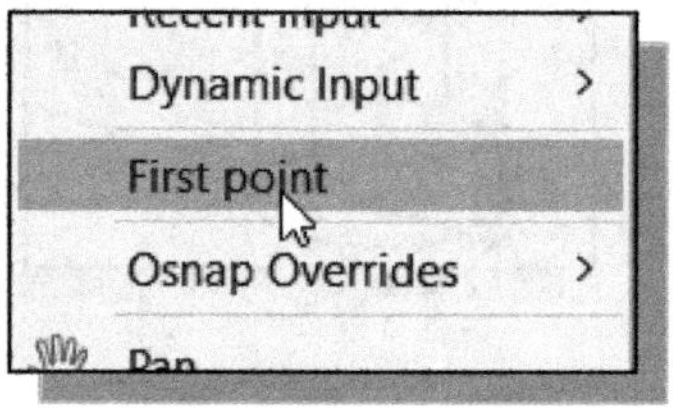

9. In the *command prompt area*, the message "*Specific second break point or [First point]:*" is displayed. Right-click once and select **First point** in the option menu.

10. In the *command prompt area*, the message "*Specific first break point:*" is displayed. Choose the top endpoint of the left vertical line as shown.

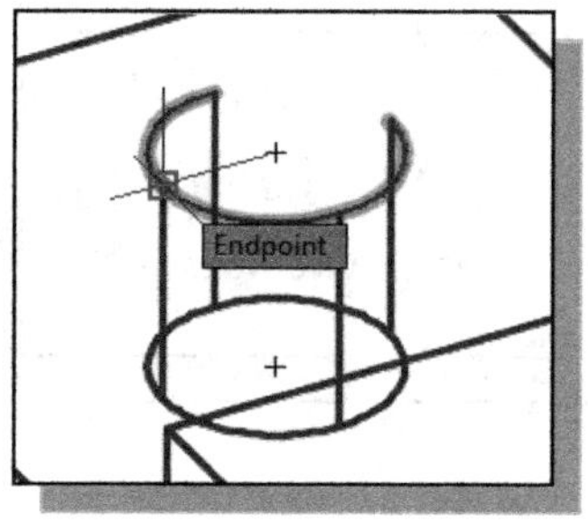

11. In the *command prompt area*, the message "*Specific second break point:*" is displayed. To split an object, choose the **same endpoint** that was previously chosen.

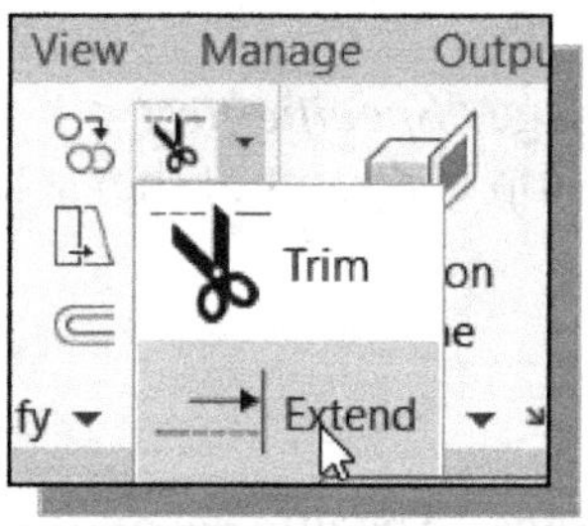

12. Select **Extend** in the *Modify* toolbar.

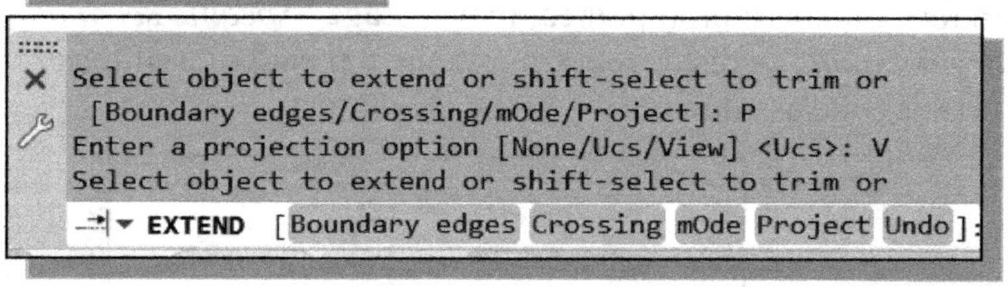

13. In the prompt window, choose *Projection* and set the option as to **View**.

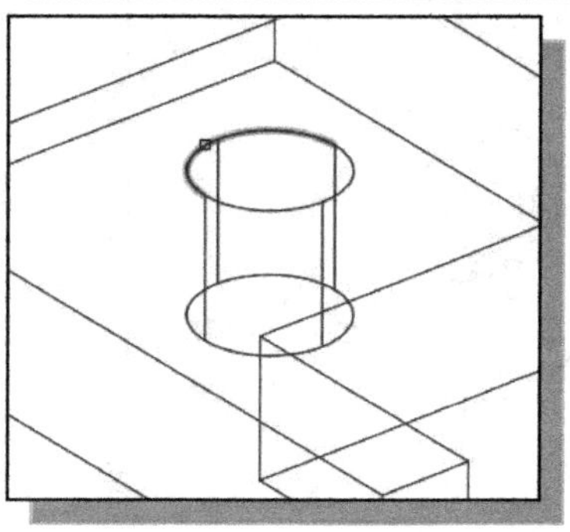

14. Pick the shorter arc near the right endpoint to extend the arc in that direction.

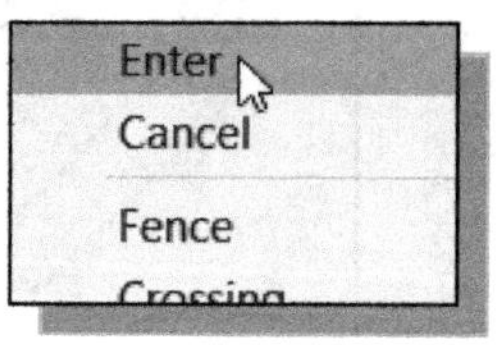

15. Inside the graphics window, right-click once to display the option menu and select **Enter** to end the Extend command.

Use the Faceted Tabulated Surface Option

In AutoCAD, the **TABSURF** command allows us to construct a polygon mesh representing a general tabulated surface defined by a path curve and a direction vector.

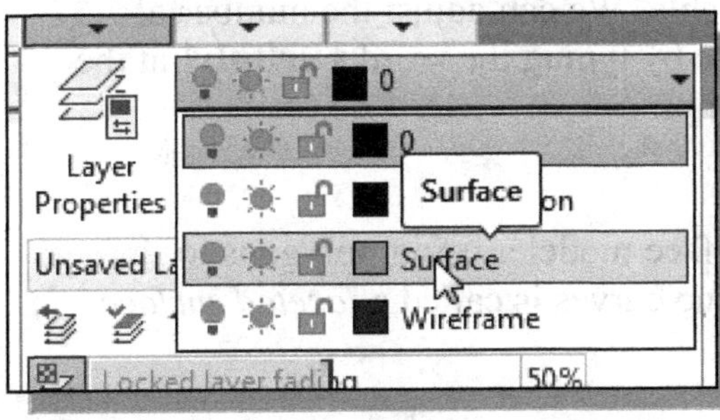

1. Set the ***Surface*** layer as the *Current Layer* by choosing the layer name in the *Layer Control* box as shown.

- We will place the surface model on a different layer than the wireframe model.

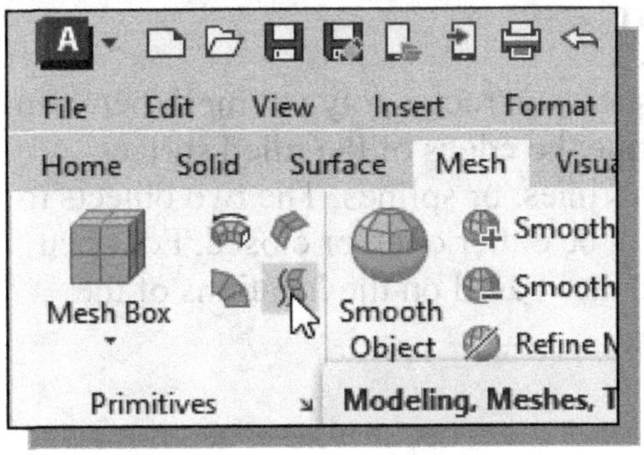

2. Click **Tabulated Surface** in the *Primitives* toolbar.

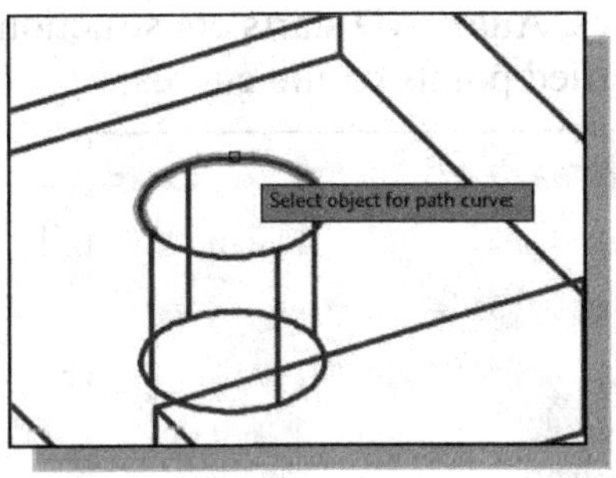

3. In the command prompt area, the message "*Select object for path curve:*" is displayed. Choose the **upper arc** as shown.

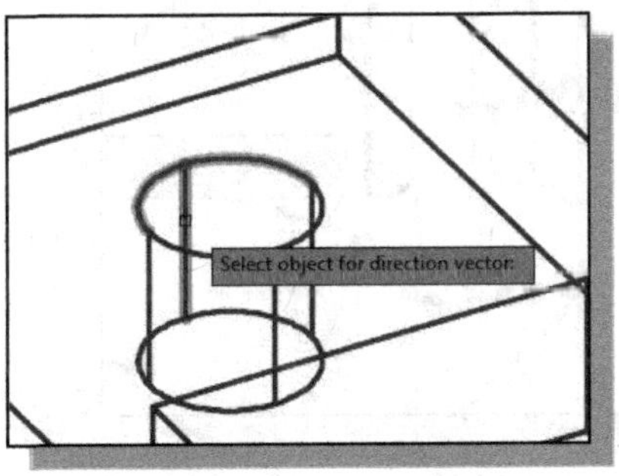

4. In the command prompt area, the message "*Select object for direction vector:*" is displayed. Choose the **vertical line** near the top endpoint as shown. Note that the endpoints of the line are used as a reference to determine the direction of the polygon mesh.

5. On your own, use the **Orbit** and **Visual Styles** commands to examine the constructed polygons.

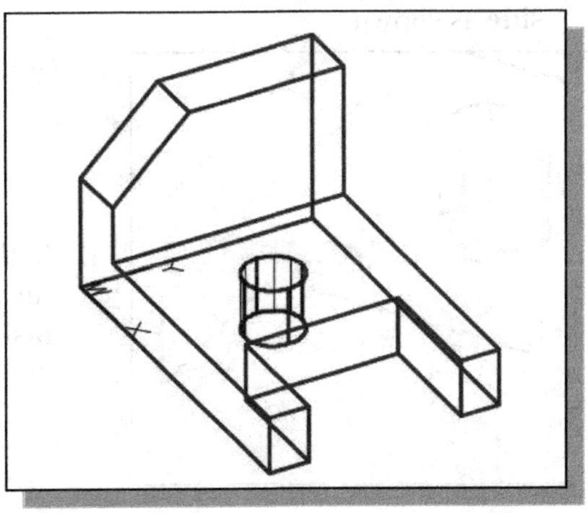

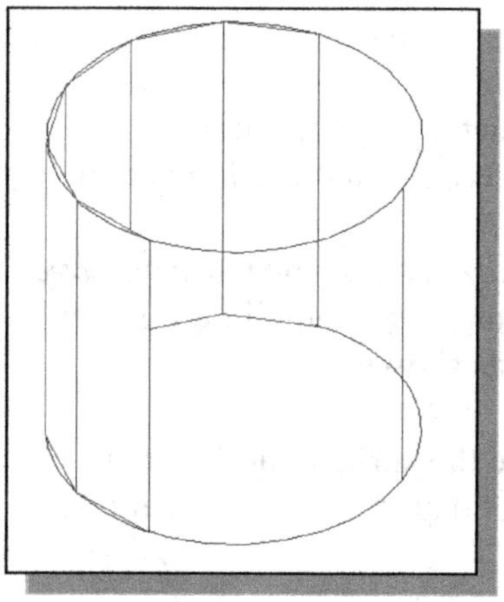

- Exactly six polygons are created and positioned along the selected *path curve*, the upper arc, with the **Tabulated Surface** command. This is set by the ***SurfTab1*** variable. We can adjust the number of segments to use by typing the word **surftab1** at the command prompt.

❖ Note that a surface modeler using polygons to approximate true curves is called a *faceted surface modeler*.

Use the Faceted Ruled Surface Option

In AutoCAD, the **RULESURF** command allows us to construct a polygon mesh between two objects. We can use two different objects to define the edges of the ruled surface: lines, points, arcs, circles, ellipses, elliptical arcs, polylines, or splines. The two objects to be used as the *rails* of a ruled surface mesh must both be either open or closed. For open curves, AutoCAD starts construction of the ruled surface based on the locations of the specified points on the curves.

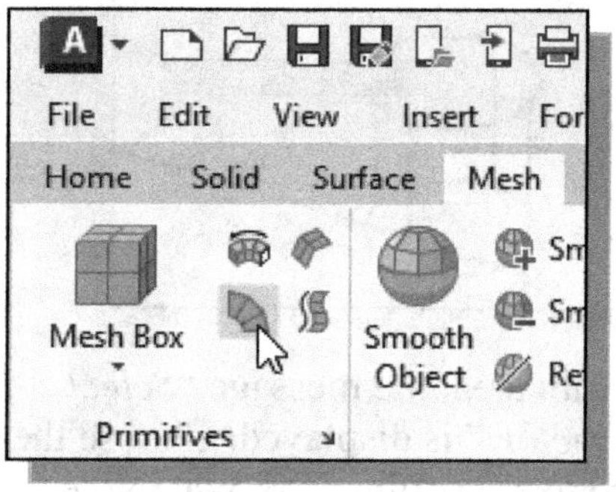

1. Pick **Ruled Surface** in the *Draw* pull-down menu.

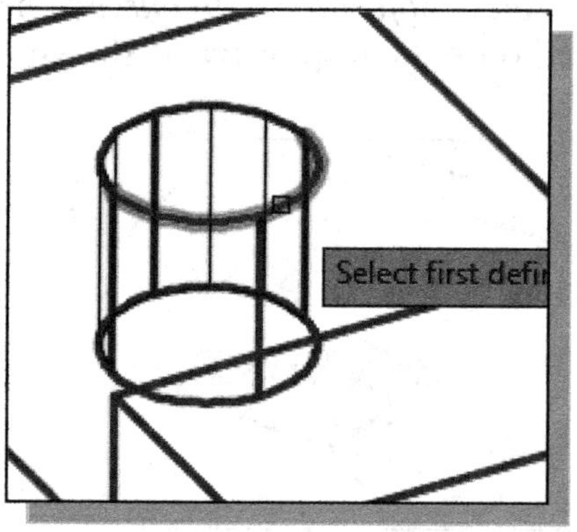

2. In the command prompt area, the message "*Select first defining curve:*" is displayed. Choose the **lower arc** by clicking on the **right side** as shown.

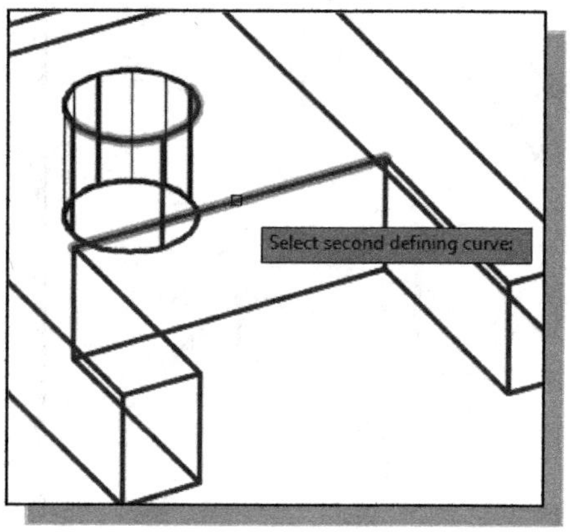

3. In the command prompt area, the message "*Select second defining curve:*" is displayed. Choose the **inside straight edge** on the **right side** as shown.

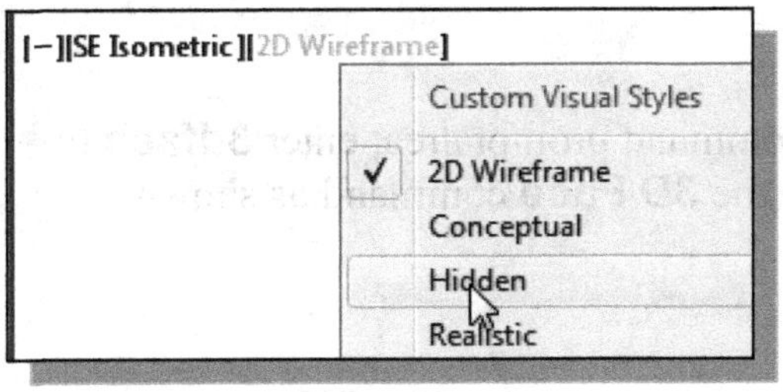

4. In the *Visual Styles* toolbar, click on the **Hidden** icon to display the model with hidden lines removed.

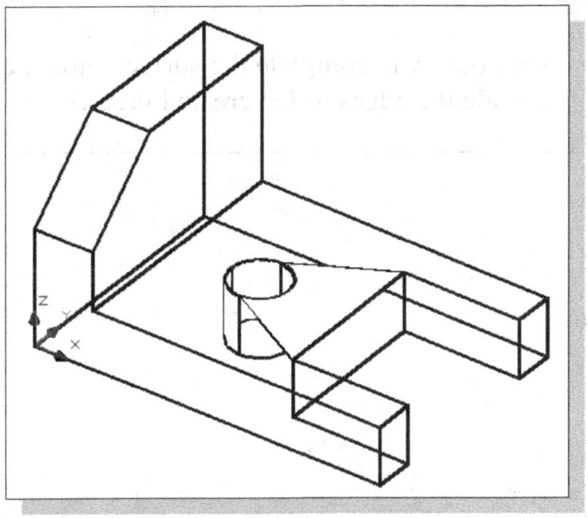

- The selected edges are removed from the display so that the face of the ruled surface appears to be more realistic.

5. On your own, repeat the above steps and create another ruled surface as shown. (Hint: Use the **Realtime Zoom** function to assist in the selection of the arc.)

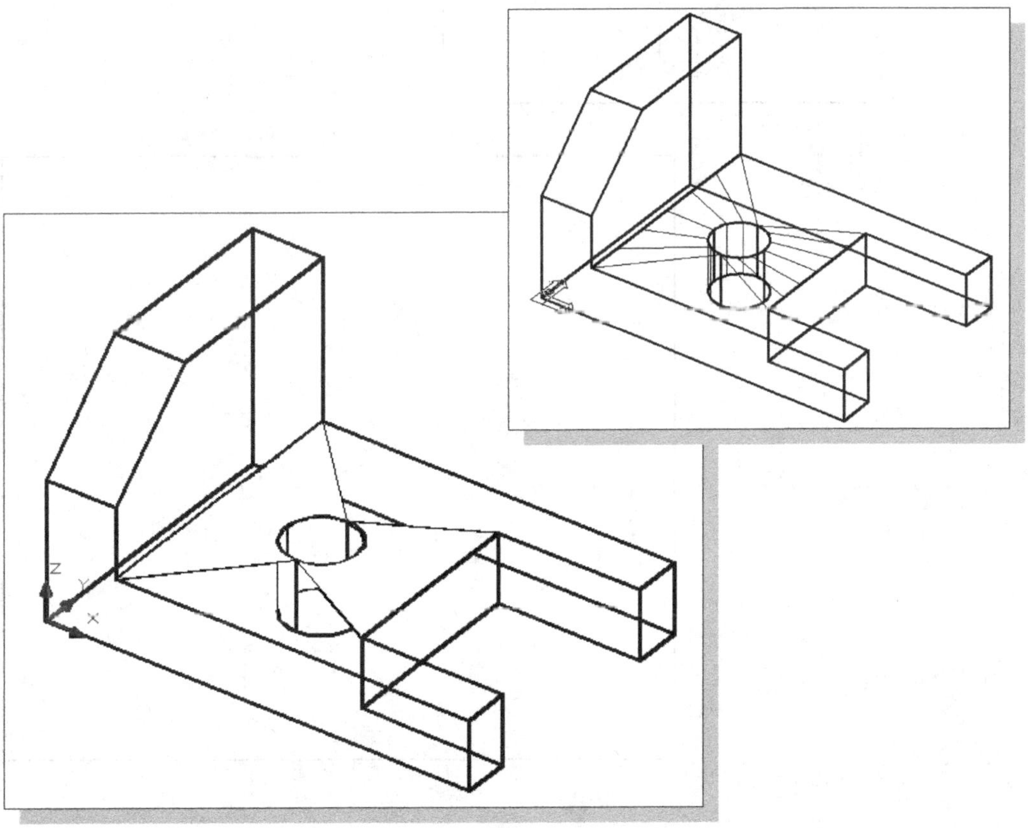

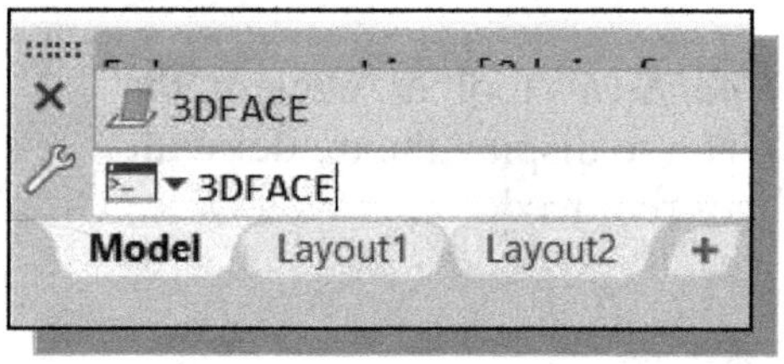

6. In the command prompt area, enter **3dface** to activate the **3D Face** command as shown.

- On your own, complete the surface model as shown. (Hint: Use the **Edge** command to hide the edges of the created faces.)

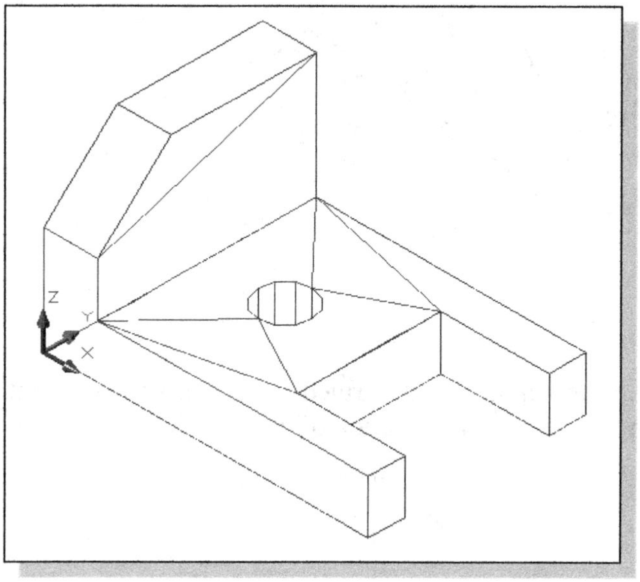

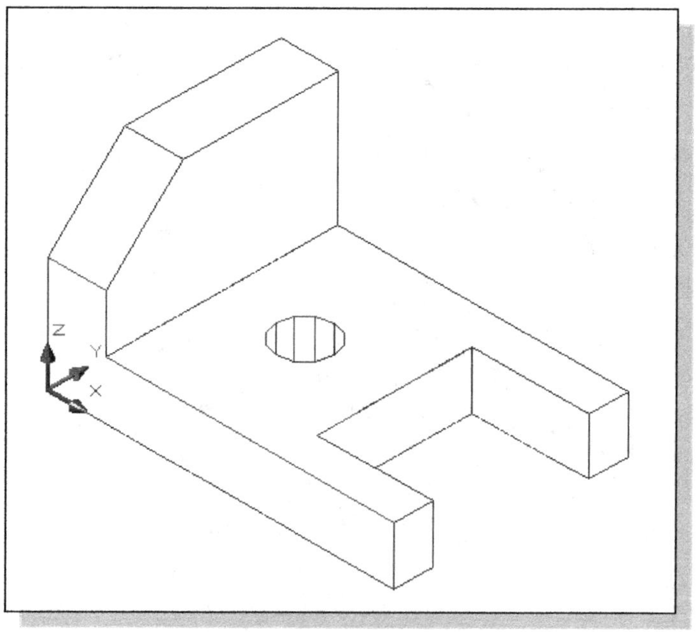

Review Questions:

1. List and describe three differences between *Wireframe models* and *Surface models.*

2. List and describe the three types of faceted surfaces available in AutoCAD.

3. List and describe two different shading options in AutoCAD.

4. What is the difference between the **2D Solid** and **3D Face** commands in AutoCAD?

5. What is the difference between **Tabulated Surface** and **Ruled Surface** in AutoCAD?

6. Identify and describe the following commands:

   a)

   b)

   c)

   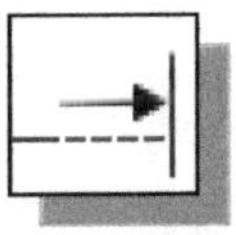

Exercises: All dimensions are in inches.

1.

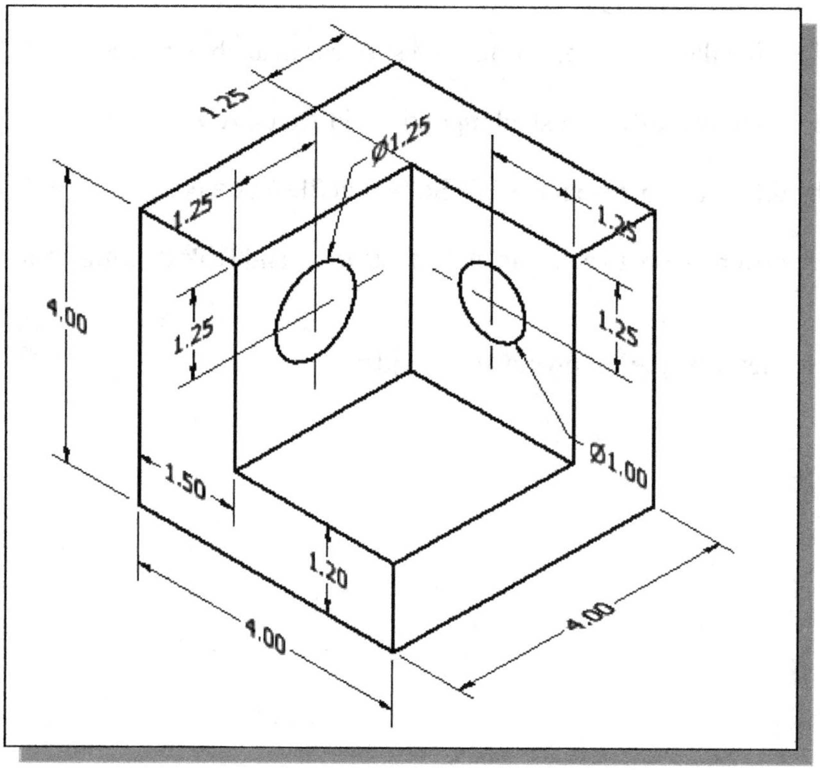

2.

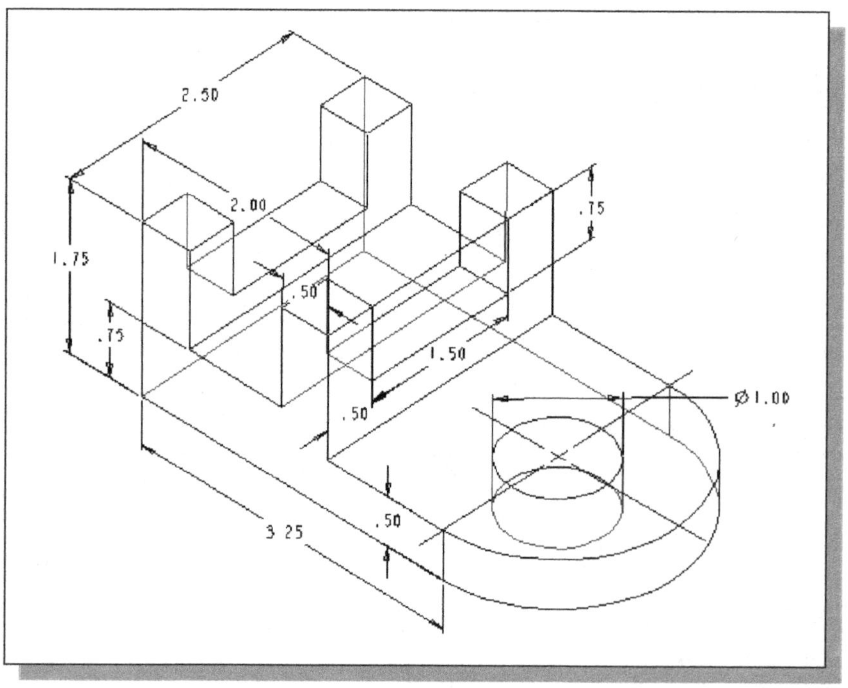

3.

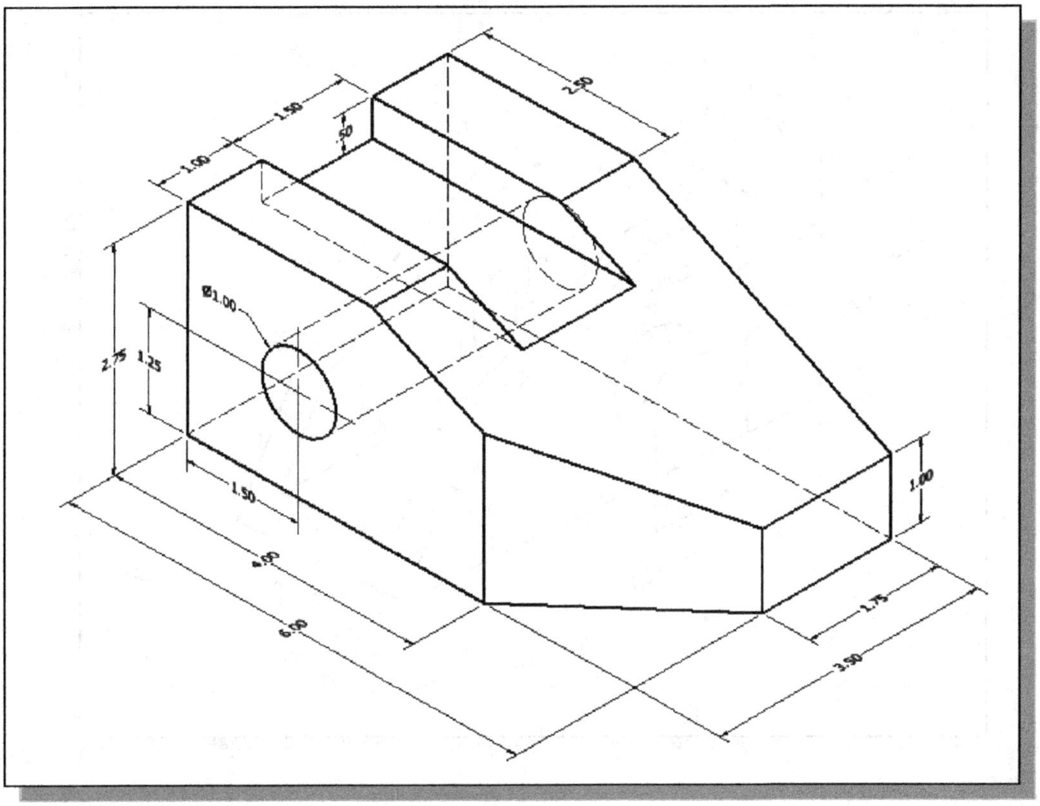
2.50
1.50
.50
1.00
Ø1.00
2.75
1.25
1.50
4.00
6.00
1.00
1.75
3.50

4.

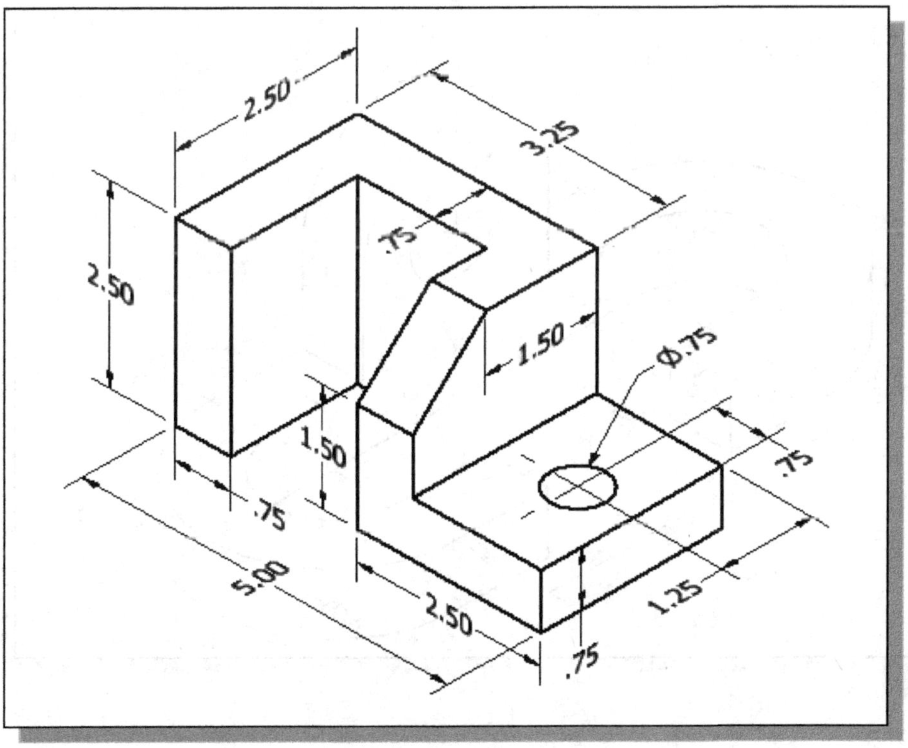
2.50
3.25
.75
2.50
1.50
Φ.75
1.50
.75
.75
5.00
2.50
1.25
.75

5.

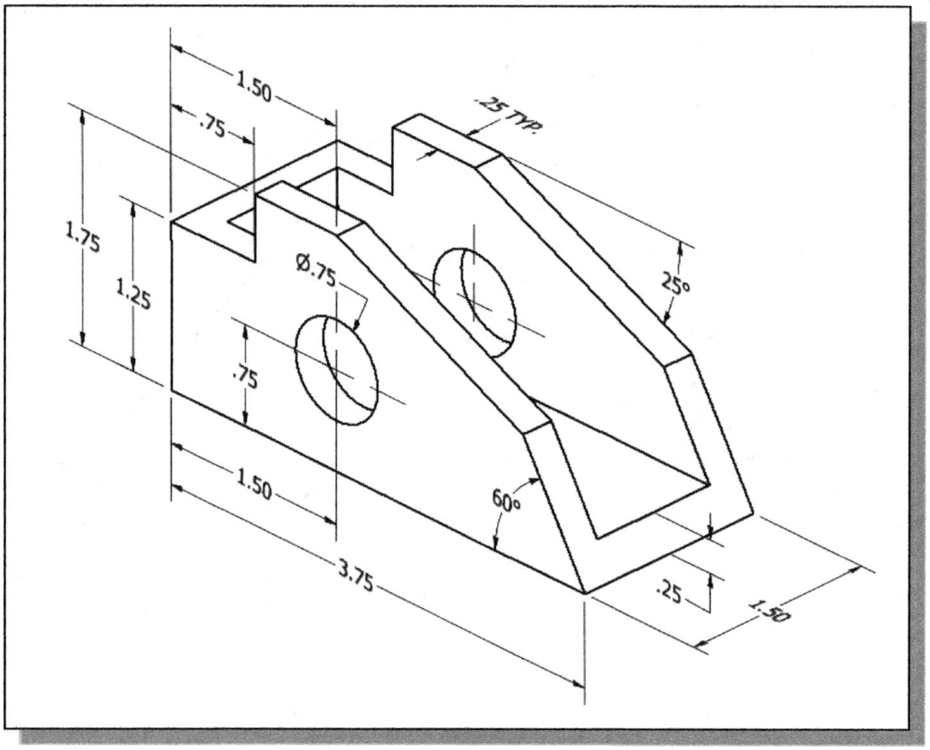
1.50
.75
.25 TYP.
1.75
1.25
Ø.75
25°
.75
1.50
60°
3.75
.25
1.50

6.

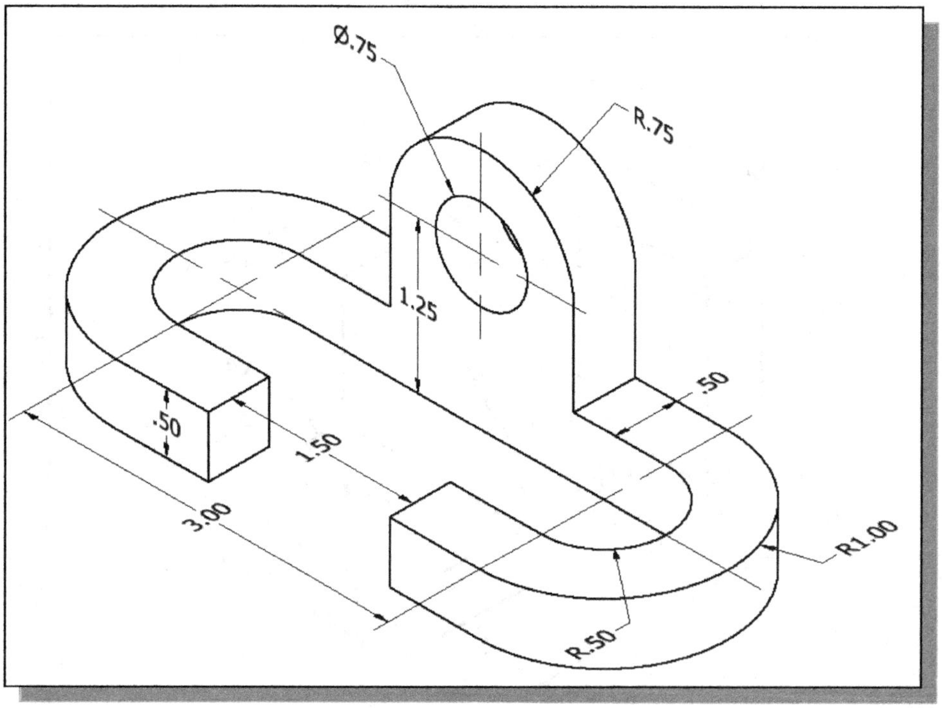
Ø.75
R.75
1.25
.50
.50
1.50
3.00
R1.00
R.50

Chapter 5
Procedural and NURBS Surface Modeling

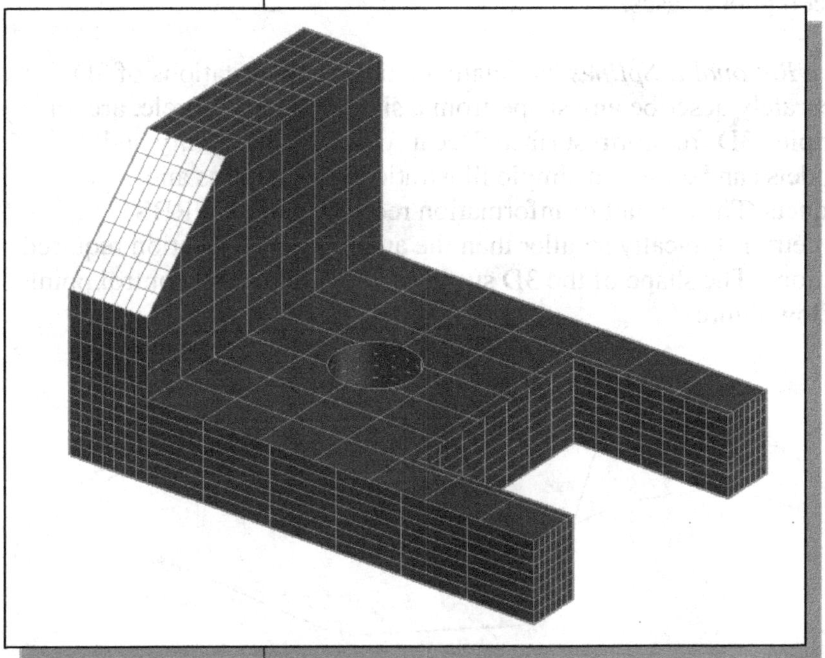

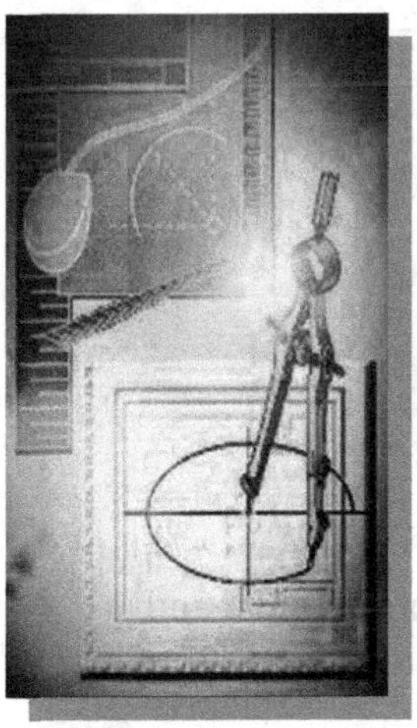

Learning Objectives

- Create Procedural Surface Models
- Understand the Different in between Spline Fit and Spline CV
- Using the Extrude, Planar and Network Commands to create surfaces
- Understand the Use of 3D NURBS Surface Editing Commands

Introduction

Besides the classical faceted surface modeling techniques, presented in the previous chapter, AutoCAD also provides two other options to create thin shell surfaces: namely **Procedural** surfaces and **NURBS** surfaces. The primary usage of 3D surface modeling in industry concentrates on creating smooth 3D surfaces, such as car bodies, ship bodies, computer mouse and cell phone cases.

NURBS, *Non-Uniform Rational B-Splines*, are mathematical representations of 3D geometry that can accurately describe any shape from a simple 2D line, circle, arc, or curve to the more complex 3D free-form surface. Because of their flexibility and accuracy, NURBS models can be used in simple illustrations, animations and manufacturing of products. The amount of information required for a NURBS representation of geometry is typically smaller than the amount of information required by faceted approximations. The shape of the 3D surface is determined by control points as illustrated in the below figure.

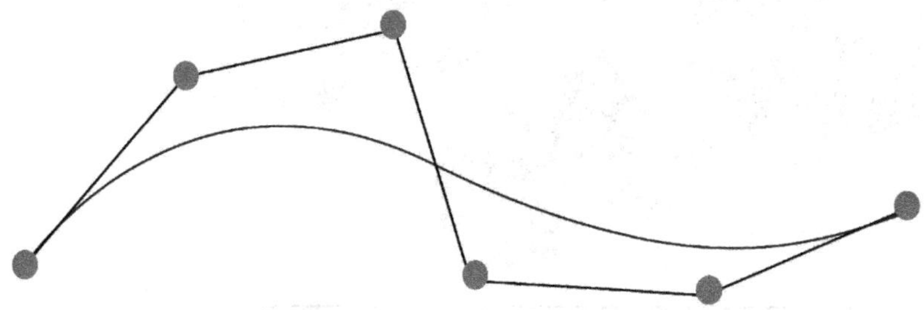

In AutoCAD, procedural surface models can be easily created from profile shapes composed of lines and curves using the *Extrude*, *Loft*, *Planar*, *Revolve, Network*, and *Sweep* commands.

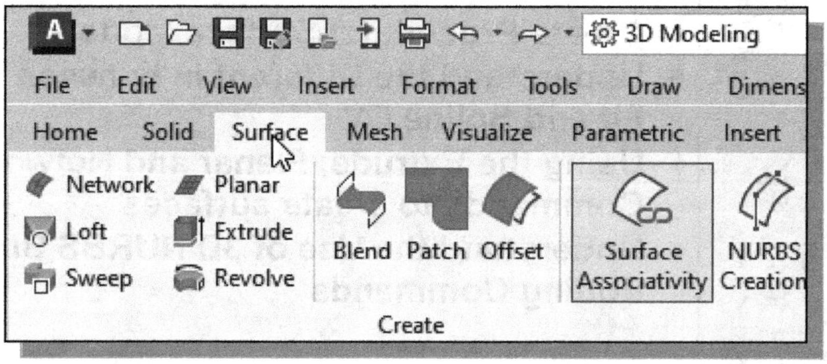

One typical modeling workflow is to create basic models using meshes, solids, and procedural surfaces, and then convert them to NURBS surfaces for additional refinements of shapes.

In this chapter, the general procedures to create **Procedural** surface models and **NURBS** surface models are illustrated.

Starting Up AutoCAD 2027

1. Select the **AutoCAD 2027** option on the *Program* menu or select the **AutoCAD 2027** icon on the *Desktop*.

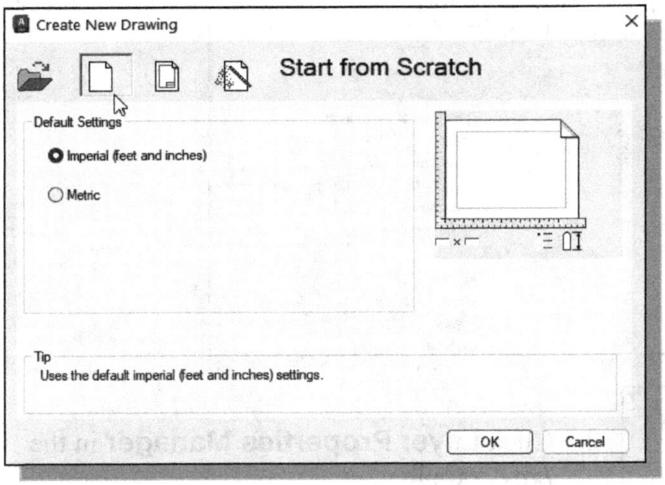

2. In the *AutoCAD Startup* dialog box, select the **Start from Scratch** option as shown in the figure.

3. Choose **Imperial** to use the *Standard English* units setting.

4. Click **OK** to accept the setting.

Turn On the UCS II Toolbar

1. In the *Menu Bar,* select **[Tools] → [Toolbars] → [AutoCAD]**.

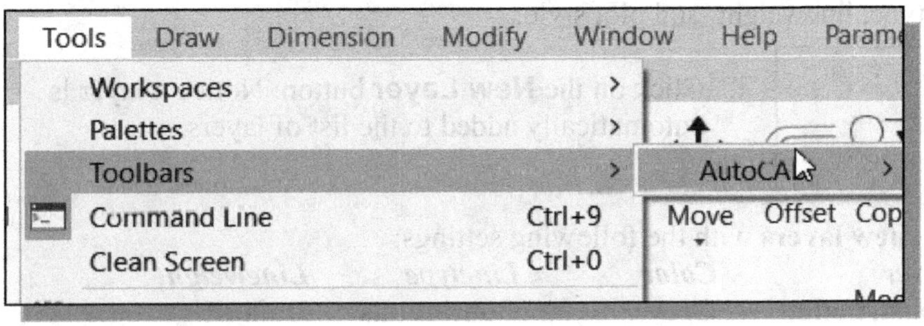

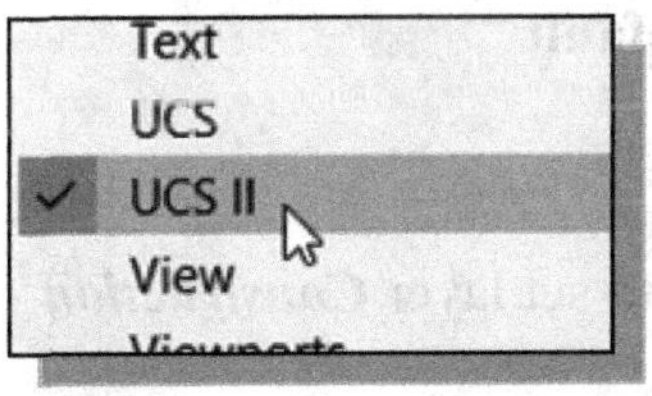

2. Select **UCSII**, with the left-mouse-button, to display the *UCSII* toolbar on the screen.

➤ The options available in the *UCSII* toolbar allow us to quickly orient and align the UCS.

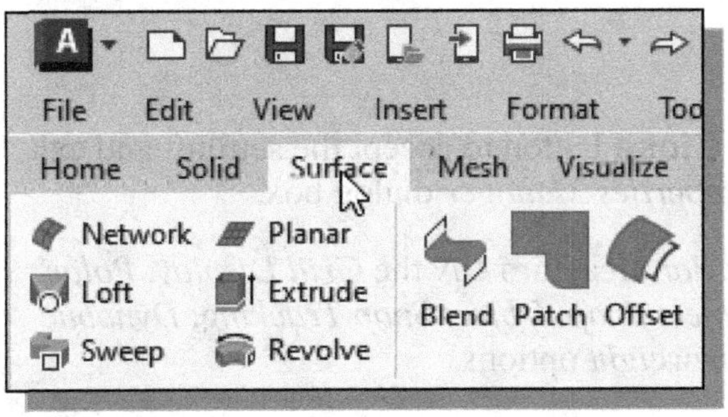

3. Click on the **Surface** tab to show the surface commands available in AutoCAD.

• Note that a variety of 2D & 3D modeling commands are available to create surface models.

Layers Setup

1. In the *Menu Bar,* select **[Tools] → [Toolbars] → [AutoCAD] → [Layers]**.

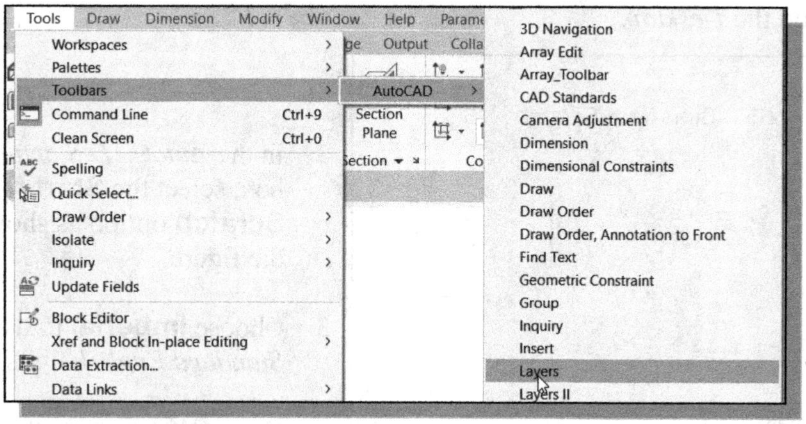

2. Click **Layer Properties Manager** in the *Layers* toolbar.

❖ In AutoCAD, we always construct entities on a layer. It may be the default layer or a layer that we create. Each layer has associated properties such as the visibility setting, color, linetype, lineweight, and plot style.

3. Click on the **New Layer** button. Notice a layer is automatically added to the list of layers.

4. Create **two new layers** with the following settings:

Layer	*Color*	*Linetype*	*Lineweight*
Construction	**Grey**	**Continuous**	**Default**
Object	**Cyan**	**Continuous**	**Default**

5. Select and highlight the layer ***Construction*** in the list of layers.

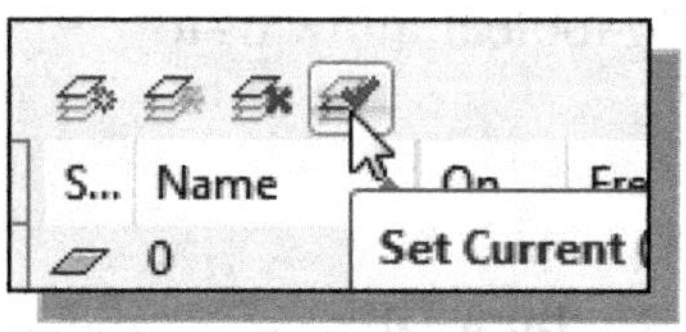

6. Click on the **Set Current** icon to set layer ***Construction*** as the *Current Layer*.

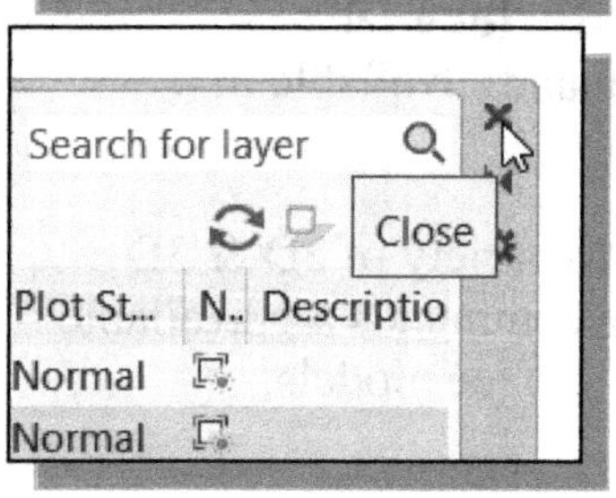

7. Click on the **Close** button to accept the settings and exit the *Layer Properties Manager* dialog box.

8. In the *Status Bar* area, turn ***ON*** the *Grid Display, Polar Tracking, Object Snap, Object Snap Tracking, Dynamic Input* and *Lineweight* options.

Create a Thin Surface Using the Extrude Command

In AutoCAD, procedural surface models can be easily created from profile shapes composed of lines and curves. The *Extrude* command allows us to quickly take a 2D profile and generate a 3D thin surface model.

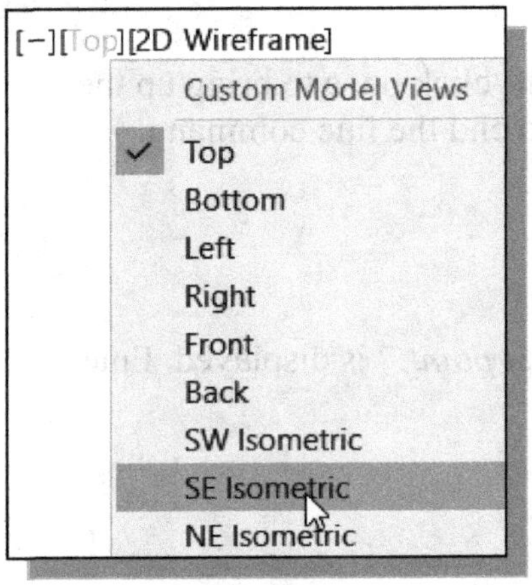

1. In the *View* option list, select **[SE Isometric].**

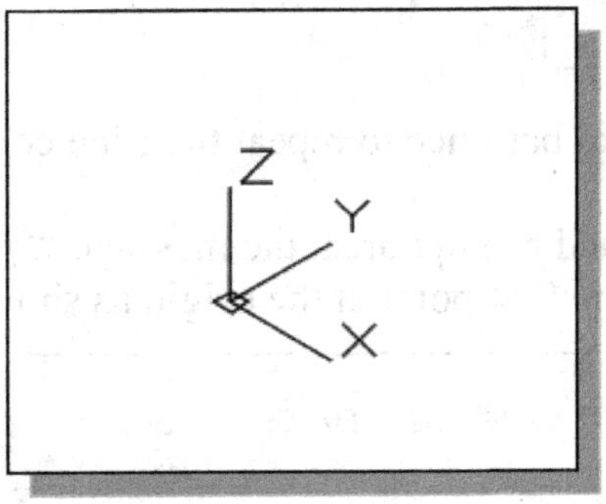

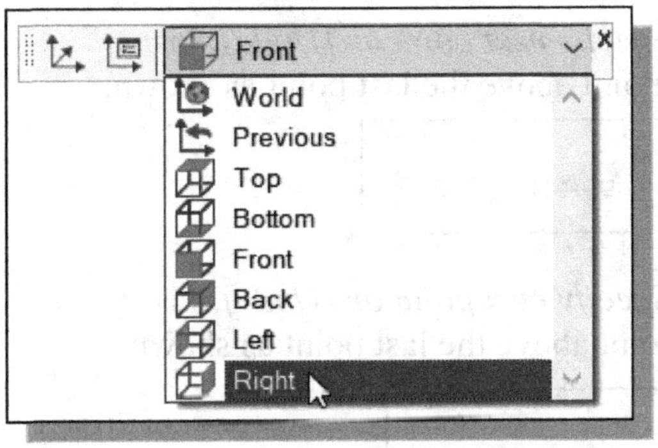

2. Note that the current *UCS* is aligned to the *World Coordinate System.* Select **Right** in the *UCS II* toolbar as shown.

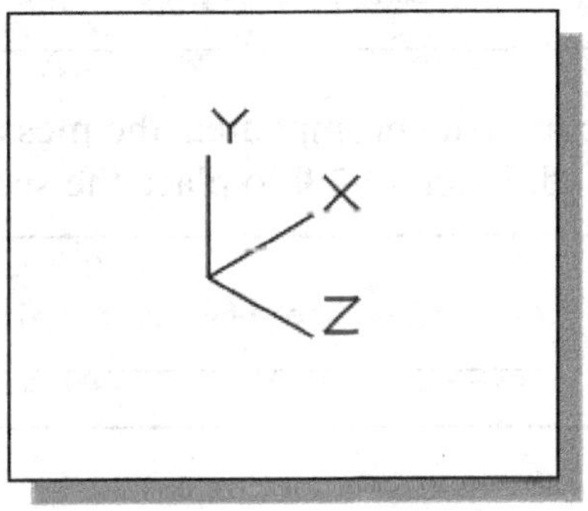

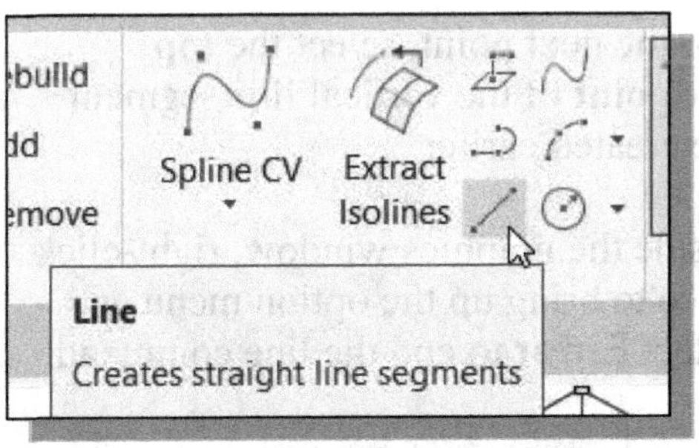

3. Select the **Line** icon in the *Curves* tab as shown.

4. In the command prompt area, the message "*Specify first point:*" is displayed. Enter **0,0** to place the first point at the origin as shown.

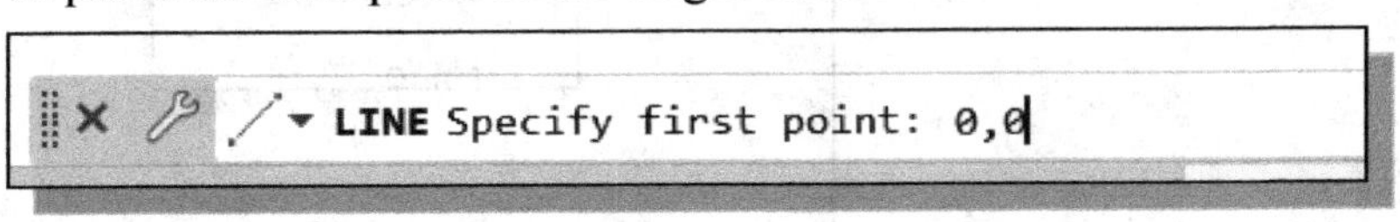

5. In the command prompt area, the message "*Specify next point or [Undo]:*" is displayed. Enter **@0,1.5** to place the second point above the last point as shown.

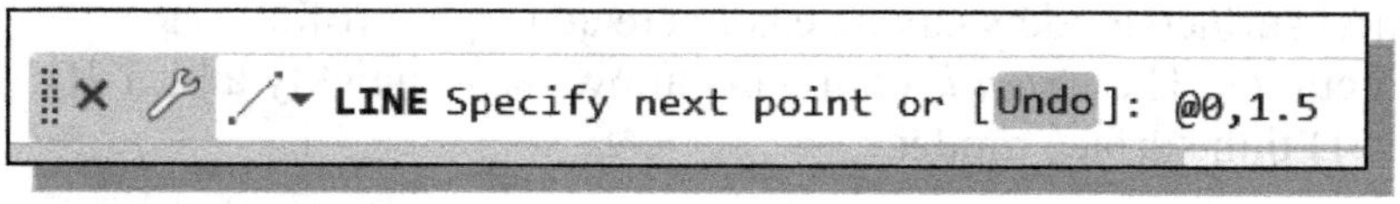

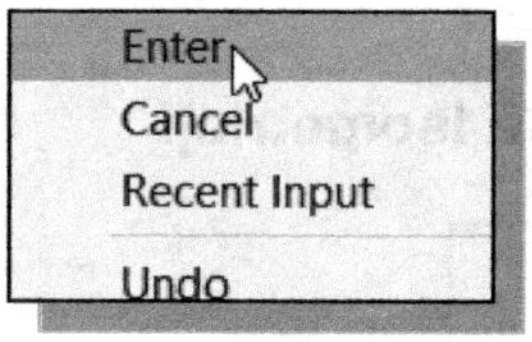

6. Inside the graphics window, right-click once to bring up the option menu and select **Enter** to end the line command.

7. Hit the [Space] bar once to repeat the Line command.

8. In the command prompt area, the message "*Specify first point:*" is displayed. Enter **3,0** to place the first point at the origin as shown.

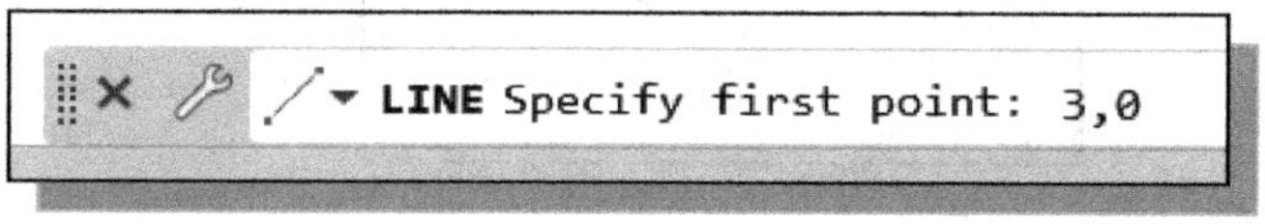

9. In the command prompt area, the message "*Specify next point or [Undo]:*" is displayed. Enter **@0,2.5** to place the second point above the last point as shown.

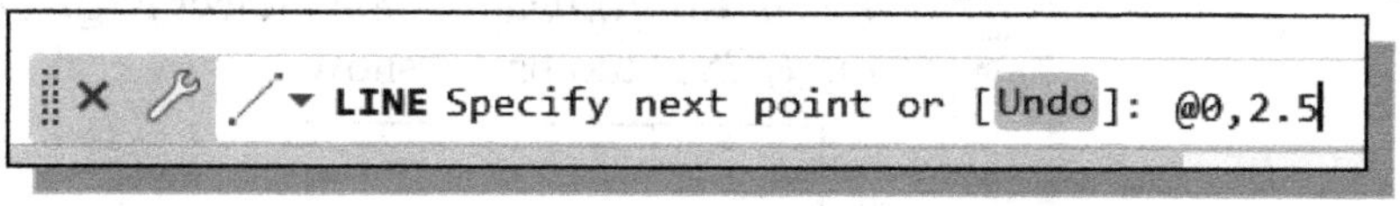

10. In the command prompt area, the message "*Specify next point or [Undo]:*" is displayed. Enter **@-2,0** to place the second point above the last point as shown.

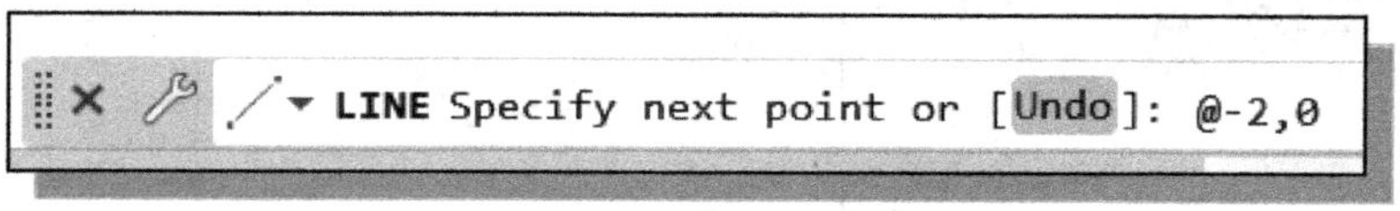

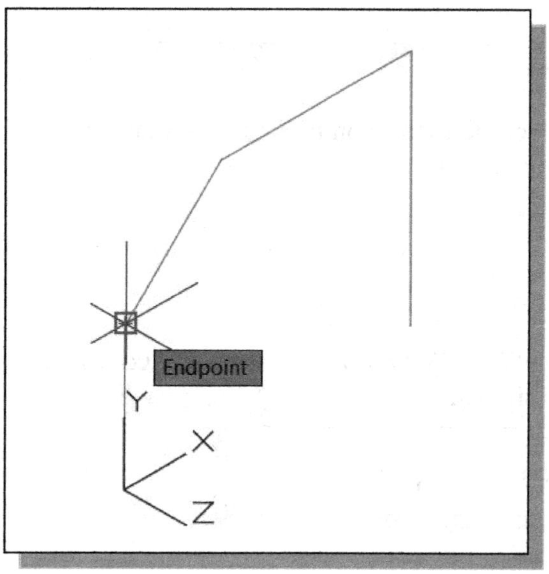

11. For the next point, select the **top endpoint** of the vertical line segment we created earlier.

12. Inside the graphics window, right-click once to bring up the option menu and select **Enter** to end the line command.

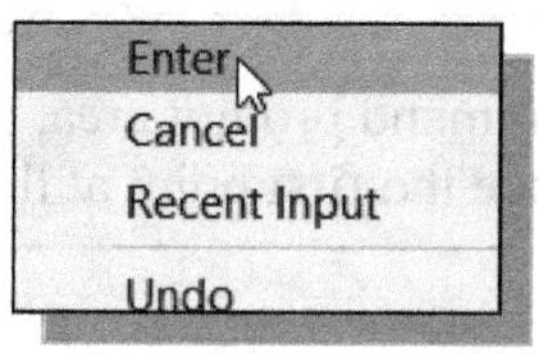

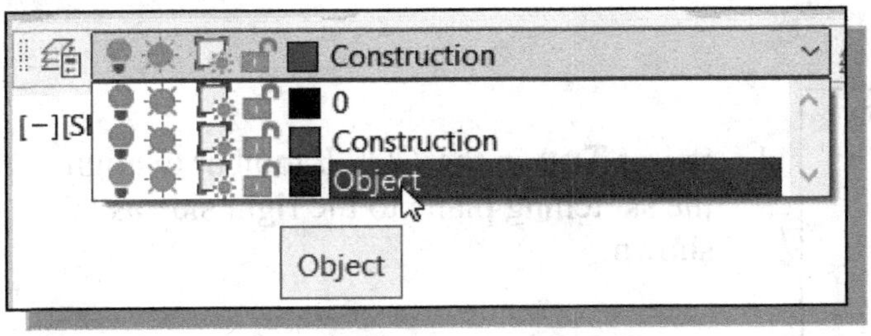

13. Activate the **Object** layer in the *Layers* toolbar as shown.

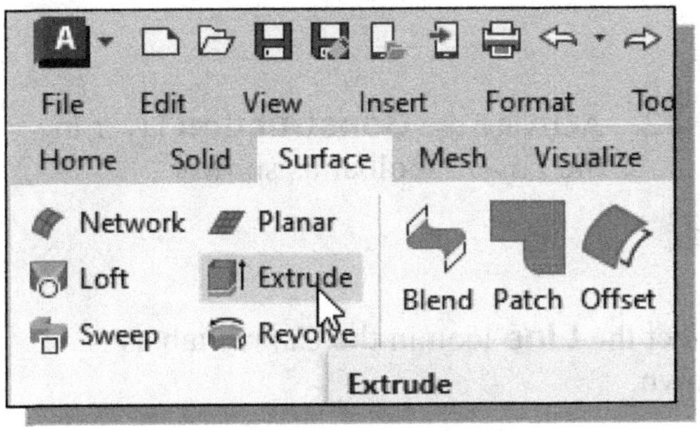

14. Select the **Extrude** icon in the *Create* tab as shown.

15. In the command prompt area, the message "*Select objects to extrude:*" is displayed. Pick all the line segments by using an enclosing window.

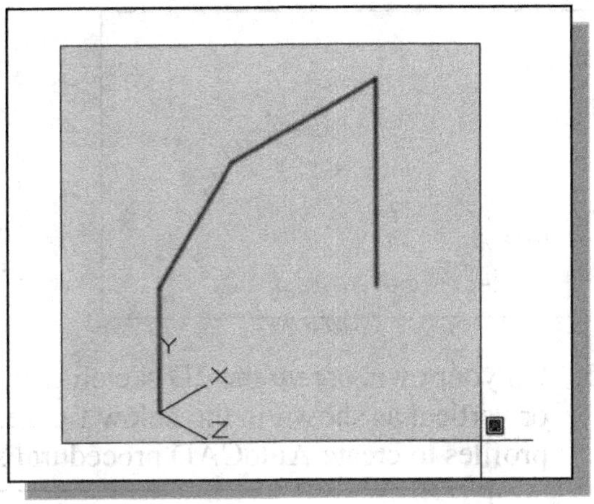

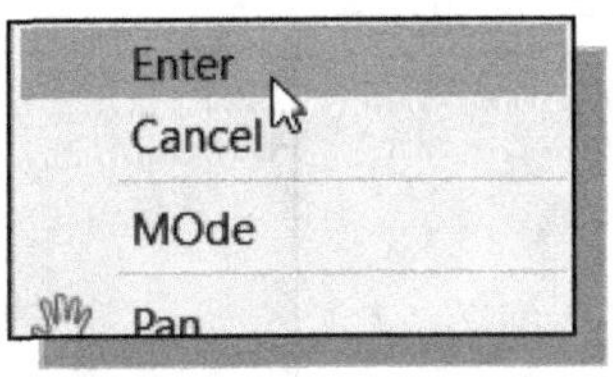

16. Inside the graphics window, **right-click once** to accept the selected entities.

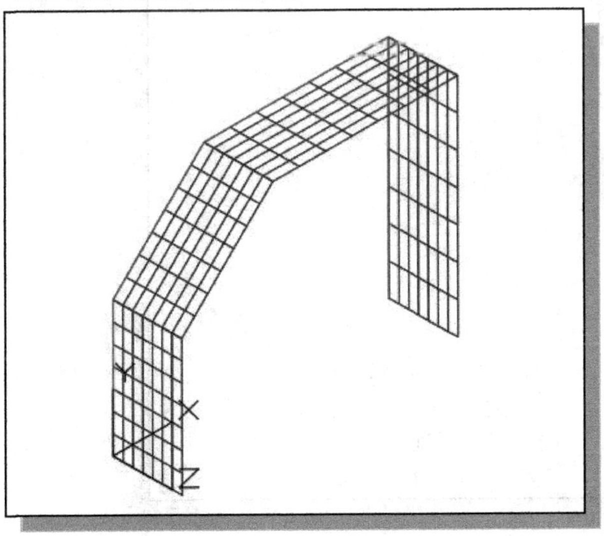

17. In the command prompt area, enter **0.75** as the extrusion height and create the surface model as shown. Note that entering a positive number will create the surface in the positive Z direction of the current coordinate system.

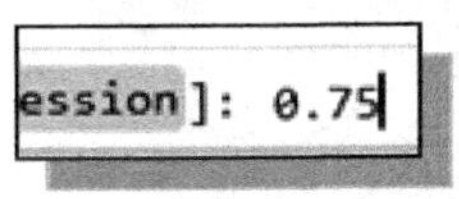

- Note that the surface model and the line segments used as the profile are on two different layers.

Create another Profile

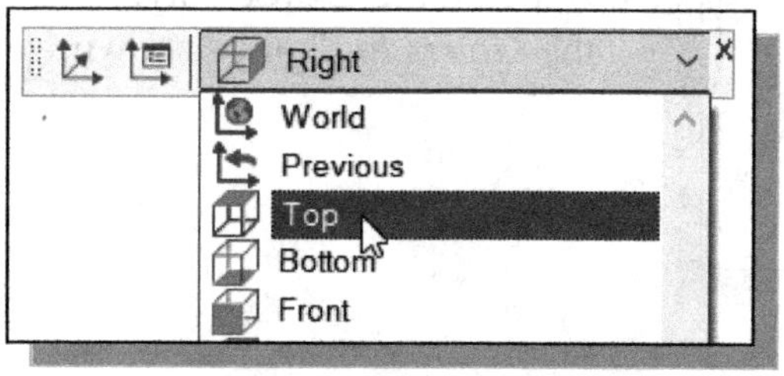

1. Select **Top** in the *UCS II* toolbar to align the sketching plane to the right side as shown.

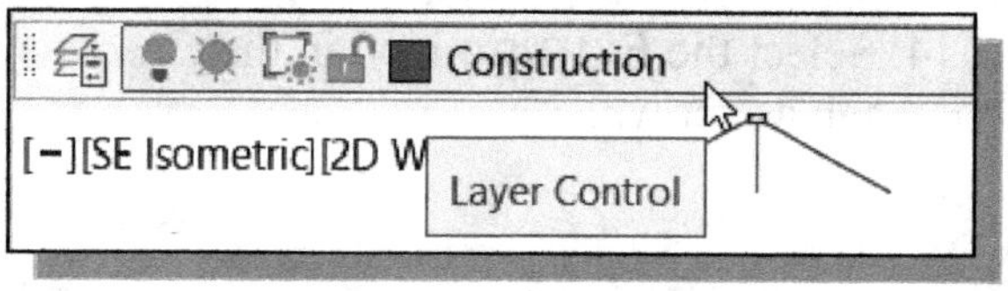

2. Activate the **Construction** layer in the *Layers* toolbar as shown.

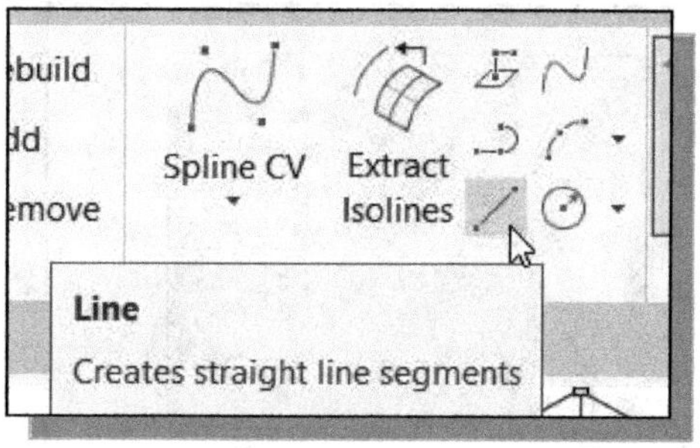

3. Select the **Line** icon in the *Curves* tab as shown.

4. In the command prompt area, the message "*Specify first point:*" is displayed. Enter **0,0** to place the first point at the origin.

5. On your own, create the 2D sketch with seven line segments that are either horizontal or vertical as shown in the below figure. Note that we can use either open or closed profiles to create AutoCAD procedural surface models.

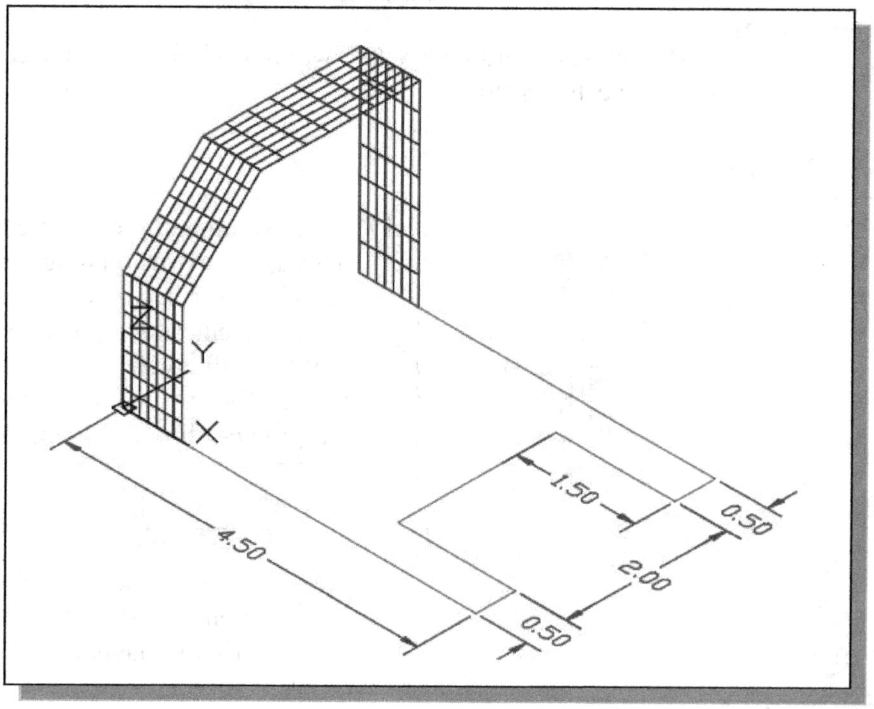

Complete the Profile Using Object Snap

1. In the *Menu Bar,* select **[Tools] → [Toolbars] → [AutoCAD]**.

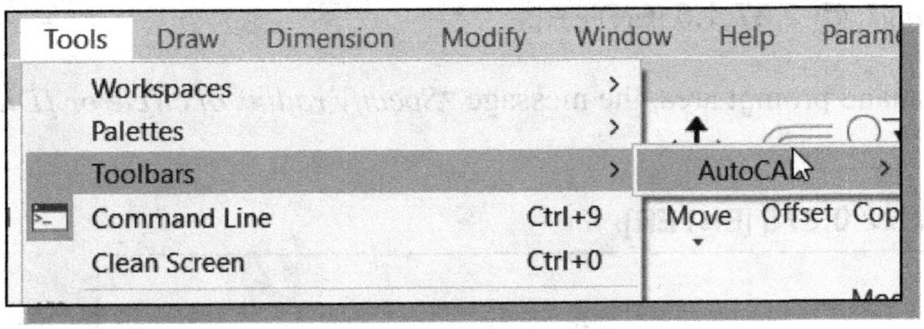

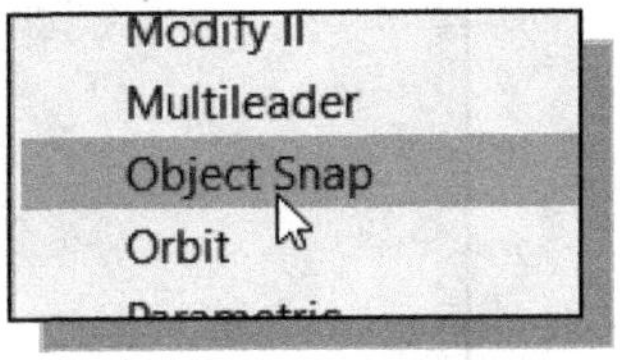

2. Select **Object Snap**, with the left-mouse-button, to display the *Object Snap* toolbar on the screen to assist the construction of the design.

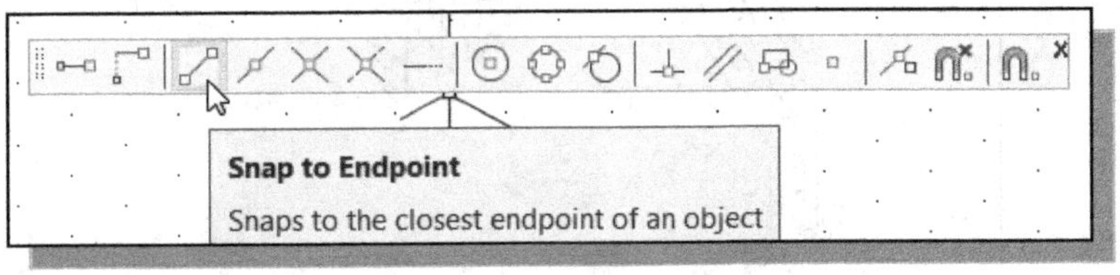

➢ ***Object Snap*** is an extremely powerful construction tool available on most CAD systems. During an entity's creation operations, we can snap the cursor to points on objects such as endpoints, midpoints, centers, and intersections.

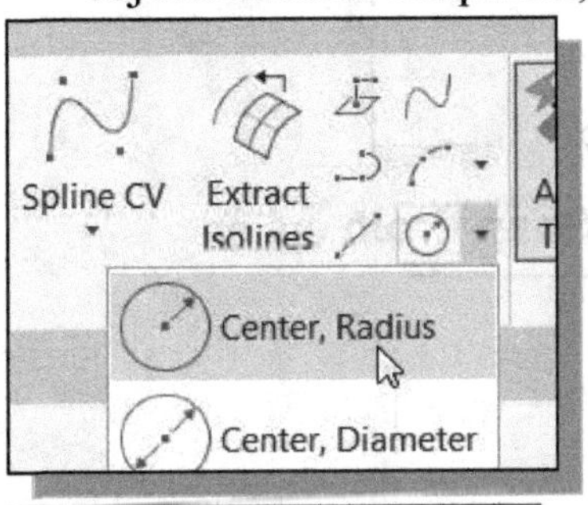

3. Activate the **Center, Radius** command in the *Curves* tab as shown.

4. In the command prompt area, the message "*_line Specify first* point:" is displayed. Select **Snap From** in the *Object Snap* toolbar.

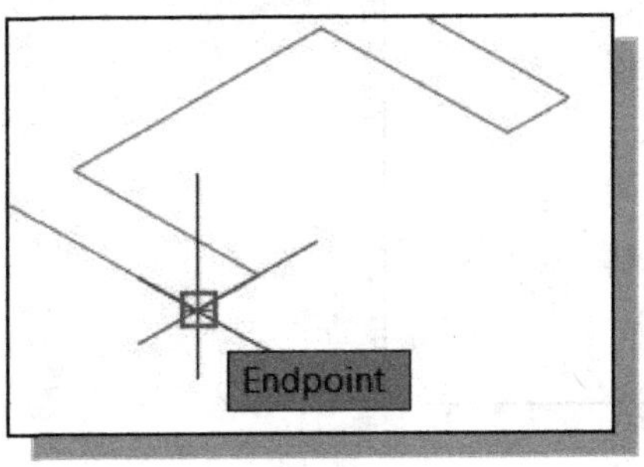

5. Select the **front right corner** as the reference point as shown.

6. In the command prompt area, the message *"Specify next point or [Close/Undo]: _from Base point <Offset>:"* is displayed.

   Command: **@-2.67,1.5 [ENTER]**.

7. In the command prompt area, the message *"Specify radius of circle or [Diameter]:"* is displayed.

   Command: **0.375 [ENTER]**.

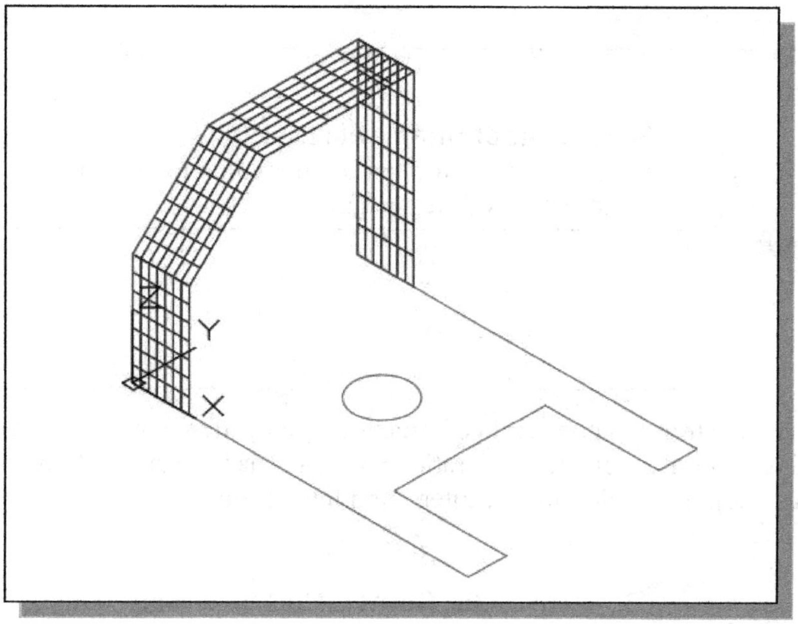

- The circle is created on the sketching plane with the **Snap From** option.

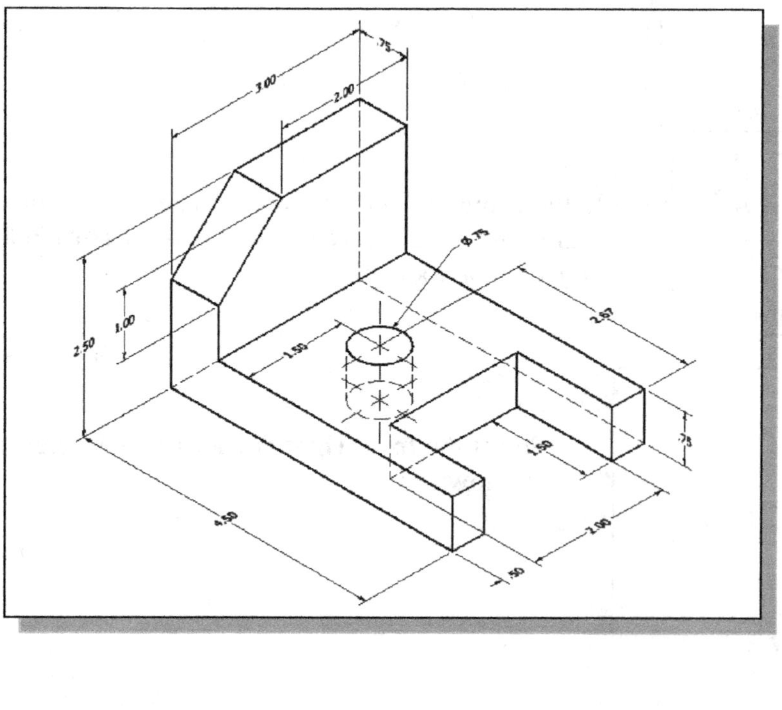

Create another Thin Surface Using the Extrude Command

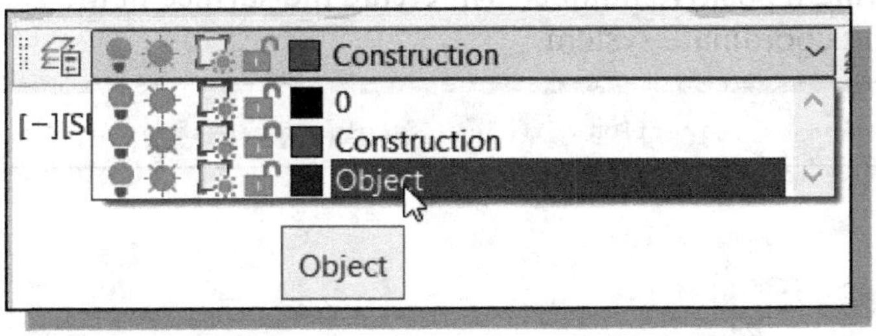

1. Activate the **Object** layer in the *Layers* toolbar as shown.

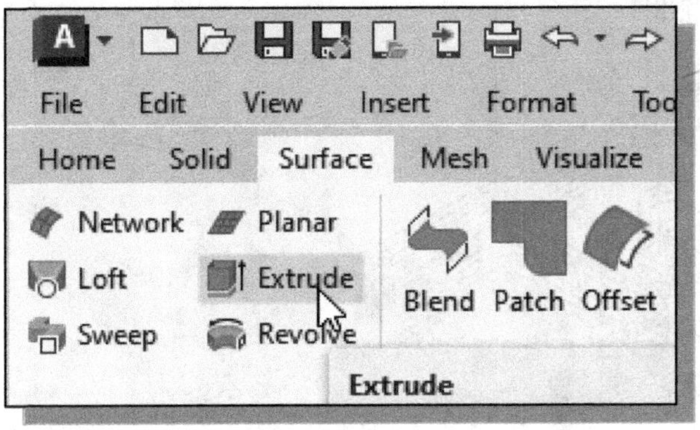

2. Select the **Extrude** icon in the *Create* tab as shown.

3. In the command prompt area, the message "*Select objects to extrude:*" is displayed. Pick all the line segments and the circle we created on the sketching plane.

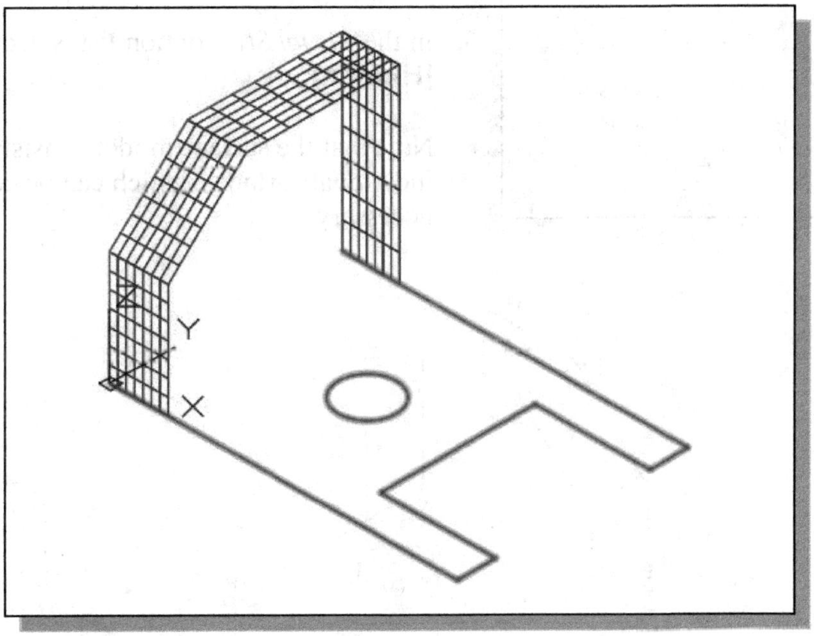

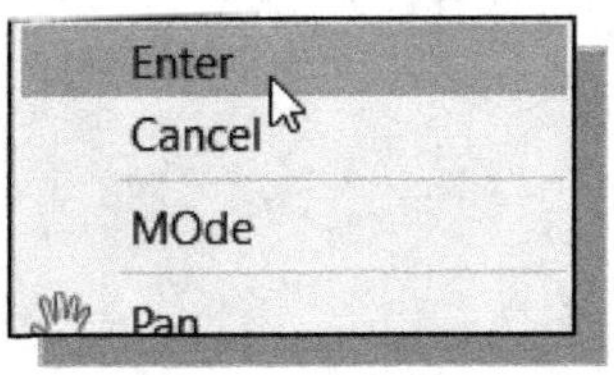

4. Inside the graphics window, **right-click once** to accept the selected entities.

5. In the command prompt area, enter **0.75** as the extrusion height and create the surface model as shown. Note that entering a positive number will create the surface in the positive Z direction of the current coordinate system.

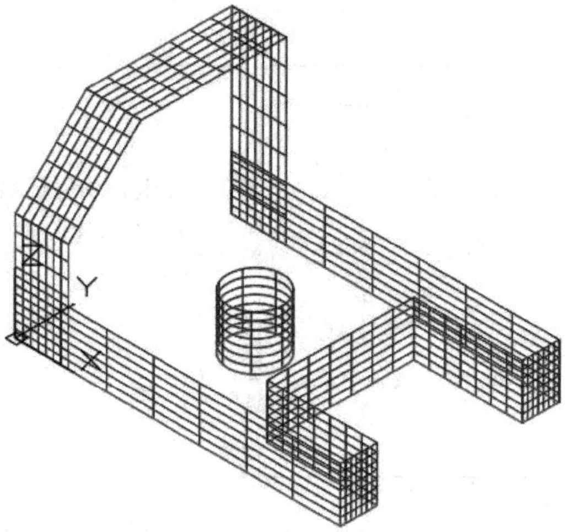

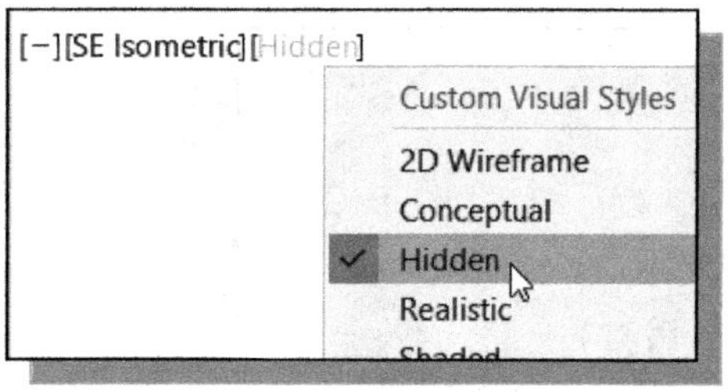

6. In the *Visual Style* option list, select **[Hidden]**.

- Note that the surface model consists of individual surfaces, which can be edited if necessary.

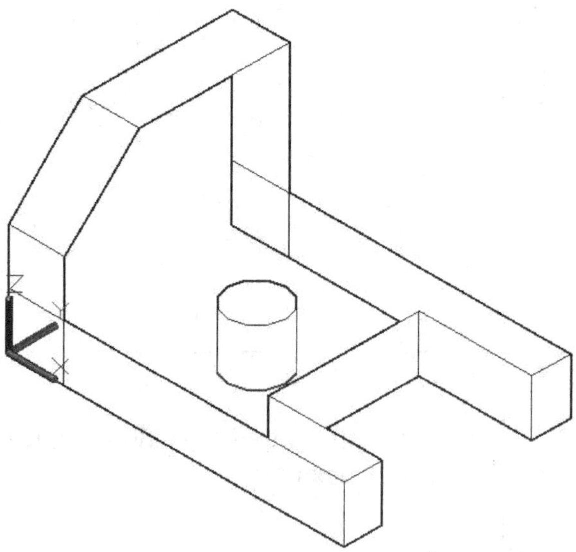

Create a Flat Planar Surface

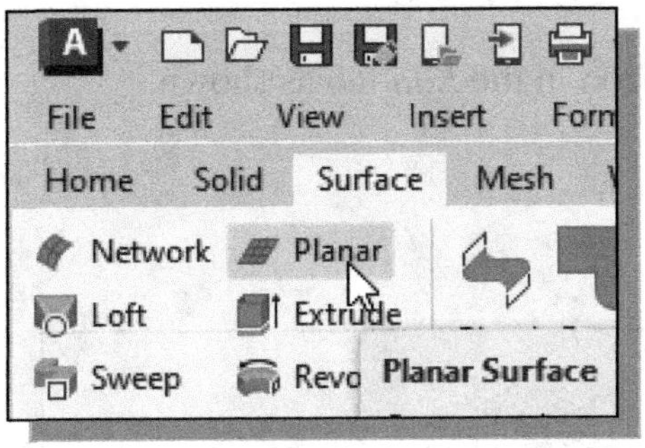

1. Select the **Planar** icon in the *Create* tab as shown.

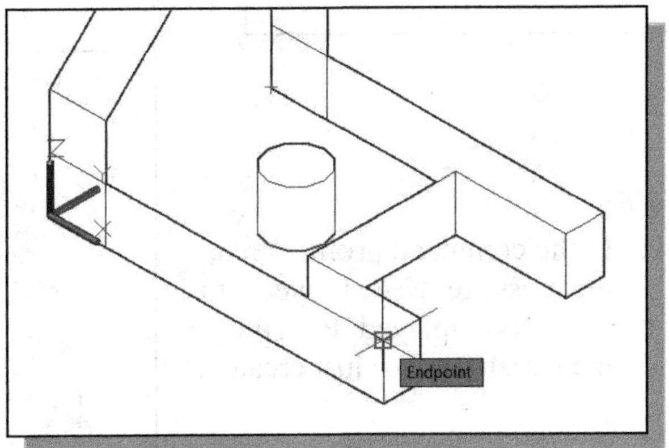

2. In the command prompt area, the message "*Specify the first corner or [object]:*" is displayed. Select the **front top right corner** as the first corner as shown.

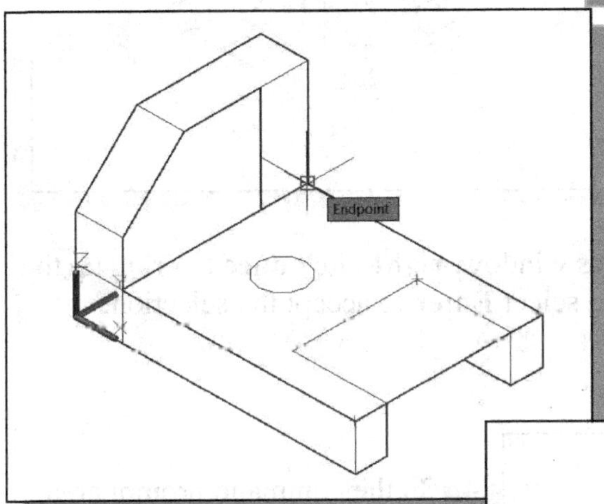

3. Select the intersection point at the **top inside corner** as the second corner as shown.

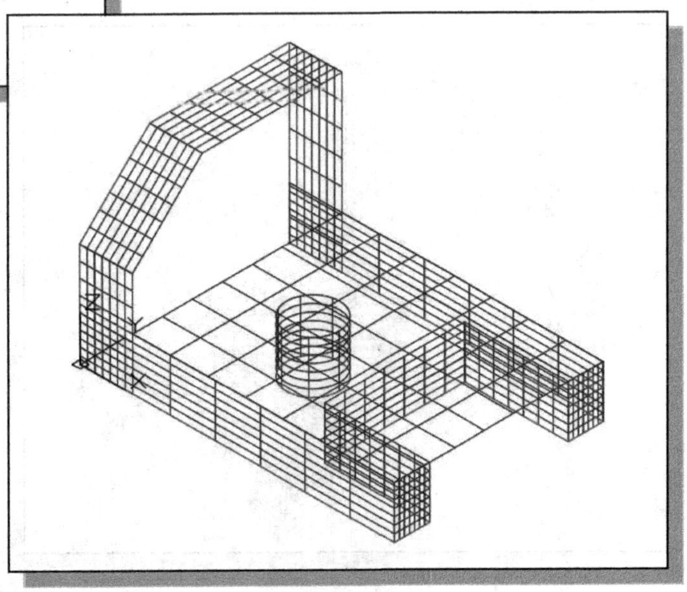

- Note that **Planar** command creates a flat planar surface.

Use the Trim option to adjust the Top Surface

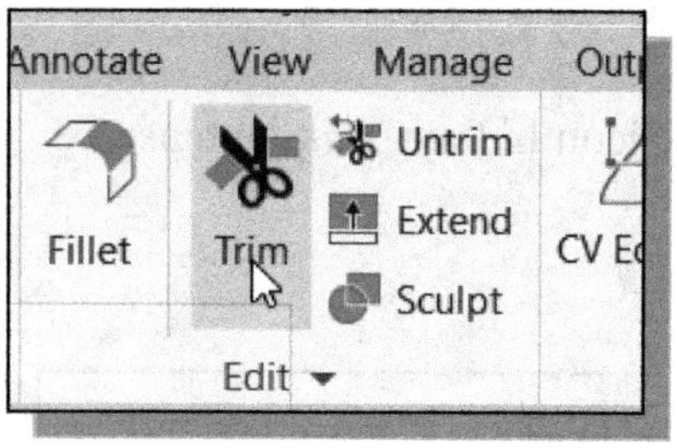

1. Select the **Trim** icon in the *Edit* tab as shown.

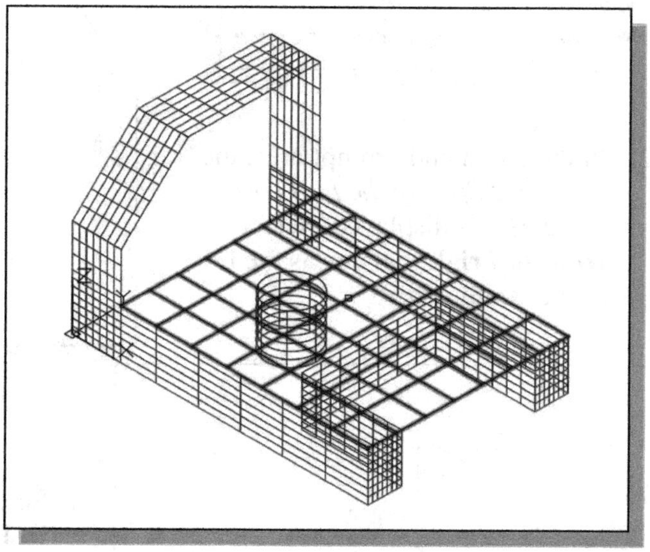

2. In the command prompt area, the message "*Select objects to trim:*" is displayed. Pick the planar surface we just created.

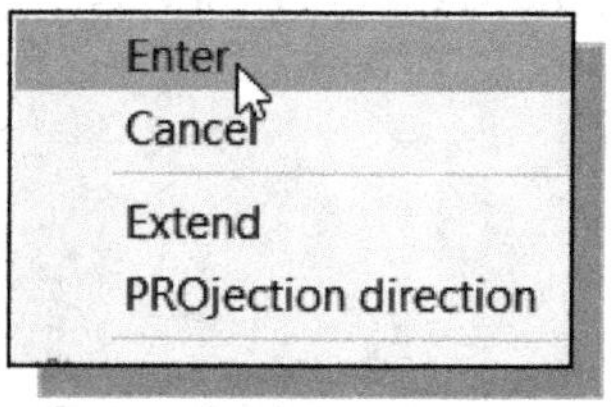

3. Inside the graphics window, **right-click once** to bring up the option menu and select **Enter** to accept the selection.

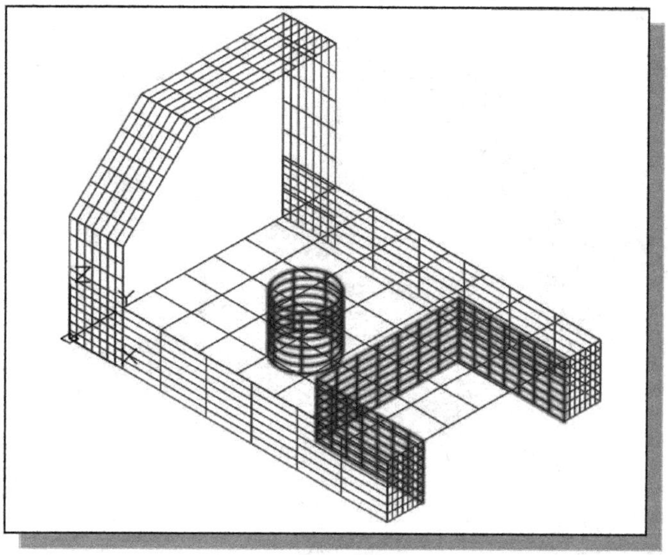

4. In the command prompt area, the message "*Select cutting curves, surfaces or regions:*" is displayed. Pick the three inside vertical surfaces and the cylindrical surface as shown.

5. Inside the graphics window, **right-click once** to accept the selection.

6. In the command prompt area, the message "*Select cutting curves, surfaces or regions:*" is displayed. Pick the inside top right area of the planar surface to trim the model as shown.

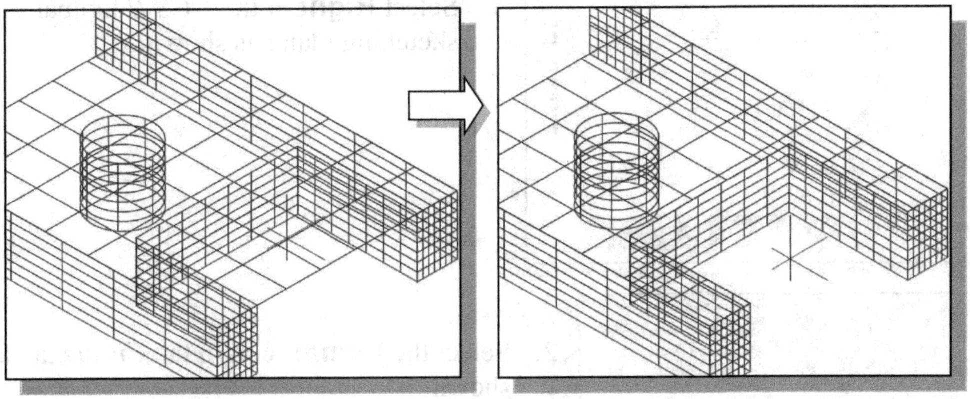

7. Pick inside the circular area on the planar surface to trim the model as shown.

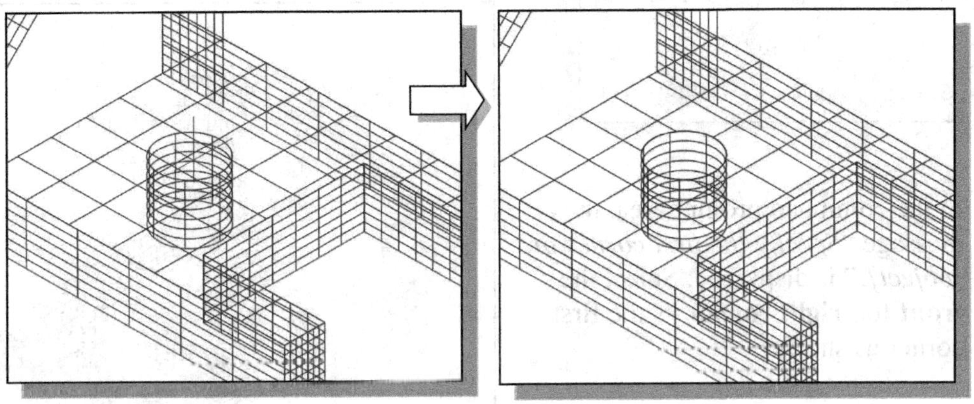

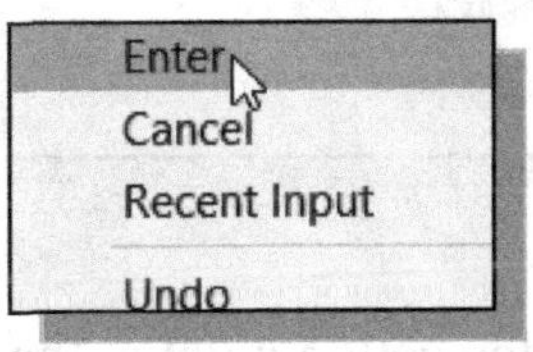

8. Inside the graphics window, **right-click once** to bring up the option menu and select **Enter** to accept the selection.

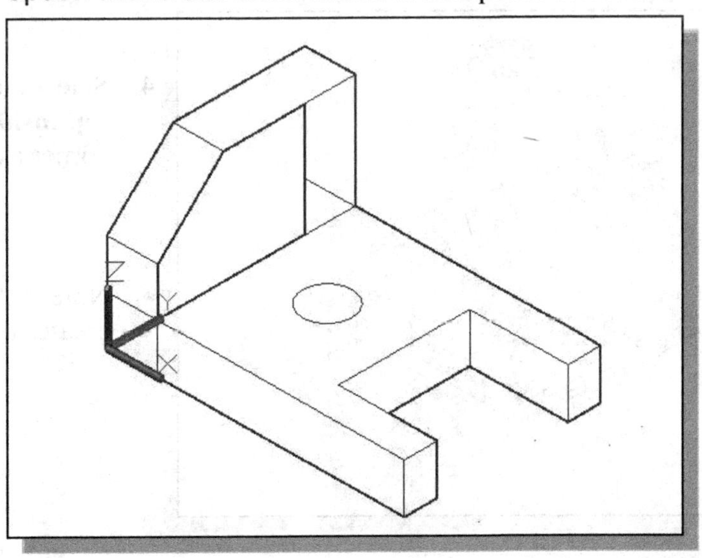

Create another Planar Surface

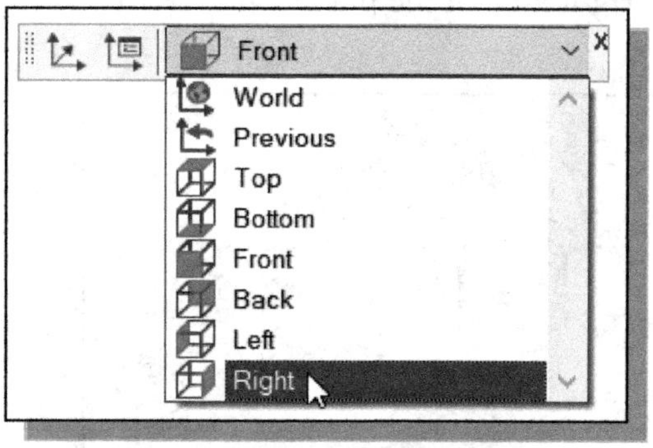

1. Select **Right** in the *UCS II* toolbar to align sketching plane as shown.

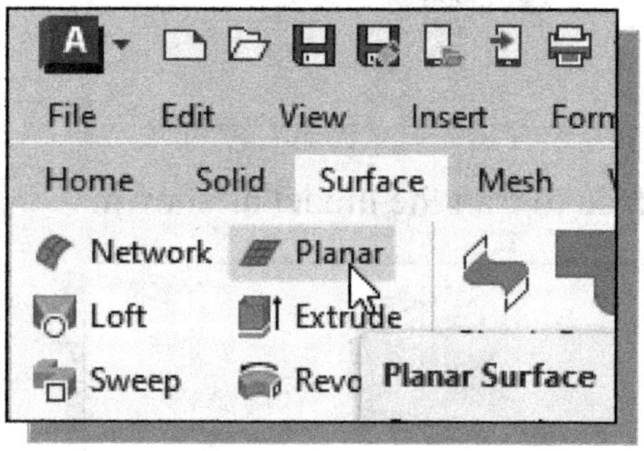

2. Select the **Planar** icon in the *Create* tab as shown.

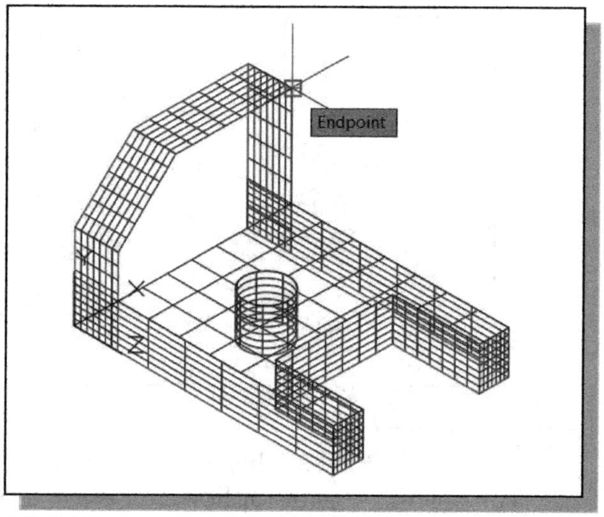

3. In the command prompt area, the message "*Specify the first corner or [object]:*" is displayed. Select the **front top right corner** as the first corner as shown.

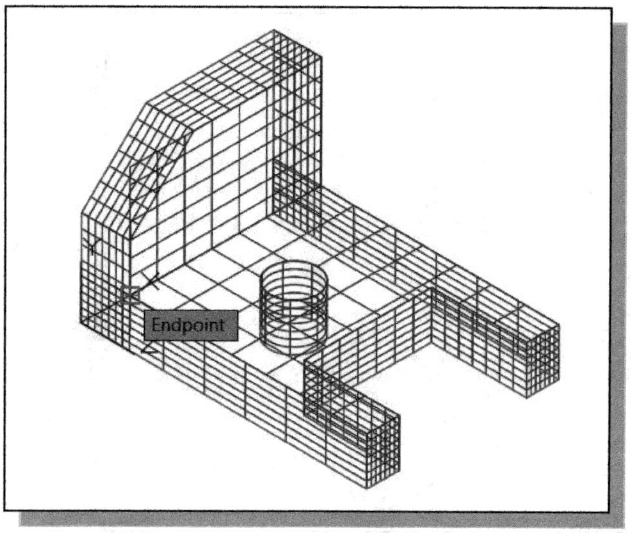

4. Select the intersection point at the **top inside corner** as the second corner as shown.

- Note that **Planar** command creates a flat planar surface.

Use the Trim option to adjust the new Surface

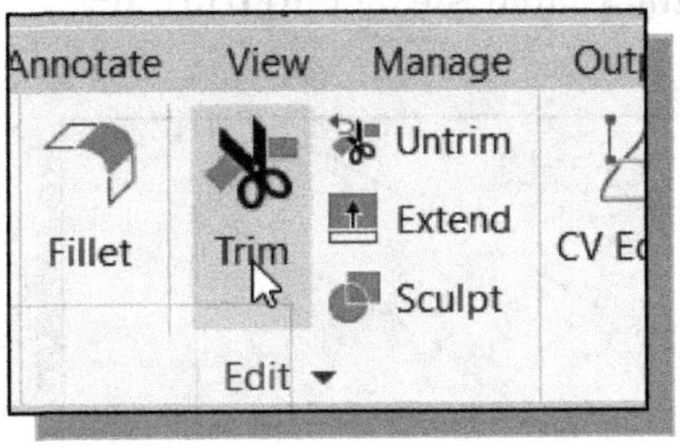

1. Select the **Trim** icon in the *Edit* tab as shown.

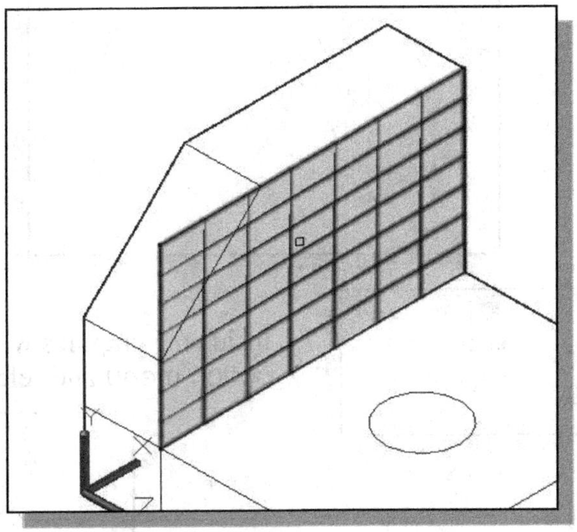

2. In the command prompt area, the message "*Select objects to trim:*" is displayed. Pick the vertical planar surface we just created.

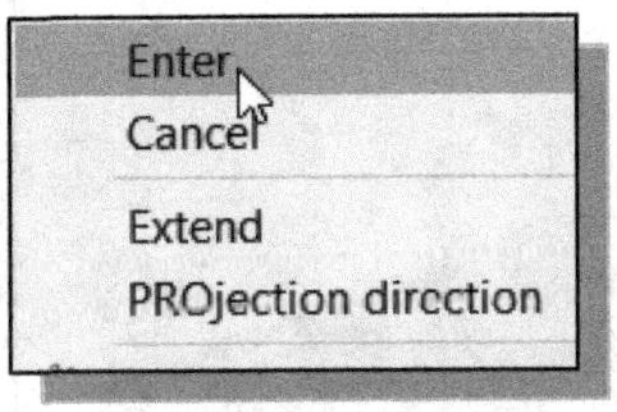

3. Inside the graphics window, **right-click once** to bring up the option menu and select **Enter** to accept the selection.

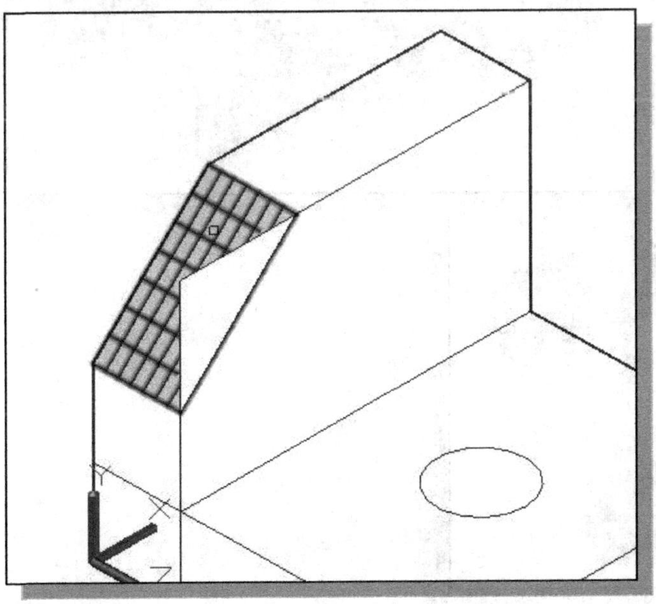

4. In the command prompt area, the message "*Select cutting curves, surfaces or regions:*" is displayed. Pick the inclined surface as shown.

5. Inside the graphics window, **right-click once** to accept the selection.

6. In the command prompt area, the message "*Select cutting curves, surfaces or regions:*" is displayed. Pick the inside top left area of the planar surface to trim the model as shown.

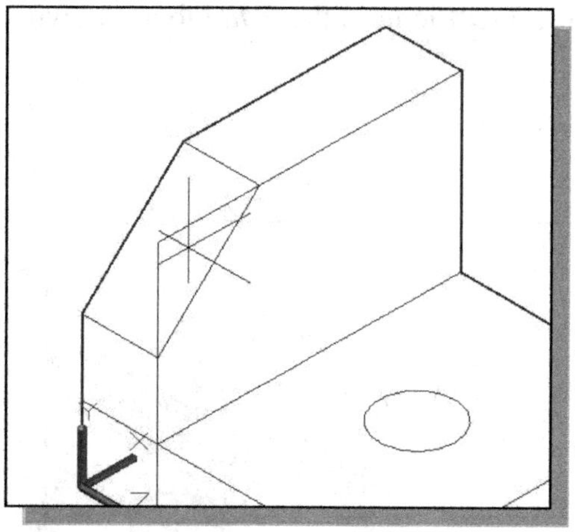

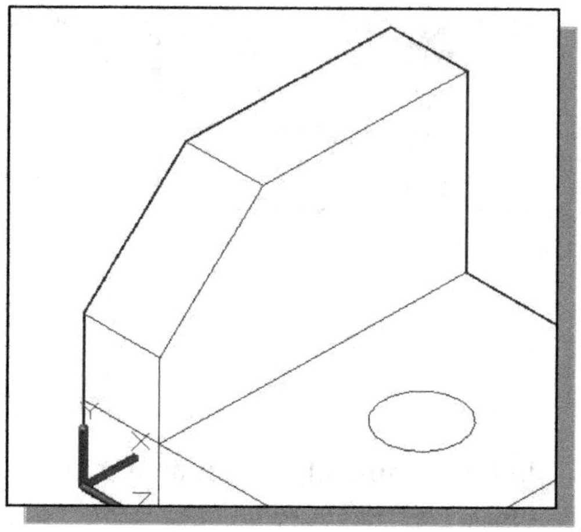

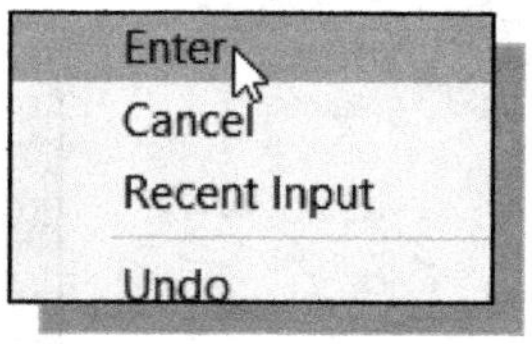

7. Inside the graphics window, **right-click once** to bring up the option menu and select **Enter** to accept the selection.

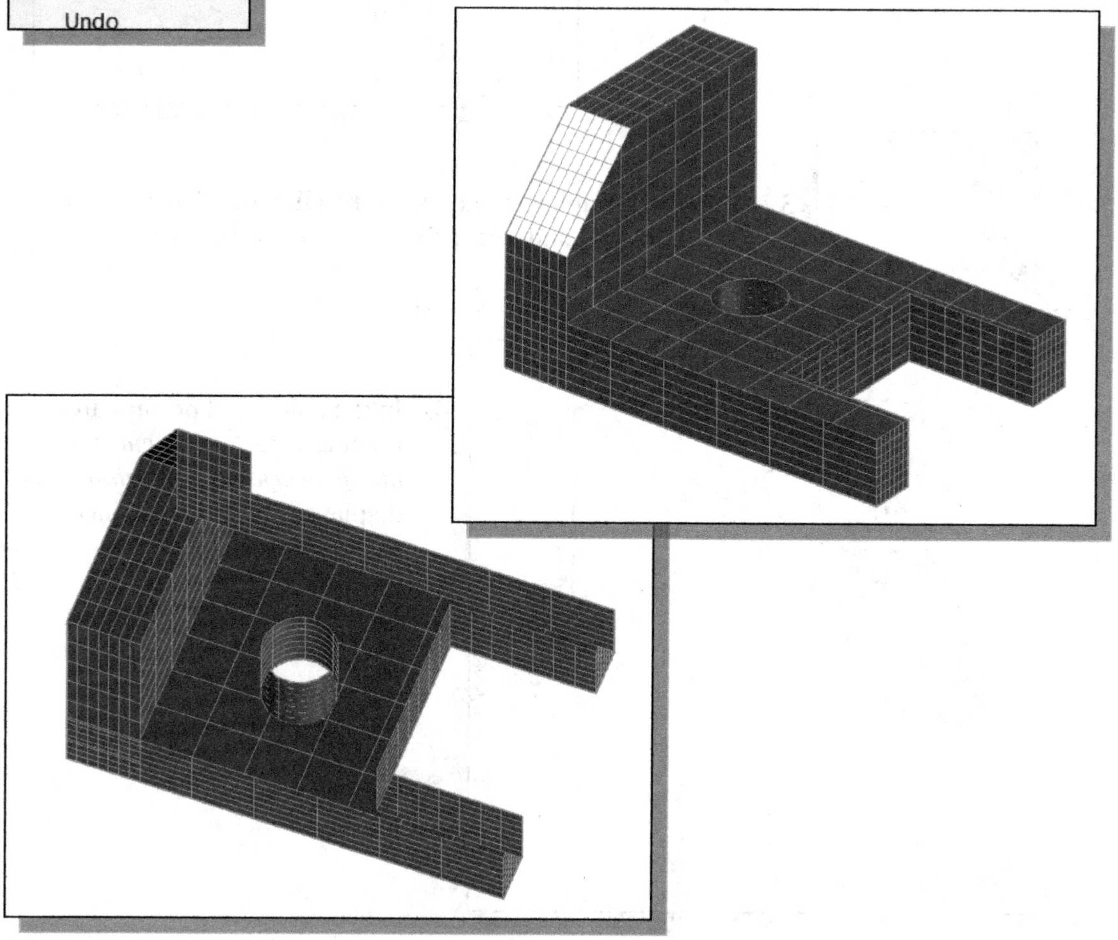

Combining two Overlapping Surfaces

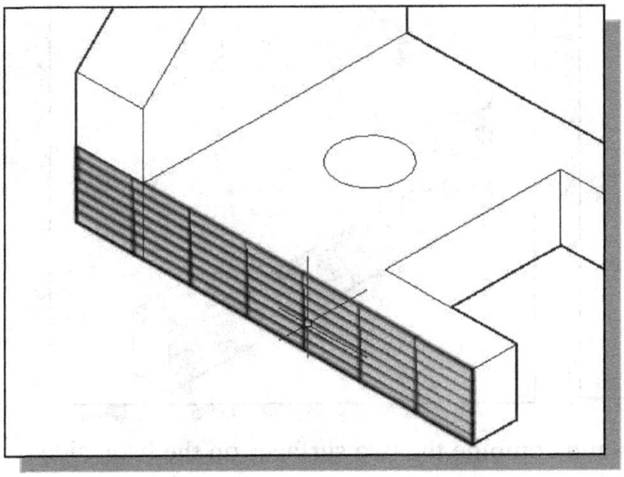

❖ Note that the front vertical surface of the base section is overlapping with the front surface of the vertical section. We will use the 3D **Union** command to combine the two surfaces into one single surface.

1. In the command prompt area, enter **UNION** to activate the *3D Union* command.

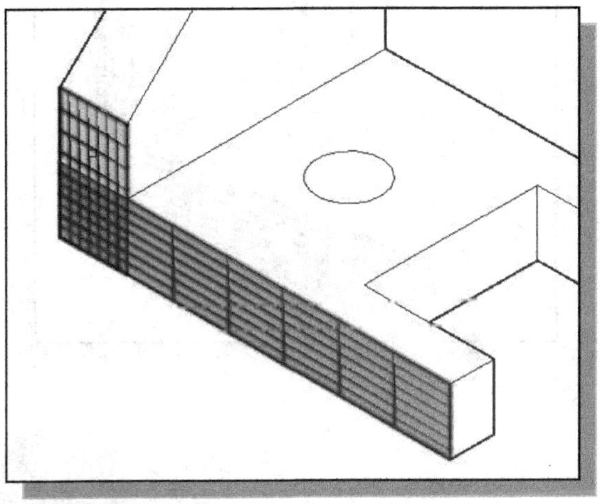

2. Pick the two overlapping surfaces as shown.

3. Inside the graphics window, **right-click once** to accept the selection.

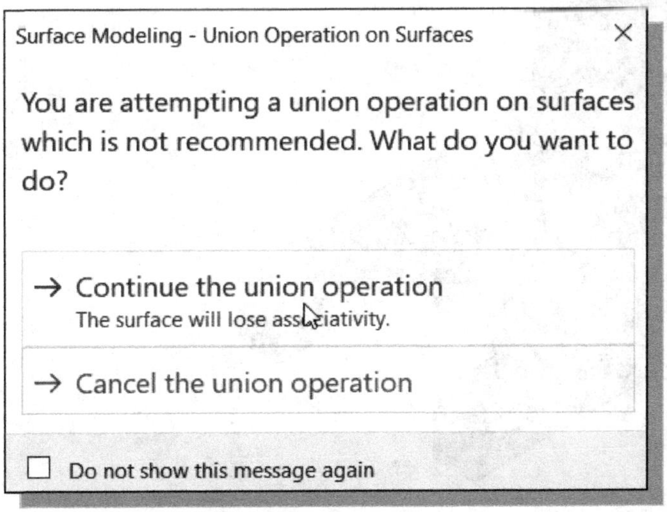

❖ By default, the *Surface Associativity* option is turned on, which means the profile and the derived surface are linked together. However, this option provides very little benefit to simple procedural surfaces.

4. Click **Continue the Union operation** to release the associated link.

❖ The two overlapping surfaces have been combined into a single surface.

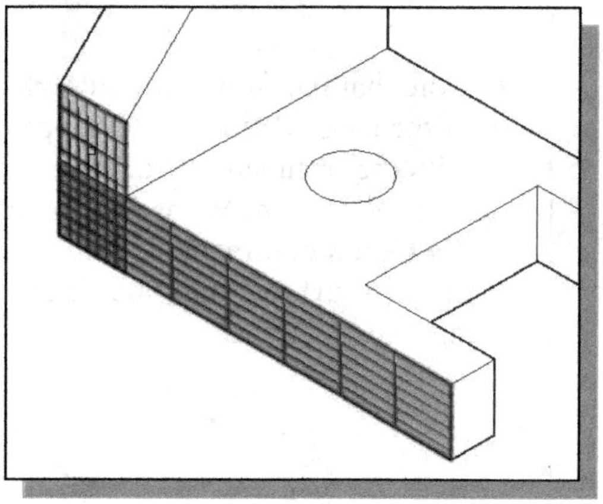

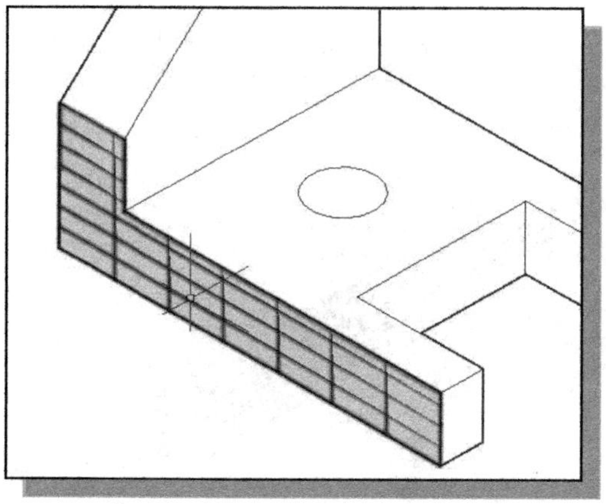

5. On your own, repeat the above steps and combine the two surfaces on the back side as shown.

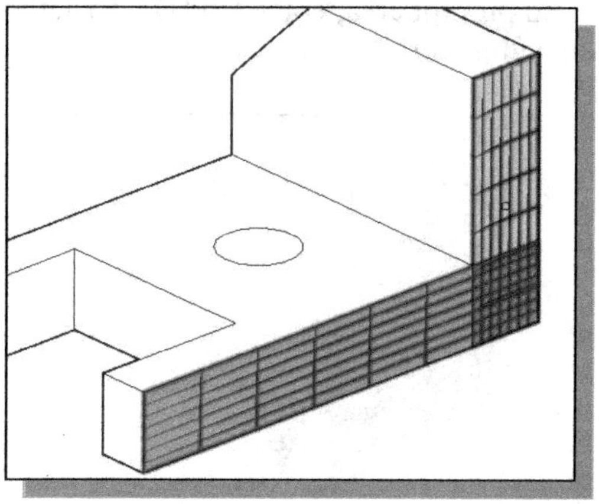

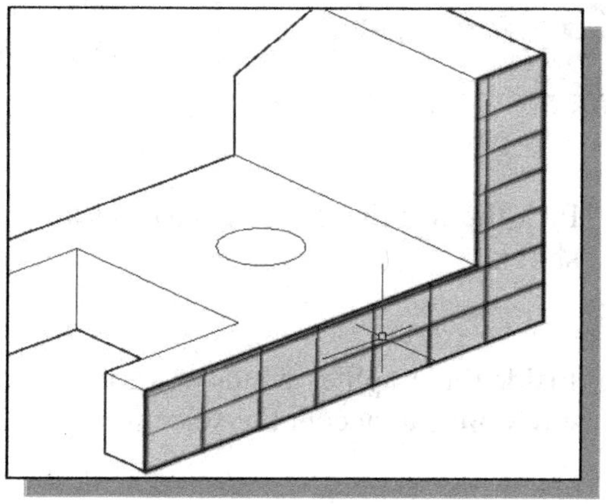

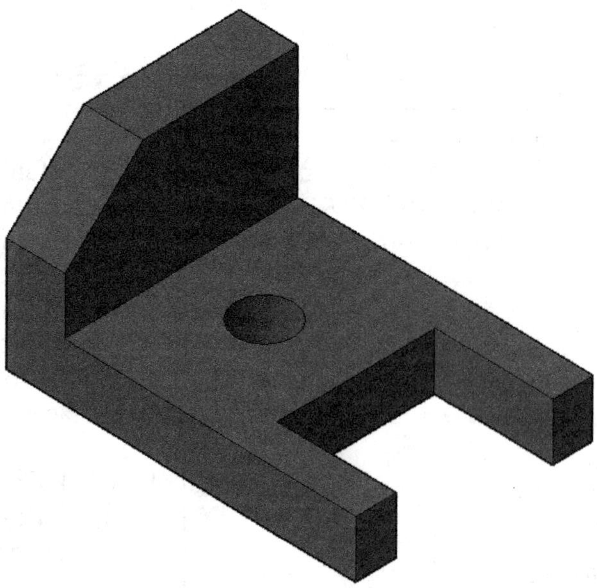

Create a 3D Free Form NURBS Surface Model

NURBS, *Non-Uniform Rational B-Splines*, are mathematical representations of 3D geometry that can accurately describe any shape from a simple 2D line, circle, arc, or curve to the more complex 3D free-form surface. Because of their flexibility and accuracy, NURBS models can be used in illustrations, animations and manufacturing of products.

NURBS are commonly used in computer-aided design (CAD), manufacturing (CAM), and engineering (CAE) and are part of numerous industry wide CAD standards, such as IGES, STEP, and ACIS. NURBS tools are also found in various general-purpose 3D modeling and animation software packages.

The main advantage of NURBS surfaces is that they can be efficiently handled by computer programs and also allow for easy human interaction. NURBS surfaces are functions of two directional mapping to a surface in three-dimensional space. The shape of the surface is determined by control points. NURBS surfaces are geometrical shapes represented in a very compact form.

In general, editing NURBS curves and surfaces is highly intuitive and predictable. Control points are either connected directly to the surface, or on construction curves. Depending on the type of user interface, editing can be done on the control points.

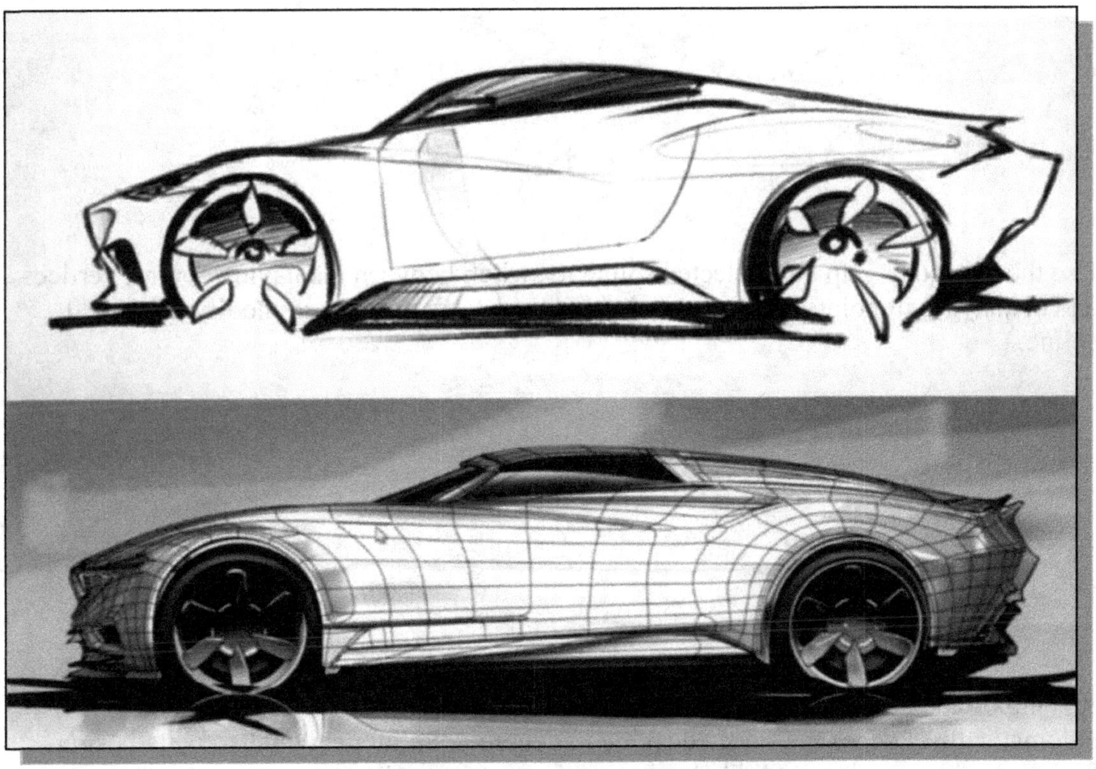

AutoCAD Spline Curves

A spline is a smooth curve that passes through or near a set of points that influence the shape of the curve. Splines are types of curves, originally developed for ship building in the days before computer modeling. Naval architects needed a way to draw a smooth curve through a set of points. The solution was to place metal weights (called knots) at the control points and bend a thin metal or wooden beam (called a spline) through the weights. The physics of the bending spline meant that the influence of each weight was greatest at the point of contact and decreased smoothly further along the spline. To get more control over a certain region of the spline, the draftsman simply added more weights. This scheme had obvious problems with data exchange! People needed a mathematical way to describe the shape of the curve. Cubic Polynomials Splines are the mathematical equivalent of the draftsman's wooden beam. Polynomials were extended to B-splines (for Basis splines), which are sums of lower-level polynomial splines. Then B-splines were extended to create a mathematical representation called NURBS.

- **Understand Control Vertices and Fit Points**

In AutoCAD, we can create or edit splines using either control vertices, or fit points. The spline on the left displays control vertices along a control polygon, and the spline on the right displays fit points.

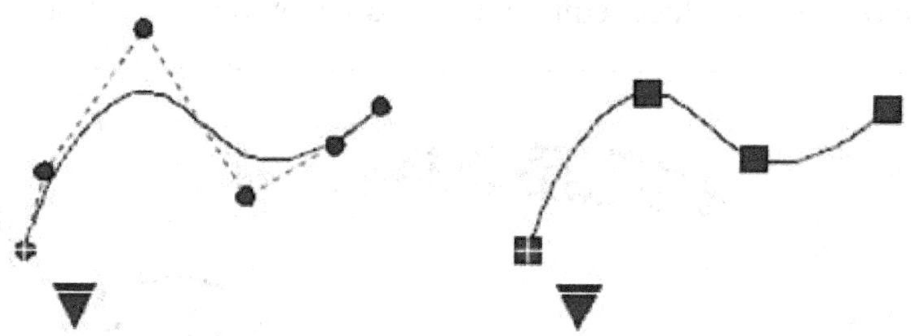

Use the triangular grip on a selected spline to switch between displaying control vertices and displaying fit points. We can use the round and square grips to modify a selected spline.

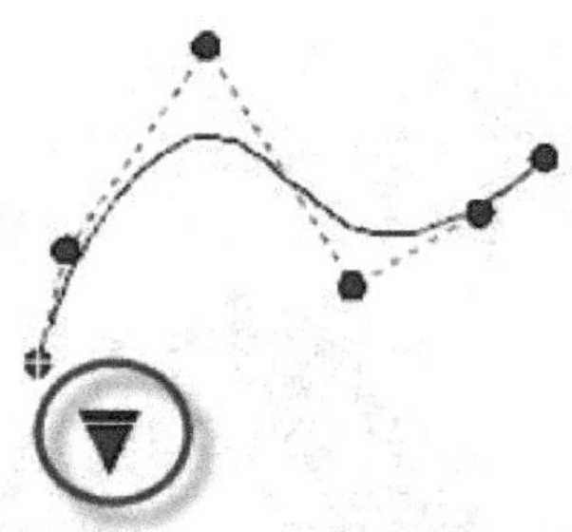

It is important to note that switching the display from control vertices to fit points automatically changes the selected spline to degree 3. Splines originally created using higher-degree equations will likely change shape as a result.

Start a New Drawing and Layers Setup

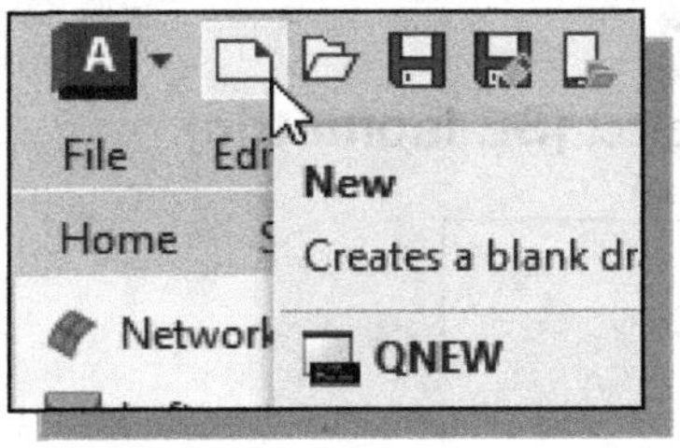

1. In the *Quick Access Bar,* select **[New]**.

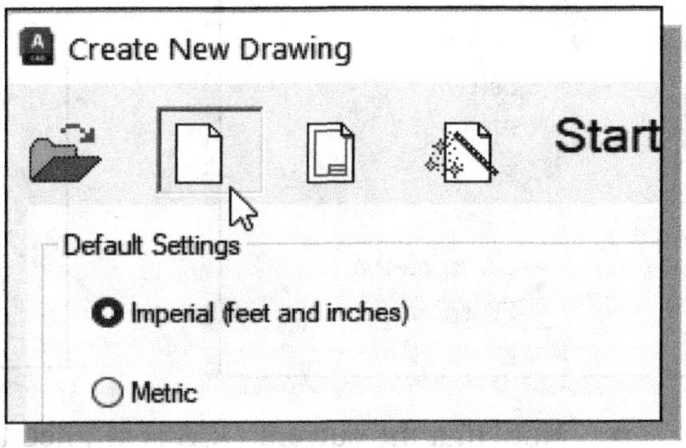

2. On your own, choose the Imperial units and start a new drawing.

3. Click **Layer Properties Manager** in the *Layers* toolbar.

❖ In AutoCAD, we always construct entities on a layer. It may be the default layer or a layer that we create. Each layer has associated properties such as the visibility setting, color, linetype, lineweight, and plot style.

4. Click on the **New Layer** button. Notice a layer is automatically added to the list of layers.

5. Create **two new layers** with the following settings:

Layer	***Color***	***Linetype***	***Lineweight***
Construction	**Grey**	**Continuous**	**Default**
Object	**Cyan**	**Continuous**	**Default**

6. Select and highlight the layer ***Construction*** in the list of layers.

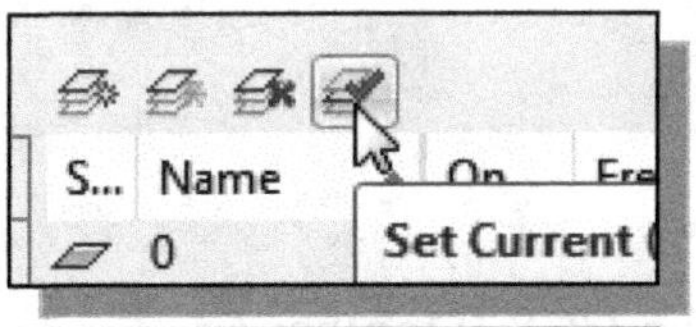

7. Click on the **Set Current** icon to set layer ***Construction*** as the *Current Layer.*

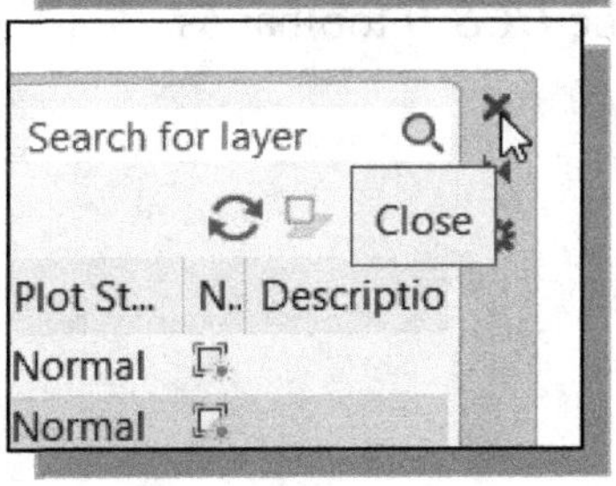

8. Click on the **Close** button to accept the settings and exit the *Layer Properties Manager* dialog box.

9. In the *Status Bar* area, turn ***ON*** the *Grid Display, Polar Tracking, Object Snap, Object Snap Tracking,* and *Dynamic Input* options.

Create Two sets of Splines

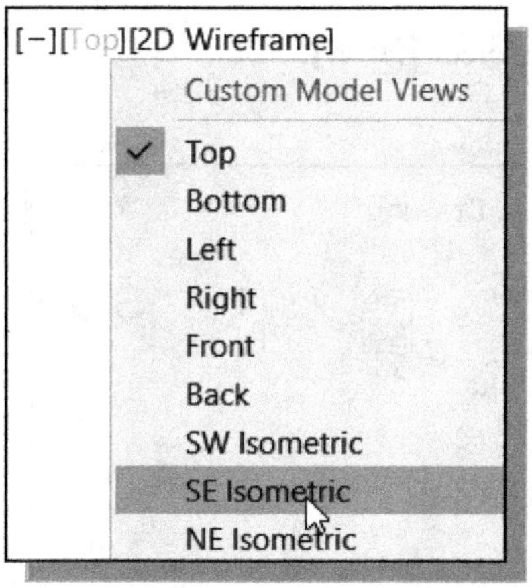

1. In the *View* option list, select **[SE Isometric].**

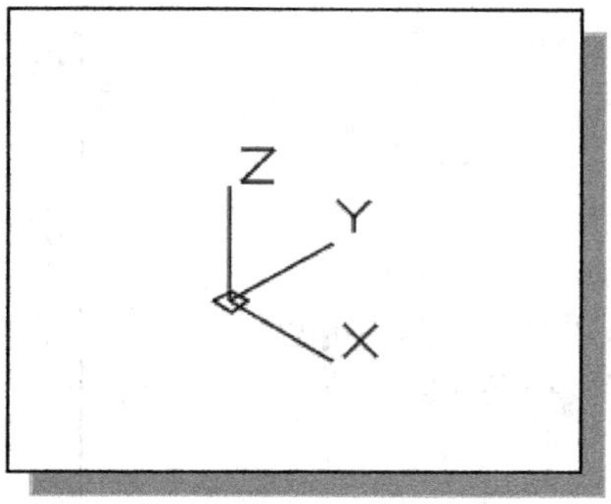

- Note that the current *UCS* is aligned to the *World Coordinate System.*

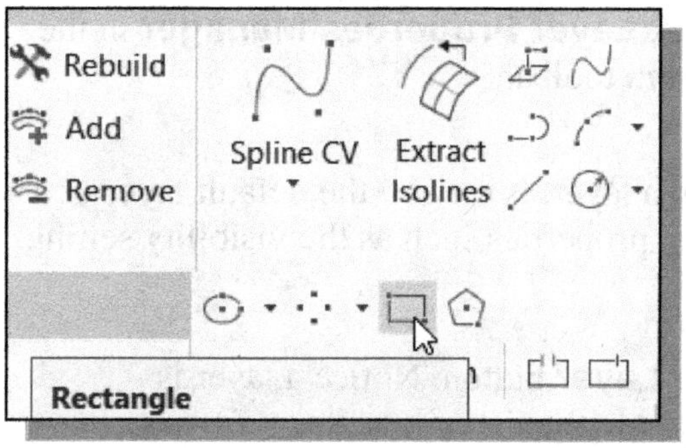

2. Select the **Rectangle** icon in the *Curves* tab as shown.

3. Enter **0,0** to place the first point at the origin as shown.

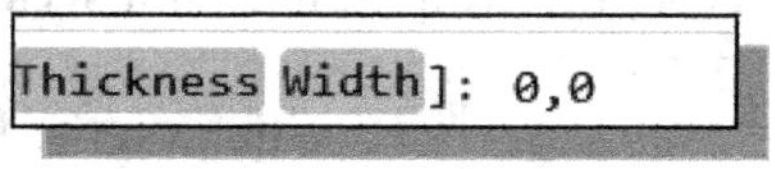

4. In the command prompt area, the message "*Specify next point or [Undo]:*" is displayed. Enter **@8,8** to place the second point above the last point as shown.

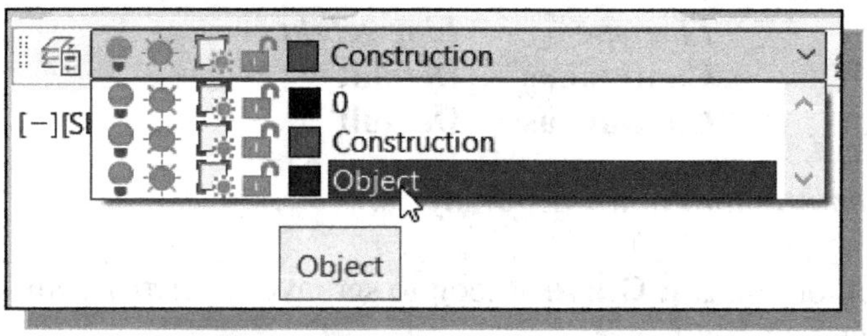

5. Activate the **Object** layer in the *Layers* toolbar as shown.

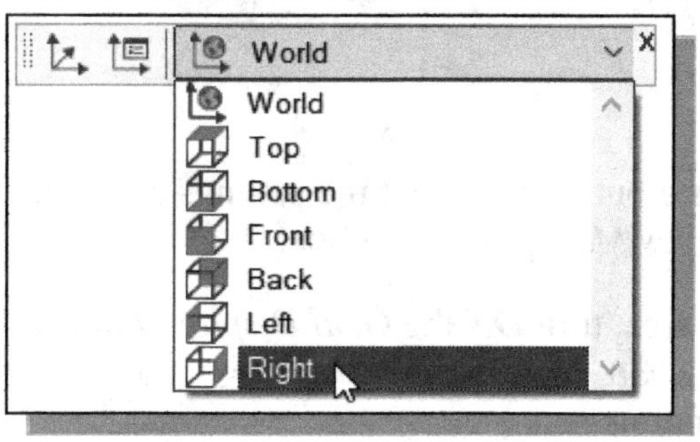

6. Select **Right** in the *UCS II* toolbar as shown.

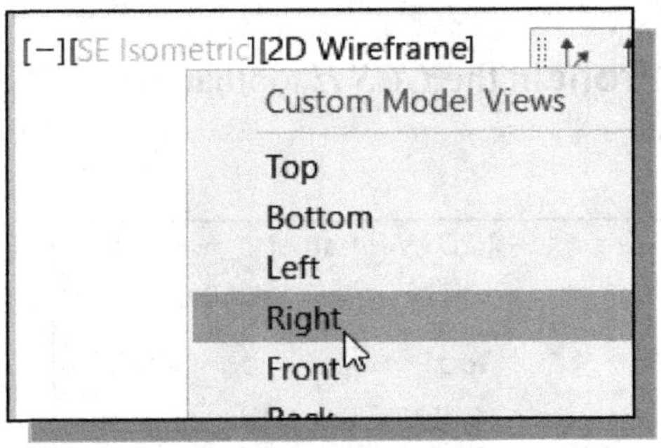

7. Select **Right** in the *View Control* toolbar as shown.

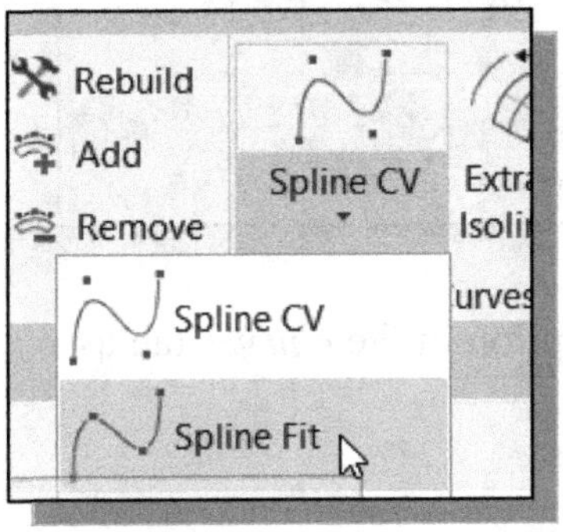

8. Select the **Spline Fit** option in the *Curves* tab as shown.

- The *Spline Fit* option means the selected points are on the created spline.

9. Start at the origin and create a spline with 5 or 6 points and end at the right endpoint as shown.

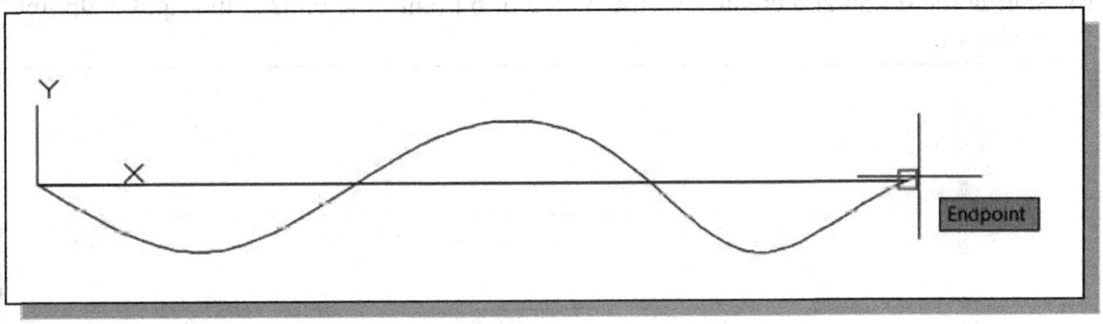

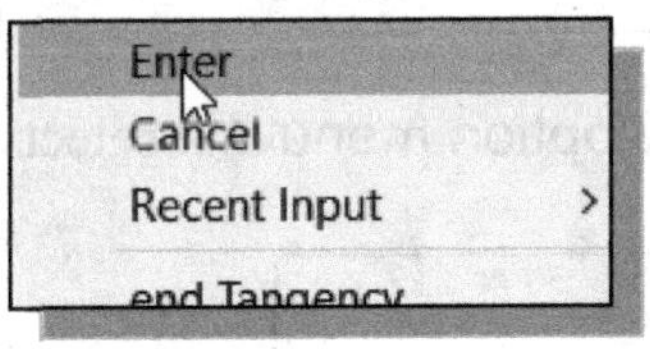

10. Inside the graphics window, **right-click once** to bring up the option menu and select **Enter** to end the command.

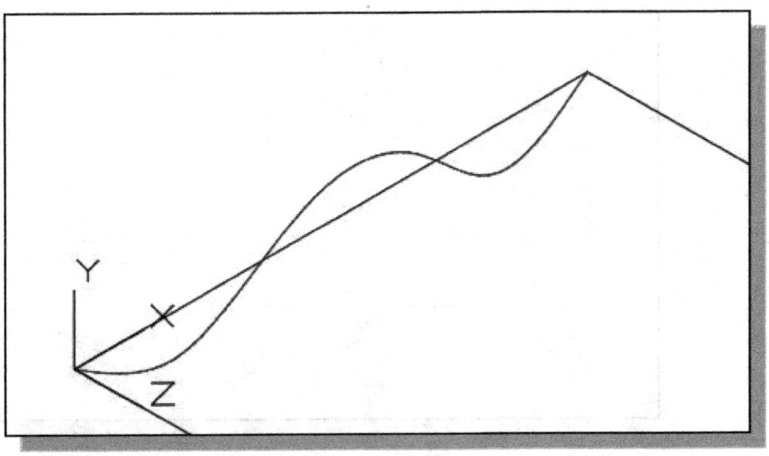

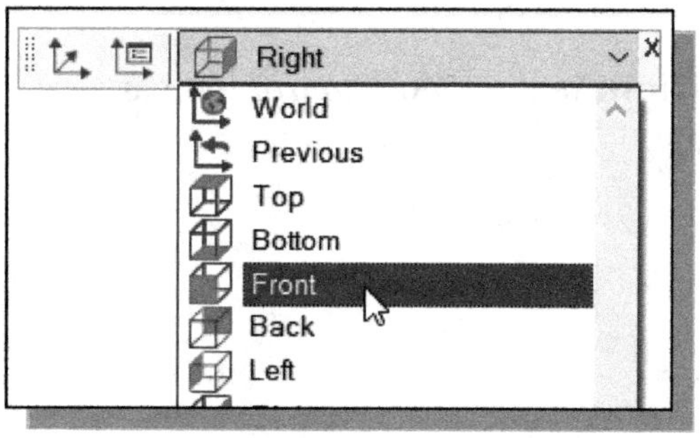

11. Select **Front** in the *UCS II* toolbar as shown.

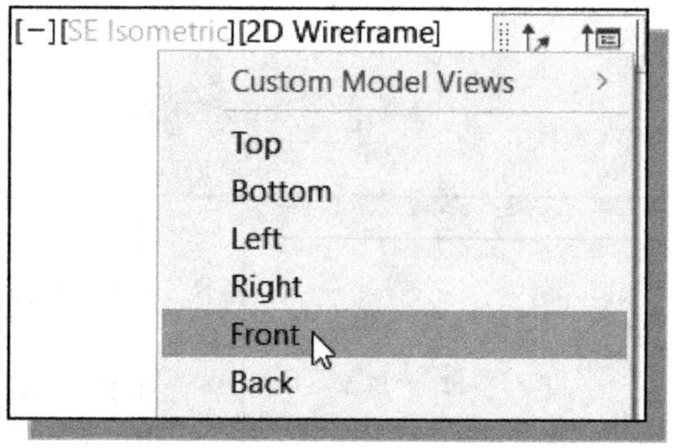

12. Select **Front** in the *View Control* toolbar as shown.

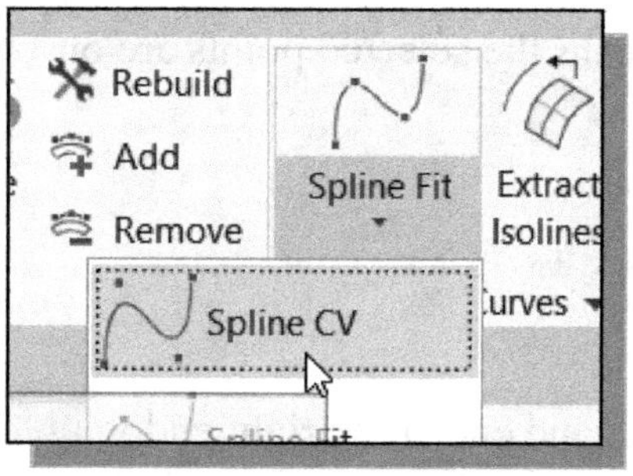

13. Select the **Spline CV** option in the *Curves* tab as shown.

14. Start at the origin and create a spline with 5 or 6 points and ends at the right endpoint as shown.

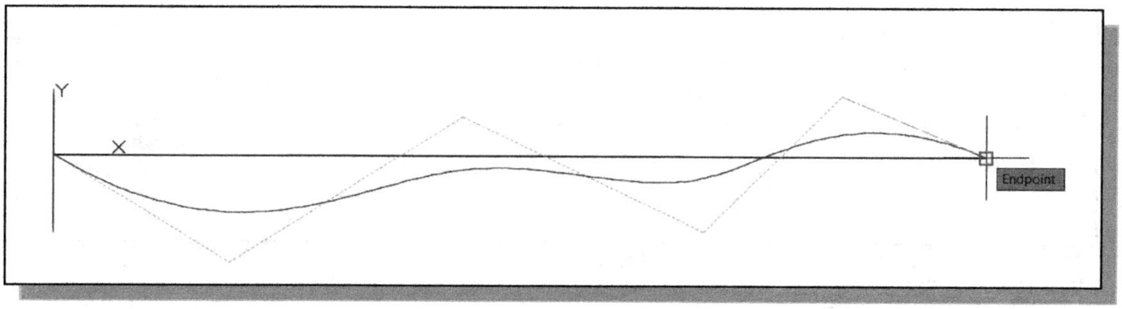

15. Inside the graphics window, **right-click once** to bring up the option menu and select **Enter** to end the command.

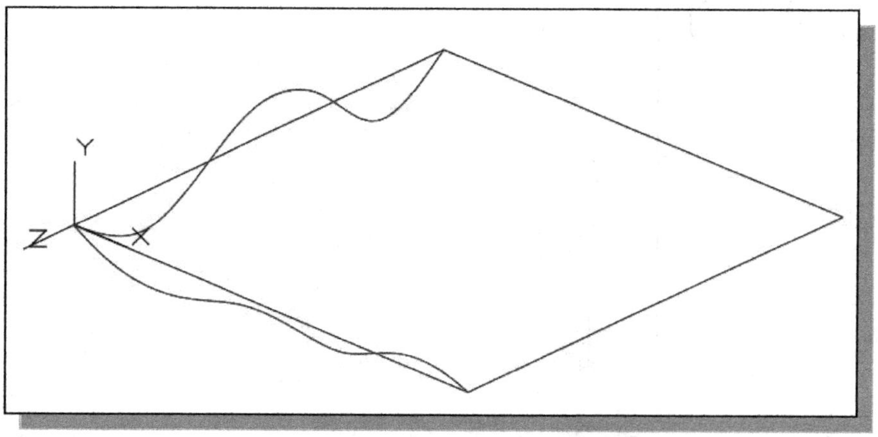

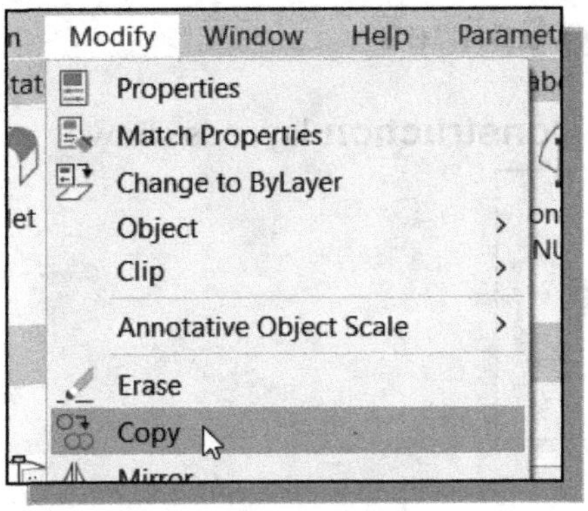

16. In the pull-down menu, select Copy as shown.

17. On your own, copy the first spline to the right side as shown.

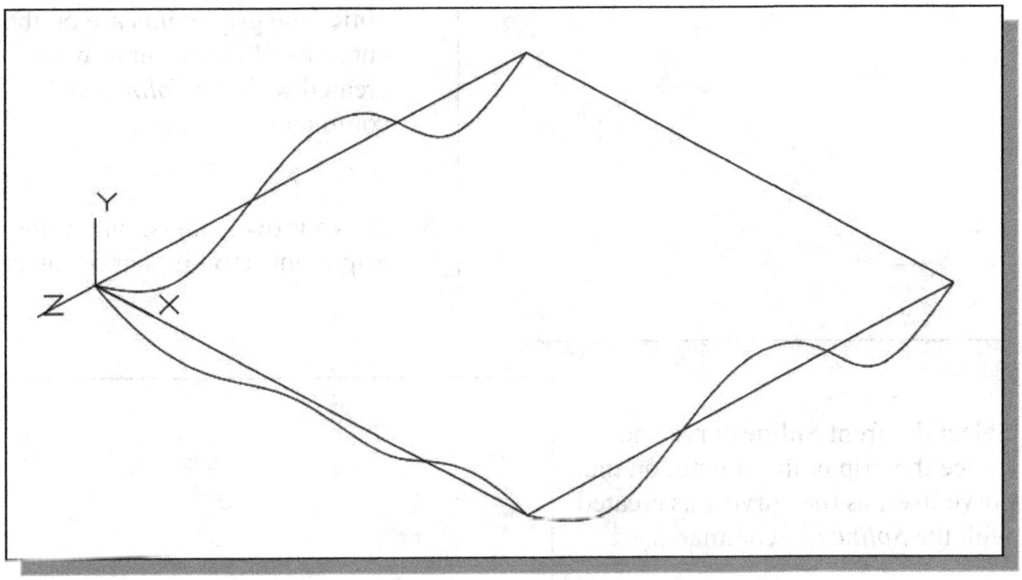

18. On your own, copy the second spline to the back side as shown.

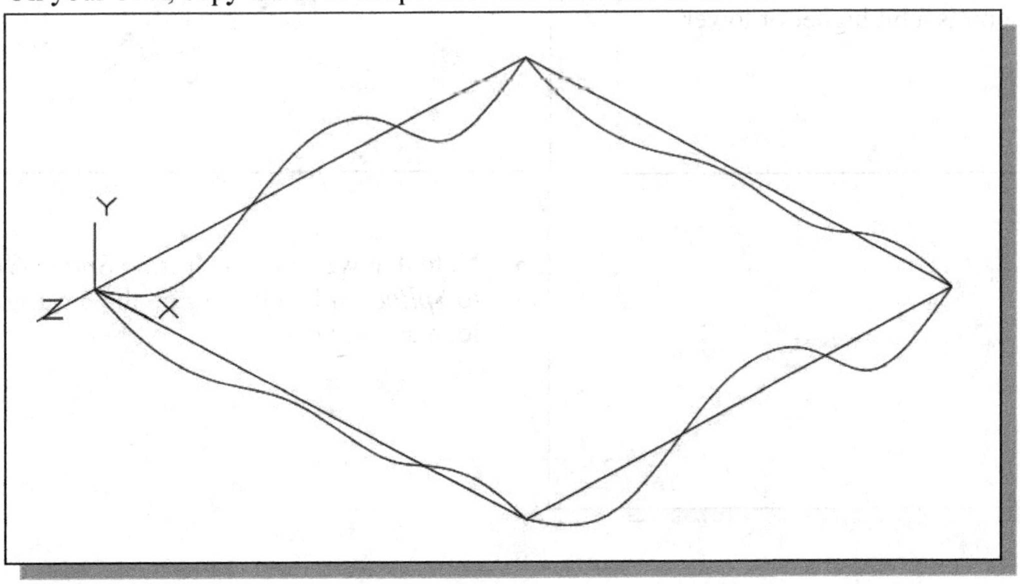

Display the Control Vertices and Edit the Splines

1. In the *Layer control* toolbar option list, turn off the **Construction** layer as shown.

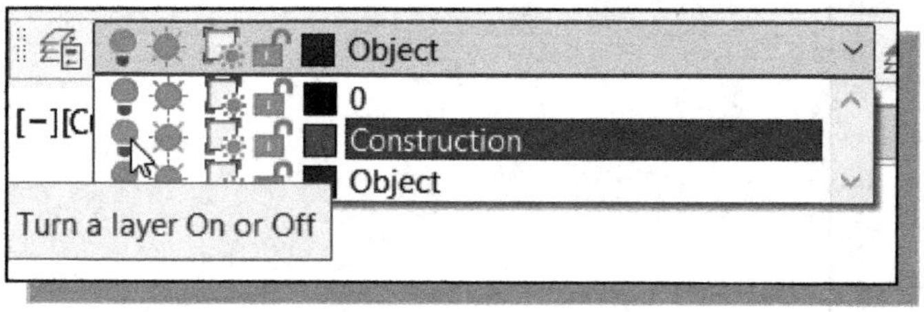

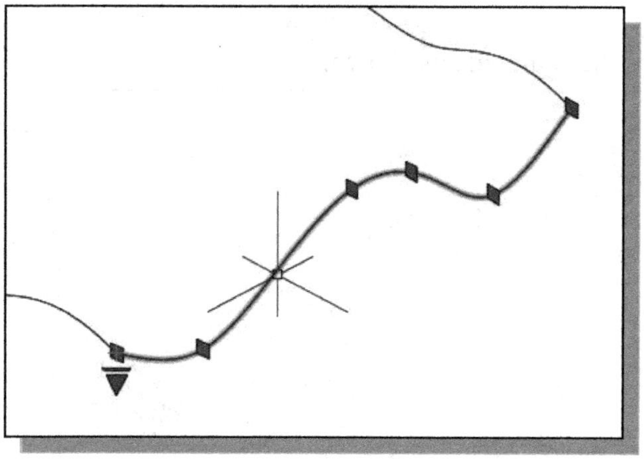

2. Select the right Spline curve and notice the grip points are on the curve itself as the curve was created with the *Spline Fit* command.

3. On your own, adjust one of the grip points a bit higher or lower.

4. Select the front Spline curve and notice the grip points are not on the curve itself as the curve was created with the *Spline CV* command.

5. On your own, adjust one of the grip points a bit higher or lower.

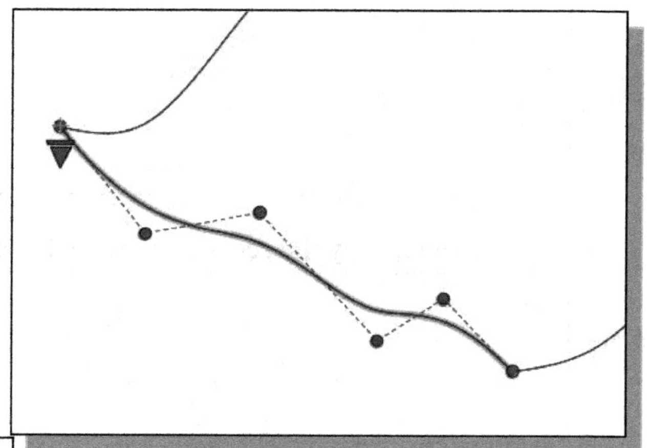

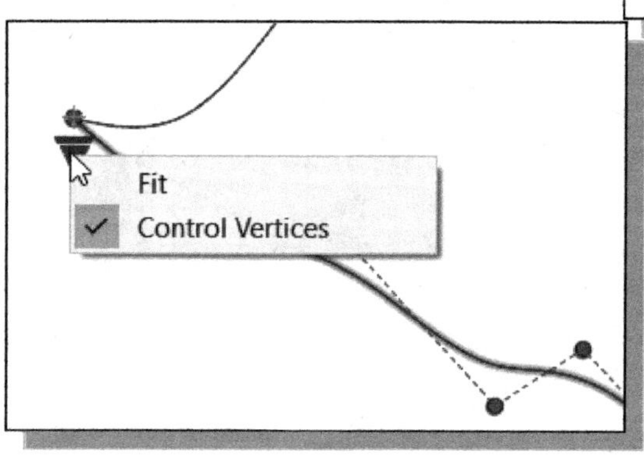

- Note that we can switch from *Spline CV* to *Spline Fit* by clicking on the **Triangle** icon as shown.

Create a Network Surface

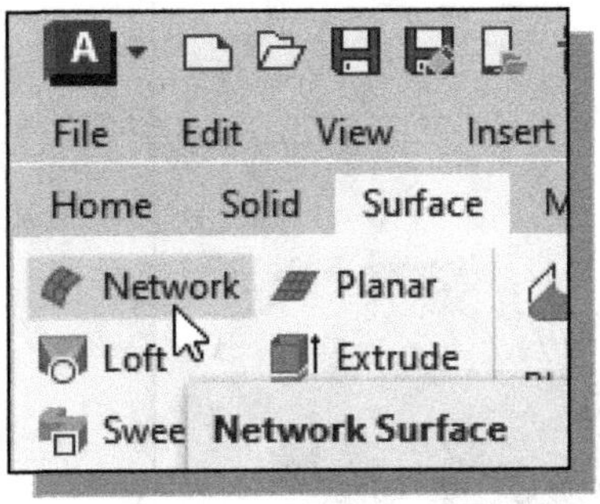

1. In the *Create* toolbar, activate the **Network Surface** command as shown.

2. In the command prompt area, the message "*Select curves or surface edges in first direction:*" is displayed. Pick the left and right curves as shown.

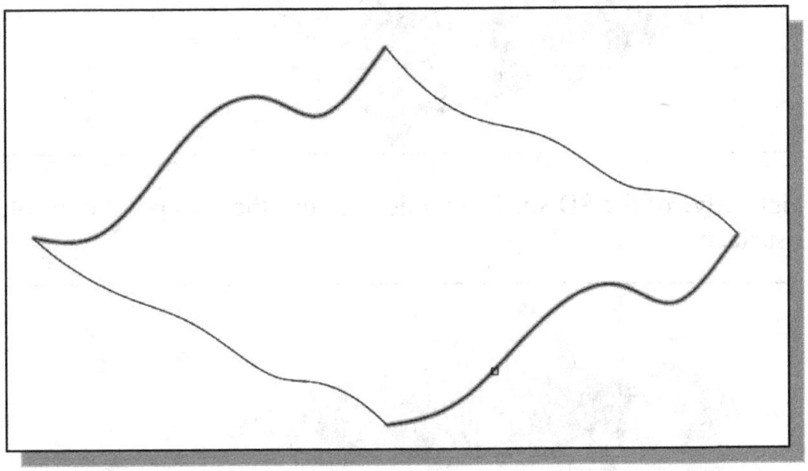

3. Inside the graphics window, **right-click once** to accept the selection.

4. In the command prompt area, the message "*Select curves or surface edges in second direction:*" is displayed. Pick the front and back curves as shown.

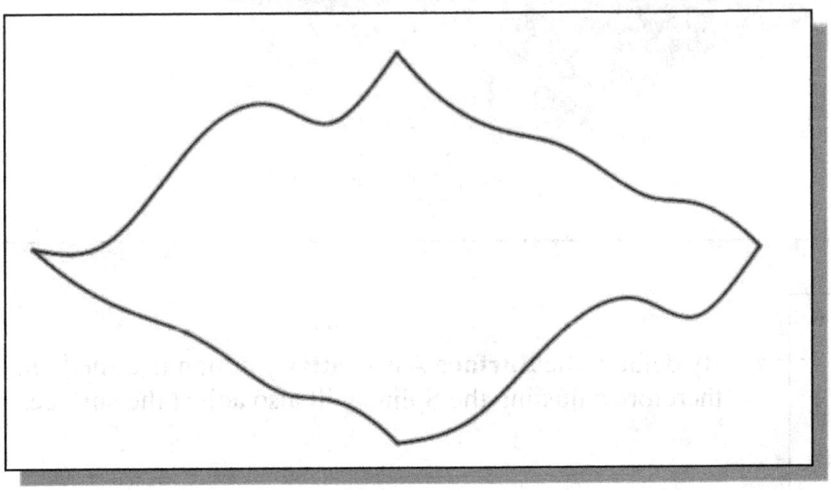

5. Inside the graphics window, **right-click once** to accept the selection.

- Note that we have created a smooth 3D surface model using four splines.

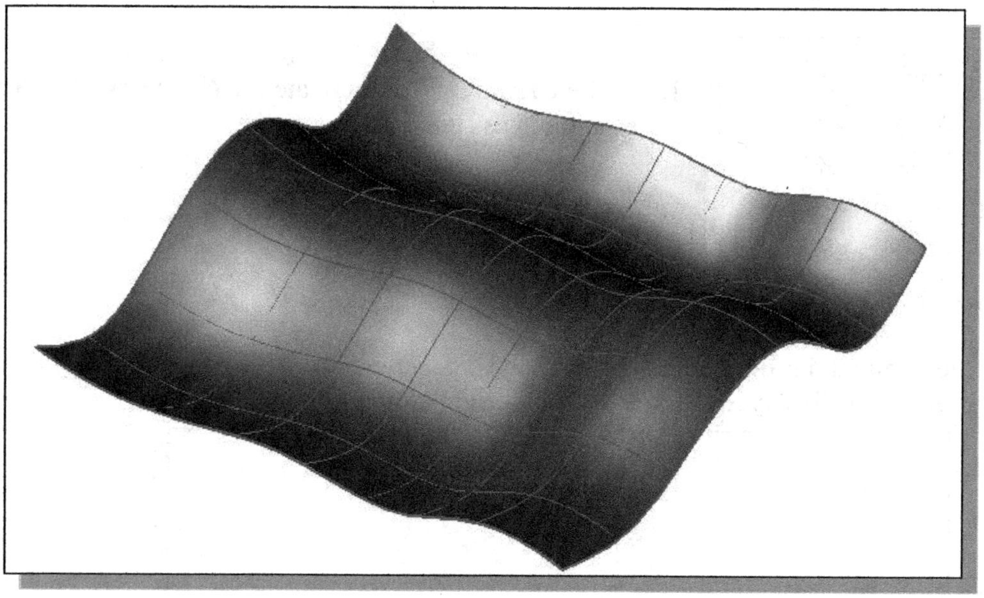

6. Click on the right edge of the 3D surface model and use the grip point control to adjust the 3D surface.

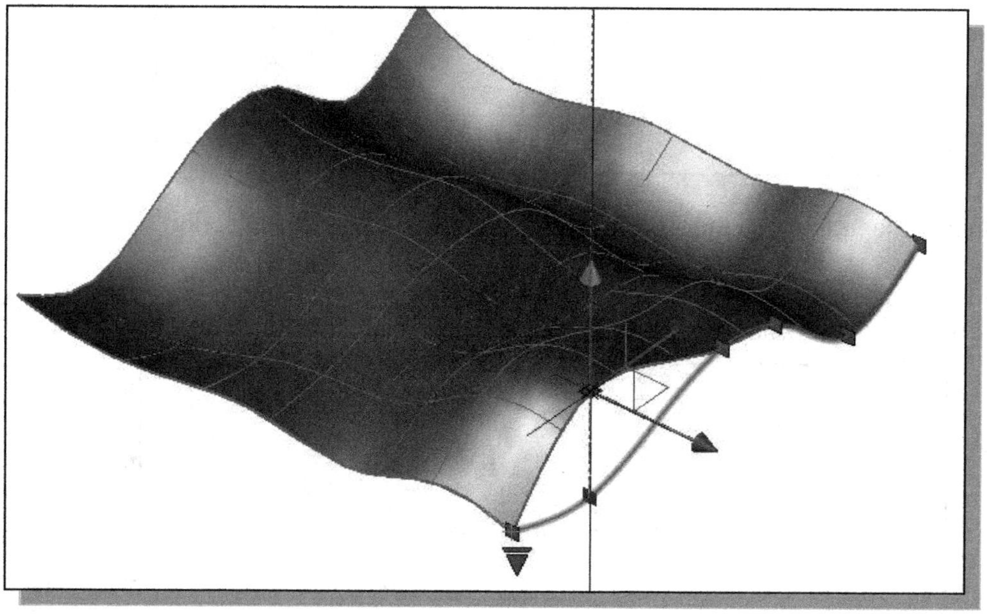

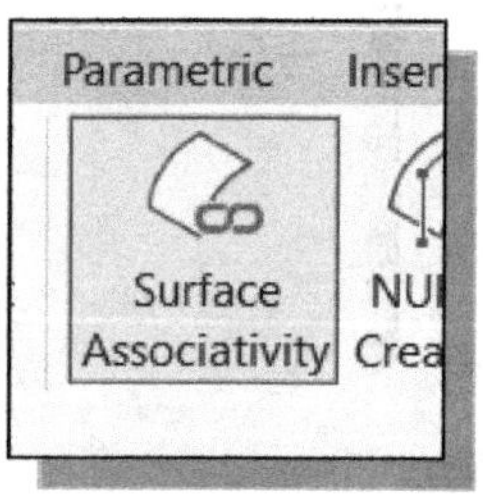

- By default, the **Surface Associativity** option is turned on, therefore adjusting the Spline will also adjust the surface.

Convert the Network surface to a NURBS surface

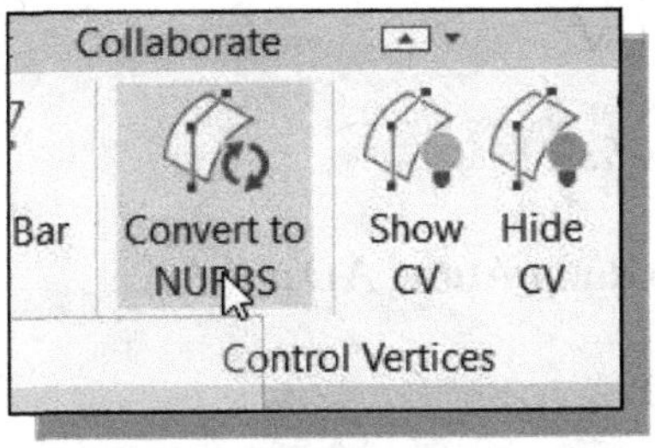

1. In the *Control Vertices* toolbar, activate the **Convert to NURBS** command as shown.

2. Select the surface and click right-mouse button once to convert the surface.

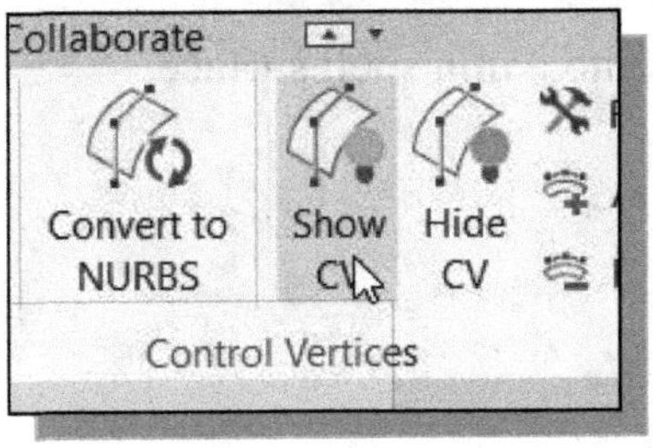

3. In the *Control Vertices* toolbar, activate the **Show CV** command as shown.

4. Select the surface and click right-mouse button once to accept the selection and display the control vertices.

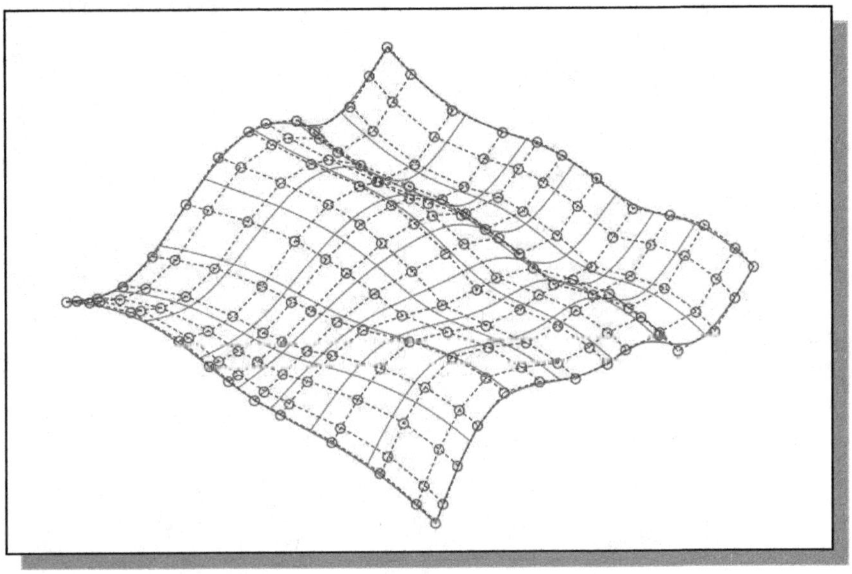

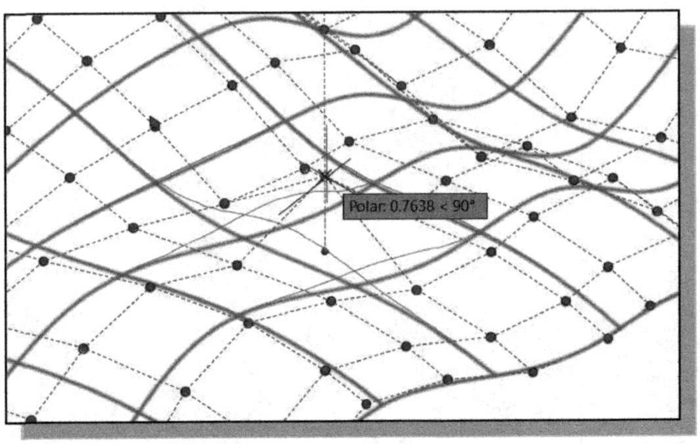

5. The NURBS surface can now be adjusted by dragging & dropping the available control vertices.

Review Questions:

1. Describe the difference between Spline Fit and Spline CV.

2. How do we convert a *Network surface* into a *NURBS surface*?

3. What does the **Surface Associativity** option allow us to do in AutoCAD?

4. Can we turn a single line into a flat surface in AutoCAD?

5. Can we use the **Extrude** command and turn a rectangle into a thin shell surface model in AutoCAD?

Exercises: All dimensions are in inches.

1.

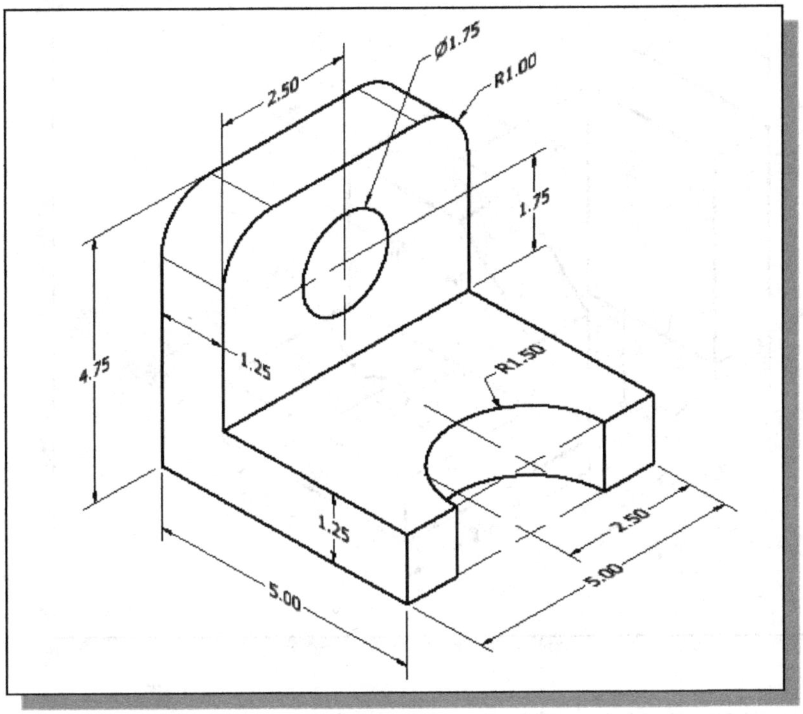

2.

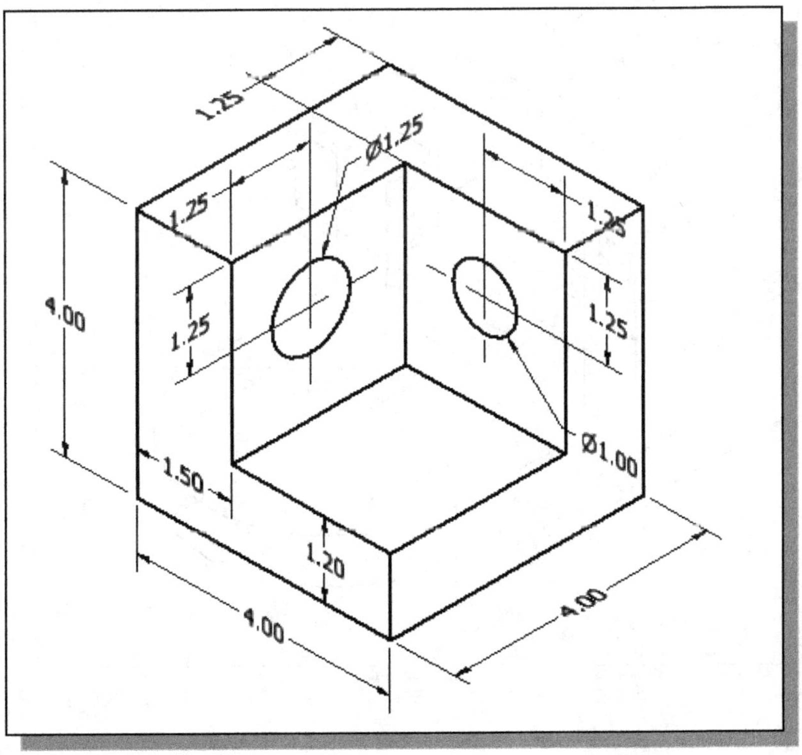

3.

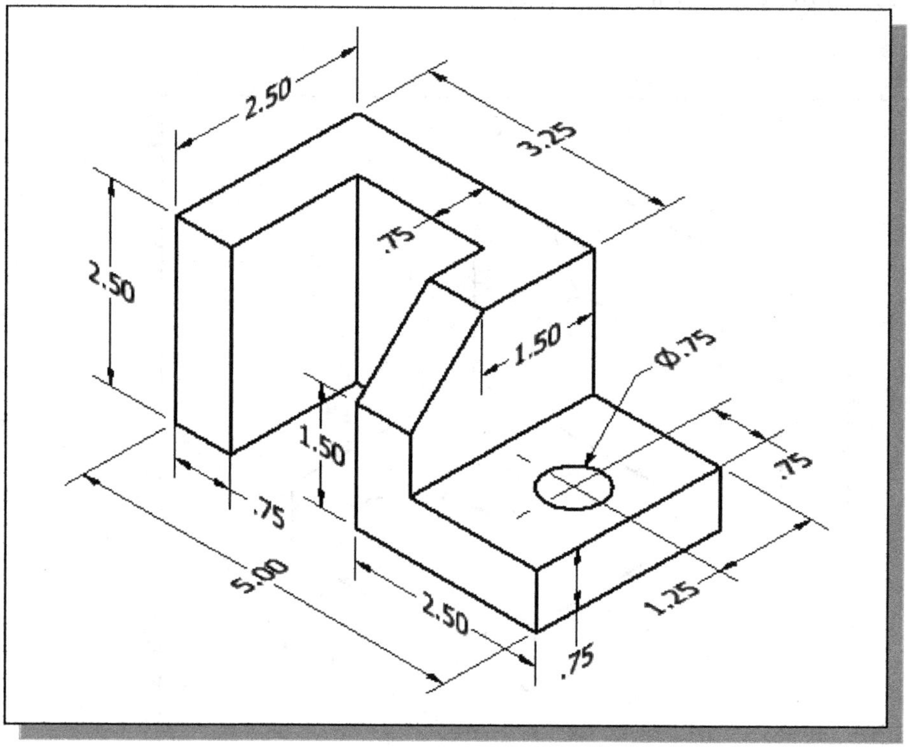
2.50
3.25
2.50
.75
1.50
Ø.75
1.50
.75
.75
5.00
2.50
1.25
.75

4.

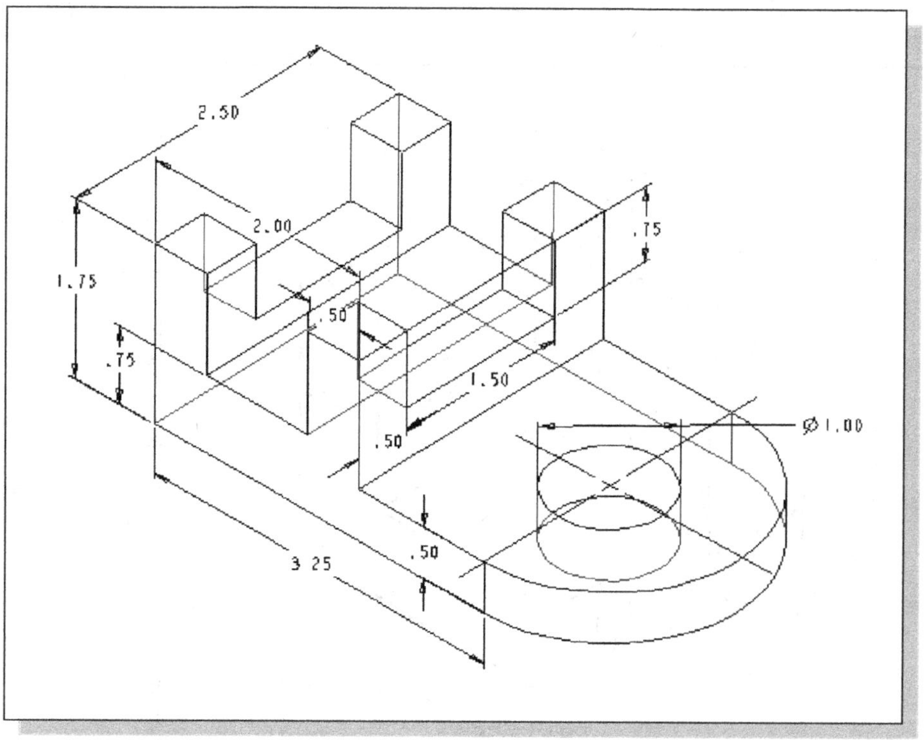
2.50
2.00
1.75
.75
.50
.75
1.50
Ø1.00
.50
3.25
.50

5.

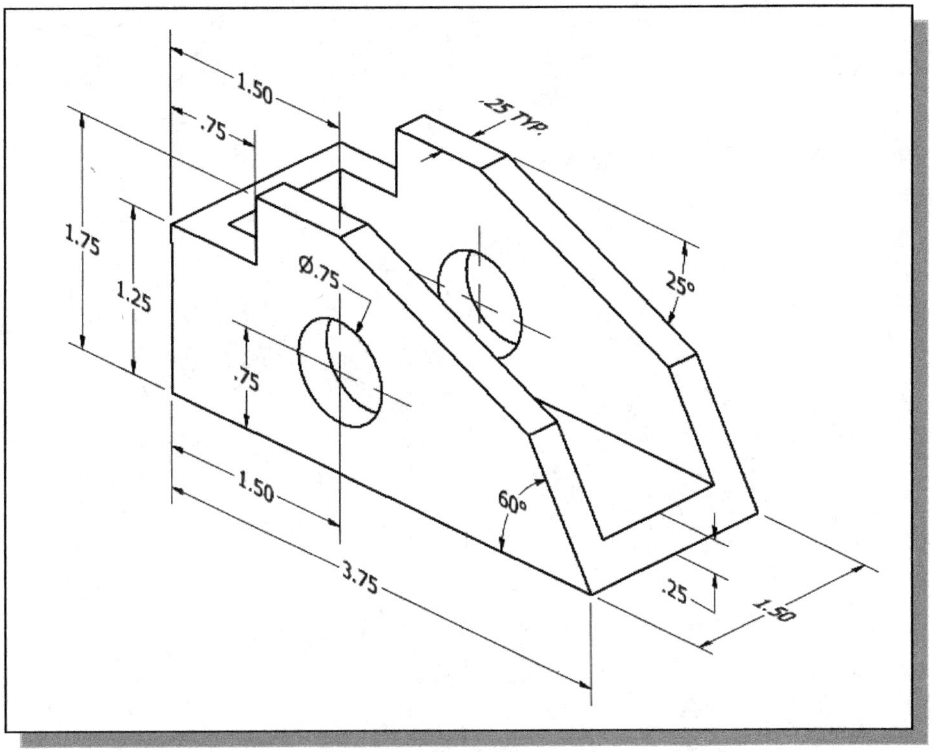
1.50
.75
.25 TYP.
1.75
1.25
Ø.75
25°
.75
1.50
60°
3.75
.25
1.50

6.

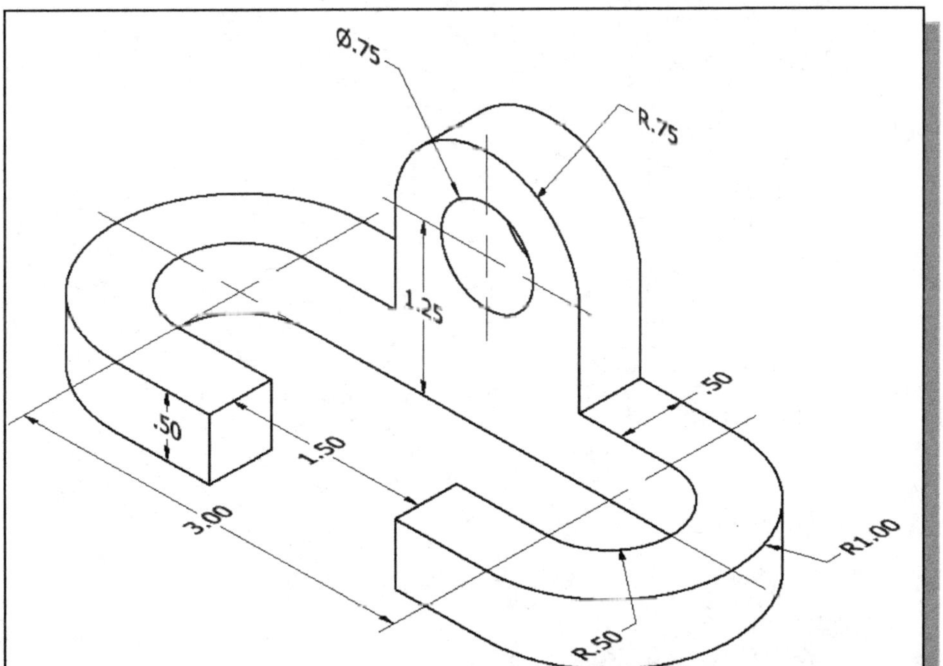
Ø.75
R.75
1.25
.50
.50
1.50
3.00
R1.00
R.50

Notes:

Chapter 6
Solid Modeling – Constructive Solid Geometry

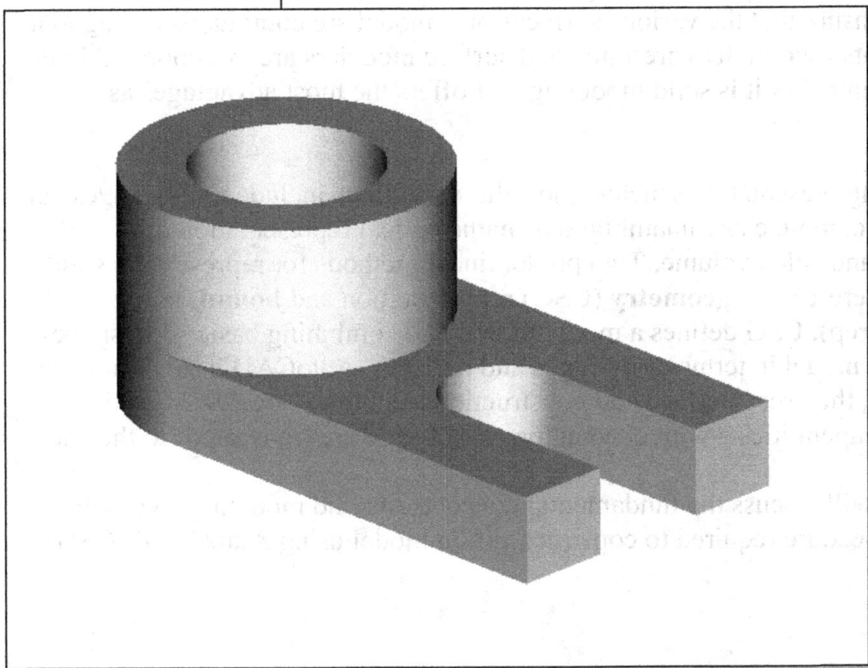

Learning Objectives

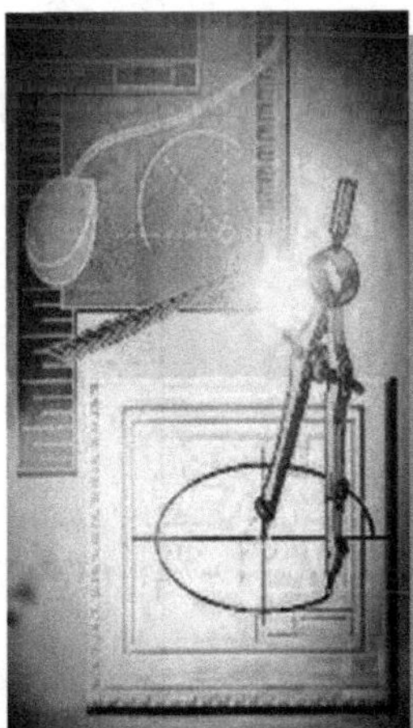

- Understand the Constructive Solid Geometry Concept
- Create a Binary Tree
- Understand the Basic Boolean Operations
- Create Solids Using AutoCAD Primitive Solids
- Generate Shaded Solid Images
- Use SteeringWheels

Introduction

In the previous chapters, we have looked at wireframe modeling and surface modeling. Wireframe modeling describes only the corners and edges of designs. Surface modeling describes part surfaces but not interiors. Although surface models are fairly good representations of the actual designs, designers are still required to interactively examine surface models to ensure that the various surfaces on a model are contiguous throughout. Many of the concepts used in 3D wireframe and surface modelers are incorporated in the solid modeling scheme, but it is solid modeling that offers the most advantages as a design tool.

In the solid modeling presentation scheme, the solid definitions include nodes, edges, and surfaces, and it is a complete and unambiguous mathematical representation of a precisely enclosed and filled volume. Two predominant methods for representing solid models are **constructive solid geometry** (CSG) representation and **boundary representation** (B-rep). CSG defines a model in terms of combining basic solid shapes and B-rep defines a model in terms of its edges and surfaces. AutoCAD's solid modeler is a hybrid modeler; the user interface and construction techniques are CSG-based, whereas the B-rep capabilities are invoked automatically and are transparent to the user.

In this chapter, we will discuss the fundamental concepts of solid modeling. We will demonstrate the procedure required to construct a solid model using AutoCAD's CSG-based user interface.

The Guide-Block Design

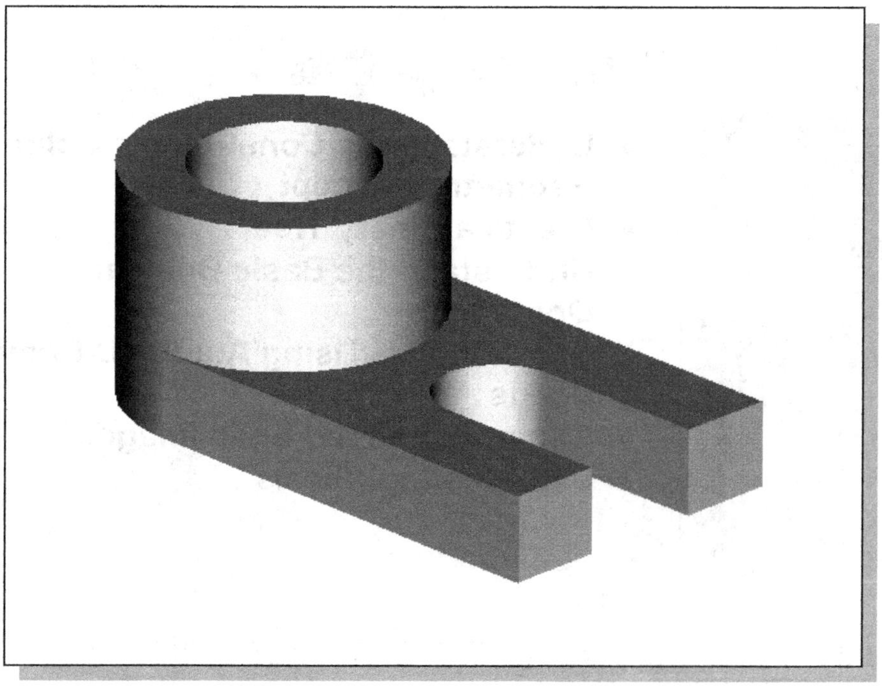

Constructive Solid Geometry Concept

In the 1980s, one of the main advancements in **Solid Modeling** was the development of the **Constructive Solid Geometry** (CSG) method. CSG describes the solid model as the combination of basic three-dimensional shapes (**primitive solids**). The basic primitive solid set typically includes Rectangular-prism (Block), Cylinder, Cone, Sphere, and Torus (Donut). Two solid objects can be combined into one object in various ways; these operations are known as **Boolean operations**. There are three basic Boolean operations: **UNION (Join), SUBTRACT (Cut),** and **INTERSECT**. The UNION operation combines the two volumes included in the different solids into a single solid. The SUBTRACT operation subtracts the volume of one solid object from the other solid object. The INTERSECT operation keeps only the volume common to both solid objects. The CSG method is also known as the **Machinist's Approach**, as the method is parallel to machine shop practices.

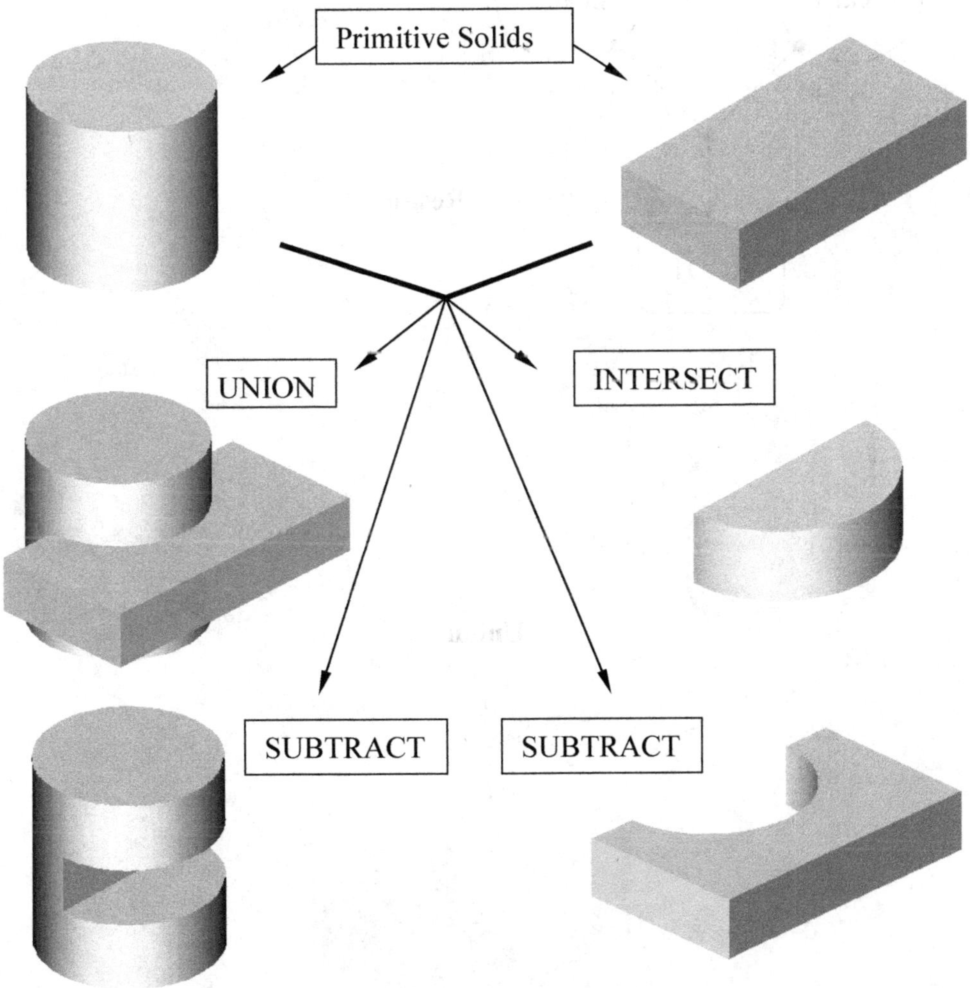

Binary Tree

CSG is also referred to as the method used to store a solid model in the database. The resulting solid can be easily represented by what is called a **binary tree**. In a binary tree, the terminal branches (leaves) are the various primitives that are linked together to make the final solid object (the root). The binary tree is an effective way to represent the steps required to construct the solid model. Complicated solid models can be modeled by considering the different combinations of Boolean operations required in the binary tree. This provides a convenient and intuitive way of modeling that imitates the manufacturing process. A binary tree is an effective way to plan your modeling strategy before you start creating anything.

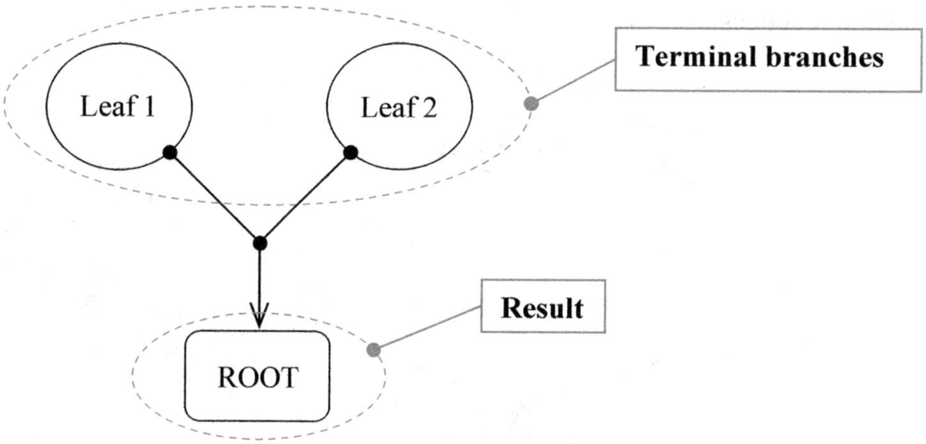

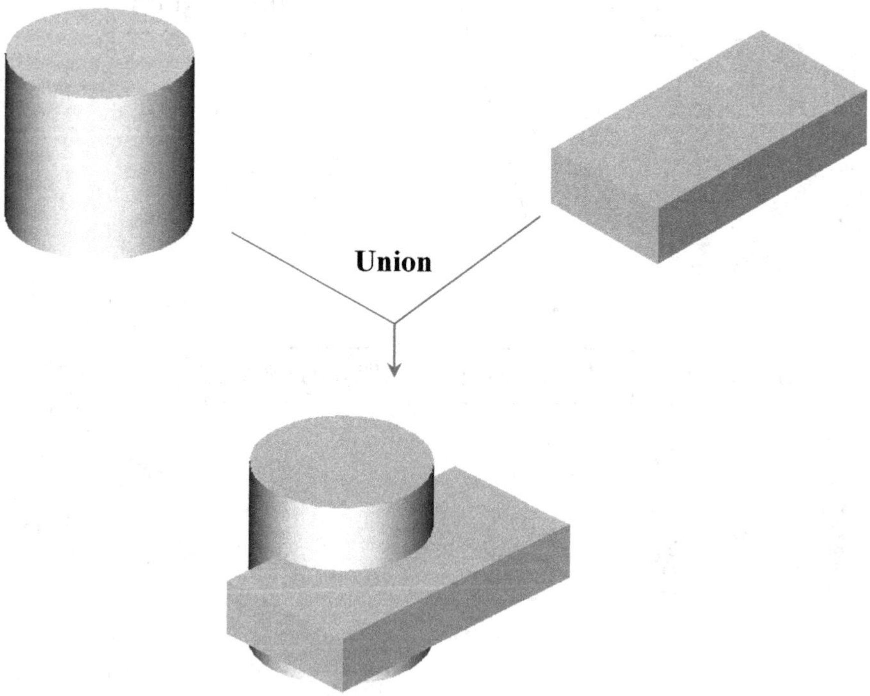

The Guide-Block CSG Binary Tree

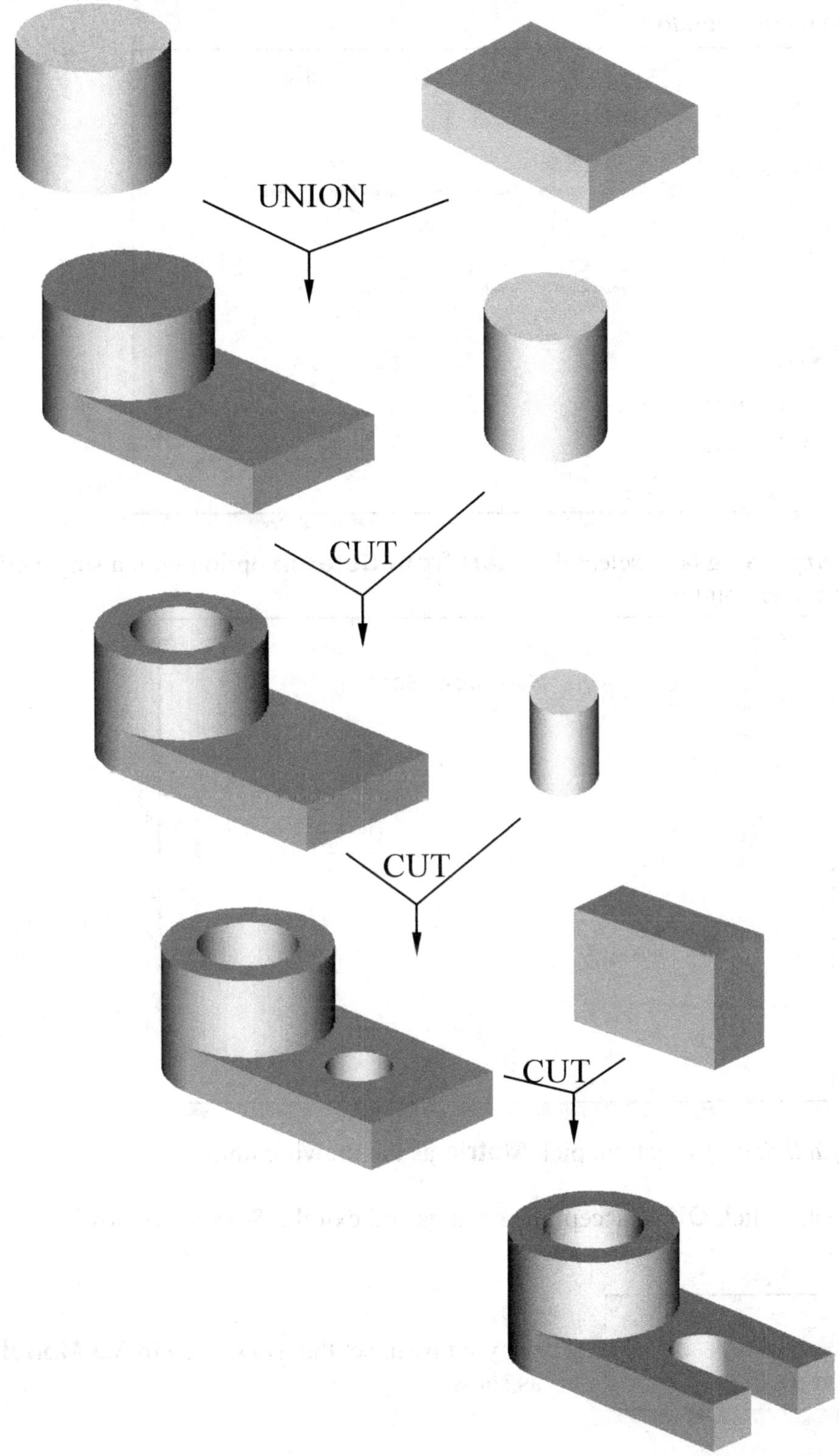

Starting Up AutoCAD 2027

1. Select the **AutoCAD 2027** option on the *Program* menu or select the **AutoCAD 2027** icon on the *Desktop*.

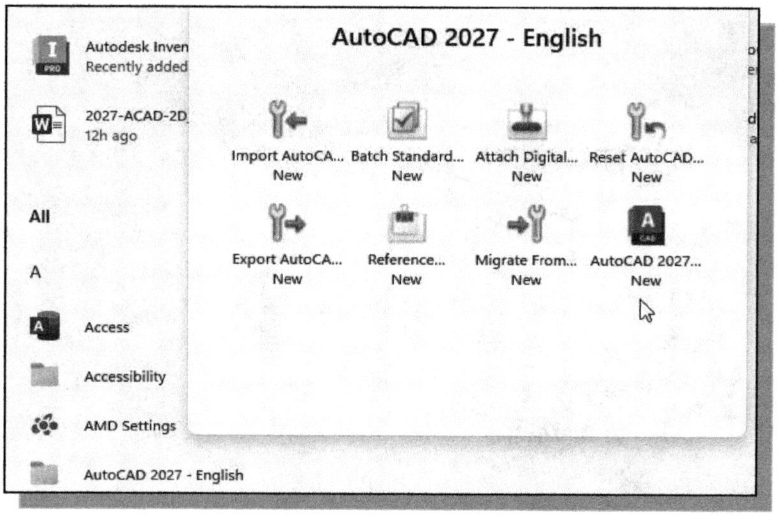

2. In the *Startup* dialog box, select the **Start from Scratch** option with a single click of the left-mouse-button.

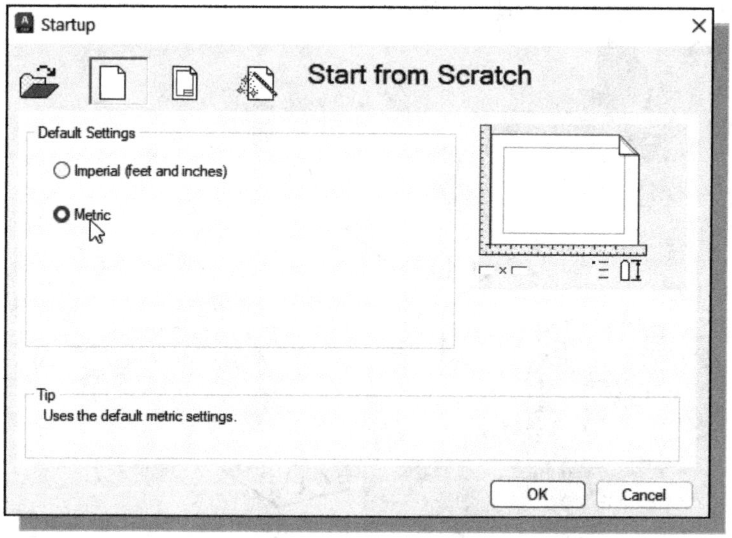

3. In the *Default Settings* section, pick **Metric** as the drawing units.

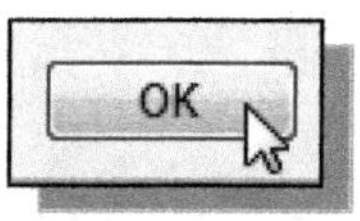

4. Click **OK** to accept the settings and exit the *Startup* window.

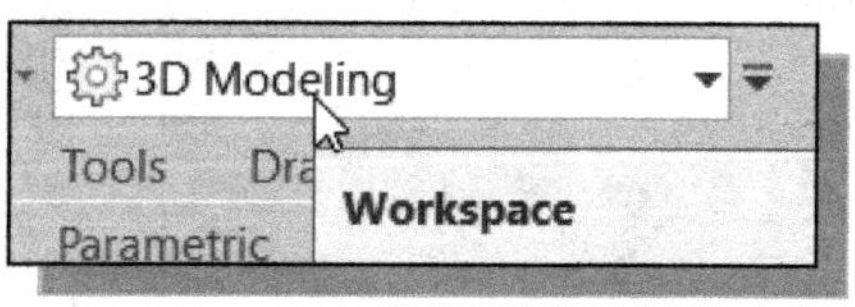

5. On your own, set the *workspace* to **3D Modeling** as shown.

Layers Setup

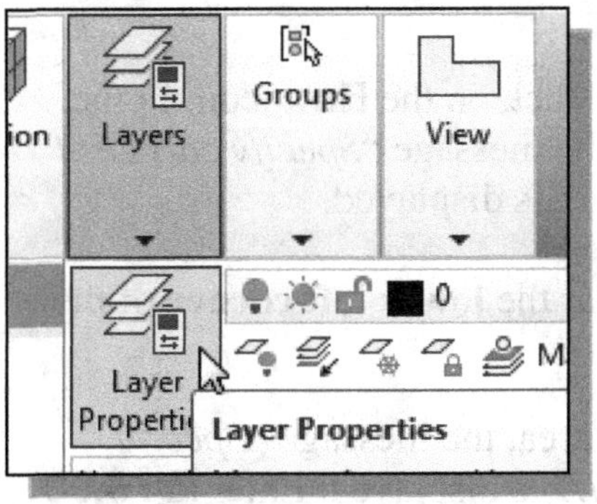

1. In the *Menu Bar,* click on the triangle symbol in the **Layers** Toolbar to display the additional options.

2. Click **Layers Properties Manager** in the *Layers* toolbar as shown.

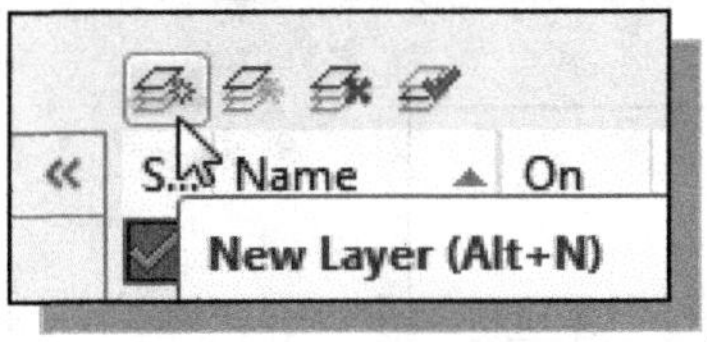

3. Click on the **New** button. Notice a layer is automatically added to the list of layers.

4. Create a **new layer** with the following settings:

Layer	*Color*	*Linetype*
Solid_Objects	**Cyan**	**Continuous**

5. Set layer ***Solid_Objects*** as the *Current Layer.*

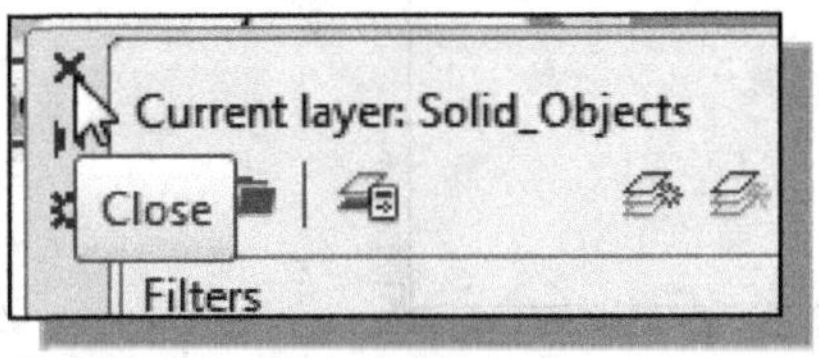

6. Click on the **Close** button to accept the settings and exit the *Layer Properties Manager* dialog box.

Create the First 3D Object

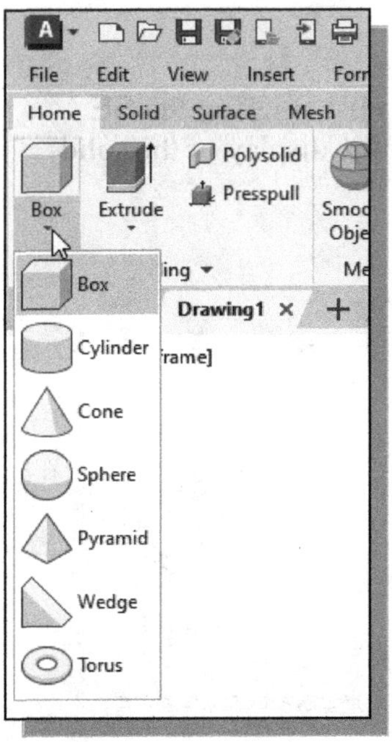

1. Click on the down arrow below the first icon of the 3D Modeling toolbar as shown.

❖ Note that the first icon of the *3DModeling* toolbar contains the basic set of pre-defined solids, primitive solids, available in **AutoCAD 2027**.

2. On your own, move the cursor on top of the different icons and examine the available options.

➢ Also note that the typical basic primitive solid set includes **Box** (**Rectangular-prism**), **Cylinder**, **Cone**, **Sphere**, and **Torus** (Donut).

- We will first create a **75** × **50** × **15** rectangular block.

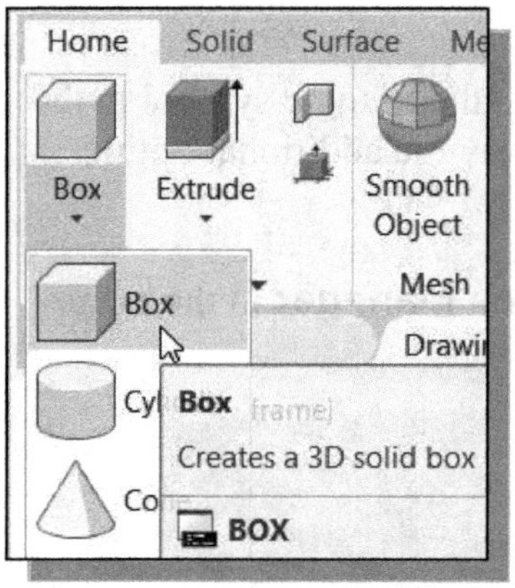

3. In the *Modeling* toolbar, click on the **Box** icon. In the command prompt area, the message "*Specify corner of box or [Center] <0,0,0>:*" is displayed.

4. Pick a location that is near the **lower left corner** of the graphics window.

5. In the command prompt area, the message "*Specify corner or [Cube/Length]:*" is displayed. Enter **@75,50 [ENTER]**.

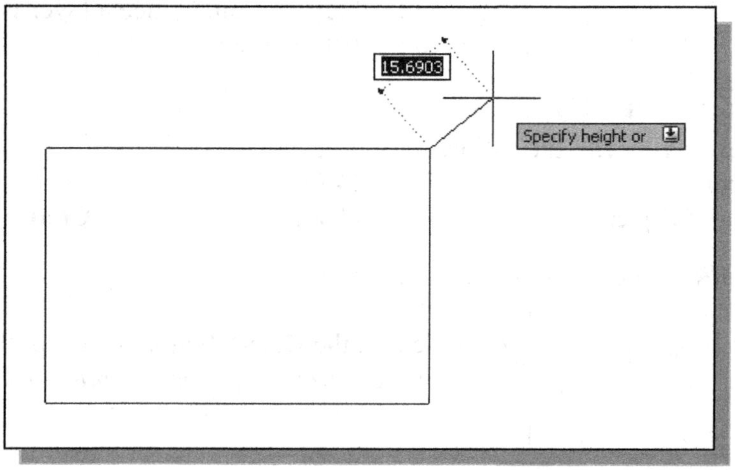

6. In the command prompt area, the message "*Specify Height:*" is displayed. Enter **15 [ENTER]**.

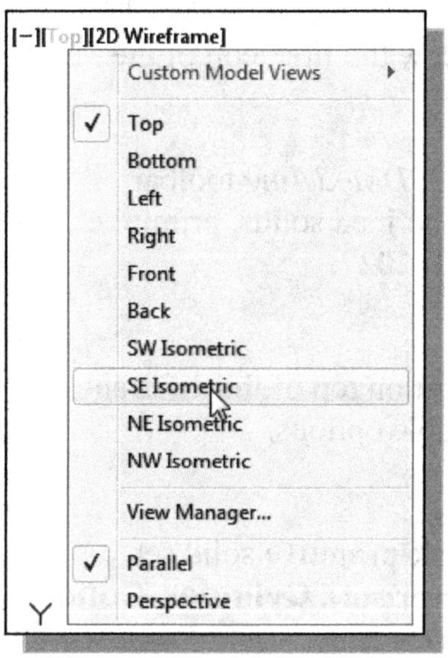

7. In the *View Display Controls* list, click on the **SE Isometric View** icon to set the display of the solid model.

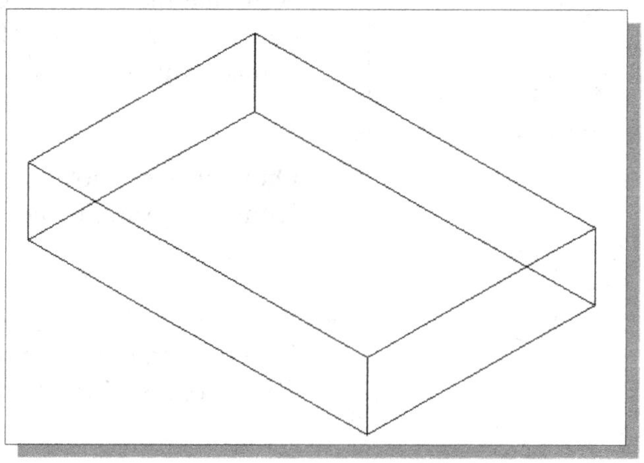

Create the Second Solid Feature

We will next create a cylinder block as the second solid feature.

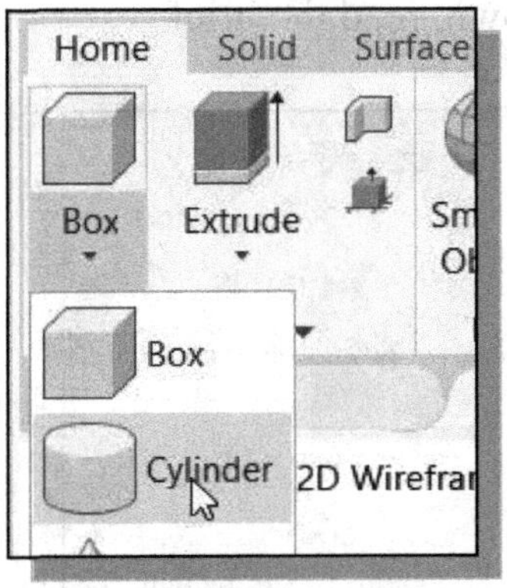

1. In the *3D Modeling* toolbar, click on the **Cylinder** icon. In the command prompt area, the message "*Specify center point for base cylinder or [Elliptical] <0,0,0>:*" is displayed.

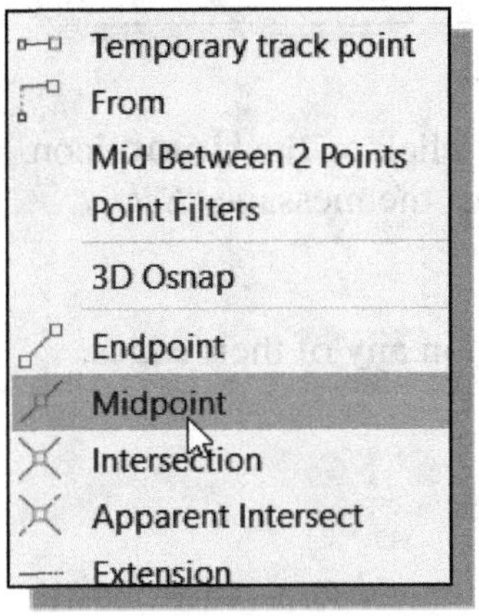

2. Inside the graphics window, press down the **[SHIFT]** key and **right-click** once to bring up the *Object Snap* shortcut menu.
3. Select the **Midpoint** option in the shortcut menu. Snap to and select the midpoint of the bottom-left edge of the rectangular block as shown in the figure below.
4. In the command prompt area, the message "*Specify radius for base of cylinder or [Diameter]:*" is displayed. Snap to and select one of the **endpoints** of the bottom edge of the rectangular block.
5. In the command prompt area, the message "*Specify height of cylinder or [Center of other end]:*" is displayed. Move the cursor up to set the height direction and enter **40 [ENTER]**.

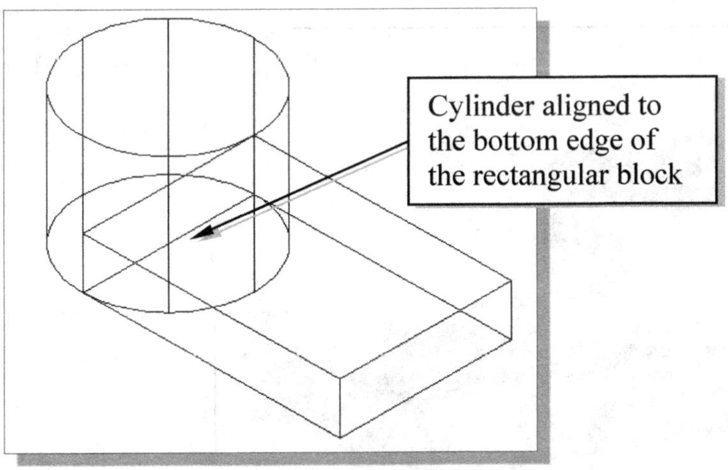

- We have created **two solid objects**, one rectangular box and one cylinder, that are displayed on the screen.

Boolean Operation – Union

1. Move the cursor on top of the third group of icons, the *Solid Editing* toolbar, which contains the basic set of Boolean operation icons. On your own, read the brief description of each of the Boolean commands.

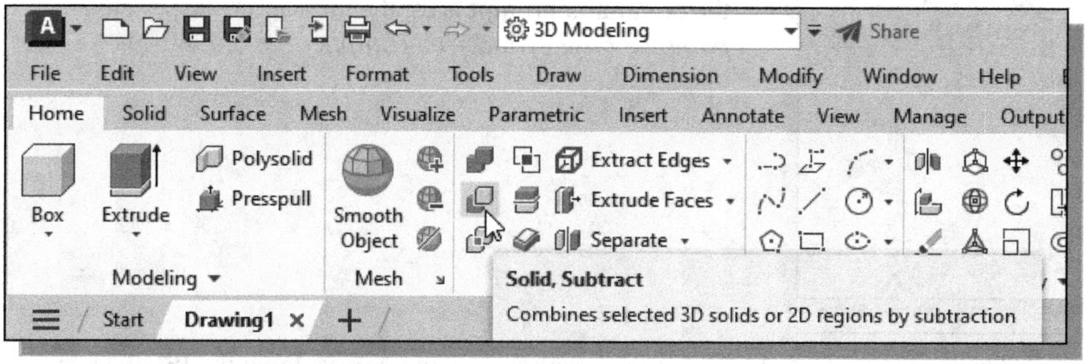

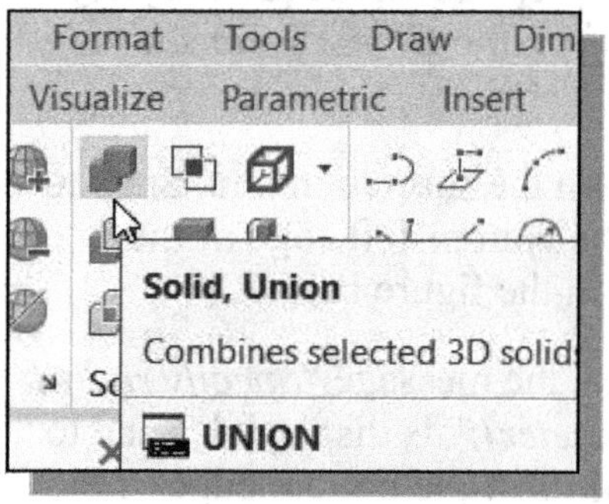

2. In the *Solid Editing* toolbar, click on the **Union** icon. In the command prompt area, the message "*Select Objects:*" is displayed.

3. Pick both solids by clicking on any of their edges.

4. Inside the *graphics window*, **right-click** to accept the selection and proceed with the Union command.

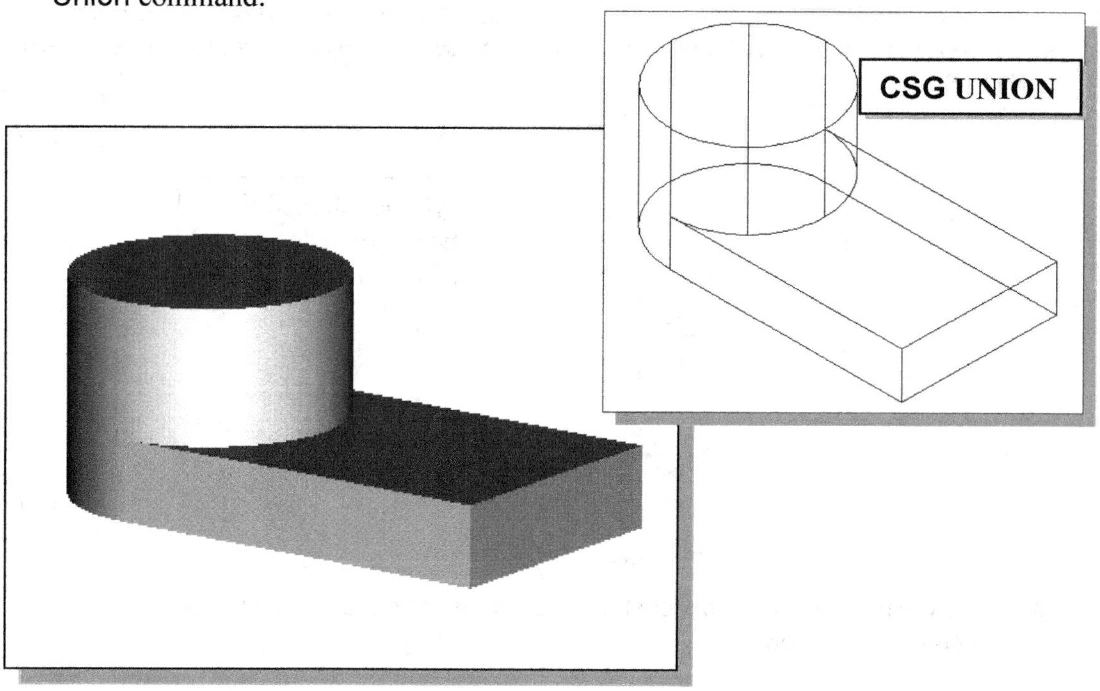

Create the Second Cylinder Feature

We will create another cylinder as the next solid feature.

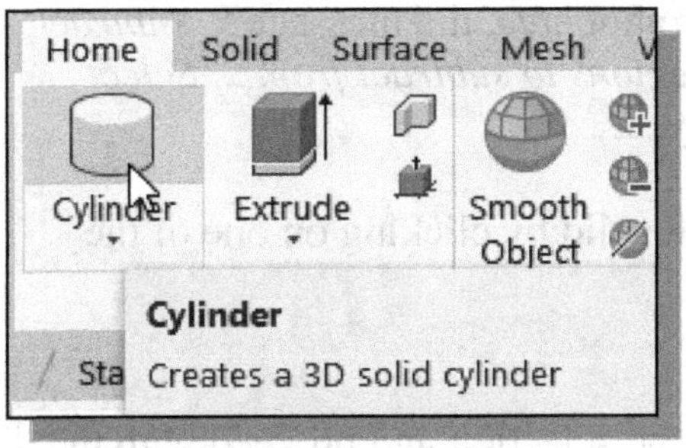

1. In the *Modeling* toolbar, click on the **Cylinder** icon. In the command prompt area, the message *"Specify center point for base cylinder or [Elliptical] <0,0,0>:"* is displayed.

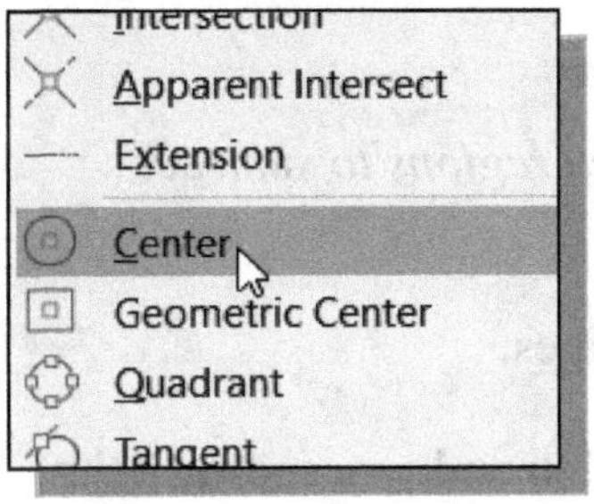

2. Inside the graphics window, press down the **[SHIFT]** key and **right-click** once to bring up the *Object Snap* shortcut menu.

3. Select the **Center** option in the shortcut menu.

4. Snap to and select the **center of the circle** that is at the **top** of the solid block.

5. In the command prompt area, the message *"Specify radius for base of cylinder or [Diameter]:"* is displayed. Enter 15 as the radius value: **15 [ENTER]**.

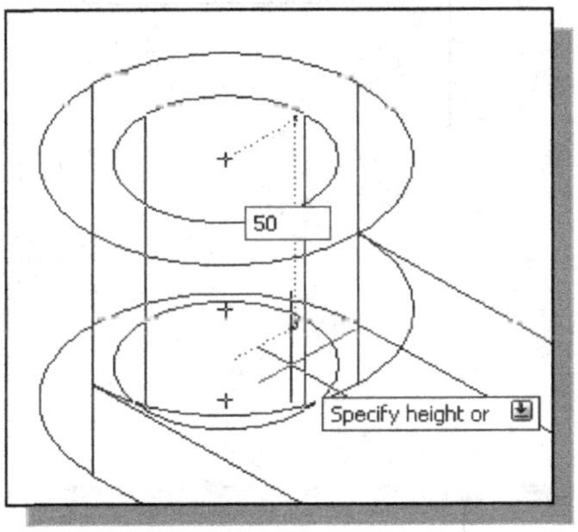

6. In the command prompt area, the message *"Specify radius for base of cylinder or [Diameter]:"* is displayed. Set the extrusion to the **downward** direction by entering a depth value: **-50 [ENTER]**.

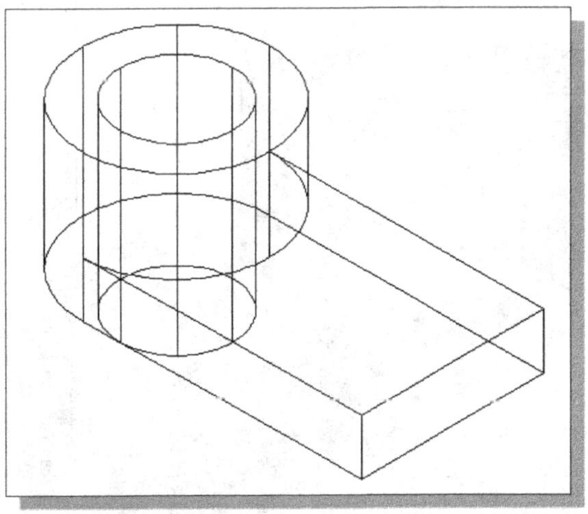

- Two solid objects, the base block and a cylinder, are displayed on the screen. On your own, use the available **Views** options to confirm the top of the two solids are aligned.

Boolean Operation – Subtract

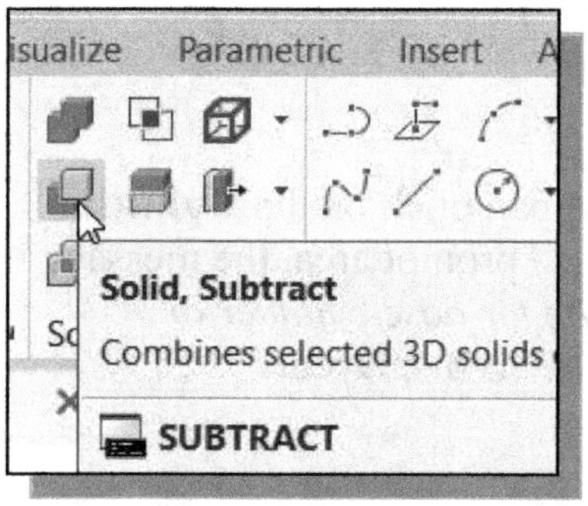

1. In the *Modeling* toolbar, click on the **Subtract** icon. In the command prompt area, the message "*_subtract Select solids and regions to subtract from ... Select Objects:*" is displayed.

2. Pick the **base block** solid by clicking on one of the straight edges.

3. Inside the graphics window, **right-click** to accept the selection and proceed with the Subtract command.

4. In the command prompt area, the message "*Select solids and regions to subtract... Select Objects:*" is displayed.

5. Pick the cylinder block by clicking on one of the circular edges.

6. Inside the graphics window, **right-click** to accept the selection and proceed with the Subtract command.

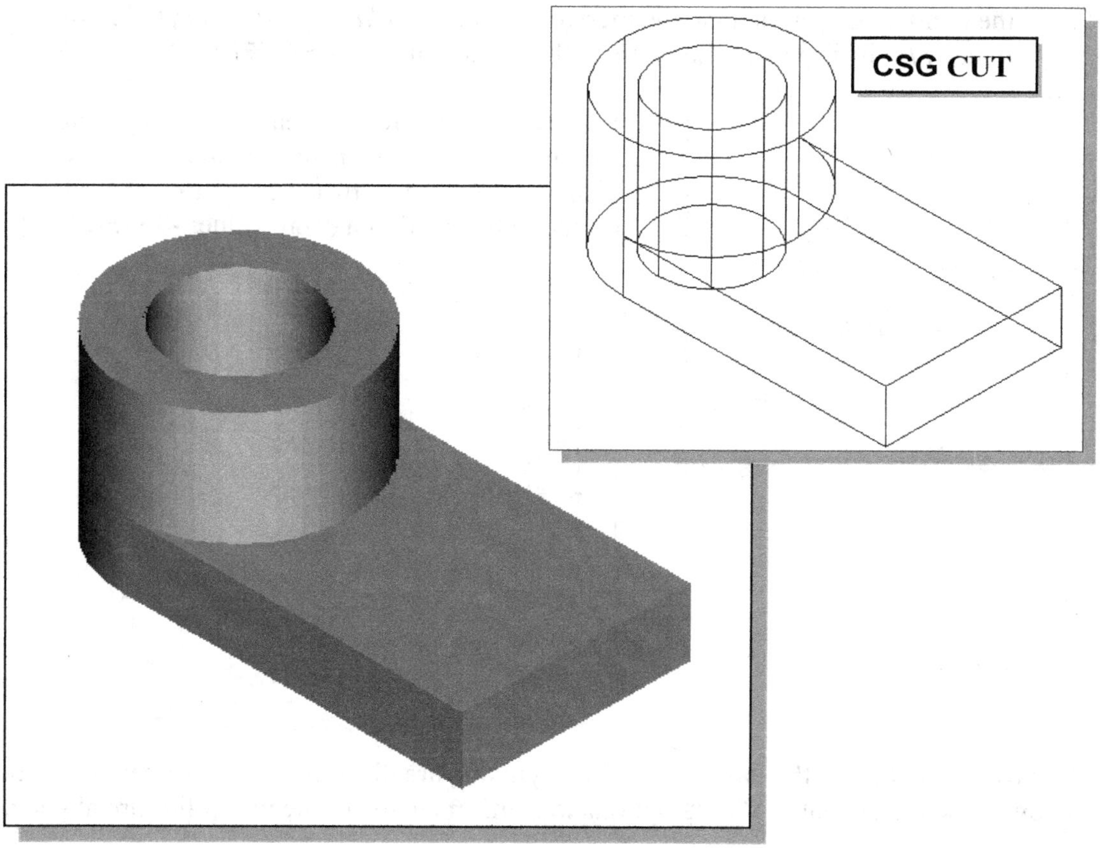

Create another Solid Feature

As can be seen, the CSG construction approach is quite straightforward. The main task is in positioning and aligning the solid blocks prior to applying a Boolean operation.

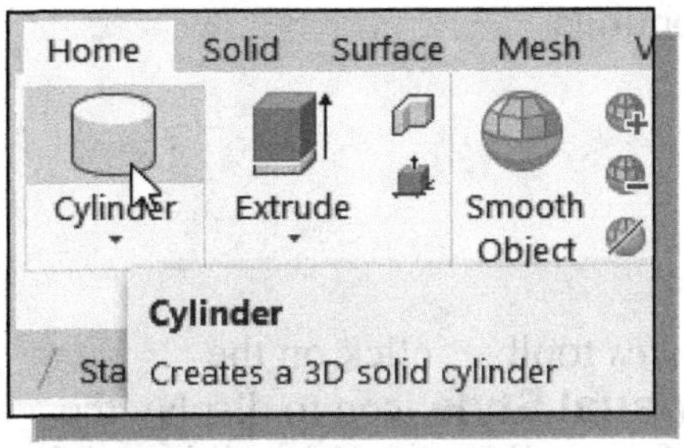

1. In the *Modeling* toolbar, click on the **Cylinder** icon. In the command prompt area, the message "*Specify center point for base cylinder or [Elliptical] <0,0,0>:*" is displayed.

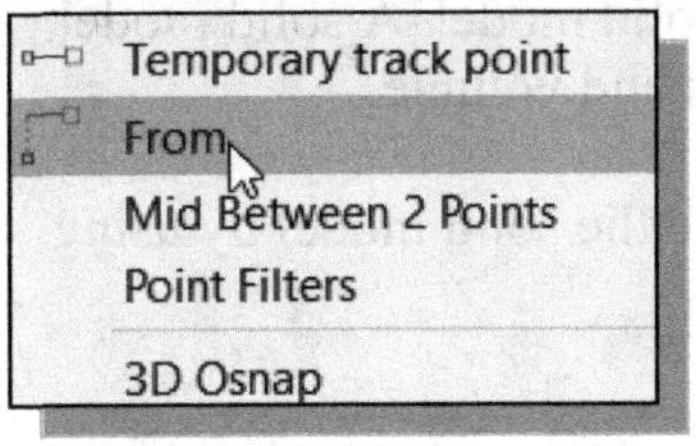

2. Inside the graphics window, press down the **[SHIFT]** key and **right-click** once to bring up the *Object Snap* shortcut menu.

3. Select the **From** option in the shortcut menu.

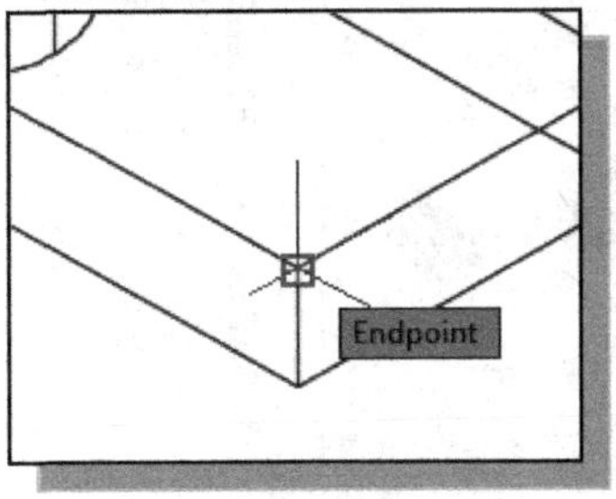

4. Snap to the **top front** corner of the base block and enter **@-30,25 [ENTER]**.

5. In the command prompt area, the message "*Specify radius for base of cylinder or [Diameter]:*" is displayed. Enter **10 [ENTER]**.

6. Move the cursor **downward** and create a cylinder that is longer than the height of the horizontal base as shown.

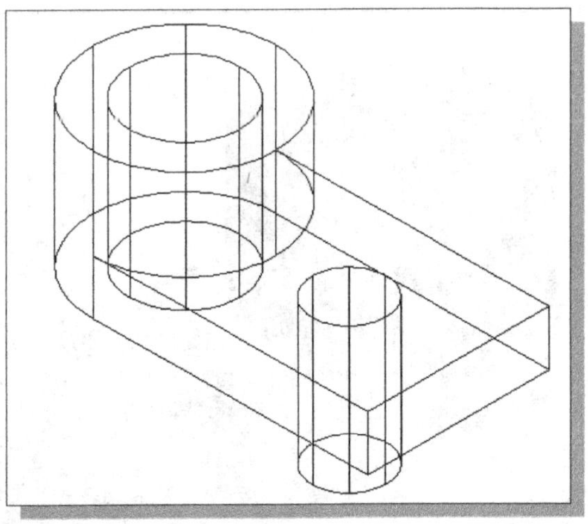

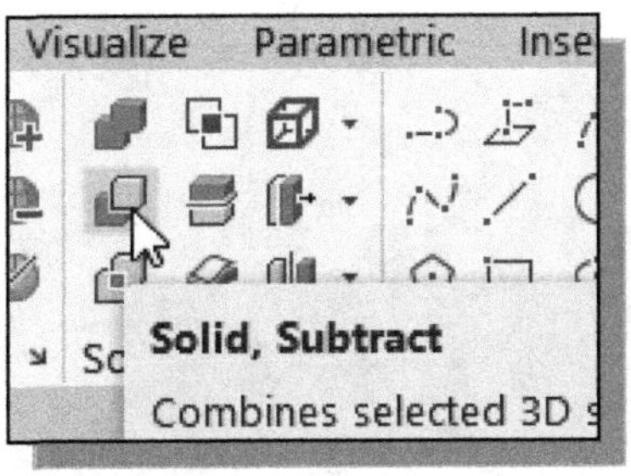

7. On your own, perform the Boolean **Subtract** operation.

Visual Styles Options

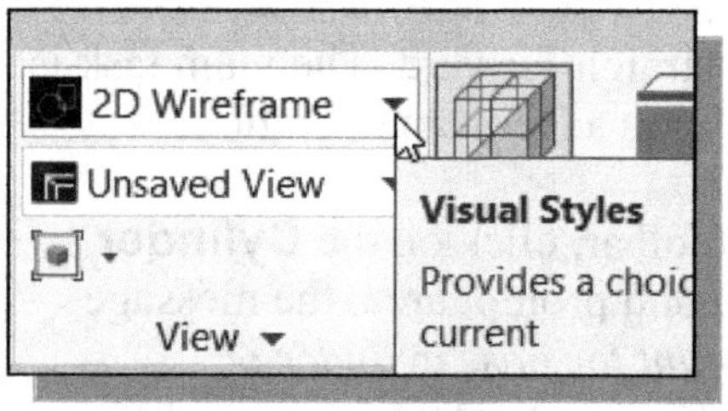

1. Move the cursor to the ***Visualize*** toolbar panel and **left-click** on the downward triangle to display a list of available options.

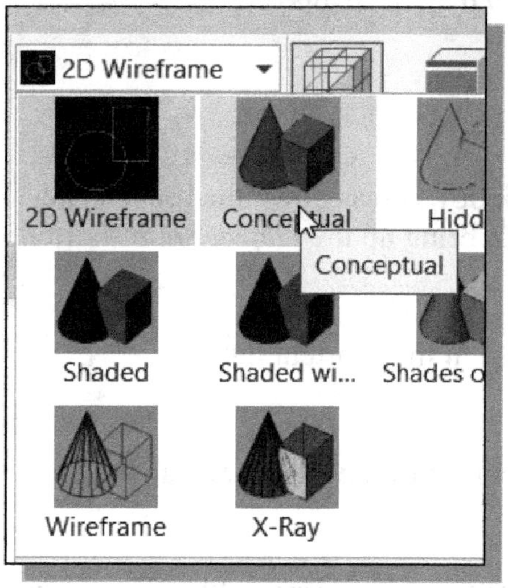

2. In the *Visual Styles* toolbar, click on the **Conceptual Visual Style** icon to display the shaded image of the solid model. A solid model contains both surfaces and volume.

➢ On your own, examine the solid model by using the **ViewCube**.

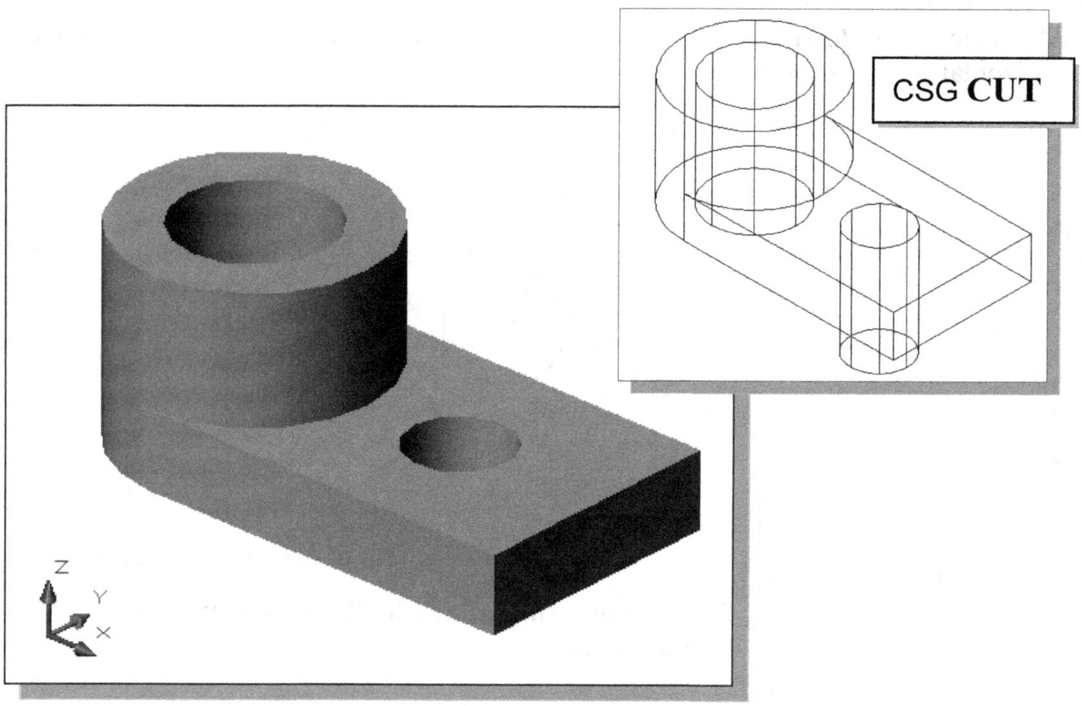

Create the Final Feature

We will create a rectangular cut as the final solid feature of the part. In the previous sections, with some careful planning, we positioned the solid blocks at the correct space locations while we were creating the solids. It is also possible to take a more general approach to orient and position solid blocks in space coordinates.

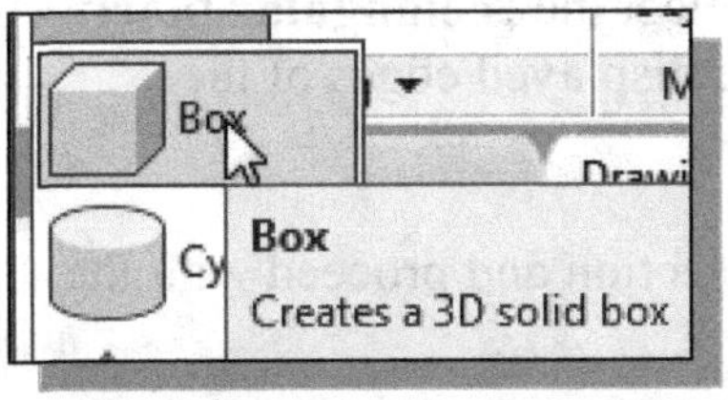

1. In the *Modeling* toolbar, click on the **Box** icon. In the command prompt area, the message "*Specify corner of box or [Center] <0,0,0>:*" is displayed.

2. In the *Status bar* area, turn **off** the **Dynamic UCS** option if it is visible, or hit the **[F6]** key once.

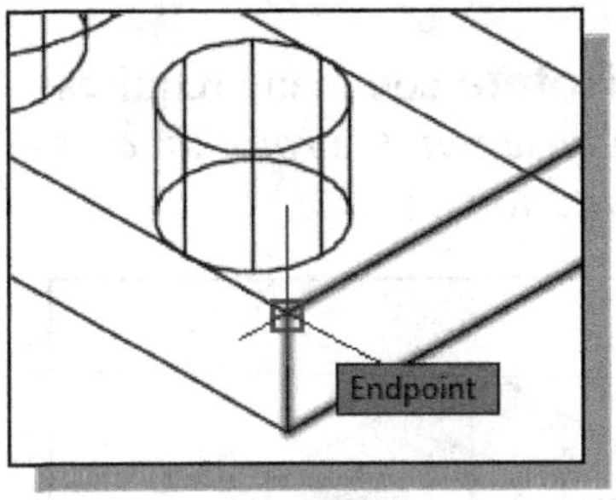

3. Snap to and select the **top front corner** of the base block.

4. In the *command prompt area*, the message "*Specify corner or [Cube/Length]:*" is displayed. Enter **@-30,30 [ENTER]**.

5. In the command prompt area, the message "*Specify height:*" is displayed. For the depth value Enter **-20 [ENTER]**.

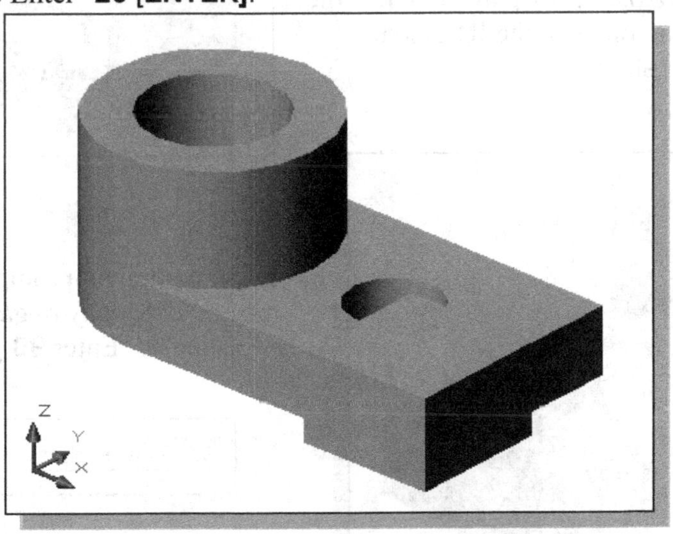

➢ Two overlapping solids appear on the screen. We will use the *editing tools* to orient the cutter, the newly created rectangular block, to its correct location.

Rotating the Rectangular Block

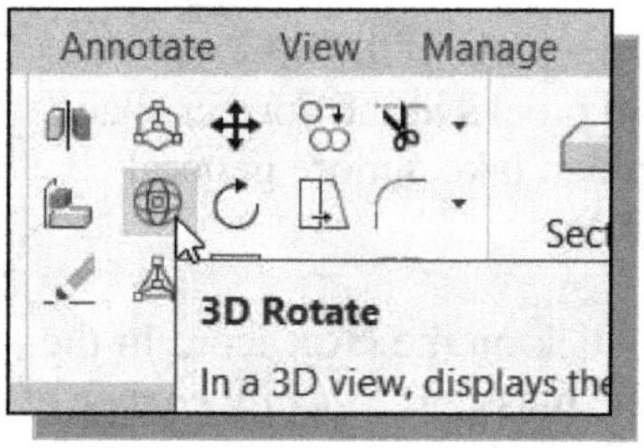

1. Select **3D Rotate** in the *Modify* toolbar as shown.

2. In the command prompt area, the message "*Select objects:*" is displayed. Select the **rectangular block** by clicking on any of the displayed edges of the model.

3. Inside the graphics window, **right-click** to accept the selection and proceed with the **3D Rotate** command.

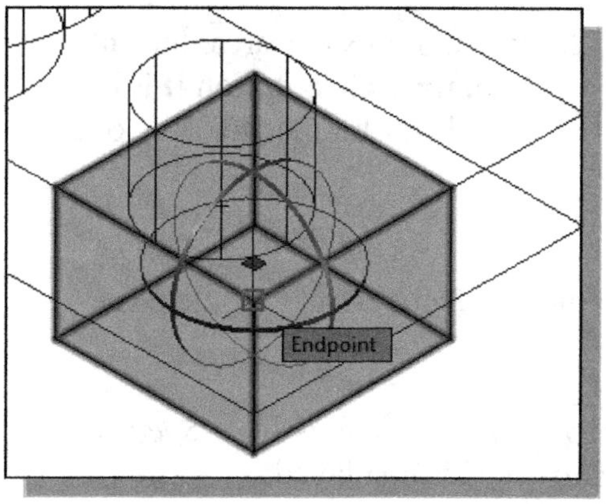

4. In the command prompt area, the message "*Specify base point:" is displayed.* Select the **top front corner** of the rectangular box as shown.

- Note that the **3D Rotate** command requires the definition of a *base point*, a *rotation axis* and the *angle of rotation.*

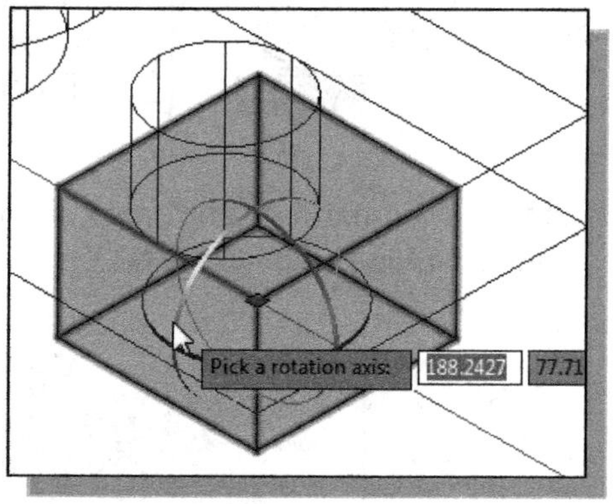

5. In the command prompt area, the message "*Pick a rotation axis:*" is displayed. Select the X-axis by clicking once on the **RED grip rotate handle** as shown.

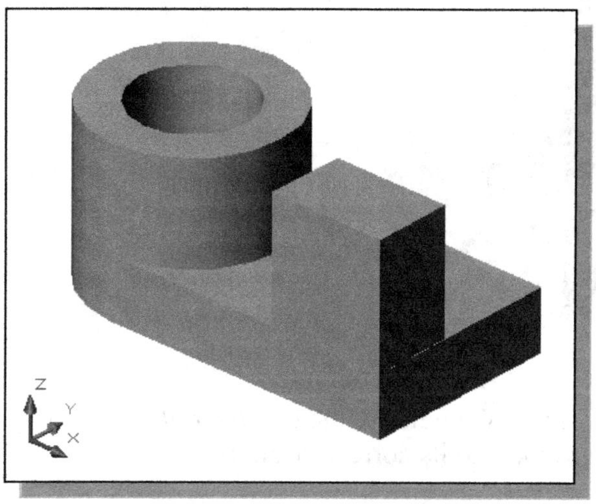

6. In the command prompt area, the message "*Specify angle start point:*" is displayed. Enter **90** [**ENTER**].

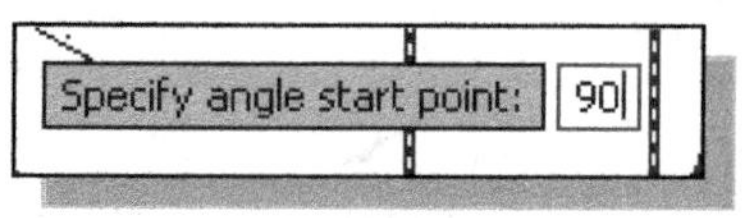

Reposition the Rectangular Block

1. **Pre-select** the rectangular block by left-clicking on any edge of the block.

2. Inside the graphics window, right-click and select **Move** in the pop-up menu. In the command prompt area, the message "*Specify base point or displacement:*" is displayed.

3. Snap to and select the **top front corner** of the rectangular block as the reference point.

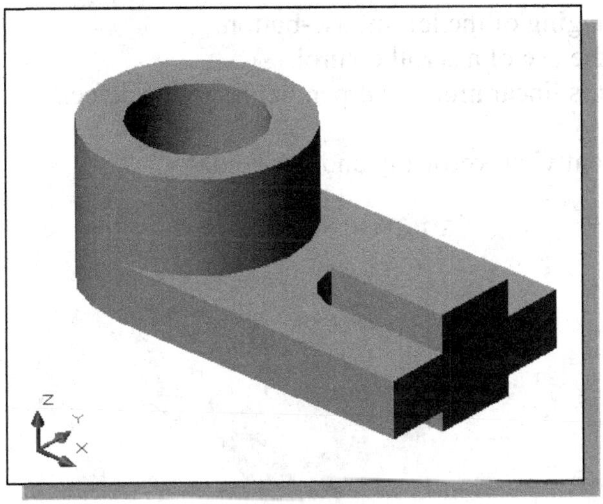

4. In the command prompt area, the message "*Specify second point of displacement or <use first point as displacement>:*" is displayed. Enter **@0,15,-20 [ENTER]**.

5. On your own, use the **Free Orbit** command to examine the constructed objects.

6. On your own, perform the Subtract Boolean operation and complete the model.

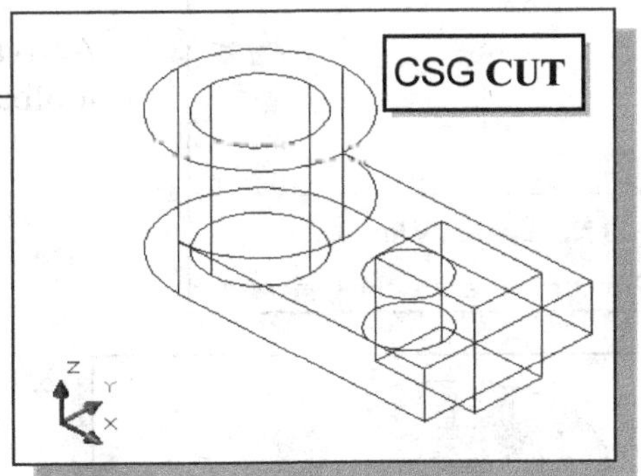

The SteeringWheels

The SteeringWheels are tracking menus that are divided into different sections known as wedges. Each wedge on a wheel represents a single navigation tool. You can pan, zoom, or manipulate the current view of a model in different ways. The 3D SteeringWheel and 2D SteeringWheel (mostly used in the 2D drawing mode) have some or all of the following options:

Zoom - Adjusts the magnification of the view.
Center - Centers the view based on the position of the cursor over the wheel.
Rewind - Restores the previous view.
Forward - Increases the magnification of the view.
Orbit - Allows 3D free rotation with the left-mouse-button.
Pan - Allows panning with the dragging of the left mouse-button.
Up/Down - Allows panning with the use of a scroll control.
Walk - Allows the *walking*, which is linear motion perpendicular to the screen, through the model space.
Look - Allows rotation of the current view vertically and horizontally.

3D Steering Wheel

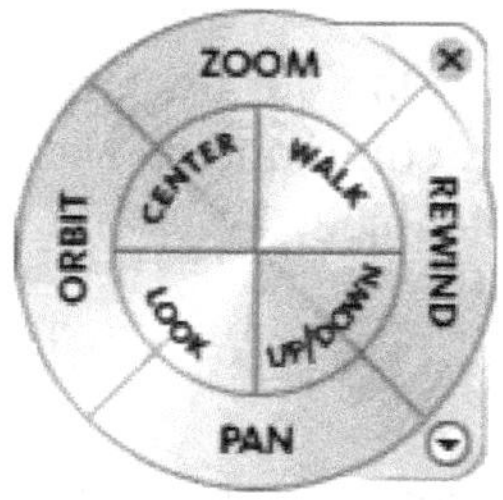

2D Steering Wheel

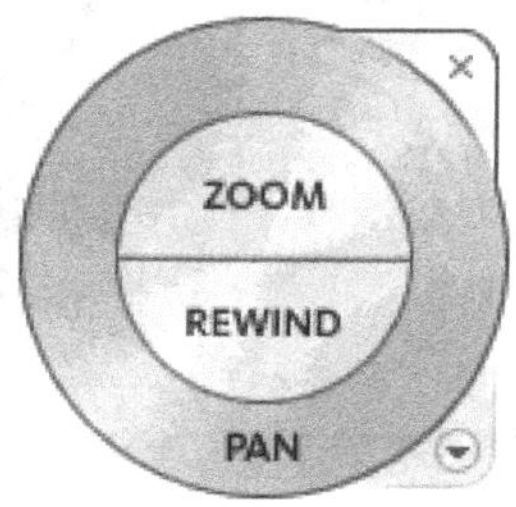

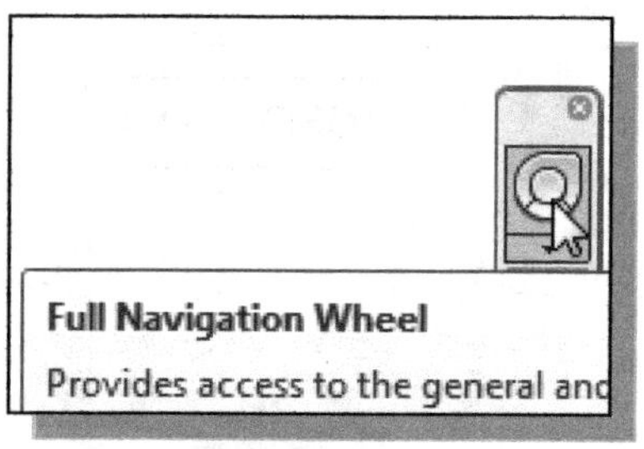

1. Activate the SteeringWheel, in the **View** display toolbar, by clicking on the icon as shown.

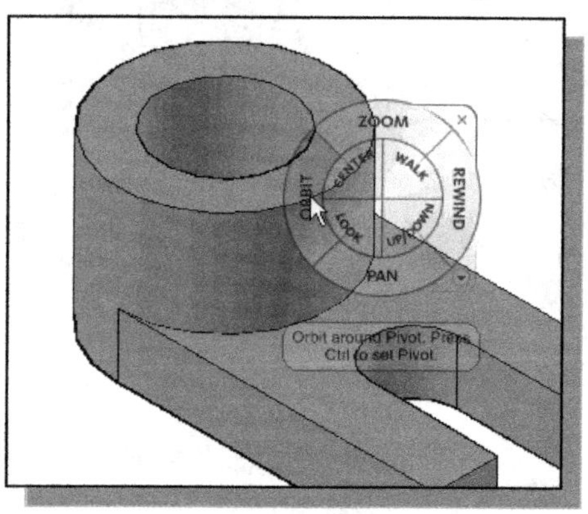

2. Move the cursor in the graphics window and notice the 3D Steering Wheel menu follows the cursor on the screen.

3. Move the cursor on the **Orbit** option to highlight the option.

4. Click and drag with the left-mouse-button to activate the **Free Rotation** option.

5. Drag with the left-mouse-button and notice the **ViewCube** also reflects the model orientation.

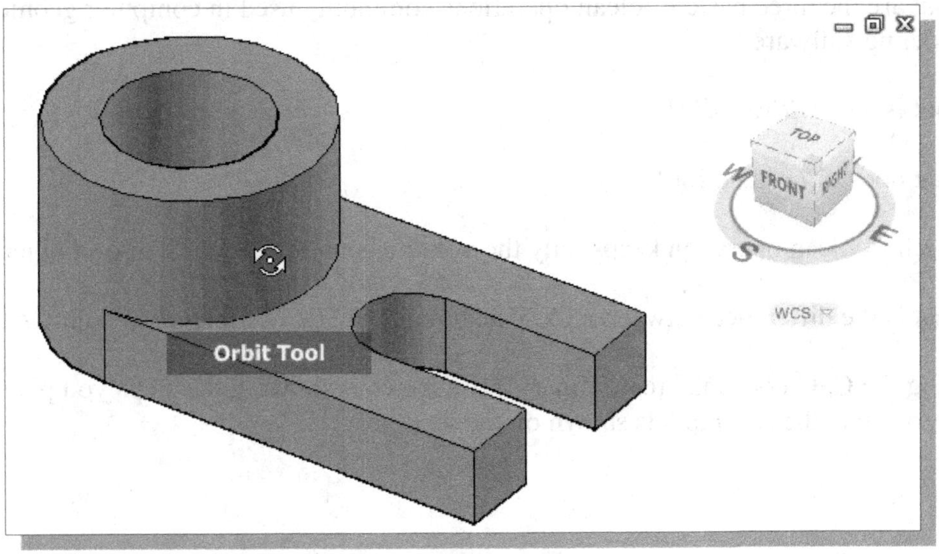

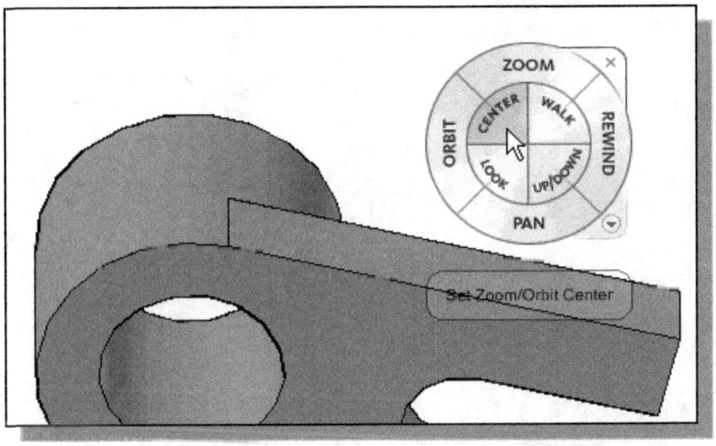

6. Move the cursor to the left side of the model and click the **Center** option as shown. The display is adjusted so the selected point is the new **Zoom/Orbit** center.

7. On your own, experiment with the other available options.

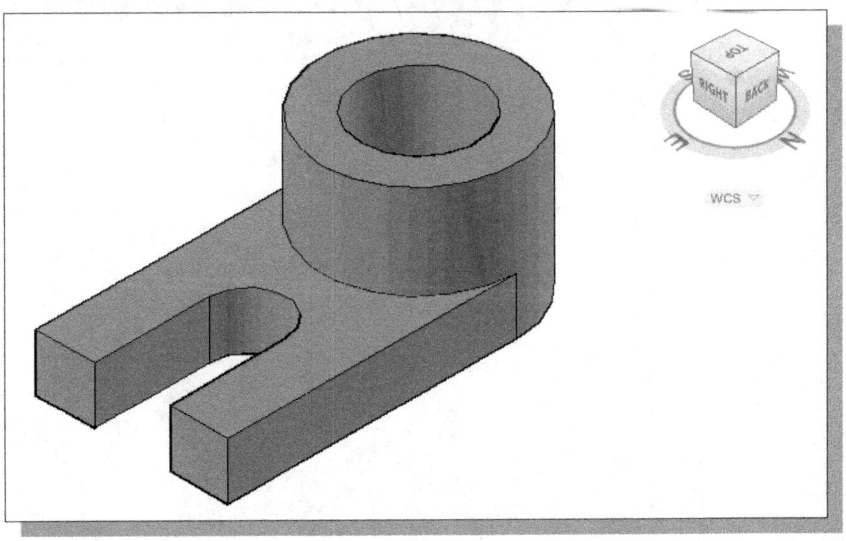

Review Questions:

1. What are the three basic Boolean operations commonly used in computer geometric modeling software?

2. What is a *primitive solid*?

3. What does *CSG* stand for?

4. Which Boolean operation keeps only the volume common to the two solid objects?

5. What is the difference between a *CUT* feature and a *UNION* feature in AutoCAD?

6. Using the CSG concept, create Binary Tree sketches showing the steps you plan to use to create the two models shown on the next page:

Ex.1)

Ex.2)

Exercises: Unless otherwise specified, all dimensions are in inches.

1.

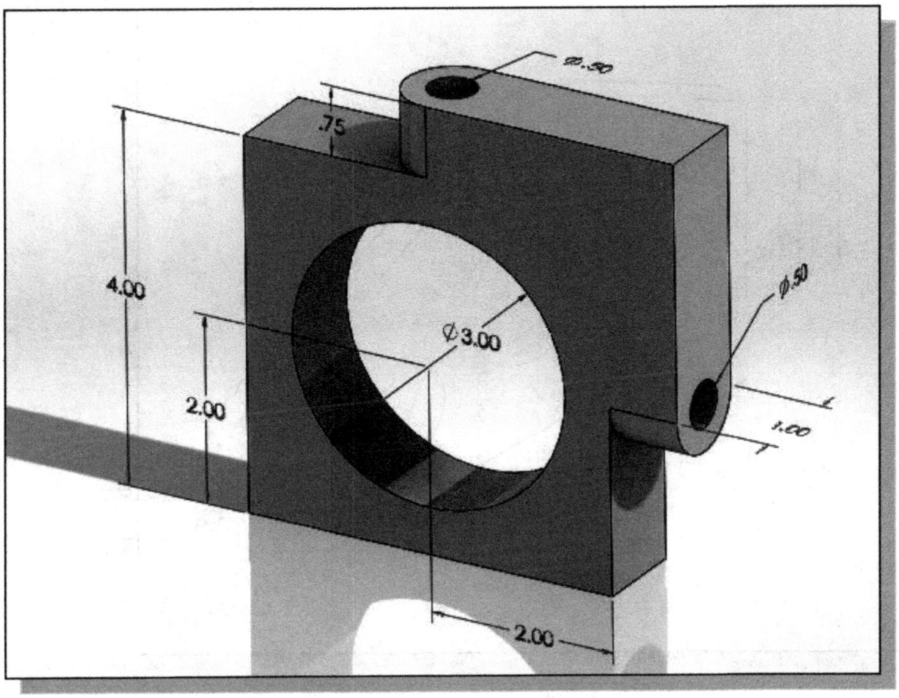

2.

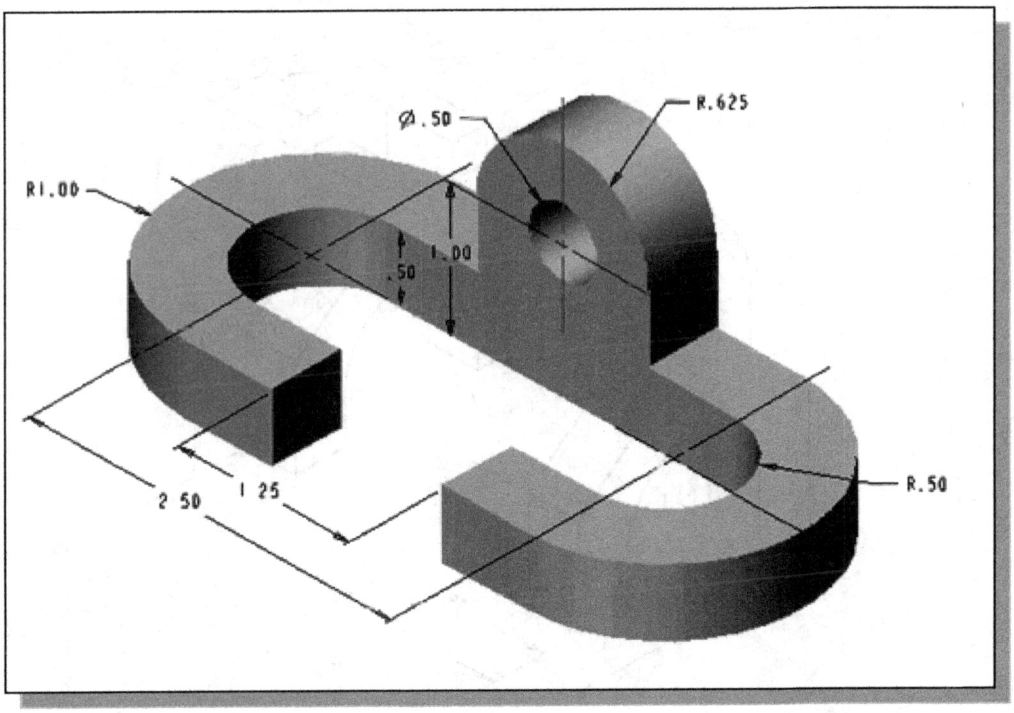

3.

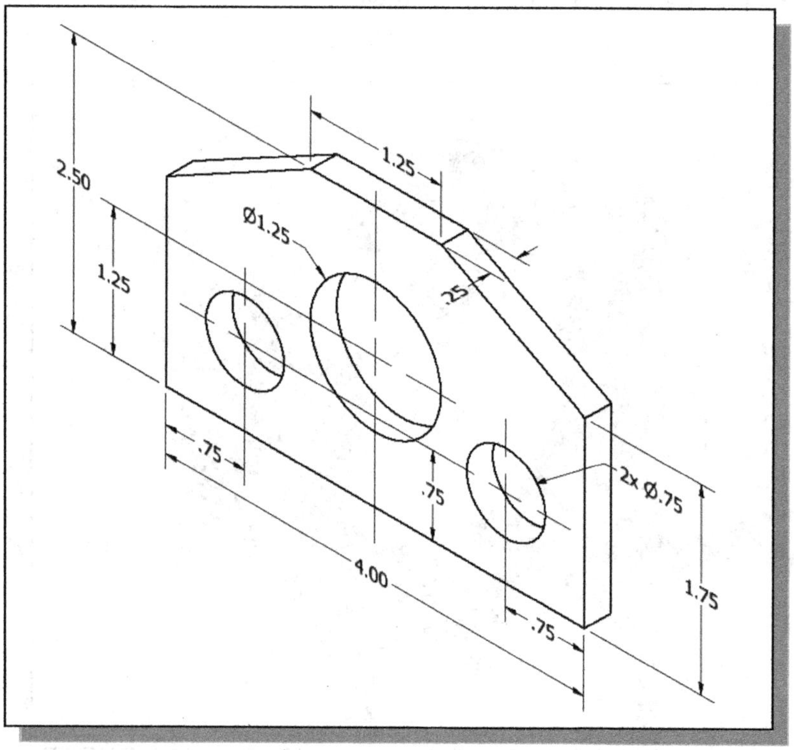
2.50
1.25
Ø1.25
.25
.75
.75
4.00
2x Ø.75
.75
1.75

4.

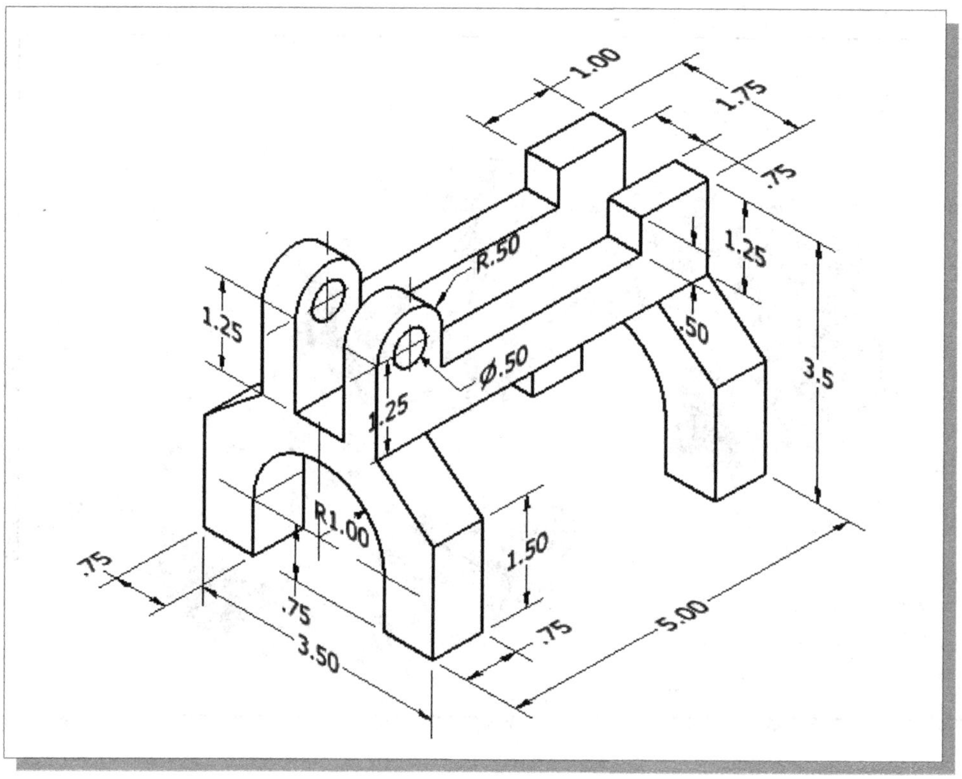
1.00
1.75
.75
1.25
R.50
1.25
.50
Ø.50
3.5
1.25
R1.00
1.50
.75
.75
3.50
.75
5.00

5. Dimensions are in mm.

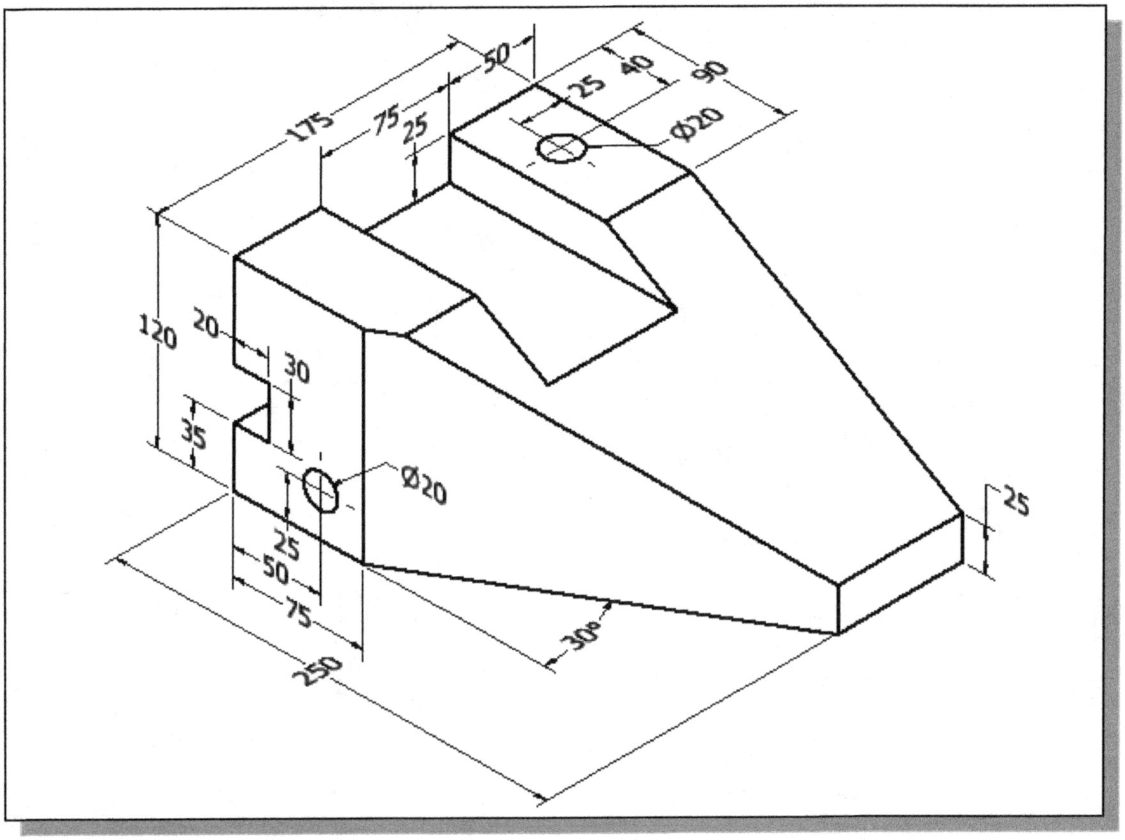

6.

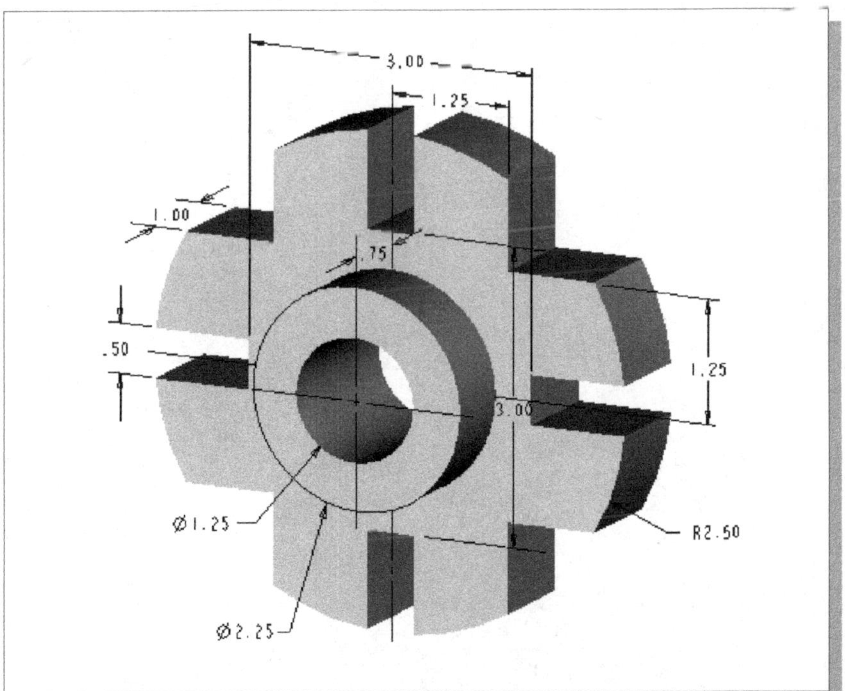

Notes:

Chapter 7
Regions, Extrude and Solid Modeling

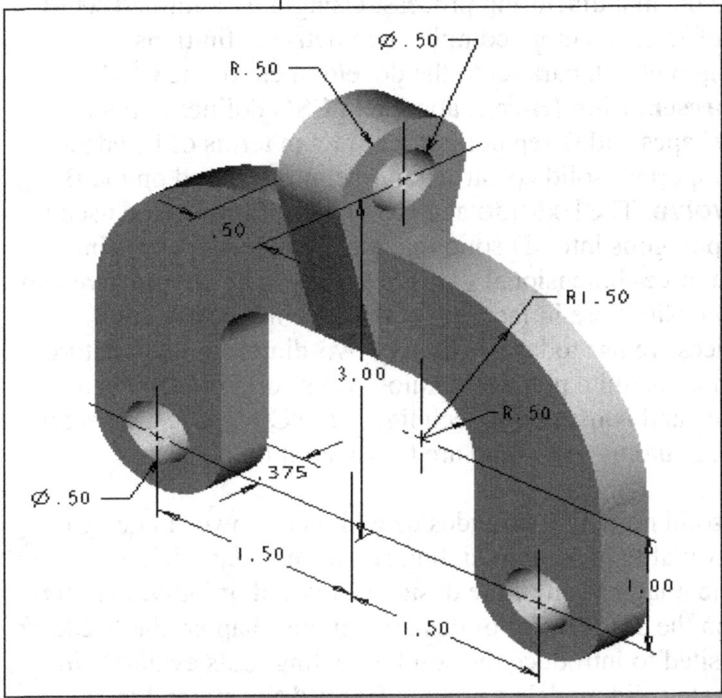

Learning Objectives

- **Use 2D Extrusion Method to Create Solid Models**
- **Understand and Create Regions**
- **Edit 3D Geometry with the Rotate and Move Commands**
- **Examine the Mass Properties of Solids**
- **Understand the Concept of Boundary-Representation Modeling Approach**

Introduction

AutoCAD provides many powerful modeling and design-tools, and there are many different approaches to accomplish solid modeling tasks. The CSG approach, as illustrated in the previous chapter, allows designers to create solid models by using a set of predefined shapes to simulate the manufacturing process. Using only a limited set of predefined solids becomes less efficient as more complex geometric definitions are involved. Another solid modeling method, parallel to the development of the CSG approach, is the **Boundary Representation (B-rep)** approach. CSG defines a model in terms of combining basic solid shapes and B-rep defines a model in terms of its edges and surfaces. Two of the most important solid construction operations based on the B-rep approach are **Extrude** and **Revolve**. The Extrude and Revolve options can be used to convert two-dimensional filled polygons into 3D solid models. This concept of using two-dimensional sketches of the three-dimensional features proves to be an effective way to construct solid models. Many designs are in fact the same shape in one direction. Computer input and output devices we use today are largely two-dimensional in nature, which makes this modeling technique quite practical. AutoCAD's solid modeler is a hybrid modeler; the user interface and construction techniques are CSG-based, whereas the B-rep capabilities are invoked automatically and are transparent to the user.

It is important to point out that solid modeling provides us with very powerful design tools. With the abundant tools available in solid modeling software, the modeling techniques are limited only to the imagination of the designer. Instead of individual 2D views, one should concentrate on the 3D features of designs. In this chapter, the *V-Block* design from chapter four is revisited to introduce the solid modeling tools available in AutoCAD. The procedure to create solid models using the **Extrude** command is demonstrated.

The V-Block-Solid Design

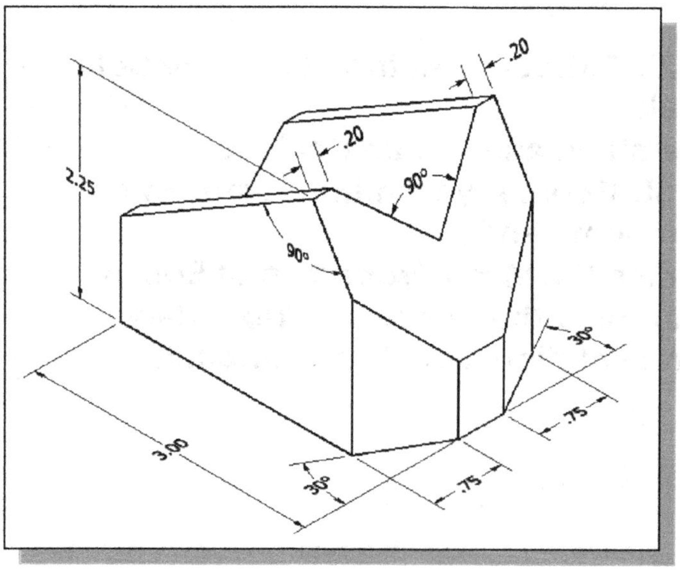

➢ Make a rough sketch of a CSG binary tree showing the steps that can be used to construct the design. What are the advantages and limitations of using the CSG approach in creating the design? What other tools could be helpful to the modeling task at hand? Take a few minutes to consider these questions. You are encouraged to construct the design on your own prior to going through the tutorial.

Starting Up AutoCAD 2027

1. Select the **AutoCAD 2027** option on the *Program* menu or select the **AutoCAD 2027** icon on the *Desktop*.

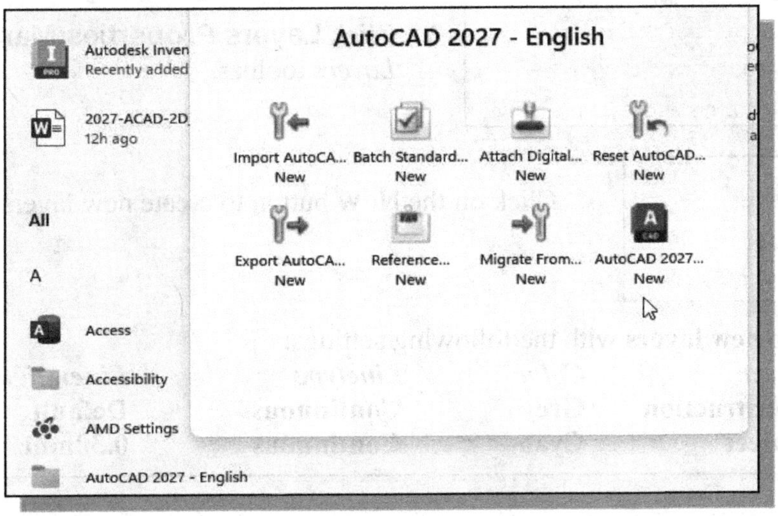

2. In the *Startup* window, select **Start from Scratch**, as shown in the figure below.

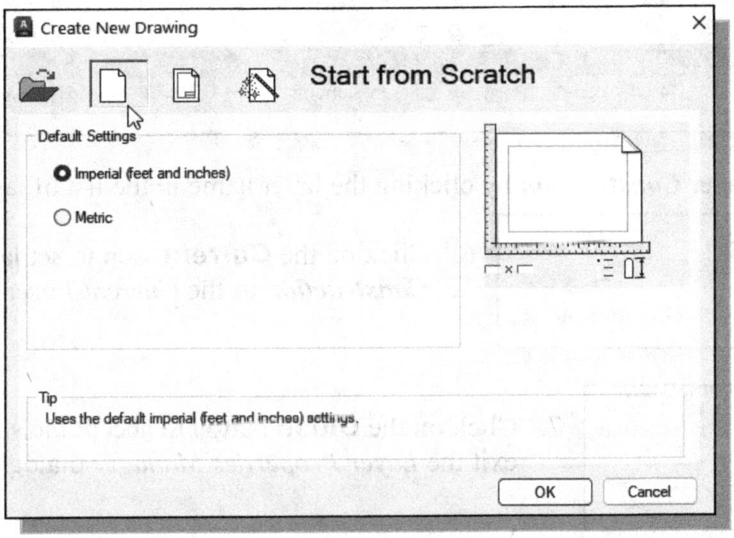

3. In the *Default Settings* section, pick **Imperial (feet and inches)** as the drawing units.

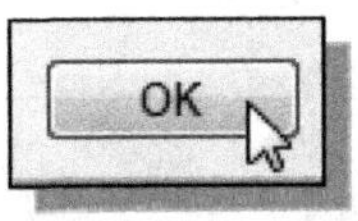

4. Pick **OK** in the *Startup* dialog box to accept the selected settings.

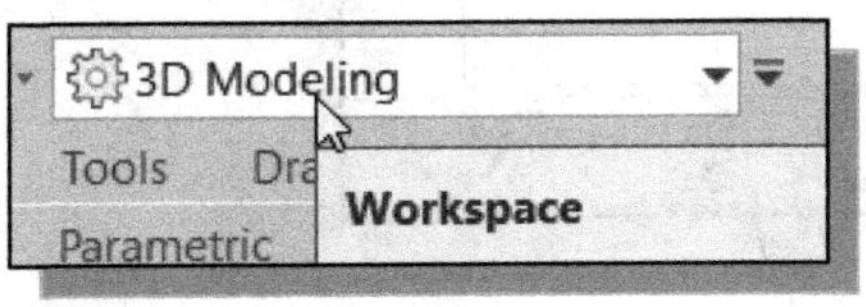

5. On your own, set the *workspace* to **3D Modeling** as shown.

Layers Setup

1. In the *Menu Bar*, select **[Tools] → Toolbars] → [AutoCAD] → [Layers]**.

2. Click **Layers Properties Manager** in the *Layers* toolbar.

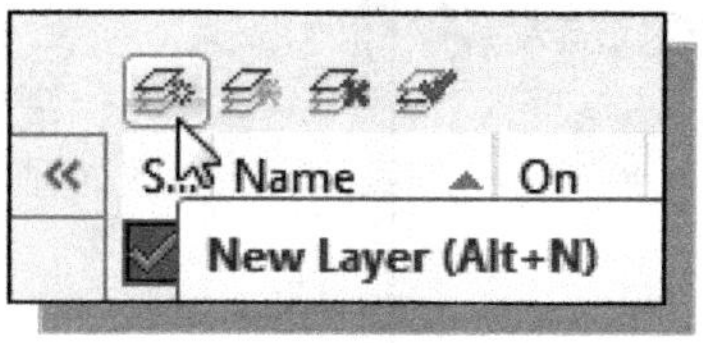

3. Click on the **New** button to create new layers.

4. Create **two new layers** with the following settings:

Layer	*Color*	*Linetype*	*Lineweight*
Construction	**Grey**	**Continuous**	**Default**
Object	**Cyan**	**Continuous**	**0.30mm**

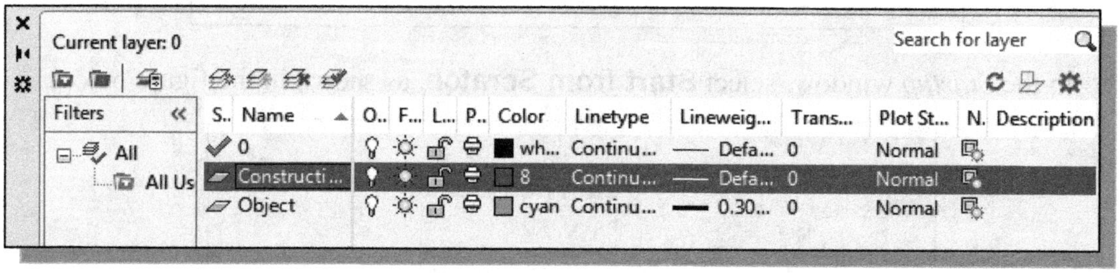

5. Select the layer ***Construction*** by clicking the layer name in the list of layers.

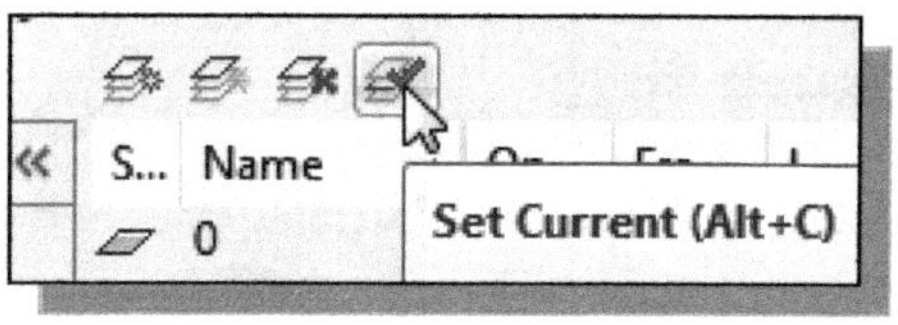

6. Click on the **Current** icon to set layer ***Construction*** as the *Current Layer*.

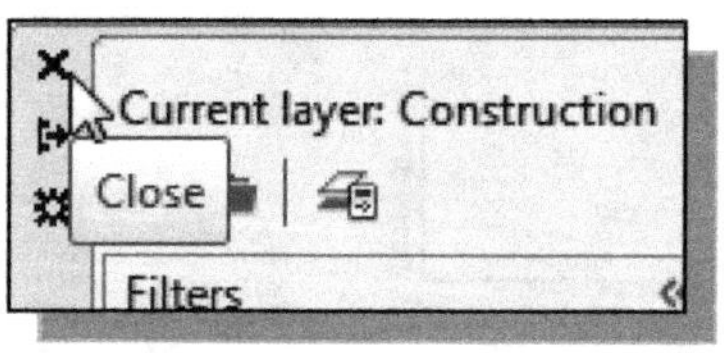

7. Click on the **Close** button to accept the settings and exit the *Layer Properties Manager* dialog box.

8. In the *Status Bar* area, reset the options and turn ***ON*** the *Grid display*, *Polar Tracking*, *Object Snap*, *Object Snap Tracking*, *Dynamic Input* and *Lineweight* options.

Setting Up a 2D Sketch

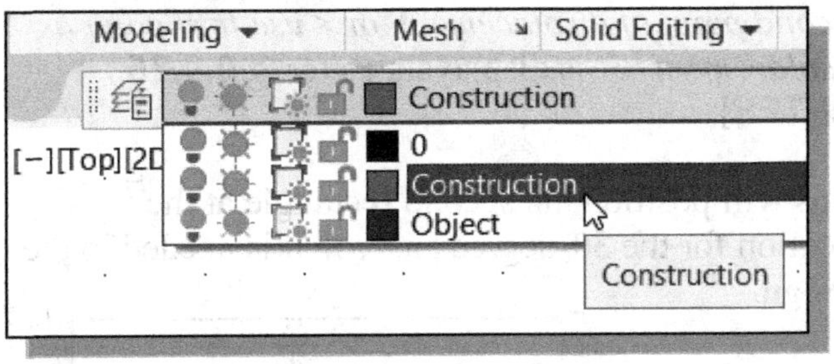

1. In the *Layer Control* box, confirm layer *Construction* is set as the *Current Layer*.

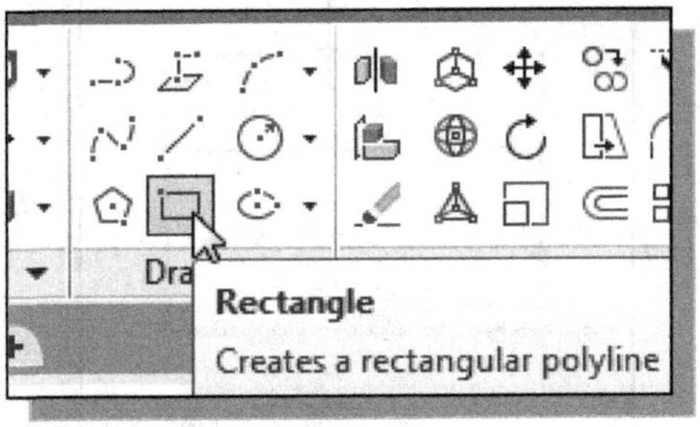

2. Select the **Rectangle** icon in the *Draw* toolbar. In the command prompt area, the message "*Specify first corner point or [Chamfer/ Elevation/Fillet/Thickness/Width]:*" is displayed.

3. Place the first corner point of the rectangle near the lower left corner of the screen. Do not be overly concerned about the actual coordinates of the selected location; the CAD drawing space is as big as you can imagine.

4. We will create a 3″ × 2.25″ rectangle. Enter **@3,2.25 [ENTER]**.

❖ The **Rectangle** command creates rectangles as *polyline* features, which means all segments of a rectangle are created as a single object.

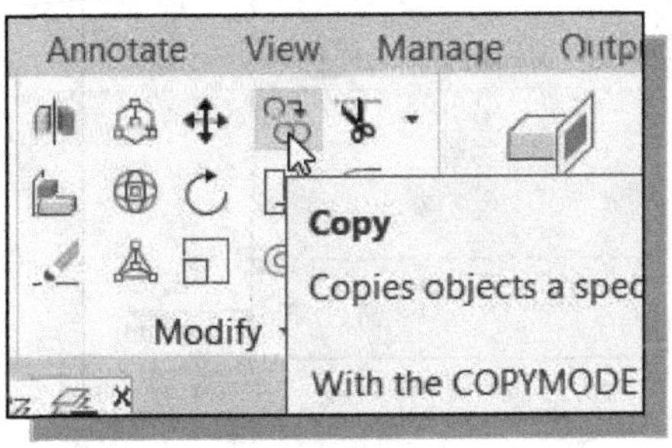

5. We will next make a copy of the rectangle. Pick **Copy Object** in the *Modify* toolbar.

6. Pick any edge of the rectangle we just created.

7. Inside the *graphics window*, **right-click** to accept the selection.

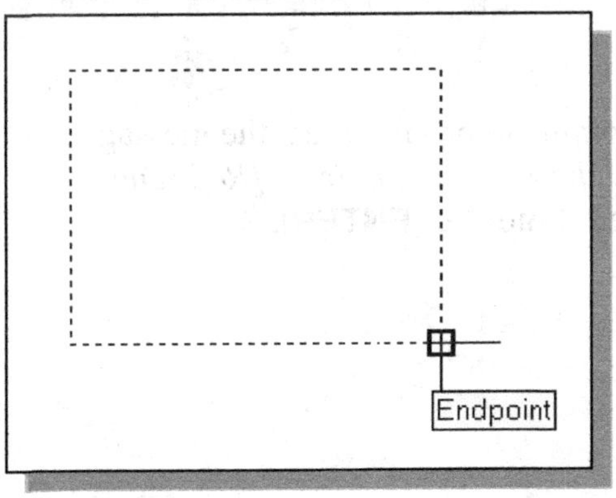

8. In the *command prompt* area, the message "*Specify base point or displacement, or [Multiple]:*" is displayed. Pick the **lower right corner** of the rectangle as the base point. A copy of the rectangle is attached to the cursor at the selected base point.

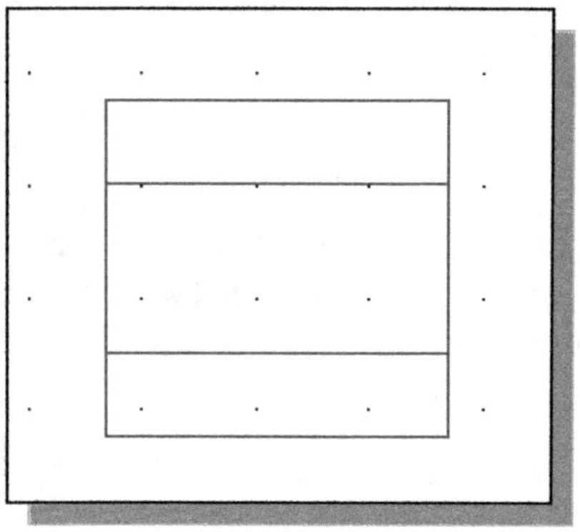

9. In the command prompt area, the message "*Specify second point of displacement, or <use first point as displacement>:*" is displayed. Enter **@0,0.75 [ENTER]**.

❖ This will position the second rectangle at the location for the 30-degree angle that is needed in the design.

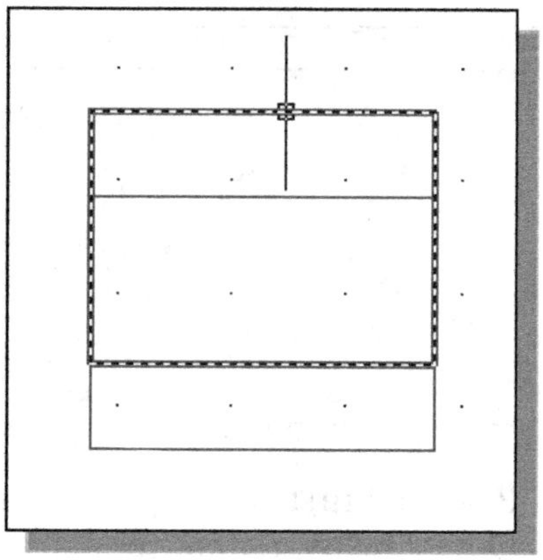

10. **Pre-select** the **copy** by picking the top horizontal line on the screen. The second rectangle, the copy we just created, is selected.

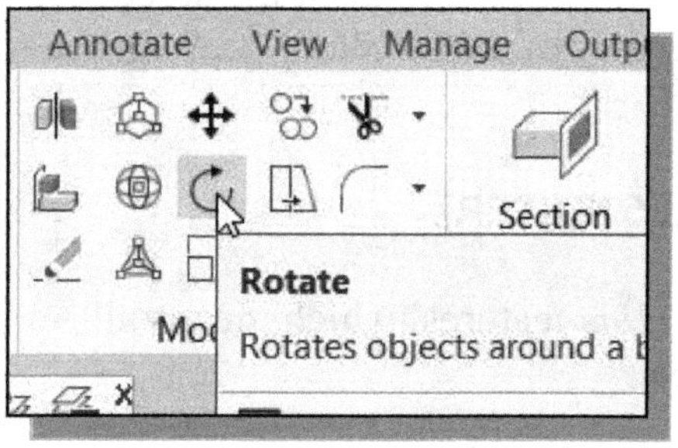

11. Pick **Rotate** in the *Modify* toolbar as shown.

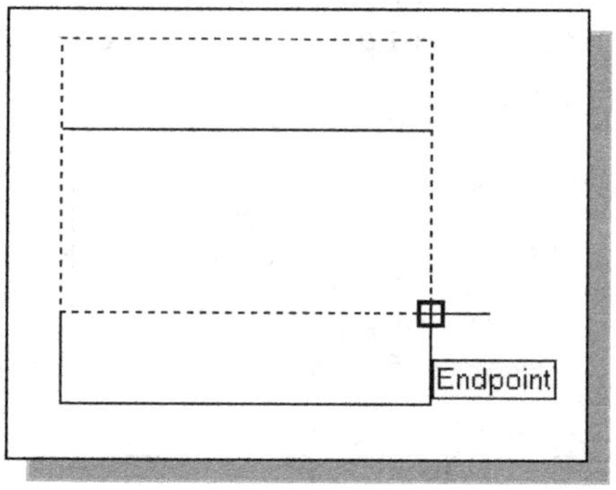

12. In the command prompt area, the message "*Specify base point:*" is displayed. Pick the lower right corner of the selected rectangle as the base point.

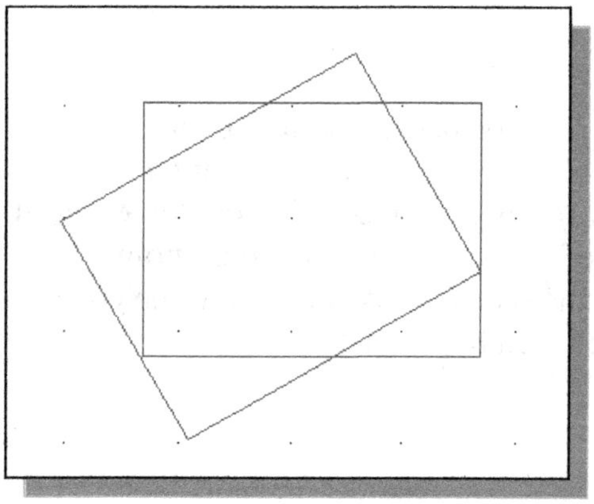

13. In the command prompt area, the message "*Specify the rotation angle or [Reference]:*" is displayed. Enter **30 [ENTER]**.

Defining the Front Edges of the Design

1. In the *Status Bar* area, **right-click** on the *POLAR* option to bring up the option menu.

2. Select **Settings** in the *option menu* as shown.

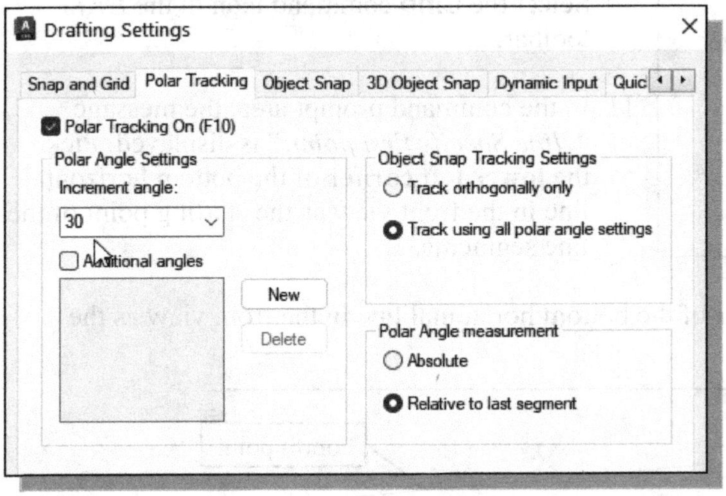

3. In the *Drafting Settings* window, confirm the *Increment angle* is set to **30** in the *Polar Angle Settings* area.

4. Switch ***ON*** the **Track using all polar angle settings** and **Relative to last segment** options as shown.

5. In the *Drafting Settings* window, click on the **Object Snap** tab to display and set the *Object Snap* options.

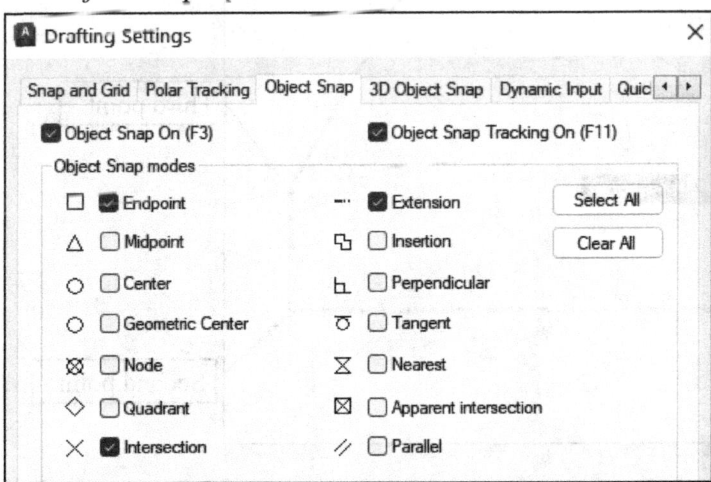

6. On your own, reset the *Object Snap modes* so that only the **Endpoint**, **Extension**, **Intersection** and **Perpendicular** are switched ***ON*** as shown in the figure.

7. In the *Drafting Settings* window, click **OK** to accept the settings.

- The AutoCAD *AutoTrack*[TM] feature includes two tracking options: *POLAR* tracking and *OBJECT SNAP* tracking. When these options are turned on, alignment markers are displayed to help us create objects at precise positions and angles.

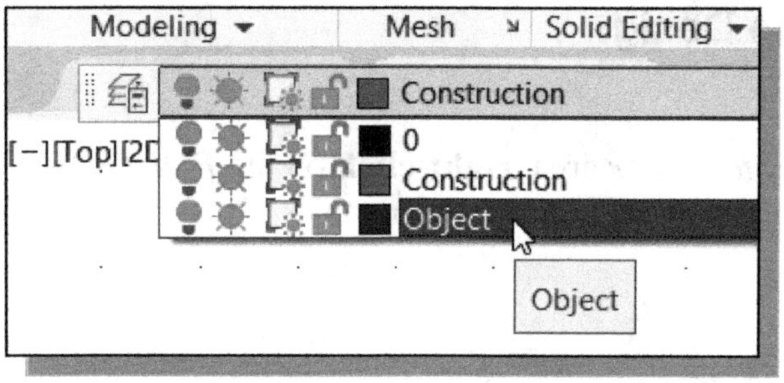

8. On the *Object Properties* toolbar, choose the *Layer Control* box with the left-mouse-button.

9. Move the cursor over the name of layer *Object*; the tool tip "*Object*" appears. **Left-click once** and layer *Object* is set as the *Current Layer*.

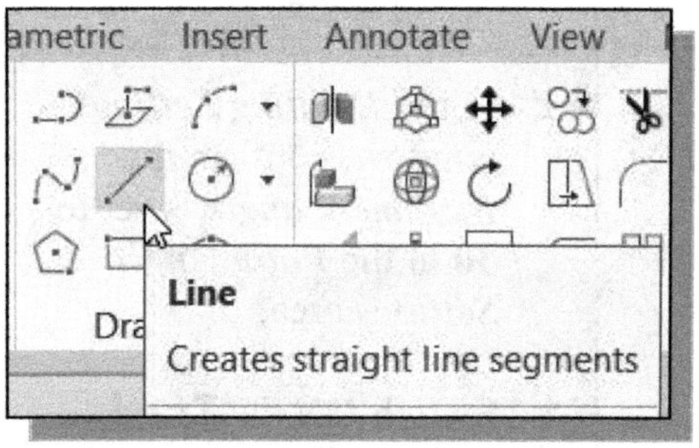

10. Select the **Line** command icon in the *Draw* toolbar.

11. In the command prompt area, the message "*_line Specify first point:*" is displayed. Pick the **lower left corner** of the bottom horizontal line in the front view as the starting point of the line segments.

12. Pick the **lower right corner** of the bottom horizontal line in the front view as the second point.

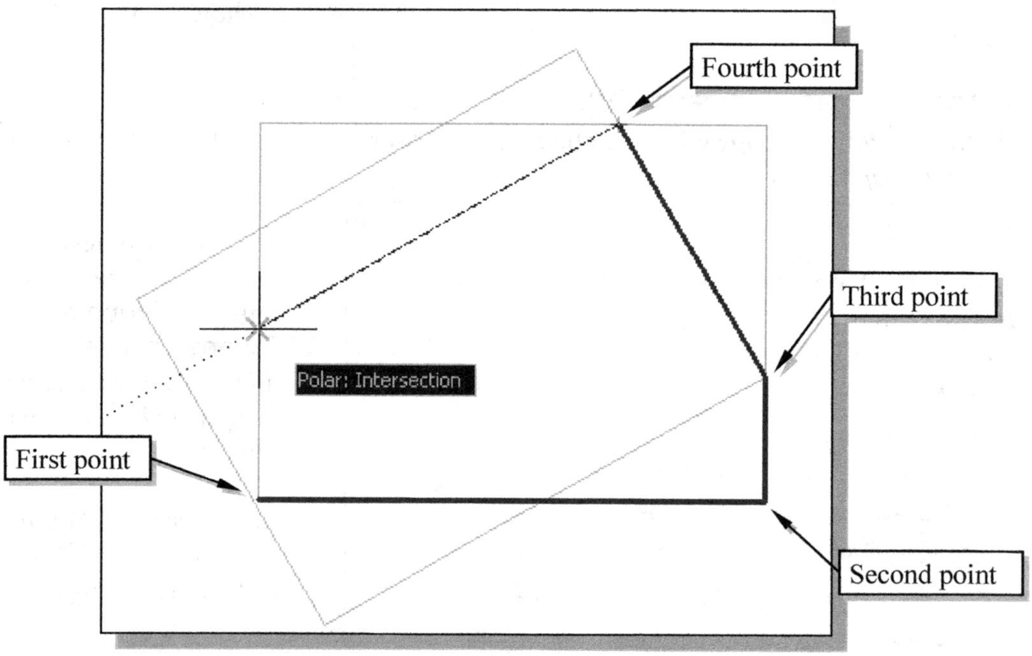

13. Select the **third** and **fourth** points as shown in the figure below.

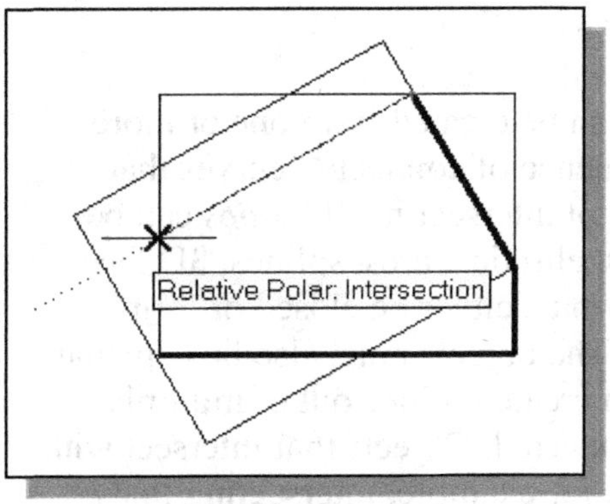

14. Move the cursor near the left vertical line and notice the *AutoTrack* feature automatically snaps the cursor to the intersection point.

15. Left-click at the intersection point as shown.

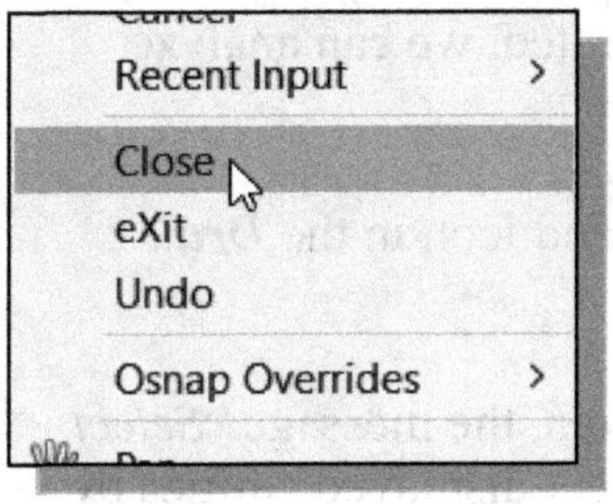

16. Inside the graphics window, right-click once to bring up the pop-up menu.

17. Pick **Close** in the pop-up menu. The Close option will create a line segment connecting the last point to the first point of the line sequence.

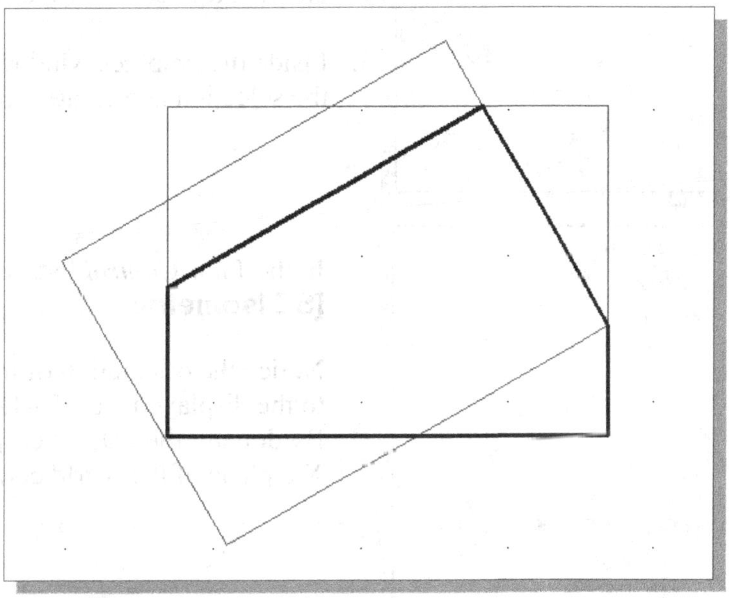

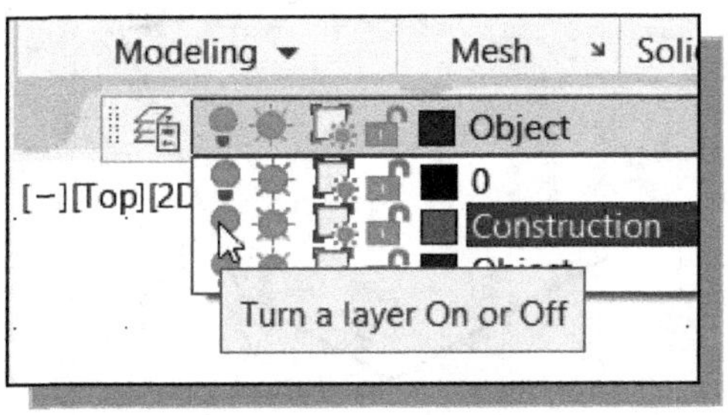

18. On your own, turn ***OFF*** the display of the ***Construction Layer*** by using the left-mouse-button.

19. Move the cursor into the graphics window and **left-click once** to accept the layer control settings.

Create a Region

In AutoCAD, **regions** are 2D enclosed areas, which can be created from one or more closed shapes called **loops**. A *loop* is a curve or a sequence of connected curves that defines an area on a plane with a boundary that does not intersect itself. *Loops* can be combinations of lines, polylines, circles, arcs, ellipses, elliptical arcs, splines, 3D faces, traces, and solids. The objects that make up the loops must either be closed or form closed areas by sharing endpoints with other objects. The objects must also be coplanar, which means they must be on the same plane. We can create regions out of multiple loops and out of open curves whose endpoints are connected. Objects that intersect with themselves or with other objects cannot form regions, for example, intersecting lines, intersecting arcs or self-intersecting curves. Once a region is created, we can analyze properties such as its area and moments of inertia.

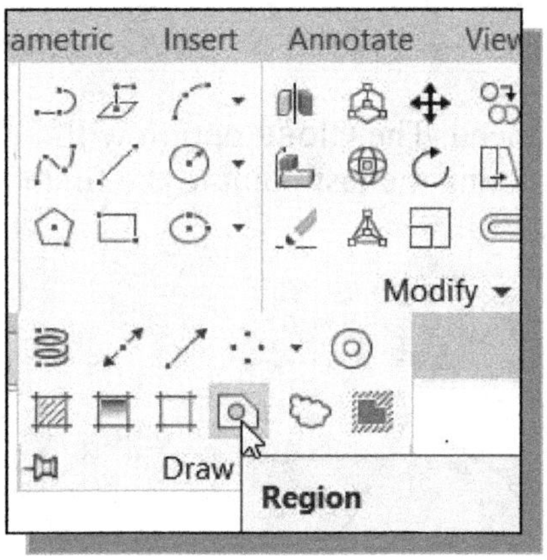

1. Select the **Region** command icon in the *Draw* toolbar.

2. In the command prompt area, the message "*Select objects:*" is displayed. Select displayed entities by creating a *selection window* enclosing **all objects.**

3. Inside the graphics window, **right-click** to accept the selection and create a region.

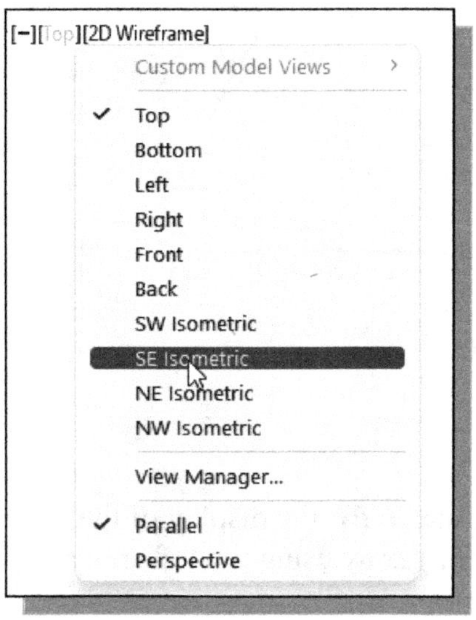

4. In the *View Control* list, select: **[SE Isometric]**

- Notice the orientation of the 2D region in relation to the displayed AutoCAD user coordinate system. By default, the 2D sketch-plane is aligned to the XY plane of the world coordinate system.

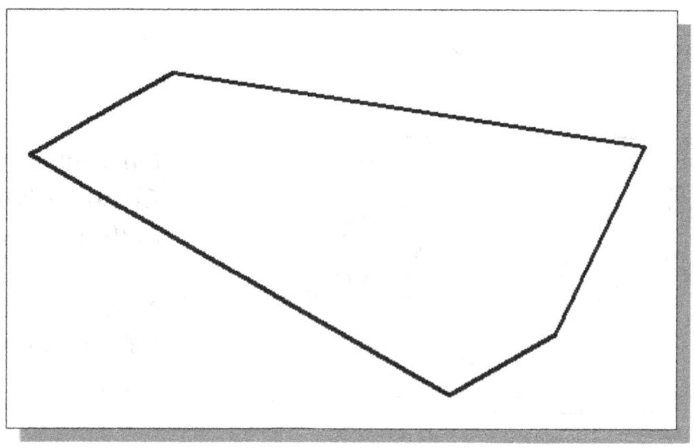

Extruding the Created Region

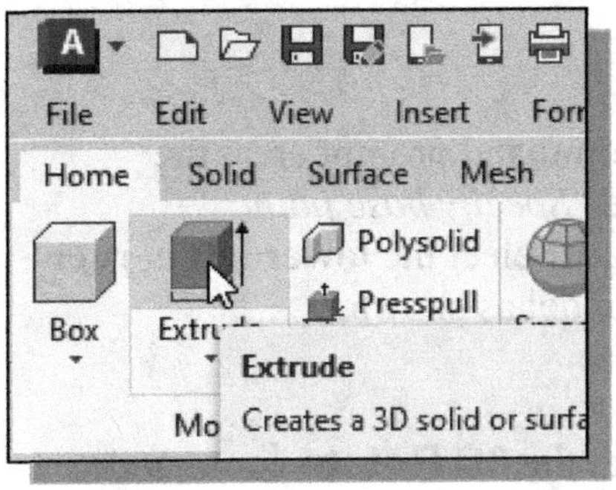

1. Select **Extrude** in the *3D Modeling* toolbar as shown.

2. In the command prompt area, the message "*Select objects:*" is displayed. Select the region by clicking on any of the displayed segments.

3. Inside the *graphics window*, **right-click** to accept the selection and select **Enter** to proceed with the extrude command.

4. In the *command prompt area*, the message "*Specify height of extrusion or [path]:*" is displayed. We will extrude the region in the upward direction; enter **2.0 [ENTER]**.

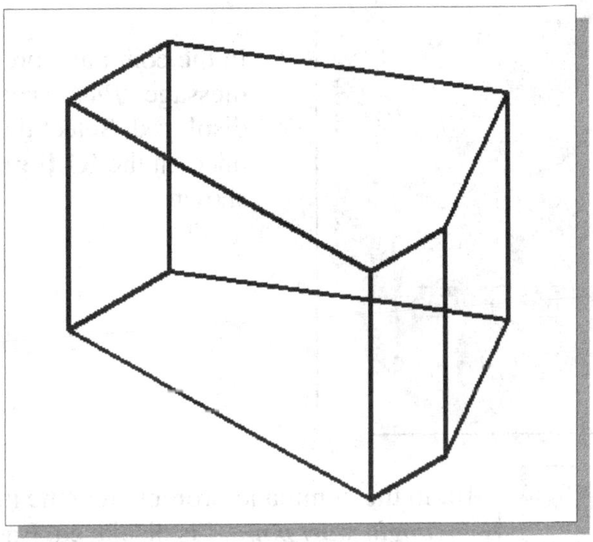

- Note that the orientation and position of solid models, in relation to the world coordinate system, can be adjusted using the Move and 3D Rotate commands.

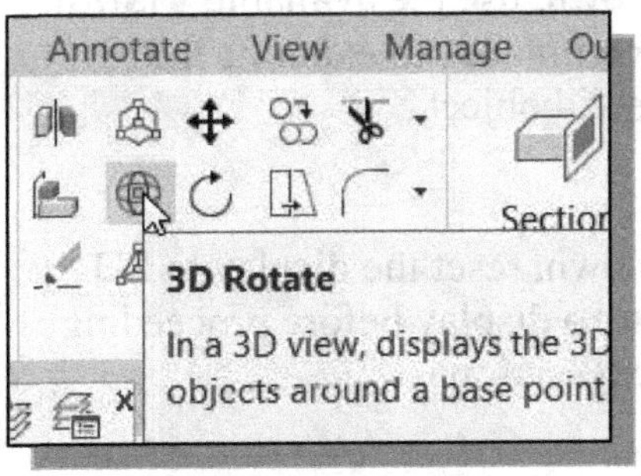

5. Select **3D Rotate** in the *Modify* toolbar as shown.

6. In the *command prompt area*, the message "*Select objects:*" is displayed. Select the solid model by clicking on any of the displayed edges of the model.

7. Inside the graphics window, **right-click** to accept the selection and proceed with the **3D Rotate** command.

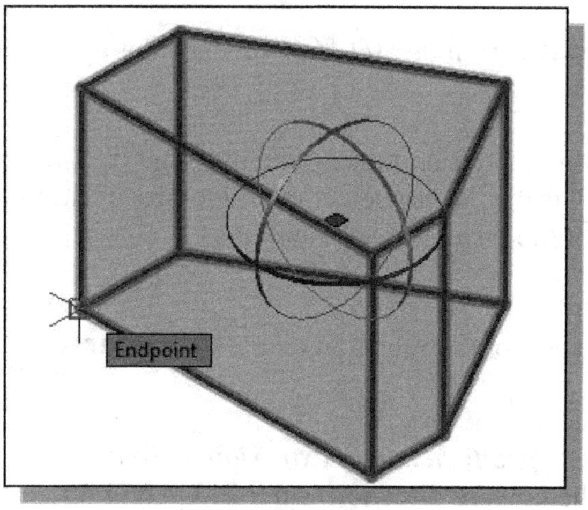

8. In the command prompt area, the message *"Specify base point:" is displayed.* Select the **lower left corner** of the model as shown.

- Note that the **3D Rotate** command requires the definition of a *base point, a rotation axis and the angle of rotation.*

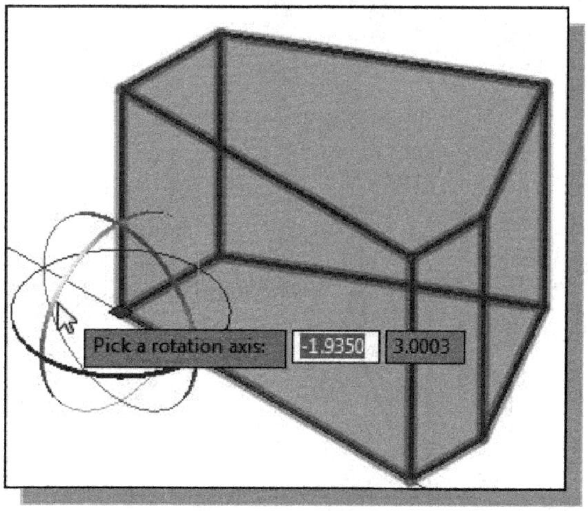

9. In the command prompt area, the message *"Pick a rotation axis:"* is displayed. Select the X-axis by clicking once on the **RED grip rotate handle** as shown.

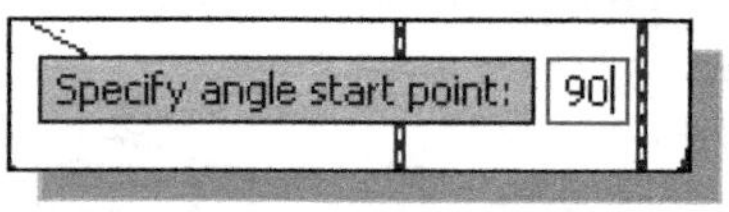

10. In the command prompt area, the message *"Specify angle start point:"* is displayed. Enter **90 [ENTER]**.

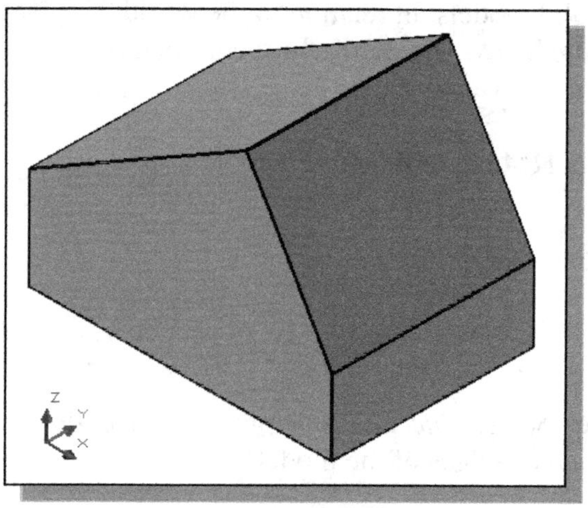

11. On your own, use the available **Visual Styles** commands to examine the created solid object.

12. On your own, reset the display to **2D Wireframe** display before proceeding to the next section.

Create a 2D Sketch at the Base of the Model

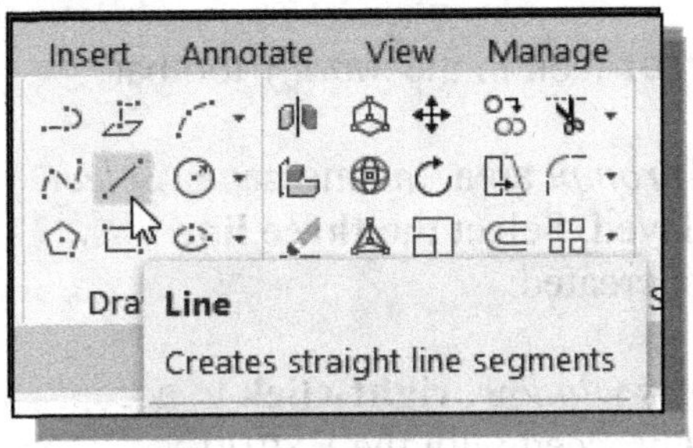

1. Select the **Line** command icon in the *Draw* toolbar. In the command prompt area, the message "*_line Specify first point:*" is displayed.

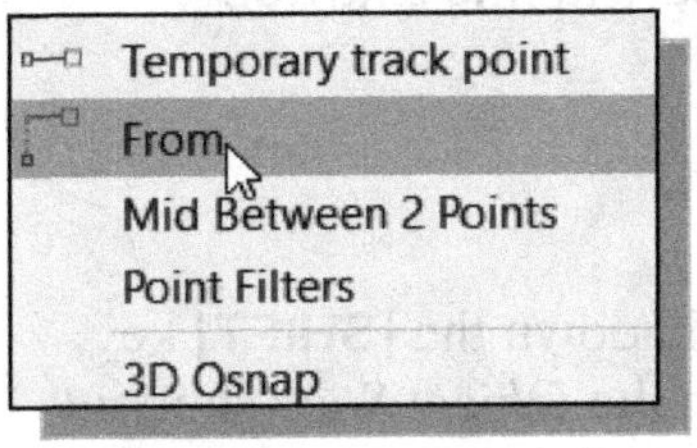

2. Inside the graphics window, hold down the **[SHIFT]** key and **right-click** once to bring up the *Object Snap* shortcut menu.

3. Select the **From** option in the pop-up window.

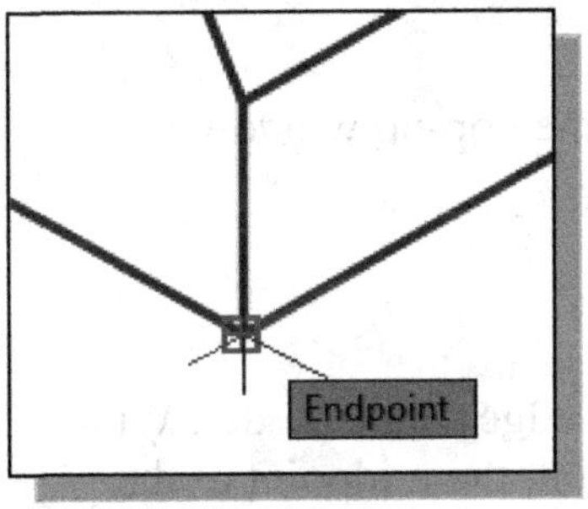

4. Pick the **lower right corner** of the solid model as the base point as shown in the figure.

5. We will place the first point above the selected corner. Enter **@0,0.75 [ENTER]**.

- Note the orientation of the world XY plane.

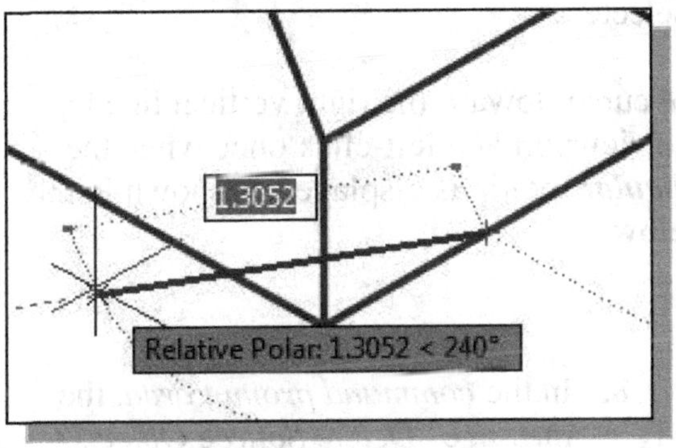

6. In the command prompt area, the message "*Specify next point or [Undo]:*" is displayed. Using the *POLAR Tracking* option (30 degrees increment), create a line that is about 1.3 inches long, as shown in the figure.

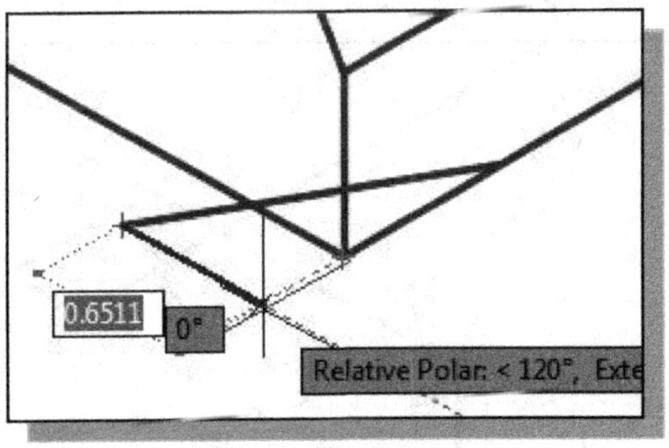

7. Move the cursor on top of the starting point of the last line to activate the *OTRACK* option and select the location that forms a 90-degrees angle as shown.

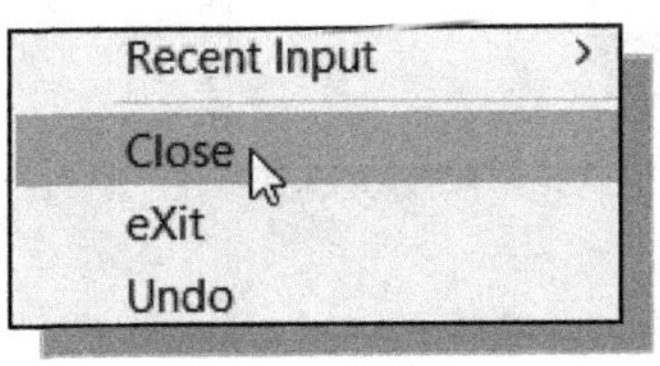

8. Inside the graphics window, right-click to activate the option menu and select **Close** with the left-mouse-button to create a line connecting to the starting point and end the **Line** command.

Create a Mirrored copy of the 2D Sketch

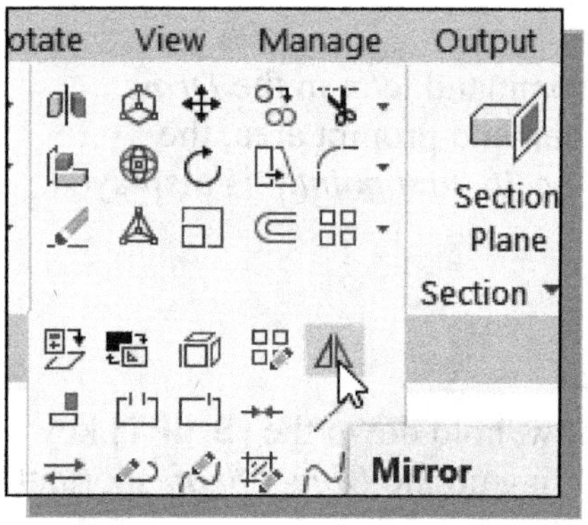

1. Click on the **Mirror** icon in the *Modify* toolbar.

2. In the *command prompt* area, the message "*Select objects:*" is displayed. Select the **three line segments** we just created.

3. Inside the *graphics window*, **right-click** to accept the selection and proceed with the Extrude command.

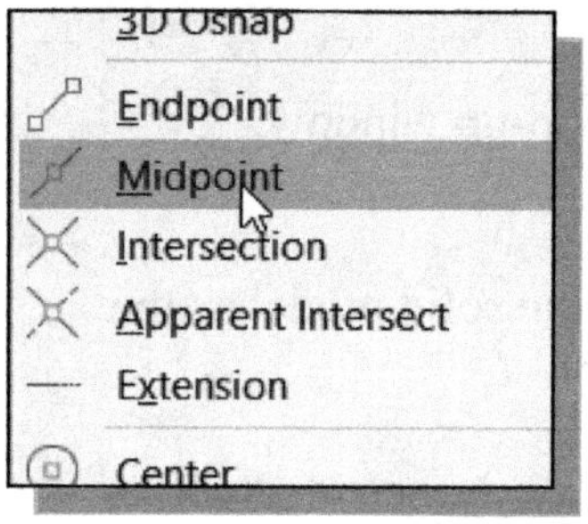

4. Inside the graphics window, hold down the [**SHIFT**] key and **right-click** once to bring up the *Object Snap* shortcut menu.

5. Select the **Midpoint** option in the pop-up window.

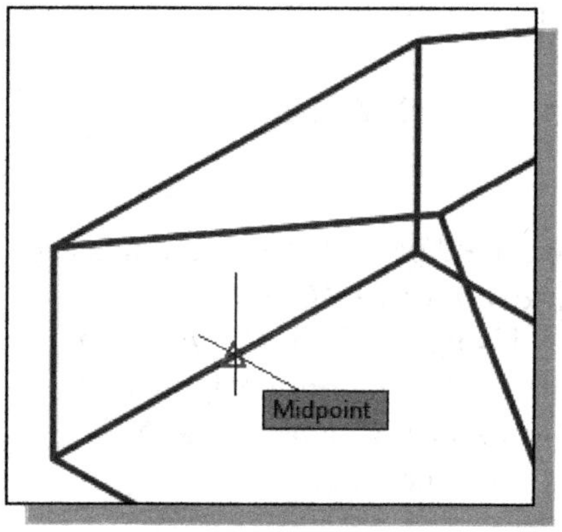

6. Click on the bottom left edge of the model. With the *Midpoint SNAP* option, the midpoint of the edge is selected.

7. Move the cursor toward the right vertical line in the active viewport and left-click once when the ***Perpendicular*** tooltip is displayed as shown in the figure below.

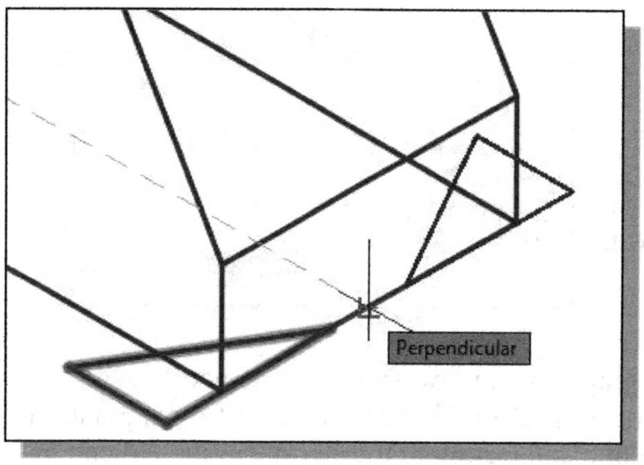

8. In the *command prompt area*, the message "*Delete Source Objects? [Yes/No] <N>:*" is displayed. In the displayed option list, select **No** to keep both sets of objects.

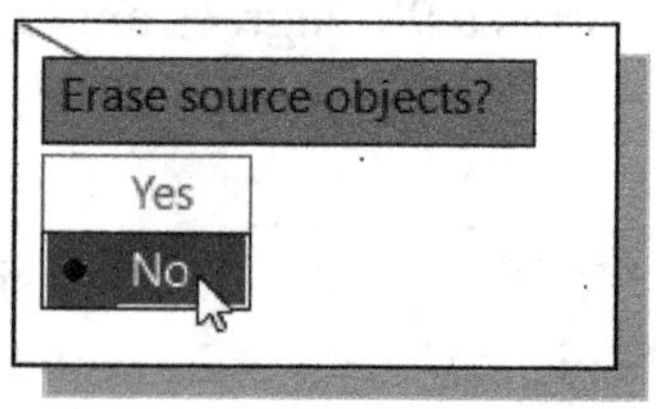

Create the Cutter Solids

The two triangular shapes will be extruded in the Z-direction to form two solids that can be used to create the two vertical cuts.

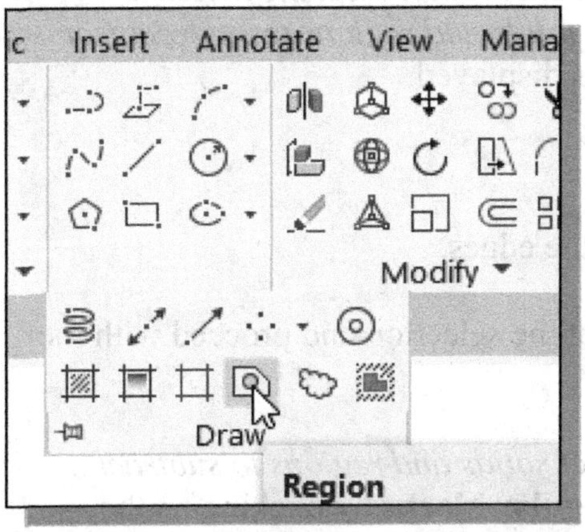

1. Select the **Region** command icon in the *Draw* toolbar.

2. In the command prompt area, the message "*Select objects:*" is displayed. Select the **six line segments** we just created by using a selection window.

3. Inside the graphics window, **right-click** to accept the selection and create two regions.

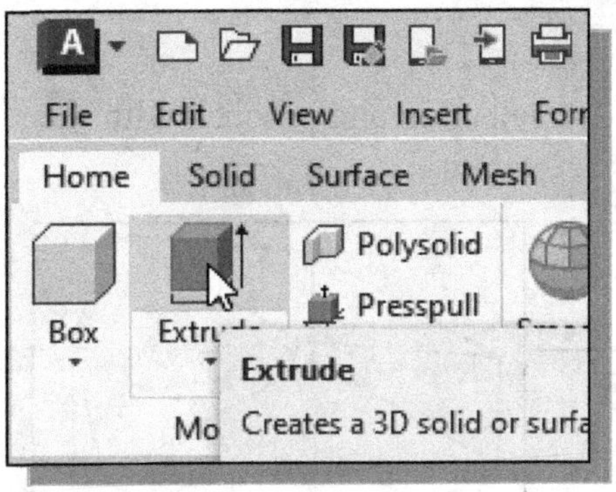

4. Select **Extrude** in the *3D Modeling* toolbar as shown.

5. In the command prompt area, the message "*Select objects:*" is displayed. Select the **two regions** by clicking on the **two triangular regions**.

6. Inside the graphics window, right-click and select **Enter** to accept the selection and procced with the Extrude command.

7. In the command prompt area, the message "*Specify height of extrusion or [path]:*" is displayed. We will extrude the regions in the upward direction; enter **2.5 [ENTER]**.

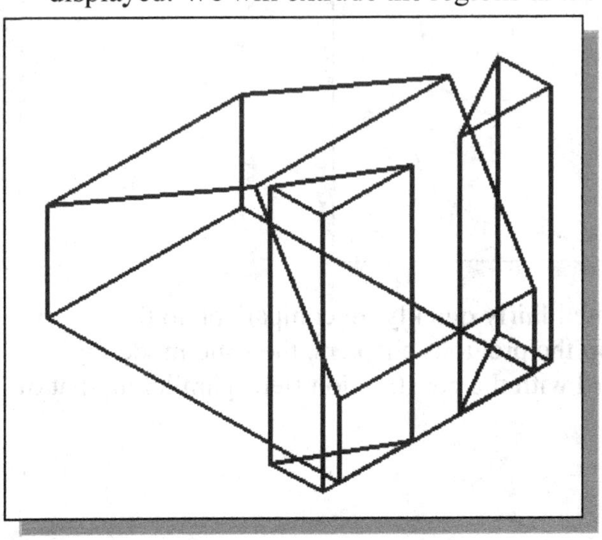

- Note that the two cutters were intentionally made larger than the dimensions shown on the design. In fact, we could create a single cutter, instead of the two we have created, provided the two triangular shapes are included and positioned at the proper locations.

Boolean Operation – Subtract

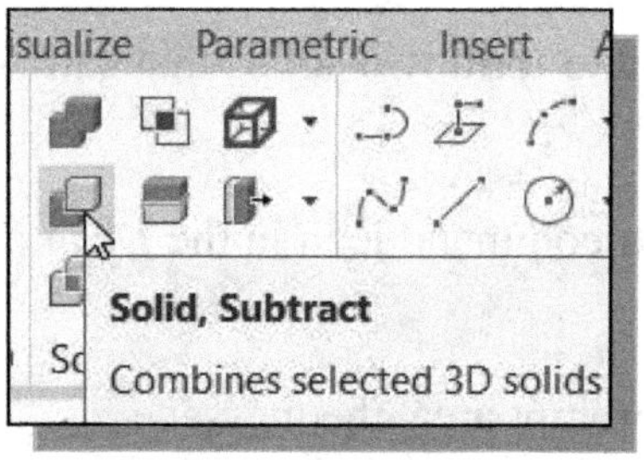

1. In the *Solid Editing* toolbar, click on the **Subtract** icon. In the command prompt area, the message "*_subtract Select solids and regions to subtract from ... Select Objects:*" is displayed.

2. Pick the **base block** solid by clicking on one of the edges.

3. Inside the *graphics window*, **right-click** to accept the selection and proceed with the **Subtract** command.

4. In the command prompt area, the message "*Select solids and regions to subtract... Select Objects:*" is displayed. Pick the **two triangular blocks** by clicking on the edges of the two cutters.

5. Inside the *graphics window*, **right-click** to accept the selection and proceed with the **Subtract** command.

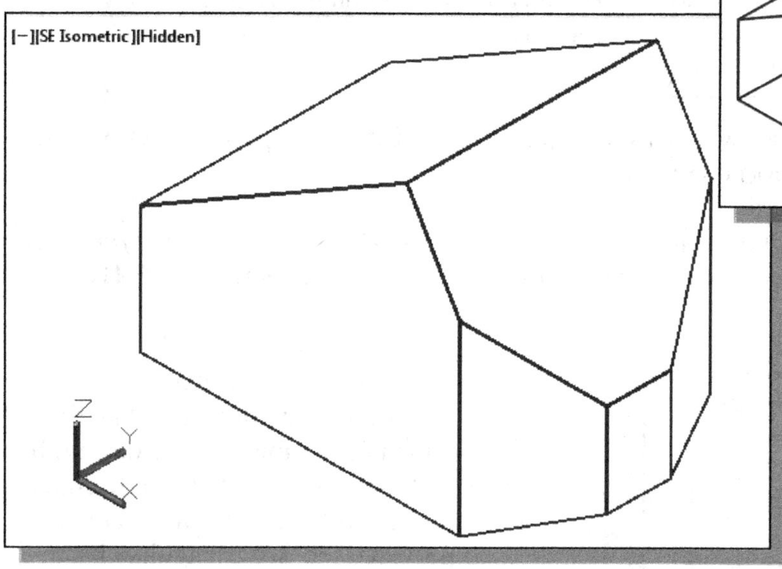

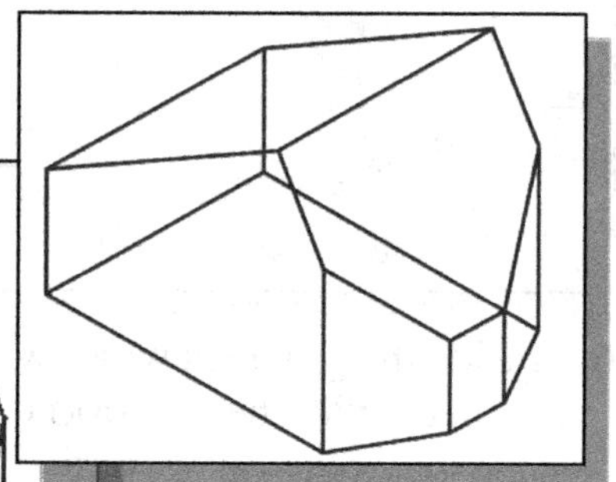

- Note that the two cut features are created fairly quickly. In comparison to the wireframe or surface models created in the previous chapters, the solid modeling approach is much more straightforward with the construction steps paralleling that of the manufacturing processes.

Mass Properties of the Solid Model

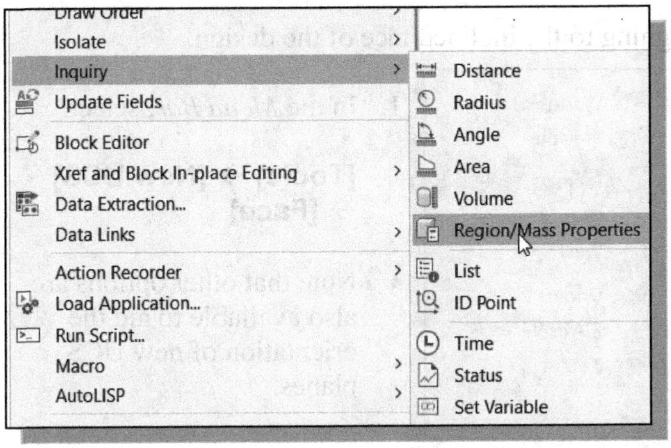

1. In the *Menu Bar*, select:

   [Tools] → [Inquiry] → [Region/Mass Properties]

2. In the *command prompt area*, the message "*Select objects:*" is displayed. Select the **solid model** by clicking on any of the displayed edges of the solid model.

3. Inside the graphics window, right-click to accept the selection and proceed with the Region/Mass Properties command.

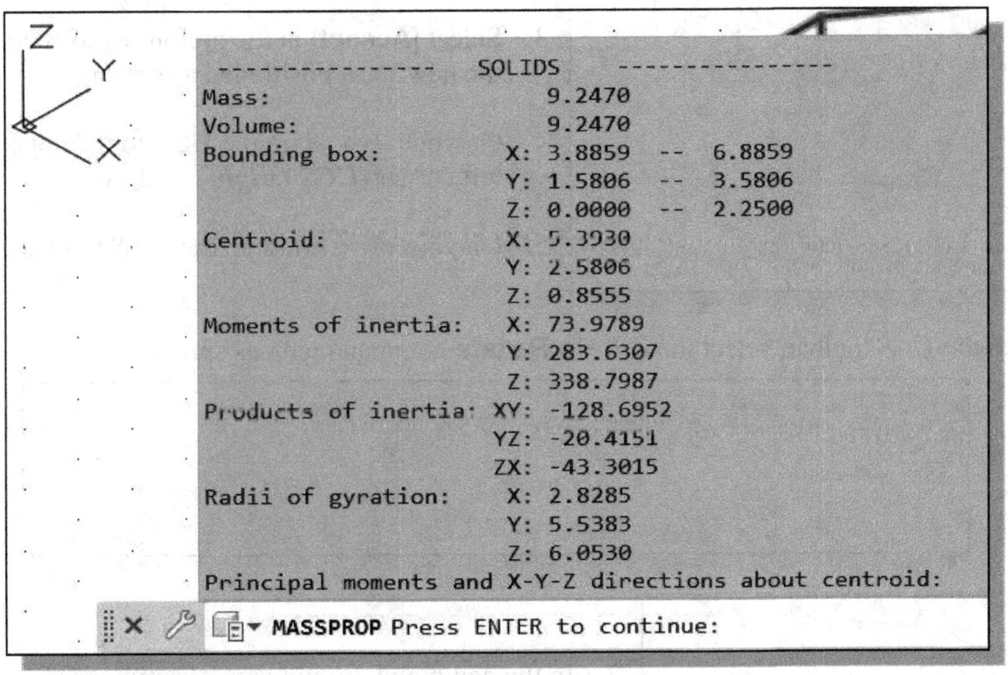

- In the *AutoCAD Text Window*, a list of properties related to the created solid model is displayed. The *Mass* and *Volume* properties are listed as the same since a mass density of one is used for the calculation.

4. Press the **[ENTER]** key twice to close the *AutoCAD Text Panel*.

Align the UCS to the Inclined Face

We will create a new UCS plane aligning to the inclined face of the design.

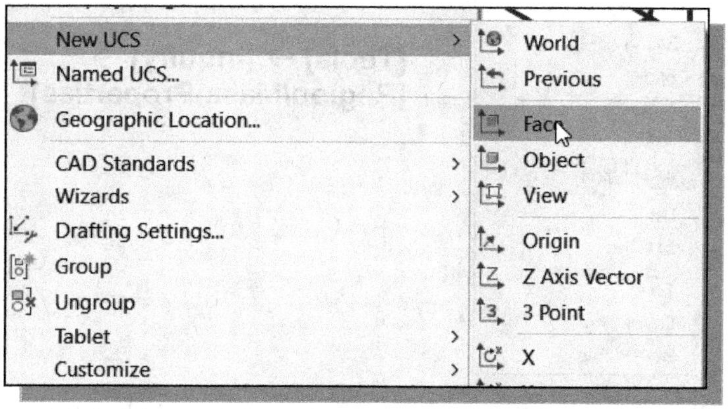

1. In the *Menu Bar*, select:

   [Tools] → [New UCS] → [Face]

- Note that other options are also available to aid the orientation of new UCS planes.

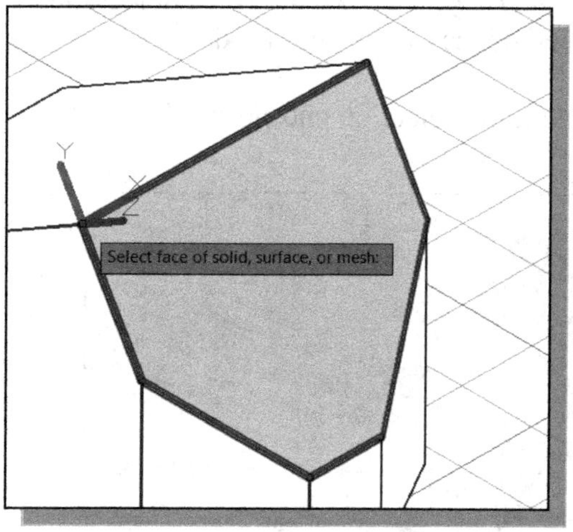

2. In the command prompt area, the message "*Select face of solid object:*" is displayed. Pick the upper left corner of the **inclined face** when the UCS is aligned as shown.

3. Select **[Accept]** in the option list to accept the new UCS positioned as shown.

4. On your own, align the UCS to the upper left corner (***UCS Origin***) as shown.

5. On your own, bring up the ***UCS*** toolbar.

6. In the *UCS* toolbar, select the **Z Axis Rotate** command icon as shown.

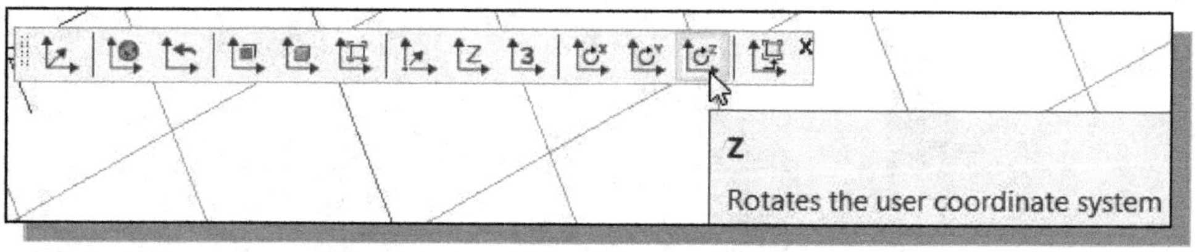

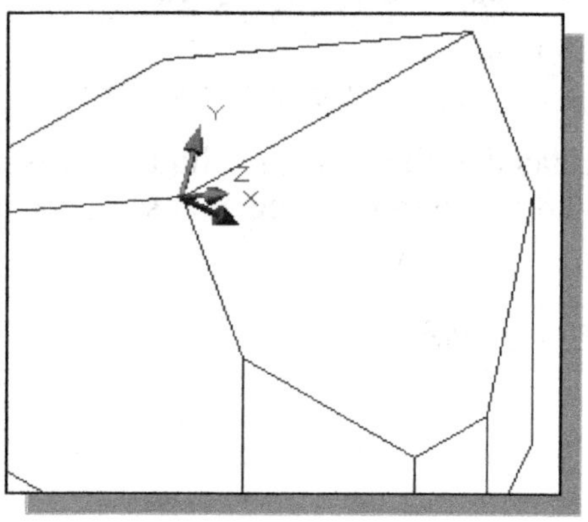

7. In the command prompt area, the message "*Specify rotation angle about Z-axis <90>:*" is displayed. Enter **-45 [ENTER]**.

- The negative value entered rotates the UCS clockwise about the current UCS Z-axis.

Create the V-Cut

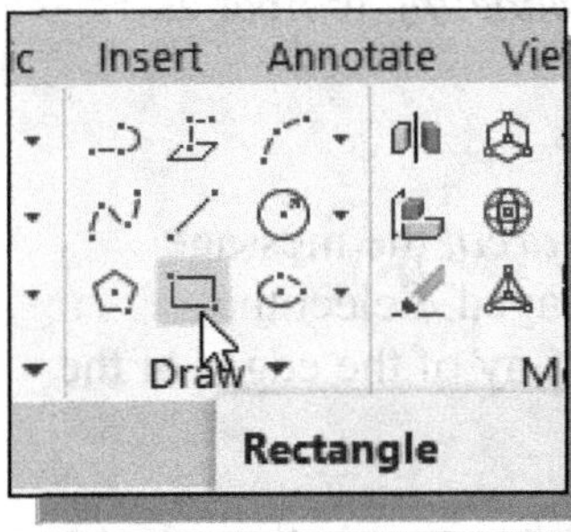

1. Select the **Rectangle** icon in the *Draw* toolbar. In the command prompt area, the message "*Specify first corner point or [Chamfer/Elevation/Fillet/Thickness/Width]:*" is displayed.

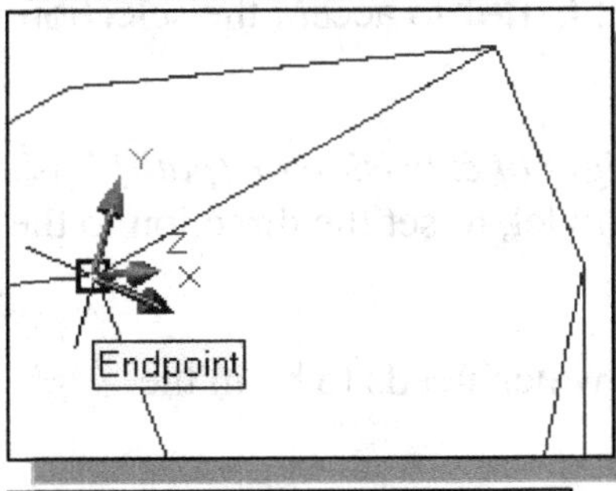

- Note that the upper left corner of the inclined surface is the origin of the current coordination.

2. We will place the first point along the top edge of the inclined face.

   Enter **0.2<45 [ENTER]**.

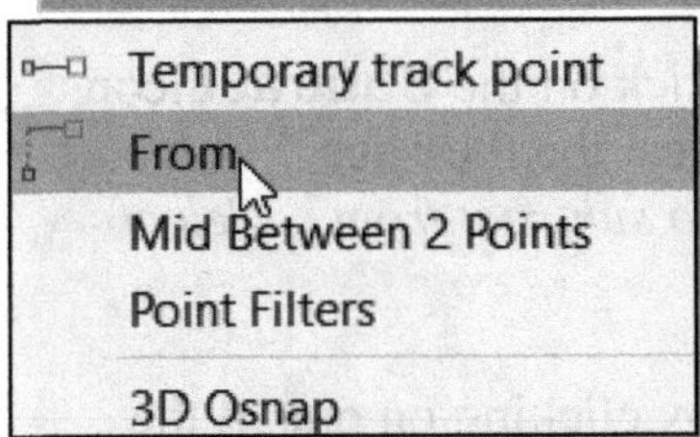

3. Inside the graphics window, hold down the **[SHIFT]** key and right-click once to bring up the *Object Snap* shortcut menu.

4. Select the **From** option in the pop-up window.

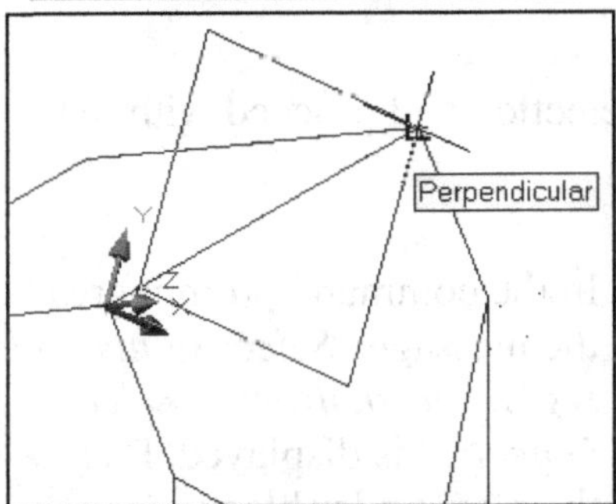

5. Pick the upper right corner of the inclined surface as the base point as shown in the figure.

6. We will place the first point above the selected corner. Enter **@0.2<-135 [ENTER]**.

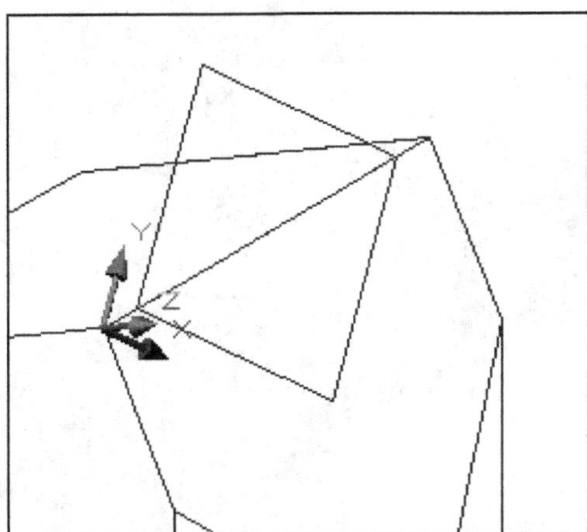

- The above procedure of creating the rectangle at the proper location is simplified by first orienting the UCS.

❖ Note that a rectangle is a valid filled polygon and therefore can be extruded into a solid object.

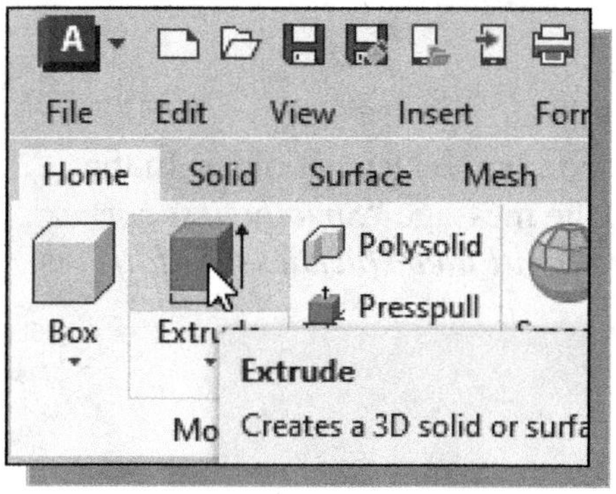

7. Select **Extrude** in the *Modeling* toolbar as shown.

8. In the *command prompt area*, the message "*Select objects:*" is displayed. Select the rectangle by clicking on any of the edges of the created rectangle.

9. Inside the *graphics window*, **right-click** once and select **Enter** to accept the selection and proceed with the Extrude command.

10. In the *command prompt area*, the message "*Specify height of extrusion or [path]:*" is displayed. We will extrude toward the left side of the model, to set the direction to the **negative** extrusion direction: **4.0 [ENTER]**.

- The negative number indicates the extrusion direction, which needs to be in the negative Z-direction of the current UCS.

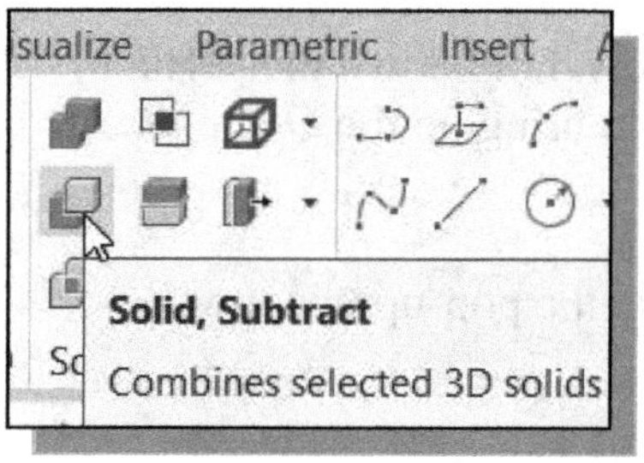

11. In the *Modeling* toolbar, click on the **Subtract** icon. In the command prompt area, the message "*_subtract Select solids and regions to subtract from ... Select Objects:*" is displayed.

12. Pick the base solid block by clicking on one of the edges.

13. Inside the graphics window, right-click to accept the selection and proceed with the **Subtract** command.

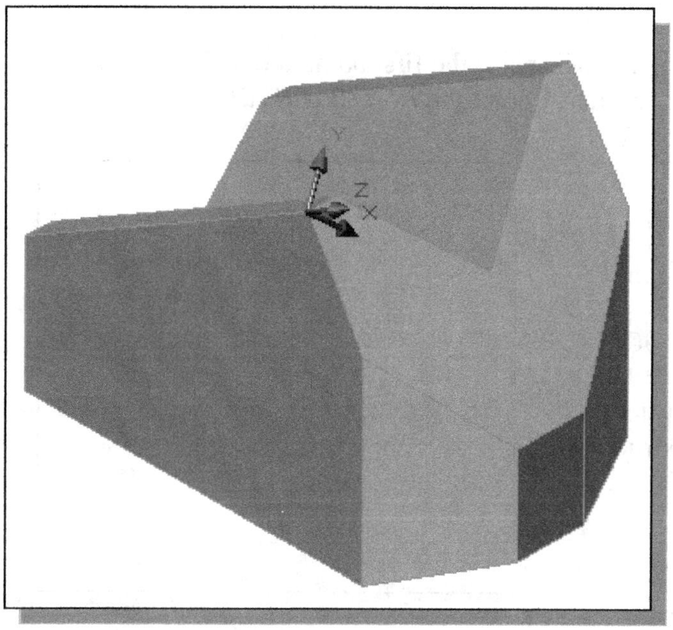

14. In the command prompt area, the message "*Select solids and regions to subtract ... Select Objects:*" is displayed. Pick the rectangular block.

15. Inside the graphics window, right-click to accept the selection and proceed with the Subtract command.

- On your own, use the dynamic viewing commands to examine the completed solid model.

16. In the *UCS* toolbar, select the **World UCS** command icon as shown.

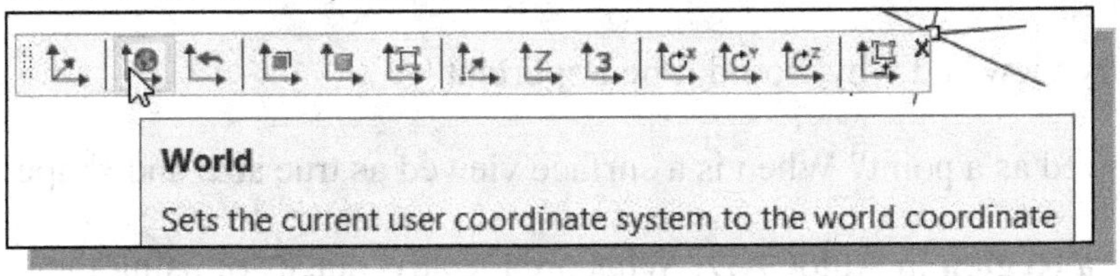

- The World UCS command aligns the UCS to the world coordinate system.

17. In the *Menu Bar*, select:
    [Tools] → [Inquiry] → [Region/Mass Properties]

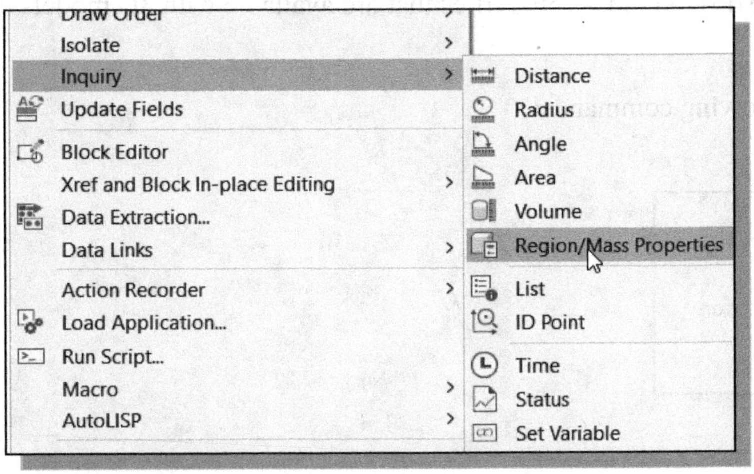

18. In the *command prompt area*, the message "*Select objects:*" is displayed. Select the solid model by clicking on any of the displayed edges of the model.

19. Inside the *graphics window*, **right-click** to accept the selection. On your own, compare the displayed values to those shown on page 7-17.

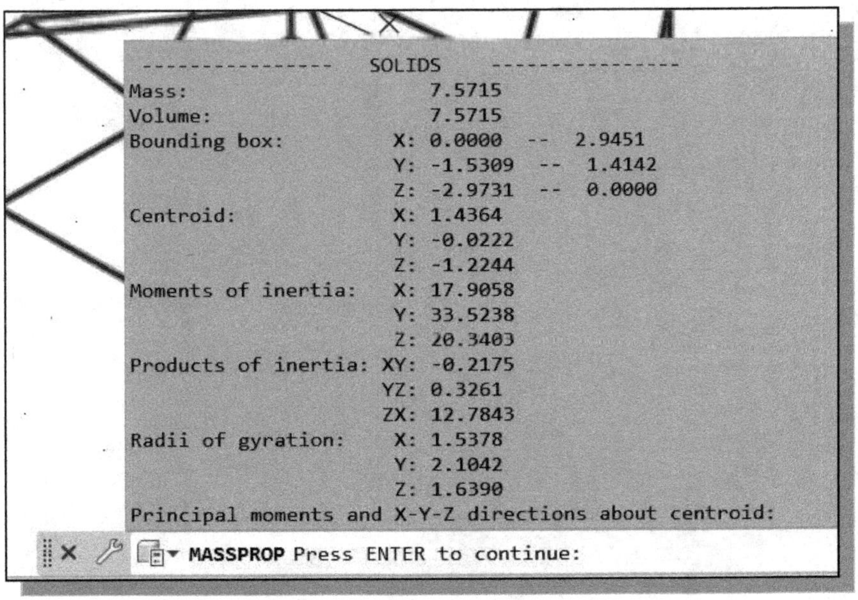

Review Questions:

1. What is an auxiliary view and why would it be important?

2. When is a line viewed as a point? When is a surface viewed as true size and shape?

3. How do we define a **Region** in AutoCAD? What are the advantages of using the Regions?

4. How is a **Solid Model** different from a **Surface Model**?

5. List some of the different mass properties that are available with 3D models in AutoCAD.

6. Identify the following commands:

(a)

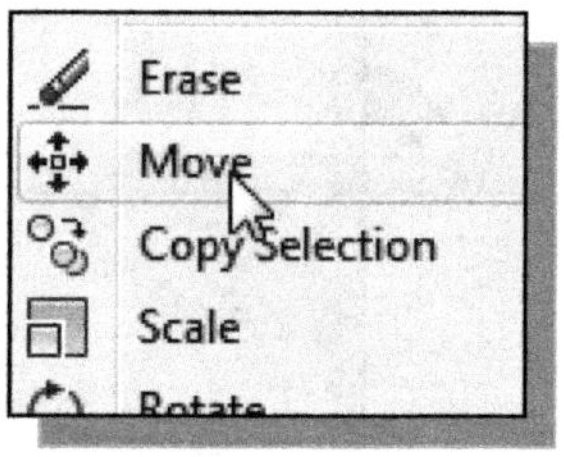

(b)

(c)

(d)

Exercises: All dimensions are in inches.

1. The overall height of the design is 2.5.

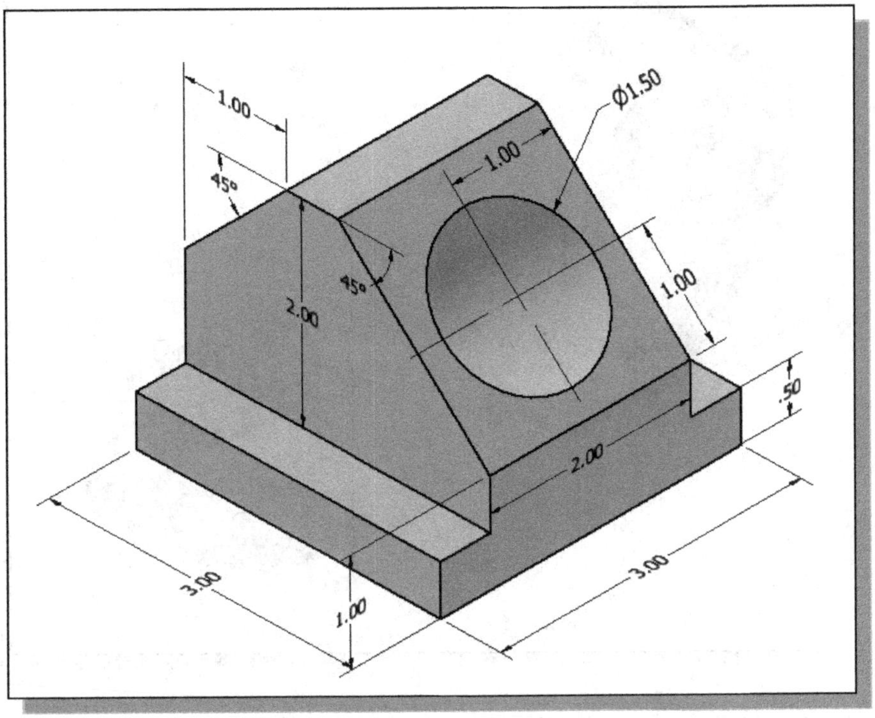

2.

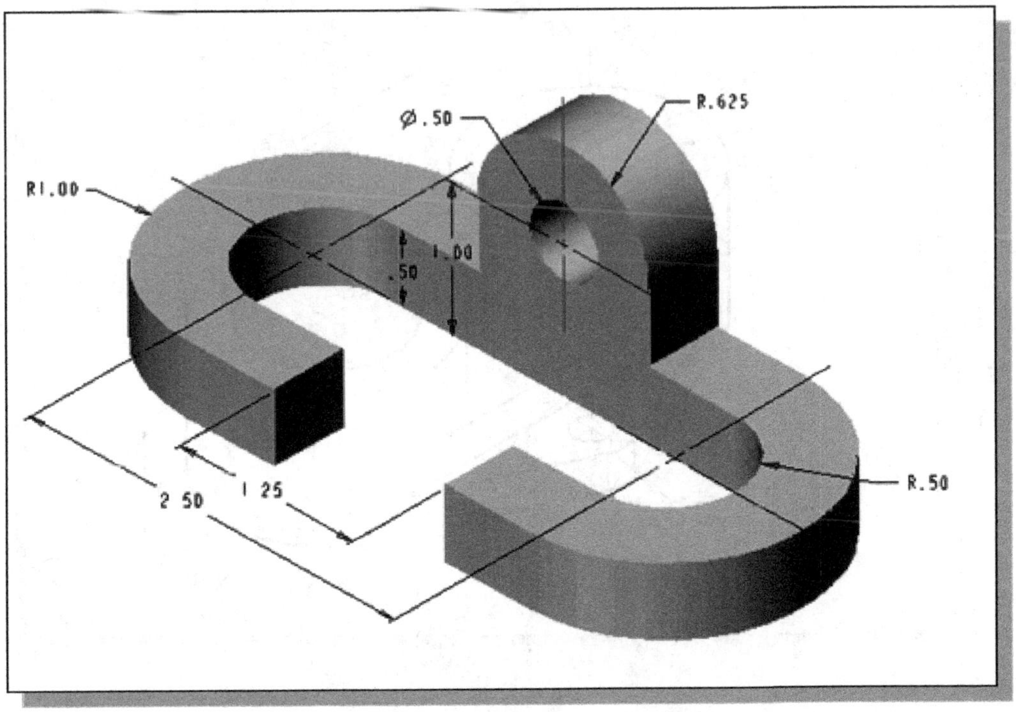

3.

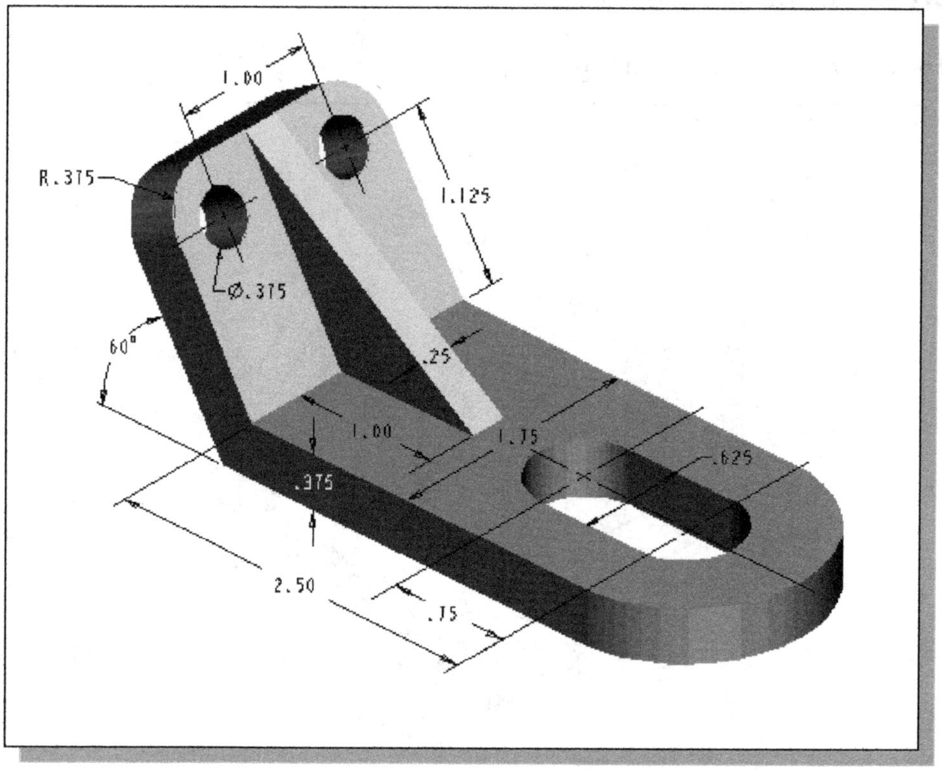
1.00
R.375
1.125
Ø.375
60°
.25
1.00
1.75
.625
.375
2.50
.75

4.

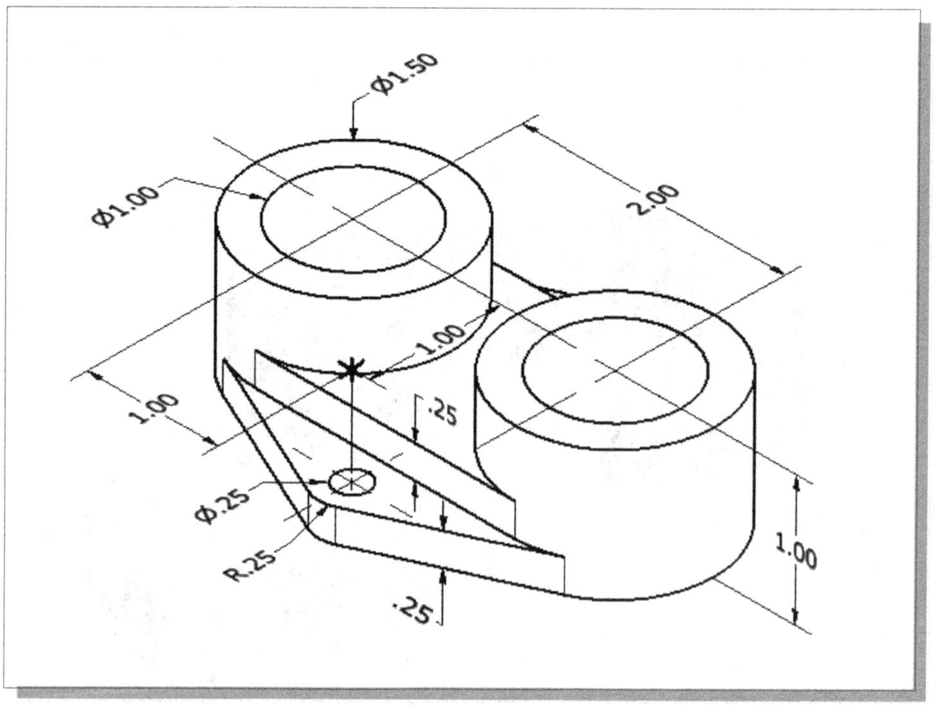
Ø1.50
Ø1.00
2.00
1.00
1.00
.25
Ø.25
R.25
1.00
.25

5.

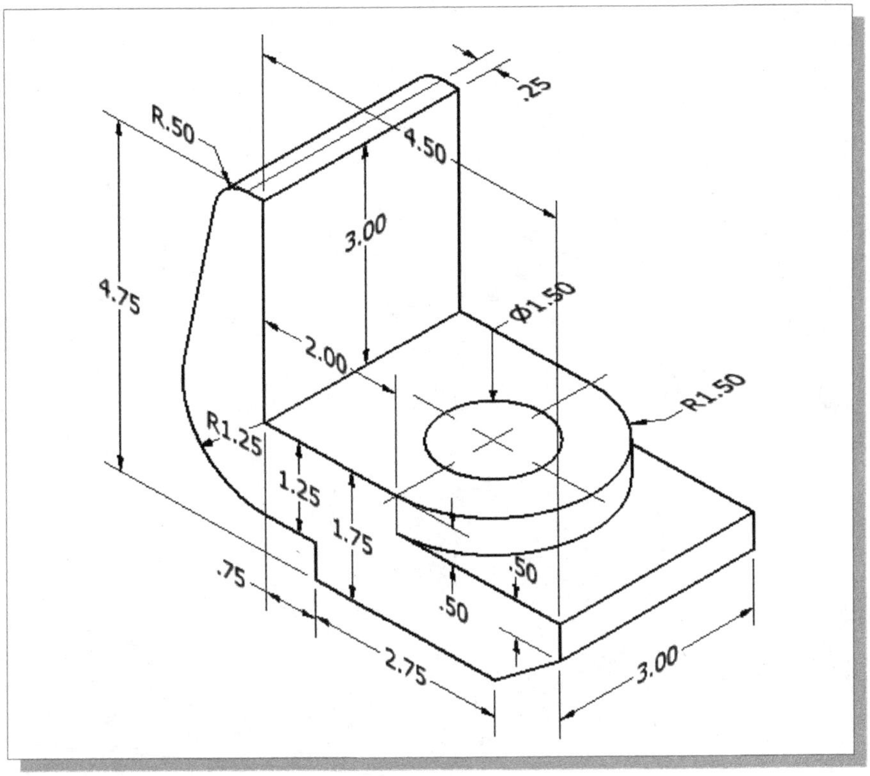
R.50
4.50
.25
3.00
4.75
Ø1.50
2.00
R1.50
R1.25
1.25
1.75
.50
.75
.50
2.75
3.00

6.

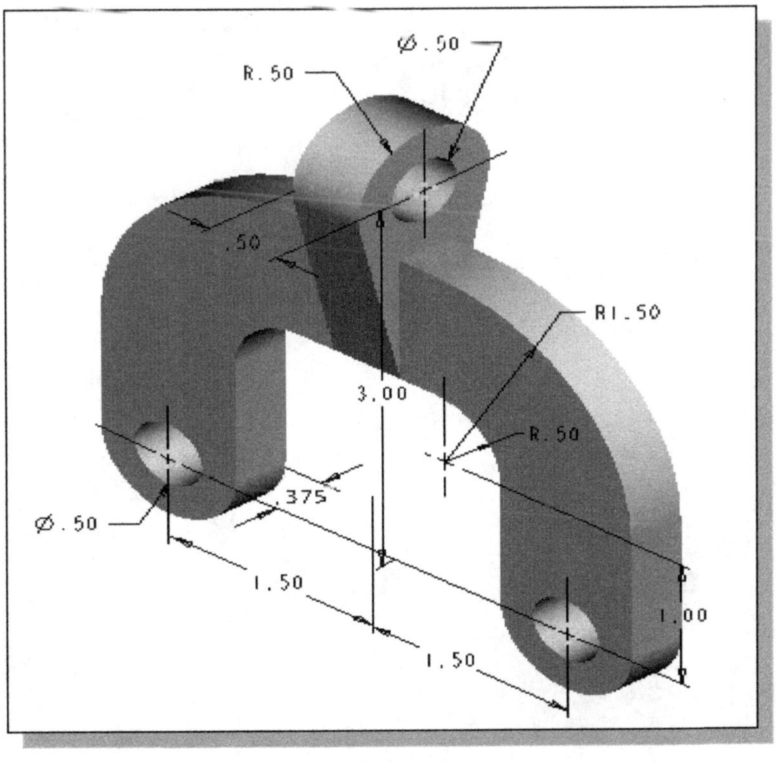
Ø.50
R.50
.50
R1.50
3.00
R.50
.375
Ø.50
1.50
1.00
1.50

Notes:

Chapter 8
Symmetrical Features in Designs

Learning Objectives

- Create Revolved Features
- Use the Mirror Part Command
- Understand and Create Construction Geometry
- Create Combined Parts
- Create and Modify Feature Arrays
- Understand the Importance of Identifying Symmetrical Features in Designs

Introduction

In solid modeling, it is important to identify and determine the features that exist in the design. *Modern solid modeling systems* enable us to build complex designs by working on smaller and simpler units. This approach simplifies the modeling process and allows us to concentrate on the characteristics of the design. Symmetry is an important characteristic that is often seen in designs. Symmetrical features can be easily accomplished by the assortments of tools that are available in feature-based modeling systems, such as AutoCAD.

The modeling technique of extruding two-dimensional sketches along a straight line to form three-dimensional features, as illustrated in the previous chapters, is an effective way to construct solid models. For designs that involve cylindrical shapes, shapes that are symmetrical about an axis, revolving two-dimensional sketches about an axis can form the needed three-dimensional features. In solid modeling, this type of feature is called a **revolved feature**.

In AutoCAD, besides using the **Revolve** command to create revolved features, several options are also available to handle symmetrical features. For example, we can create multiple identical copies of symmetrical features with the **Array** command or create mirror images of models using the **Mirror** command. In this chapter, the construction and modeling techniques of these more advanced features are illustrated.

A Revolved Design: Pulley

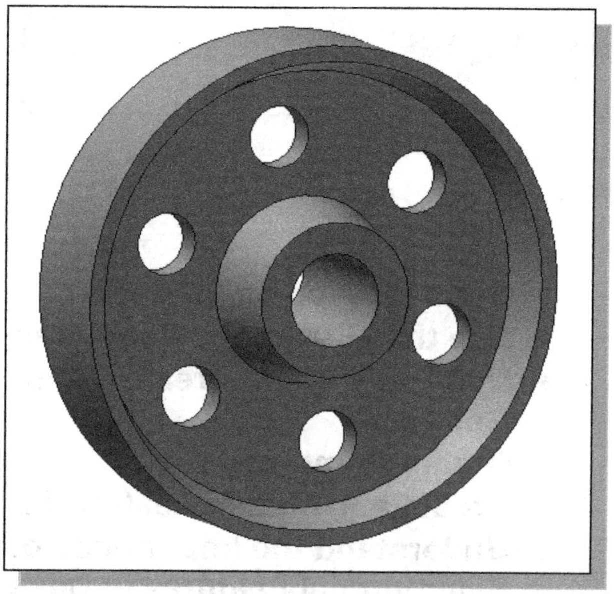

❖ Based on your knowledge of AutoCAD, how many features would you use to create the design? Which feature would you choose as the starting point for creating the model? Identify the symmetrical features in the design and consider other possibilities in creating the design. You are encouraged to create the model on your own prior to following through the tutorial.

Modeling Strategy – A Revolved Design

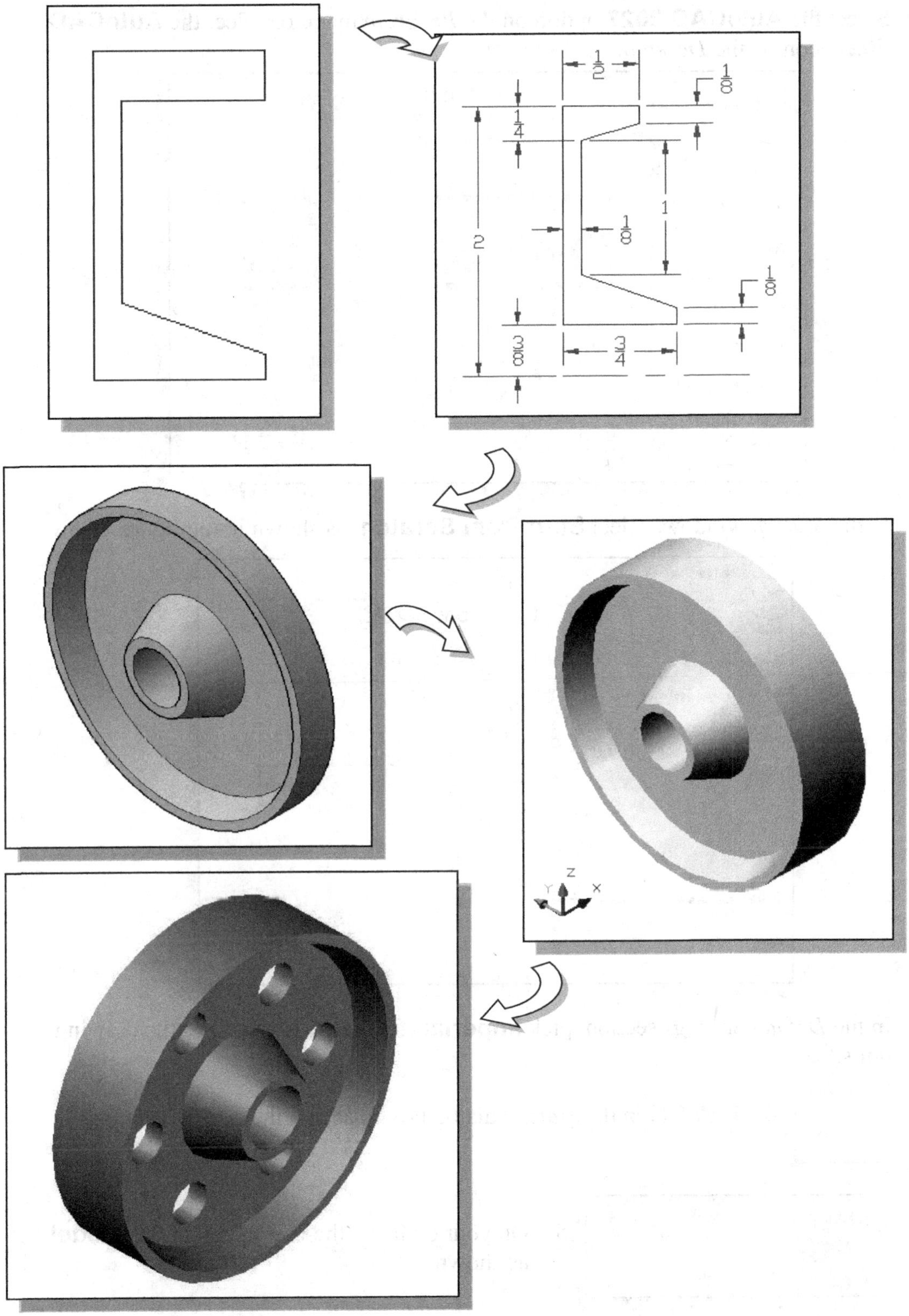

Starting Up AutoCAD 2027

1. Select the **AutoCAD 2027** option on the *Program* menu or select the **AutoCAD 2027** icon on the *Desktop*.

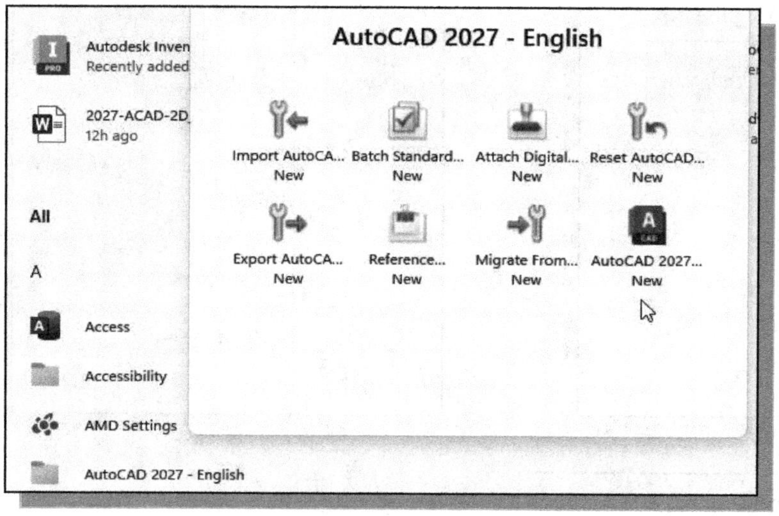

2. In the *Startup* window, select **Start from Scratch**, as shown in the figure below.

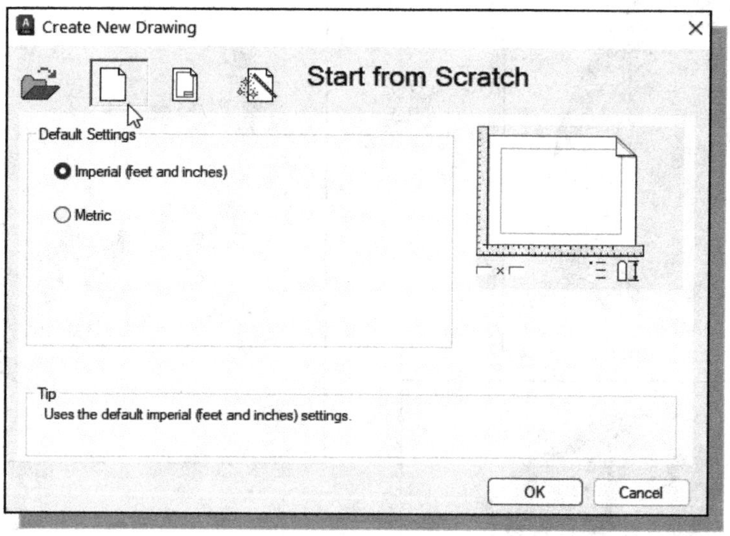

3. In the *Default Settings* section, pick **Imperial (feet and inches)** as the drawing units.

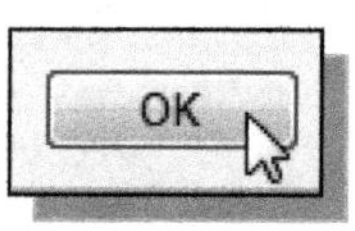

4. Pick **OK** in the *Startup* dialog box to accept the selected settings.

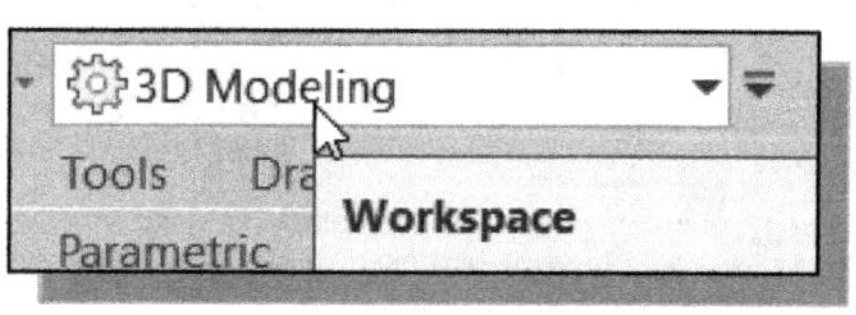

5. On your own, set the *workspace* to **3D Modeling** as shown.

Layers Setup

1. In the *Menu Bar,* select **[Tools] → [Toolbars] → [AutoCAD] → [Layers]**.

2. Click **Layers Properties Manager** in the *Layers* toolbar.

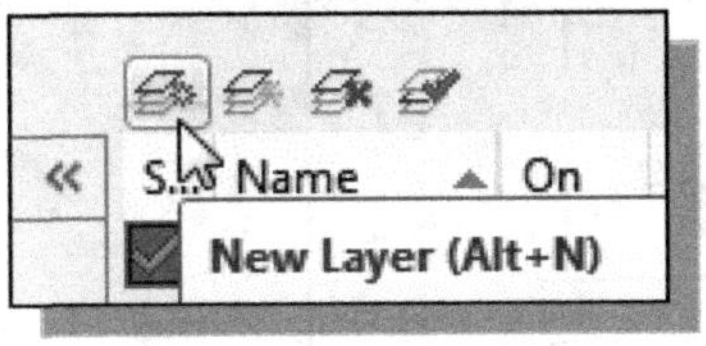

3. Click on the **New** button to create new layers.

4. Create **three new layers** with the following settings:

Layer	*Color*	*Linetype*	*Lineweight*
Center_lines	**Red**	**Center**	**Default**
Dimensions	**Magenta**	**Continuous**	**Default**
Object_lines	**Cyan**	**Continuous**	**0.3mm**

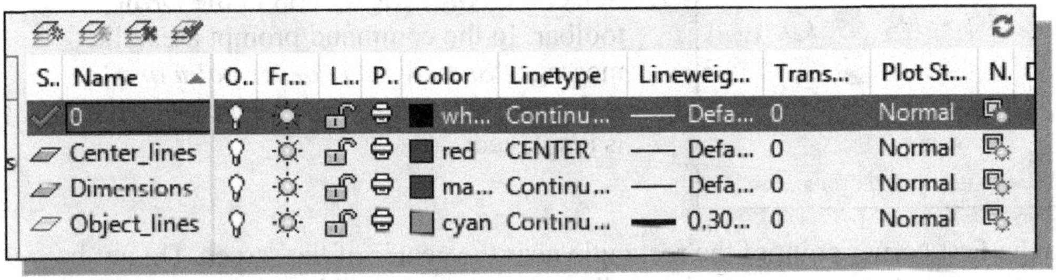

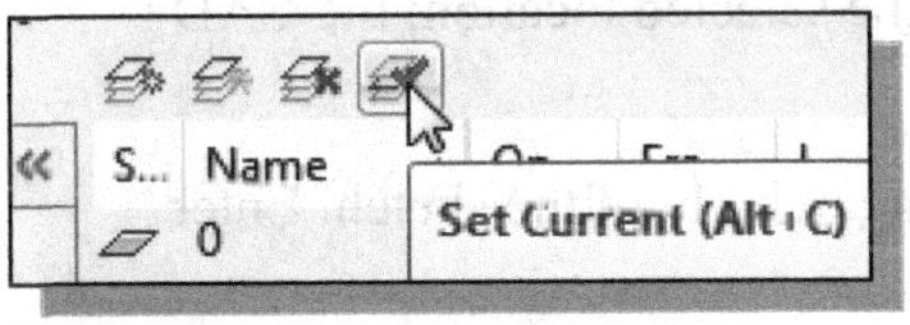

5. Select ***Object_lines*** layer in the list of layers.

6. Click on the **Current** button to set layer ***Object_lines*** as the *Current Layer*.

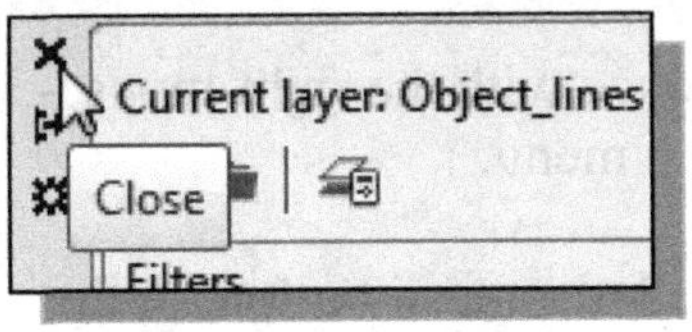

7. Click on the **Close** button to accept the settings and exit the *Layer Properties Manager* dialog box.

8. In the *Status Bar* area, reset the options and turn ***ON*** the *Grid Display, Polar Tracking*, *Object Snap*, *Object Snap Tracking*, and *Dynamic Input* options.

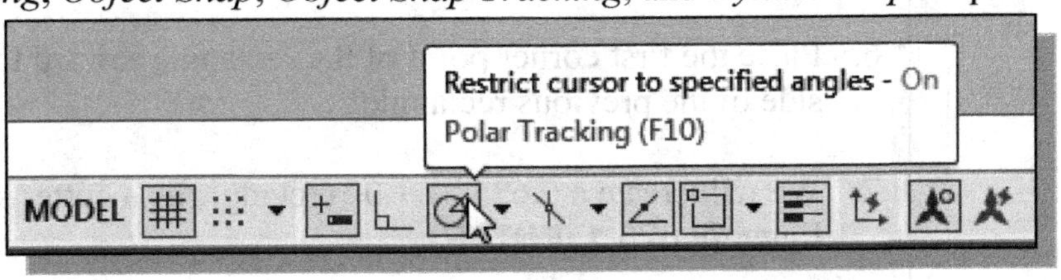

Set Up a 2D Sketch for the Revolved Feature

Note that the *Pulley* design is symmetrical about a horizontal axis as well as a vertical axis, which allows us to simplify the 2D sketch as shown below. Instead of creating the 2D sketch by the **Line** command, we will use some of the more advanced editing options available with the **Region** command.

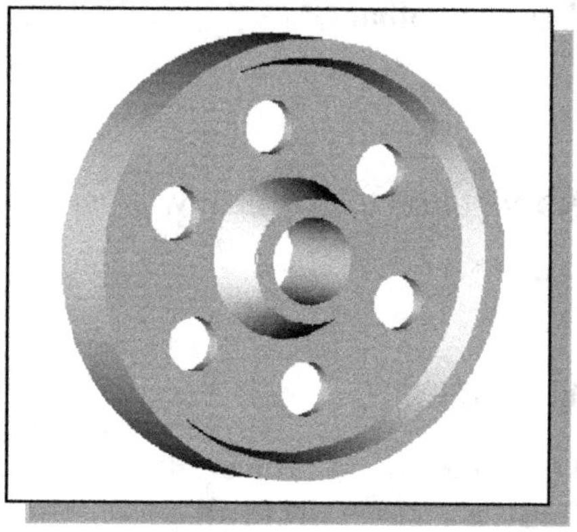

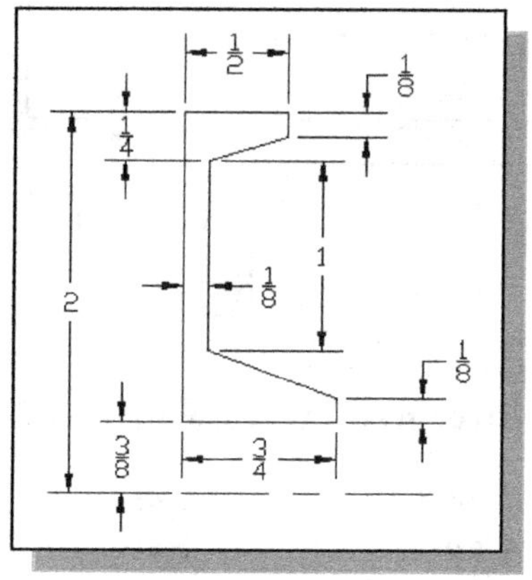

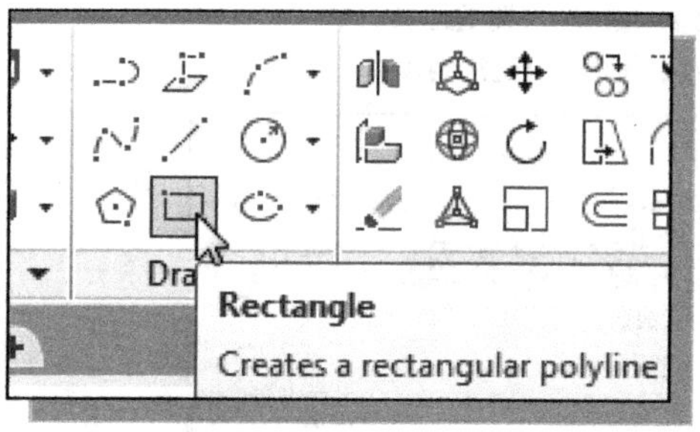

1. Select the **Rectangle** icon in the *Draw* toolbar. In the command prompt area, the message "*Specify first corner point or [Chamfer/ Elevation/Fillet/ Thickness/Width]:*" is displayed.

2. Place the first corner point of the rectangle near the center of the screen. Do not be overly concerned about the actual coordinates of the selected location; the CAD drawing space is as big as you can imagine.

3. We will create a 0.75″ × 1.625″ rectangle for the main body of the sketch. Enter **@.75,1.625 [ENTER]**.

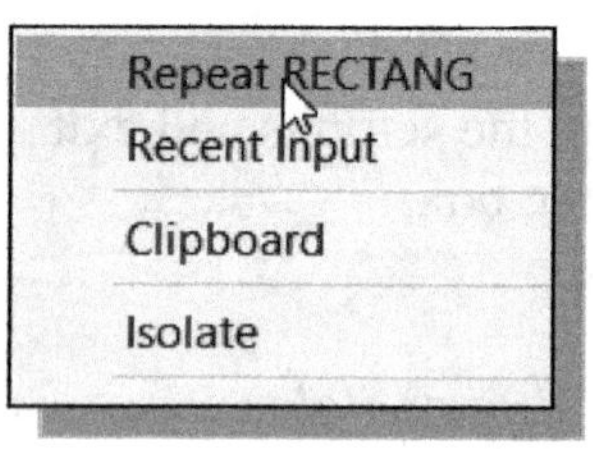

4. Inside the graphics window, click once with the right-mouse-button to bring up the pop-up option menu.

5. Pick **Repeat Rectangle**, with the left-mouse-button, in the pop-up menu to repeat the last command.

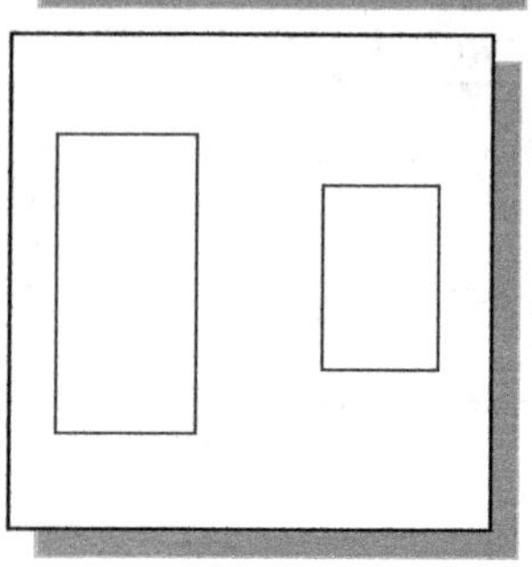

6. Place the first corner point of the rectangle toward the right side of the previous rectangle.

7. We will create a 0.625″ × 1.0″ rectangle as a cutter sketch. Enter **@.625,1 [ENTER]**.

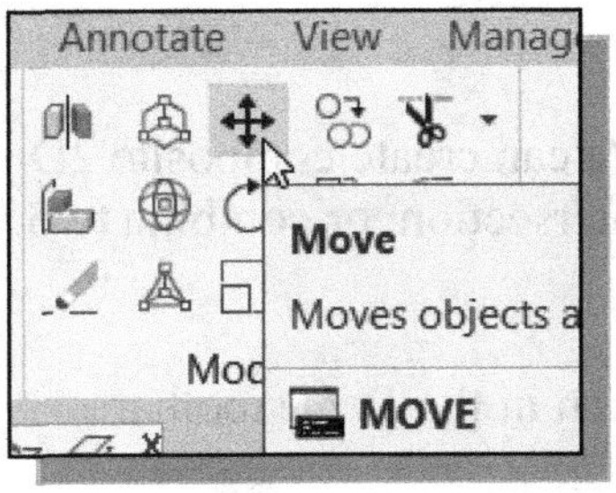

8. Select the **Move** icon in the *Modify* toolbar.

9. In the command prompt area, the message "*Select Objects:*" is displayed. Pick the cutter rectangle, **the smaller rectangle**, to move.

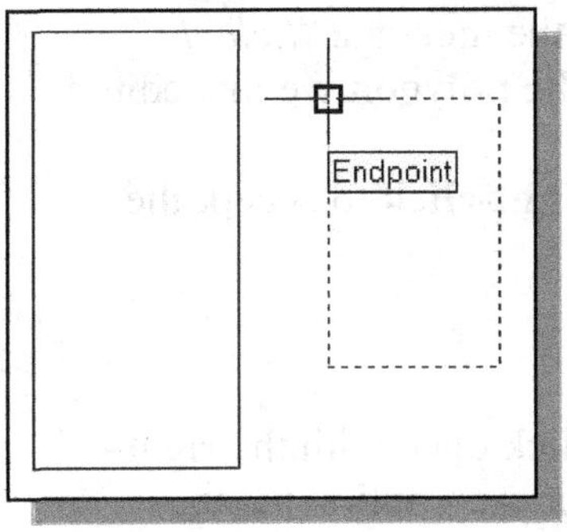

10. Inside the graphics window, **right-click** to accept the selection.

11. In the command prompt area, the message "*Specify base point or displacement:*" is displayed. Pick the **upper left corner** of the smaller rectangle as shown.

12. Inside the graphics window, hold down the **[SHIFT]** key and **right-click** once to bring up the *Object Snap* shortcut menu.

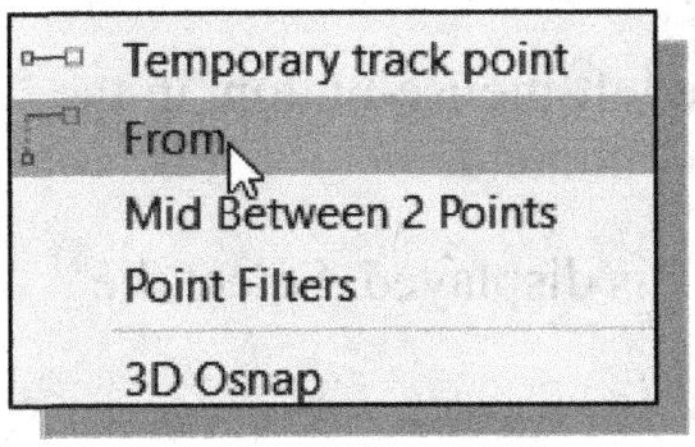

13. Select the **From** option in the pop-up window.

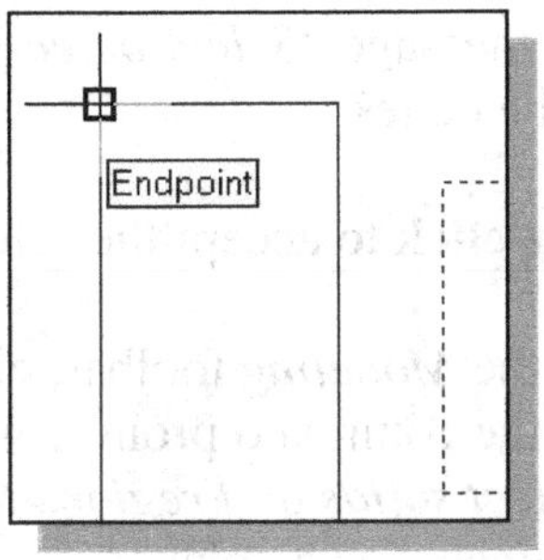

14. Pick the upper left corner of the larger rectangle as shown.

15. In the command prompt area, the message "*Specify base point or displacement: _from Base point: <Offset>:*" is displayed. Enter **@.125,-.25 [ENTER]**.

16. Pre-select the **smaller rectangle** to activate the grip-editing function.

17. Pick the **lower right grip point** displayed along the right vertical edge.

18. Inside the graphics window, hold down the **[SHIFT]** key and **right-click** once to bring up the *Object Snap* shortcut menu.

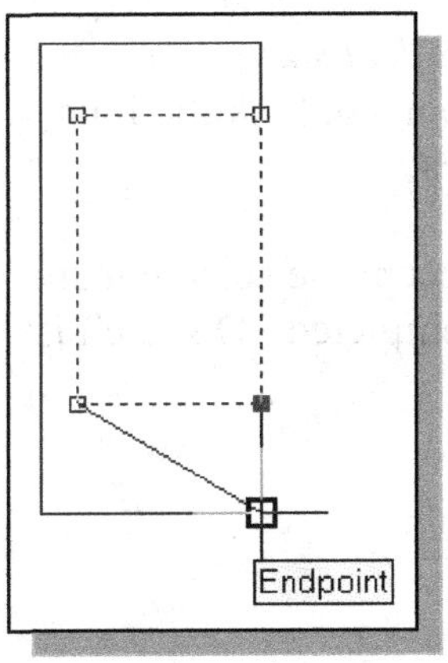

19. Select the **From** option in the pop-up window.

20. Pick the **lower right corner** of the larger rectangle.

21. At the command prompt: **@0,.125 [ENTER]**.

22. Press the **[Esc]** key once to deselect any selected entities.

Perform 2D Boolean Operations

AutoCAD's 2D regions are special types of filled polygons. We can create composite 2D regions by applying *Boolean operations* to subtract, find the intersection, or combine two or more regions.

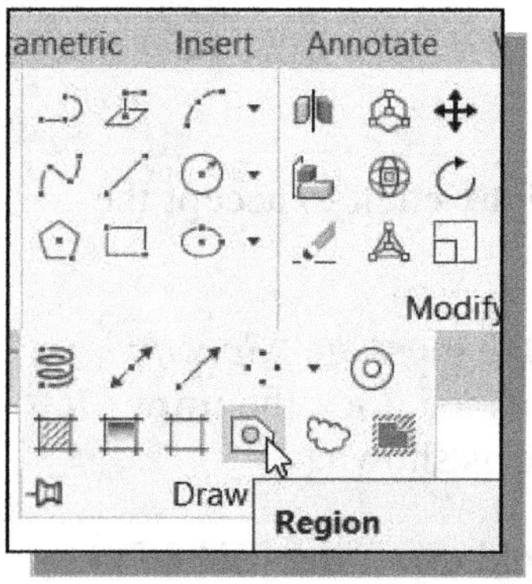

1. Select the **Region** command icon in the *Draw* toolbar.

2. In the *command prompt area,* the message "*Select objects:*" is displayed. Select the **polygon** we just edited.

3. Inside the *graphics window*, **right-click** to accept the selection and create a region.

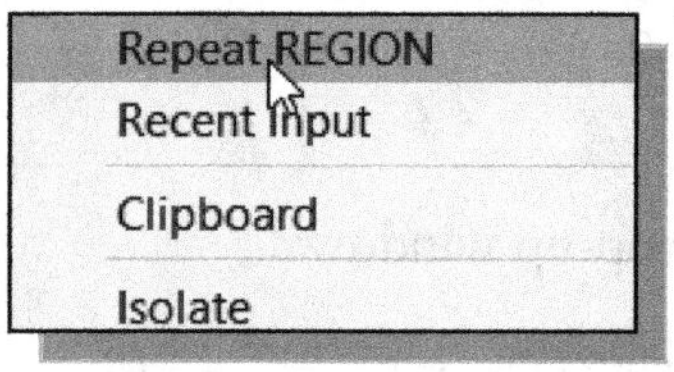

4. Inside the *graphics window*, click once with the right-mouse-button to bring up the pop-up option menu.

5. Pick **Repeat Region**, with the left-mouse-button, in the pop-up menu to repeat the last command.

6. In the command prompt area, the message "*Select objects:*" is displayed. Select the **rectangle** by clicking on one of the edges.

7. Inside the graphics window, **right-click** to accept the selection and create a region.

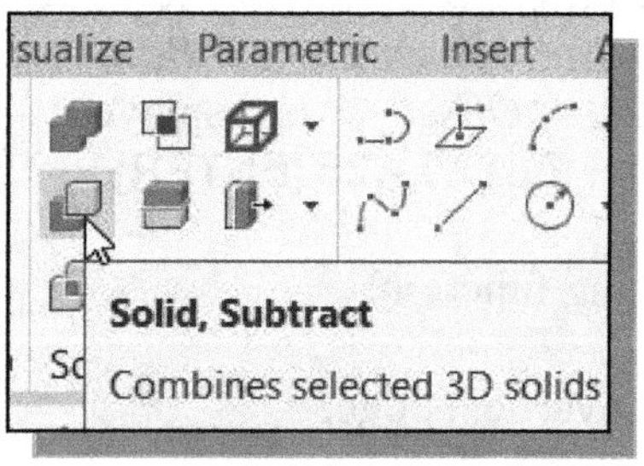

8. In the *Modeling* toolbar, click on the **Subtract** icon. In the command prompt area, the message "*_subtract Select solids and regions to subtract from ... Select Objects:*" is displayed.

9. Pick the **rectangle** by clicking on one of the edges.

10. Inside the *graphics window*, right-click to accept the selection and proceed with the Subtract command.

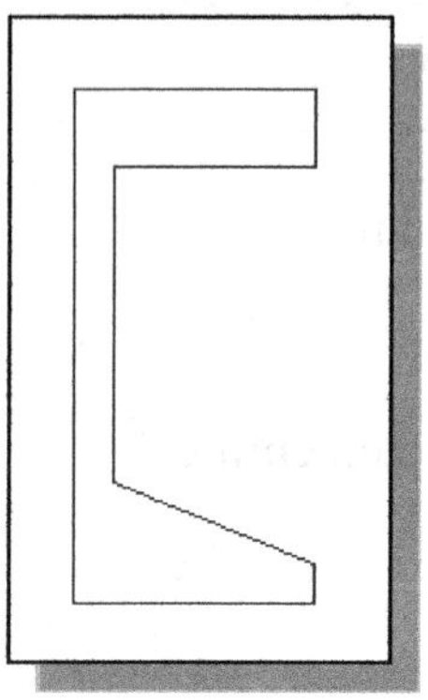

11. In the *command prompt area,* the message "*Select solids and regions to subtract ... Select Objects:*" is displayed. Pick the four-sided **polygon** by clicking on one of the edges.

12. Inside the *graphics window*, **right-click** to accept the selection and proceed with the Subtract command. The completed 2D sketch is as shown.

AutoCAD's region is a special type of geometric entity. It was developed based on the CSG solid modeling technique and is valuable in the sense that it provides a different method to construct complex geometric shapes. In many cases, the Boolean operations are more efficient than creating geometry by entering point-to-point coordinates.

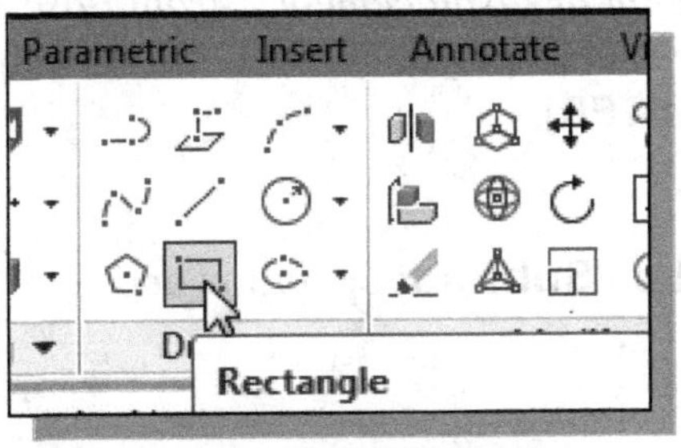

13. Select the **Rectangle** icon in the *Draw* toolbar.

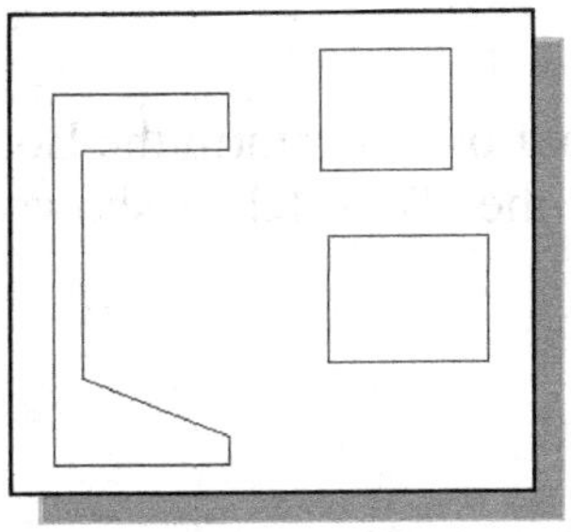

14. On your own, create two arbitrary rectangles roughly positioned as shown. We will use these two rectangles to shape the upper regions of the design.

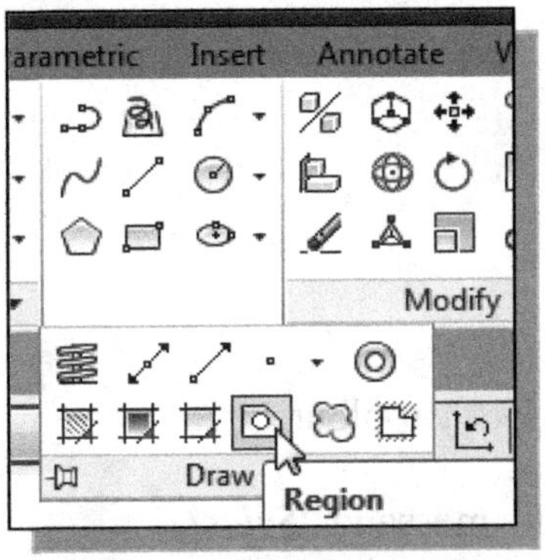

15. On your own, convert the two rectangles into **two regions.**

16. Select the **Move** icon in the *Modify* toolbar.

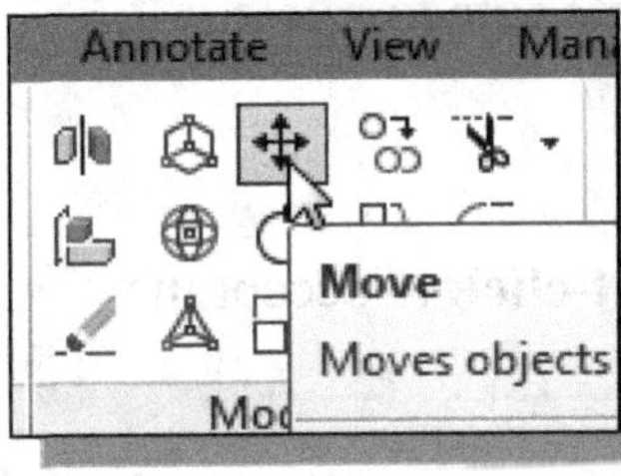

17. In the *command prompt area*, the message "*Select Objects:*" is displayed. Pick **one of the rectangles** to move.

18. Inside the *graphics window*, **right-click** to accept the selection.

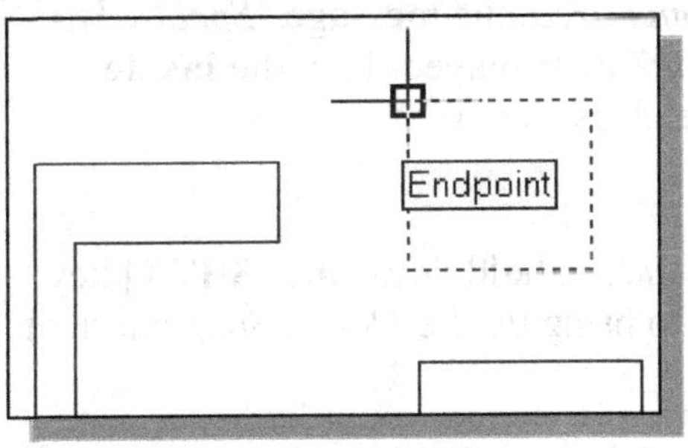

19. In the *command prompt area*, the message "*Specify base point or displacement:*" is displayed. Pick the **upper left corner** of the selected rectangle as shown.

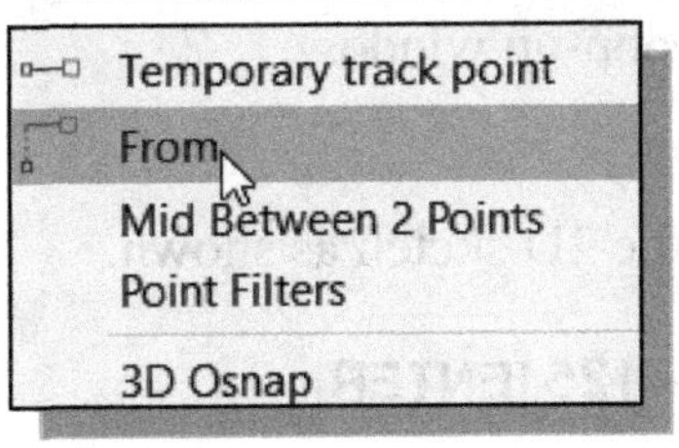

20. Inside the *graphics window*, hold down the **[SHIFT]** key and **right-click** once to bring up the *Object Snap* shortcut menu.

21. Select the **From** option in the pop-up window.

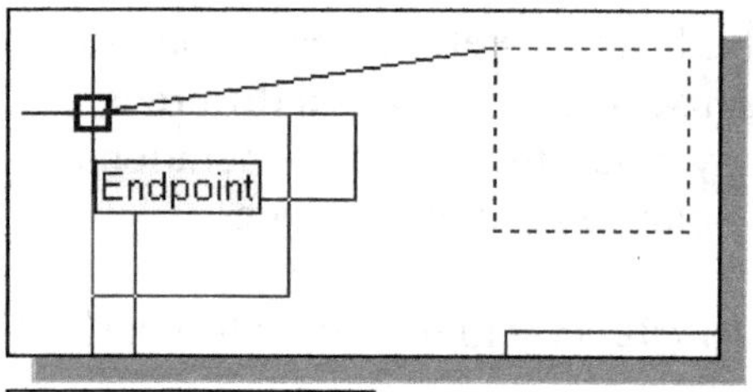

22. Pick the upper left corner of the larger rectangle as shown.

23. In the *command prompt area*, the message "*Specify base point or displacement: _from Base point: <Offset>:*" is displayed.
    Enter **@.5,0 [ENTER]**.

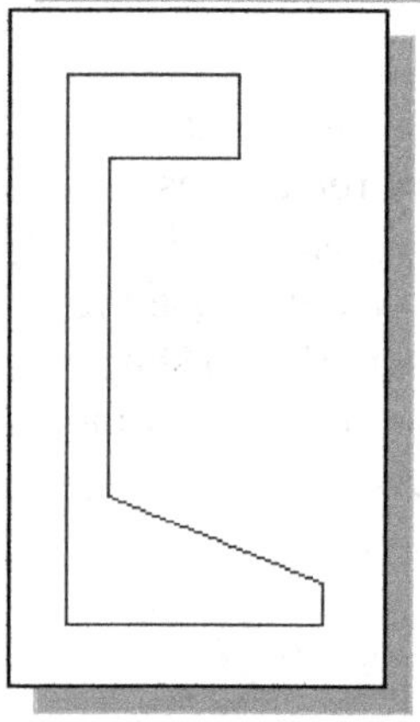

24. On your own, perform the Boolean **Subtract** operation and create the 2D sketch as shown.

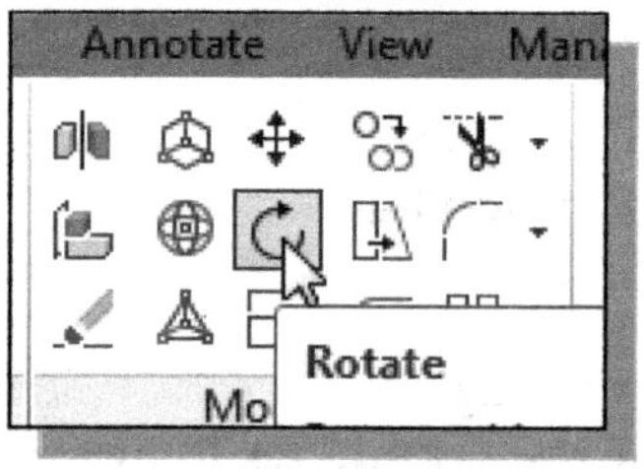

25. Select the **Rotate** icon in the *Modify* toolbar.

26. In the *command prompt area*, the message "*Select Objects:*" is displayed. Pick the **rectangle** to rotate.

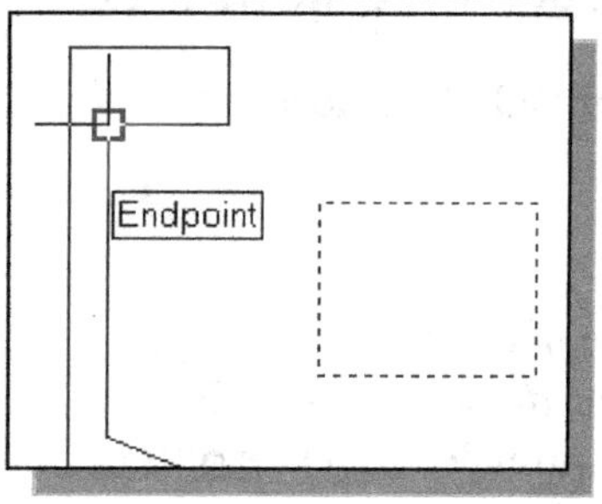

27. Inside the *graphics window*, **right-click** to accept the selection.

28. In the *command prompt area*, the message "*Specify base point or displacement:*" is displayed. Pick the **inside corner** of the 2D sketch as shown.

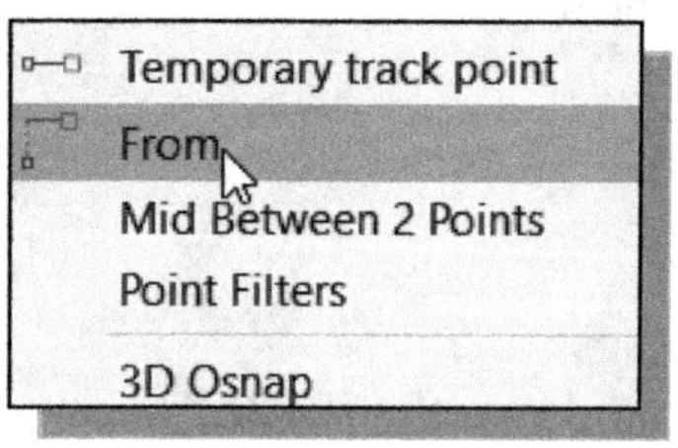

29. Inside the *graphics window*, hold down the **[SHIFT]** key and **right-click** once to bring up the *Object Snap* shortcut menu.

30. Select the **From** option in the pop-up window.

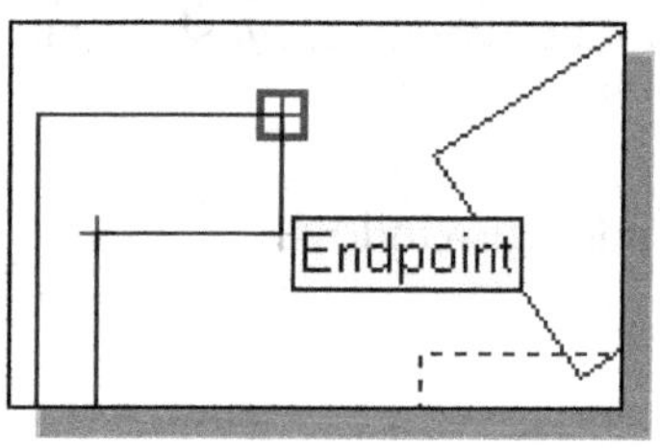

31. Pick the upper right corner of the 2D sketch as shown.

32. At the *command prompt*: **@0,-.125 [ENTER]**.

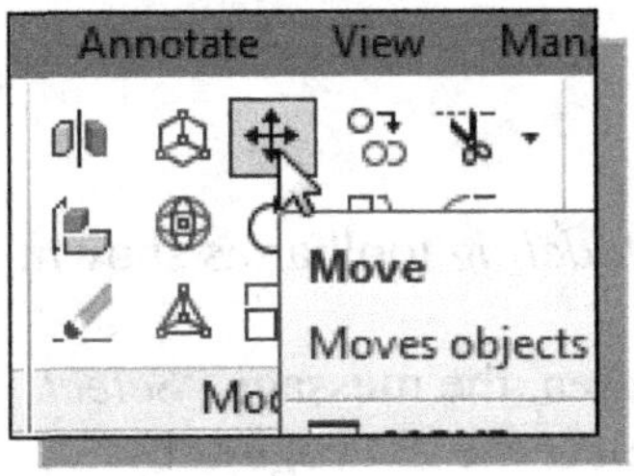

33. Select the **Move** icon in the *Modify* toolbar.

34. In the command prompt area, the message "*Select Objects:*" is displayed. Pick the rotated rectangle to move.

35. Inside the graphics window, right-click to accept the selection.

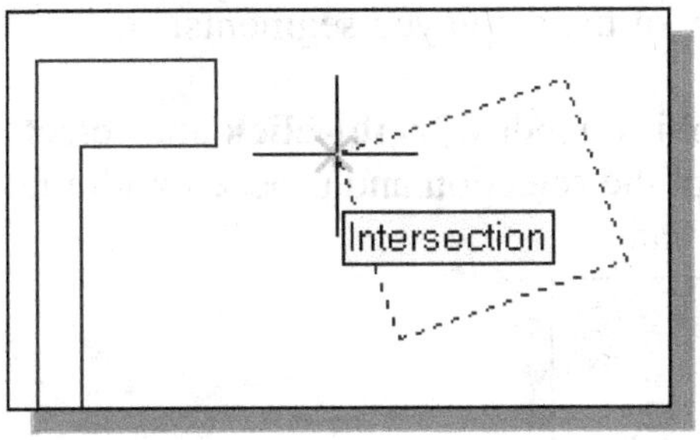

36. In the command prompt area, the message "*Specify base point or displacement:*" is displayed. Pick the upper left corner of the selected rectangle as shown.

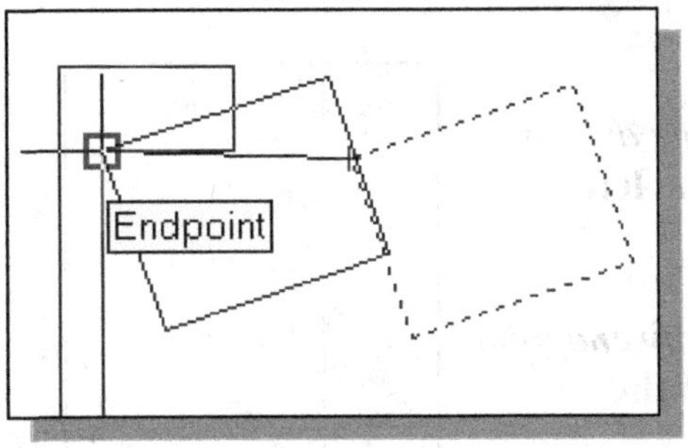

37. In the command prompt area, the message "*Specify base point or displacement:*" is displayed. Pick the inside corner of the 2D sketch as shown.

38. On your own, perform the Boolean **Subtract** operation and complete the 2D sketch as shown.

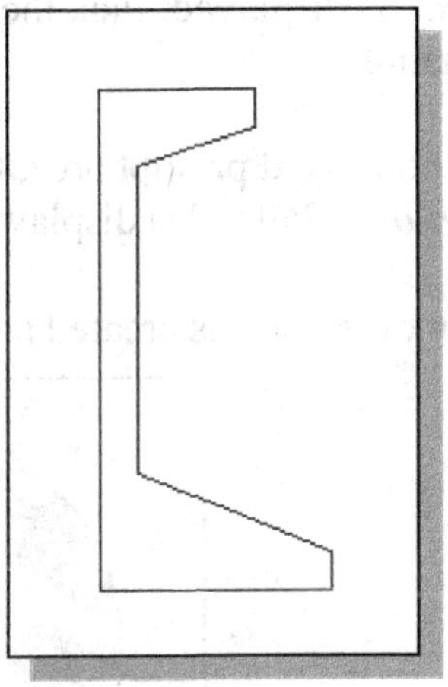

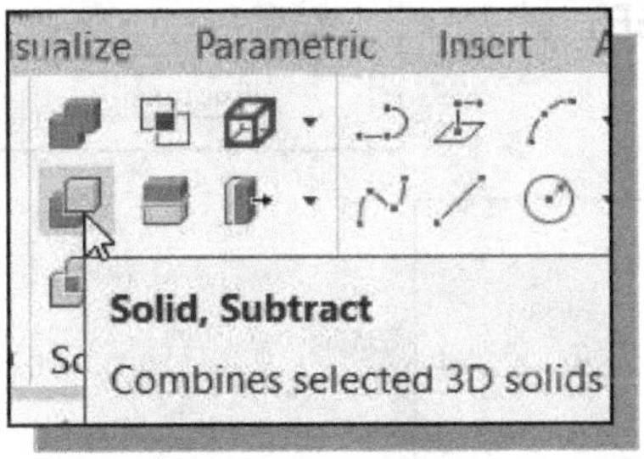

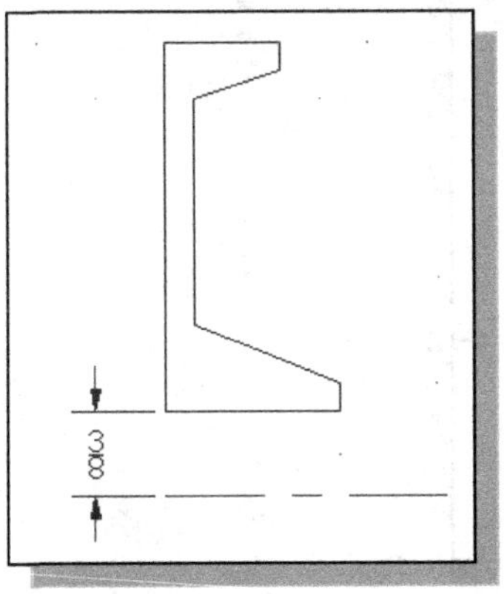

39. On your own, create a center line that is ⅜ below the 2D sketch as shown. This line will be used as the axis of rotation for the revolved feature. **Trim** the line so that the **left endpoint is aligned to the left edge of the 2D sketch**.

Create the Revolved Feature

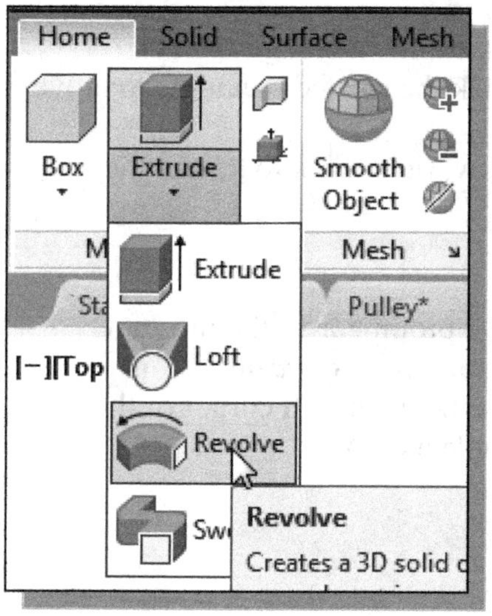

1. Select **Revolve** in the *Modeling* toolbar as shown.

2. In the command prompt area, the message "*Select objects:*" is displayed. Select the **2D region** by clicking on any of the displayed segments.

3. Inside the graphics window, **right-click** and select **Enter** to accept the selection and proceed with the Revolve command.

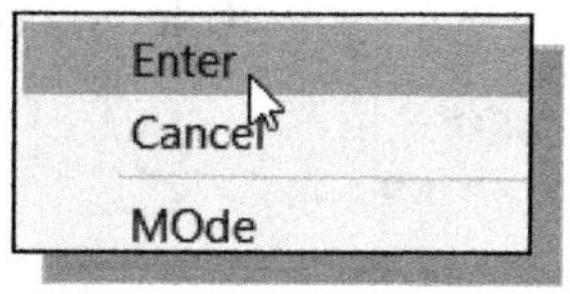

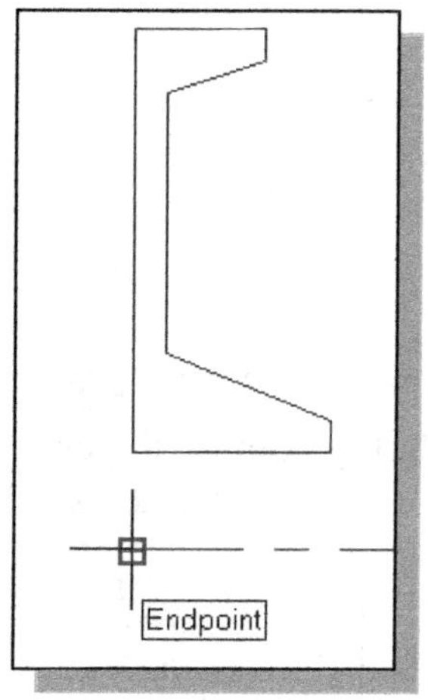

4. In the command prompt area, the message "*Define axis by [Object/X (axis)/Y (axis)}]:*" is displayed. Pick the **left endpoint of the centerline** as shown.

5. In the command prompt area, the message "*Specify endpoint of axis:*" is displayed. Pick the **right endpoint of the centerline.**

6. In the command prompt area, the message "*Specify angle of revolution <360>:*" is displayed. Enter **360 [ENTER]**.

- The revolved part is created as shown.

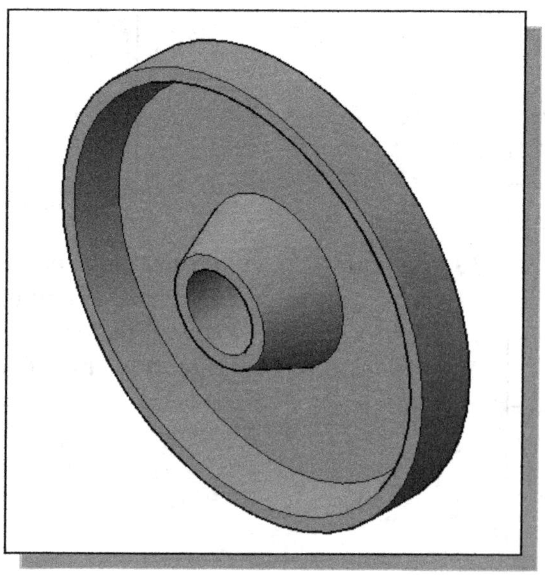

Mirrored Image of the Part

In AutoCAD, we can mirror a 2D sketch or a 3D part about a line or a specified surface. We can define the line by selecting existing points or by picking locations on the screen. We can physically flip the part about a reference plane or create a new mirrored part.

1. On your own, change the display to **SW Isometric View** or use the **Free Orbit** command to display the flat face of the solid model as shown.

2. In the *Modify* toolbar, select **3D Mirror**.

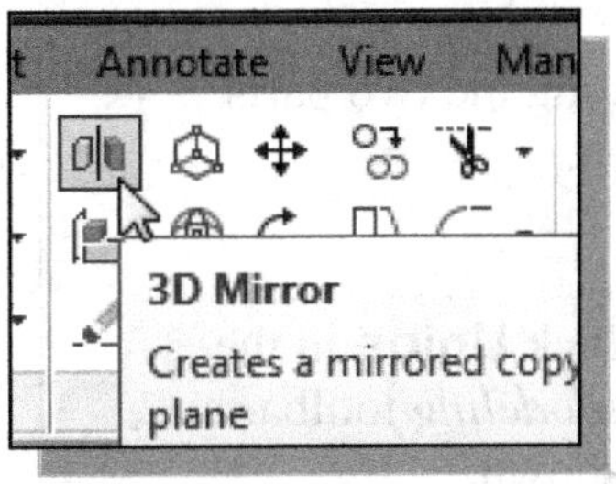

3. In the *command prompt area*, the message "*Select objects:*" is displayed. Select any edge of the **3D model**.

4. Inside the *graphics window*, **right-click** to accept the selection.

5. In the *command prompt area*, the message "*Specify first point of mirror plane (3 points) or [Object/Last/Zaxis/View/XY/YZ/ZX/3points] <3points>:*" is displayed. Choose the YZ plane by selecting **YZ** in the *prompt area* or enter **YZ [ENTER]**.

6. In the *command prompt area*, the message "*Select point on YZ plane <0,0,0>:*" is displayed. Pick the **left endpoint of the centerline**.

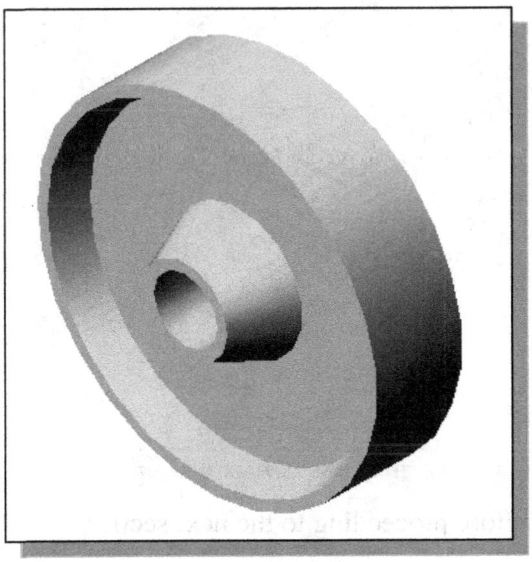

7. In the *command prompt area*, the message "*Delete source objects? [Yes/No] <N>:*" is displayed. In the displayed option list, select **No** to create a new part.

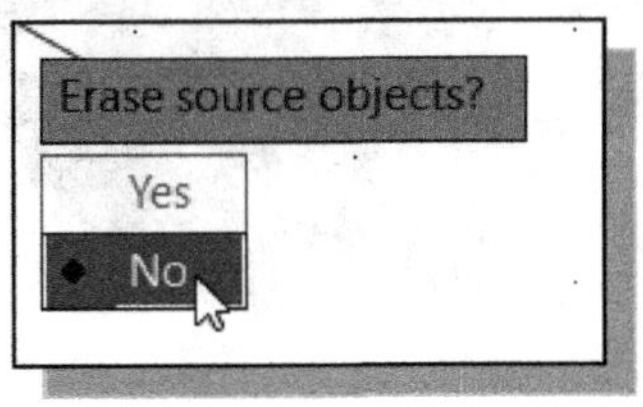

Combine Two Parts into One

We have created a separate part with the Mirror 3D command. We will combine the two parts into a single part using the CSG *Boolean operations*.

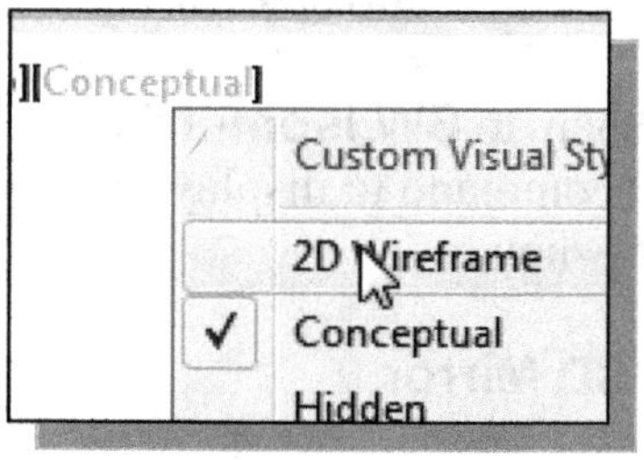

1. Select **2D Wireframe** by left-clicking once on the icon in the *Visual Style* controls list.

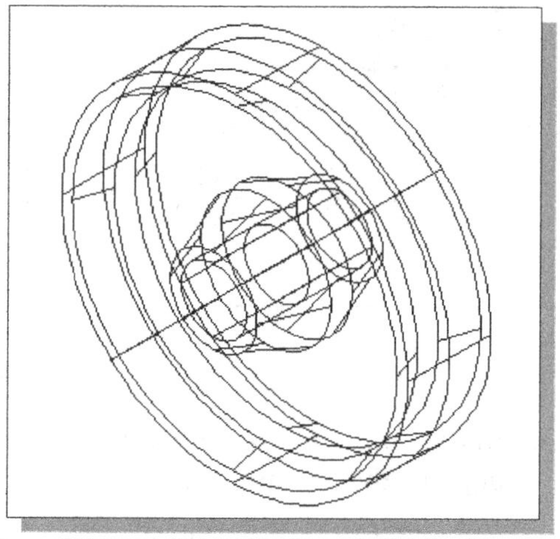

- Note the edges separating the two parts displayed on the screen.

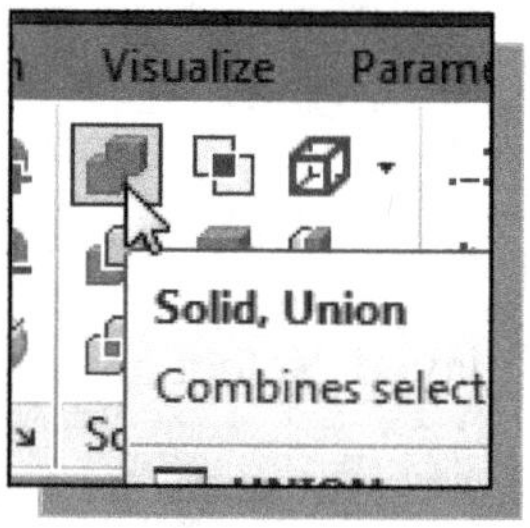

2. Pick **Union** in the *Modeling* toolbar as shown.

3. In the *command prompt area,* the message "*Select Objects:*" is displayed. Pick the two parts.

4. Inside the *graphics window*, right-click to accept the selection and proceed with the Union command to combine the two parts into a single part.

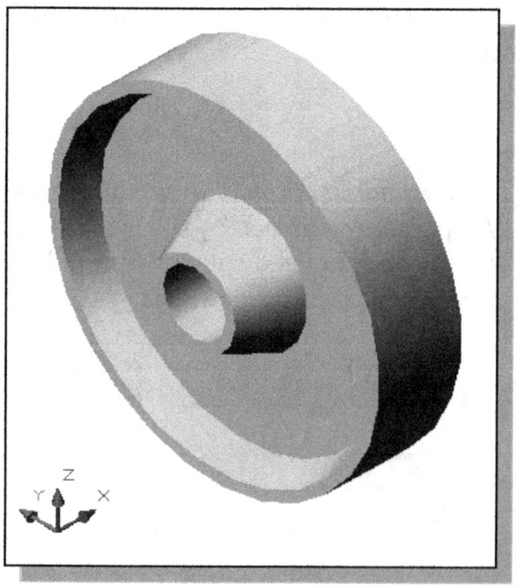

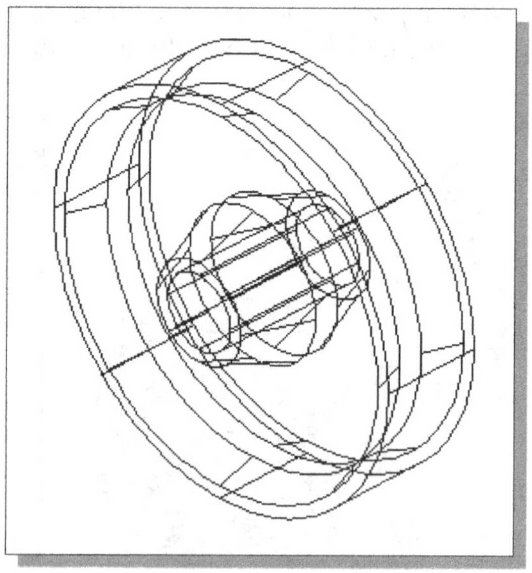

- Reset the display to **2D Wireframe** mode before proceeding to the next section.

Use the 3D Array Command

In AutoCAD, existing 2D and/or 3D features can be easily duplicated. The **Array** command allows us to create both rectangular and polar arrays of features.

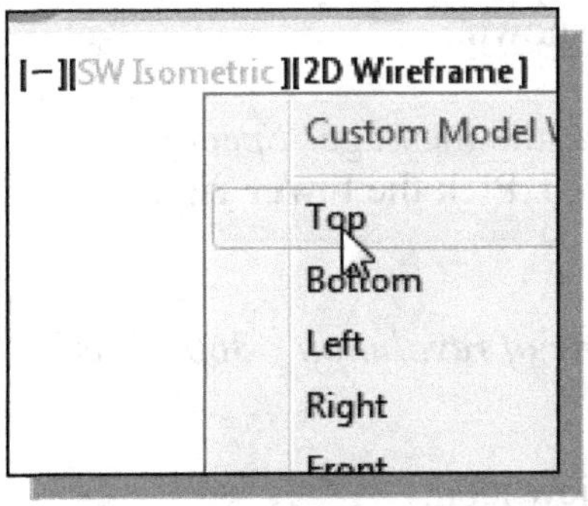

1. In the *View* toolbar, select the **Top** view option to reset the display.

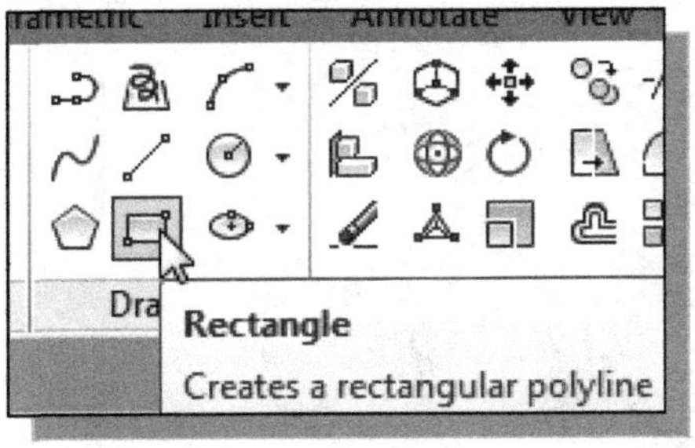

2. Select the **Rectangle** icon in the *Draw* toolbar.

3. On your own, create a rectangle that is **1.0″** × **.25″** toward the right side of the solid model.

4. On your own, convert the rectangle into a ***region***.

- The rectangle will be used to create a cylindrical solid model. The cylinder will be used to generate a polar array using the Array command.

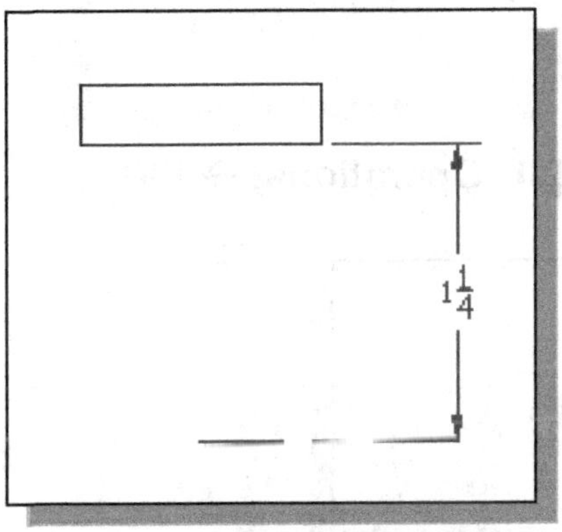

5. On your own, create a centerline that is **1¼″** below the rectangle with the **left endpoint aligned to the center of the rectangle** as shown.

- The centerline will be used as the axis of rotation to create the *polar array*.

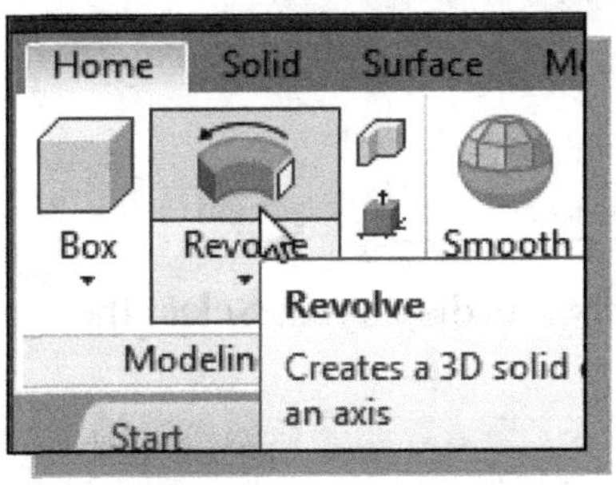

6. Select **Revolve** in the *Modeling* toolbar as shown.

7. In the *command prompt area*, the message "*Select objects:*" is displayed. Select the **rectangular region** by clicking on any of the displayed segments.

8. Inside the graphics window, **right-click** and pick **Enter** to accept the selection and proceed with the Revolve command.

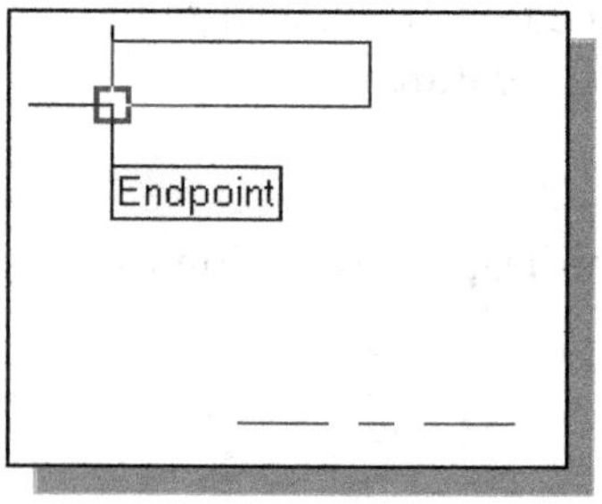

9. In the command prompt area, the message "*Define axis by [Object/X (axis)/Y (axis)}]:*" is displayed. Pick the **lower left corner** of the region as shown.

10. In the command prompt area, the message "*Specify endpoint of axis:*" is displayed. Pick the **lower right corner** of the region.

11. In the command prompt area, the message "*Specify angle of revolution <360>:*" is displayed. Enter **360.0** **[ENTER]**.

12. In the *View Controls* list, click on the **SE Isometric** view icon.

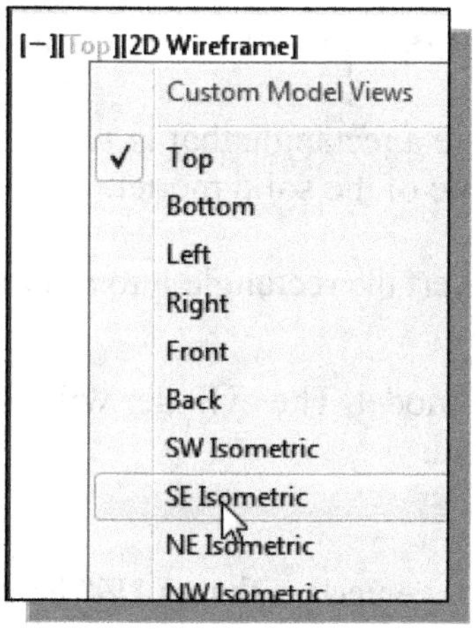

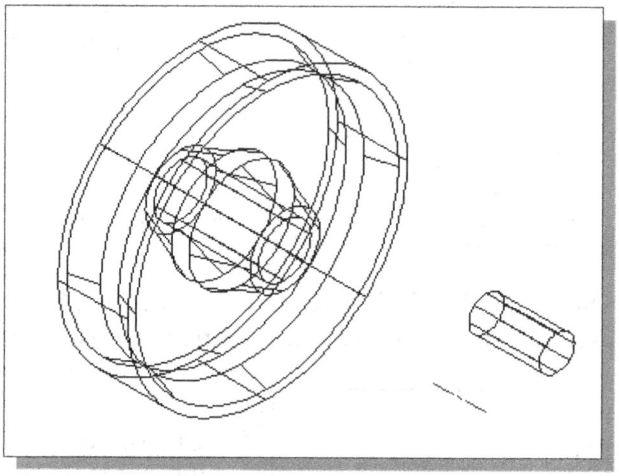

13. In the standard pull-down menu, select **[Modify] → [3D Operations] → [3D Array]**.

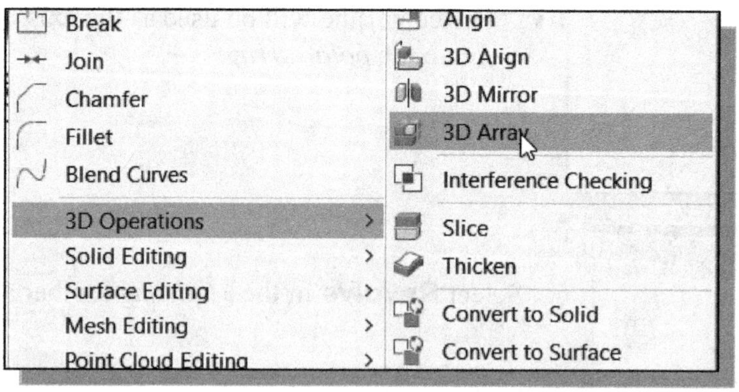

14. In the command prompt area, the message "*Select objects:*" is displayed. Select the **small cylinder** by clicking on any edge of the cylinder.

15. Inside the graphics window, **right-click** to accept the selection.

16. In the command prompt area, the message "*Enter the type of array [Rectangular/ Polar] <R>:*" is displayed.
    Choose the *Polar* option by selecting **Polar** in the *prompt area* or enter **P [ENTER]**.

17. In the command prompt area, the message "*Enter the number of items in the array:*" is displayed. We will create 6 items by entering **6 [ENTER]**.

18. In the command prompt area, the message "*Specify the angle to fill (+=ccw, -=cw) <360>:*" is displayed. Enter **360 [ENTER]**.

19. In the command prompt area, the message "*Rotate arrayed objects?[Yes/No] <Y>:*" is displayed. Click **No** in the prompt area or enter **N [ENTER]**.

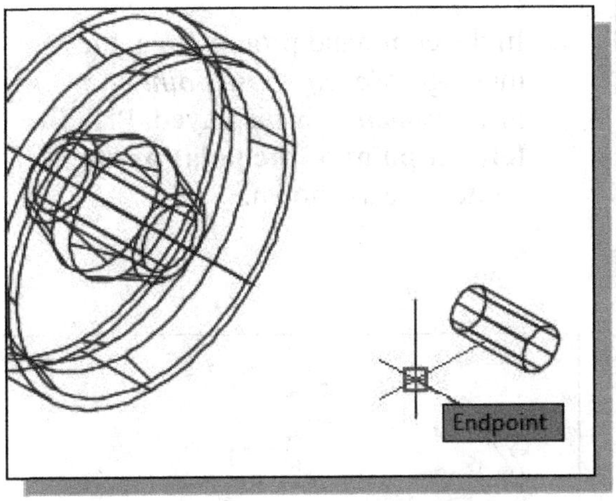

20. In the command prompt area, the message "*Specify center point of array:*" is displayed. Pick the **left endpoint of the centerline** as shown.

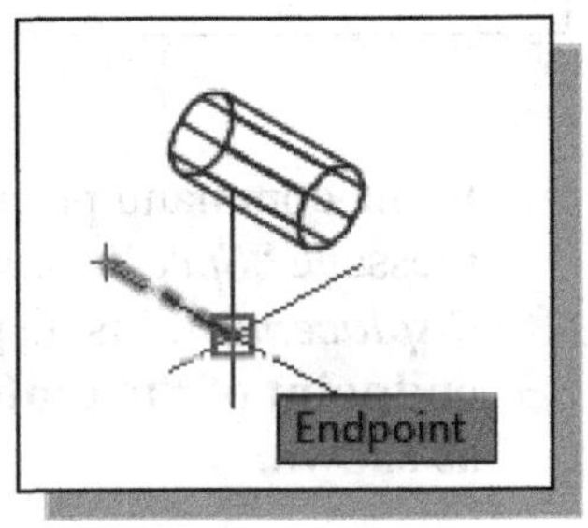

21. In the command prompt area, the message "*Specify second point on axis of rotation:*" is displayed. Pick the right endpoint of the centerline as shown.

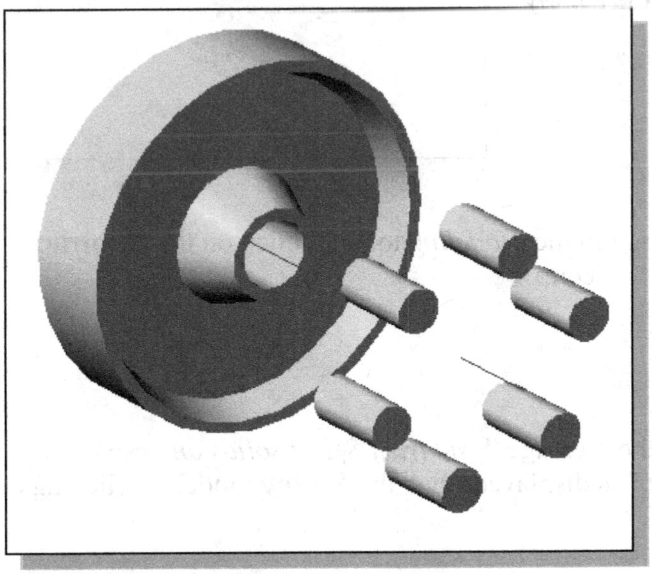

Position and Perform the Cut

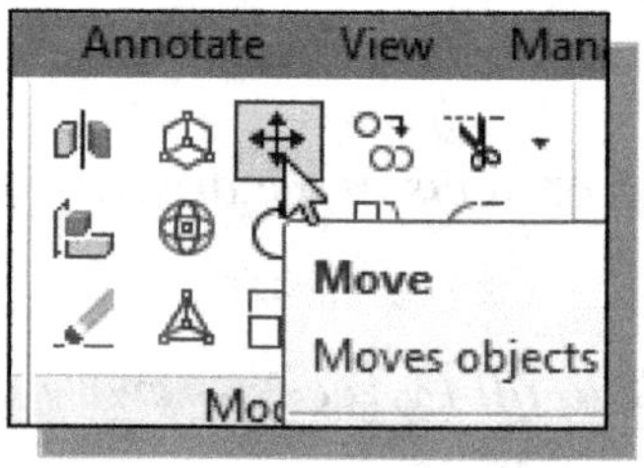

1. Select the **Move** icon in the *Modify* toolbar.

2. In the command prompt area, the message "*Select Objects:*" is displayed. Pick the **six cylinders** we just created.

3. Inside the graphics window, **right-click** to accept the selection.

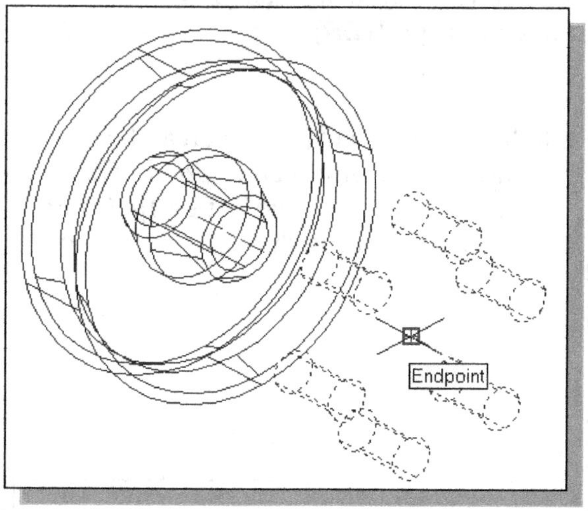

4. In the command prompt area, the message "*Specify base point or displacement:*" is displayed. Pick the **left endpoint of the polar array centerline** as shown.

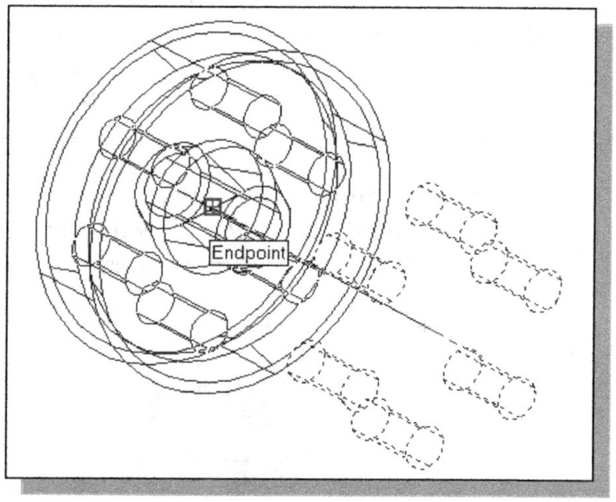

5. In the command prompt area, the message "*Specify base point or displacement:*" is displayed. Pick the **left endpoint of the centerline** of the *Pulley* as shown.

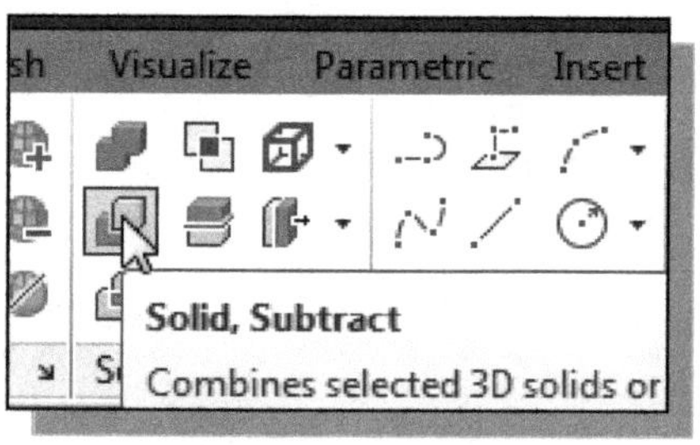

6. In the *Modeling* toolbar, click on the **Subtract** icon.

7. In the *command prompt area*, the message "*_subtract Select solids and regions to subtract from ... Select Objects:*" is displayed. Pick the ***Pulley*** model by clicking on one of the edges.

8. Inside the graphics window, **right-click** to accept the selection and proceed with the Subtract command.

9. In the command prompt area, the message "*Select solids and regions to subtract… Select Objects:*" is displayed.

10. Pick the **six cylinder** blocks by clicking on their circular edges.

11. Inside the graphics window, right-click to accept the selection and proceed with the Subtract command.

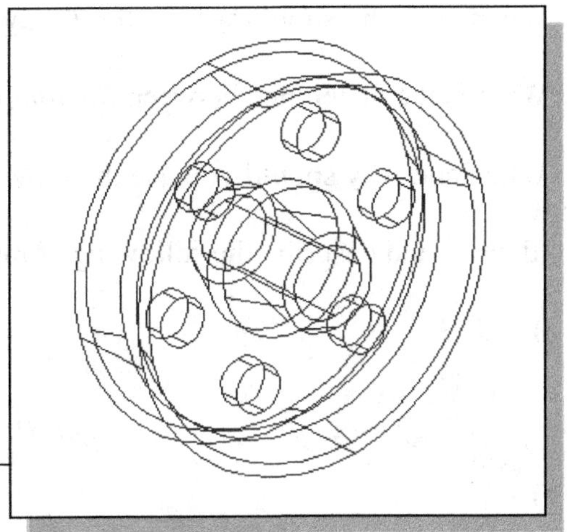

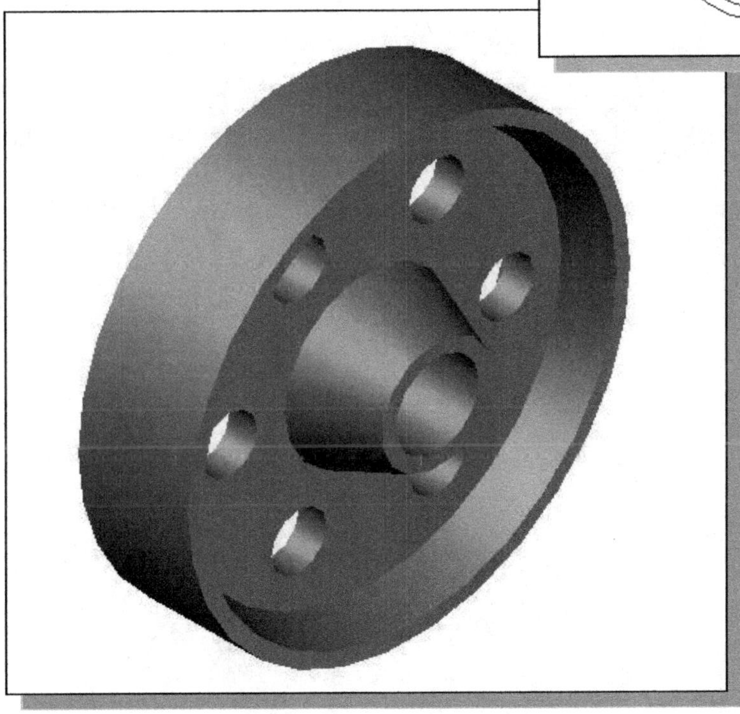

- Note that the Pulley 3D model will be used again in Chapter 9 and Chapter 12.

Review Questions:

1. List the different symmetrical features created in the *Pulley* design.
2. What are the advantages of using *regions*?
3. Describe the steps required in using the **Mirror Part** command.
4. Why is it important to identify symmetrical features in designs?
5. When and why should we use the **Array** option?
6. What is the difference between *Rectangular Array* and *Polar Array*?
7. When and why should you use the **Revolve** command in AutoCAD?
8. Identify and describe the following commands:

(a)

(b)

(c)

(d)

Exercises:

1. Dimensions are in inches.

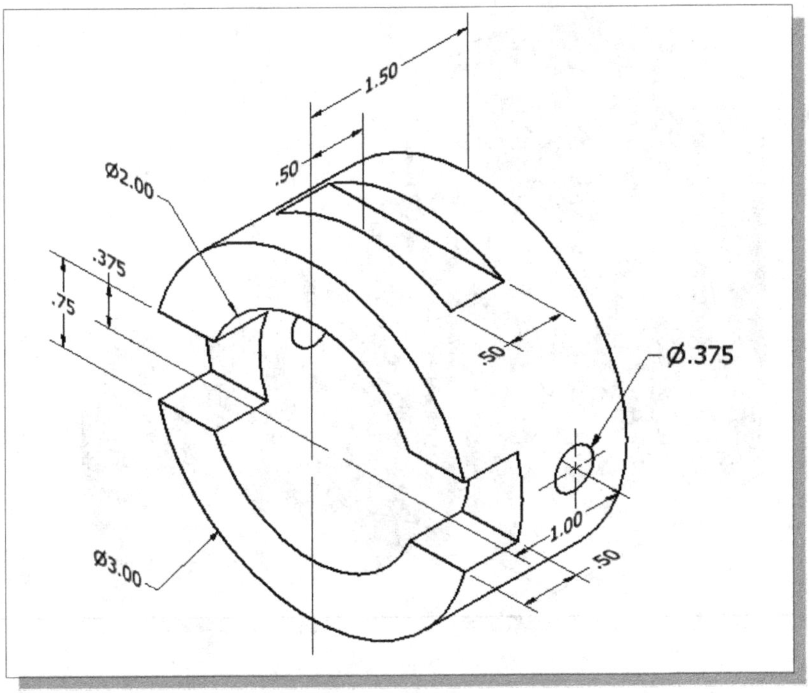

2. Dimensions are in inches. Plate thickness: 0.25 inch

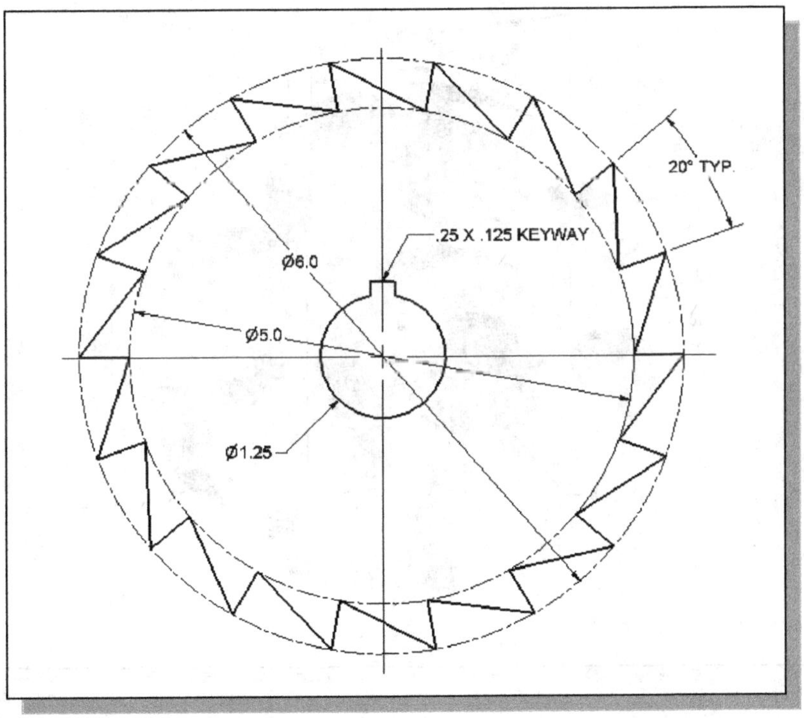

3. Dimensions are in inches.

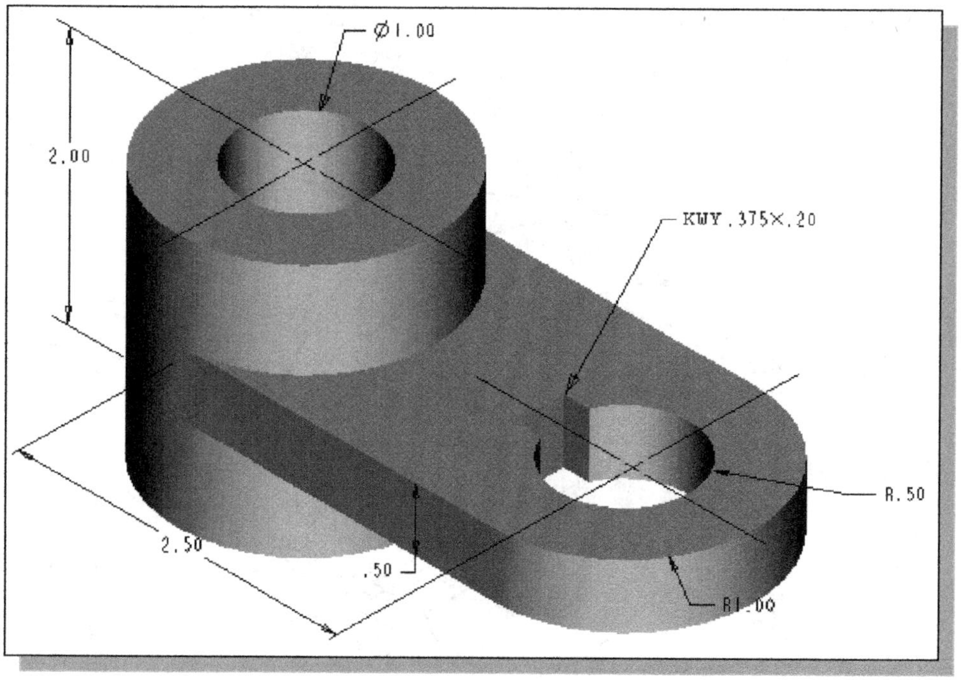

4. Dimensions are in inches.

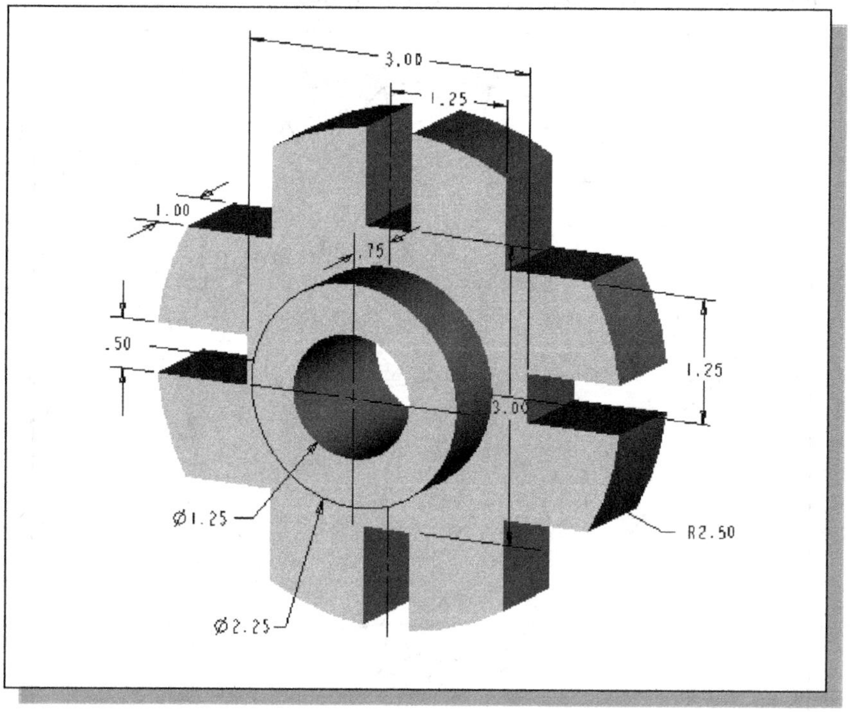

5. Dimensions are in inches.

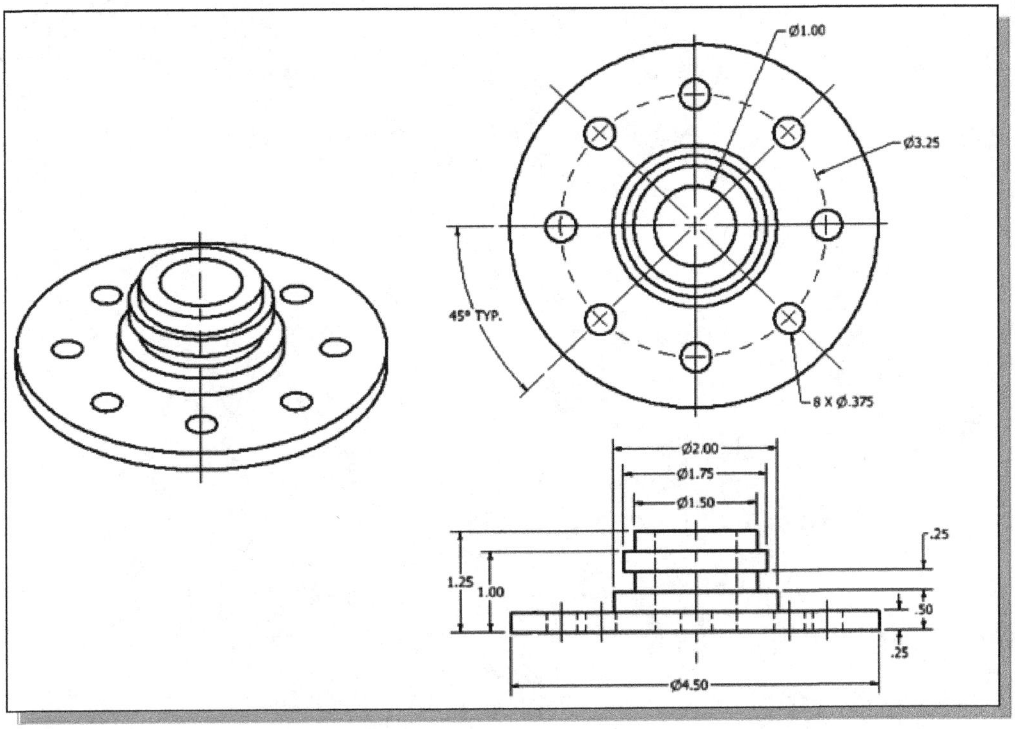

6. Dimensions are in inches.

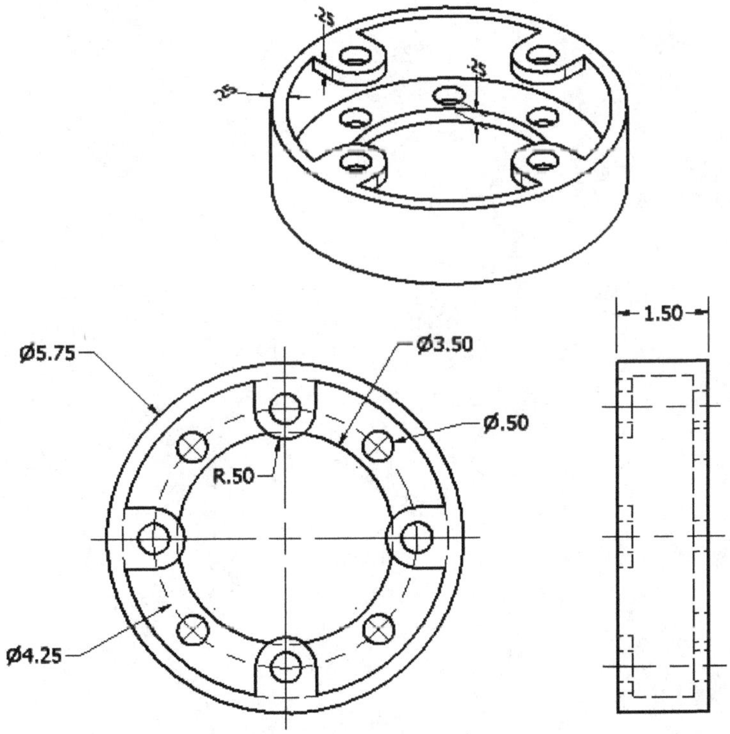

Notes:

Chapter 9
Multiview Drawings from 3D Models

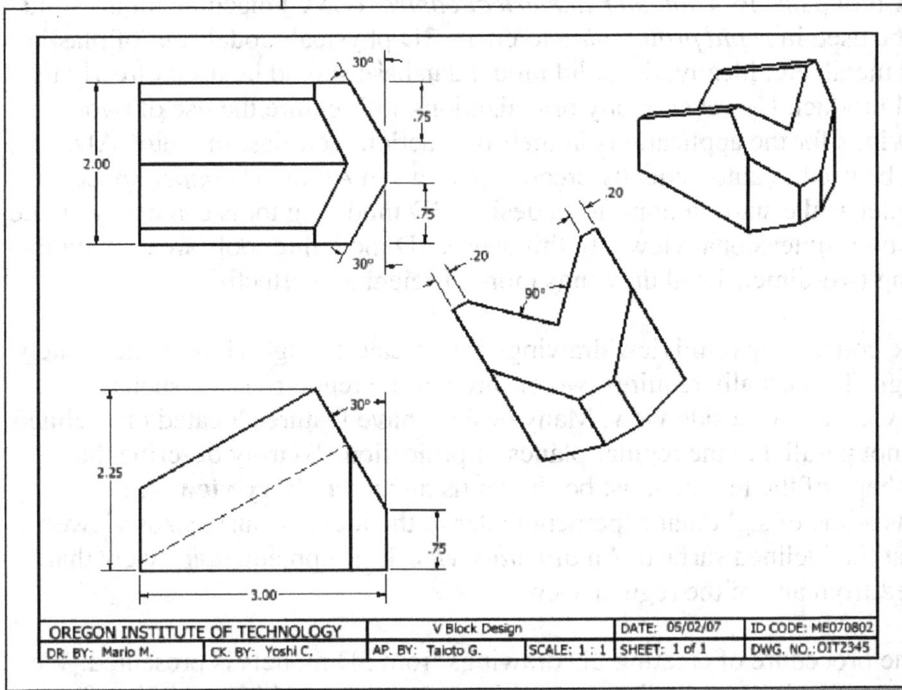

Learning Objectives

- **Create Multiview Drawings from 3D Models**
- **Create Borders and Title Block in the Layout Mode**
- **Create 2D Projections from 3D Models**
- **Create Auxiliary and Section views with the Section option**
- **Align and Position 2D Projected Views in Layout Mode**

Introduction

With the capabilities of solid modeling software, the importance of two-dimensional drafting is decreasing. Drafting is now considered as one of the downstream applications of using solid modeling. In many production facilities, solid models are being used to generate machine tool paths for *computer numerical control* (CNC) machine tools. Solid models can also be used in *rapid prototyping* to create 3D physical models out of plastic resins, powdered metal, etc. Ideally, the solid model database should be used directly to generate the final product. However, many organizations still require the use of two-dimensional drawings for the applications in their production facilities. In AutoCAD, model views can be used to automatically create 2D views in AutoCAD *paper space*. Using the 3D model as the starting point for a design, 3D modeling tools can easily create all the necessary two-dimensional views. In this sense, 3D modeling tools are making the process of creating two-dimensional drawings more efficient and effective.

An important rule concerning multiview drawings is to create enough views to accurately describe the design. This usually requires two or three of the regular views, such as a front view, a top view and/or a side view. Many designs have features located on inclined surfaces that are not parallel to the regular planes of projection. To truly describe the feature, the true shape of the feature must be shown using an **auxiliary view**. An *auxiliary view* has a line of sight that is perpendicular to the inclined surface, as viewed looking directly at the inclined surface. An *auxiliary view* is a supplementary view that can be constructed from any of the regular views.

In this chapter, the procedure of creating 2D drawings from 3D models is presented. We will create orthographic views, including an auxiliary view, of the *V-block* design from Chapter 7 and a section view for the Pulley design from Chapter 8.

The V-Block Design

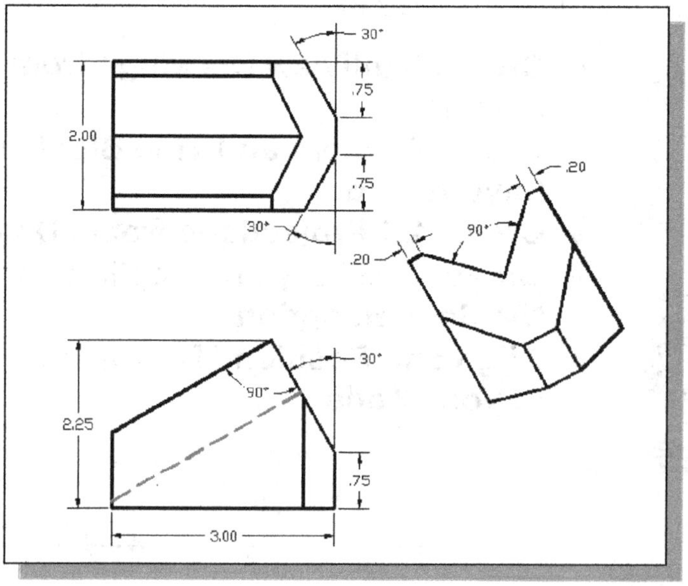

Starting Up AutoCAD 2027

1. Select the **AutoCAD 2027** option on the *Program* menu or select the **AutoCAD 2027** icon on the *Desktop*.

2. In the AutoCAD *Startup* dialog box, select the **Open a Drawing** option with a single click of the left-mouse-button.

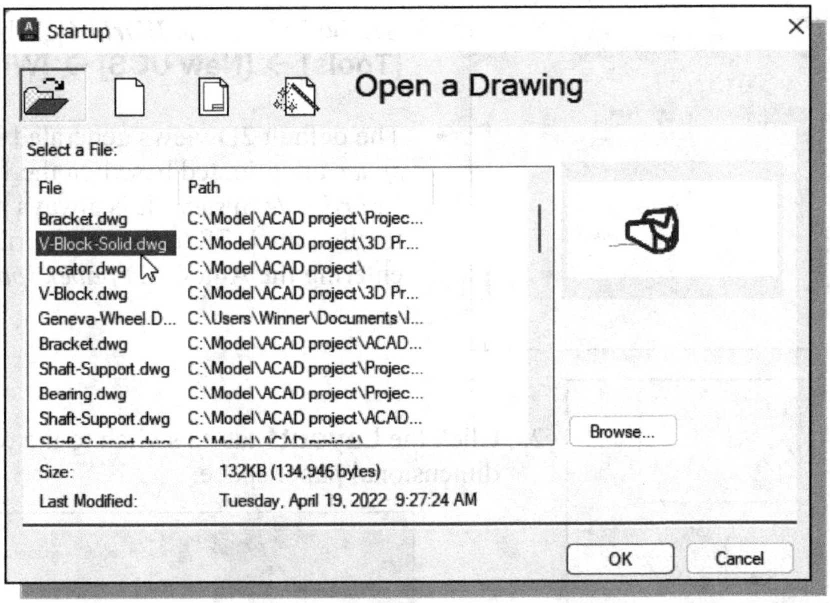

3. Open the *V-Block-Solid* solid model created in the previous chapter by clicking on the corresponding filename. (Use the **Browse** option to locate the solid model file if it is not displayed.)

- The *V-Block-Solid* solid model is retrieved and displayed in the graphics window.

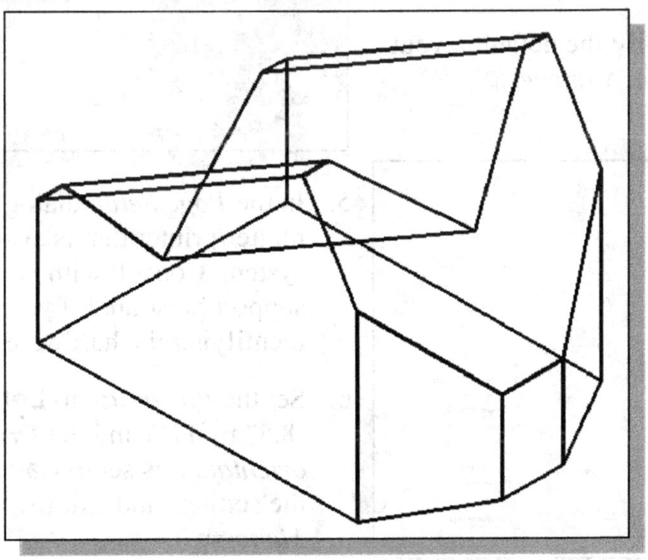

AutoCAD Paper Space

Until now, we have been working in ***model space*** to create our design in **full size**. Once the 3D model is constructed, we can arrange our design on a two-dimensional sheet of paper so that the plotted hardcopy is exactly what we want. This two-dimensional sheet of paper is known as ***paper space*** in AutoCAD. We can place borders and title blocks, the objects that are less critical to our design, on *paper space*.

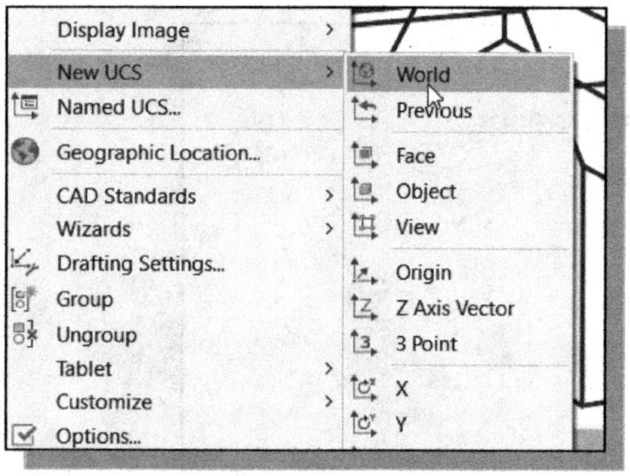

1. Set the UCS to the ***World UCS*** by selecting:
   [Tools] → [New UCS] → [World]

- The default 2D views generated in *paper space* are oriented based on the *World Coordinate System*. It is always a good idea to align the UCS to the WCS prior to entering the AutoCAD *paper space*.

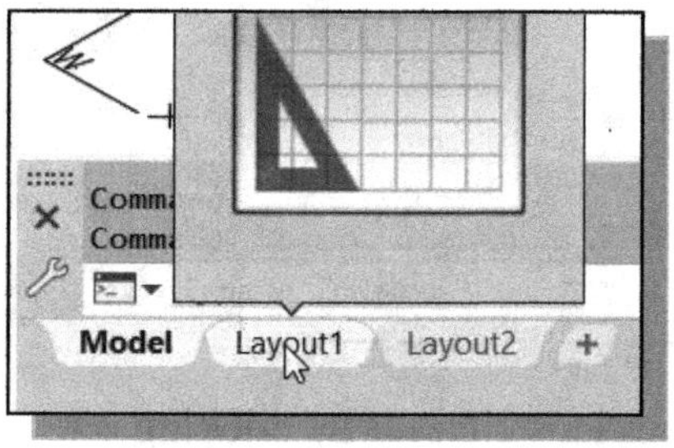

2. Click the **Layout1** tab to switch to the two-dimensional paper space.

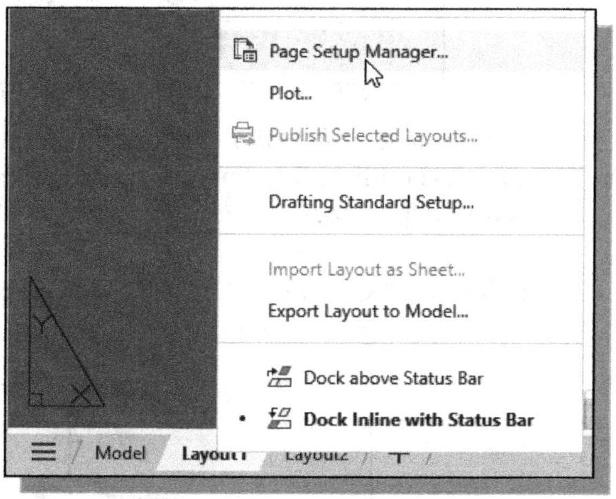

3. To adjust any *Page Setup* options, **right-click** once on the Layout1 tab and select **Page Setup Manager**.

4. Choose to **modify** the default layout in the *Page Setup Manager*.

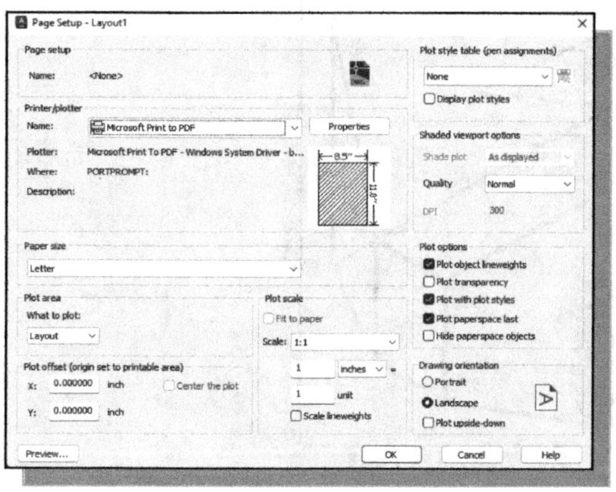

5. In the *Page Setup* dialog box, select a plotter/printer that is available to your system. Consult with your technical support personnel if you have difficulty identifying the hardware.

6. Set the *Paper size* to **Letter** or equivalent (8.5″ by 11″) and the *Drawing orientation* is set to **Landscape**. Accept the settings and exit the *Page Setup Manager*.

❖ In the *graphics window*, a rectangular outline on a gray background indicates the paper size. The 3D model appears inside a solid rectangle, which is known as a **viewport**. Note that the orientation of the model is identical to that of the model space.

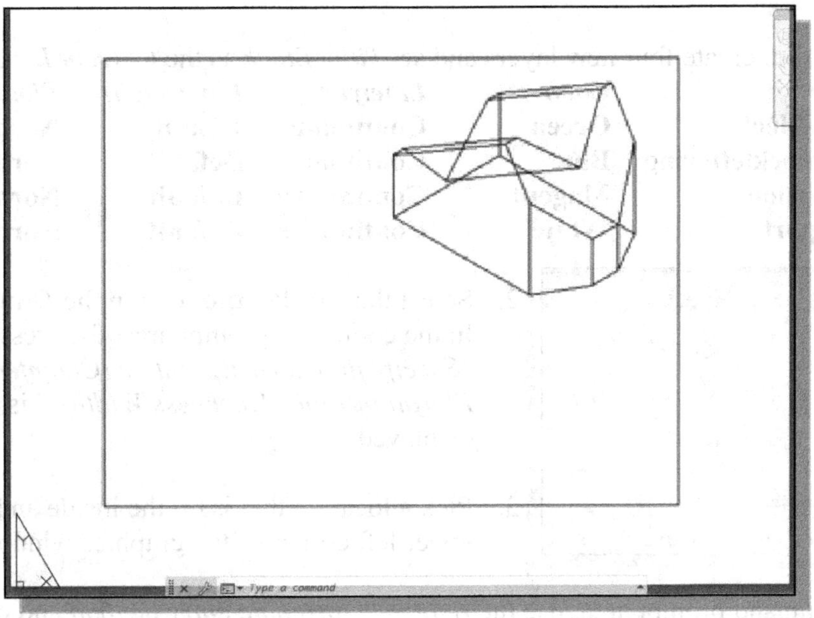

Delete the Displayed Viewport

Viewports can be considered as objects with a view into model space that we can move and resize. Floating viewports can be overlapping or separated from one another. We can also create new viewports, as well as delete them.

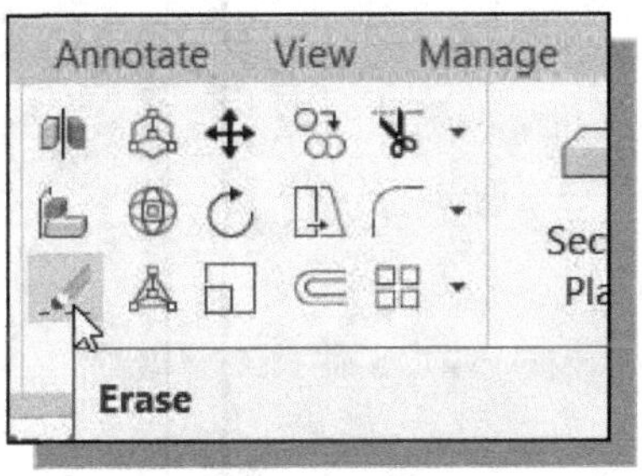

1. Pick **Erase** in the *Modify* toolbar.

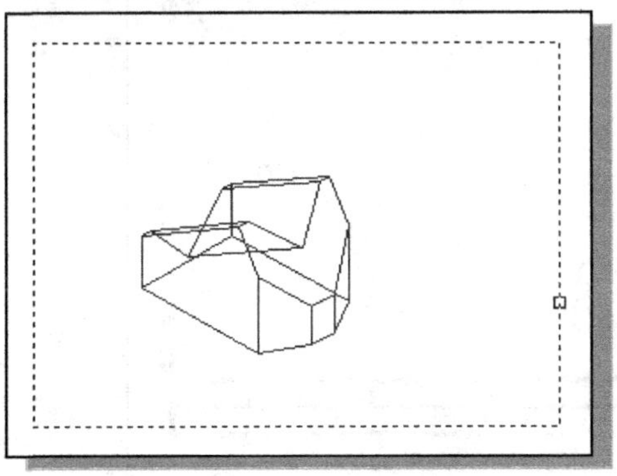

2. Pick the **viewport** by clicking on one of the edges of the viewport border.

3. Inside the graphics window, **right-click** to accept the selection and delete the viewport.

Add Borders and Title Block in the Layout

AutoCAD 2027 allows us to create plots/prints to any exact scale on the paper. We can place borders and title blocks, the objects that are less critical to our design, on *paper space*.

1. On your own, create four new layers and set *Title_Block* as the *Current Layer*.

Layer	*Color*	*Linetype*	*Lineweight*	*Plot Style*
Title_Block	**Green**	**Continuous**	**1.2mm**	**Normal**
Titleblocklettering	**Blue**	**Continuous**	**Default**	**Normal**
Dimensions	**Magenta**	**Continuous**	**Default**	**Normal**
Viewport	**White**	**Continuous**	**Default**	**Normal**

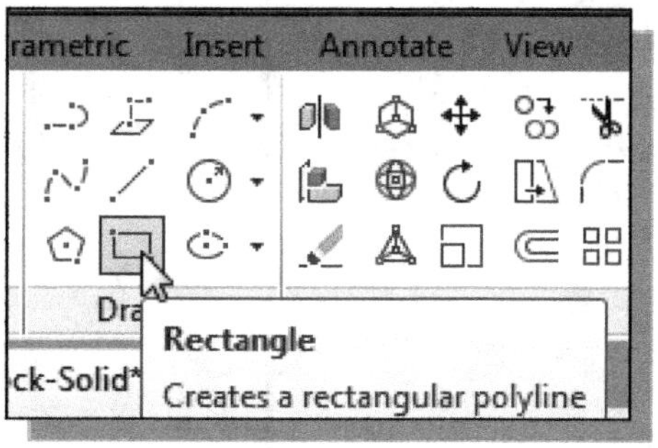

2. Select the **Rectangle** icon in the *Draw* toolbar. In the command prompt area, the message "*Specify first corner point or [Chamfer/ Elevation/Fillet/Thickness/Width]:*" is displayed.

3. Pick a location that is on the inside and near the lower left corner of the graphics window.

4. In the command prompt area, use the *relative coordinate entry method* and create a **10.25″** × **7.75″** rectangle.

5. Complete the title block as shown in the figure below. (Place the ***text*** in the *Titleblocklettering* layer.)

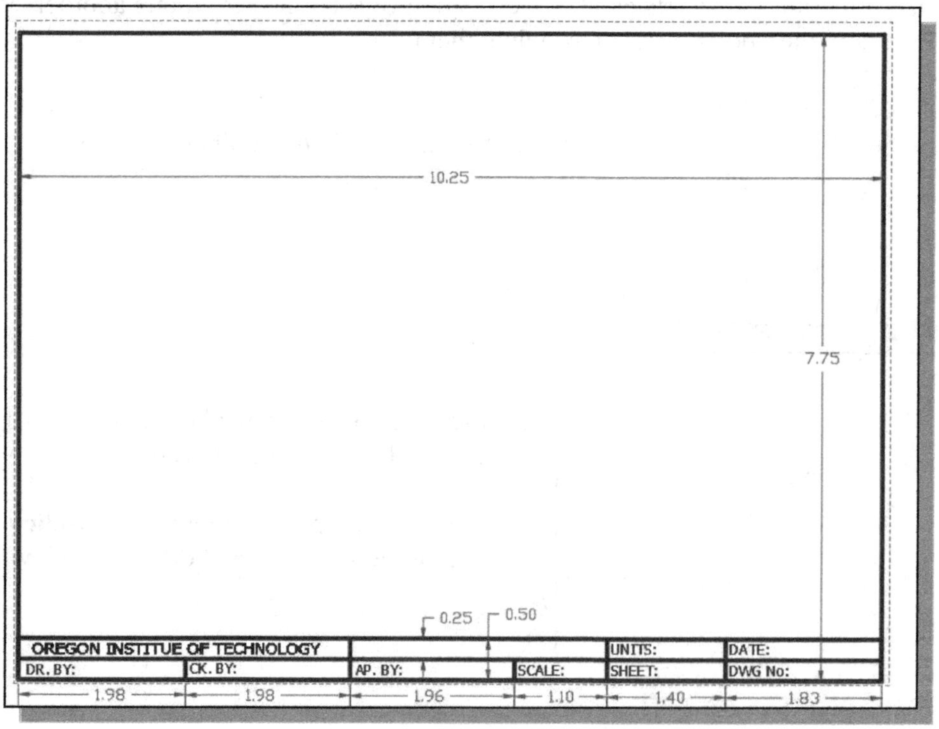

Setting Up the Standard Views

AutoCAD allows us to generate 2D views directly from models within AutoCAD or from existing Autodesk Inventor models. The default orientation of the standard views is based on the Top View being aligned to the World XY plane, and the Front View being aligned to the World ZX plane. Note that AutoCAD allows us to change the 2D view orientation in paper space, but it is less confusing to set the solid model orientation in the model space.

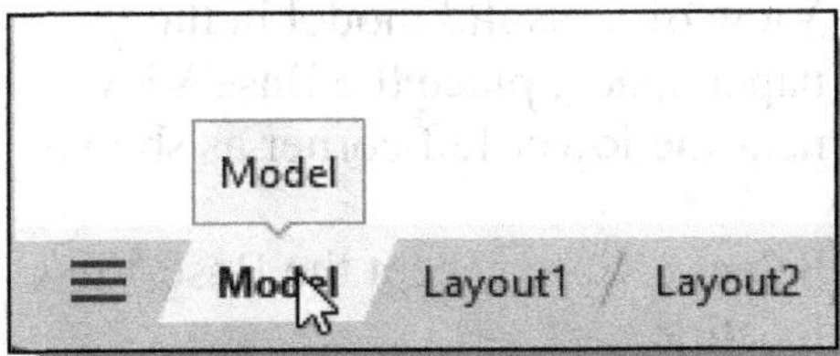

1. Click the **Model** tab to switch back to *model Space* as shown.

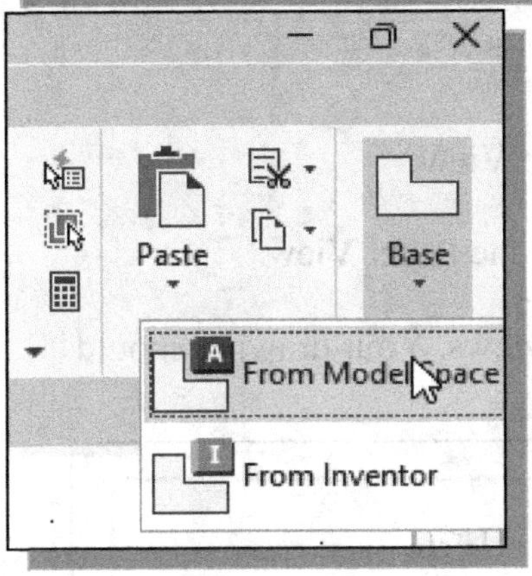

2. Activate the **Base View** command by clicking with the left-mouse-button, **Base →From Model Space** as shown. (Hint: the Base command is on the right side of the ribbon toolbar.)

3. Pick the **Solid Model** in the graphics area as shown.

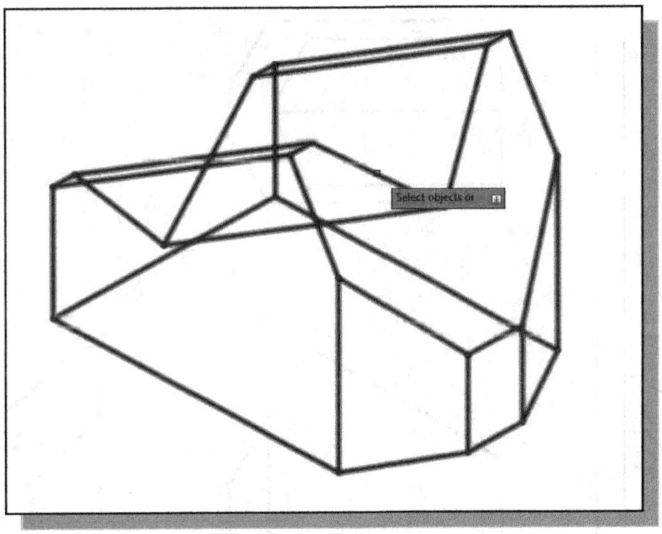

4. Click on the Entire Model option to accept the selected object as shown.

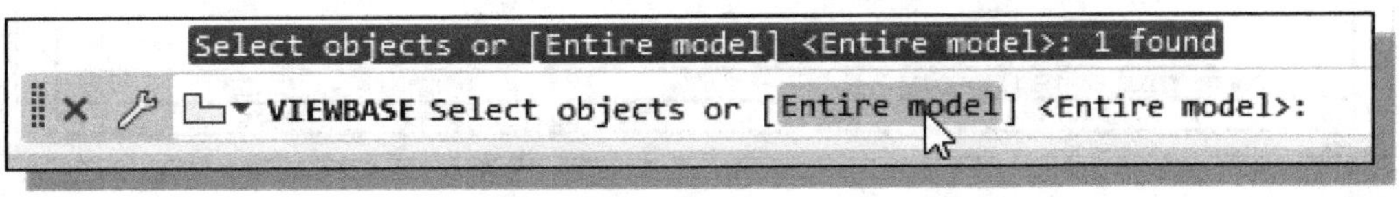

5. Press the **[Enter]** key once to accept using Layout1 to place the Base View.

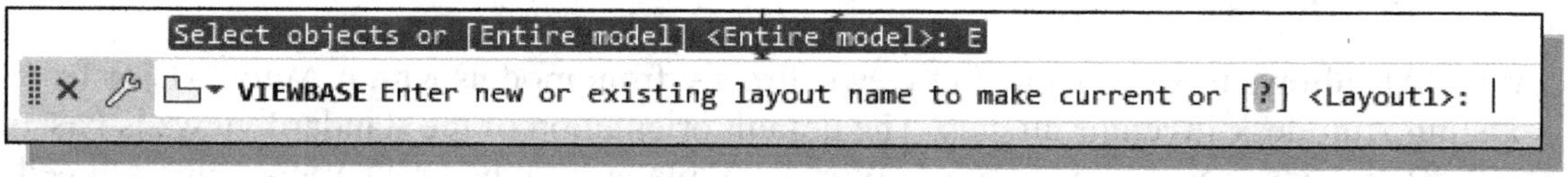

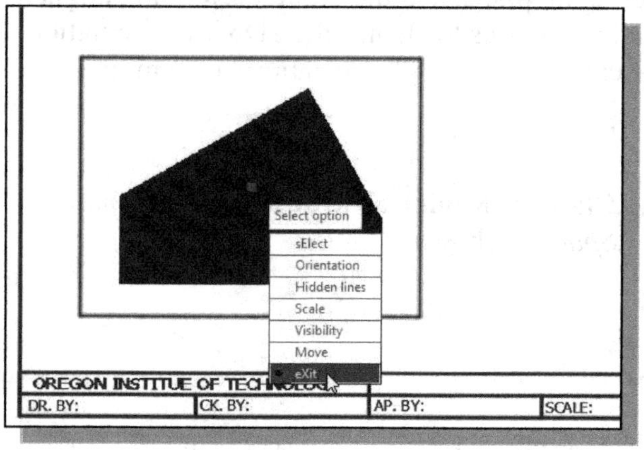

6. Note that the **View-Base** command now displays the Front View of the solid model in the paper space; place the Base View near the lower left corner as shown.

7. Select eXit to accept the Base View location.

8. Move the cursor above the Base View to place the Top View.

9. Move the cursor to the right of the Base View to place the Right View.

10. Press the **[Enter]** key once to accept the placed three views. Your drawing should appear as shown in the below figure.

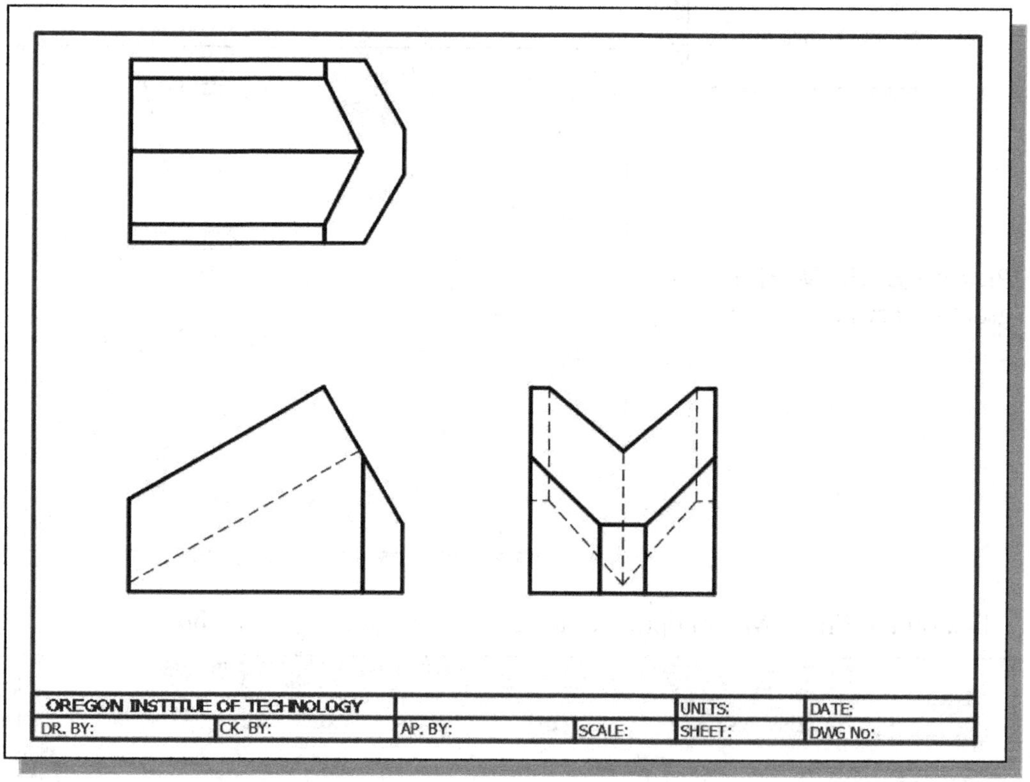

Determine the Necessary 2D Views

Multiview drawings usually require two or three of the regular views, such as a front view, a top view and/or a side view. Many designs have features located on inclined surfaces that are not parallel to the regular planes of projection. For the *V-block* design, to truly describe the V-cut feature, the true shape of the feature must be shown using an **auxiliary view**. An *auxiliary view* has a line of sight that is perpendicular to the inclined surface, as viewed looking directly at the inclined surface. An *auxiliary view* is a supplementary view that can be constructed from any of the regular views.

Examining the current four standard views, we can conclude that the right side view provides no crucial information on the design. Instead, an *auxiliary view* is needed to truly describe the V-cut feature.

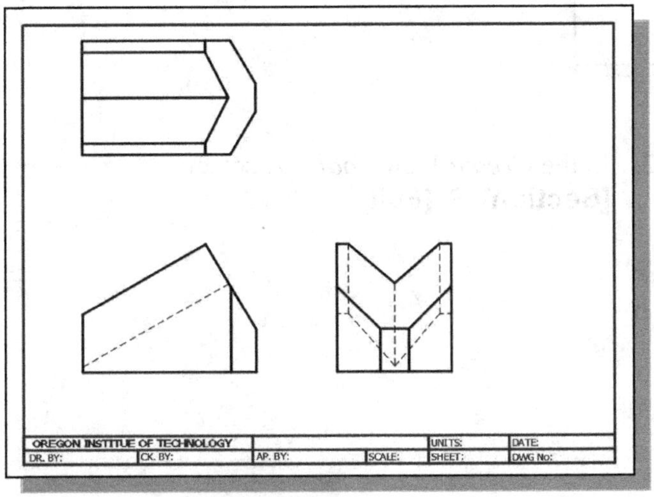

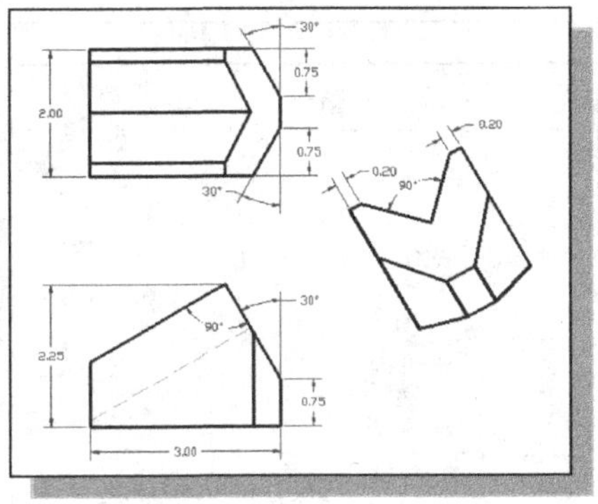

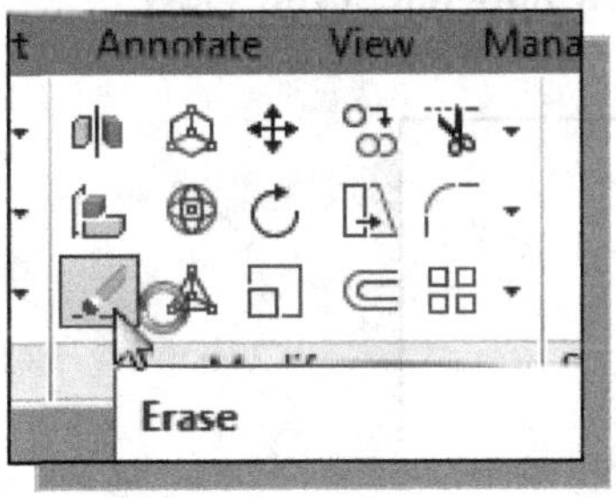

1. Pick **Erase** in the *Modify* toolbar.

2. The message "*Select objects*" is displayed in the *command prompt area* and AutoCAD awaits us to select the objects to erase. Pick the **lower right view** by clicking on any edge of the view.

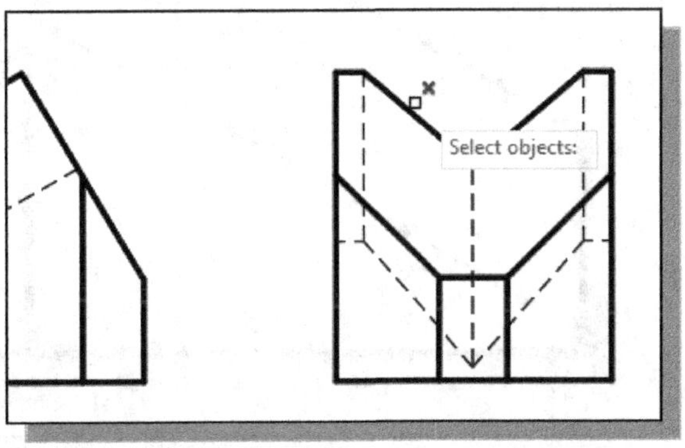

3. Inside the *graphics window*, **right-click** to accept the selection and delete the selected view.

Establish an Auxiliary View

AutoCAD provides us with many options to establish new views in the paper space. The easiest approach to create an auxiliary view is to use the **Section View** command. Note that an Auxiliary View is established following the same rules of orthographic projection for standard views; however, the alignment direction is always perpendicular to the edge view of the surface.

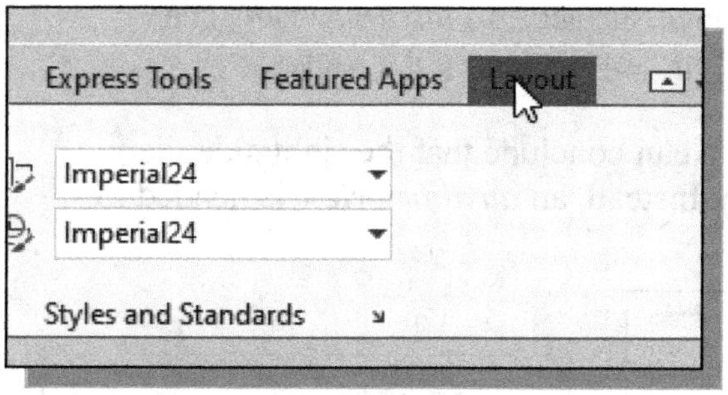

1. Click the **Layout** tab to switch to *model space*.

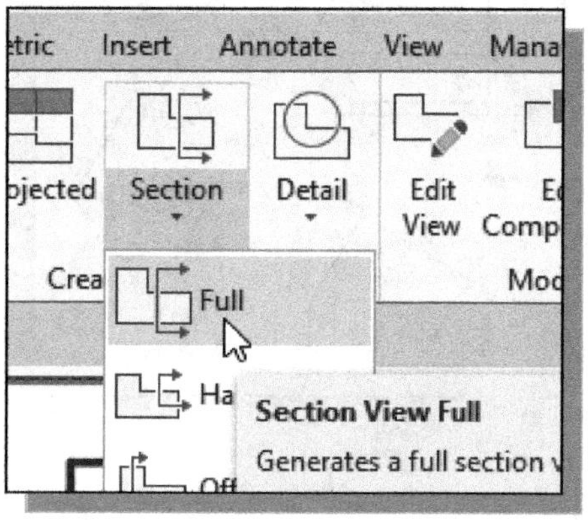

2. In the *Create View ToolBar*, select: **[Section] → [Full]**

3. Pick the **Base View** by moving the cursor on top of the view and select the view when the dashed box appears as shown.

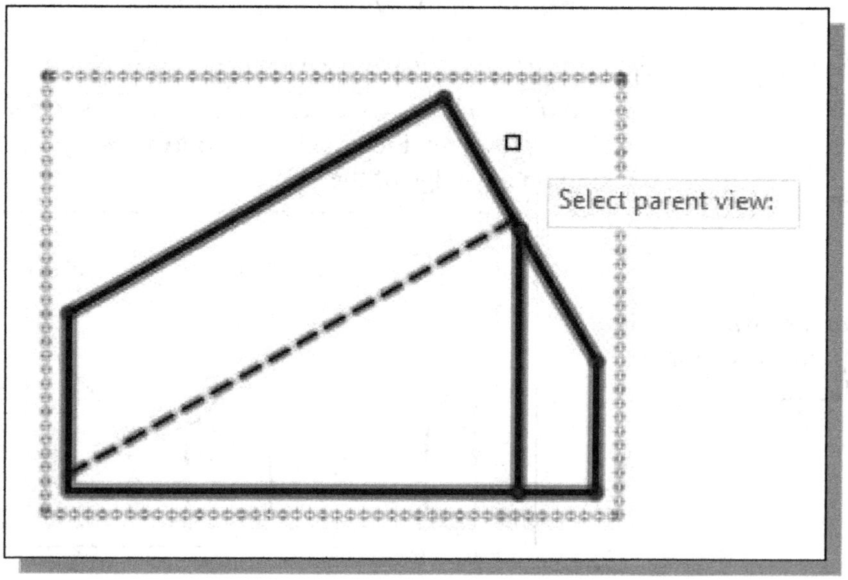

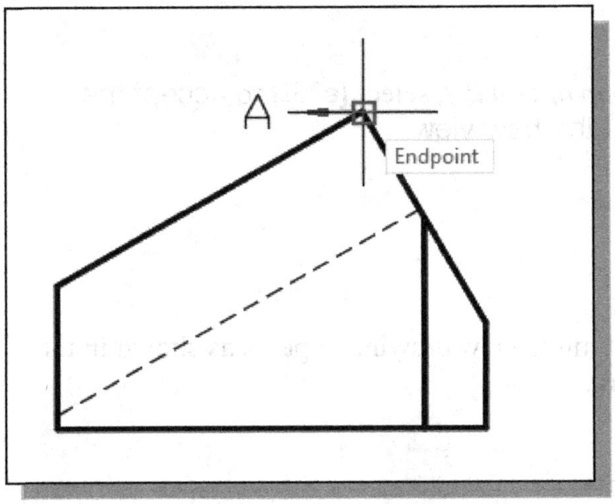

4. Select the top corner of the base view to align the first point of the cutting plane line.

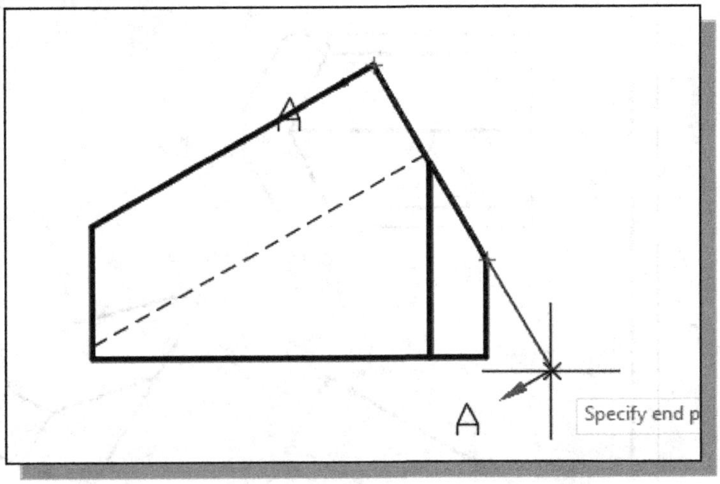

5. Move the cursor along the inclined line and accept a point that is below the bottom horizontal line as shown.

6. Move the cursor to the right and notice an auxiliary view following the orthographic projection rules is generated. Select a location to the right as shown.

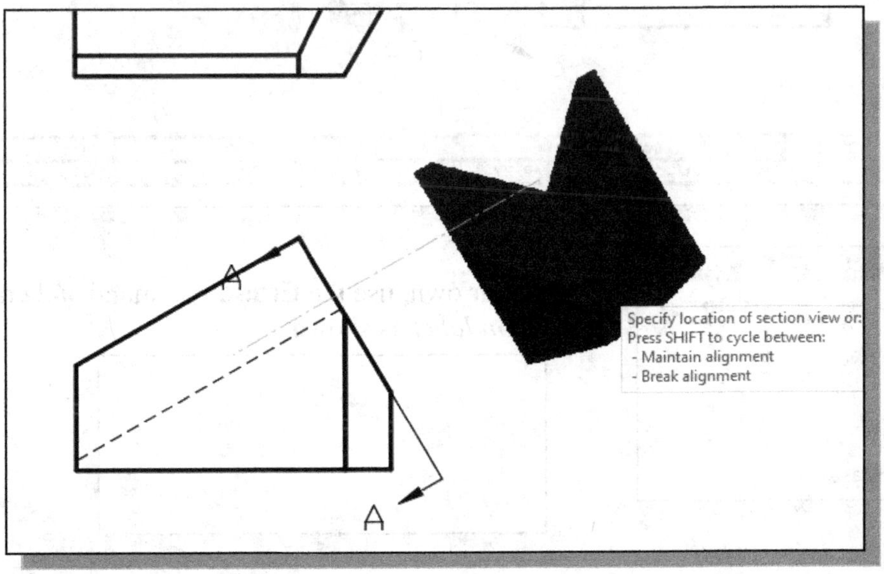

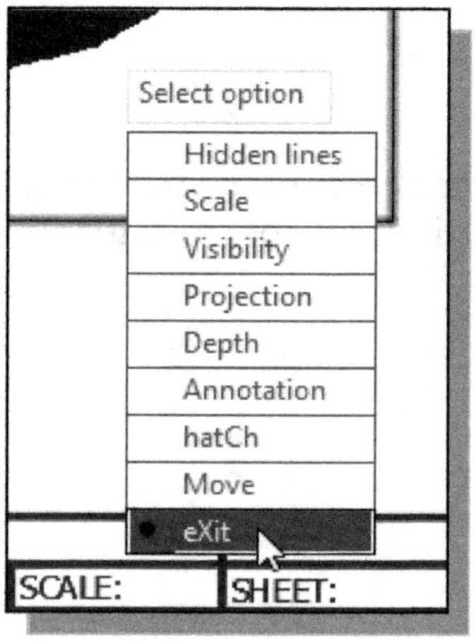

7. In the *pop-up option list*, select **[eXit]** to accept the creation of the new view.

- The current multi-view drawing appears as shown in the below figure.

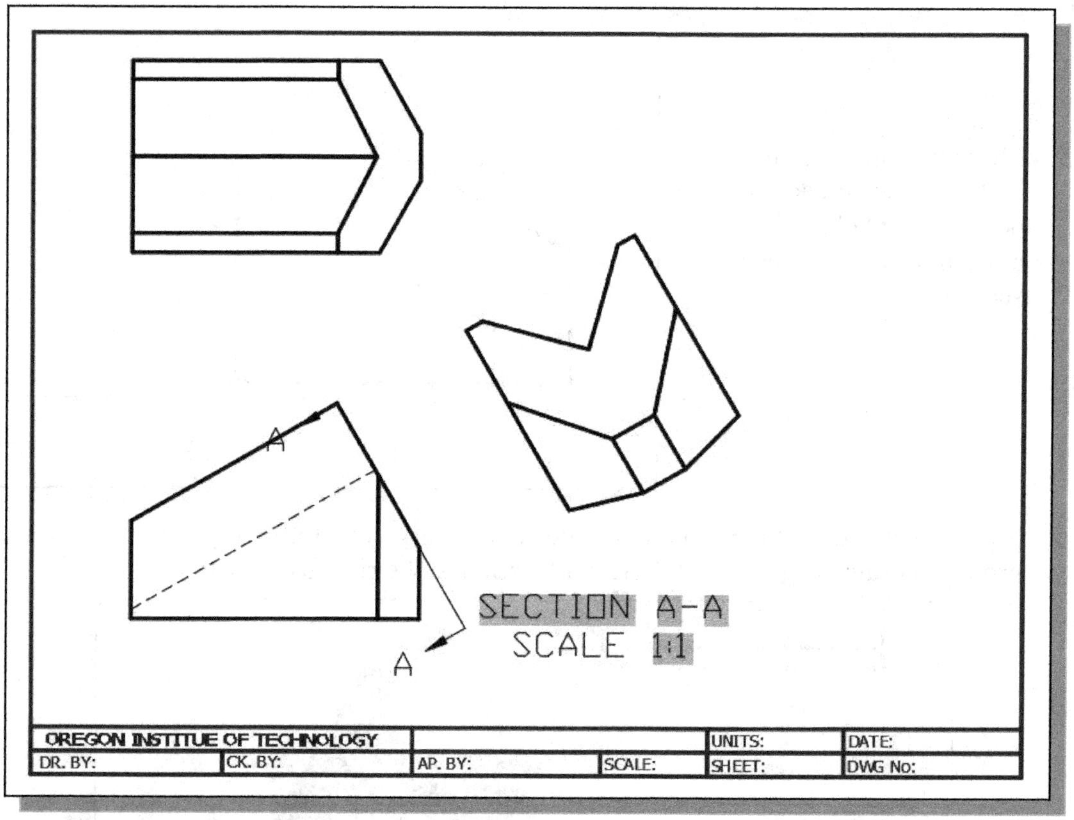

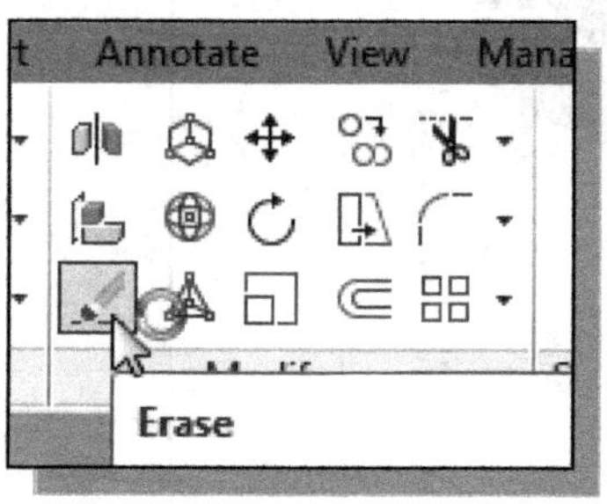

8. On your own, use the **Erase** command and erase the *Section label* as shown.

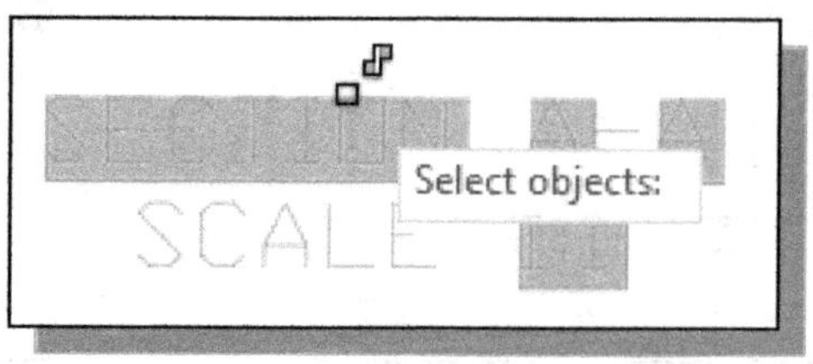

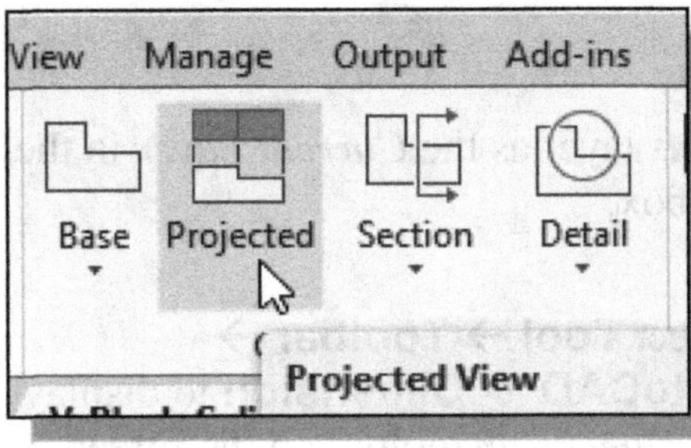

9. In the *Create View Toolbar*, select the **Projected** button to create a new projected view.

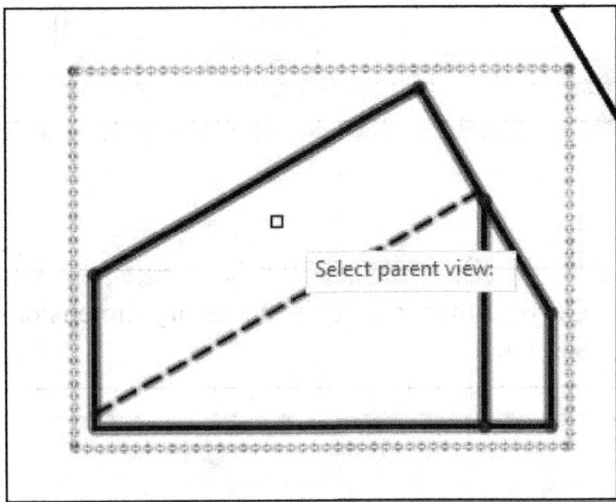

10. Select the **Front View** as the parent view as shown.

11. On your own, place an isometric view at the **upper right corner**.

12. Click **eXit** to end the projected view command.

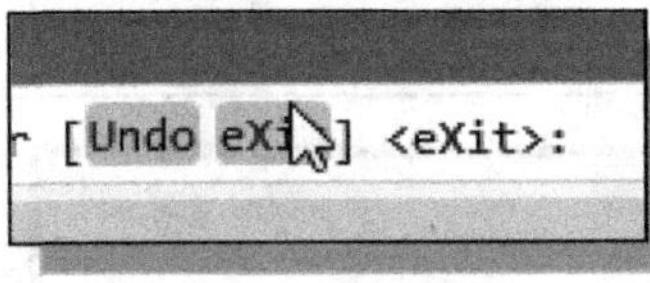

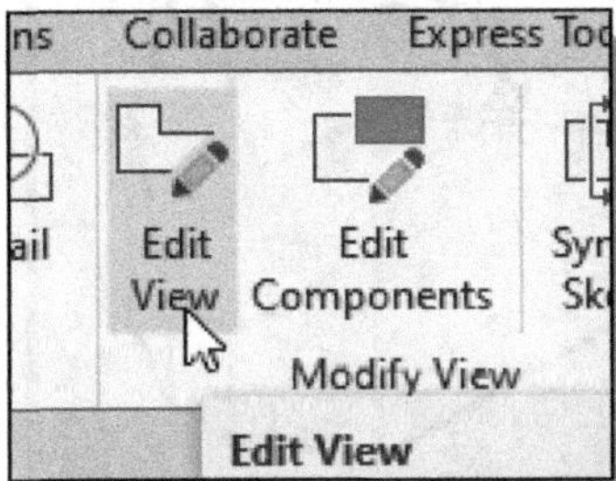

13. Select the **Edit View** button to adjust the properties of a view.

14. Select the *Isometric view*.

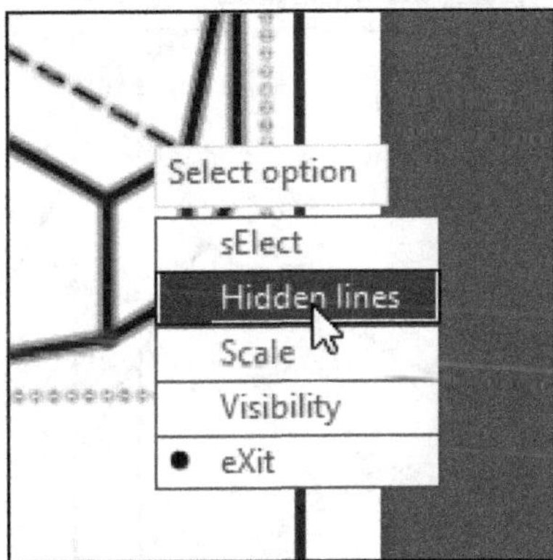

15. Select the **Hidden lines** option.

16. Select the **Visible Lines** option.

17. Click **eXit** to end the command

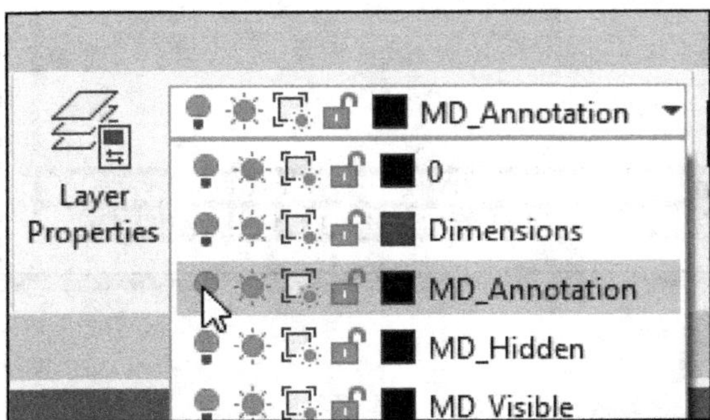

18. On your own, turn off the display of the *MD Annotation* layer as shown. (Hint, Switch back to the Home tab.) This will turn off the arrows on the Front View.

Complete the 2D Drawing

1. Set the ***Dimensions*** layer as the *Current Layer* in the *Layer Properties* box.

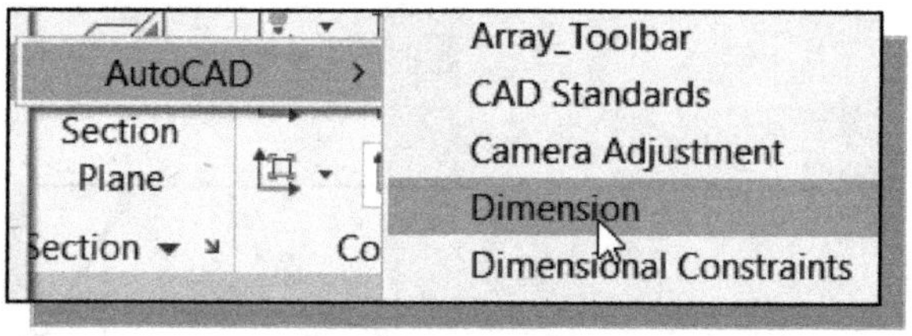

2. Select **Tool → Toolbar → AutoCAD → Dimension** to display the *Dimension* toolbar on the screen.

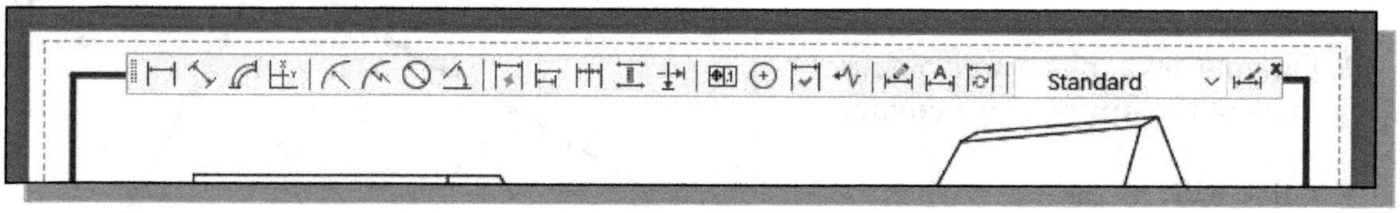

3. On your own, create the necessary dimensions and complete the 2D drawing as shown.

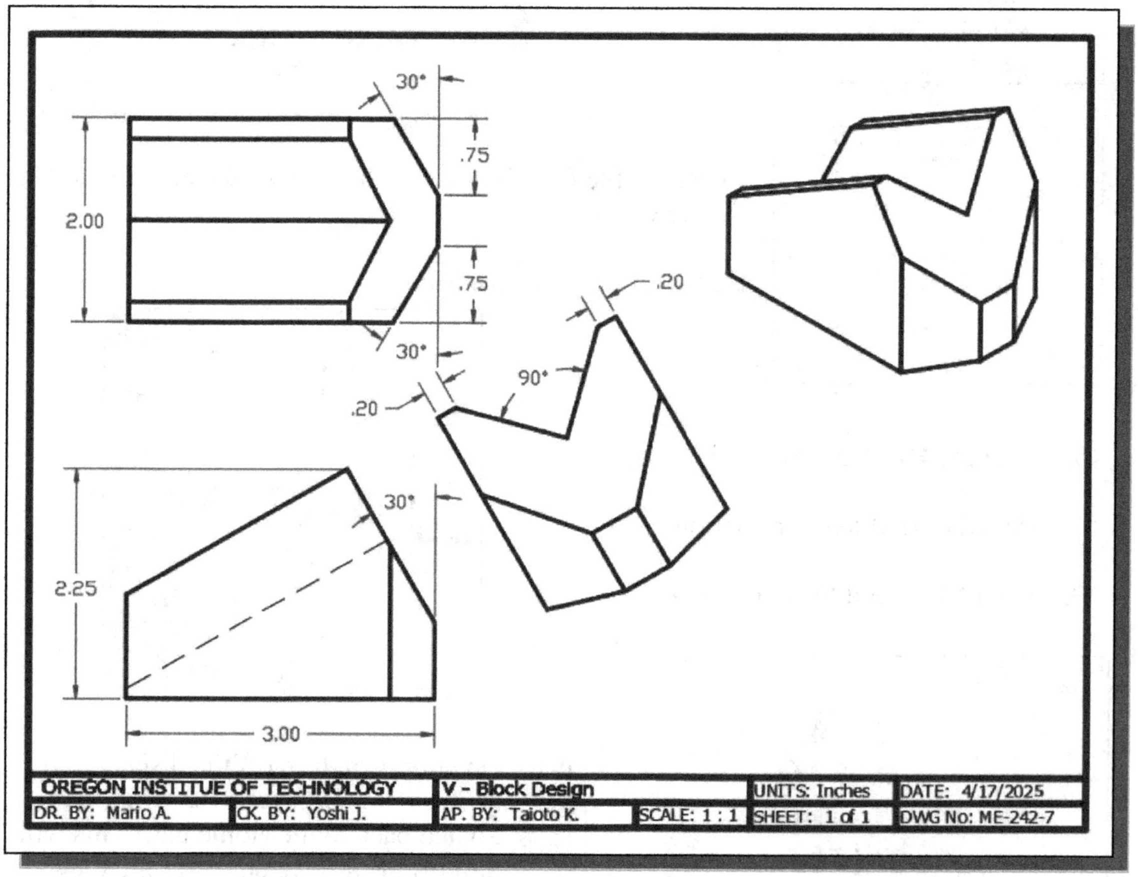

Open the Pulley Solid Model

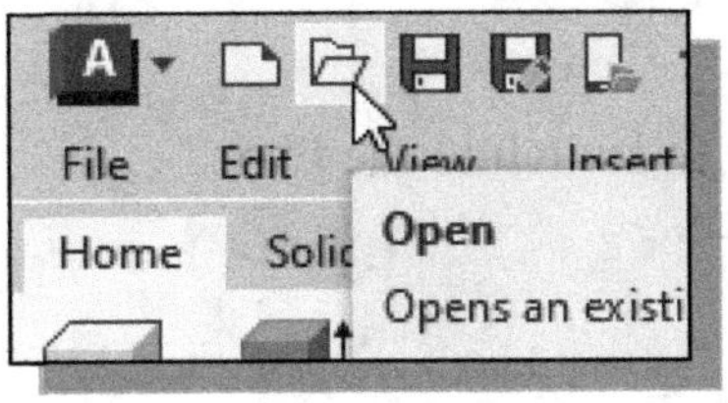

1. Select the **Open** option in the *Quick Access* menu as shown.

2. In the AutoCAD *Select Files* dialog box, open the **Pulley.dwg** *V-Block-Solid* solid model created in the previous chapter by clicking on the corresponding filename.

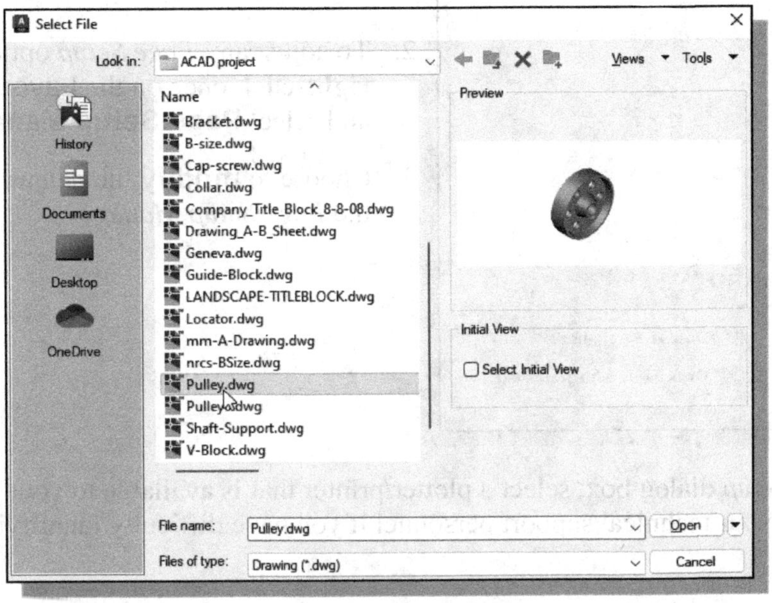

- The *Pulley* solid model is retrieved and displayed in the graphics window.

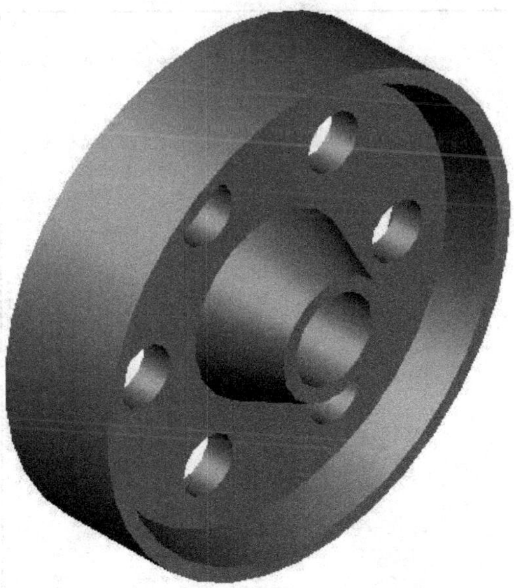

AutoCAD Paper Space Setup

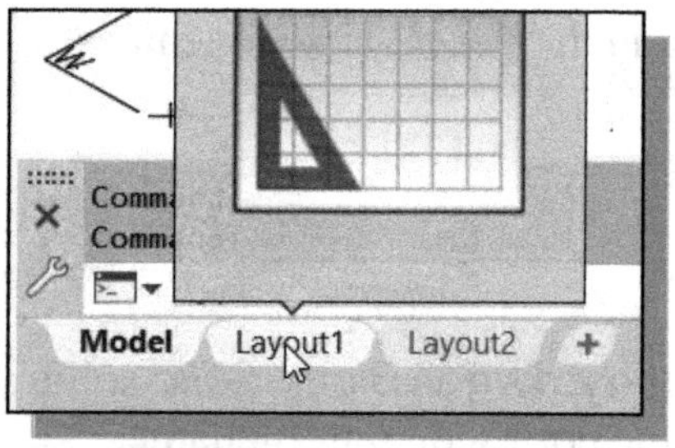

1. Click the **Layout1** tab to switch to the two-dimensional paper space.

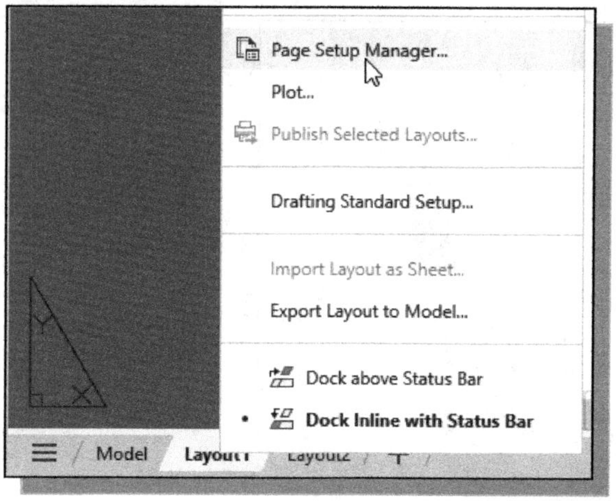

2. To adjust any *Page Setup* options, **right-click** once on the **Layout1** tab and select **Page Setup Manager**.

3. Choose to **modify** the default layout in the *Page Setup Manager*.

4. In the *Page Setup* dialog box, select a plotter/printer that is available to your system. Consult with your technical support personnel if you have difficulty identifying the hardware.

5. Set the *Paper size* to **Letter** or equivalent (8.5″ by 11″) and the *Drawing orientation* is set to **Landscape**. Accept the settings and exit the *Page Setup Manager*.

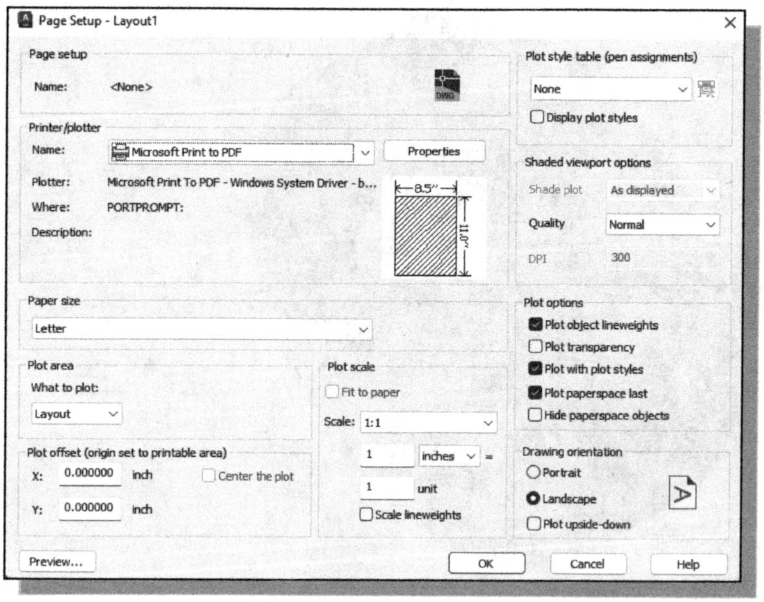

Delete the Displayed Viewport

Viewports can be considered as objects with a view into model space that we can move and resize. Floating viewports can be overlapping or separated from one another. We can also create new viewports, as well as delete them.

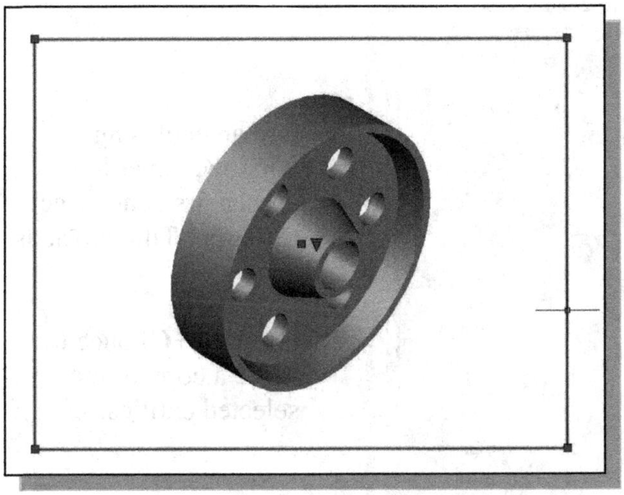

1. Pick the **viewport** by clicking on one of the edges of the viewport border.

2. Press the [Delete] key once to delete the viewport.

Add Borders and Title Block by Copy & Paste

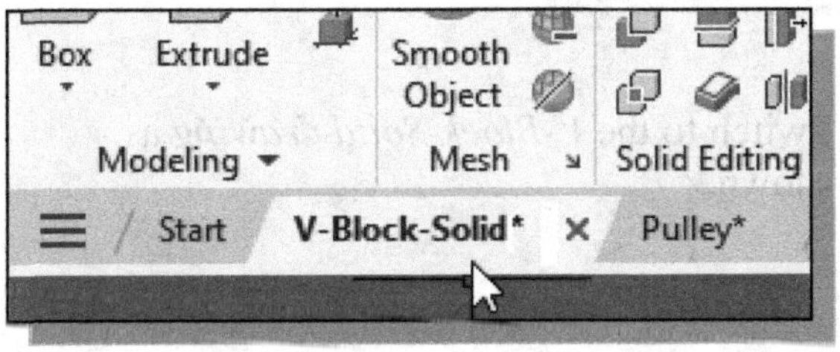

1. On your own, switch to the *V-Block-Solid drawing* as shown.

2. In the *Layer Properties,* turn off the **MD Hidden**, **MD Visible** layers as shown.

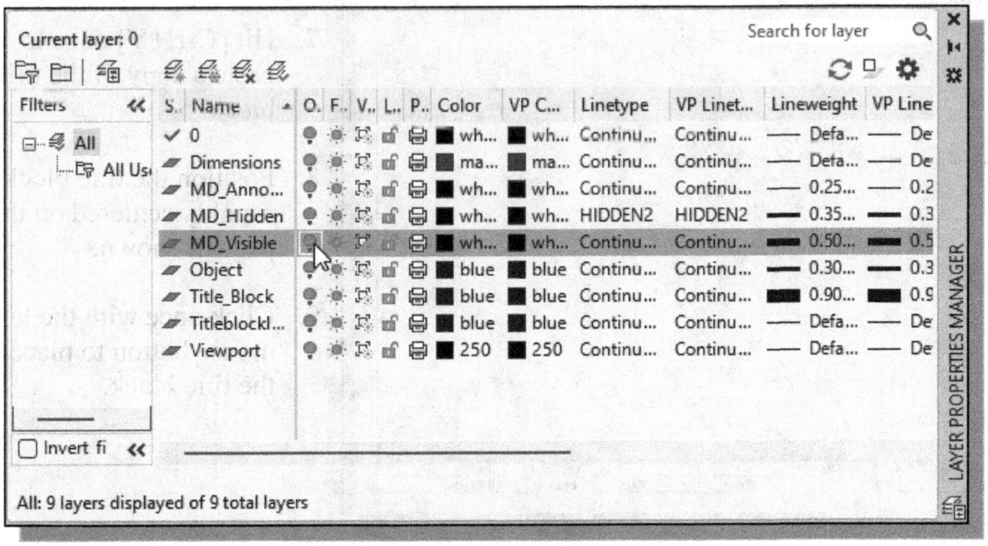

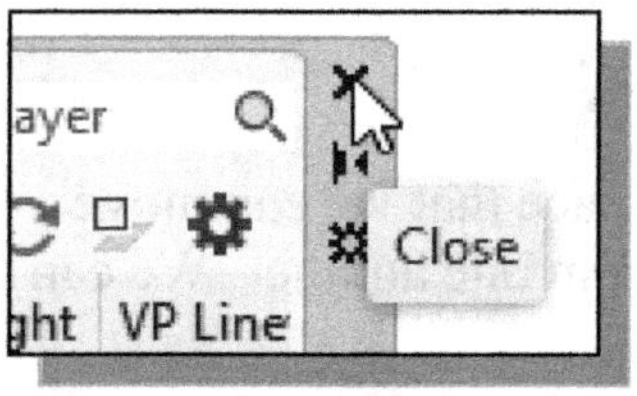

3. Click **Close** to exit the *Layer properties* dialog box.

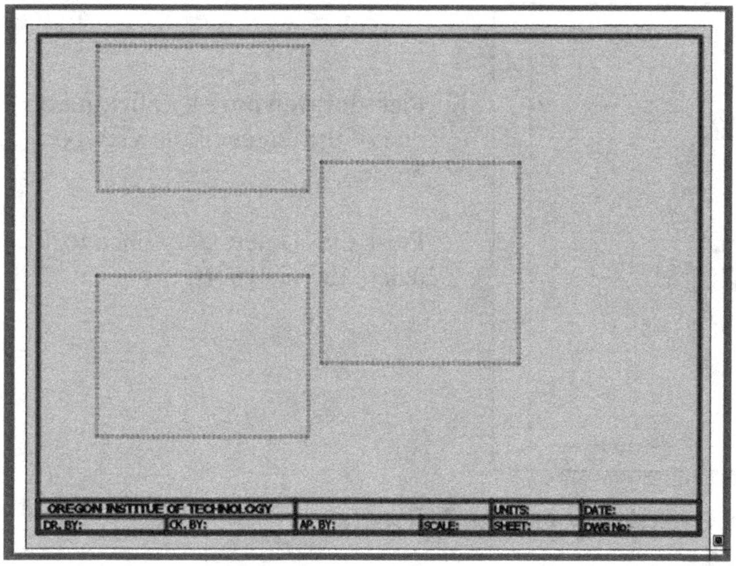

4. Use an enclosing window, upper left corner first, and select the entire Title block as shown.

5. Hit [**Ctrl+C**] once to make a copy of the selected entities.

6. Switch to the *V-Block-Solid drawing* as shown.

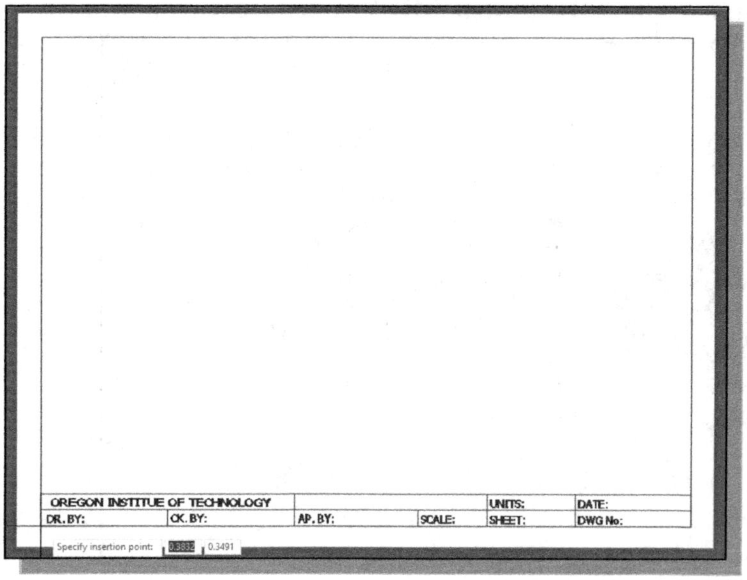

7. Hit [**Ctrl+V**] once to paste a copy of the title block.

8. Position the title block roughly centered on the page as shown.

9. Click once with the left-mouse button to place the title block.

Setting Up the Standard Views

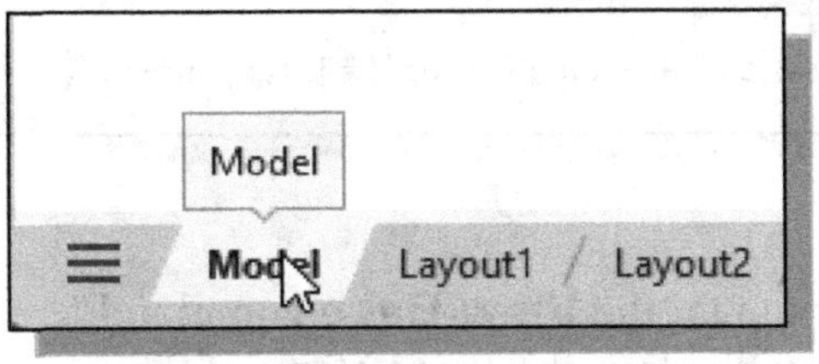

1. Click the **Model** tab to switch back to *model Space* as shown.

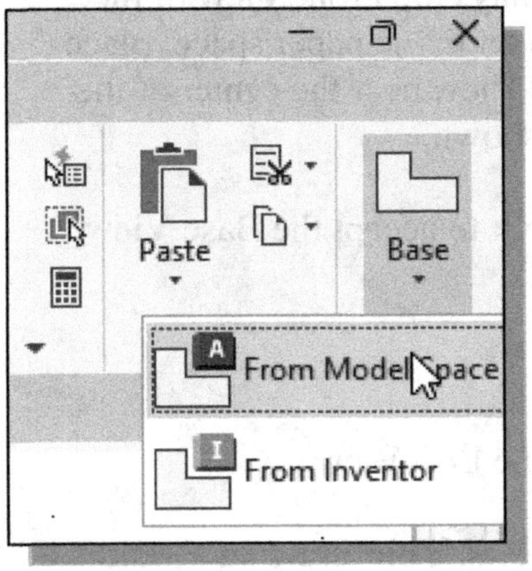

2. Activate the **Base View** command by selecting with the left-mouse-button **Base →From Model Space** as shown.

3. Pick the **Solid Model** in the graphics area as shown.

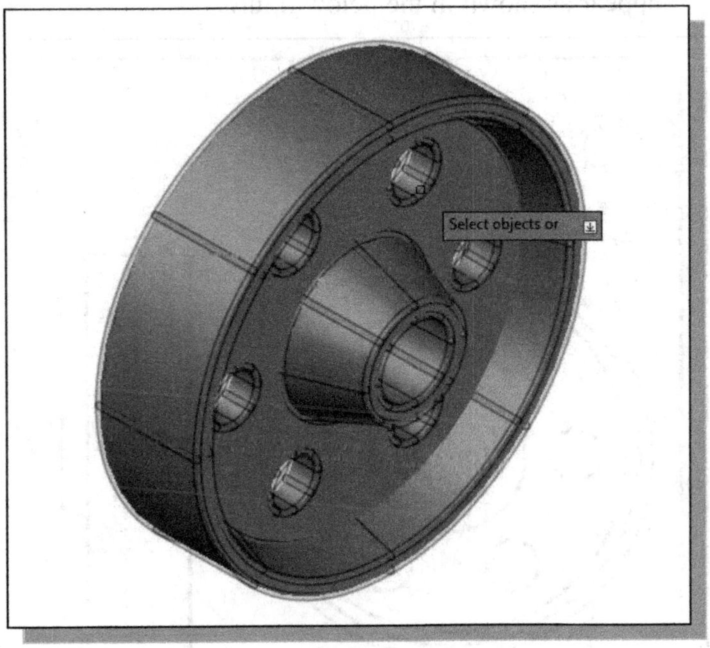

4. Click on the **Entire Model** option to accept the selected object as shown.

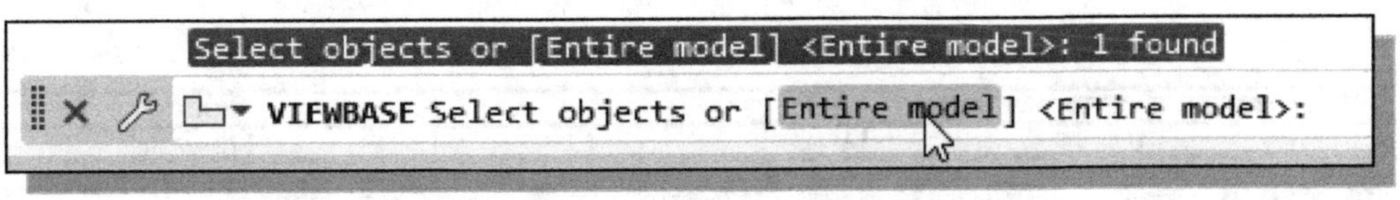

5. Press the [**Enter**] key once to accept using Layout1 to place the Base View.

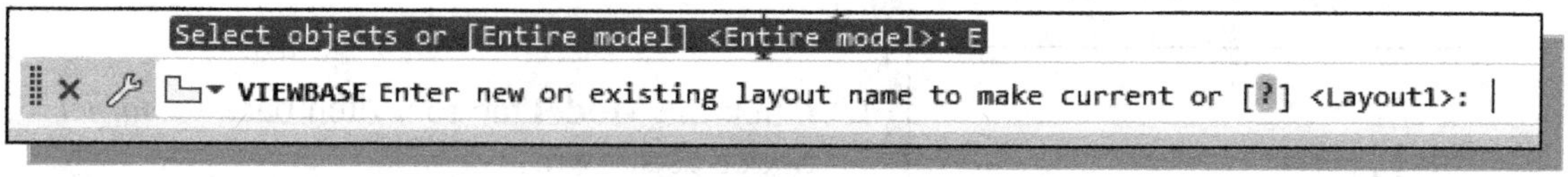

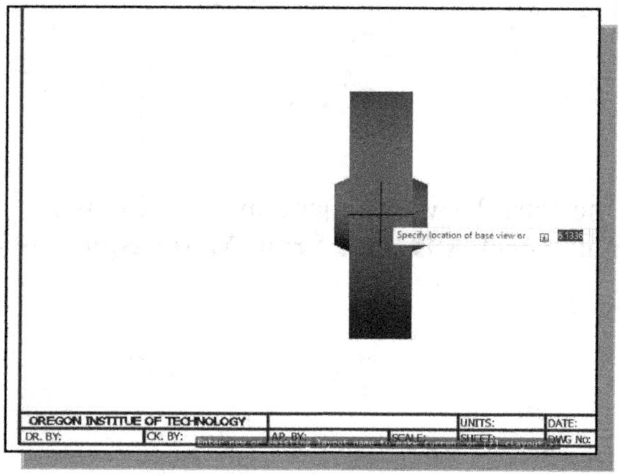

6. Note that the **View-Base** command now displays the Front View of the solid model in the paper space; place the Base View near the center of the page as shown.

7. Select eXit to accept the Base View location.

8. Move the cursor to the left of the Base View to place the Left View.

9. Press the [**Enter**] key once to accept the placed two views. Your drawing should appear as shown in the below figure.

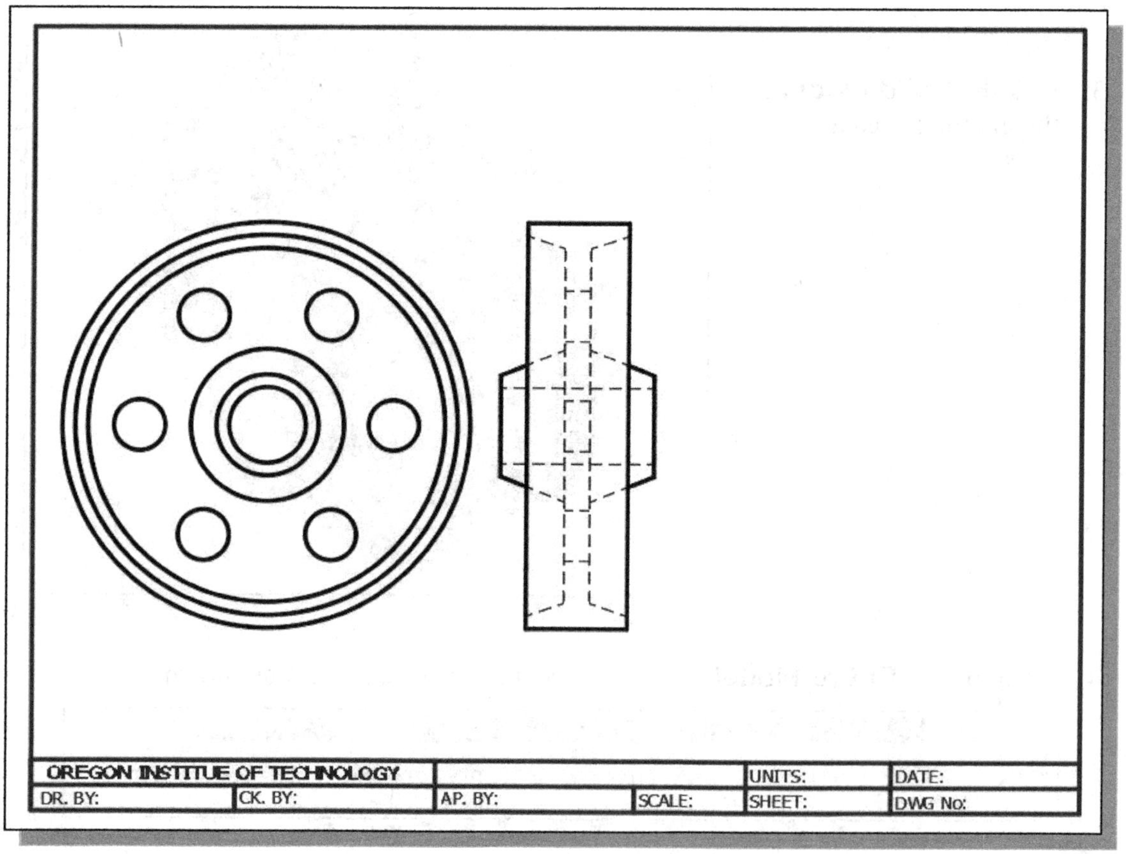

Determine the Necessary 2D Views

Multiview drawings usually require two or three of the regular views, such as a front view, a top view and/or a side view. Many designs may have features located on the interior that are not easily seen through standard views. For the *Pulley* design, the true shape of the interior features can be shown using a **section view**. In AutoCAD, a *section view* is constructed by referencing an existing view.

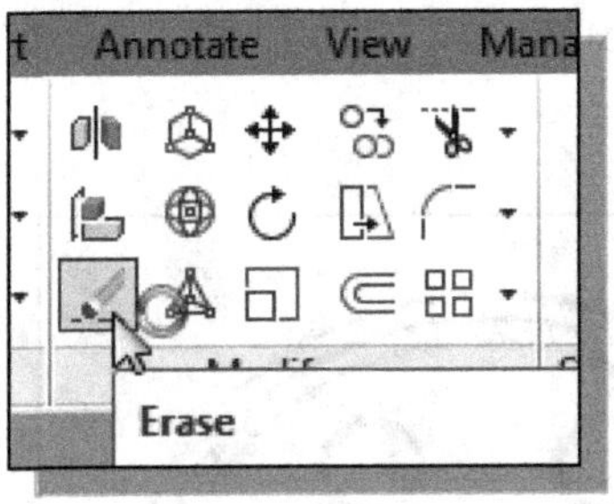

1. Pick **Erase** in the *Modify* toolbar.

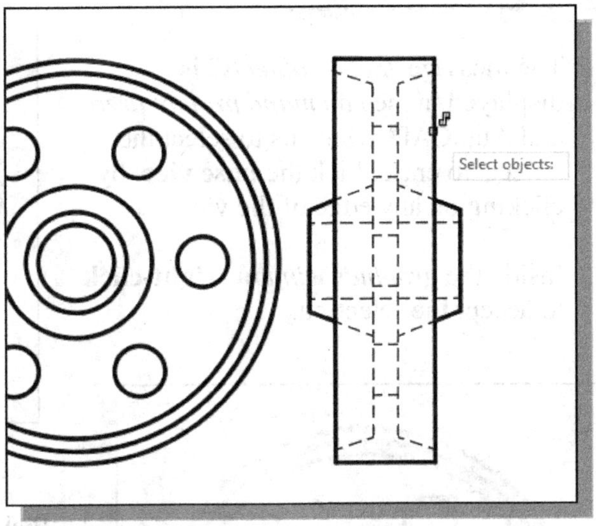

2. The message "*Select objects*" is displayed in the *command prompt area* and AutoCAD awaits us to select the objects to erase. Pick the **lower right view** by clicking on any edge of the view.

3. Inside the *graphics window*, **right-click** to accept the selection and delete the selected view.

4. On your own, use the left-mouse-button to reposition the view by drag & drop.

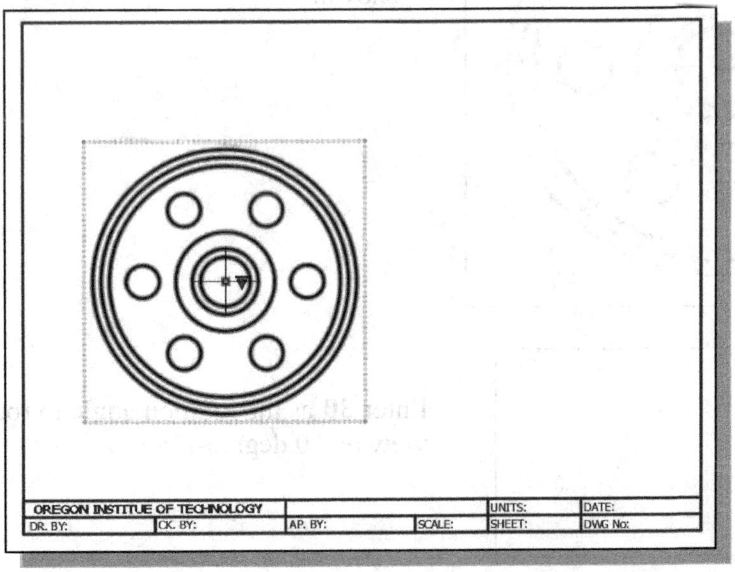

Rotate the Base View

The current Base view is showing the two center points of the six holes are aligned to the center of the design horizontally; we will first adjust the alignment to be in the vertical direction prior to creating a section view.

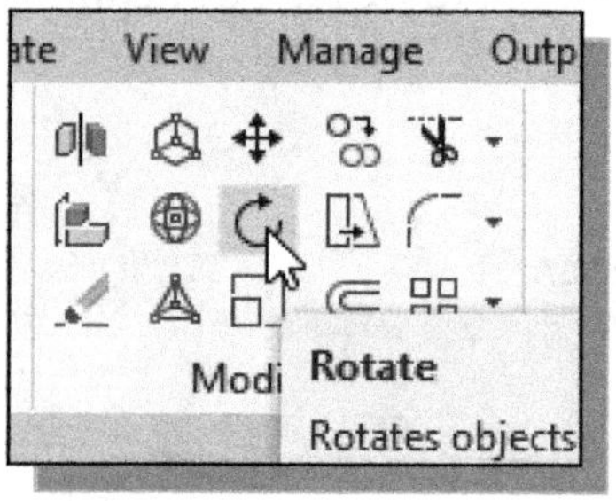

1. Pick **Rotate** in the *Modify* toolbar.

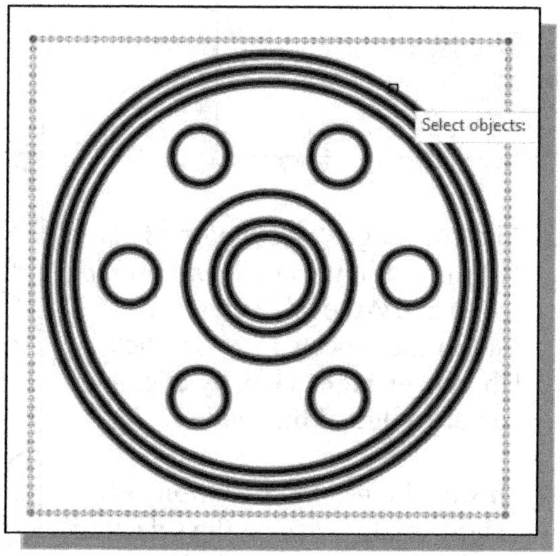

2. The message "*Select objects*" is displayed in the *command prompt area* and AutoCAD awaits us to select the objects to erase. Pick the **base view** by clicking on any edge of the view.

3. Inside the *graphics window*, **right-click** to accept the selection.

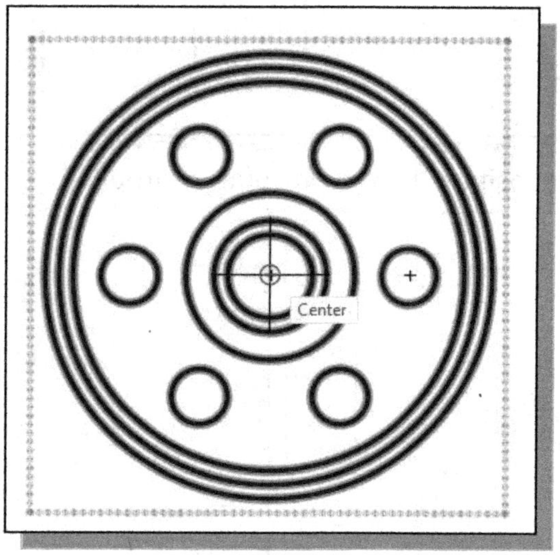

4. Pick the center point of the design as shown.

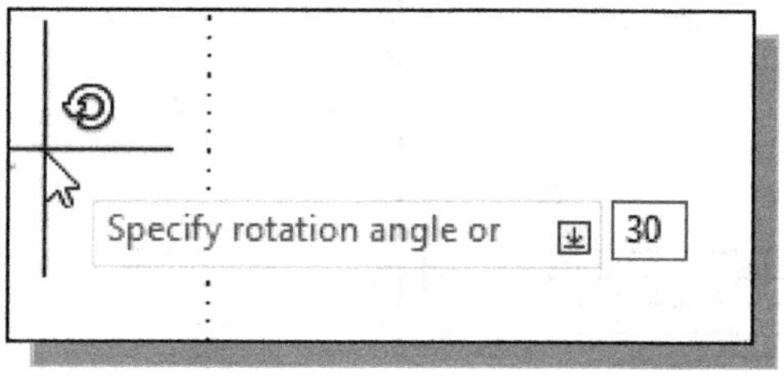

5. Enter **30** as the rotation angle to rotate the view by 30 degrees.

Establish a Section View

AutoCAD provides us with many options to establish a section view in the paper space. We will use the full section option for the pulley design available in the **Section View** command.

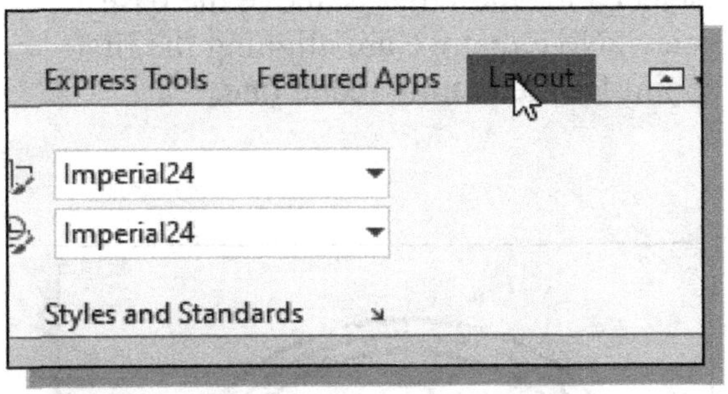

1. Click the **Layout** tab to switch to *model space*.

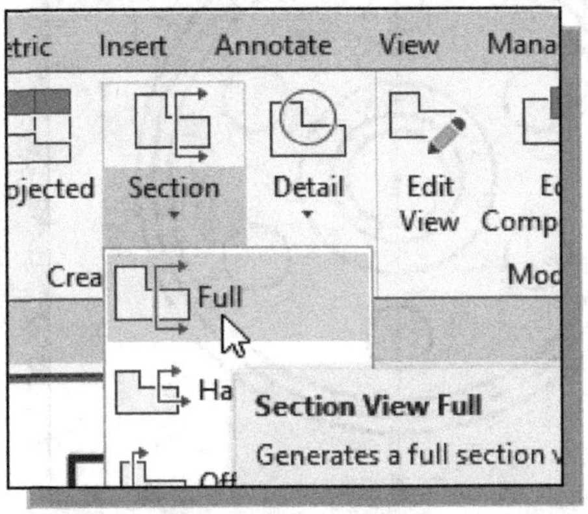

2. In the *Create View ToolBar*, select: **[Section] → [Full]**

3. Pick the **Base View** by moving the cursor on top of the view and select the view when the dashed box appears as shown.

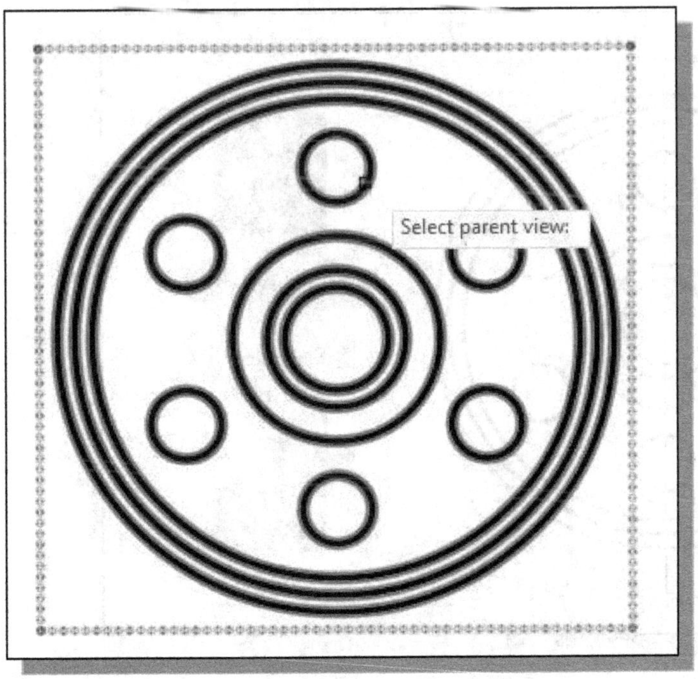

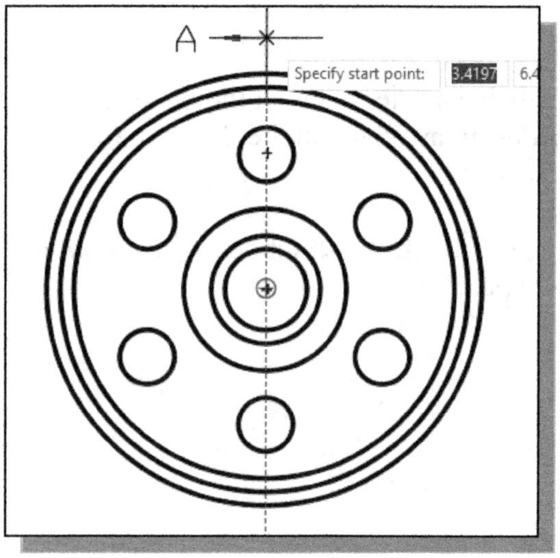

4. Pause the cursor on top of the center point of design, then move the cursor upward to select a location that is above the base view. Note that we are aligning the first point for the cutting plane line.

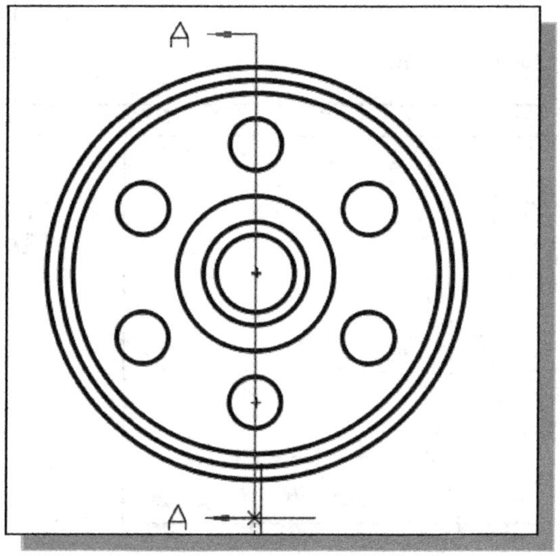

5. Move the cursor downward and select a point that is below the base view as shown.

6. Move the cursor to the right and notice a section view following the orthographic projection rules is generated. Select a location to the right as shown.

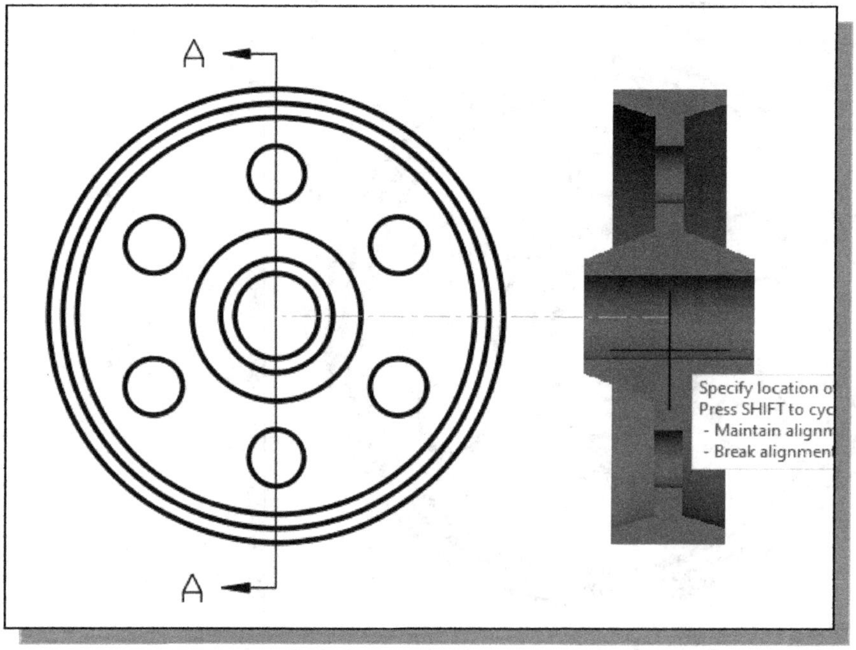

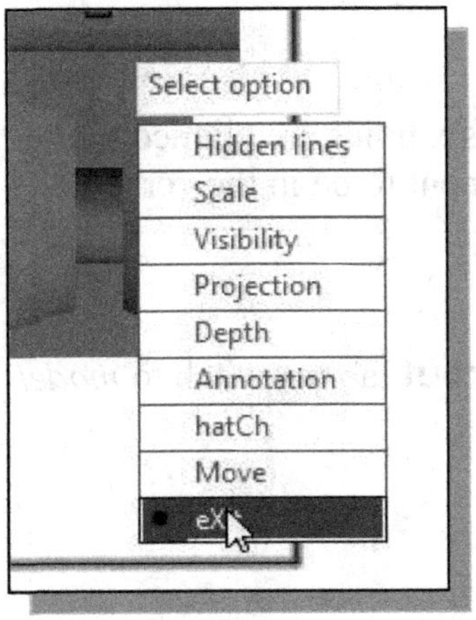

7. In the *pop-up option list*, select **[eXit]** to accept the creation of the new view.

- The current multi-view drawing appears as shown in the below figure.

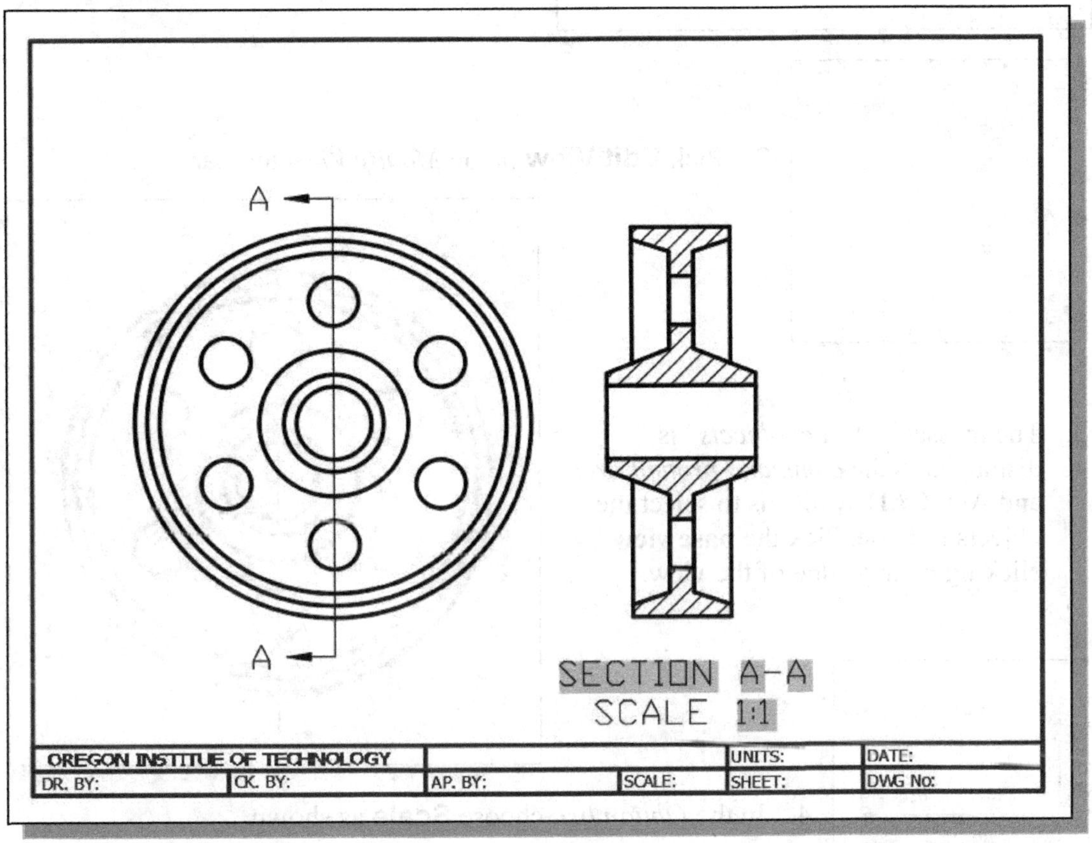

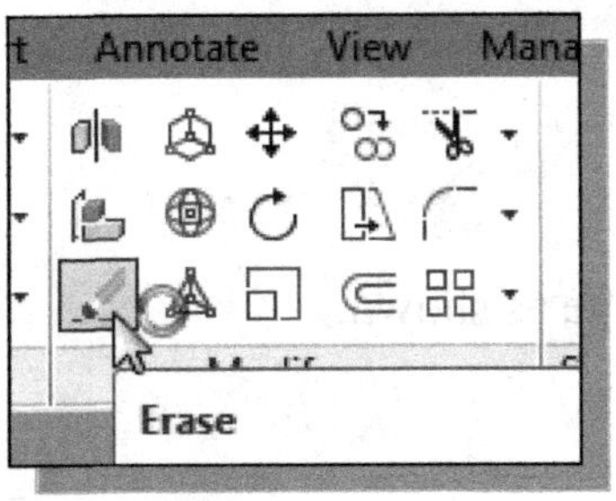

8. On your own, use the **Erase** command and erase the *Section label* as shown.

Adjust the Scale of the Base View

The current Base view is showing the two center points of the six holes are aligned to the center of the design horizontally; we will first adjust the alignment to be in the vertical direction prior to creating a section view.

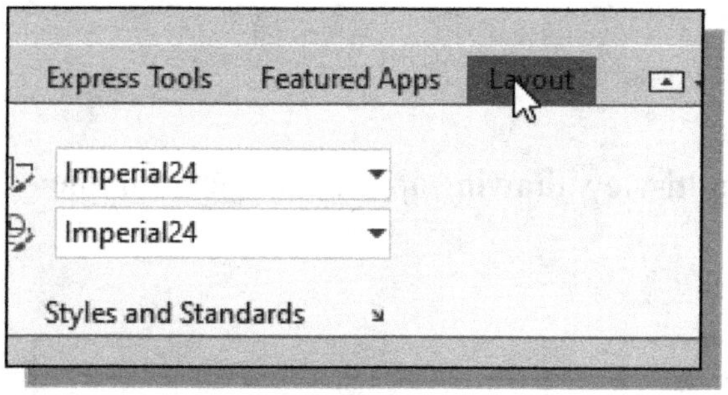

1. Click the **Layout** tab to switch to *model space*.

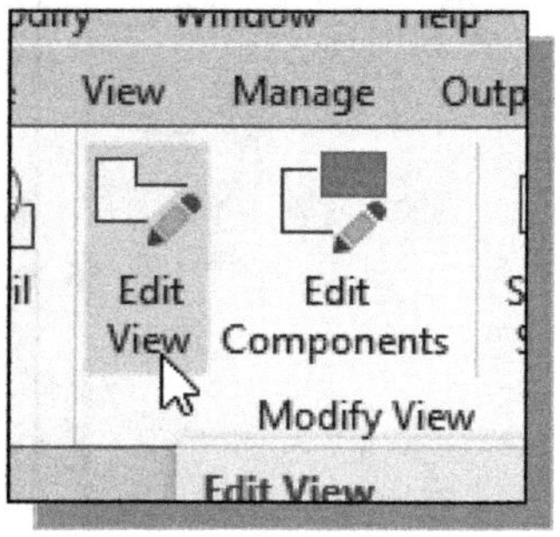

2. Pick **Edit View** in the *Modify View* toolbar.

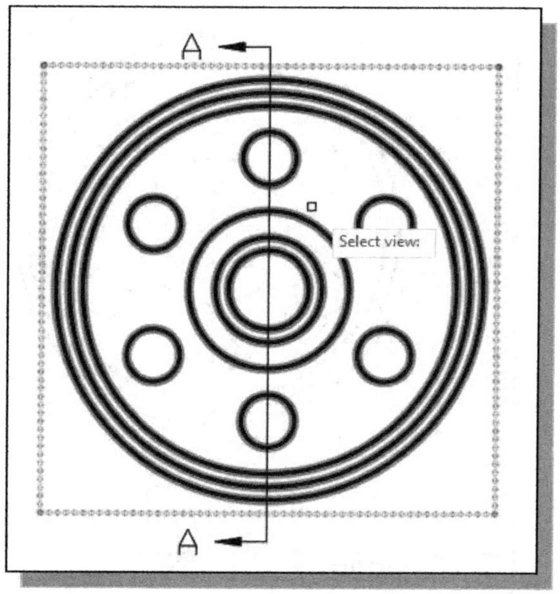

3. The message "*Select objects*" is displayed in the *command prompt area* and AutoCAD awaits us to select the objects to erase. Pick the **base view** by clicking on any edge of the view.

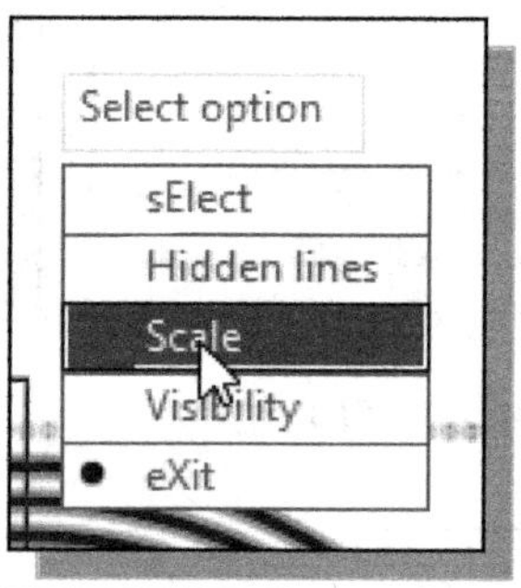

4. In the *Option list*, choose **Scale** as shown.

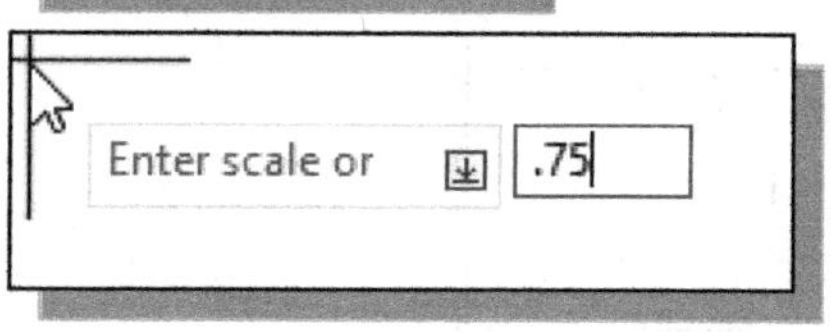

5. Enter **0.75** as the scale value as shown.

6. In the *pop-up option list*, select **[eXit]** to accept the adjustment of the scale.

Add an Isometric View

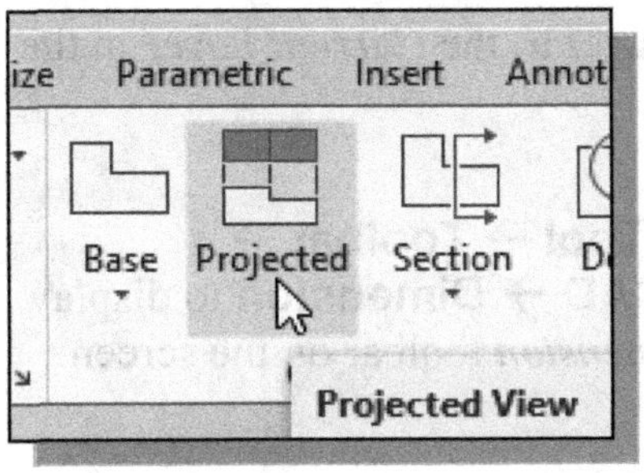

1. Pick **Projected** in the *CreateView* toolbar.

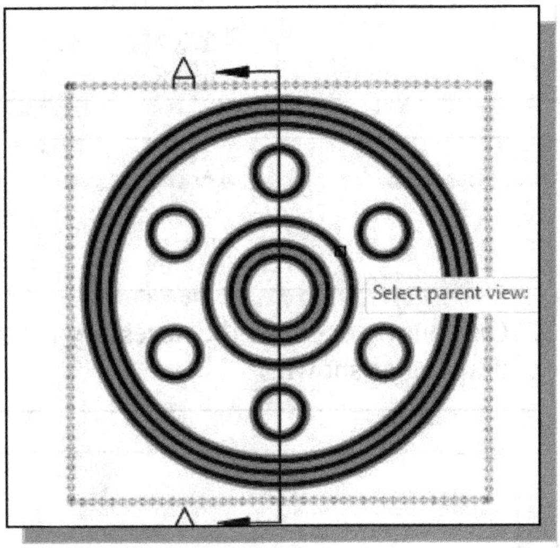

2. The message "*Select objects*" is displayed in the *command prompt area* and AutoCAD awaits us to select the objects to erase. Pick the **base view** by clicking on any edge of the view.

3. Move the cursor to the upper right corner of the page and create an isometric view as shown.

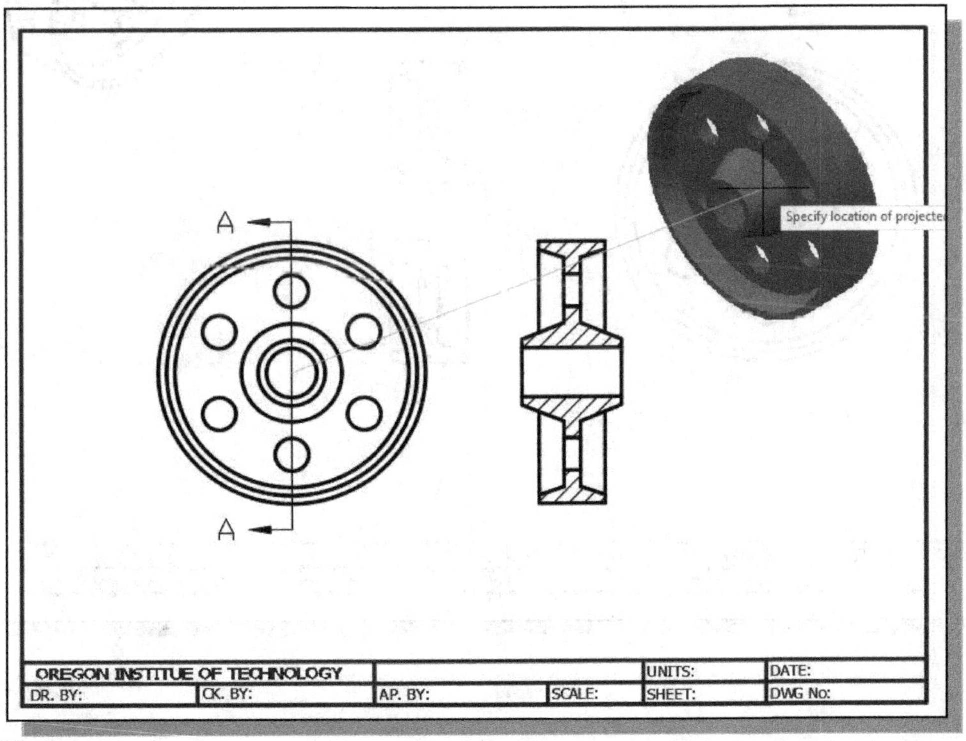

Complete the 2D Drawing

1. Set the ***Dimensions*** layer as the *Current Layer* in the *Layer Properties* box.

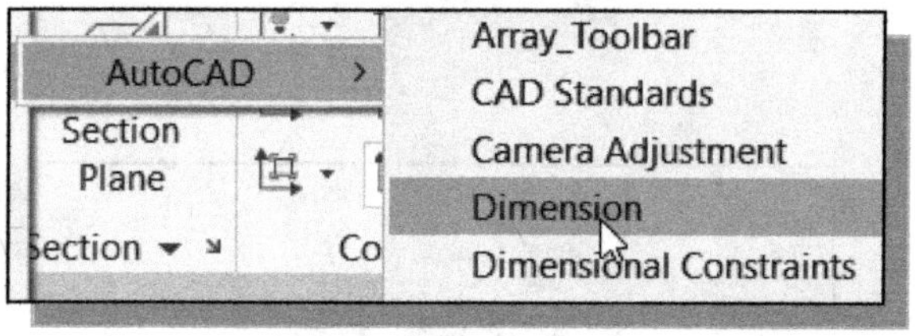

2. Select **Tool → Toolbar → AutoCAD → Dimension** to display the *Dimension* toolbar on the screen.

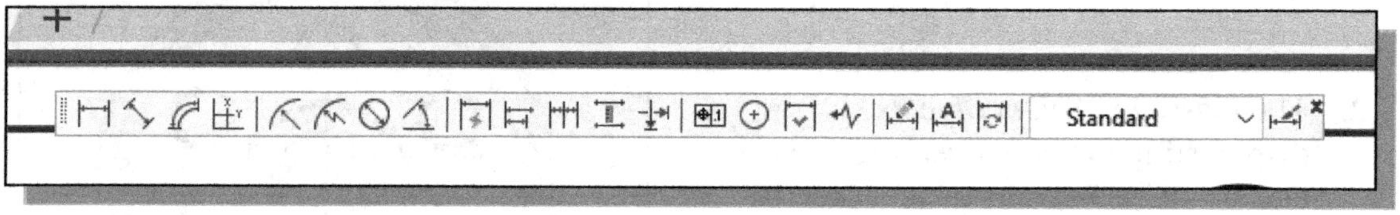

3. On your own, create the necessary center lines, dimensions and complete the 2D drawing as shown.

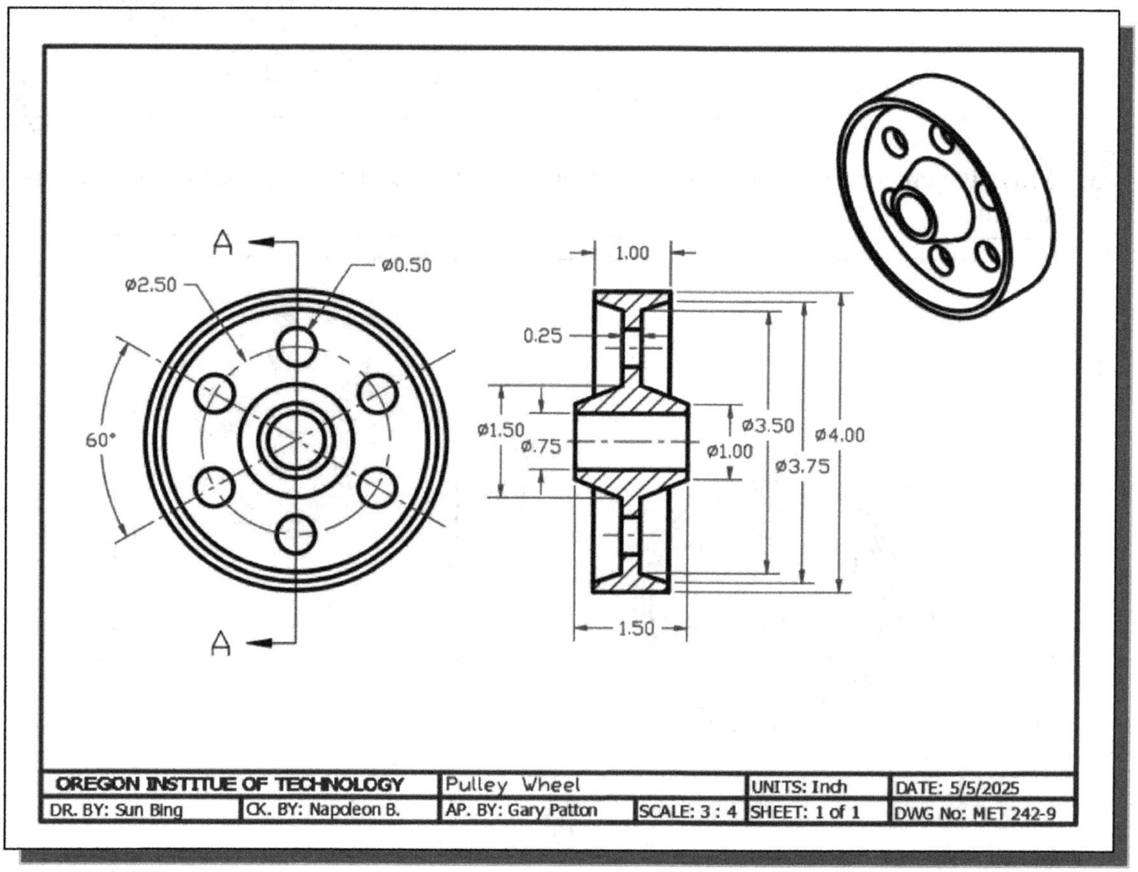

Review Questions:

1. What is an auxiliary view and why would it be important?
2. List and describe the types of 2D views used in the lesson.
3. How do you switch Paper Space to Model space in a layout?
4. What is the difference between *model space* and *paper space* in AutoCAD?
5. Identify the following commands:

(a)

(b)

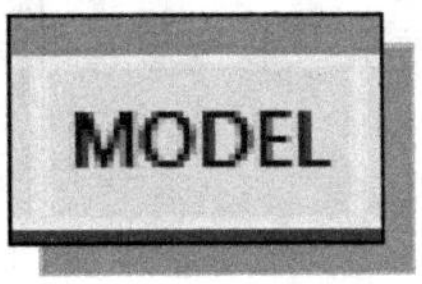

(c)

(d)

Exercises: Create the following solid models and generate multiview drawings from the 3D models. (All dimensions are in inches.)

1. (The overall height of the design is 2.5.)

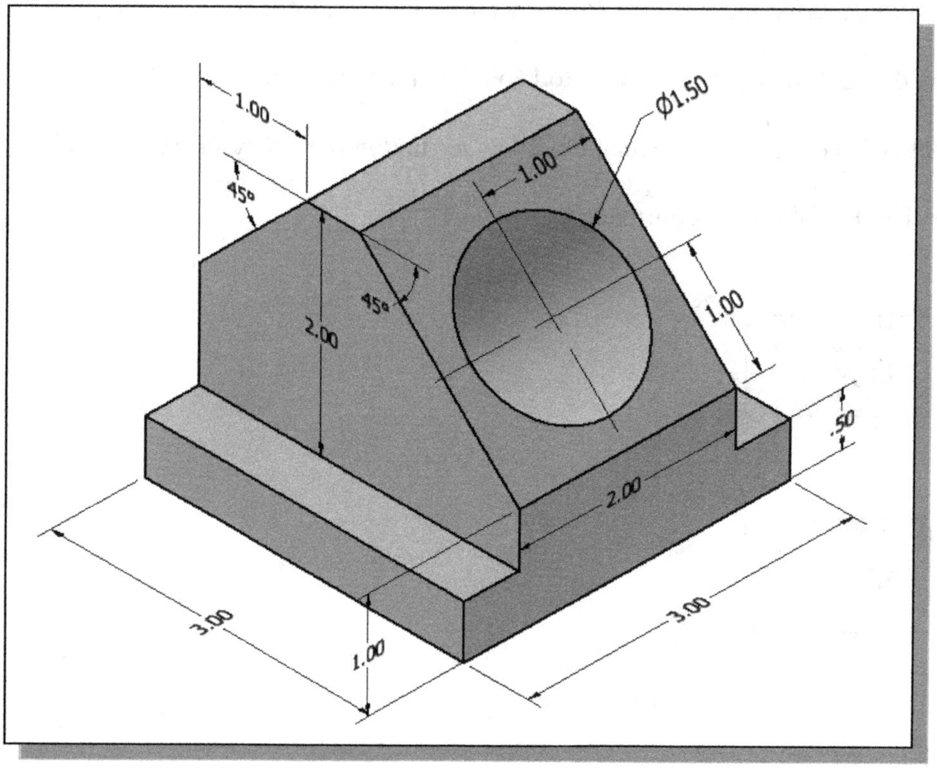

2.

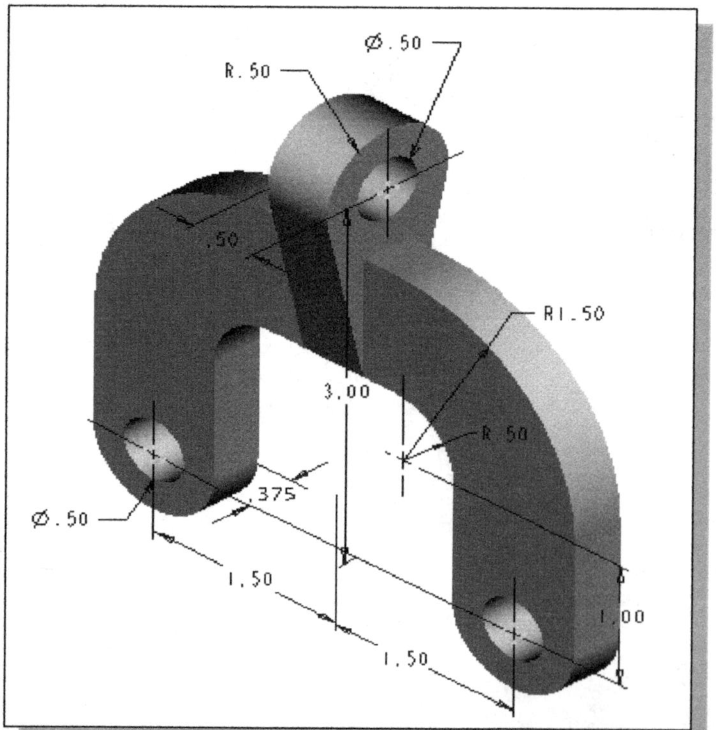

3.

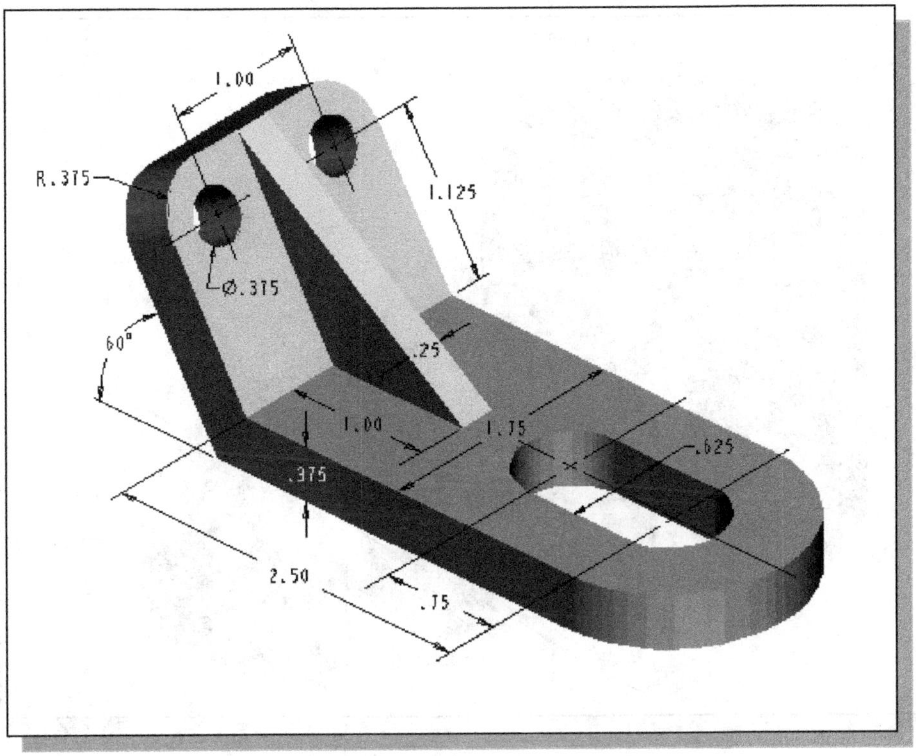
1.00
R.375
1.125
Ø.375
60°
.25
1.00
1.75
.625
.375
2.50
.75

4.

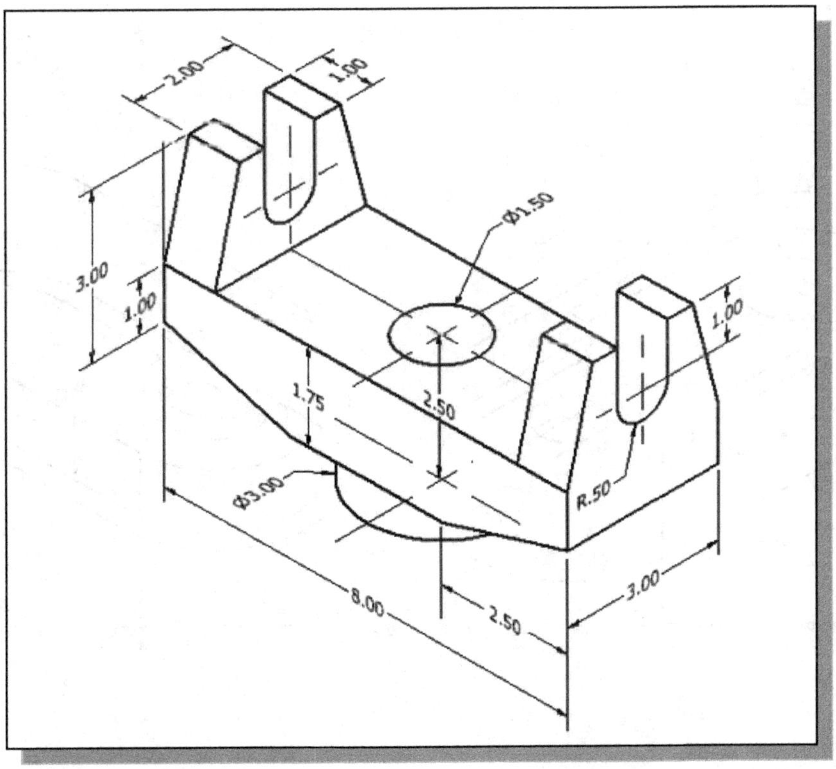
2.00
1.00
Ø1.50
3.00
1.00
1.00
1.75
2.50
Ø3.00
R.50
8.00
2.50
3.00

5.

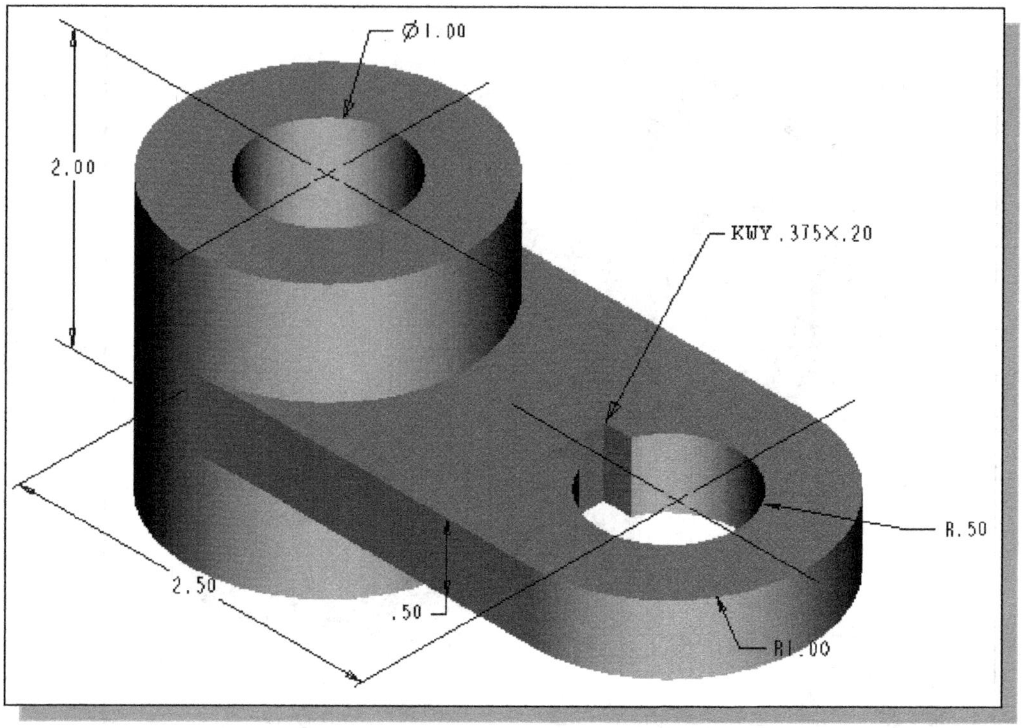

Ø1.00
2.00
KWY .375×.20
R.50
2.50
.50
R1.00

6.

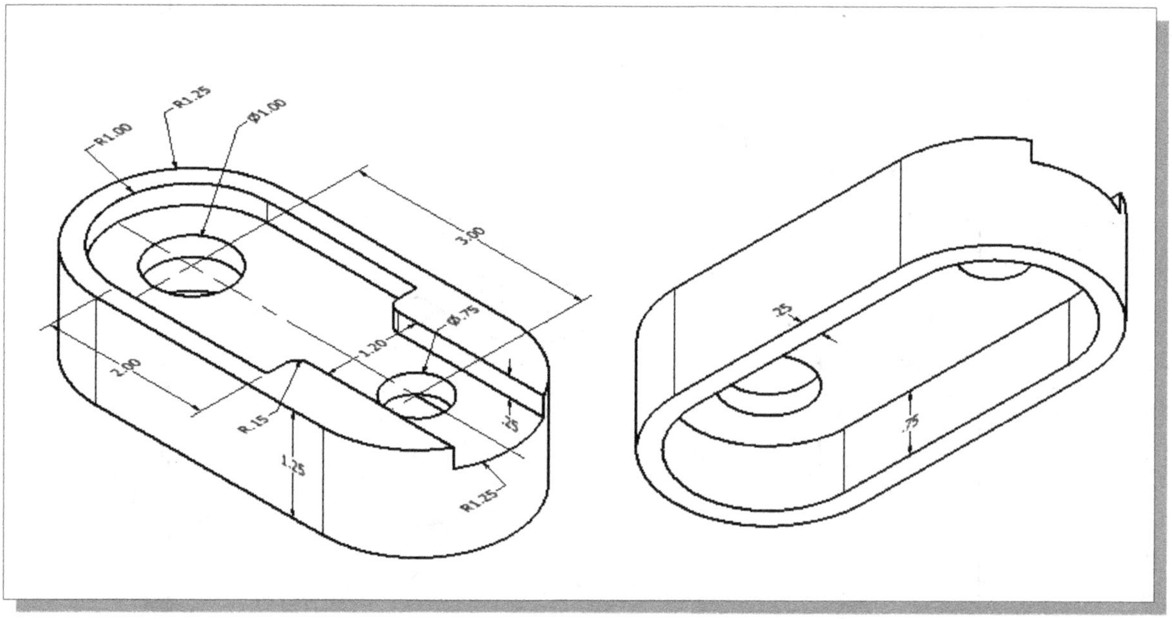

R1.00
R1.25
Ø1.00
3.00
Ø.75
1.20
2.00
R.15
1.25
R1.25
.25
.25
.75

Chapter 10
Advanced Modeling Tools & Techniques

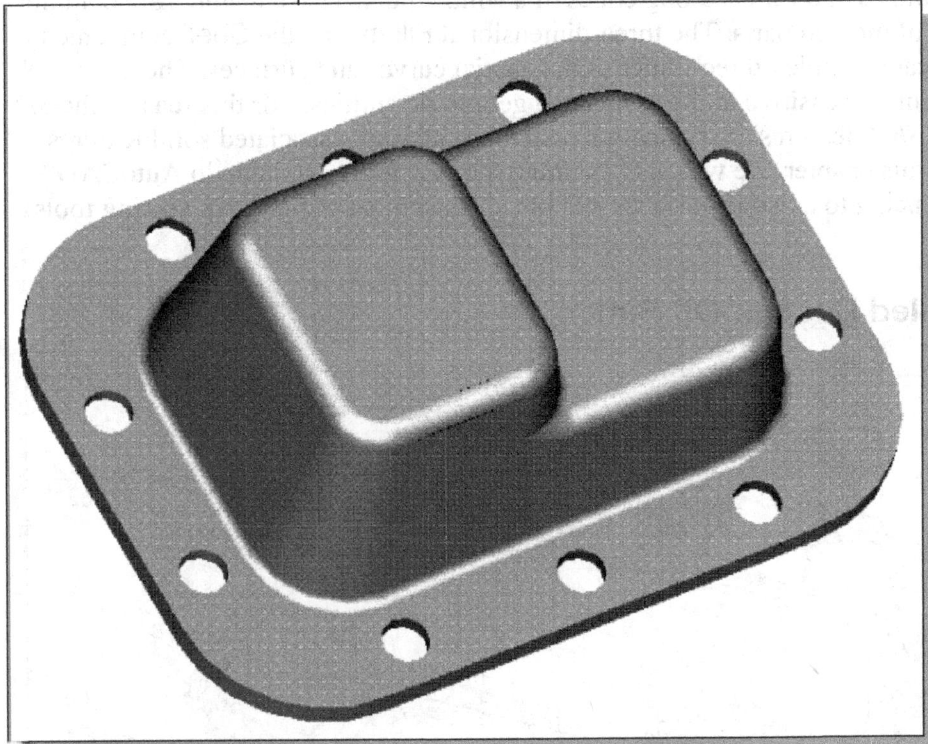

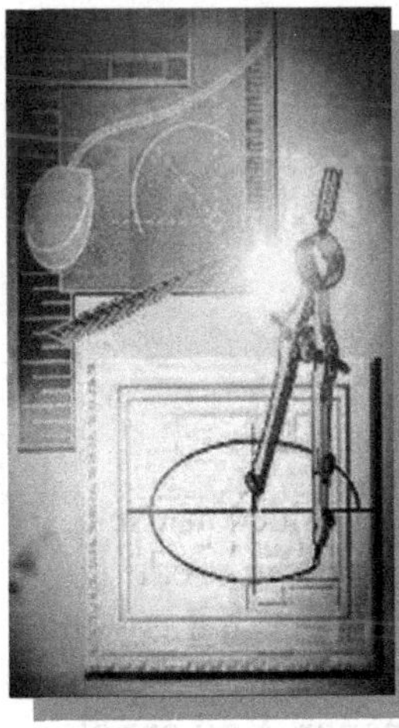

Learning Objectives

- Use More Advanced Solid Modeling Construction Tools
- Create Draft Angle Features
- Use the 3D Rounds & Fillets Command
- Create Rectangular Patterns
- Use the Shell Command
- Use the Copy Faces Command
- Use the DUCS Option

Introduction

AutoCAD provides an assortment of three-dimensional construction tools to make the creation of solid models easier and more efficient. In this chapter, we will examine the procedures to create the *Draft Angle* feature, the *Shell* feature and also for creating three-dimensional *Rounds* and *Fillets* along edges of a solid model. These features are common characteristics of molded parts. The three-dimensional Fillets and the Shell commands will usually create complex three-dimensional spatial curves and surfaces. These commands are more sensitive to the associated geometric entities. For this reason, the *3D Fillets* and the *Shell* features are typically created last after all associated solid features are created. In this chapter, we will also examine the new tools available in AutoCAD 2027 for referencing to existing surfaces and the enhancement of the **Grip editing** tools.

A Thin-Walled Design: Oil Sink

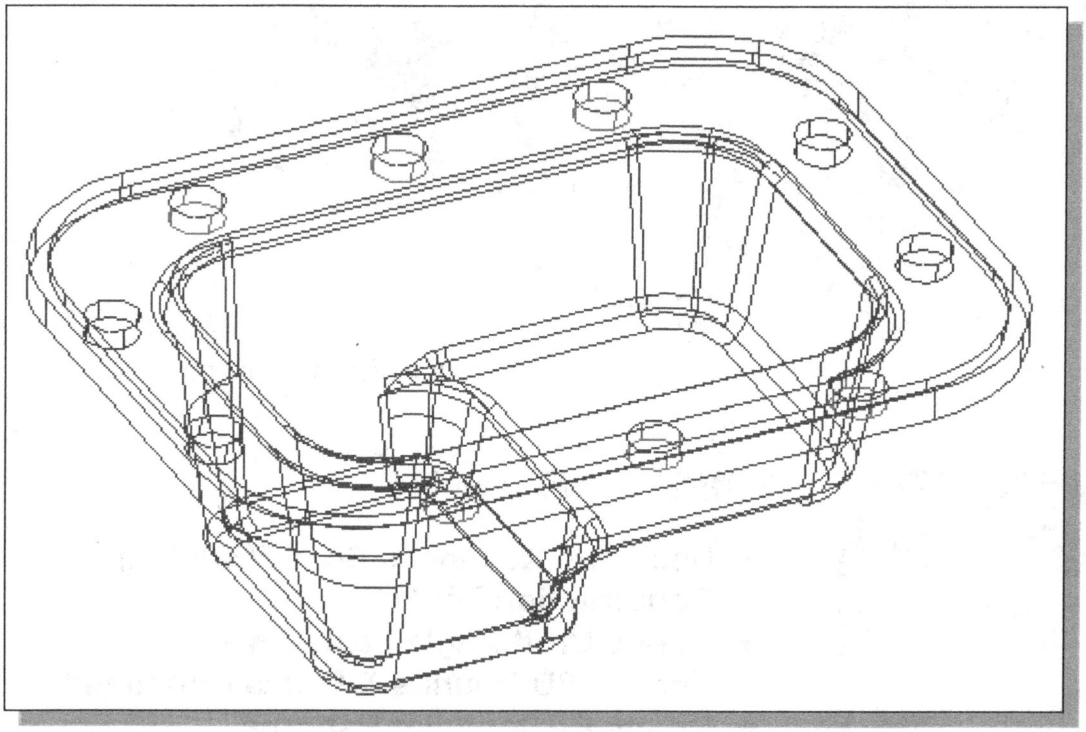

- Based on your knowledge of AutoCAD so far, how many features would you use to create the design? Which feature would you choose as the starting point in creating the model? What are the more difficult features involved in the design? What is your choice in arranging the order of the features? Take a few minutes to consider these questions and do preliminary planning by sketching on a piece of paper. You are also encouraged to create the design on your own prior to following through the tutorial.

Modeling Strategy

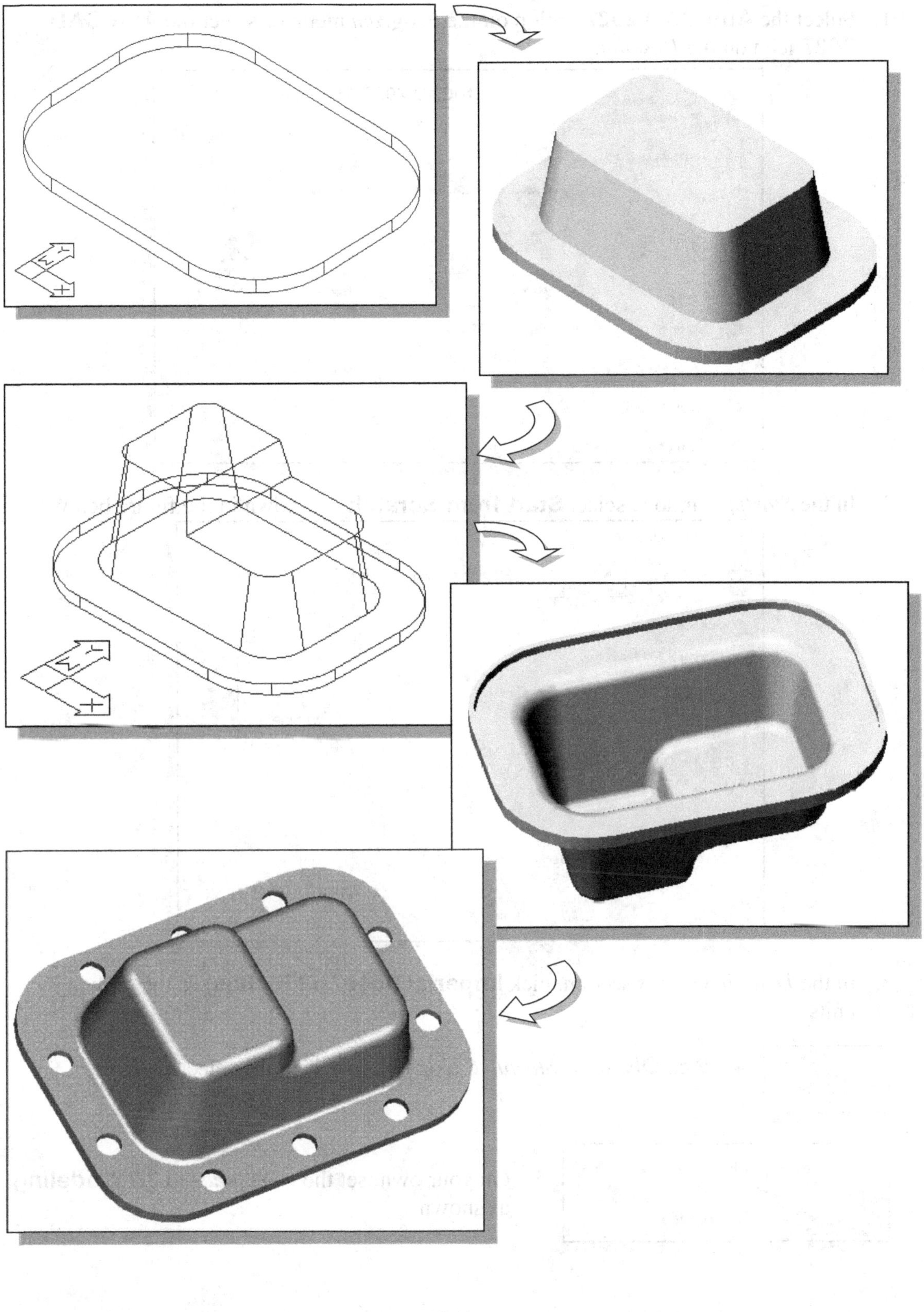

Starting Up AutoCAD 2027

1. Select the **AutoCAD 2027** option on the *Program* menu or select the **AutoCAD 2027** icon on the *Desktop*.

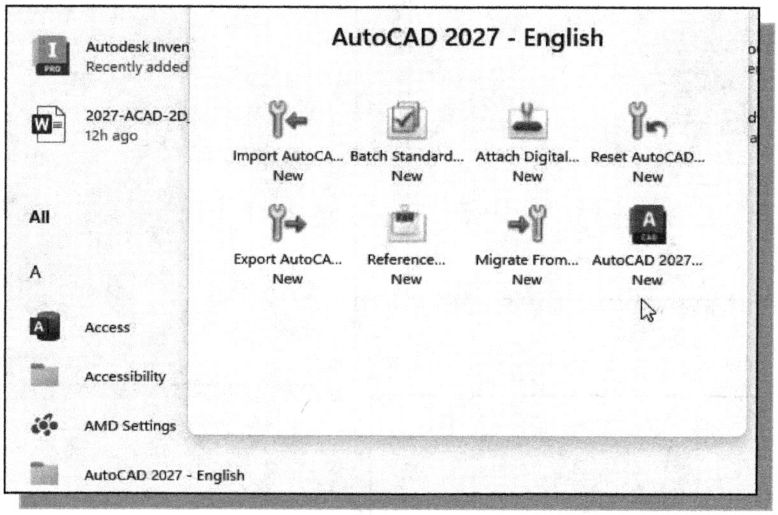

2. In the *Startup* window, select **Start from Scratch**, as shown in the figure below.

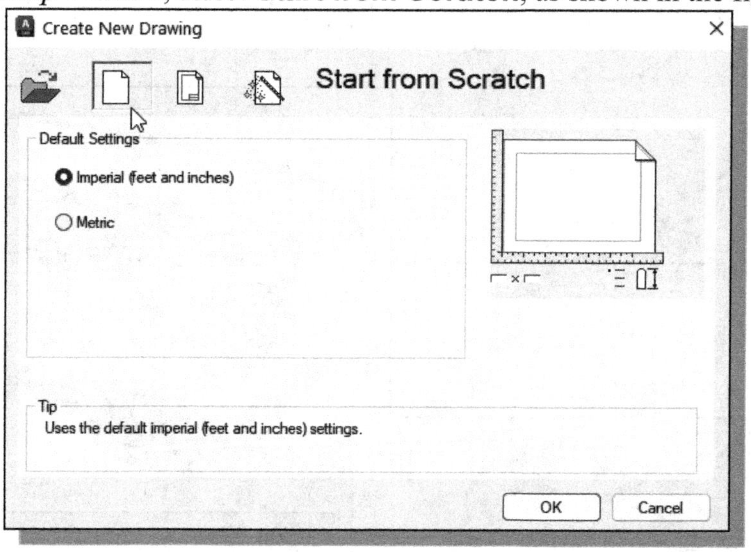

3. In the *Default Settings* section, pick **Imperial (feet and inches)** as the drawing units.

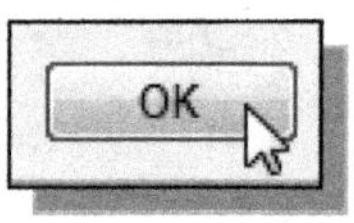

4. Pick **OK** in the *Startup* dialog box to accept the selected settings.

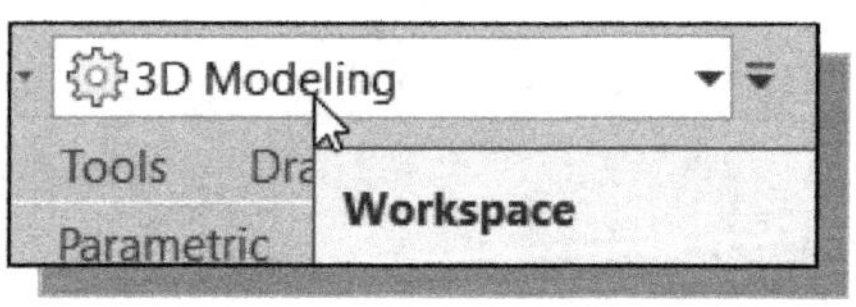

5. On your own, set the *workspace* to **3D Modeling** as shown.

Layers Setup

1. In the *Menu Bar,* select **[Tools] → [Toolbars] → [AutoCAD] → [Layers]**.

2. Click **Layers Properties Manager** in the *Layers* toolbar.

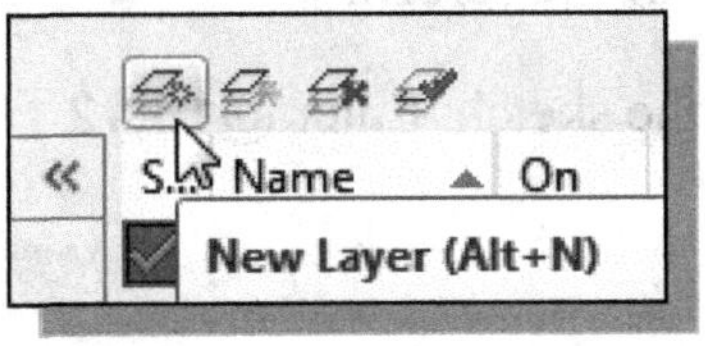

3. Click on the **New** button to create new layers.

4. Create **three new layers** with the following settings:

Layer	*Color*	*Linetype*	*Lineweight*
Center_lines	**Red**	**Center**	**Default**
Dimensions	**Magenta**	**Continuous**	**Default**
Object_lines	**Cyan**	**Continuous**	**0.3mm**

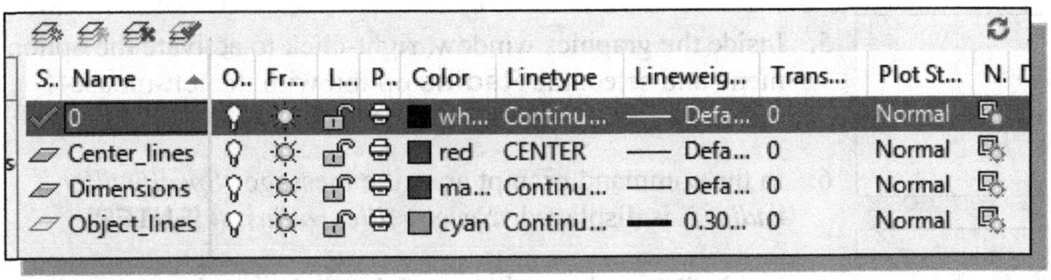

5. Select ***Object_lines*** layer in the list of layers.

6. Click on the **Current** button to set layer ***Object_lines*** as the *Current Layer*.

7. Click on the **Close** button to accept the settings and exit the *Layer Properties Manager* dialog box.

8. In the *Status Bar* area, reset the options and turn ***ON*** the *Grid Display, Polar Tracking*, *Object Snap*, *Object Snap Tracking*, and *Dynamic Input* options.

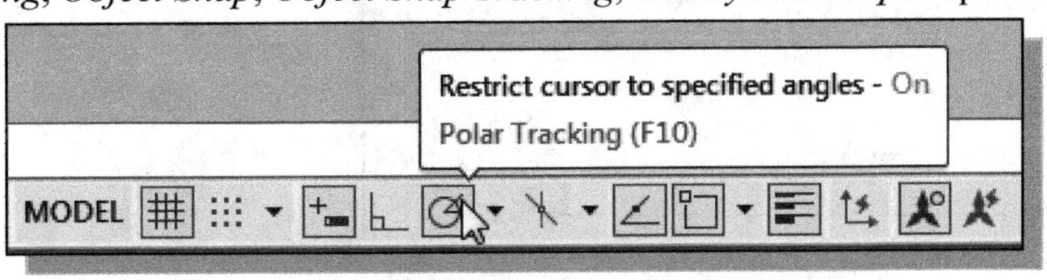

The First Extruded Feature

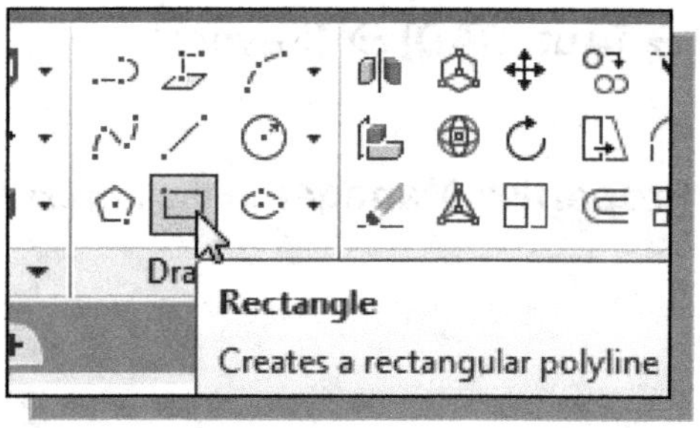

1. Select the **Rectangle** icon in the *Draw* toolbar. In the command prompt area, the message "*Specify first corner point or [Chamfer/ Elevation/Fillet/Thickness/Width]:*" is displayed.

2. Place the first corner point of the rectangle near the lower left corner of the screen.

3. We will create a 16″ x 12″ rectangle for the main body of the sketch. Enter **@16,12 [ENTER]**.

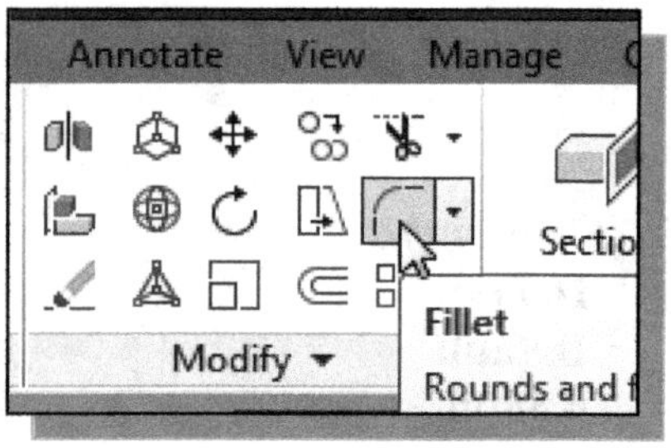

4. Select the **Fillet** command icon in the *Modify* toolbar. In the command prompt area, the message "*Select first object or [Polyline/Radius/Trim]:*" is displayed.

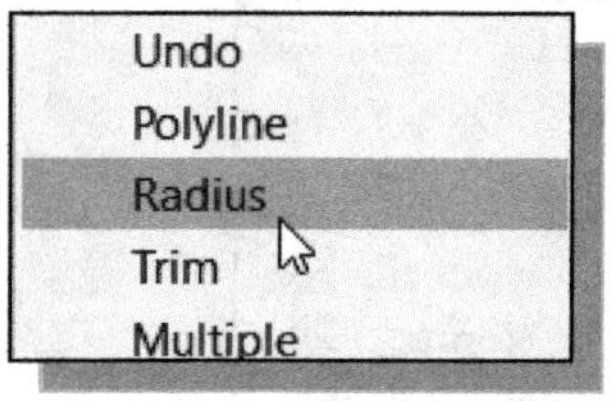

5. Inside the graphics window, right-click to activate the option menu and select the **Radius** option with the left-mouse-button to specify the radius of the fillet.

6. In the command prompt area, the message "*Specify fillet radius:*" is displayed. *Specify fillet radius:* **4 [ENTER]**.

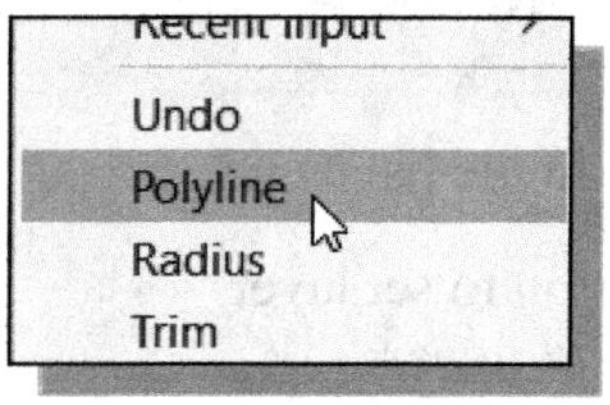

7. Inside the graphics window, right-click to activate the option menu and select the **Polyline** option.

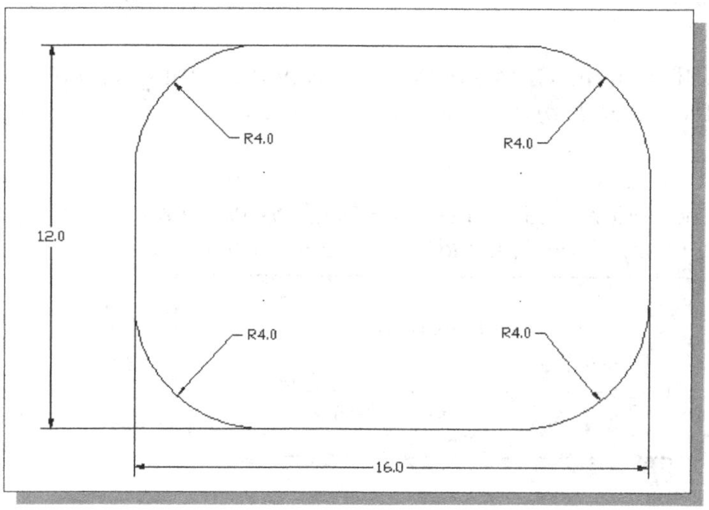

8. Pick the rectangle to create the **four rounded corners** as shown.

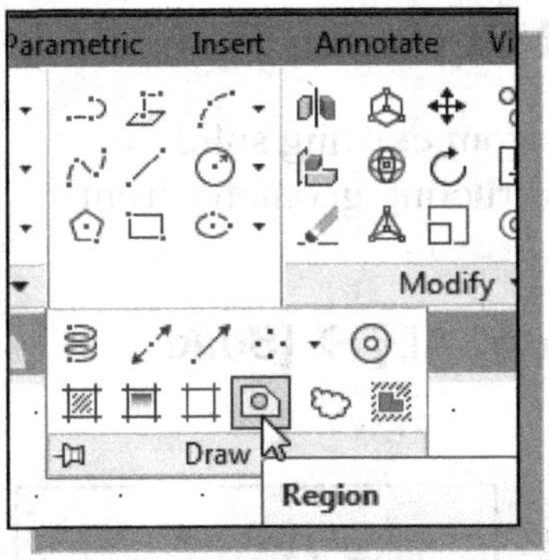

9. Select the **Region** command icon in the *Draw* toolbar.

10. In the command prompt area, the message "*Select objects:*" is displayed. Select the **polyline** by clicking on any segments of the 2D sketch.

11. Click once with the right-mouse-button to accept the selection and create a new region.

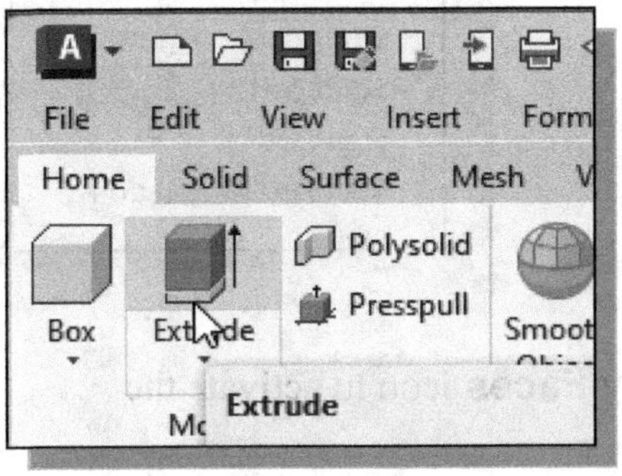

12. Select **Extrude** in the *Modeling* toolbar as shown.

13. In the *command prompt area*, the message "*Select objects:*" is displayed. Select the region by clicking on any of the displayed segments.

14. Inside the *graphics window*, **right-click** and select **Enter** to accept the selection and proceed with the **Extrude** command.

15. In the command prompt area, the message "*Specify height of extrusion or [Direction/Path/Taper Angle]:*" is displayed. Enter **0.625 [ENTER]**.

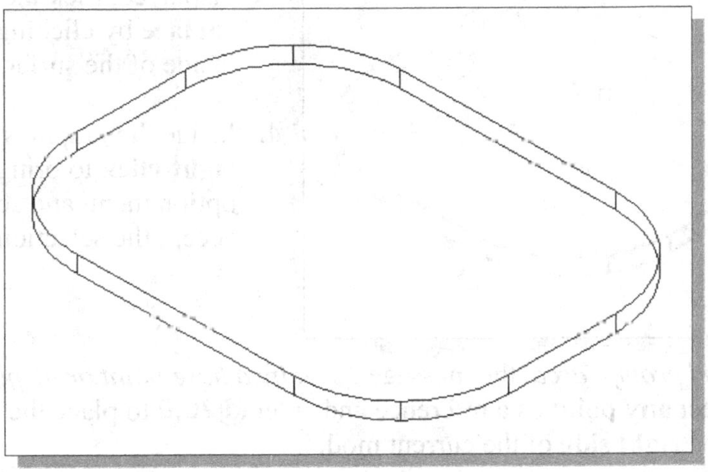

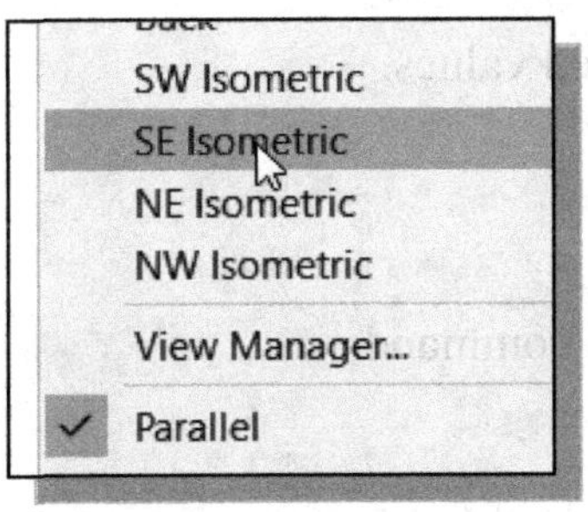

16. Set the *view display* to **SE Isometric** as shown.

Create an Offset Geometry from an Extracted Surface

In AutoCAD, several options are available to create geometry from existing solid features. We will use the **Copy Faces** command to assist constructing geometry from the existing surfaces.

1. In the *Menu Bar* area, select **[Tools] → [Toolbar] → [AutoCAD] → [Solid Editing]** as shown.

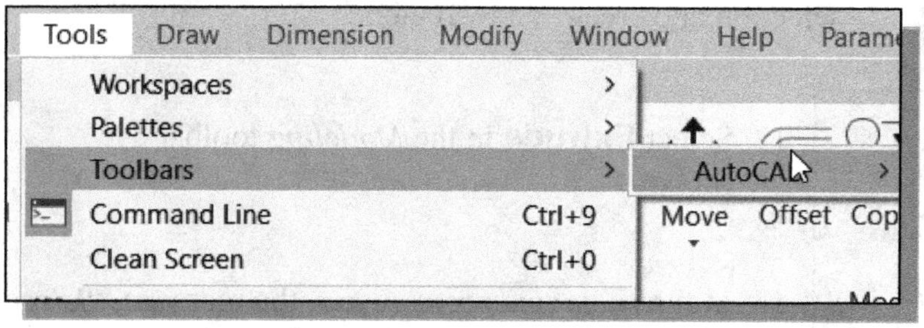

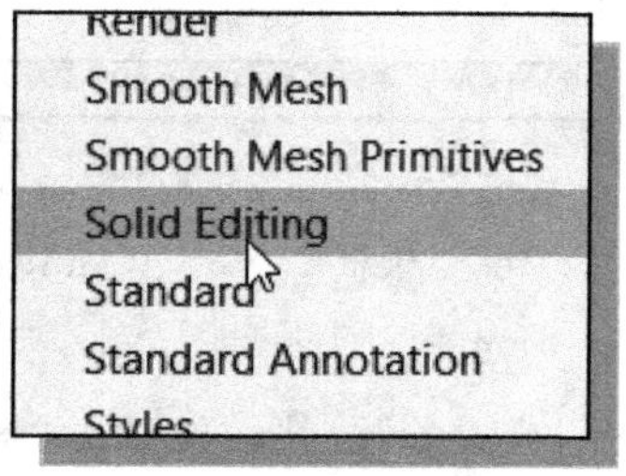

2. Click on the **Copy Faces** icon to activate the command.

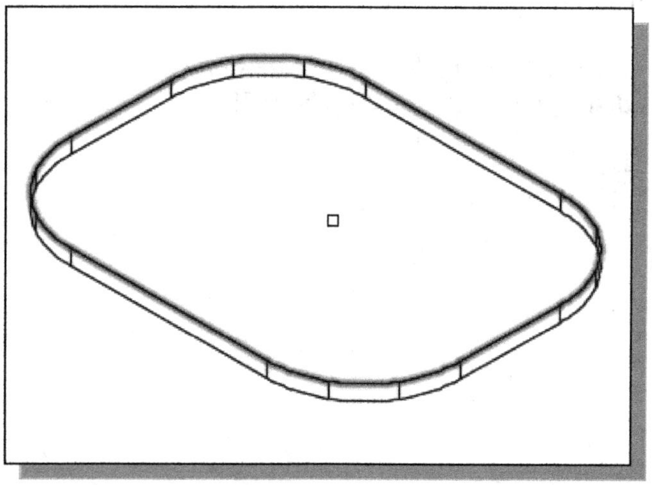

3. In the *command prompt area*, the message "*Select faces or [Undo/ Remove/ All]:*" is displayed. Pick the **upper surface** by clicking on the inside of the surface as shown.

4. Inside the graphics window, **right-click** to bring up the option menu and select **Enter** to accept the selection.

5. In the *command prompt area*, the message "*Specify a base point or displacement:*" is displayed. Select **any point** as a reference and enter **@20,0** to place the copy about **20** inches to the **right side** of the current model.

6. Inside the *graphics window*, **right-click** to accept the entered values.

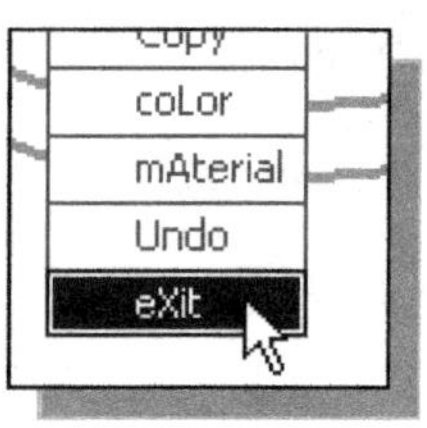

7. In the *option menu* select **Exit**.

8. Select **Exit** again to end the Copy Faces command.

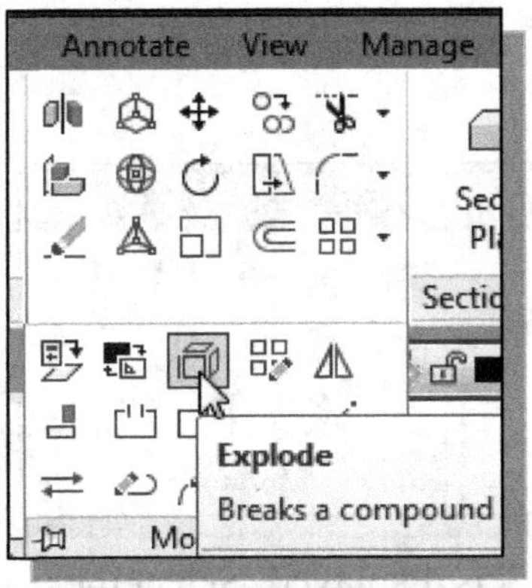

9. Select the **Explode** command icon in the *Modify* toolbar. In the command prompt area, the message "*Select objects:*" is displayed.

10. Pick the **new surface** we just created.

11. Inside the graphics window, **right-click** to end the Explode command.

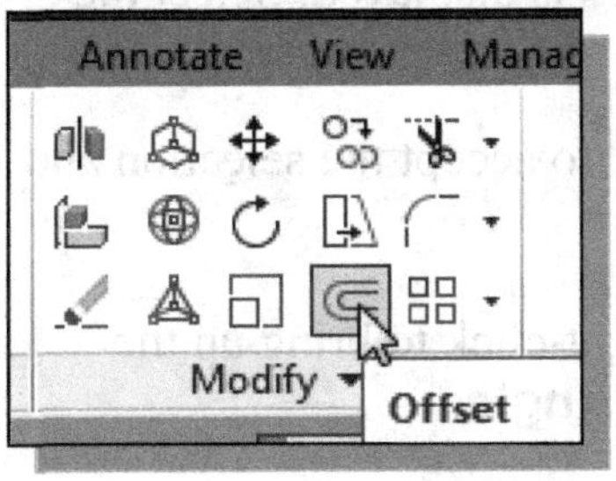

12. Select the **Offset** command icon in the *Modify* toolbar. In the command prompt area, the message "*Specify offset distance or [Through]:*" is displayed.
Specify offset distance or [Through]: **2 [ENTER]**.

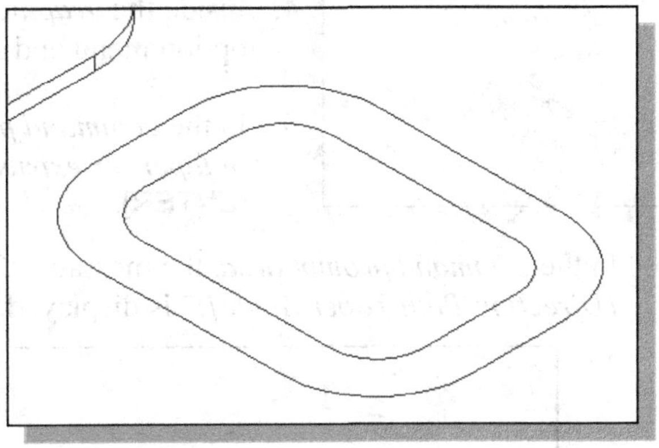

13. On your own, create a set of entities on the **inside** of the exploded surface as shown.

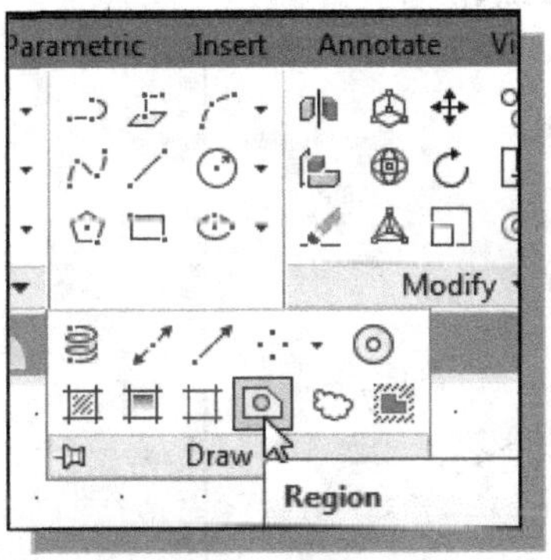

14. Select the **Region** command icon in the *Draw* toolbar.

15. In the *command prompt area*, the message "*Select objects:*" is displayed. Select the **entities** we just created with the **Offset** command (the objects that form the inside loop).

16. Inside the *graphics window*, **right-click** to accept the selection and create a region.

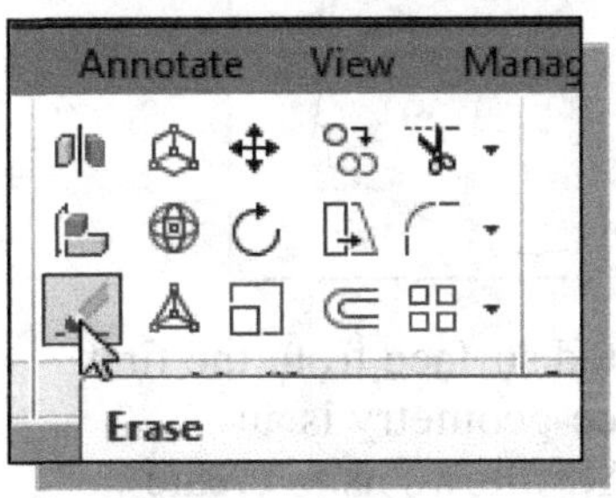

17. Select the **Erase** command icon in the *Modify* toolbar.

18. In the *command prompt area*, the message "*Select objects:*" is displayed. Select the **outer loop entities** that were created with the *Copy Faces* command.

19. Inside the *graphics window*, **right-click** to accept the selection and end the Erase command.

Extrude with Draft Angle

1. Select **Extrude** in the *Modeling* toolbar as shown.

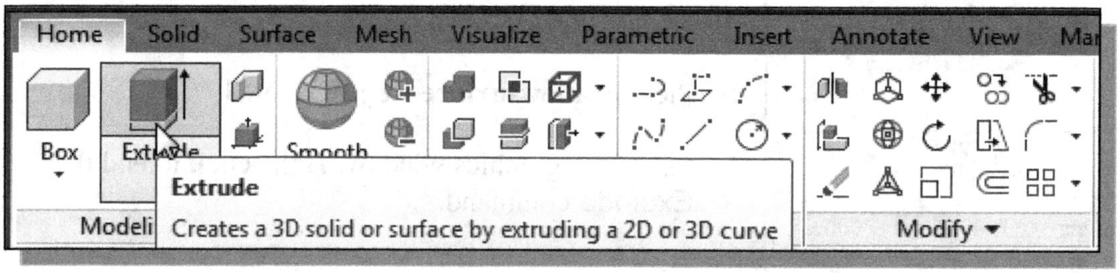

2. In the *command prompt area*, the message "*Select objects:*" is displayed. Select the **2D region** by clicking on any of the displayed segments.

3. Inside the *graphics window*, **right-click** and choose **Enter** to accept the selection and proceed with the Extrude command.

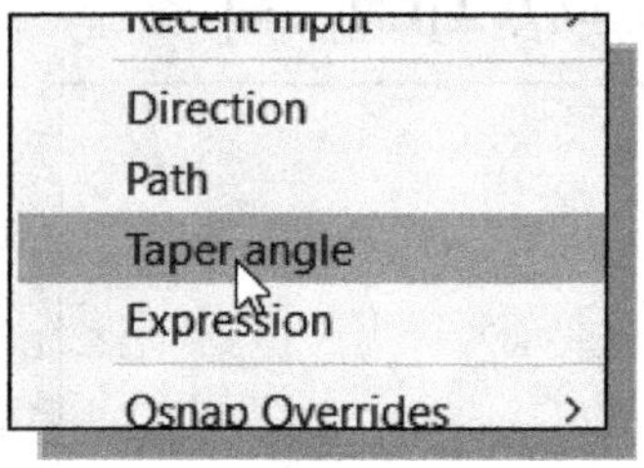

4. Inside the *graphics window*, right-click to bring up the option menu and select **Taper Angle**.

5. In the *command prompt area*, the message "*Specify angle of taper for extrusion <0>:*" is displayed. Enter **10 [ENTER]**.

6. In the *command prompt area*, the message "*Specify height of extrusion or [Direction/Path/Taper Angle]:*" is displayed. Enter **4 [ENTER]**.

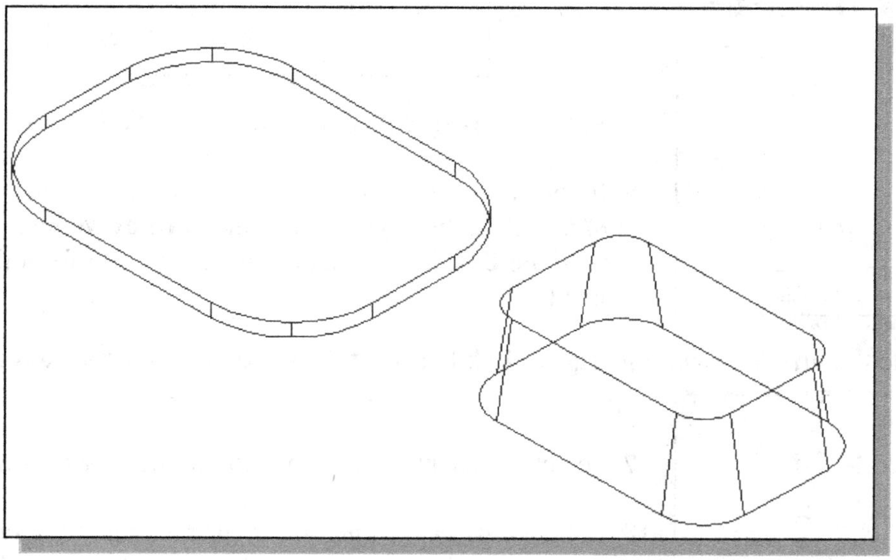

- Note that the second part is created by extruding an extracted surface from the first solid model. The ability to extract and reuse existing surface-geometry is an important aspect of solid modeling. Also note that AutoCAD allows us to create multiple parts in a single drawing file, which allows us to create assembly models under the same design environment.

Align the Parts

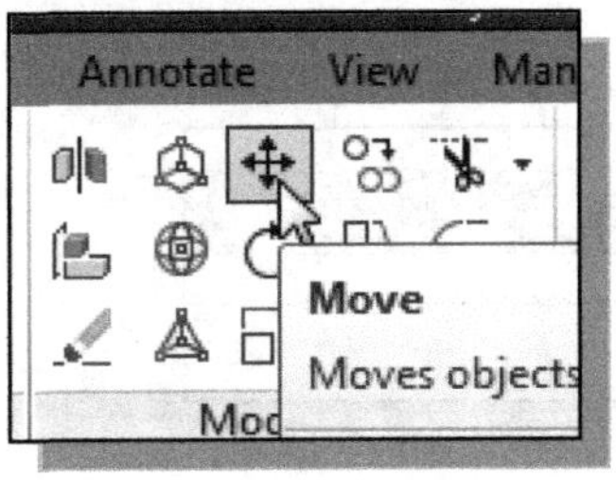

1. Select the **Move** icon in the *Draw* toolbar.

2. In the command prompt area, the message "*Select Objects:*" is displayed. Pick the **second part** we just created.

3. Inside the graphics window, right-click to accept the selection.

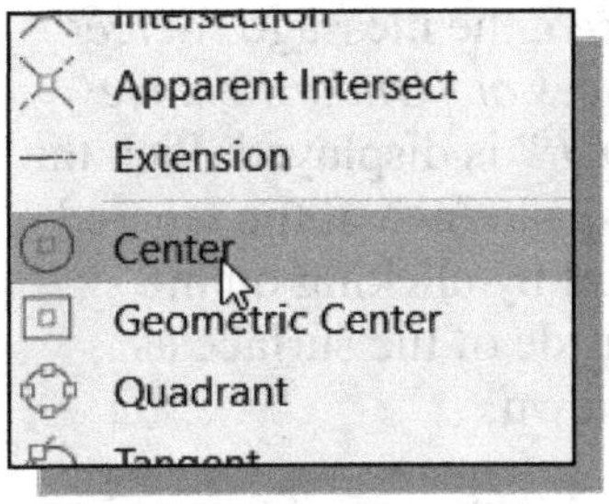

4. Inside the graphics window, hold down the **[SHIFT]** key and **right-click** once to bring up the *Object Snap* shortcut menu.

5. Select the **Center** option in the pop-up window.

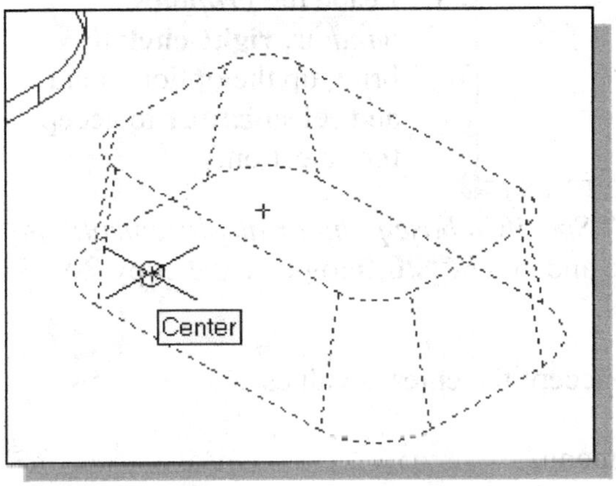

6. Pick the **center** of the bottom left arc as shown in the figure.

7. Inside the graphics window, hold down the **[SHIFT]** key and **right-click** once to bring up the *Object Snap* shortcut menu.

8. Select the **Center** option in the pop-up window.

9. Pick the corresponding center point on the **top surface** of the solid model as shown.

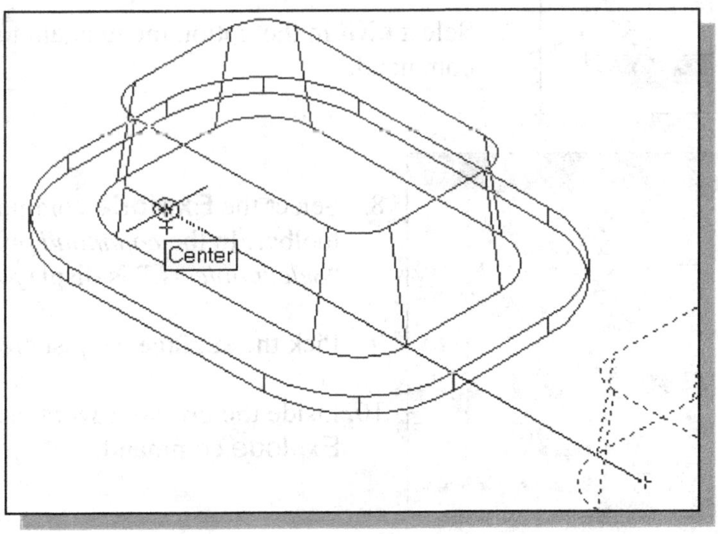

Create another Extracted Surface

1. Click on the **Copy Faces** icon to activate the command.

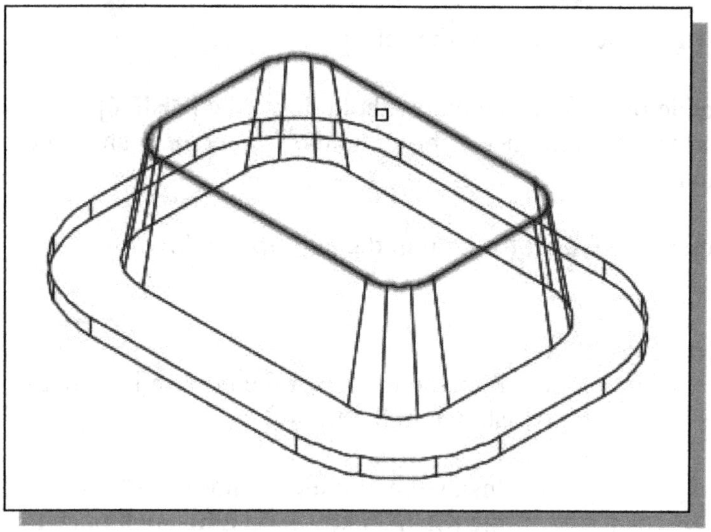

2. In the *command prompt area*, the message "*Select faces or [Undo/ Remove/ All]:*" is displayed. Pick the **top surface** of the tapered part by clicking on the inside of the surface as shown.

3. Inside the *graphics window*, **right-click** to bring up the option menu and select **Enter** to accept the selection.

4. In the *command prompt area*, the message "*Specify a base point or displacement:*" is displayed. Select **any corner** as a reference and enter **@20,0** to place the copy **20** inches to the right side of the current model.

5. Inside the *graphics window*, **right-click** to accept the entered values.

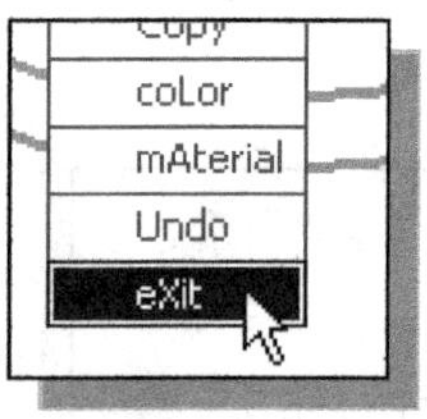

6. Select **eXit** in the option menu.

7. Select **eXit** in the option menu again to end the Copy Faces command.

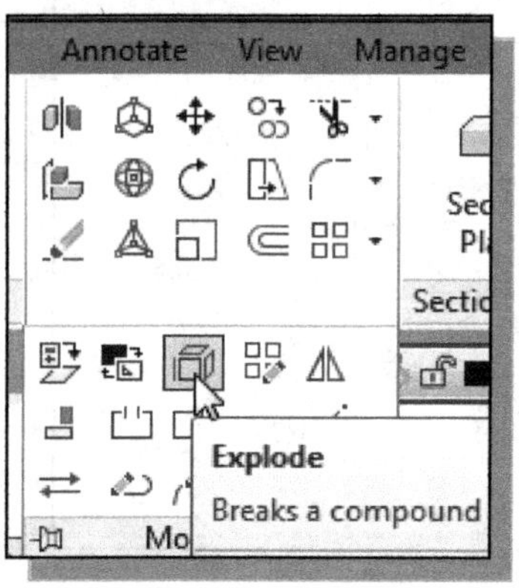

8. Select the **Explode** command icon in the *Modify* toolbar. In the *command prompt area*, the message "*Select objects:*" is displayed.

9. Pick the **surface** we just created.

10. Inside the *graphics window*, right-click to end the Explode command.

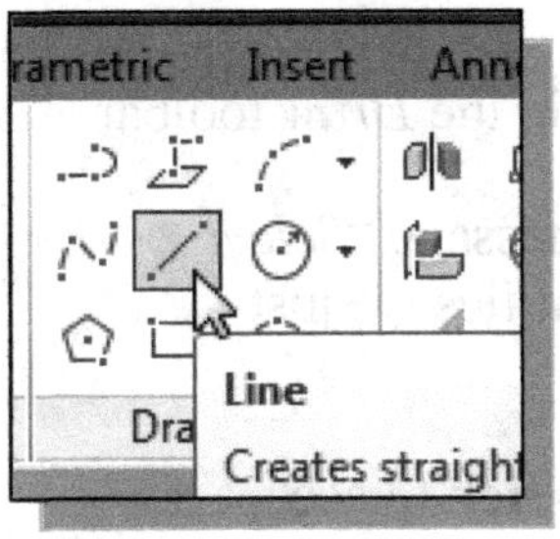

11. Select the **Line** command icon in the *Draw* toolbar.

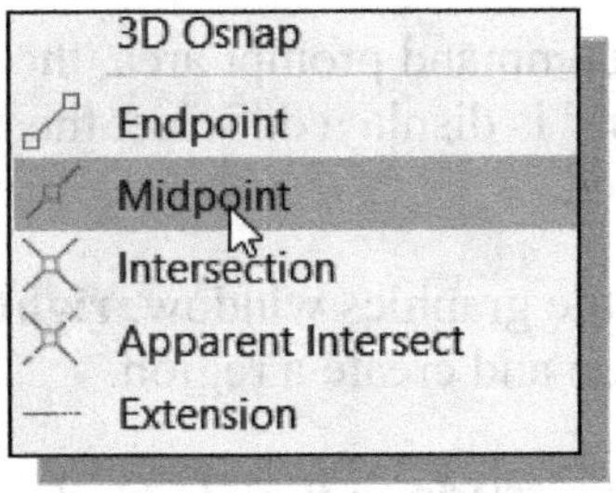

12. Inside the graphics window, hold down the [**SHIFT**] key and **right-click** once to bring up the *Object Snap* shortcut menu.

13. Select the **Midpoint** option in the pop-up window.

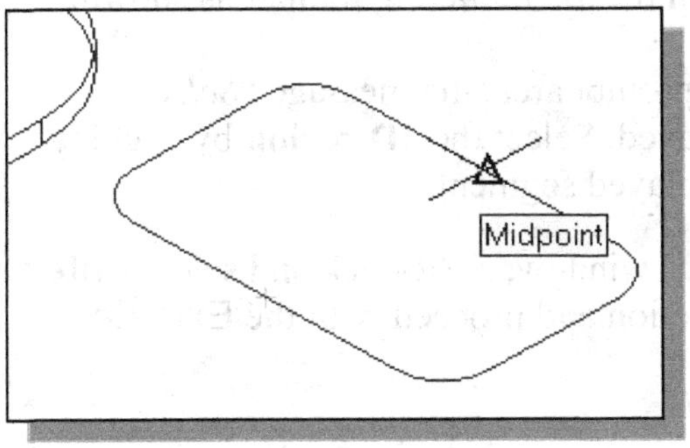

14. In the command prompt area, the message "*_line Specify first point:*" is displayed. Pick the **line segment** on the extracted surface as shown.

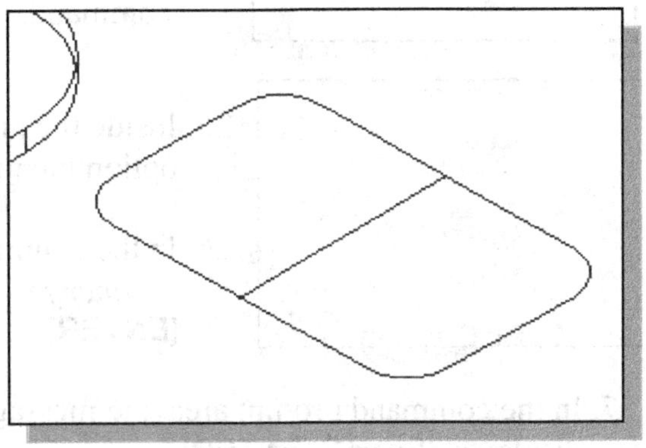

15. On your own, repeat the **Midpoint** ***SNAP*** option and create a line as shown.

16. Inside the *graphics window*, right-click once and select **Enter** to end the Line command.

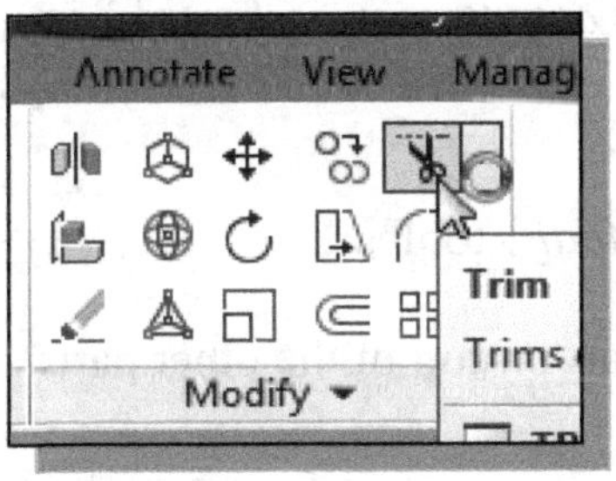

17. Select the **Trim** command icon in the *Modify* toolbar.

18. Trim the two lines of the exploded geometry as shown.

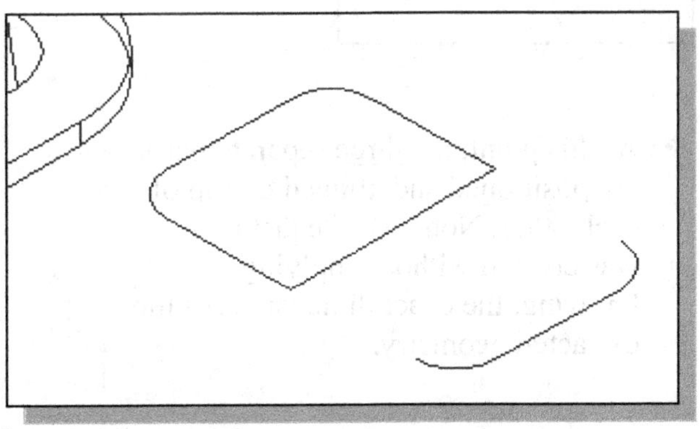

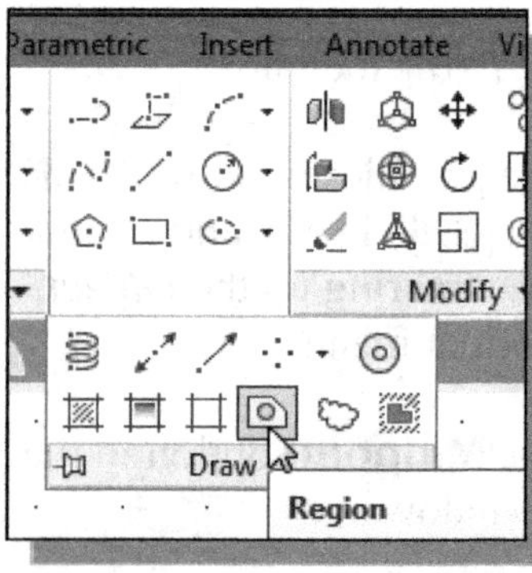

19. Select the **Region** command icon in the *Draw* toolbar.

20. In the command prompt area, the message "*Select objects:*" is displayed. Select the entities we just modified.

21. Inside the graphics window, **right-click** to accept the selection and create a region.

22. Select **Extrude** in the *3D Modeling* toolbar as shown.

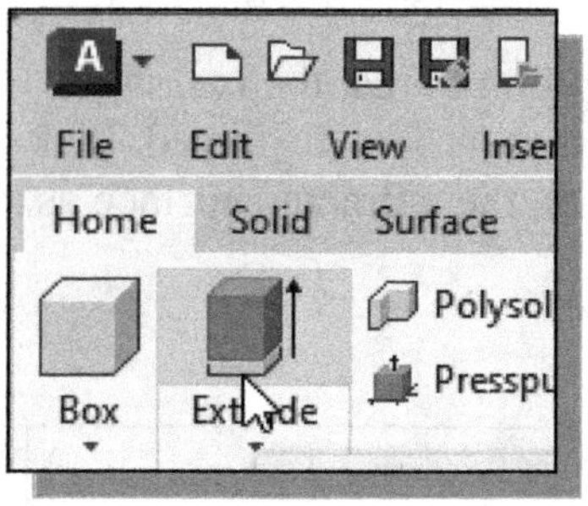

23. In the command prompt area, the message "*Select objects:*" is displayed. Select the **2D region** by clicking on any of the displayed segments.

24. Inside the graphics window, right-click and select **Enter** to accept the selection and proceed with the Extrude command.

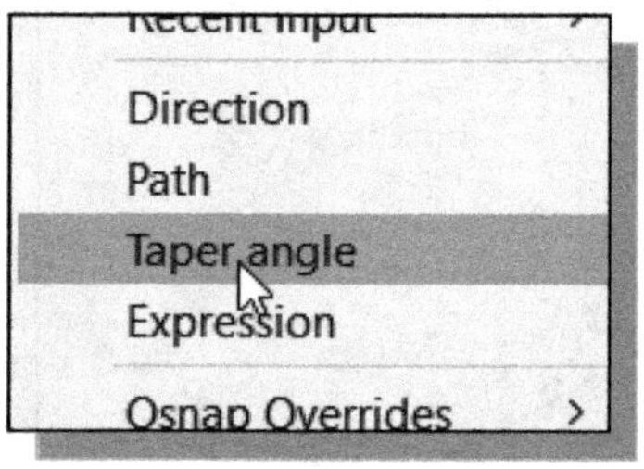

25. Inside the graphics window, right-click to bring up the option menu and select **Taper Angle.**

26. In the command prompt area, the message "*Specify angle of taper for extrusion <0>:*" is displayed. Enter **10 [ENTER]**.

27. In the command prompt area, the message "*Specify height of extrusion or [path]:*" is displayed. Enter **2 [ENTER]**.

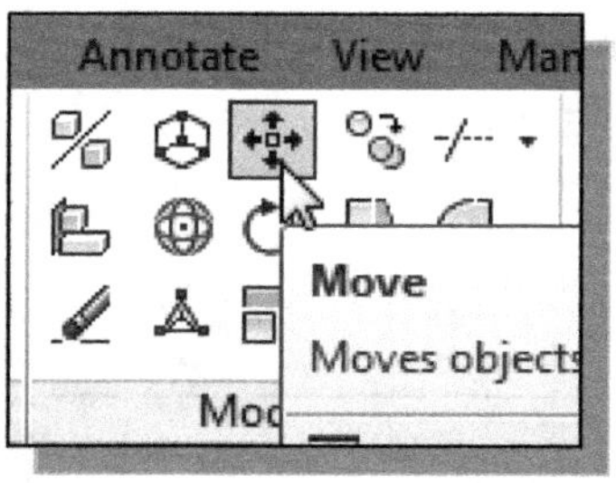

28. Select the **Move** icon in the *Modify* toolbar.

29. On your own, reposition the part on **top** of the other parts as shown.

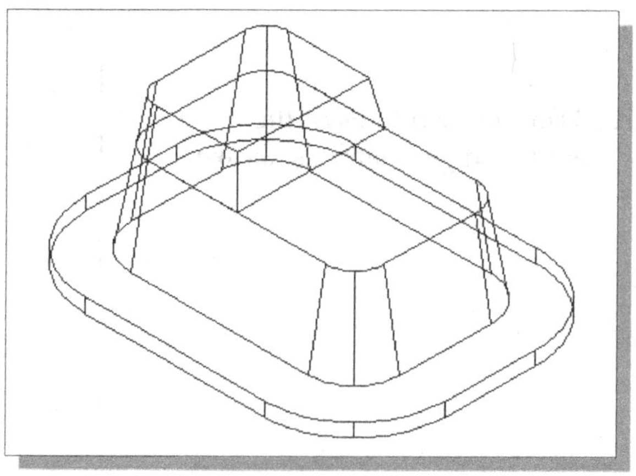

❖ At this point, the three separate parts are positioned and aligned on top of each other. Note that the last part was created without applying, or knowing, the exact dimensions of the extracted geometry.

Combining Parts – Boolean Union

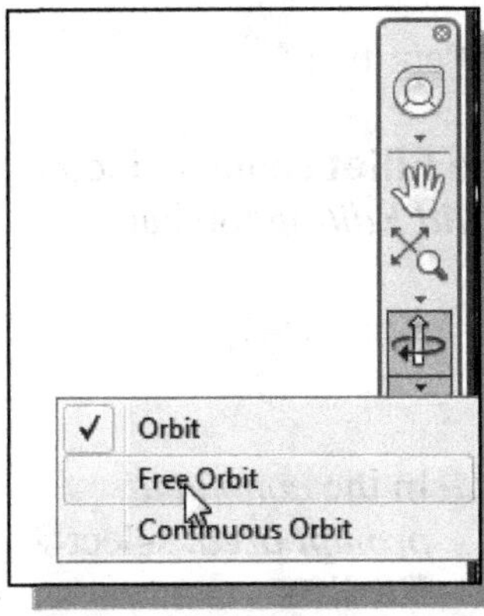

1. Select **Free Orbit** in the *Navigation* toolbar:
   [Orbit] → [Free Orbit].

2. On your own, rotate the created models in 3D space and confirm the three parts are positioned on top of each other. Readjust the positions of the parts if necessary.

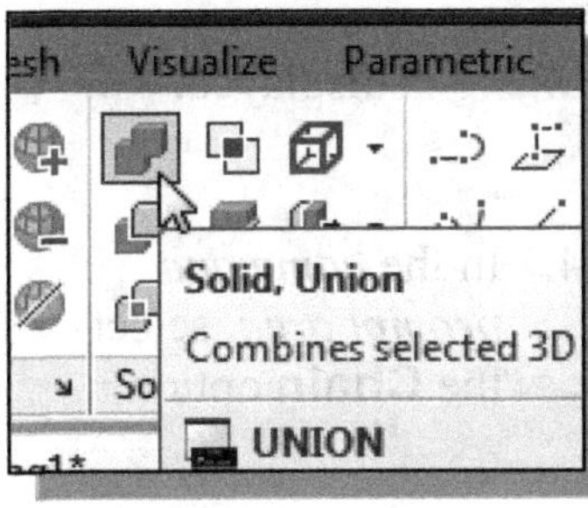

3. In the *Solid Editing* toolbar, click on the **Union** icon. In the command prompt area, the message "*Select Objects:*" is displayed.

4. Pick all the solid models by clicking on their edges.

5. Inside the graphics window, **right-click** to accept the selection and proceed with the Union command.

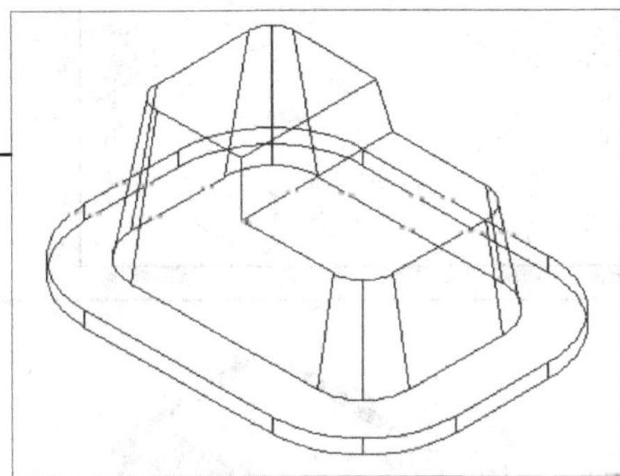

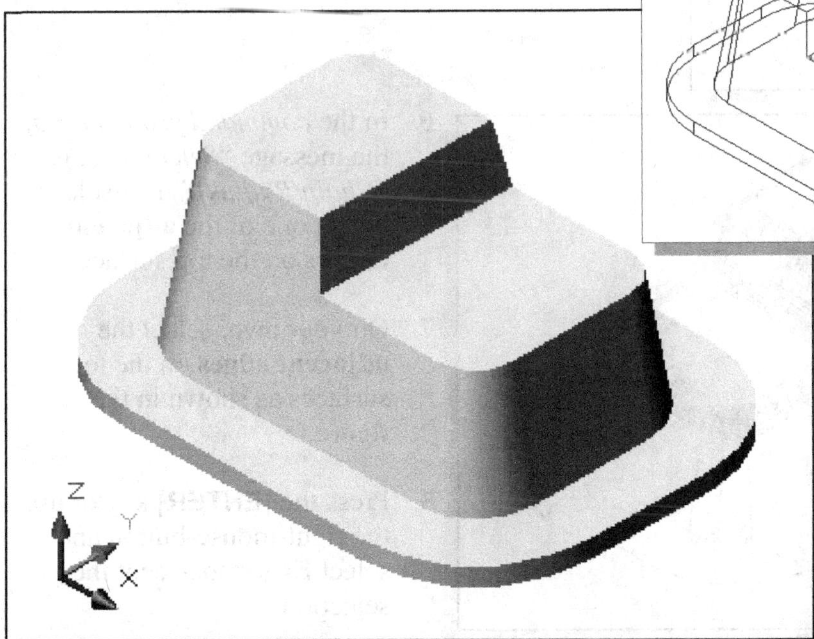

Create 3D Rounds and Fillets

In **AutoCAD 2027**, there are two **Fillet** commands for 2D and 3D entities.

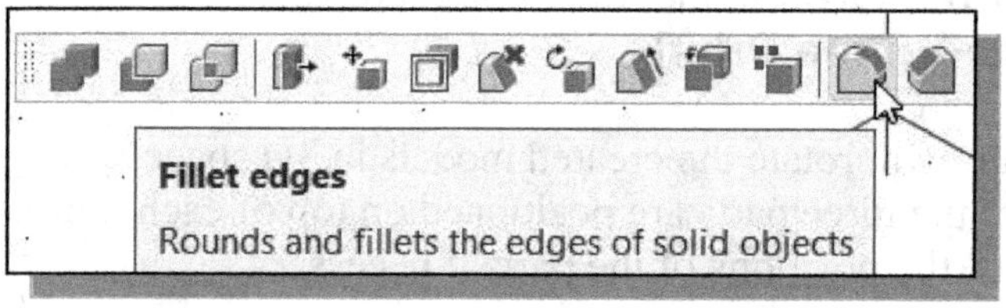

1. Select the **Fillet** command icon in the *Solid Editing* toolbar.

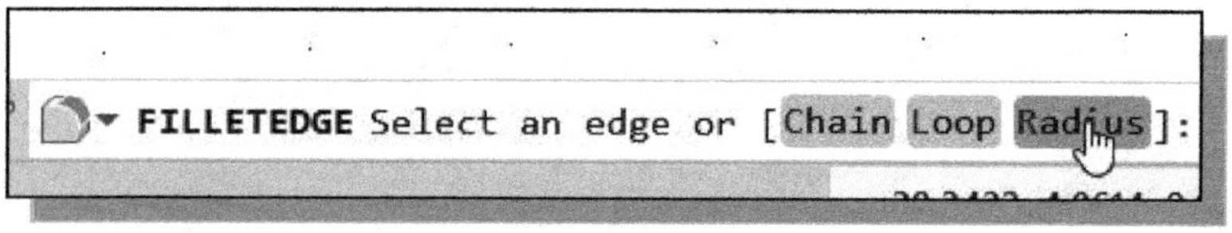

2. In the *command prompt area*, select **Radius**.

3. In the *command prompt area*, the message "*Specify fillet radius:*" is displayed. *Specify fillet radius:* **.75 [ENTER]**.

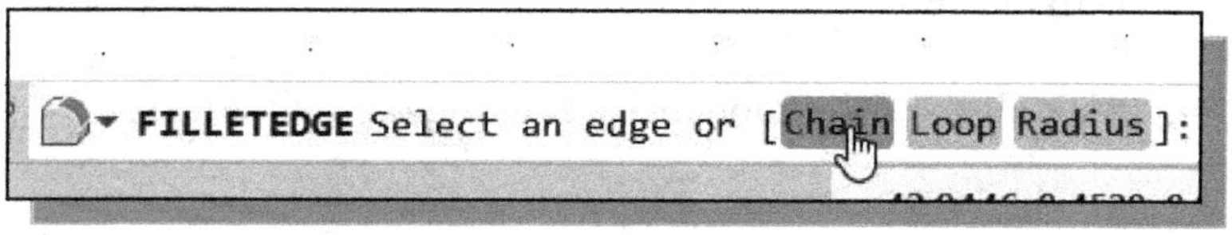

4. In the *command prompt area*, select the **Chain** option.

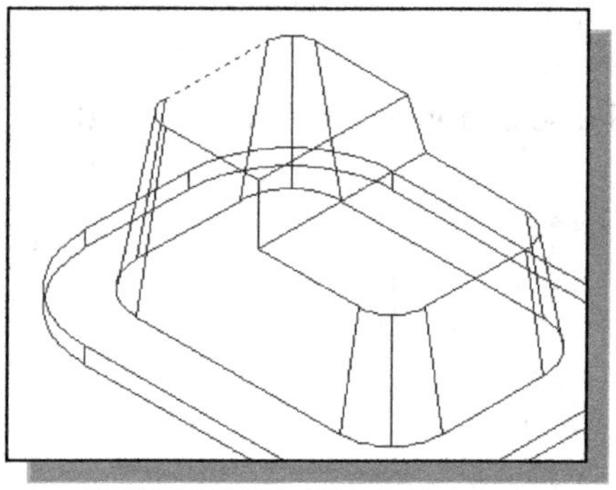

5. Pick the **top back edge** as shown.

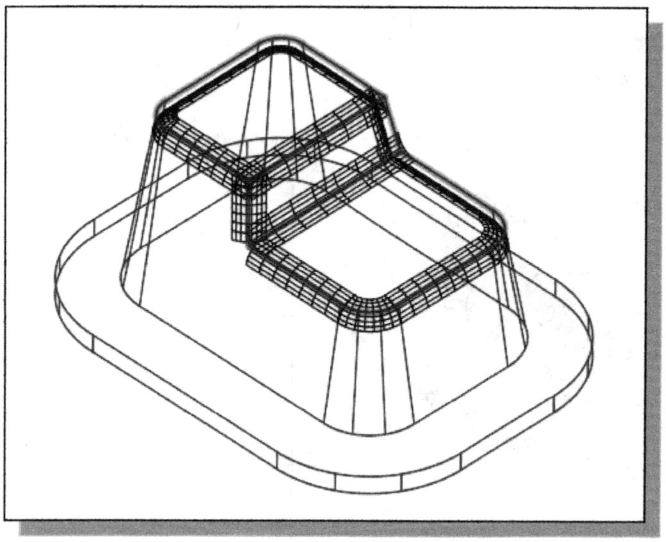

6. In the *command prompt area*, the message "*Select an edge or [Chain/Radius]:*" is displayed. Select one of the **adjacent curves** on the top surface.

7. On your own, select the **adjacent edges** on the top surfaces as shown in the figure.

8. Press the **[ENTER]** key or use the right-mouse-button and select **Enter** to accept the selection.

- The **Fillet** command can be used to create complex 3D curves and surfaces as shown in this example.

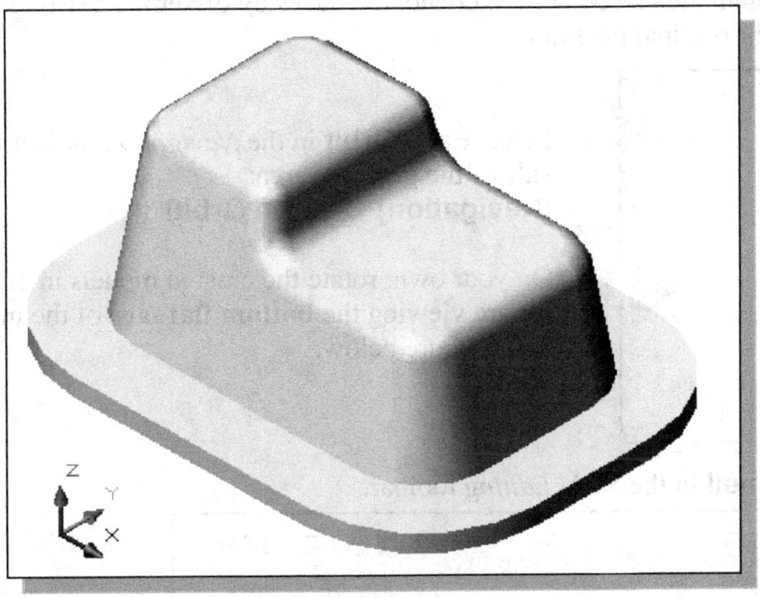

- On your own, create a *chained fillet* of **0.625 radius** at the bottom edges as shown.

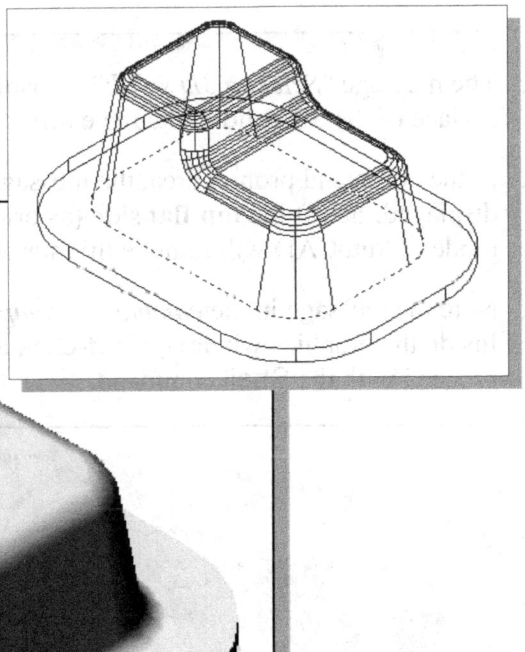

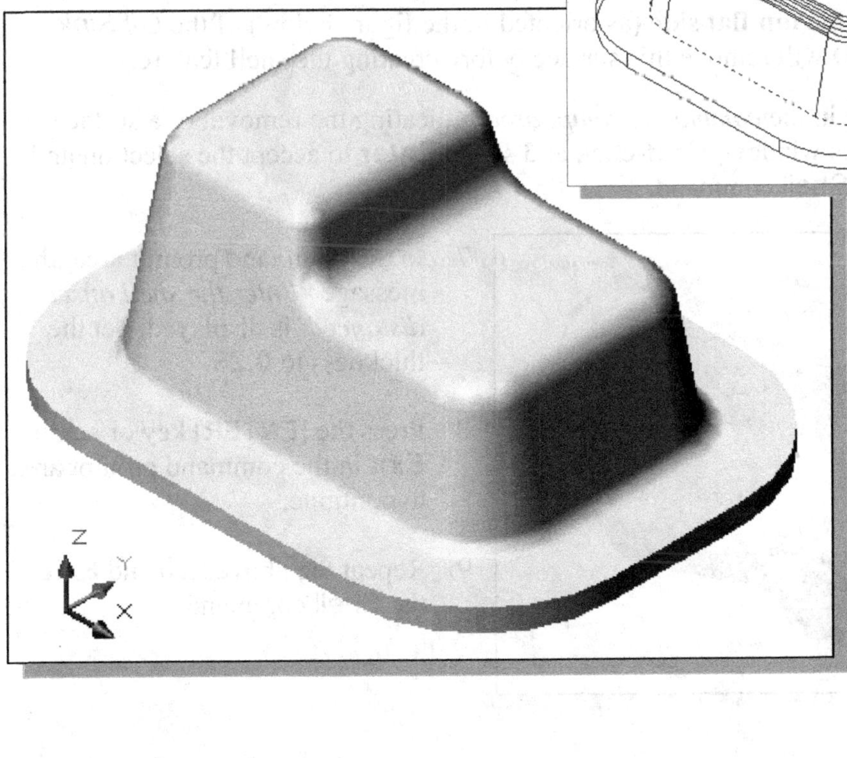

Create a Shell Feature

The **Shell** command can be used to create new faces by offsetting existing ones inside or outside of their original positions.

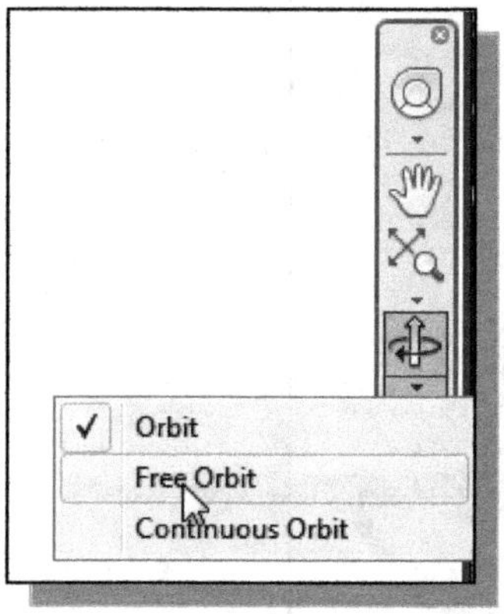

1. Select **Free Orbit** in the *Navigation* toolbar to the right side of the graphics area:
   [Navigation] → [Free Orbit]

2. On your own, rotate the created models in 3D space so that we are viewing the **bottom flat face** of the model as shown in the figure below.

3. Choose **Shell** in the *Solid Editing* toolbar.

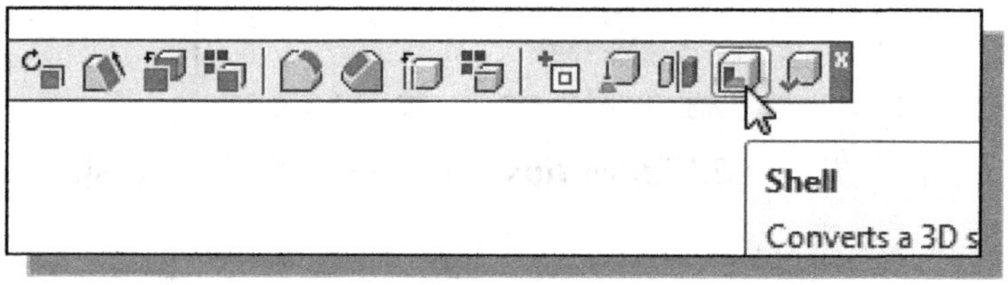

4. The message "*Select a 3D solid:*" is displayed in the command prompt area. Pick any surface of the **3D solid**. Note the entire solid is selected.

5. In the command prompt area, the message "*Remove faces or [Undo /Add /All]:*" is displayed. Select the **top flat side** (as oriented in the figure below) of the *Oil Sink* model. (AutoCAD will remove this surface before creating the shell feature.)

6. Note the message in the *command prompt area* indicating the removal of a surface. Inside the graphics window, **right-click** and select **Enter** to accept the selection and proceed with the Shell command.

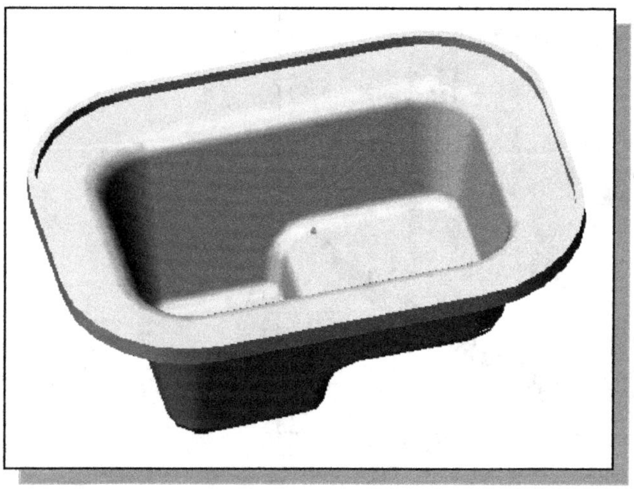

7. In the command prompt area, the message "*Enter the shell offset distance:*" is displayed. Set the thickness to **0.25**.

8. Press the **[ENTER]** key or select **Exit** in the command prompt area to continue.

9. Repeat the above step and **Exit** the Shell command.

Create a Rectangular Array Cut Feature

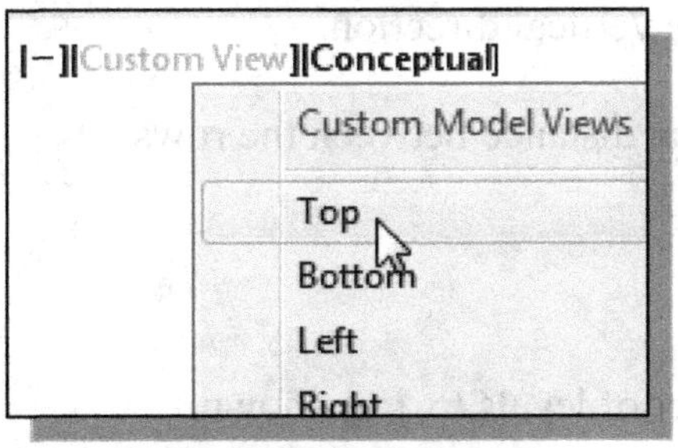

1. In the *View* control list, select the **Top** view option to reset the display to the XY plane of the coordinate system.

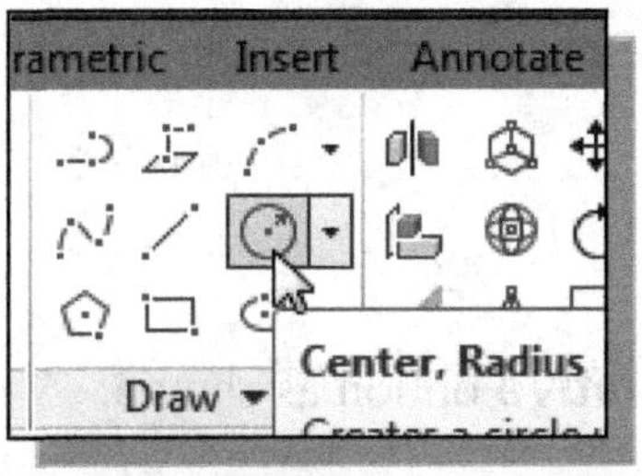

2. Select the **Circle** icon in the *Draw* toolbar.

3. On your own, create a circle (radius **0.375**) that is toward the right side of the solid model. Note that, in AutoCAD, ***circles*** are created as valid ***regions***.

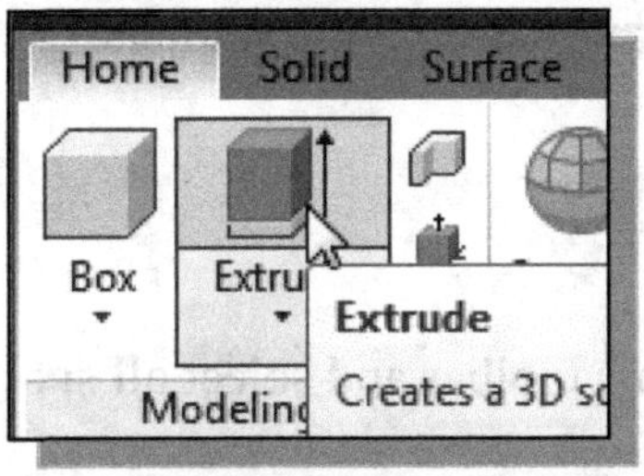

4. On your own, extrude the region into a **1″** high cylinder. (*Taper angle* set to **0**.)

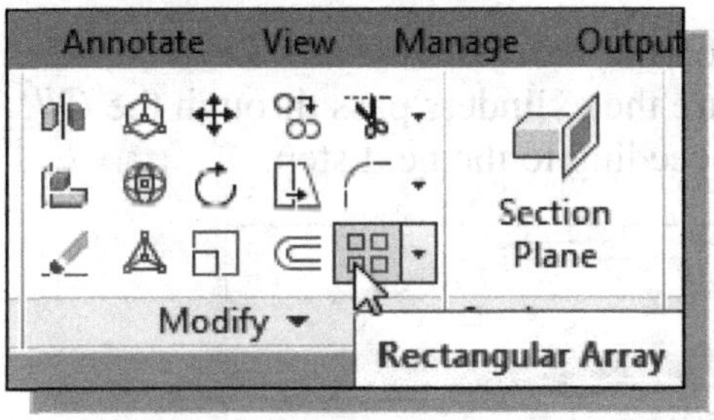

5. Select **Rectangle Array** in the *Modify* toolbar as shown.

6. Select the **cylinder** we just created.

7. Inside the *graphics window*, **right-click** to accept the selection and proceed to use the Array command.

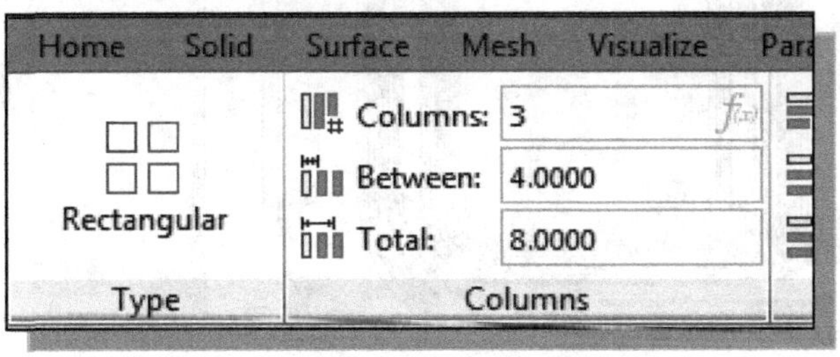

8. In *Columns control panel*, enter **3** as the number of items in the horizontal direction.

9. Enter **4** as the spacing between items in the horizontal direction as shown.

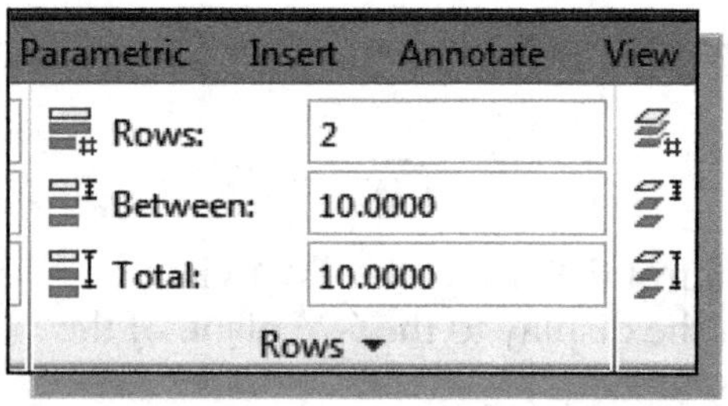

10. In *Columns control panel*, enter **2** as the number of items in the vertical direction.

11. Enter **10** as the distance between the rows.

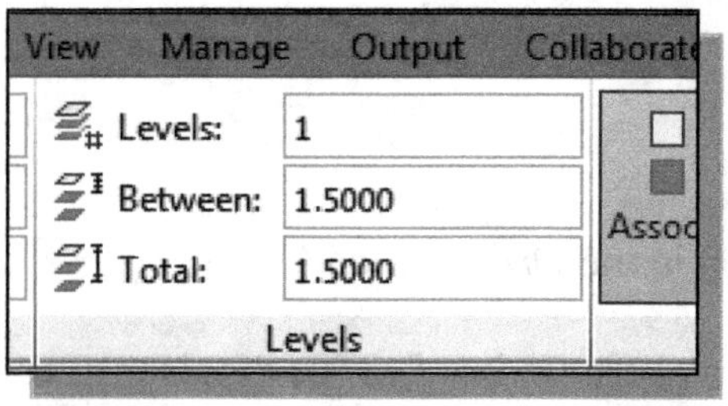

12. Set the number of levels to **1** as shown.

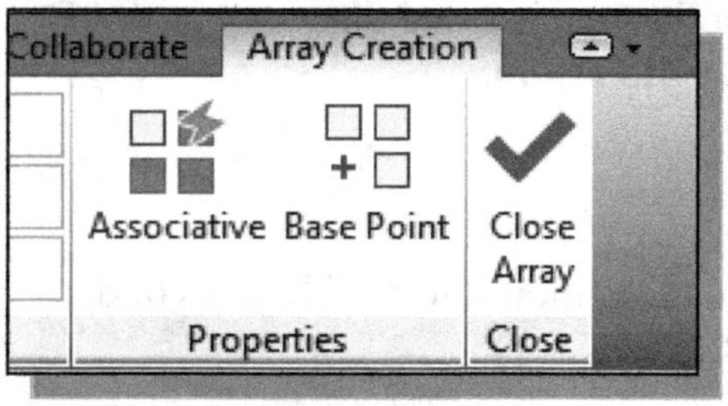

13. Turn **Off** the **Associative** option as shown.

14. Click on **Close Array** to accept the settings and create the array.

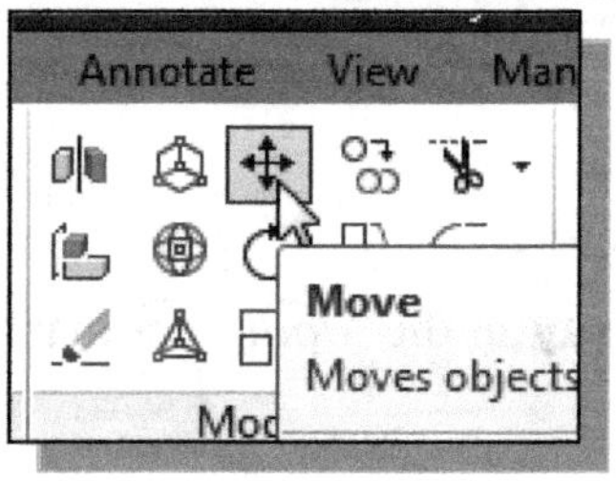

15. Select the **Move** icon in the *Draw* toolbar and select all six cylinders to move.

16. On your own, reposition the six cylinders as shown in the figure below. Make sure the cylinders pass through the *Oil Pan* model before proceeding to the next step.

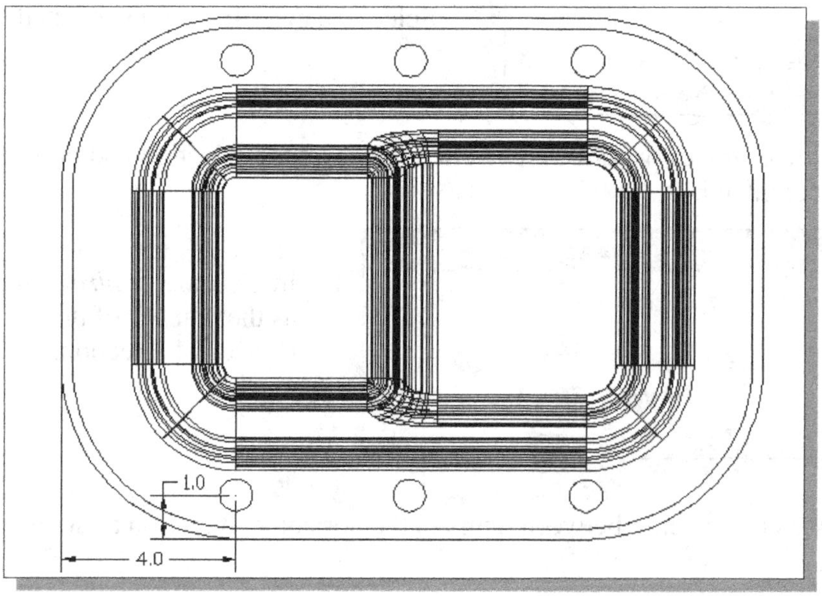

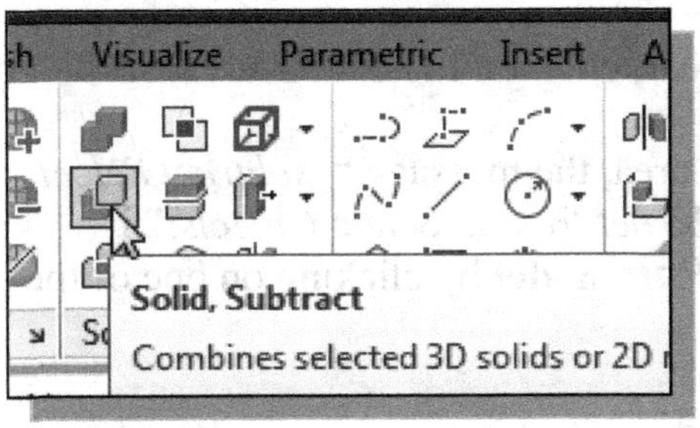

17. In the *Solid Editing* toolbar, click on the **Subtract** icon.

18. In the *command prompt area*, the message "*_subtract Select solids and regions to subtract from ... Select Objects:*" is displayed. Pick the ***Oil Pan*** **model** by clicking on one of the edges.

19. Inside the *graphics window*, **right-click** to accept the selection and proceed with the Subtract command.

20. Pick all **six cylinder blocks** by clicking on the circular edges.

21. Inside the *graphics window*, **right-click** to accept the selection and proceed with the Subtract command.

Create another Rectangular Array Cut Feature

1. On your own, repeat the above steps and create another rectangular array as shown (circular hole: radius **0.375**, ***Rectangular array***, **2** ***Columns*** with **14"** ***Column spacing,*** and **2** ***Rows*** with **4"** ***Row spacing***).

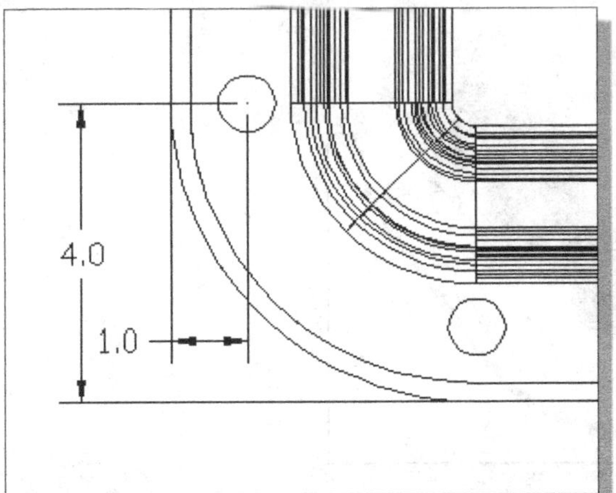

2. On your own, reposition the rectangular array so that the lower left cylinder is located 4.0 inches away from the bottom edge of the base feature and 1.0 inch away from the left edge of the *Oil Pan* model.

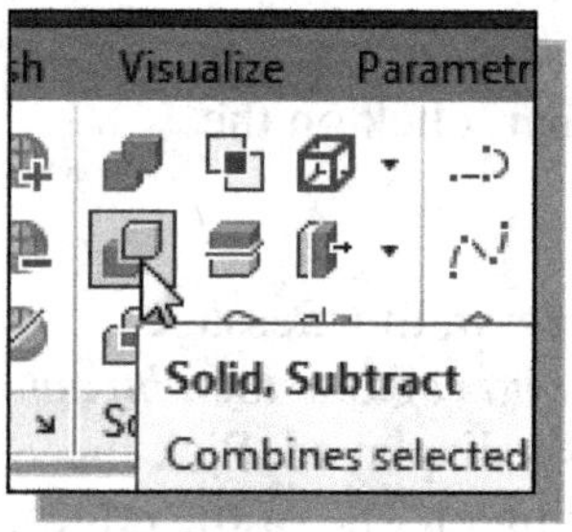

3. In the *Solid Editing* toolbar, click on the **Subtract** icon.

4. In the command prompt area, the message "*_subtract Select solids and regions to subtract from ... Select Objects:*" is displayed. Pick the ***Oil Pan* model** by clicking on one of the edges.

5. Complete the model with the **Subtract** command.

6. Inside the graphics window, **right-click** to accept the selection and proceed with the Subtract command.

7. In the command prompt area, the message "*Select solids and regions to subtract ... Select Objects:*" is displayed.

8. Pick all **six cylinder blocks** by clicking on the circular edges.

9. Inside the graphics window, right-click to accept the selection and proceed with the Subtract command.

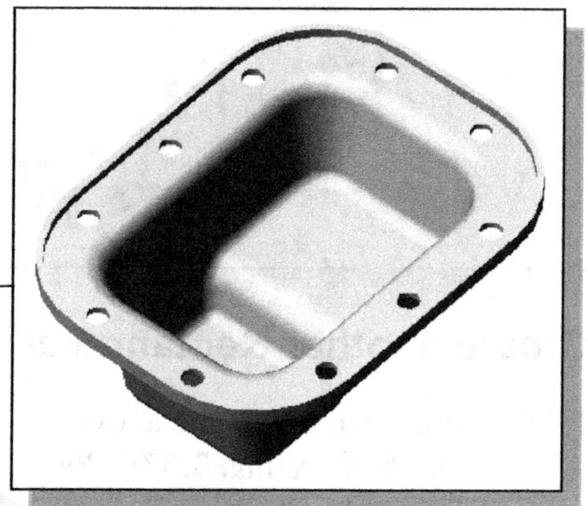

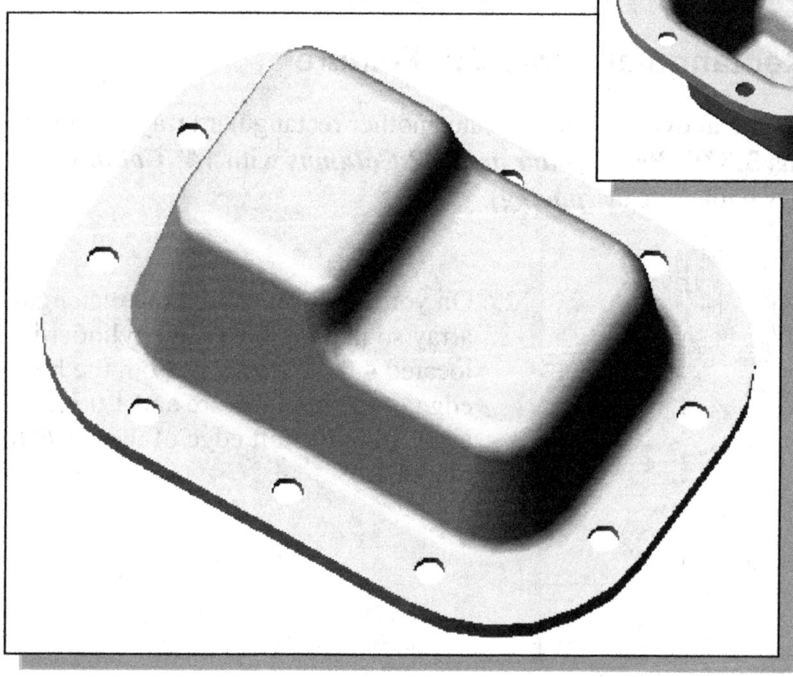

Making a Design Change

Engineering designs usually go through many revisions and changes before they go into production. In AutoCAD 2027, an assortment of 3D tools has been implemented to handle design changes more quickly. In this section, two different approaches to perform a simple design change are illustrated: (1) modifying with the *Grip Editing* tools, and (2) creating with *Dynamic UCS*.

Grip Editing Approach: One of the main 3D editing enhancements in AutoCAD 2027 is the Grip Editing Tools. We can now use grips to manipulate original solid primitive forms that were used to make up ***composite solids***. **Composite solids** are solids created from two or more individual solids through any of the *Boolean* commands: **UNION**, **SUBTRACT**, and **INTERSECT**. To select an individual form of a composite solid, press and hold the **[CTRL]** key while selecting. We will reposition the location of one of the holes using this approach.

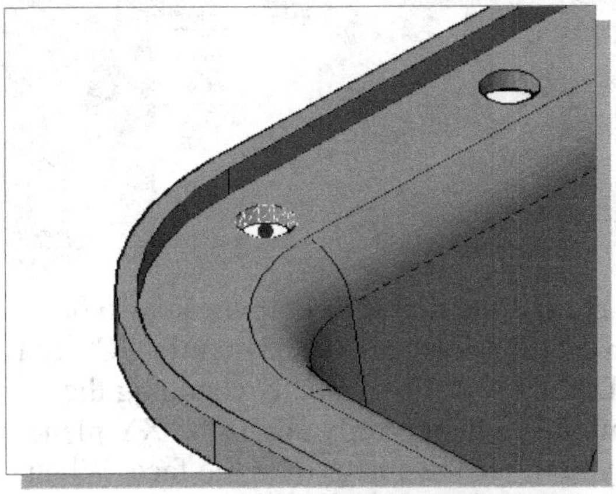

1. Select one of the hole features by pressing down the **[CTRL]** key and clicking on one of the hole cylindrical surfaces as shown.

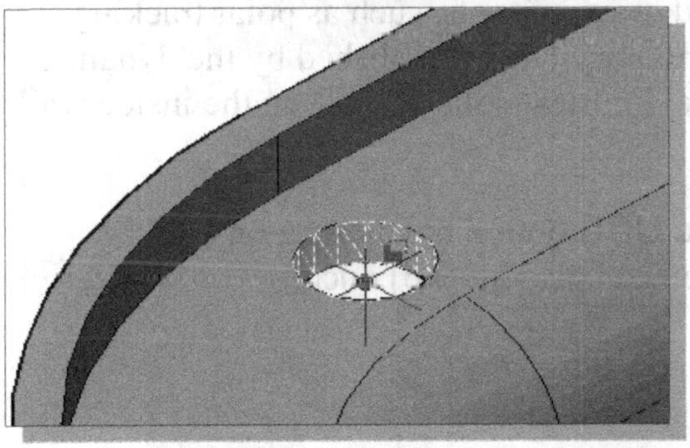

2. **Click** on the *center grip point* that is located at the center of the hole feature. This will activate the **Stretch** option of *Grip Editing*.

3. In the *command prompt area*, the message *"Specify stretch point or [Base point/Undo/eXit]:"* is displayed. Enter **@1.5,0 [ENTER]**.

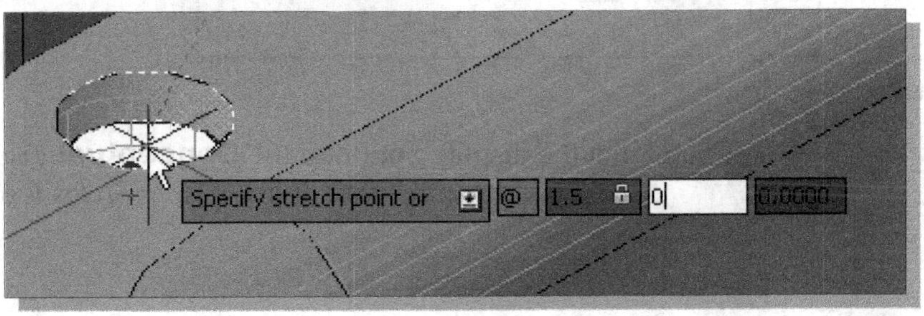

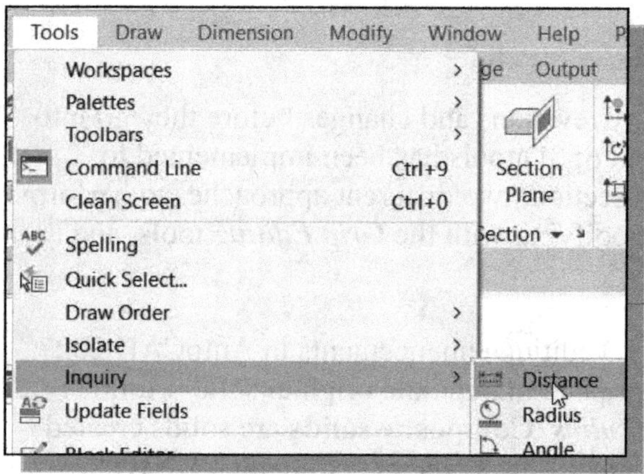

4. On your own, use the **[Tools] → [Inquiry] → [Distance]** command to confirm the design change has been performed correctly.

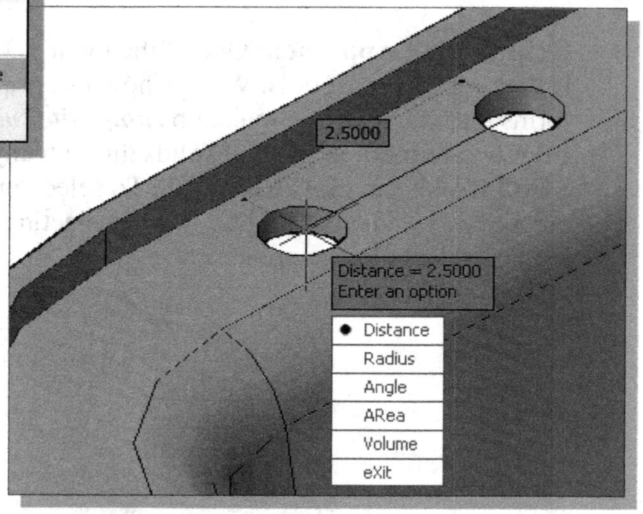

Dynamic UCS Approach: In AutoCAD 2027, the **Dynamic UCS** option can also be used to quickly change the alignment of UCS to existing surfaces. The dynamic UCS can be used to create objects on a planar face of a 3D solid without manually changing the UCS orientation. During a command, the dynamic UCS temporarily aligns the XY plane of the UCS to a planar face of a 3D solid when you move the cursor over the face. When the dynamic UCS is active, specified points, and drawing tools, such as polar tracking and the grid, are all measured relative to the temporary UCS established by the dynamic UCS. In this section, we will add an additional cylindrical solid feature on the inside wall using this approach.

5. In the *Status Bar* area, activate the Dynamic UCS option by clicking on the **UCSDETECT** option button as shown. (You can also hit [F6] once.)

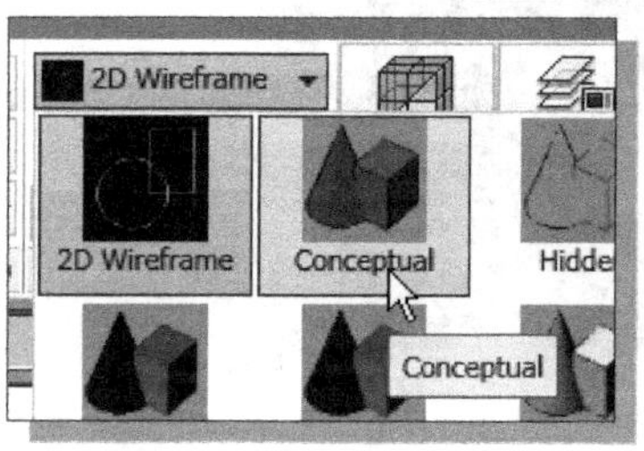

6. Set the display option to the **Conceptual** visual style by clicking on the icon in the *Visual Styles* toolbar as shown.

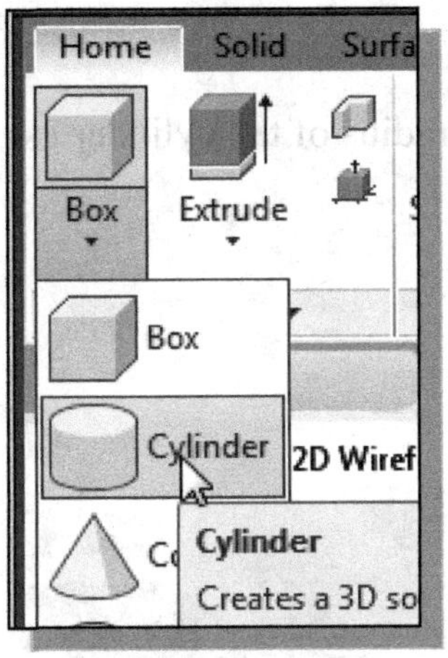

7. Click on the **Cylinder** icon to activate the **Create Cylinder** command.

8. Move the cursor on top of any planar surface and notice the displayed dashed edges signifying the alignment of the *XY plane* of the temporary UCS to the surface.

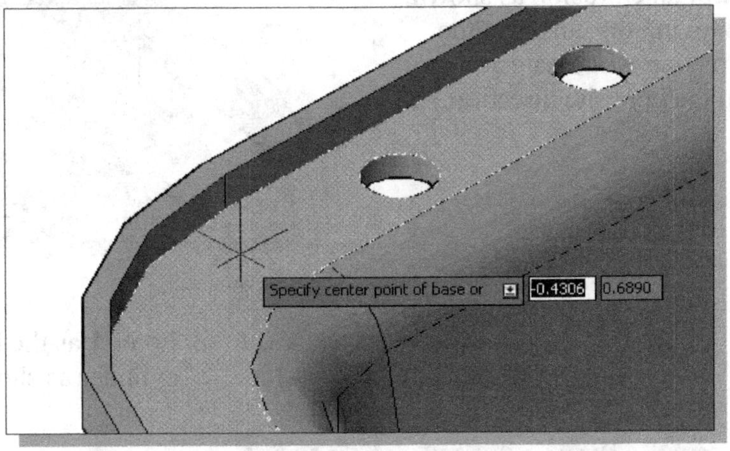

9. Pick an arbitrary location on the surface to use as the center point of the cylinder. Note the display of the alignment of the temporary UCS.

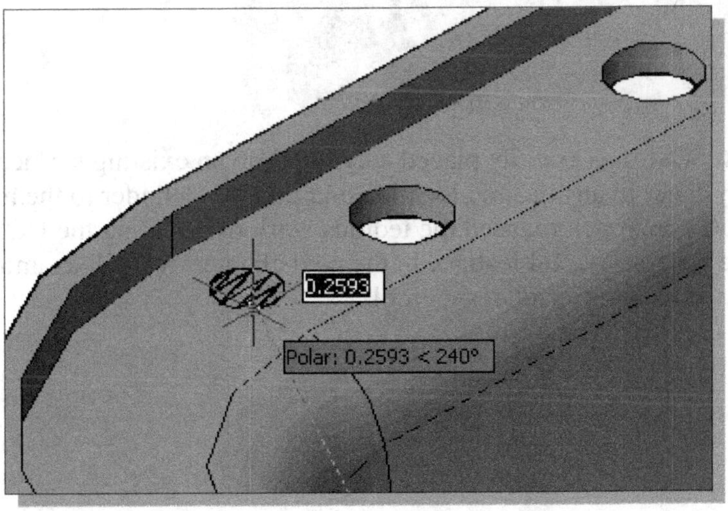

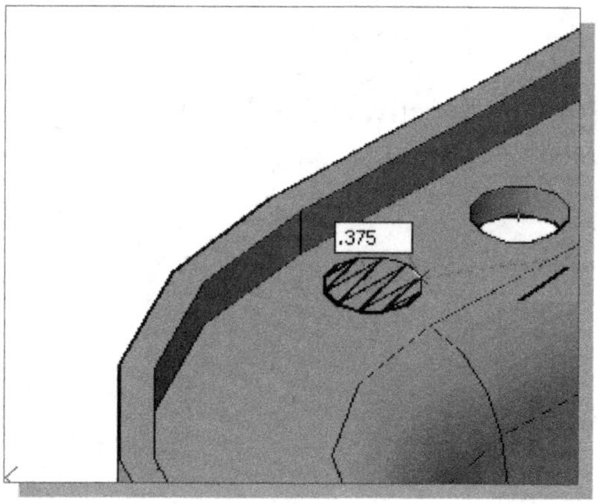

10. Enter **0.375** as the radius of the cylinder as shown.

11. Move the cursor upward and observe the preview of an extrusion as shown. (Note that moving the cursor in the opposite direction will create an extrusion in the opposite direction.)

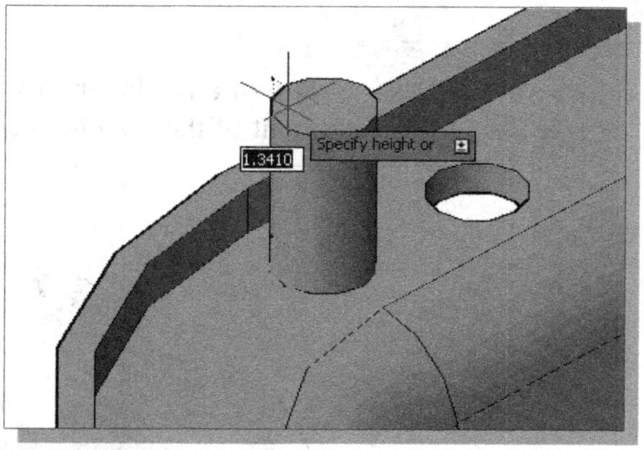

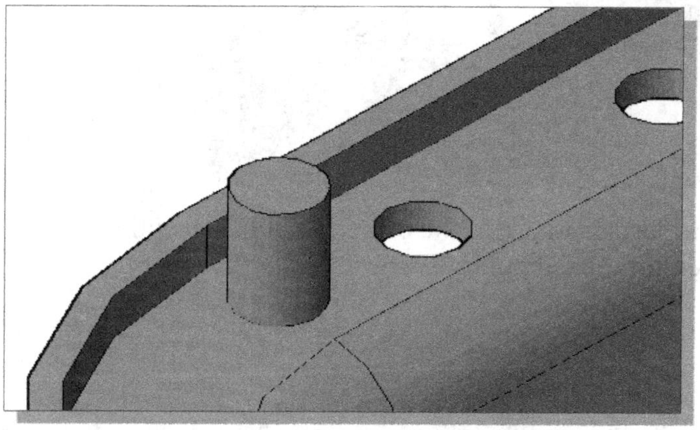

12. Enter **1** as the height of the cylinder as shown.

- Note that we have successfully placed a cylinder on an existing surface. We can now move the cylinder to any desired location and join the cylinder to the main body. The Dynamic UCS approach reduced the tedious work of orienting the UCS prior to creating the necessary solid feature. In the next chapter, we will examine the use of Dynamic UCS as a powerful design tool.

Review Questions:

1. Describe the method used in the tutorial to create *Draft Angle* features in AutoCAD.

2. List and describe the differences between *Cut with a Pattern* and *Cut Each One Individually*.

3. Which command is used to create 3D rounded corners in AutoCAD?

4. What elements are required to define a *Rectangular Array* in AutoCAD?

5. How do we create a thin-walled part in AutoCAD? What elements are required to perform the operation?

6. Identify the following commands:

(a)

(b)

(c)

(d)

Exercises:

1. Dimensions are in inches.

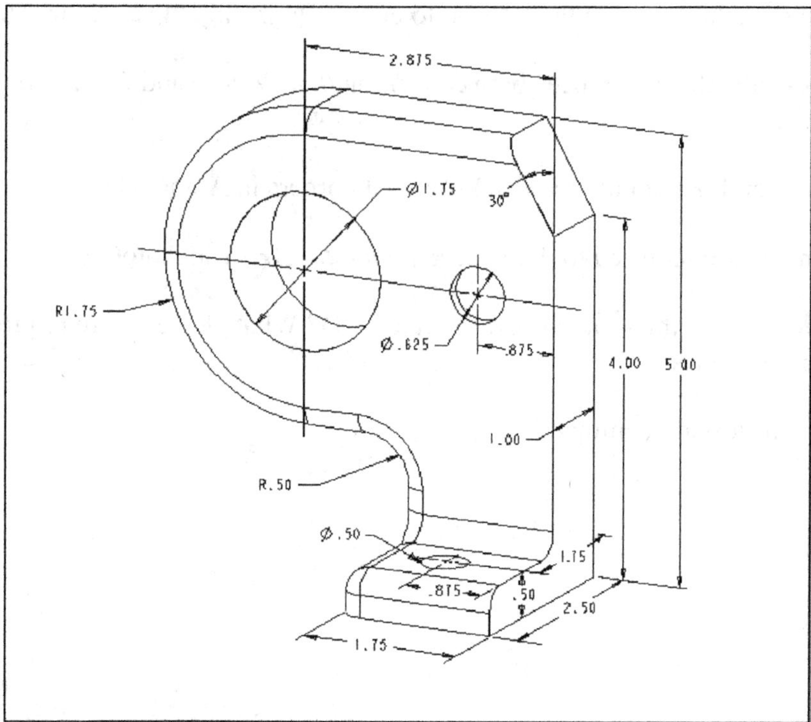

2. Dimensions are in millimeters. (Note the two R40 arcs at the base share the same center.)

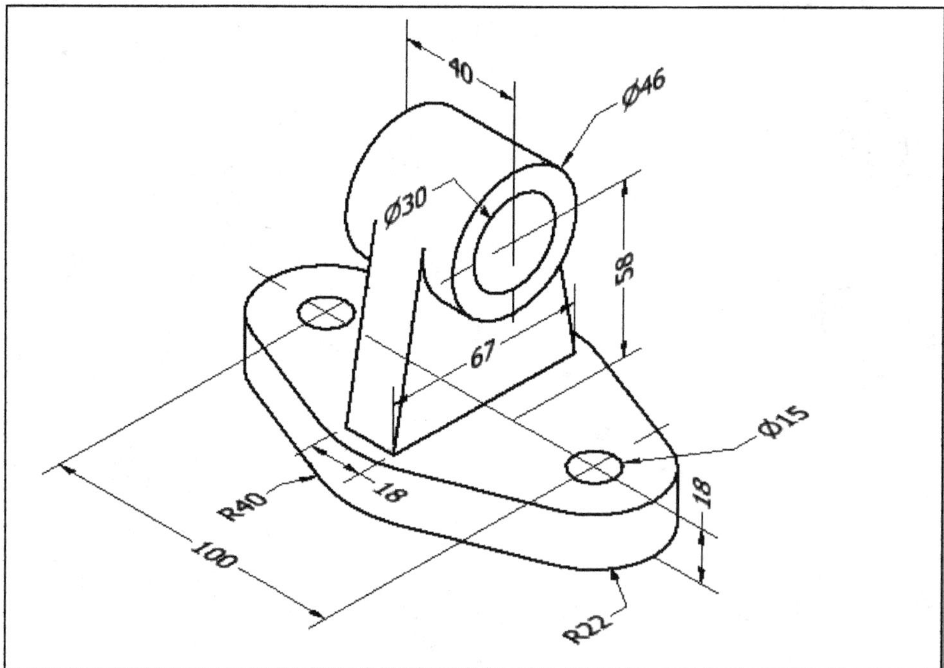

3. Dimensions are in inches.

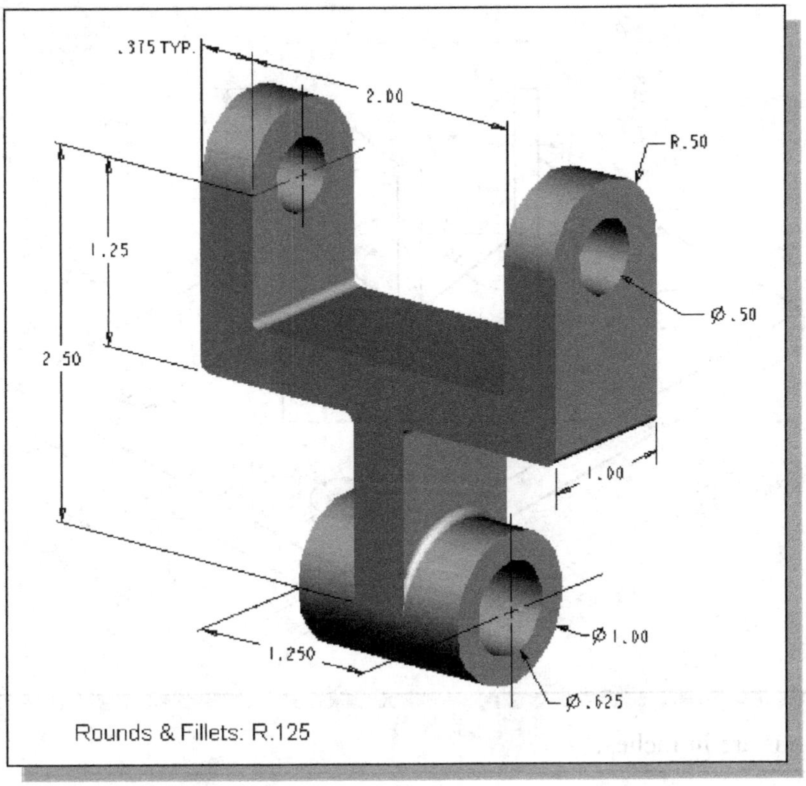

4. Dimensions are in inches.

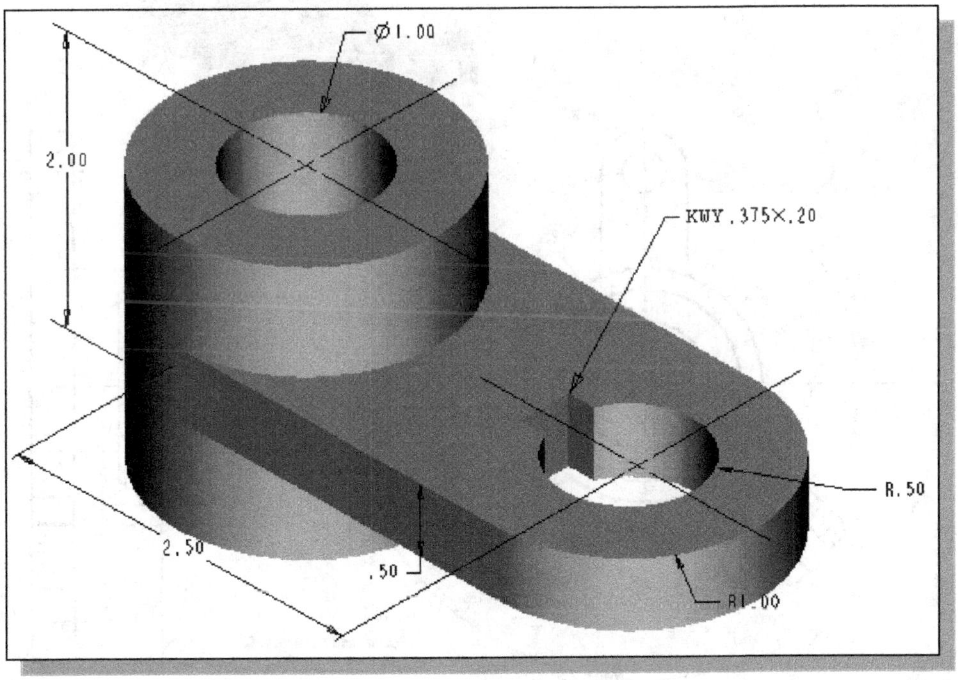

5. Dimensions are in inches.

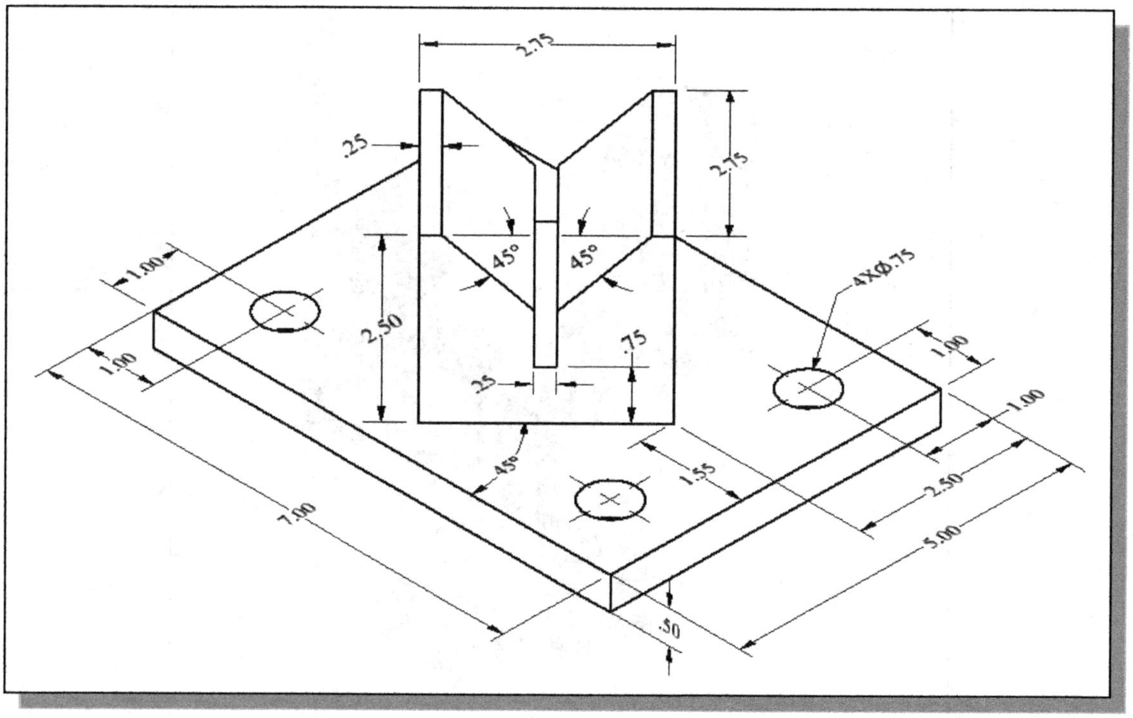

6. Dimensions are in inches.

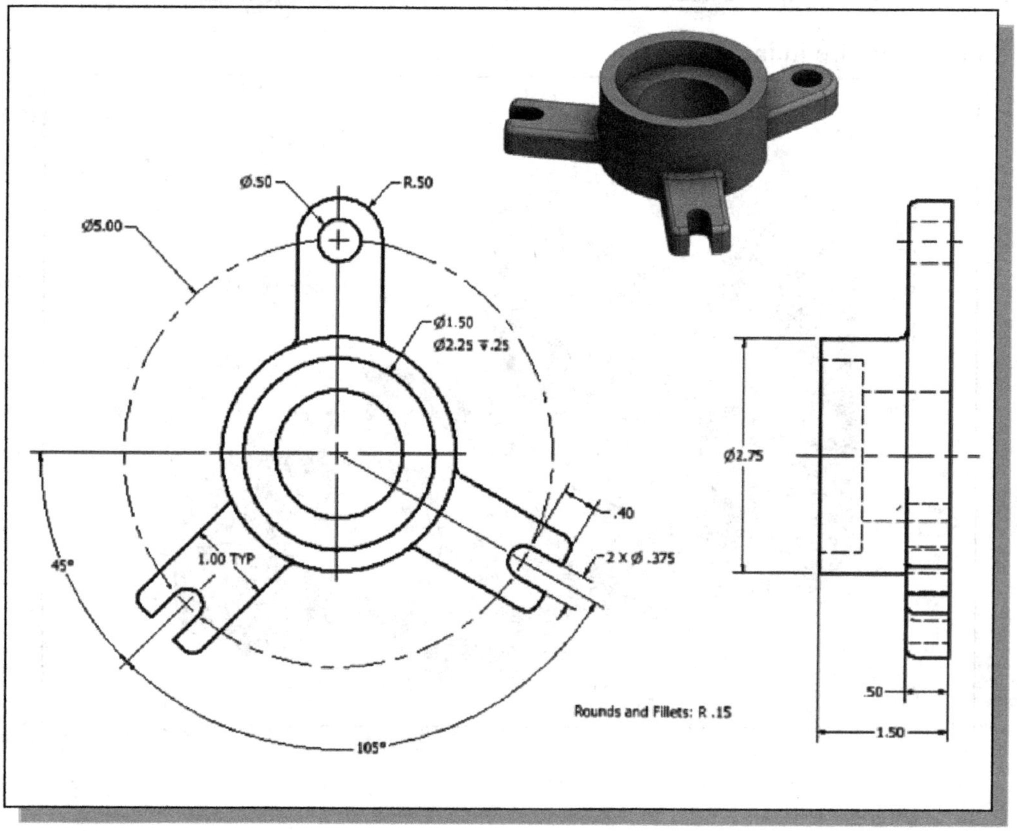

Chapter 11
Conceptual Design Tools & Techniques

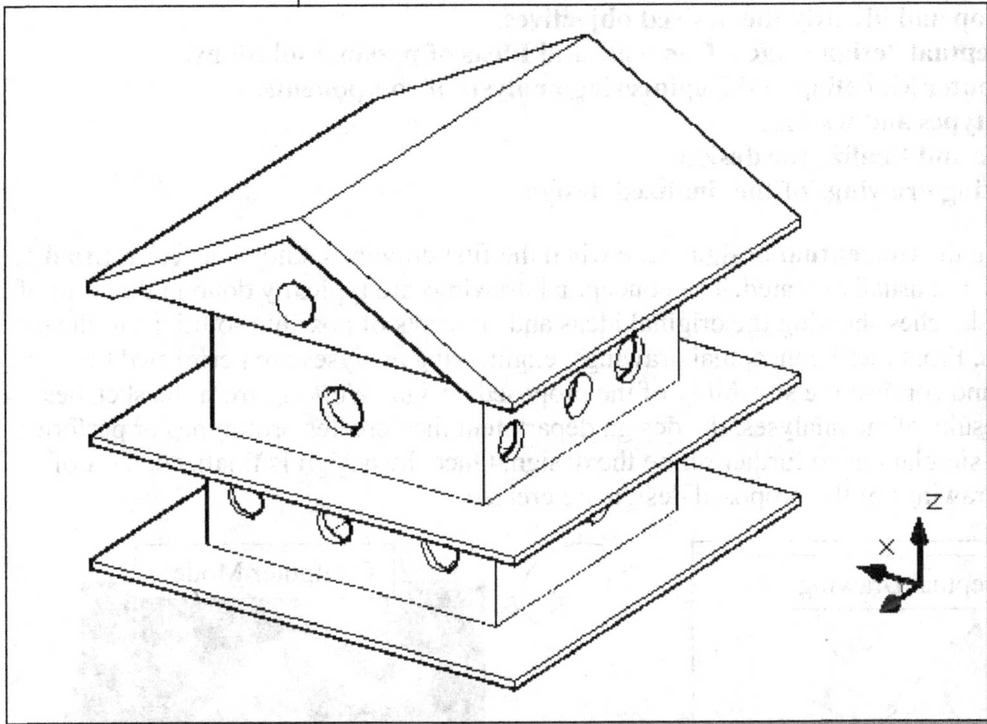

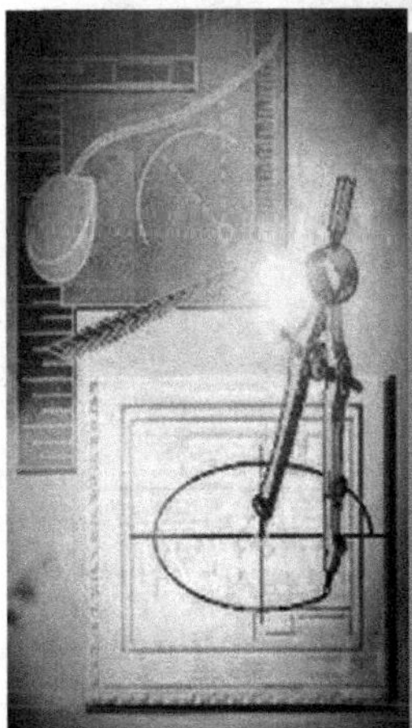

Learning Objectives

- ♦ **Use the Conceptual Modeling Construction Tools**
- ♦ **Use the Dynamic UCS Option**
- ♦ **Use the Press/Pull Command**
- ♦ **Create Rectangular Patterns**
- ♦ **Use the Shell Command**
- ♦ **Use the Copy Faces Command**

Introduction

Engineering design is the ability to create and transform ideas and concepts into a product definition that meets the desired objective. The general procedure for the design of a new product, or improving an existing product, involves the following six stages:

1. **Develop and identify the desired objectives.**
2. **Conceptual design stage – Concepts and Ideas of possible solutions.**
3. **Computer Modeling and Engineering analysis of components.**
4. **Prototypes and testing.**
5. **Refine and finalize the design.**
6. **Working drawings of the finalized design.**

It is during the **conceptual design** stage when the first drawings, known as **conceptual drawings**, are usually created. The conceptual drawings are typically done in the form of freehand sketches showing the original ideas and concepts of possible solutions to the set objectives. From these conceptual drawings, engineering analyses are performed to improve and confirm the suitability of the proposed design. Working from the sketches and the results of the analyses, the design department then creates prototypes or performs computer simulations to further refine the design. Once the design is finalized, a set of detailed drawings of the proposed design are created.

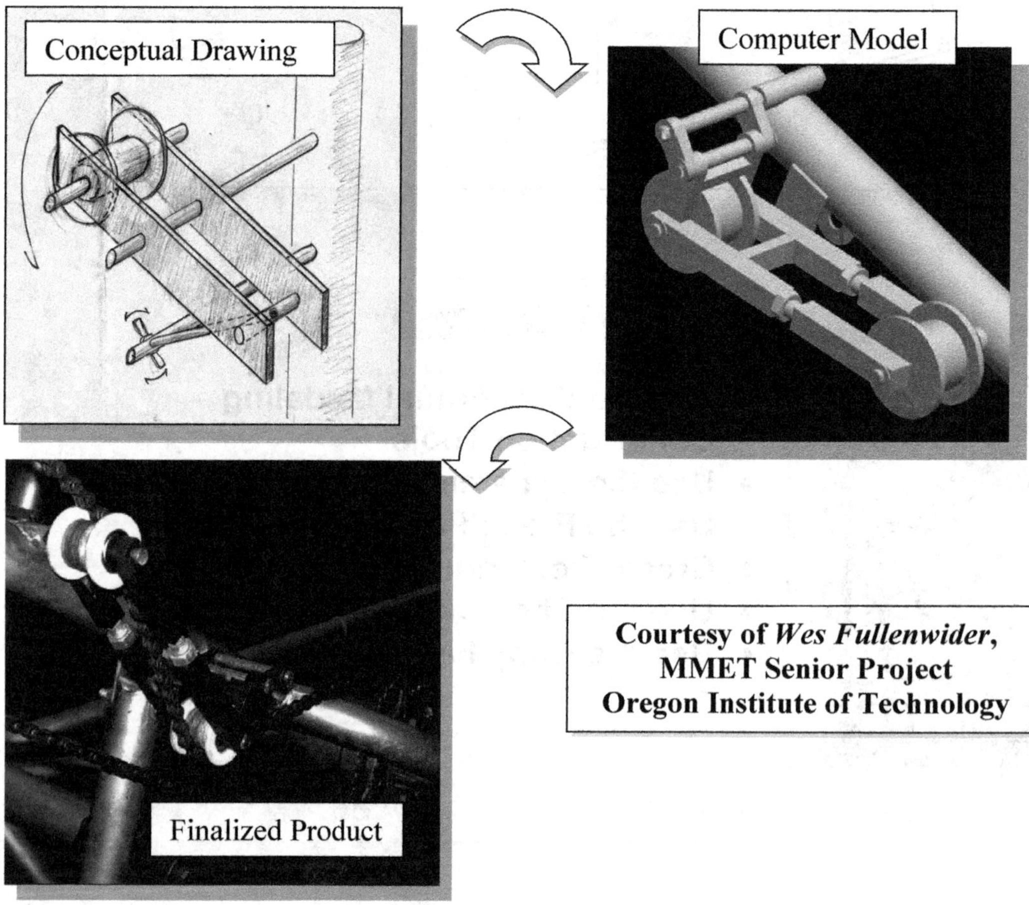

Courtesy of *Wes Fullenwider*,
MMET Senior Project
Oregon Institute of Technology

During the **conceptual design** stage of the design process, the main emphasis is typically placed on the conceptualization of problems and solutions. Also, very little emphasis is placed on the finer details of the design during the conceptual design stage; only a few rough estimates of the actual sizes are considered.

The initial conceptual drawings and sketches represent the idea or essence of what the designer is trying to communicate. Getting the conceptual design correct at the beginning avoids the risk of costly redesign further down the line. Think about how expensive it would be to add a second bathroom once all the plumbing has been done.

One of the main enhancements of AutoCAD in recent years was the introduction of the 3D conceptual modeling tools, which allow the users to very quickly create 3D conceptual models. With the 3D conceptual computer models, the ideas and concepts of a design can be further examined and options explored. The introduction of the 3D conceptual modeling tools has made AutoCAD not just a drafting tool, but a very powerful design tool.

In this chapter, we will use a relatively simple design to illustrate the conceptual modeling tools that are available in AutoCAD 2027.

A Bird House Design

In this tutorial, we will create a 3D conceptual model of a *Bird House* design, based on the rough sketches shown below. Note that detailed dimensions are not of great concern during the conceptual design phase; only rough sizes are noted. This approach is also known as the **shape before size** design philosophy, where the primary concern is the shapes and forms of the design.

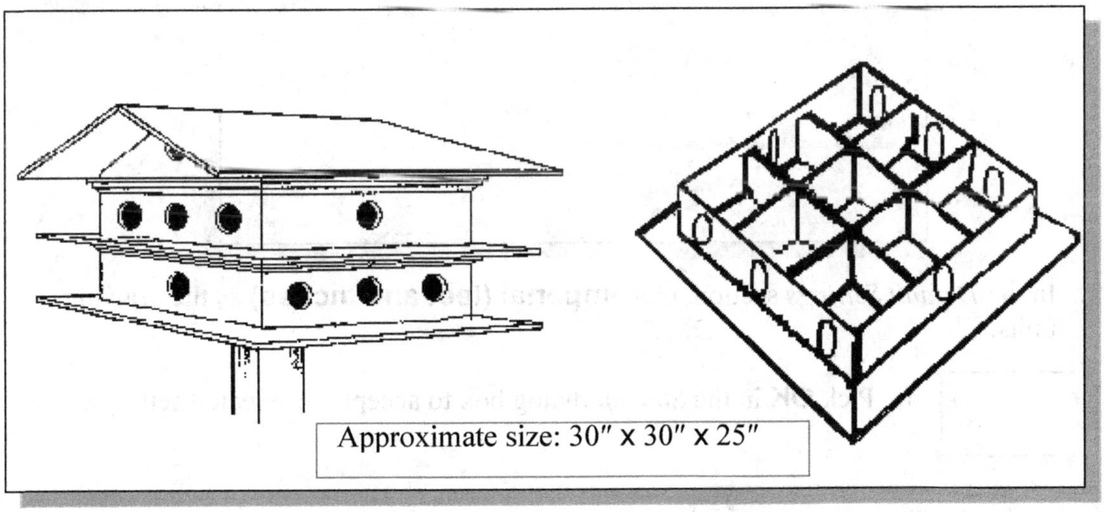

Starting Up AutoCAD 2027

1. Select the **AutoCAD 2027** option on the *Program* menu or select the **AutoCAD 2027** icon on the *Desktop*.

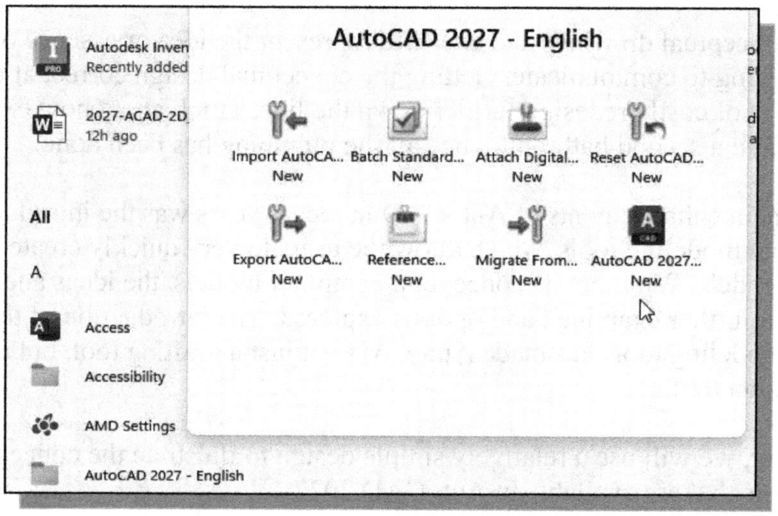

2. In the *Startup* window, select **Start from Scratch**, as shown in the figure below.

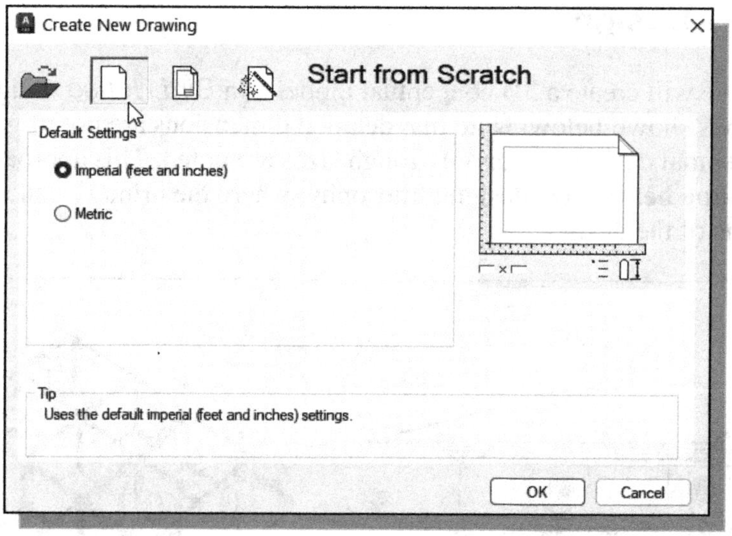

3. In the *Default Settings* section, pick **Imperial (feet and inches)** as the drawing units.

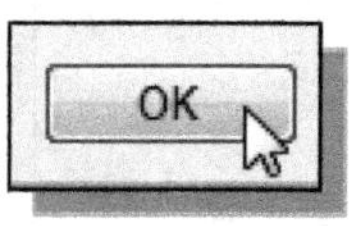

4. Pick **OK** in the *Startup* dialog box to accept the selected settings.

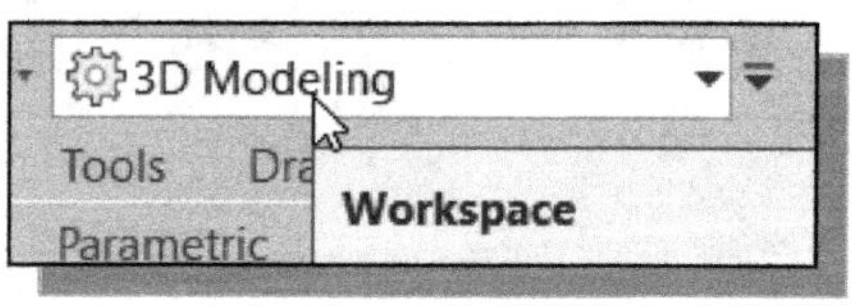

5. On your own, set the *workspace* to **3D Modeling** as shown.

Layers Setup

1. In the *Menu Bar,* select **[Tools] → [Toolbars] → [AutoCAD] → [Layers]**.

2. Click **Layers Properties Manager** in the *Layers* toolbar.

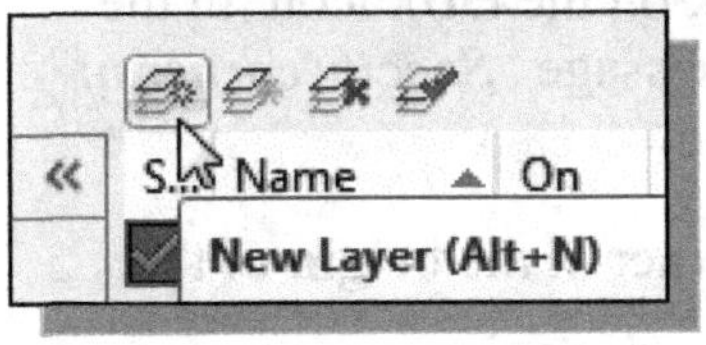

3. Click on the **New** button to create new layers.

4. Create **two new layers** with the following settings:

Layer	***Color***	***Linetype***	***Lineweight***
Base	**Cyan**	**Continuous**	**Default**
Roof	**Blue**	**Continuous**	**Default**

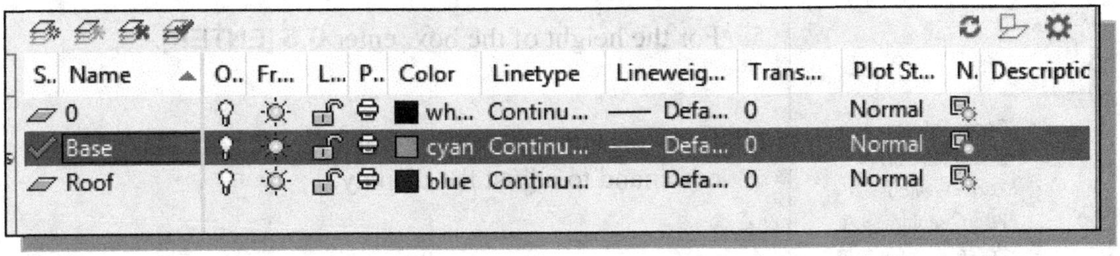

5. Highlight the layer ***Base*** in the list of layers.

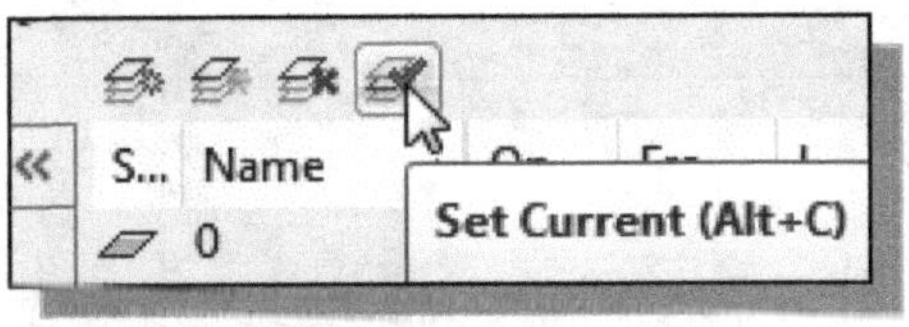

6. Click on the **Current** button to set layer ***Base*** as the *Current Layer*.

7. Click on the **Close** button to accept the settings and exit the *Layer Properties Manager* dialog box.

8. In the *Status Bar* area, reset the options and turn ***ON*** only the *Dynamic Input* option.

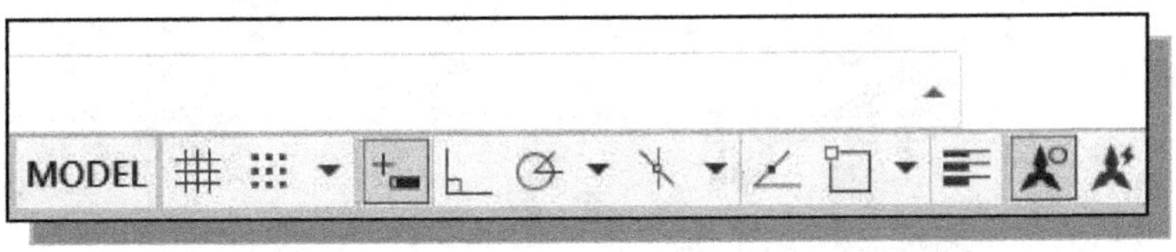

The Base Plate

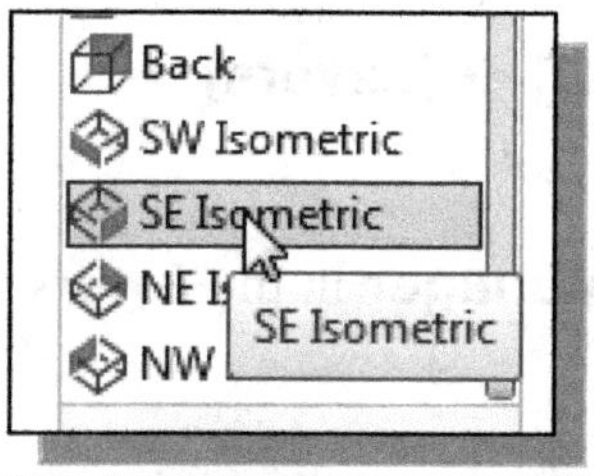

1. Move the cursor to the *View* control list and click on the **SE Isometric** view icon as shown.

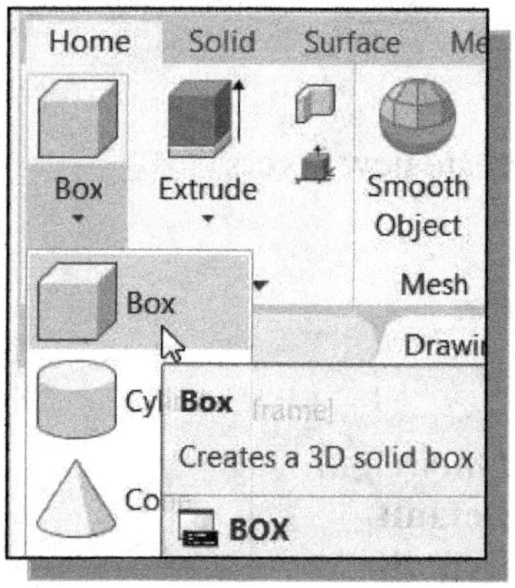

2. In the *Modeling* toolbar, click on the **Box** icon. In the command prompt area, the message "*Specify corner of box or [Center]:*" is displayed.

3. Enter **0,0** to place the first corner at the **origin** of the world coordinate system.

4. In the command prompt area, the message "*Specify corner or [Cube/Length]:*" is displayed. Enter **@30,30 [ENTER]**.

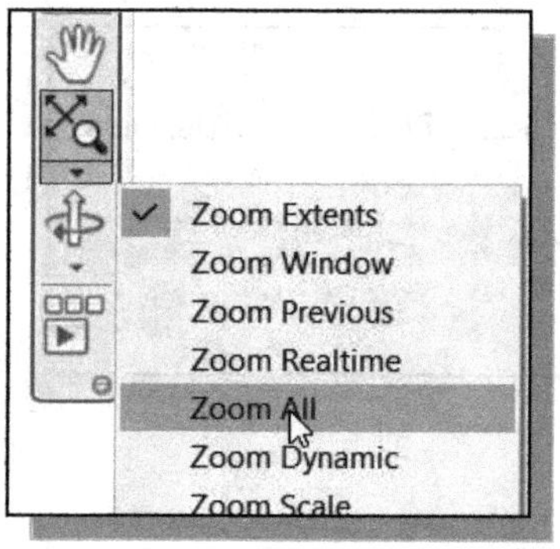

5. For the height of the box, enter **0.5 [ENTER]**.

6. In the *Navigation* toolbar, select the **Zoom All** command to adjust the display.

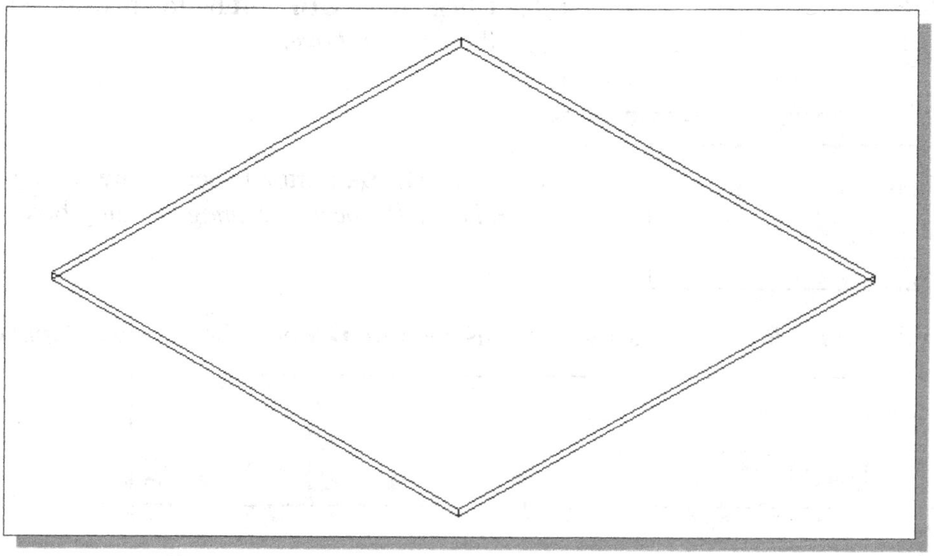

Create the Compartments for the 1st Floor

In AutoCAD, the **Dynamic UCS** option can be used to quickly align UCS to existing surfaces. The dynamic UCS can be used to create objects on a planar face of a 3D solid without manually changing the UCS orientation.

1. Activate the *Dynamic UCS* option by clicking on the **associated** icon in the *Status Bar* as shown. (Use the **Customization** button to switch **on** the display.)

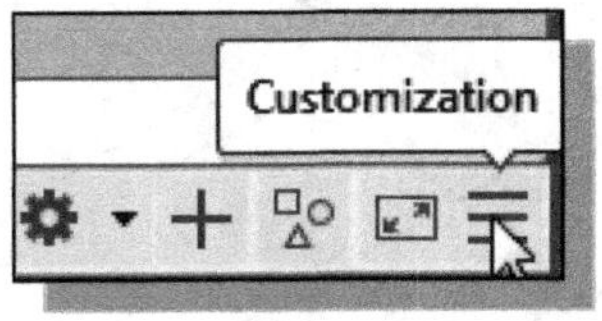

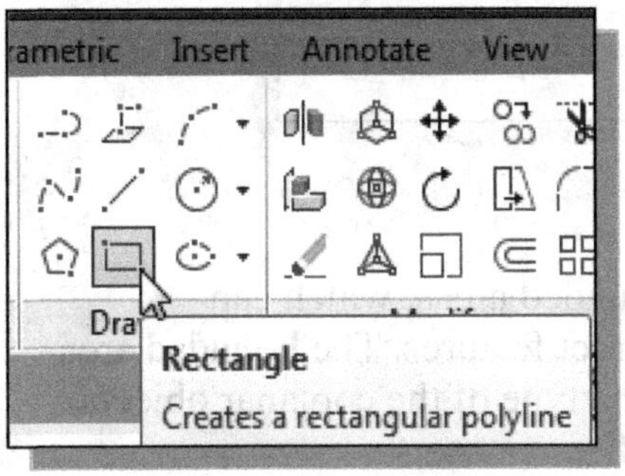

2. Select the **Rectangle** icon in the *Draw* toolbar. In the *command prompt area*, the message "*Specify first corner point or [Chamfer/Elevation/Fillet/Thickness/Width]:*" is displayed.

3. Move the cursor on the top plan of the 3D base and notice the dynamic UCS option automatically aligns the UCS to the top plane as shown.

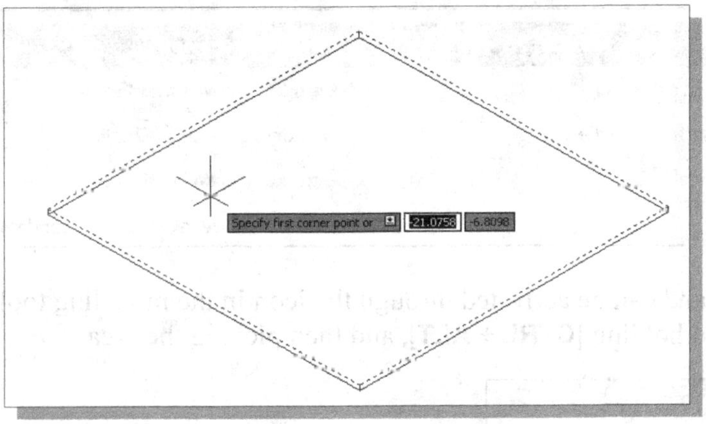

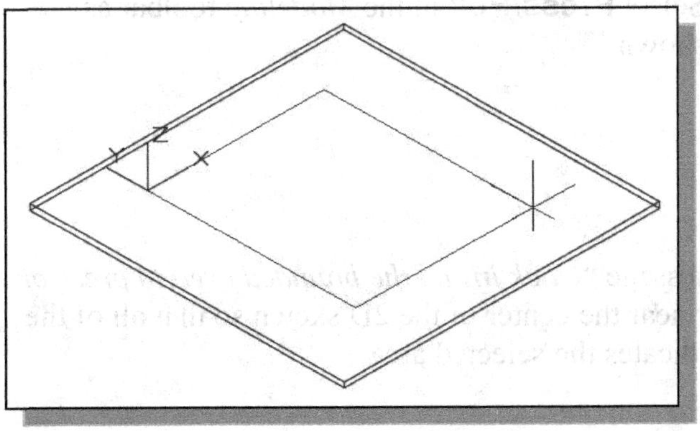

4. On your own, create a rectangle that is roughly ⅔ the size of the base as shown.

5. On your own, repeat the above steps and create four additional rectangles as shown in the figure below. Do not be overly concerned with the actual sizes and dimensions of the sketch; the main goal is "fast and loose" for conceptual models.

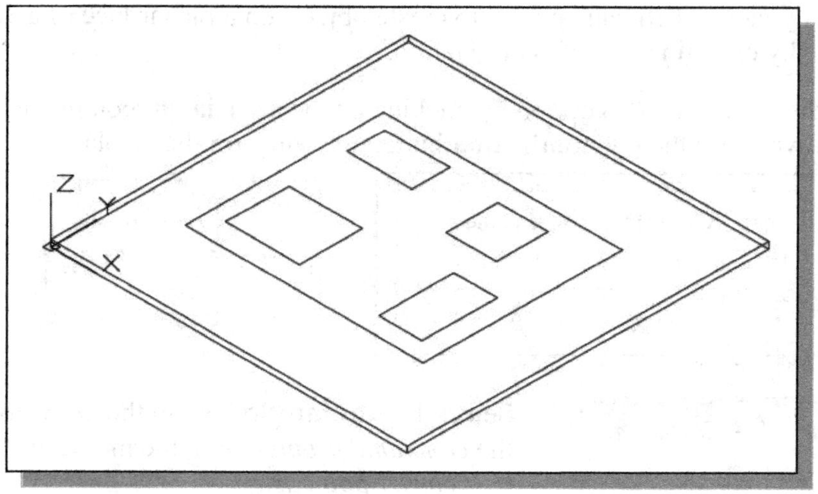

Using the Press/Pull Command

The **Press/Pull** command allows us to press or pull bounded areas, which can automatically form either Boolean Join or Boolean Subtract features. The bounded area must be bounded by coplanar lines or edges. Based on the type of the coplanar objects, the Press/Pull command can produce the following results:

Selection	Presspull behavior
Open 2D object (such as an arc)	Extrudes to create a surface
Closed 2D object (such as a circle)	Extrudes to create a 3D solid
Inside a bounded area	Extrudes to create a 3D solid
3D solid face	Offsets the face, expanding or condensing the 3D solid

- This command can be activated through the icon in the modeling toolbar panel or by pressing and holding **[CTRL + ALT]**, and then picking the area.

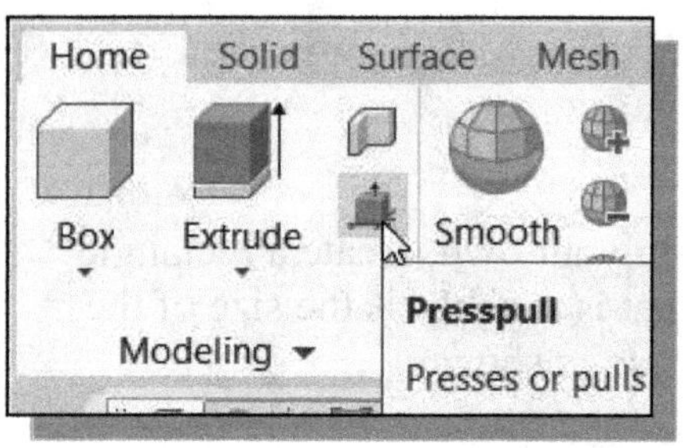

1. Select **Press/Pull** in the *Modeling* toolbar as shown.

2. In the *command prompt area,* the message "*Click inside the bounded area to press or pull:*" is displayed. Move the cursor near the center of the 2D sketch so that all of the rectangles are highlighted, which indicates the selected area.

3. Inside the graphics window, use the **left-mouse-button** and **pull** the selection upward as shown. Note that the large rectangle (the outside loop) indicates the boundary of adding material to the base, while the smaller rectangles (the inside loops) indicate the boundaries of holes.

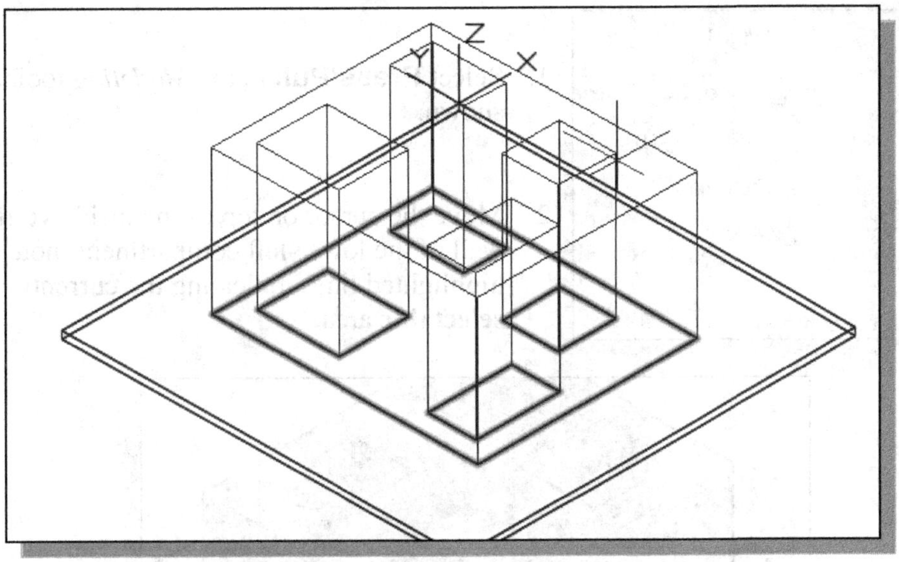

4. Inside the graphics window **left-click** once to create the solid feature.

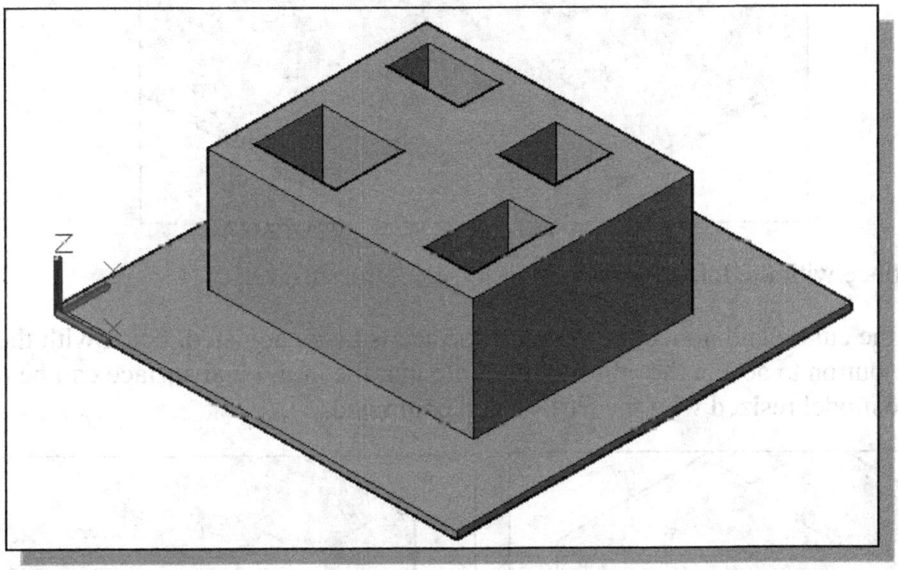

- Note that the solid feature created with the **Press/Pull** command automatically joins the new feature to the existing solid model. The **Press/Pull** command allows us the ability to create solids from sketched 2D geometry. Note that this is a totally different approach than the **Region** command. This new approach was first introduced by the @Last Software Co. (now part of Trimble, Inc.) in their *SketchUp* software.

Using the Press/Pull Command as an Editing Tool

The **Press/Pull** command can also be used as an editing tool. This command enables us to quickly resize any of the existing solid features.

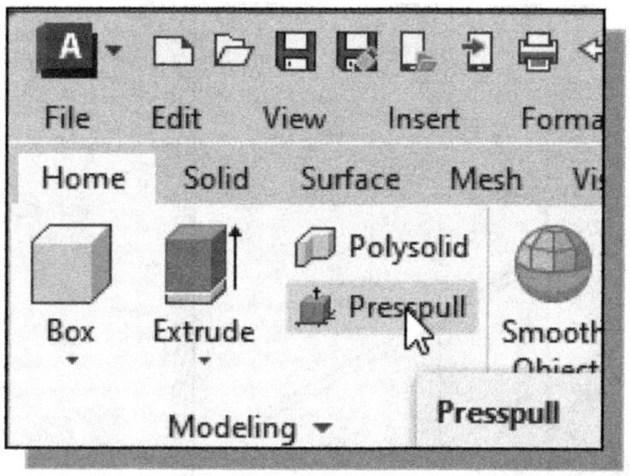

1. Select **Press/Pull** in the *Modeling* toolbar as shown.

2. Move the cursor on top of the inside vertical wall of the lower-left compartment; note the highlighted lines indicating the currently **selectable** area.

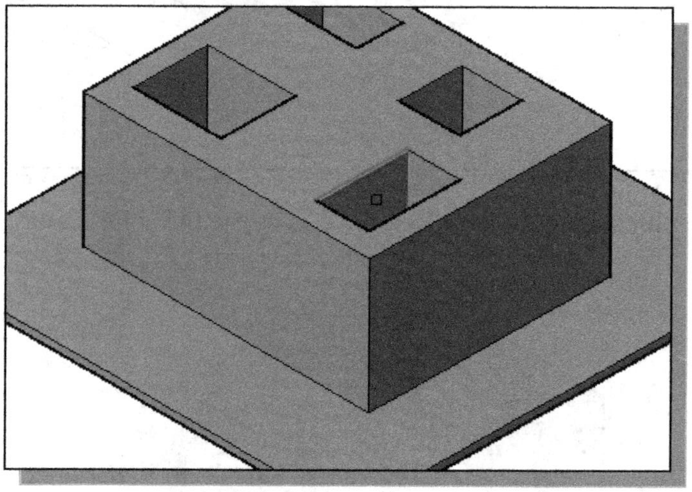

3. Click once with the **left-mouse-button** to select the surface.

4. Move the cursor and notice the selected surface is being adjusted. Click with the left-mouse-button to accept the adjustment. Note that the individual surface can be moved and the model resized with the Press/Pull command.

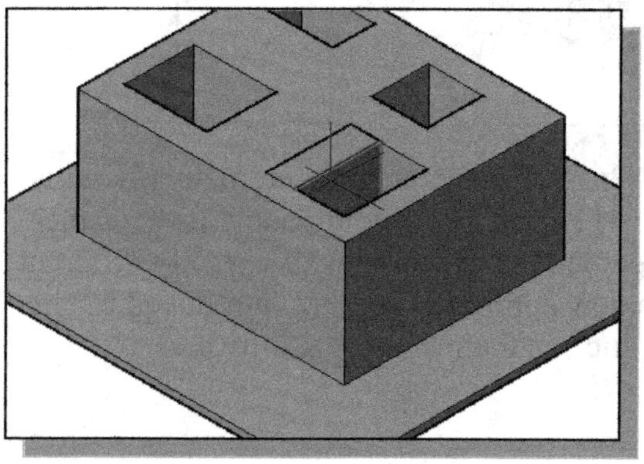

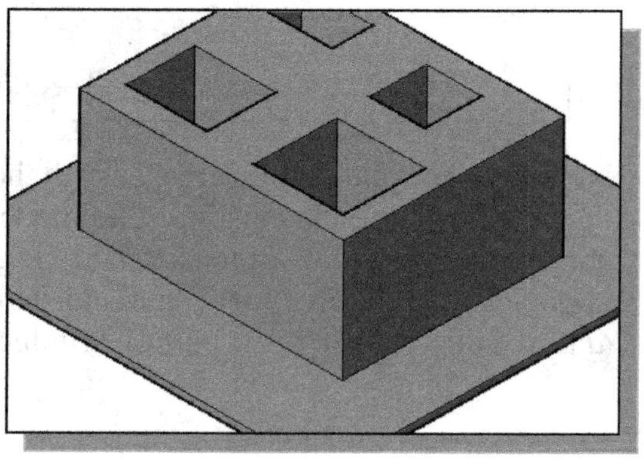

Create another Cut Feature

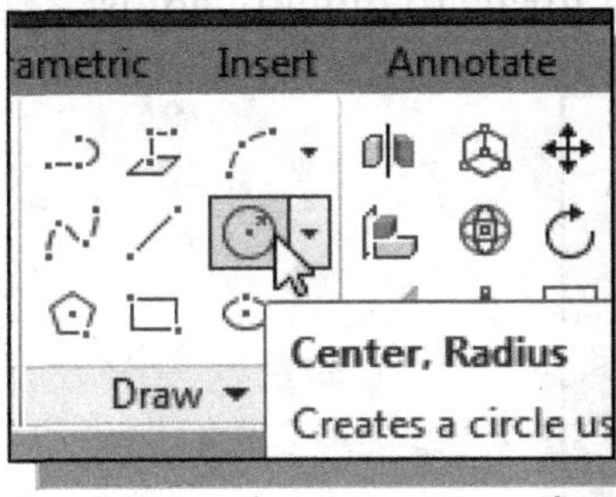

1. In the *Draw* toolbar, click on the **Circle** icon to activate the circle command. In the command prompt area, the message "*Specify center point for circle or [3P/2P/Ttr]:*" is displayed.

2. Move the cursor on the front plane of the 3D base and notice the dynamic UCS option automatically aligns the UCS to the front plane as shown.

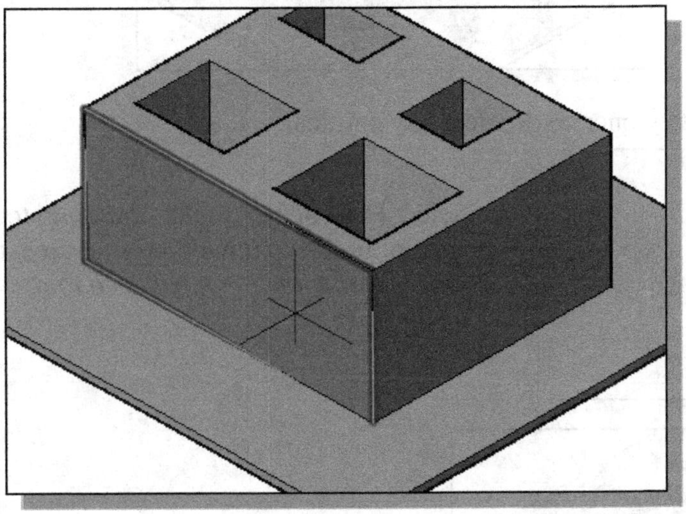

3. Pick a location to place the center point so that it is aligned to the center of the square opening.

4. Create a circle that is about half of the width of the square opening as shown in the figure below.

5. Inside the graphics window, select the circle by clicking once with the left-mouse-button. Notice that the 2D grip editing tool is also available for us to quickly adjust the size and location of the sketched 2D geometry.

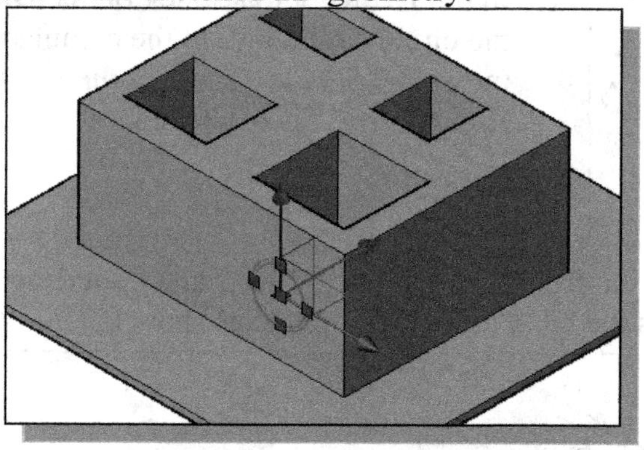

6. Press the [**Esc**] key once to deselect any entities.

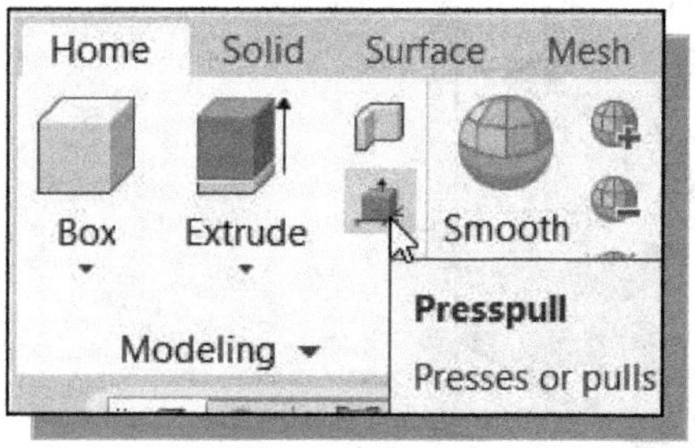

7. Select **Press/Pull** in the *Modeling* toolbar as shown. In the command prompt area, the message "*Click inside the bounded area to press or pull:*" is displayed.

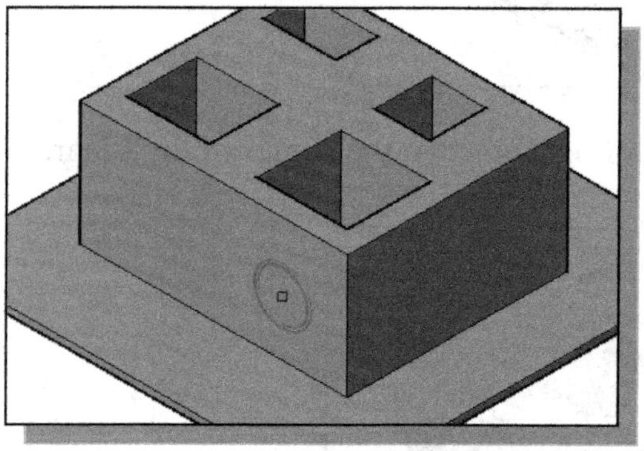

8. Move the cursor near the center of the circle we just created and notice the highlighted lines indicating the selected area. (Hint: Use the **Zoom** functions to assist this operation.)

9. Inside the *graphics window*, press down the left-mouse-button and press the selection toward the right side and create the cut feature (Boolean Subtract) as shown.

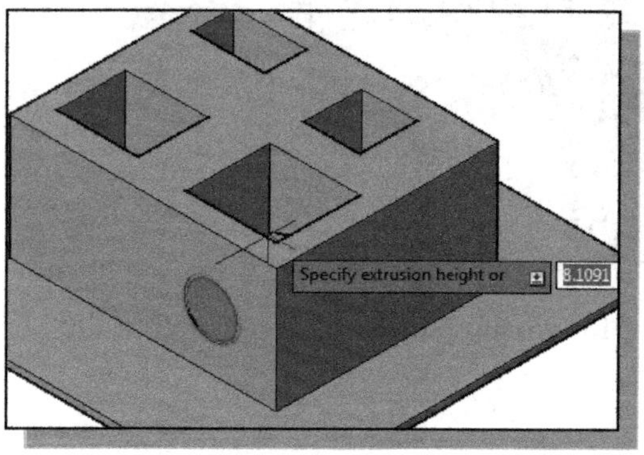

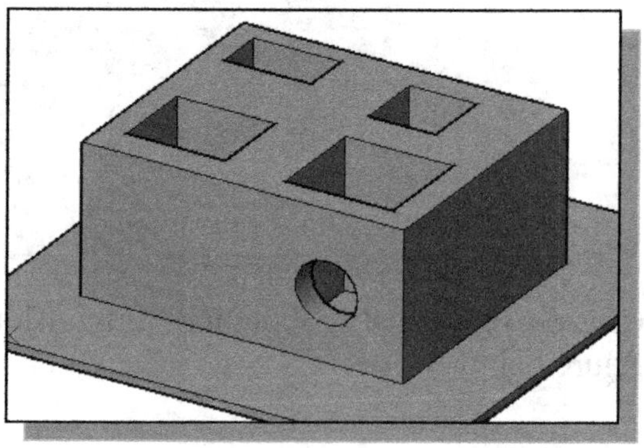

Adjust the Compartments

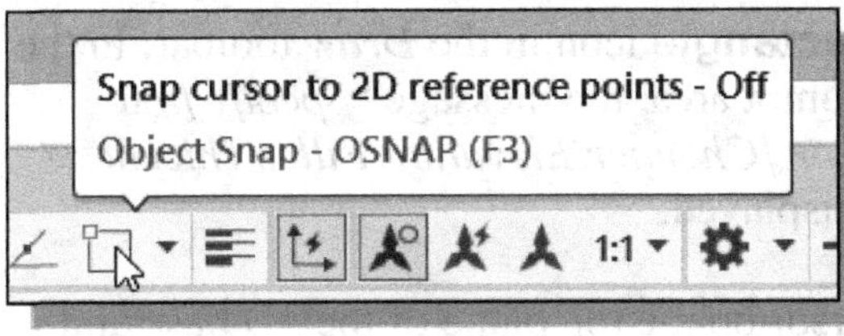

1. Confirm the *Object Snap* option is turned off in the *Status Bar* as shown.

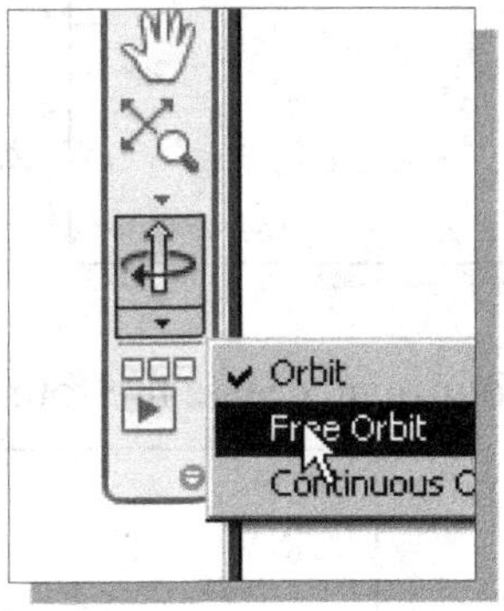

2. On your own, use the **Free Orbit** option to view the current 3D solid model.

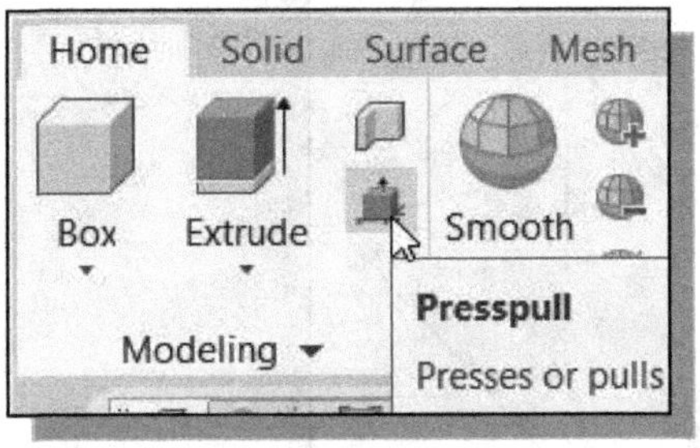

3. Select **Presspull** in the *Modeling* toolbar as shown. In the command prompt area, the message "*Click inside the bounded area to press or pull:*" is displayed.

4. On your own, adjust the compartments so that we can add additional compartments in between the existing ones, as shown in the figure below.

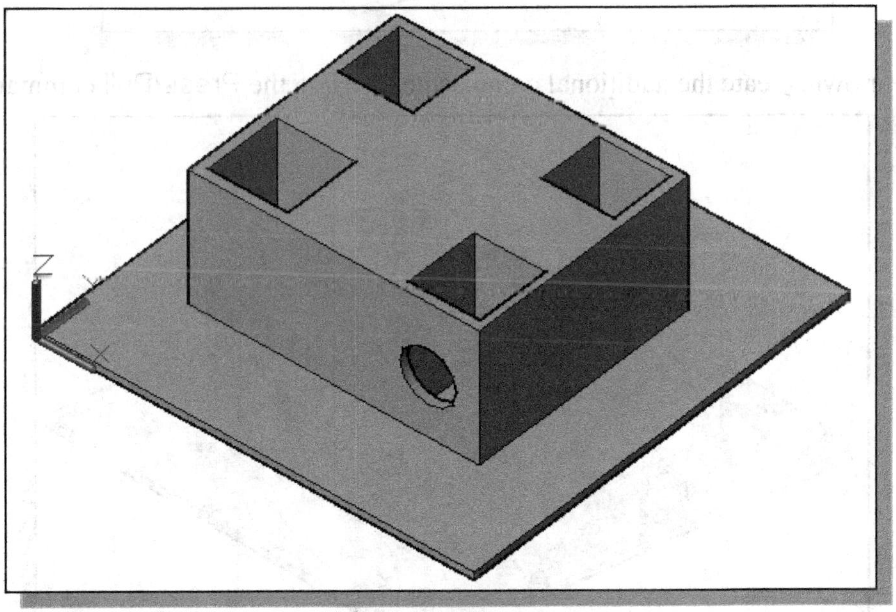

- The **Press/Pull** command enables us to perform fast and loose adjustments of existing surfaces, which conforms to the basic concept of conceptual design.

Add Additional Compartments

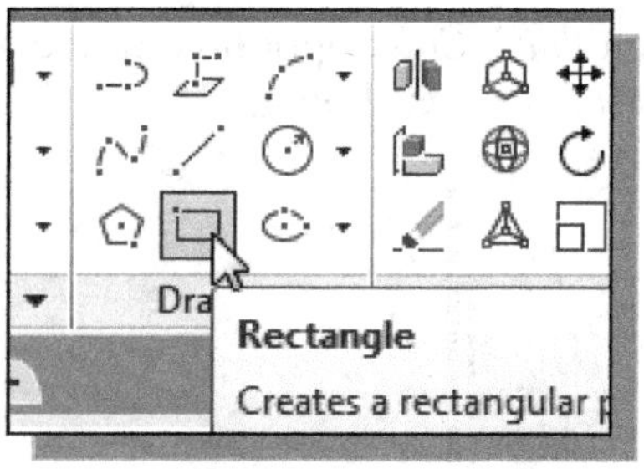

1. Select the **Rectangle** icon in the *Draw* toolbar. In the command prompt area, the message "*Specify first corner point or [Chamfer/Elevation/Fillet/Thickness/Width]:*" is displayed.

2. Move the cursor on the top plane of the 3D base and notice the dynamic UCS option automatically aligns the UCS to the top plane.

3. On your own, create the four additional rectangles as shown in the figure below.

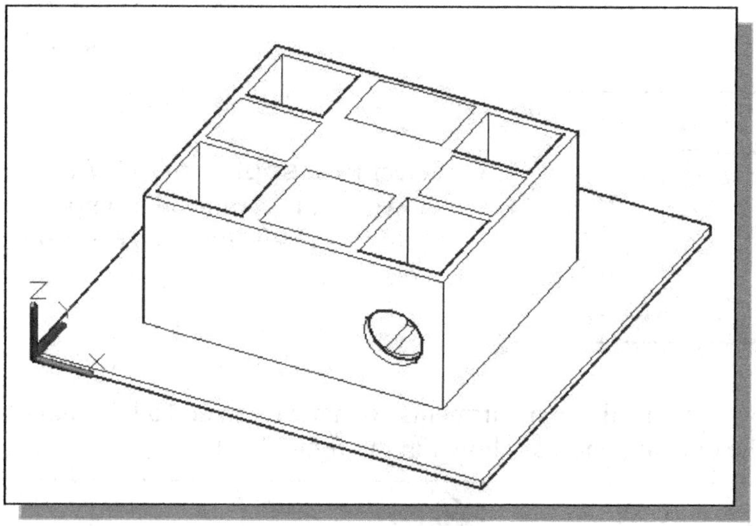

4. On your own, create the additional compartments using the **Press/Pull** command.

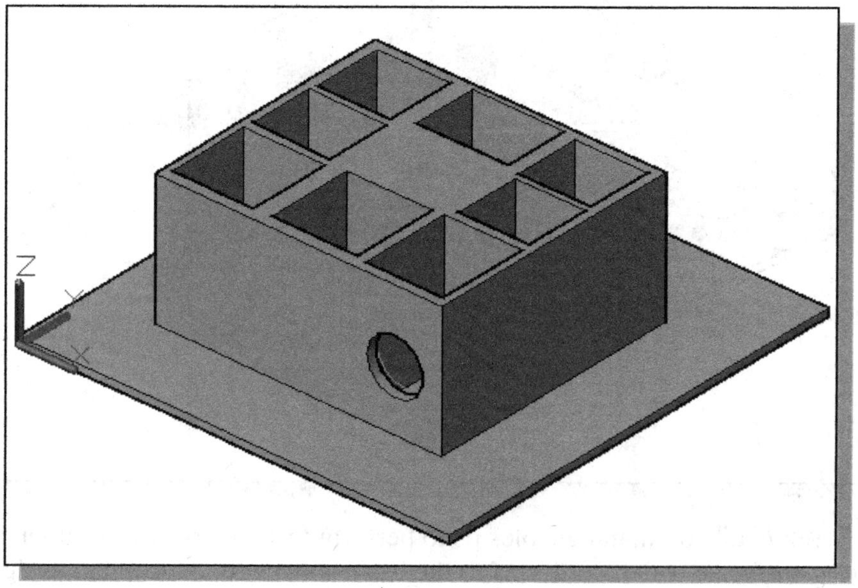

Create the Doors

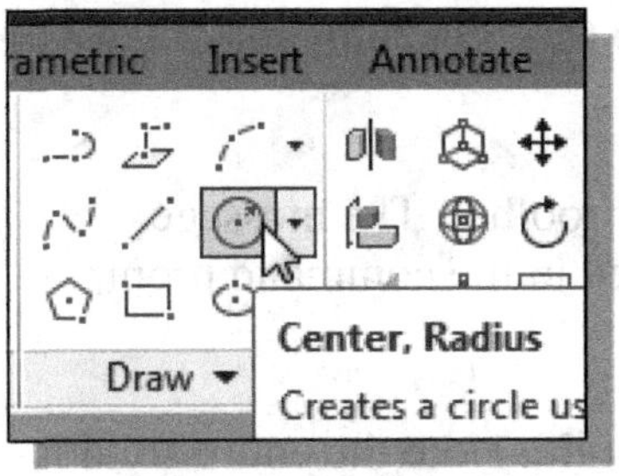

1. Click on the **Circle** icon to activate the Circle command. In the command prompt area, the message "*Specify center point for circle or [3P/2P/Ttr]:*" is displayed.

2. Move the cursor on the front plan of the 3D base and notice the dynamic UCS option automatically aligns the UCS to the front plan as shown.

3. On your own, create the additional circles as shown in the figure below.

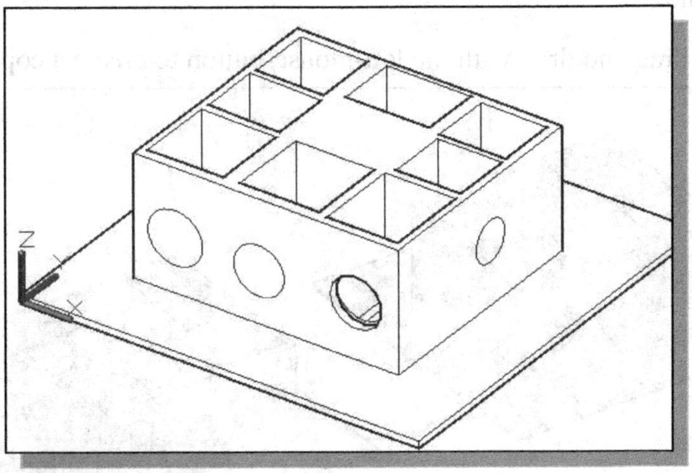

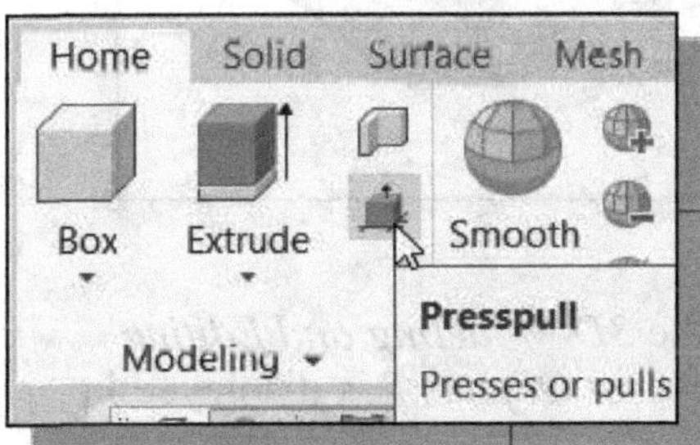

4. On your own, use the **Press/Pull** command and create the doors as shown in the figure below.

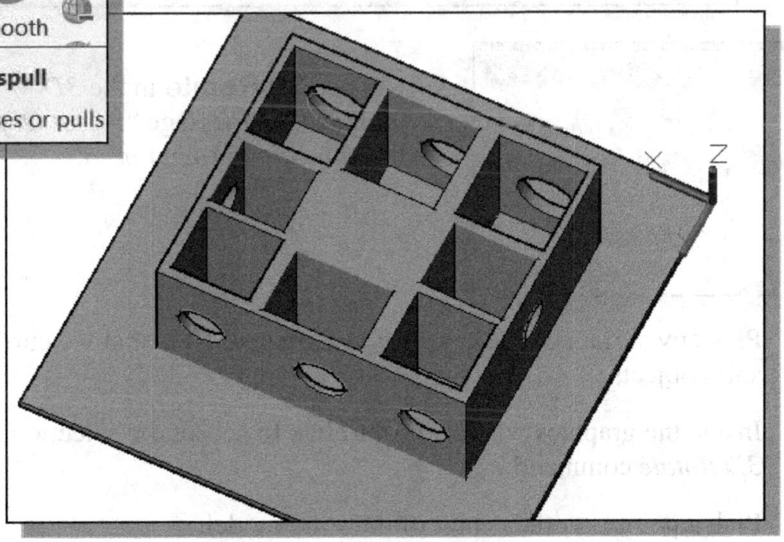

Create the 2nd Floor

We will next create the 2nd floor of the bird house; we will do this by simply making a copy of the 1st floor model.

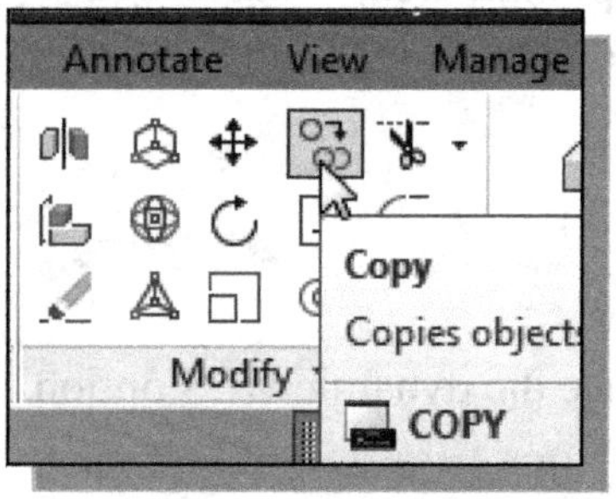

1. Choose **Copy** in the *Modify* toolbar. The message "*Select Objects:*" is displayed in the command prompt area.

2. Pick any surface of the 3D solid. Note the entire solid is selected.

3. Inside the *graphics window*, **right-click** to accept the selection and proceed with the Copy command.

4. On your own, drag and drop with the left-mouse-button to create a copy as shown.

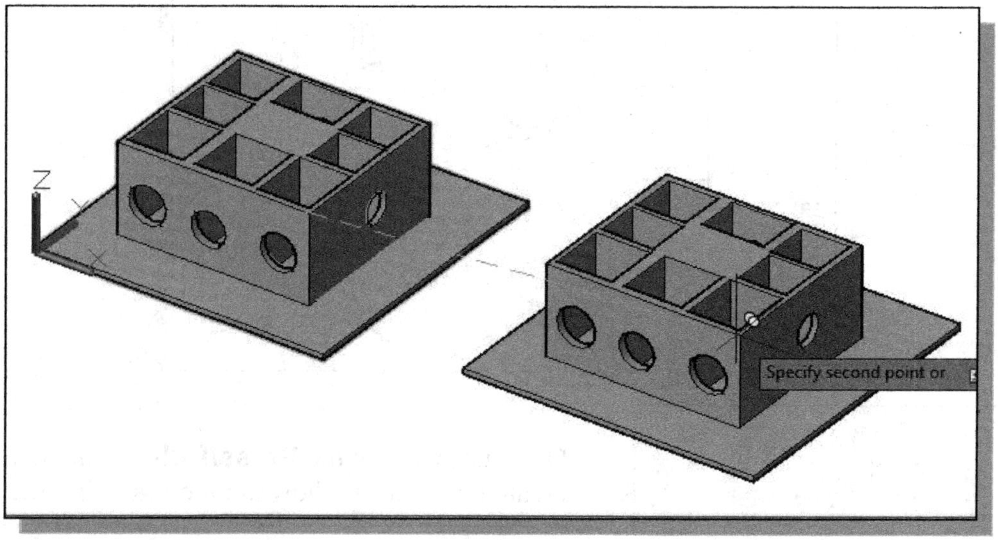

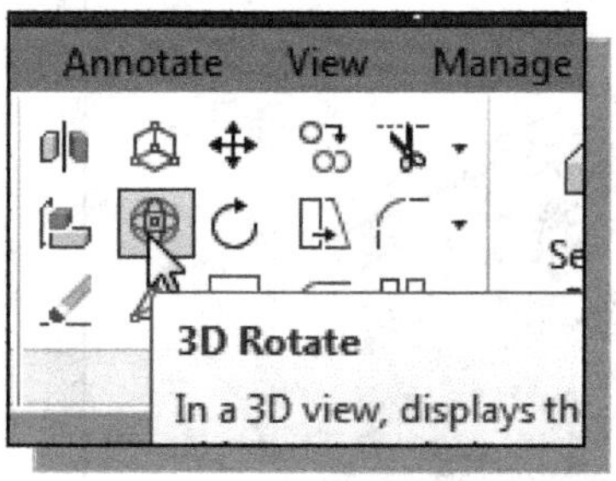

5. Choose **3D Rotate** in the *3D Modeling and Editing* toolbar. The message "*Select Objects:*" is displayed in the *command prompt area.*

6. Pick any surface of the copy we just created. Note that we currently have two separate solid objects.

7. Inside the graphics window, right-click to accept the selection and proceed with the *3D Rotate* command.

8. Pick a point near the center of the solid model.

9. Select the **horizontal ring** that is associated with the **Z** rotation axis as shown.

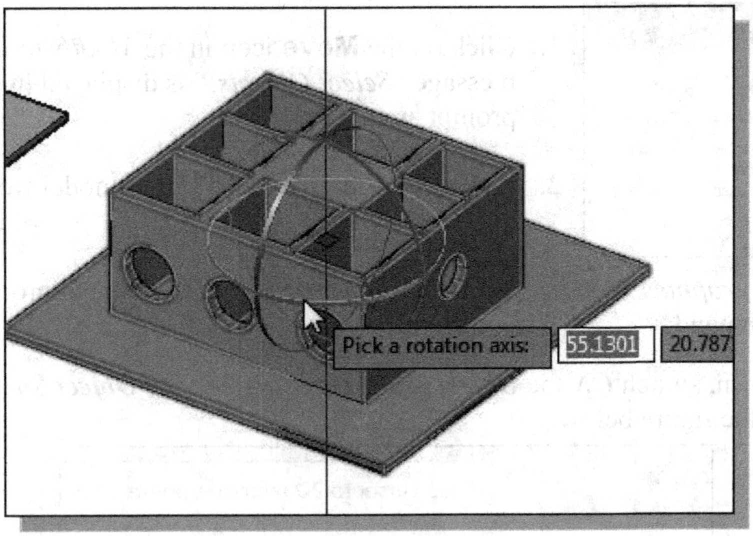

10. We will rotate the model 90 degrees about the Z-axis. Enter **90** as the rotation angle as shown.

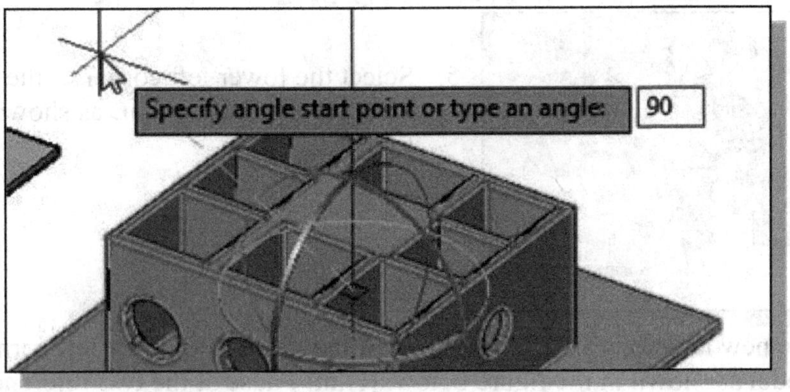

11. The 2nd floor is now rotated 90 degrees; note that all the AutoCAD solid modeling tools are also available for conceptual modeling.

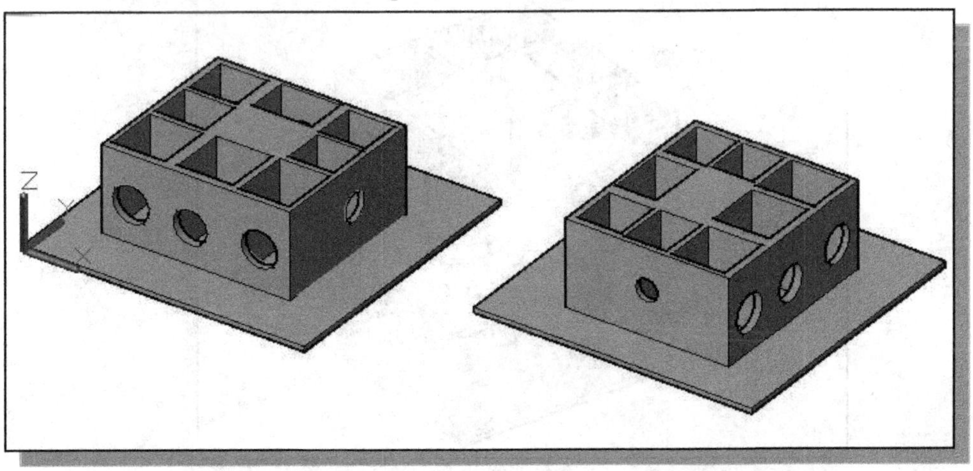

Reposition the 2nd Floor

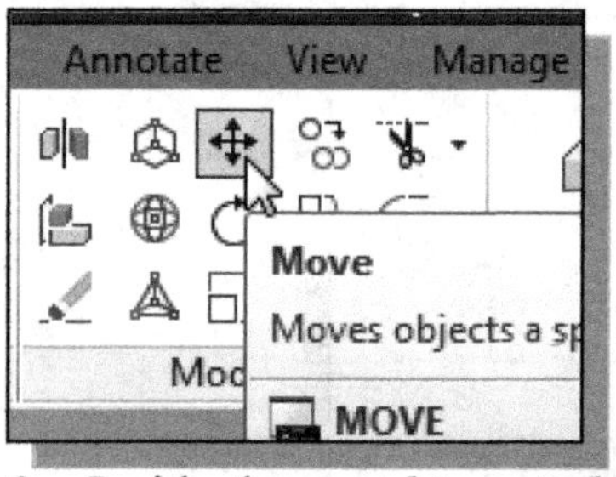

1. Click on the **Move** icon in the *Modify* toolbar. The message "*Select Objects:*" is displayed in the command prompt area.

2. Pick any surface of the 2nd floor model we just rotated.

3. Inside the *graphics window*, **right-click** to accept the selection and proceed with the **Move** command.

4. On your own, switch *ON* the ***Object Snap Tracking*** and the ***Object Snap*** options as shown in the figure below.

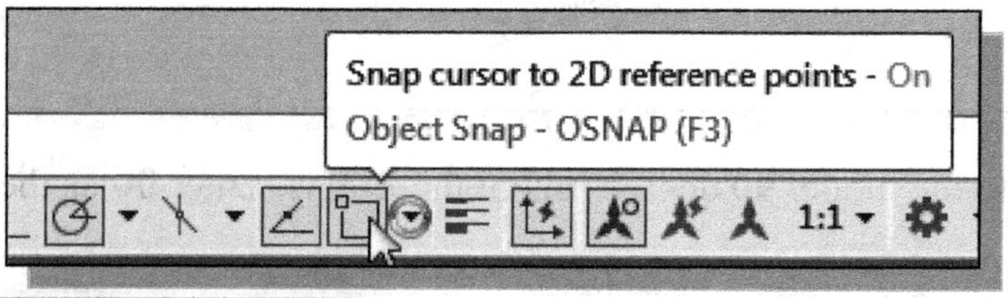

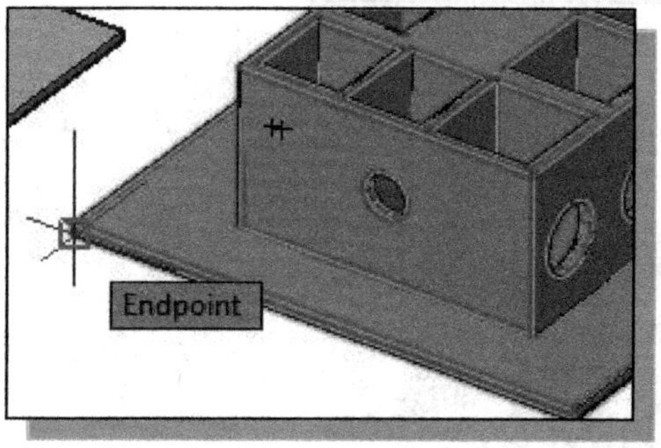

5. Select the lower left corner of the 2nd floor model as the **base point**, as shown in the figure.

6. Align the new location to the intersection of the lower and upper left corners of the 1st floor model as shown in the figure below. (Hint: Pause at the two reference corners and observe the dashed lines showing alignments.)

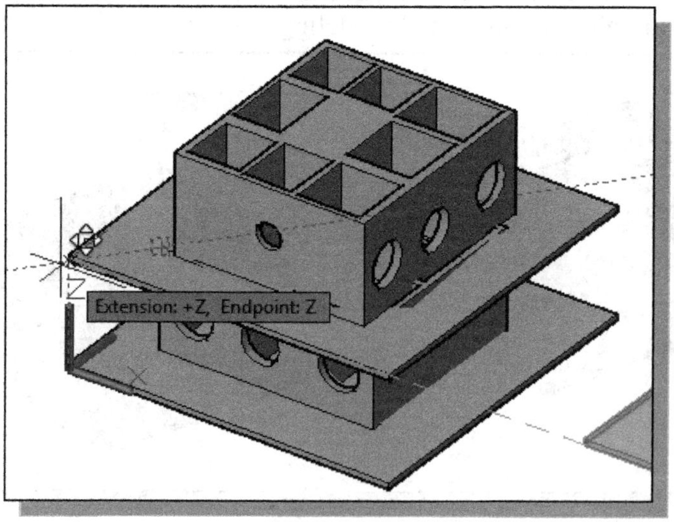

Modeling the Roof Section with the Press/Pull Command

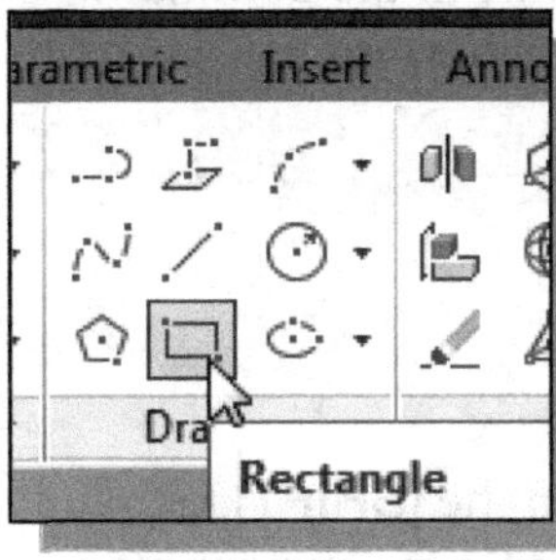

1. Select the **Rectangle** icon in the *Draw* toolbar. In the command prompt area, the message "*Specify first corner point or [Chamfer/Elevation/Fillet/Thickness/Width]:*" is displayed.

2. Place the first corner point of the rectangle to the right side of the current 3D model.

3. We will create a rectangle that is the same size as the base of the model. Enter **@30,30 [ENTER]**.

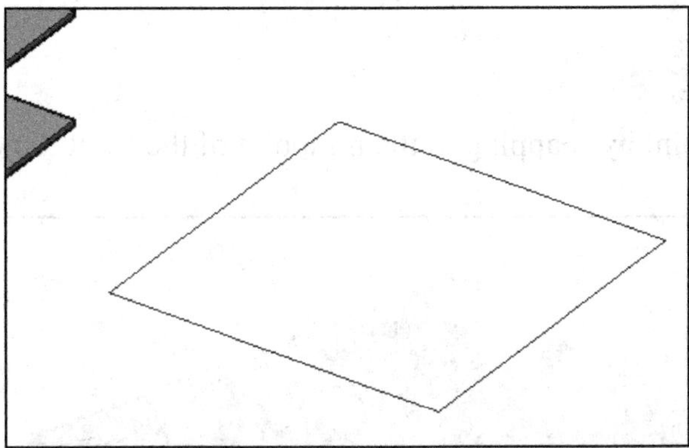

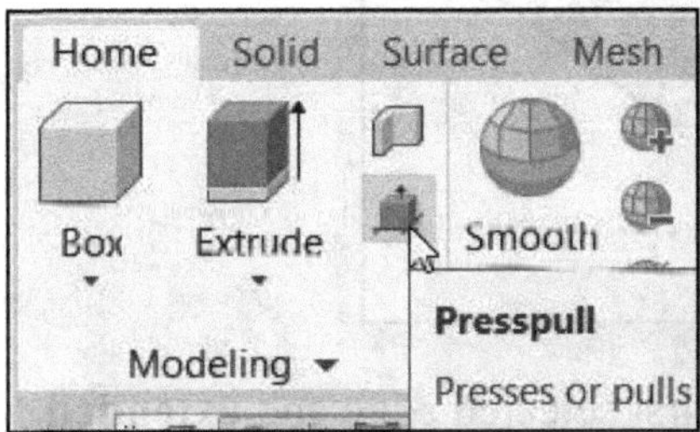

4. Pick the **Presspull** icon in the *Solid* editing toolbar as shown in the figure.

5. Pick a location inside the rectangle we just created.

6. Move the cursor upward and enter **.5** as the height value as shown in the figure below.

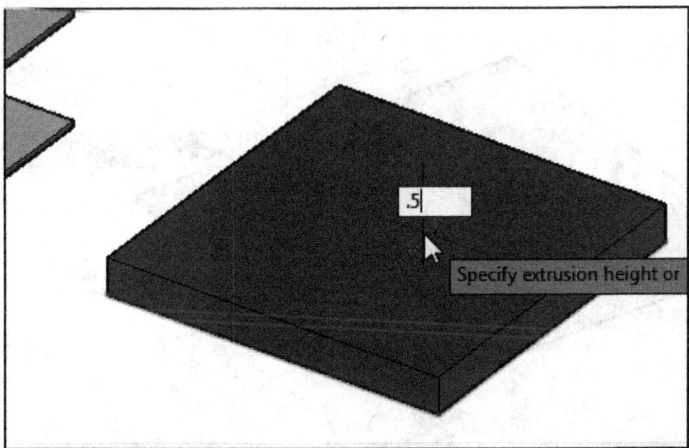

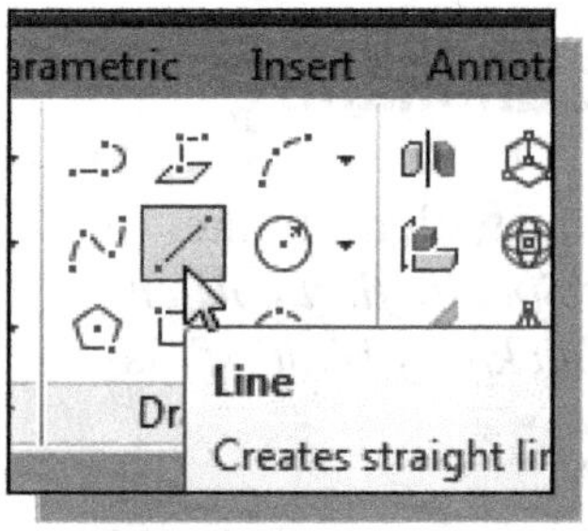

7. Select the **Line** icon in the *Draw* toolbar. In the command prompt area, the message "*_line Specify first point:*" is displayed.

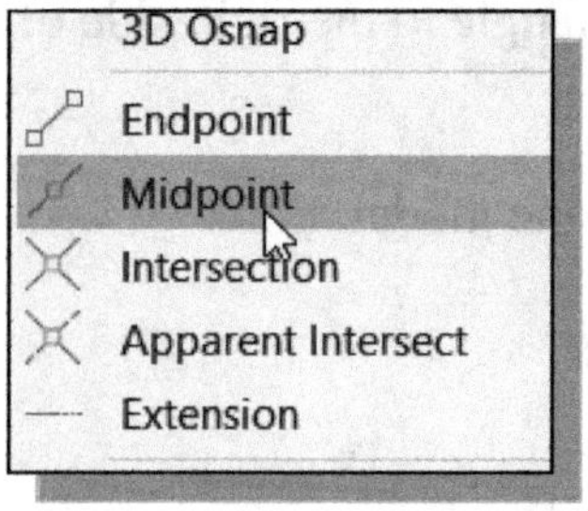

8. Inside the graphics window, hold down the **[SHIFT]** key and **right-click** once to bring up the *Object Snap* shortcut menu.

9. Select the **Midpoint** option in the pop-up window.

10. Place the first endpoint by snapping to the midpoint of the front top edge of the new model as shown.

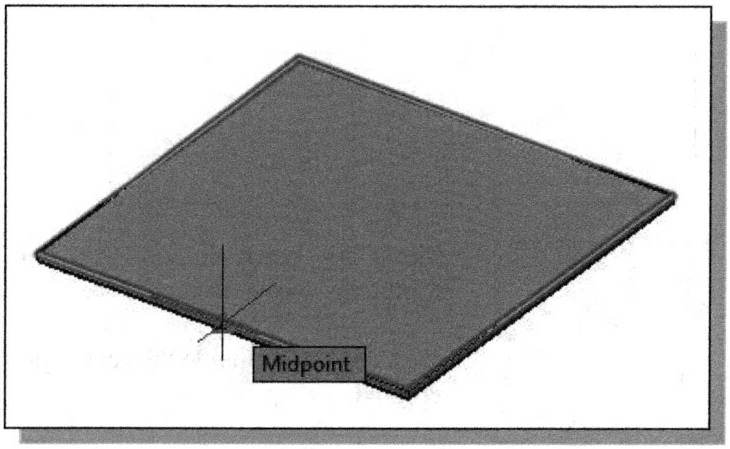

11. Complete the line by making it perpendicular to the first selected edge and **extended beyond** the top of the rectangular block as shown.

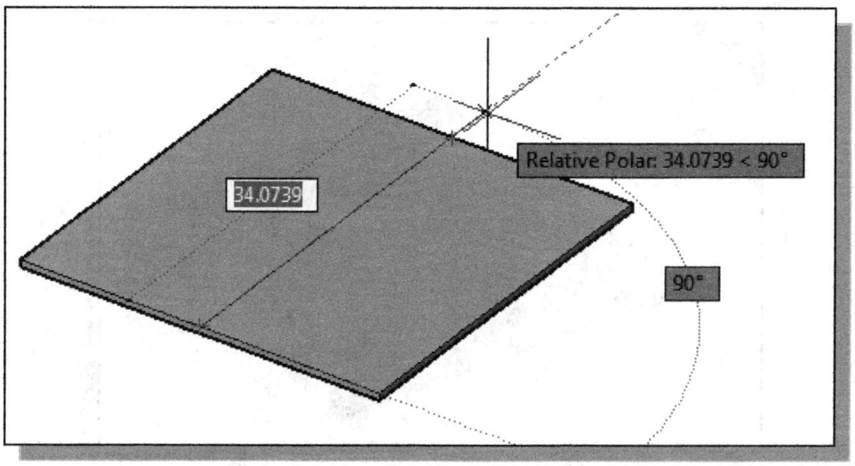

Use the Imprint Command

In AutoCAD, the appearance of a surface on a 3-D solid can be adjusted by imprinting the surface with an object that intersects with it. Imprinting combines the object with the surface, creating a new edge.

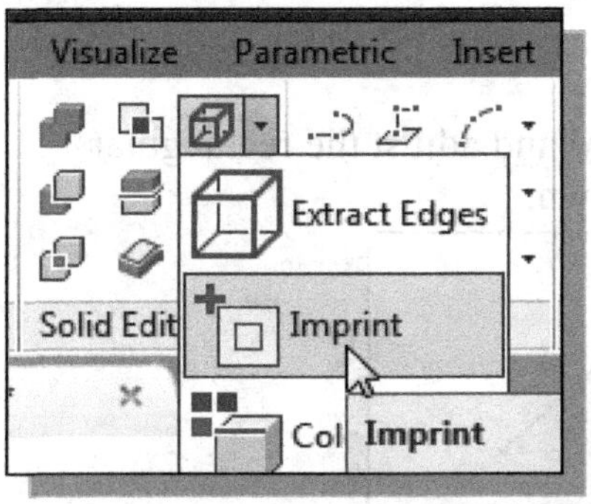

1. In the *Solid Editing toolbar*, click on the **Imprint** icon. In the command prompt area, the message "*Select a 3D Object:*" is displayed.

2. Select the **rectangular block** as the solid object to be adjusted.

3. In the *command prompt area*, the message "*Select an object to imprint:*" is displayed. Select the **line** we just created.

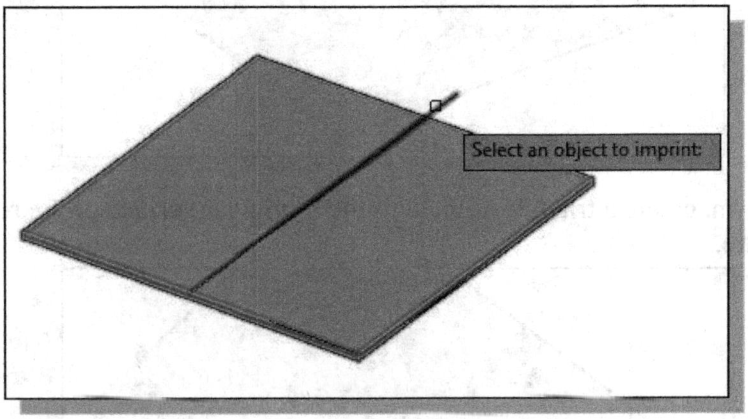

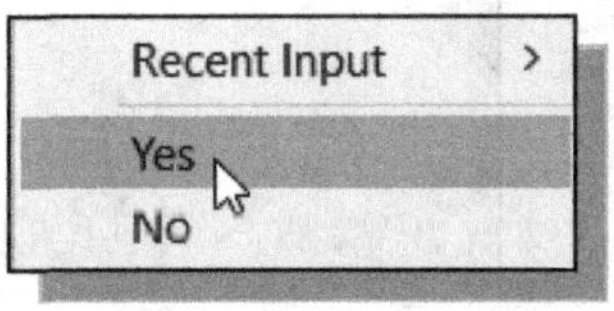

4. In the *command prompt area*, the message "*Delete the source object [Yes/No]:*" is displayed. Click once with the **right-click** to bring up the option menu and select **Yes** as shown.

5. In the *command prompt area*, the message "*Select an object to imprint:*" is displayed. Click once with the **right-mouse-button** to **end** the Imprint command.

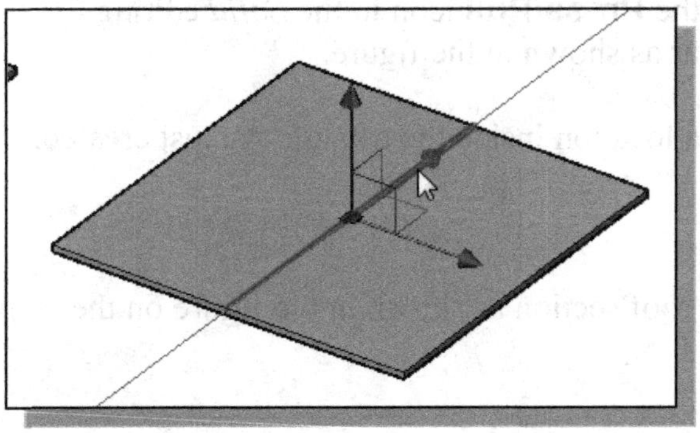

6. Hold down the **[CTRL]** key and move the cursor on top of the imprinted line we just created. Note that the two surfaces are also selectable; move the cursor around to cycle through the possible selections. Select the **line** when it is highlighted as shown.

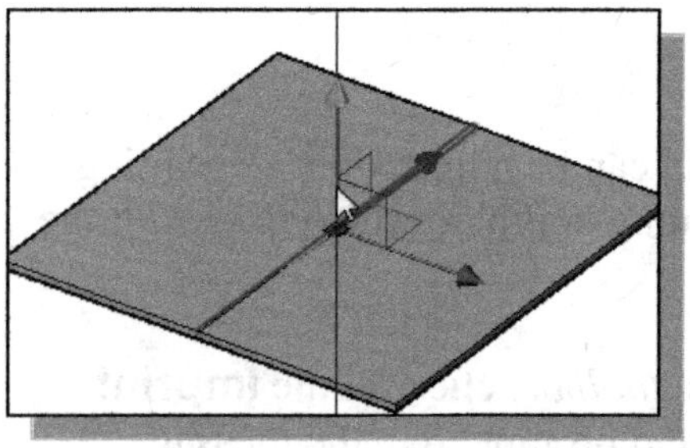

7. Move the cursor on top of the **vertical axis** near the center.

8. Drag the cursor **upward** to pull the center edge upward and adjust the rectangular shape of the solid model into a triangular shape as shown.

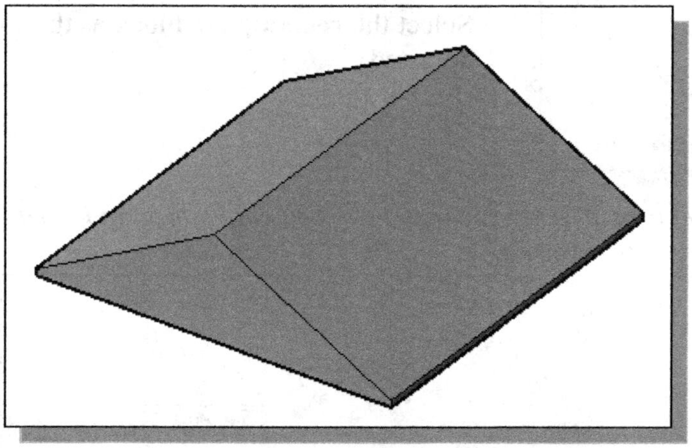

9. On your own, create a triangle aligned to the triangular surface of the roof as shown in the figure.

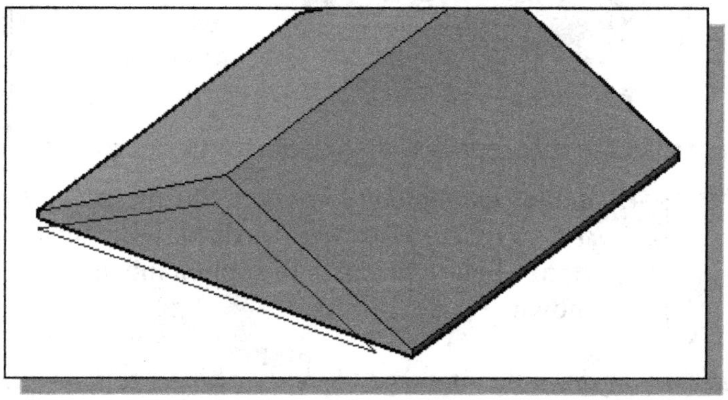

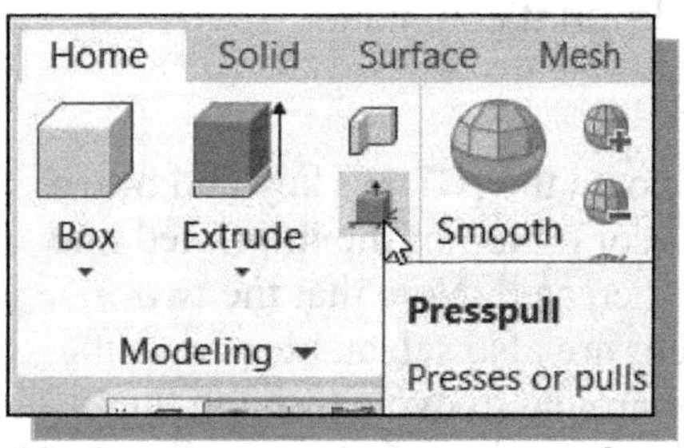

10. Pick the **Press/Pull** icon in the *Solid* editing toolbar as shown in the figure.

11. Pick a location inside the triangle we just created.

12. On your own, create a cut feature on the roof section as shown in the figure on the next page.

13. On your own, create a circular cut feature on the roof section as shown in the figure.

14. On your own, repeat the above steps to create similar features on the back side of the roof.

15. On your own, position the roof section on top of the 2nd floor model to complete the conceptual model of the bird house design as shown.

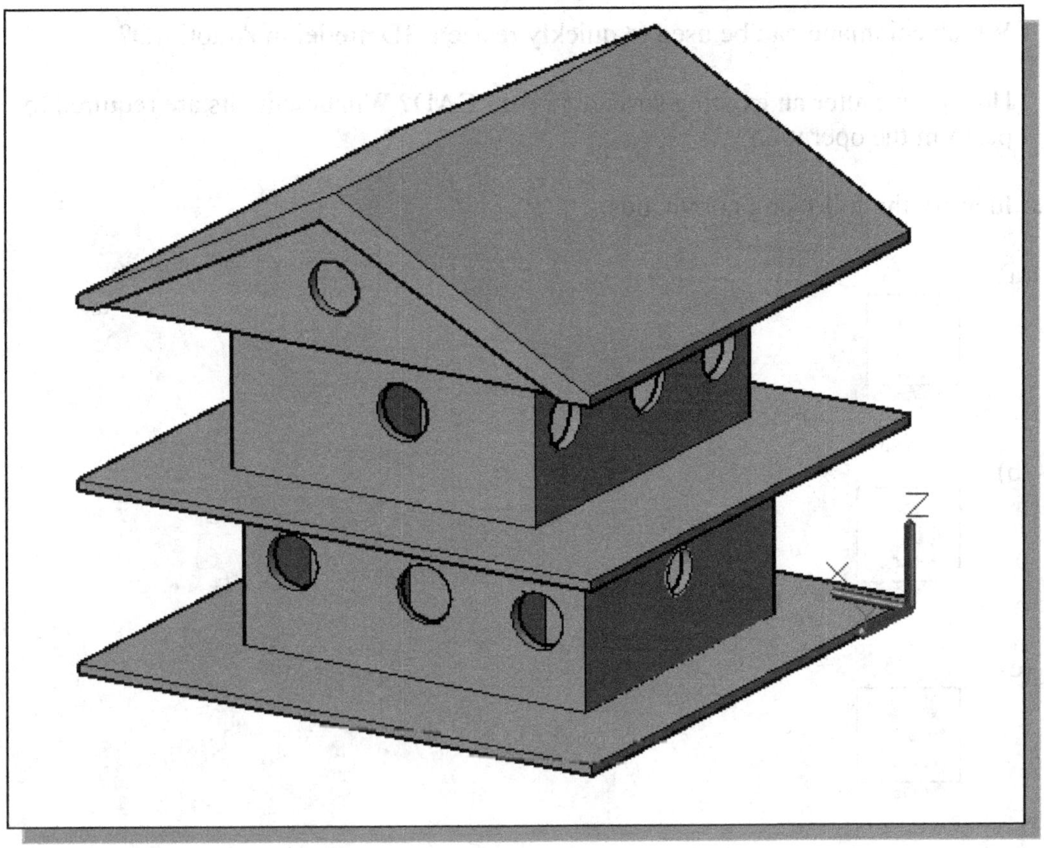

Review Questions:

1. Describe the general stages involved in an engineering design procedure.

2. What is the purpose of creating a *Conceptual Model*?

3. What are the main differences between a conceptual drawing and a detail drawing?

4. Which command can be used to quickly resize a 3D model in AutoCAD?

5. How do we alter an existing surface in AutoCAD? What elements are required to perform the operation?

6. Identify the following commands:

(a)

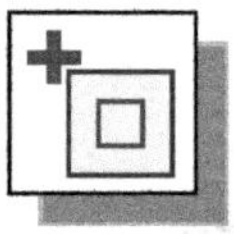

(b)

(c)

(d)

Exercises:

Create conceptual sketches and conceptual models of the following design projects:

1. A better mousetrap.
2. A walking robot with four legs.
3. A rocket launcher.
4. A vehicle powered by birthday candles.
5. A hand-launched glider aircraft.
6. A catapult for water balloons.
7. A vehicle to carry an egg safely down an inclined surface into a wall.
8. A vehicle to be powered solely by a hamster.
9. A rubber band powered all-terrain vehicle.

Notes:

Chapter 12
Introduction to Photorealistic Rendering

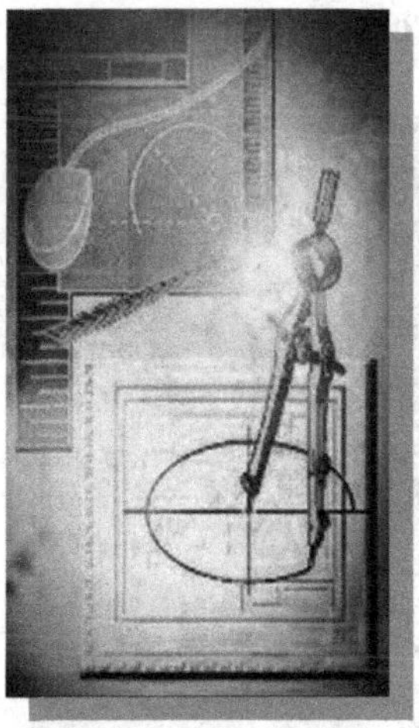

Learning Objectives

- Use the Basic Rendering Tools
- Use the Lighting Simulation Options
- Add Individual Lights to the Scene
- Create and Modify Materials
- Use the Sun & Sky Background Command

Introduction

In this chapter, we will examine the tools available in AutoCAD to perform photorealistic rendering. The purpose of photorealistic rendering is to help the engineers/designers communicate their design concepts. In AutoCAD we can use the different rendering options to create 2D photorealistic images based on the constructed 3D models and scenes. Using Render, it is possible to add realistic materials and lighting to get the most realistic view of the design. AutoCAD will generate photorealistic images by applying the selected materials to the models, adding effects of environmental settings, such as background images, or the effects of fog and shadows can be included in the rendering.

It is important to note that rendering can be a very time-consuming task. For example, if multiple light sources are included in the setup, and each of them casts shadows, a considerable amount of computing power will be required. One can also spend a lot of time adjusting materials, camera and lighting positions/angles. With AutoCAD 2027 it is now possible to preview many aspects of the final image before actually performing the rendering. And it is also feasible to do initial renderings at lower quality settings or render just a portion of the final image to check the effects before creating a final high-resolution rendering.

The process of creating a computerized photorealistic rendering usually involves the five steps below:

1. **Create the 3D models of the design.**
2. **Create and adjust the environmental settings.**
3. **Attach materials to the models.**
4. **Create and place lights.**
5. **Render the photorealistic image.**

Once the CAD objects are drawn, you have to decide which materials to use. AutoCAD comes with a basic materials library that you can use to apply to the objects. Applying the materials is a relatively easy process, but getting them to look exactly the way we want can be a skill in itself. There are three types of lights in AutoCAD: **Point**, **Spotlight** and **Distant**. We will examine how each one is created and adjusted.

Start Up AutoCAD 2027 and Retrieve the Pulley Design

1. Select the **AutoCAD 2027** option on the *Program* menu or select the **AutoCAD 2027** icon on the *Desktop*.

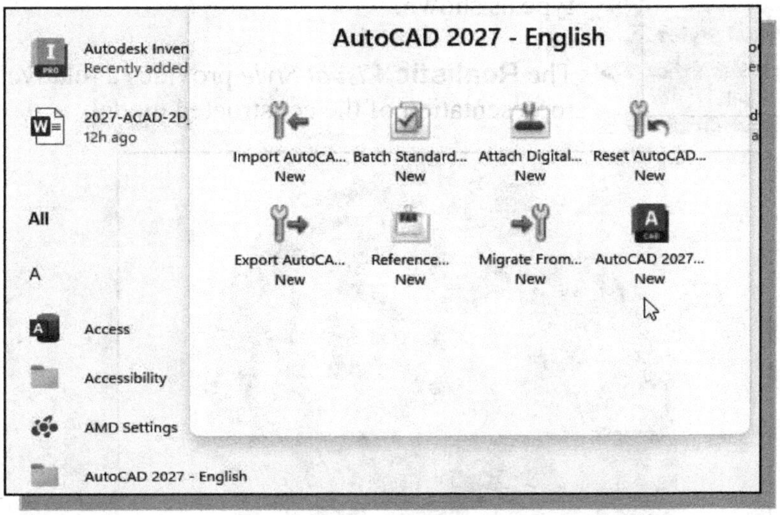

2. In the *Startup* window select **Open a Drawing**, as shown in the figure below.

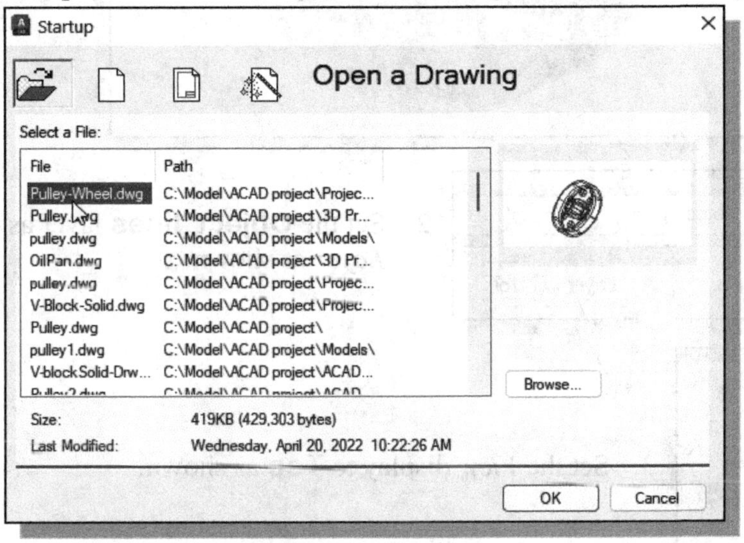

3. Select the **Pulley design** from chapter 8 to be opened. Use the **Browse** button to search for the file if it is not displayed in the files list.

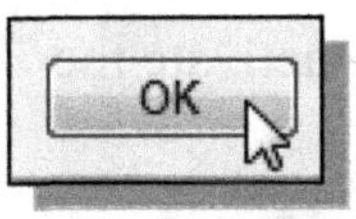

4. Pick **OK** in the *Startup* dialog box to accept the selected drawing.

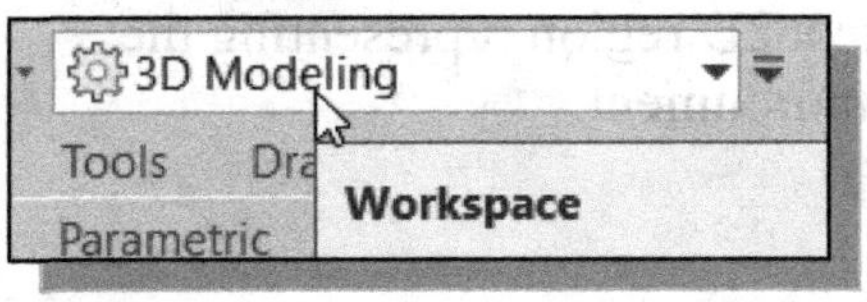

5. On your own, set the *workspace* to **3D Modeling** as shown.

Environment Setup

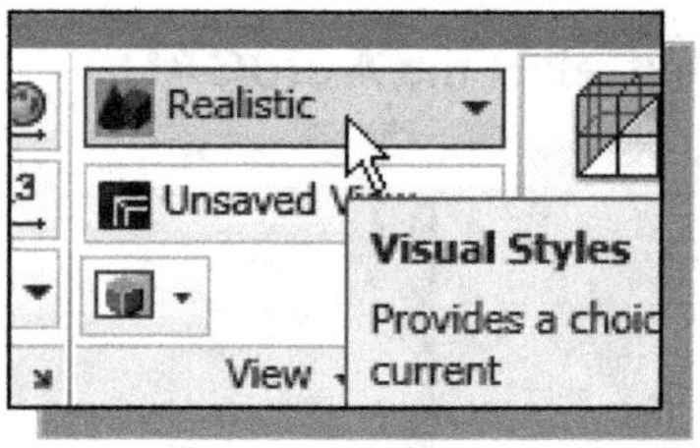

1. In the *View* toolbar, select **Realistic** as the *Visual Styles* type as shown.

➢ The **Realistic** *Visual Style* provides a relatively good representation of the constructed model.

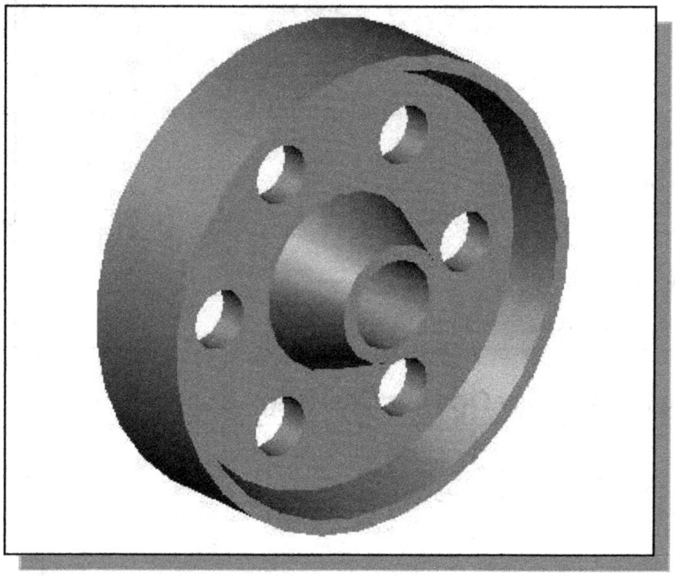

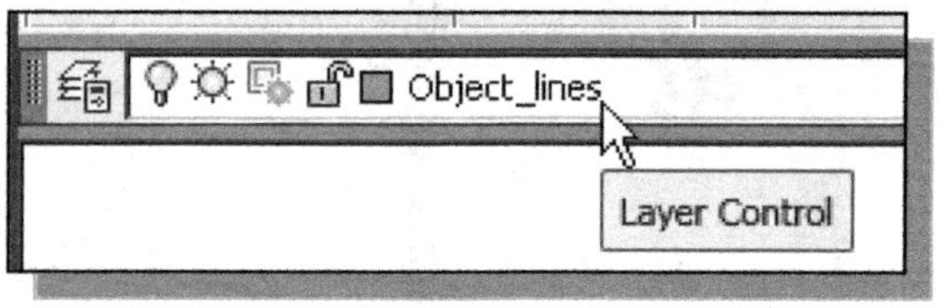

2. Set the **Object_lines** layer as the current *Layer* as shown.

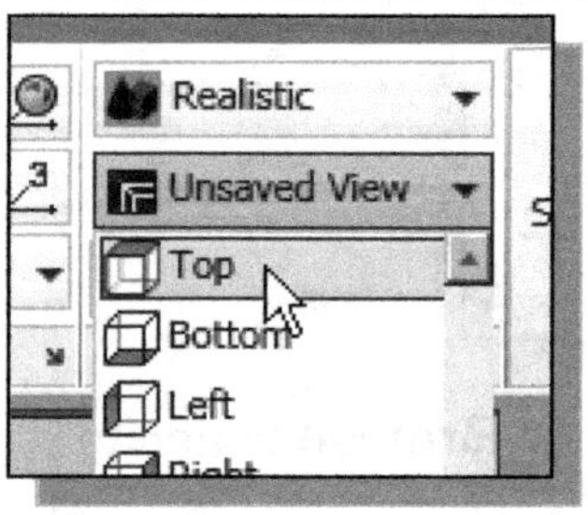

3. Set the *View* display to **Top** as shown.

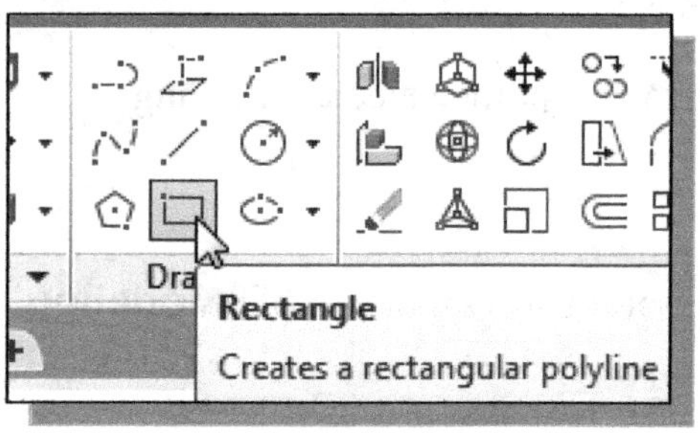

4. Click on the **Rectangle** button to activate the Rectangle command.

➢ We will create a 2D region representing the floor of the environment.

5. On your own, create a rectangle so that the *Pulley* sits roughly near the center of the floor as shown.

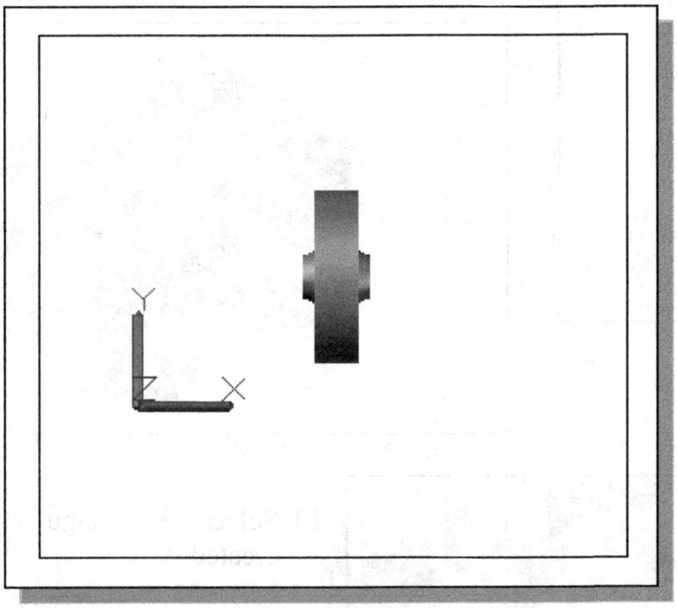

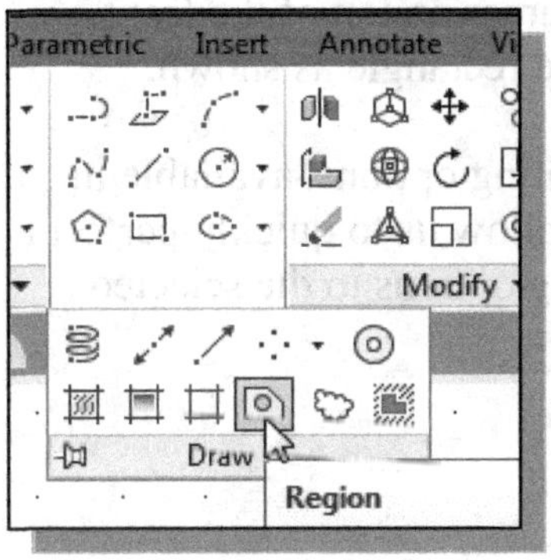

6. Activate the **Region** command by clicking on the button in the *Draw* toolbar as shown.

7. Select the **rectangle** we just created.

8. Inside the *graphics area*, **right-click** once to accept the selection.

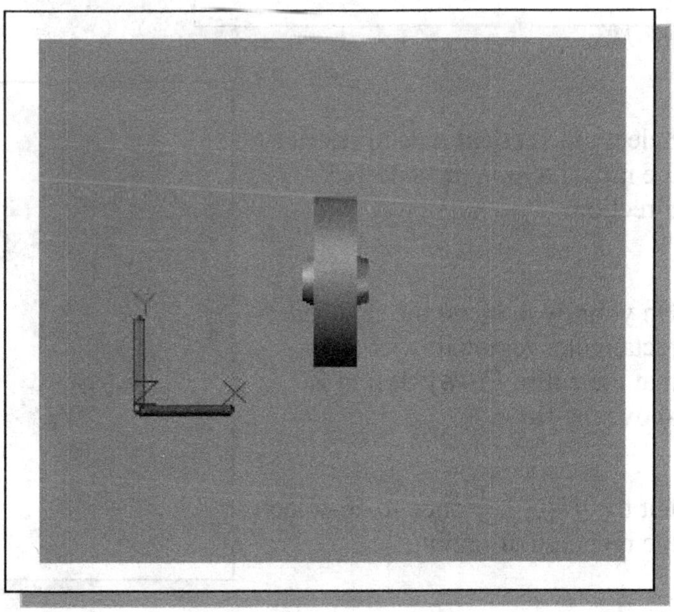

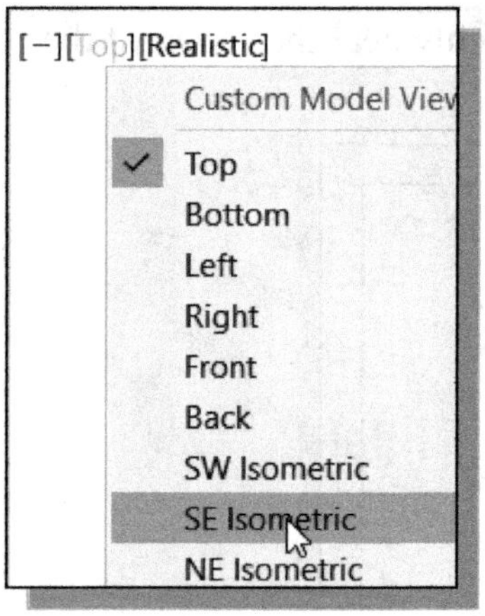

9. Set the *View* display to **SE Isometric** as shown.

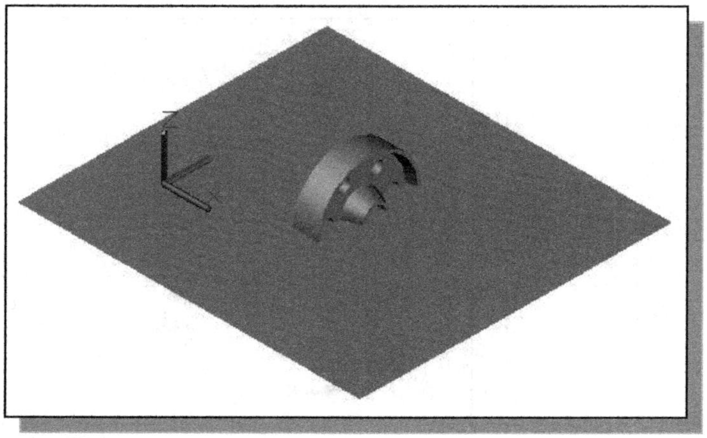

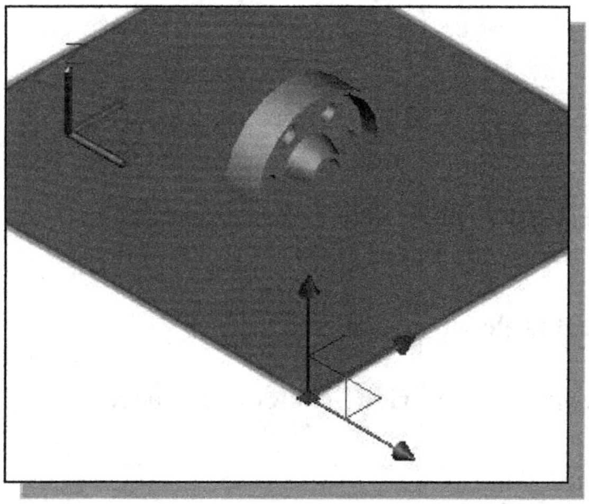

10. Select the rectangular **region** we just created.

11. Move the cursor on top of the front corner of the rectangle as shown.

➢ The grip editing options, available in AutoCAD, allow us to quickly perform many editing options to the selected geometry.

12. Select the **vertical axis** to restrict the movement in the selected direction.

13. On your own, move the selected rectangular region downward so that the entire *Pulley* design is above the floor.

14. Hit the **[Esc]** key once to de-select the rectangular region.

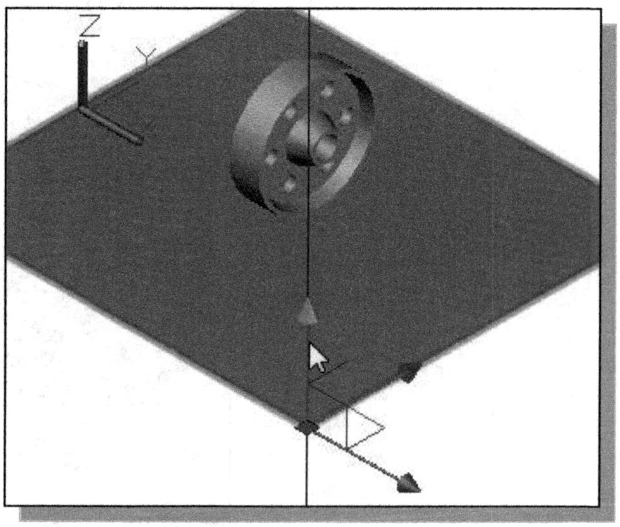

Use the Render Command

To illustrate the effects of the different rendering options, we will first execute the **Render** command using the default setups and without applying any materials or lights.

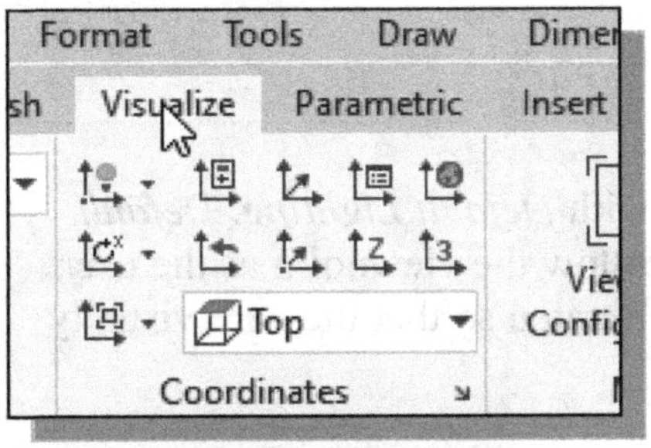

1. Click on the **Visualize** tab in the *Ribbon* toolbar area to display the render related toolbars as shown.

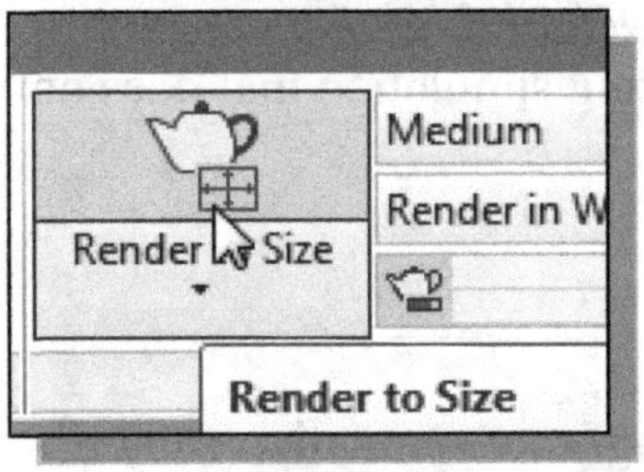

2. In the *Render* toolbar, click on the **Render** icon. Note that we are using the default settings.

➢ A separate *Render* window appears on the screen.

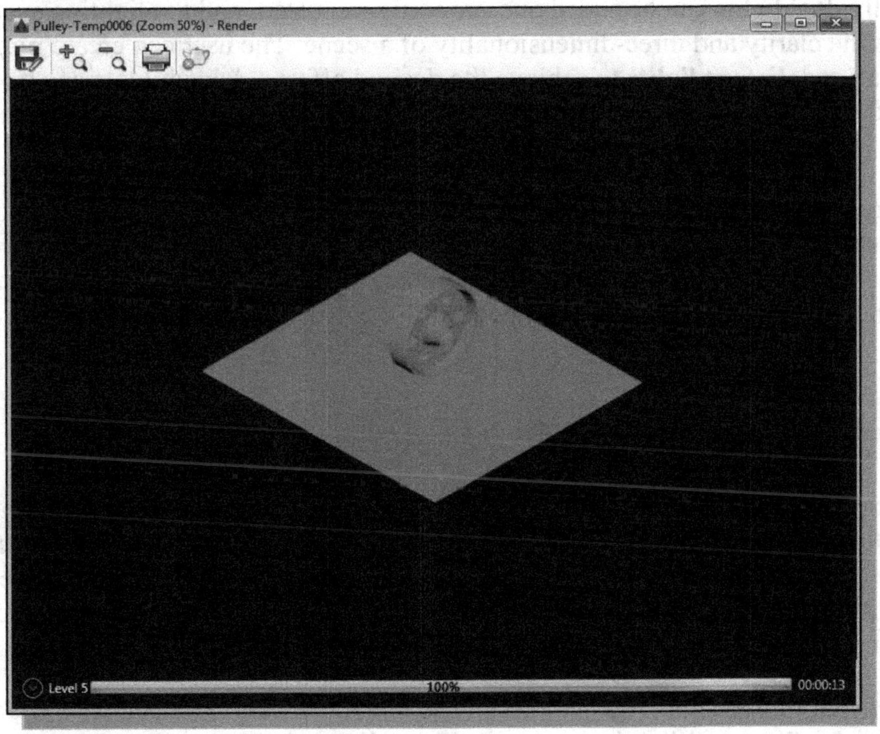

➢ The default lighting system is a fast and simple system where the rendered image is very rough and does not have any realistic feel to it.

3. Hit the **[Esc]** key once to close the *Render* window.

Available Lighting Simulation Modes in AutoCAD

Three types of lighting simulations are available in AutoCAD; each offers their own advantages and disadvantages.

Default Lighting Simulation Mode

When there are no lights in a scene, the scene is shaded with *Default Lighting. Default Lighting* mode is derived from two distant sources that follow the viewpoint as the user moves around the model. All faces in the model are illuminated so that they are visually discernible.

When custom lights or sunlight are added into the scene, the *Default Lighting* can be disabled. The *Default Lighting* mode is a fast and simple lighting simulation that does not require much computing power to render.

Standard Lighting Simulation Mode

To give the scene a more realistic appearance, the *Standard Lighting* simulation can be used. Individual lights can be added and properties adjusted, and the lighting system enhances the clarity and three-dimensionality of a scene. The user can create **point lights**, **spotlights**, and **distant lights** to achieve the desired effects. Added lights can be moved or rotated with grip editing tools; they can be turned *ON* and *OFF*, and properties can be changed. The effects of changes are visible in the viewport in real time.

Spotlights and *point lights* are each represented by a different light glyph (a symbol in the drawing showing the location of the light). Distant lights and the sun are not represented by glyphs in the drawing because they do not have a discrete position and affect the entire scene. The light glyphs can be used to control the position and properties of the related lights.

Photometric Lighting Simulation Mode

For more precise control over lighting, the *Photometric Light* simulation mode can be used to illuminate the scene. *Photometric Lighting* simulation mode uses ***photometric*** (light energy) values that define lights more accurately as they would be in the real world. Lights with various distribution and color characteristics can be created, and specific photometric files available from lighting manufacturers can be imported into the scene.

Photometric Lighting simulation mode can use manufacturers' ***IES*** standard file format. By using manufacturers' lighting data, commercially available lighting can be simulated in the model. This provides the most realistic lighting results. We can experiment with different fixtures, and by varying the light intensity and color temperature, we can design a lighting system mode that produces the desirable results. Note that it may require a considerable amount of computing power with this simulation mode.

Use the Materials Options

In AutoCAD, the ***Dynamic UCS*** option can be used to quickly align the UCS to existing surfaces. The *Dynamic UCS* can be used to create objects on a planar face of a 3D solid without manually changing the UCS orientation.

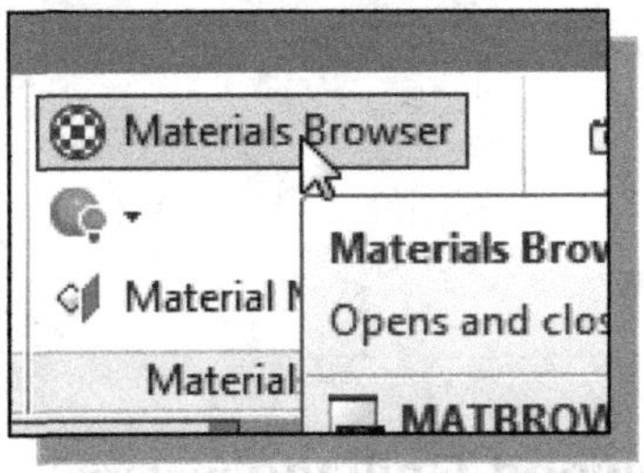

1. Select the **Materials Browser** icon in the *Materials* toolbar to open the AutoCAD *Materials Browser.*

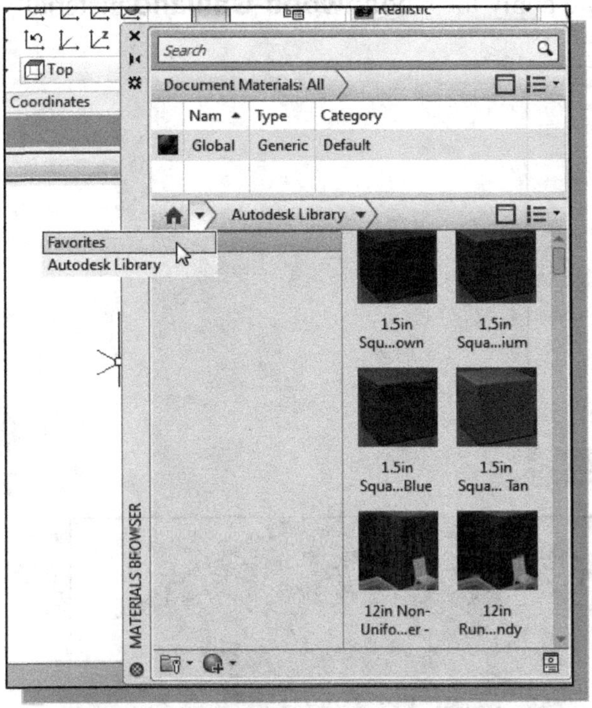

- In the *Materials Browser* window, two libraries are available as default. The **Autodesk Library** contains the pre-defined materials that are commonly used for Architectural and Mechanical Engineering designs. The other library available is **Favorites**, which is currently empty; this is for user-defined materials.

2. Select the **Autodesk Library** by clicking on the icon if necessary.

3. On your own, use the scrollbar and the list options to examine the different materials available.

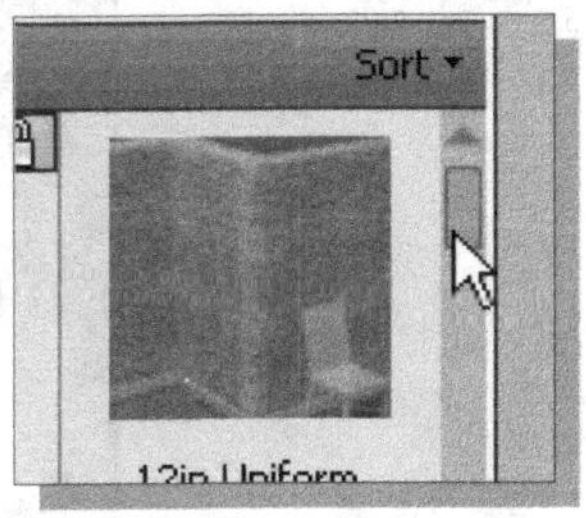

4. Click on the **add material to document** button on **1in Square-Ivory** in the materials list. Note that the selected material is now listed in the ***Document Materials*** section near the top of the *Materials Browser* window.

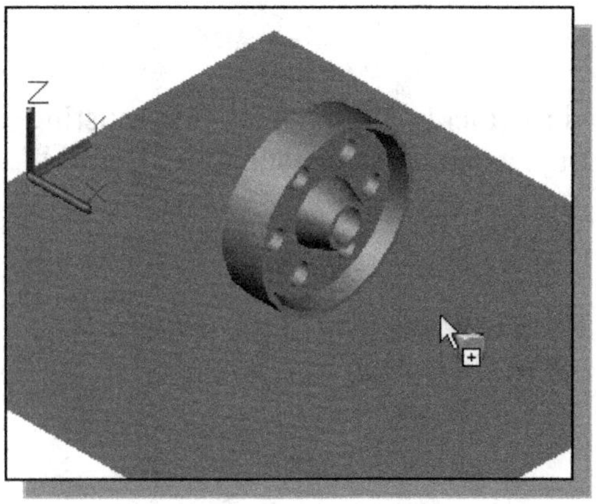

5. *Drag and drop* the **1in Square-Ivory** material, the icon shown in the *Document Materials* section, on top of the floor region as shown.

6. On your own, repeat the above steps and apply the **Beechwood-Galliano** material to the *Pulley* design.

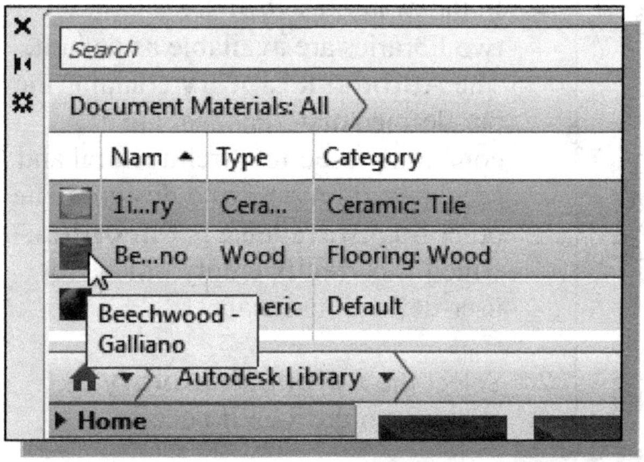

Activate the Sun & Sky Background Option

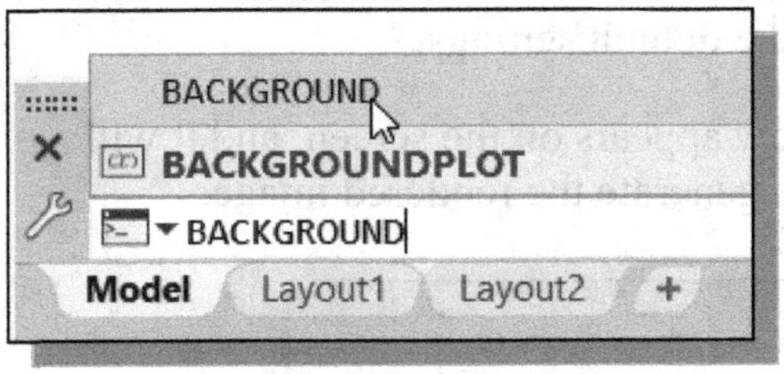

1. Type **Background** in the *command prompt area* as shown.

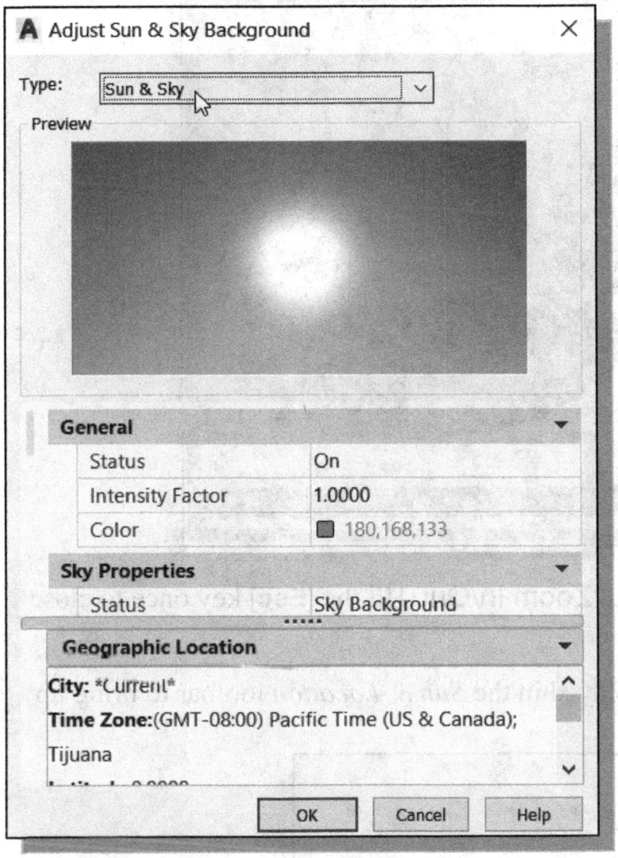

2. In the ***Adjust Sun & Sky Background*** window, set the background *Type* to **Sun & Sky**.

➢ Note that the *Sun & Sky* background can be used to simulate a 3D outdoor environment. The geographic location and time are initially set based on the user's computer settings.

3. Click **OK** to accept the settings.

➢ Notice the ***Sun and Sky Background*** options become activated in the *Ribbon* toolbar area.

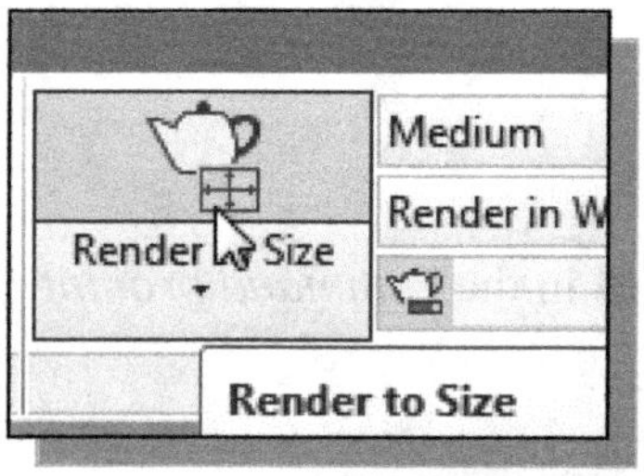

4. In the *Render* toolbar, click on the **Render** icon. Note that we are using the default settings.

➢ The ***Render*** window appears on the screen, and it will take a bit longer to generate the rendered image.

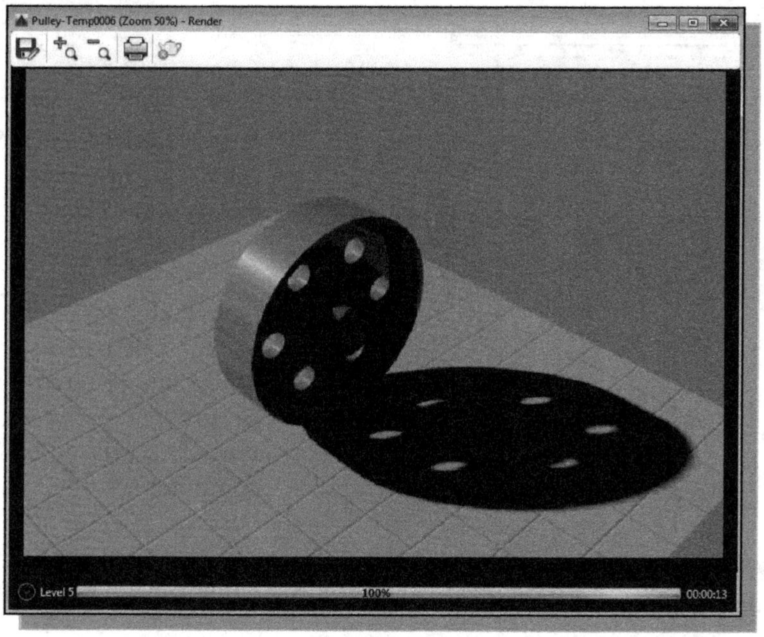

5. On your own, use the mouse-wheel to **Zoom In/Out**. Hit the **[Esc]** key once to close the *Render* window.

6. Click on the small **down arrow** displayed in the *Sun & Location* toolbar to bring up the ***Sun Properties*** dialog box.

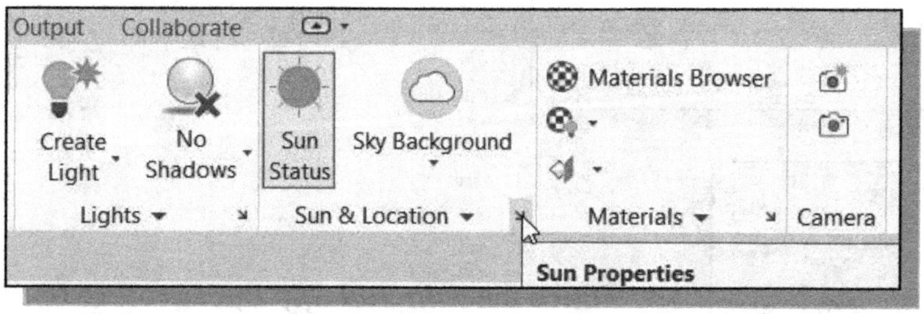

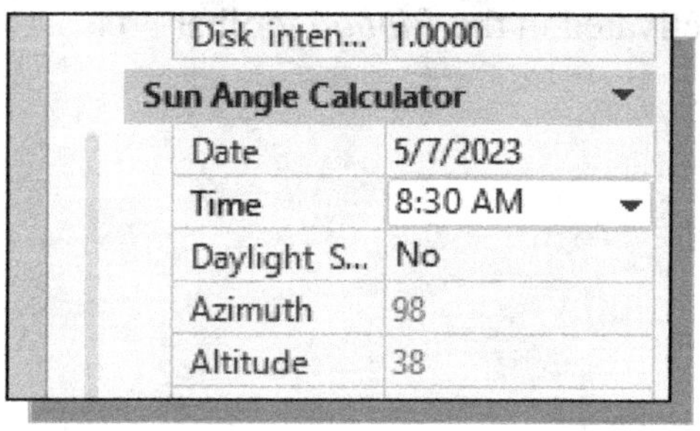

7. Set the *Time* to earlier in the morning, such as **8:30 AM**, by selecting the time list as shown.

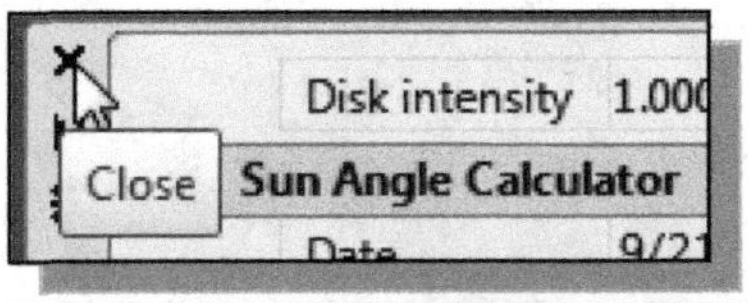

8. Click **Close** to exit the ***Sun Properties*** dialog box.

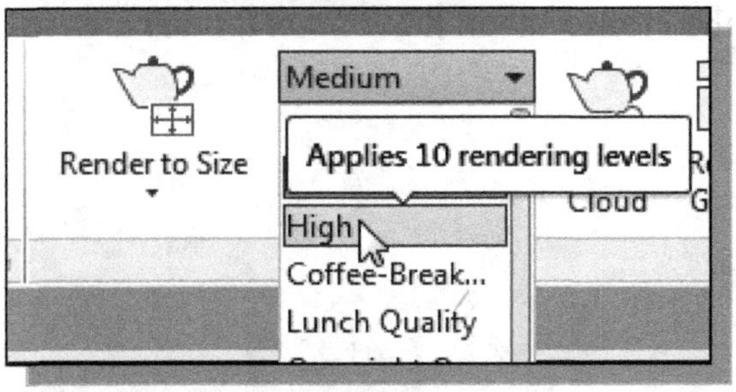

9. In the *Render* toolbar, set the *Render resolution* option to **High** as shown.

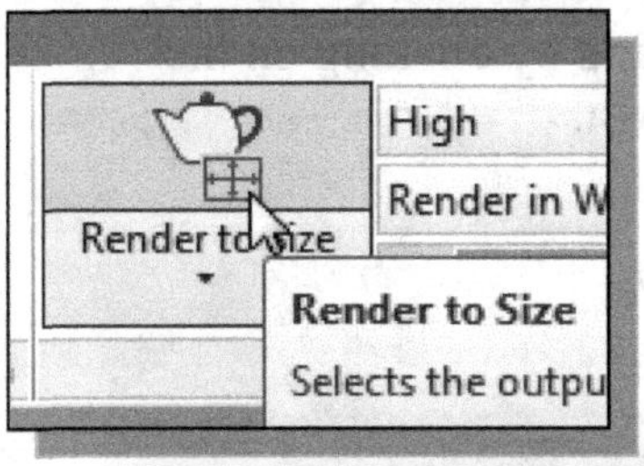

10. In the *Render* toolbar, click on the **Render** icon to start the Render command.

11. Hit the **[Esc]** key once to close the *Render* window.

12. On your own, adjust the ***Time*** and ***Date*** settings to see the different effects.

➢ Setting the ***Time*** to earlier in the day, or later in the afternoon, will produce longer shadows than at midday.

Add Additional Walls

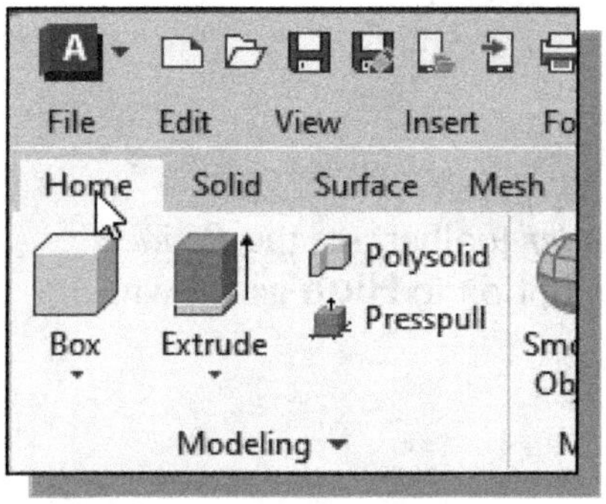

1. Click on the **Home** tab in the *Ribbon* toolbar area as shown.

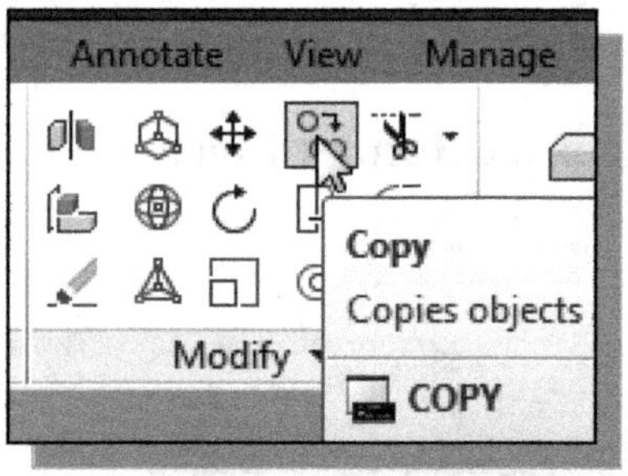

2. Activate the **Copy** command by clicking on the corresponding icon as shown.

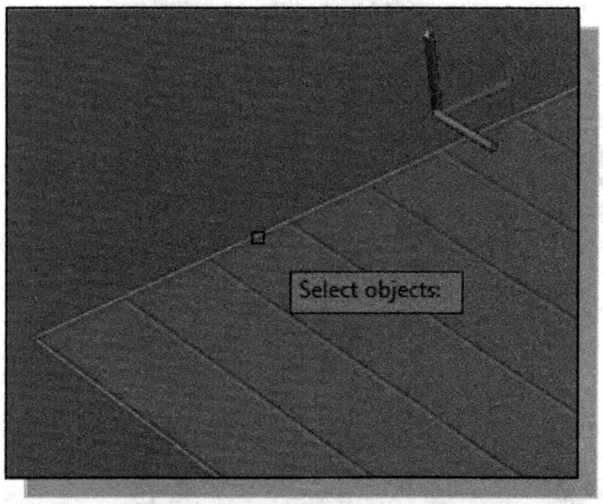

3. Select the **floor** as the object to be copied.

4. Click once with the **right-mouse-button** to accept the selection.

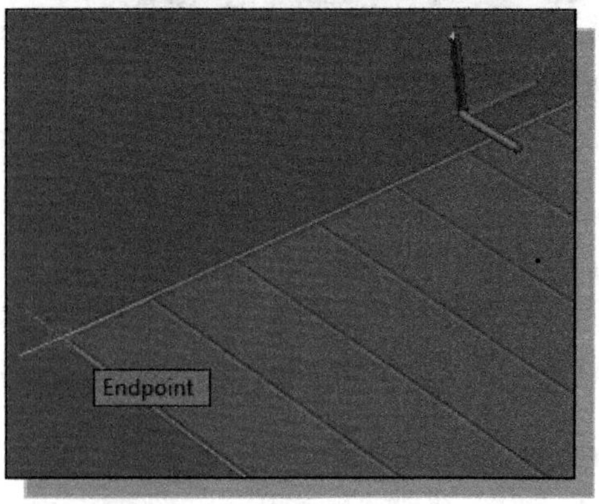

5. Select the **left corner** of the rectangular region as a reference point.

6. Select the **same location** again. We have created a copy at the same location of the original rectangular region.

7. **Right-click** once to bring up the option list.

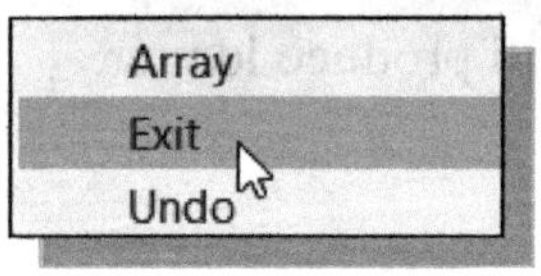

8. Select **Exit** to end the Copy command.

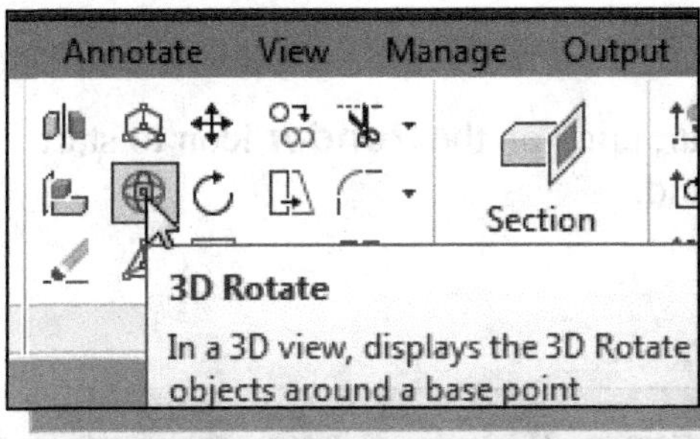

9. Activate the **3D Rotate** command by clicking on the corresponding icon as shown.

10. Select one copy of the overlapping rectangular regions.

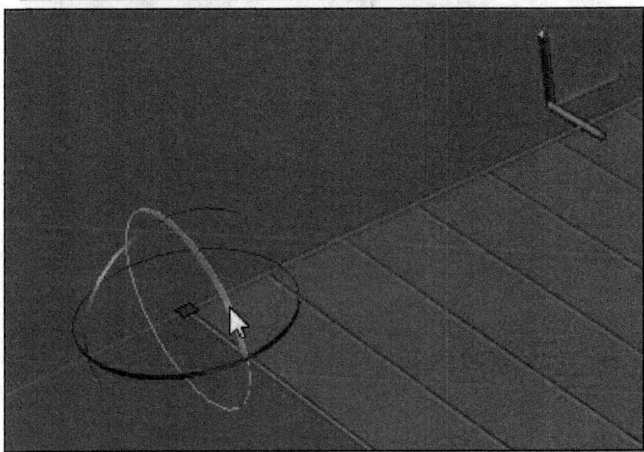

11. Click once with the **right-mouse-button** to accept the selection.

12. Select the **left corner** as the base point for the rotation operation.

13. Select the **green circle** to set the rotation axis.

14. Enter **90** as the rotation angle as shown.

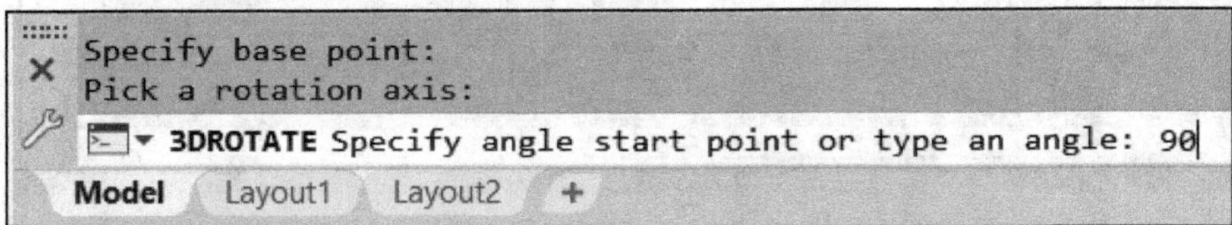

15. On your own, repeat the above steps and create the other side wall.

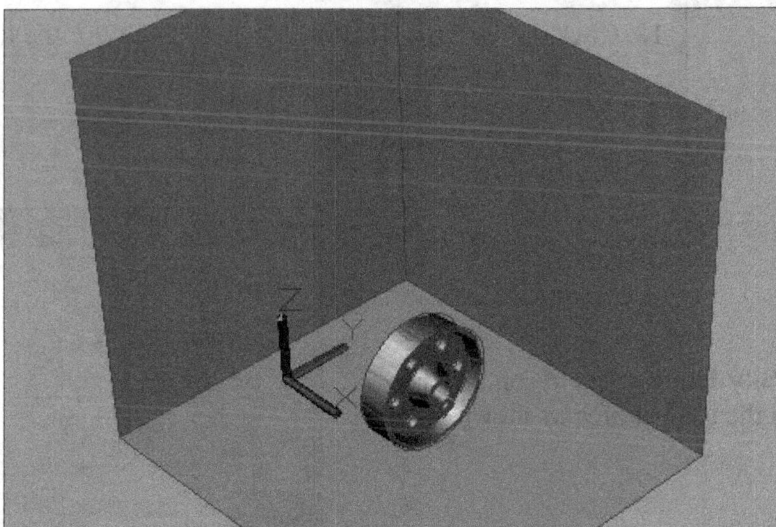

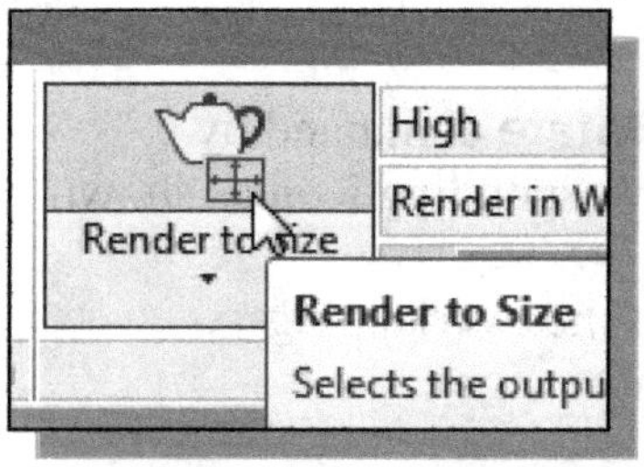

16. In the *Render* toolbar, click on the **Render** icon to start the Render command.

17. Hit the **[Esc]** key once to close the *Render* window.

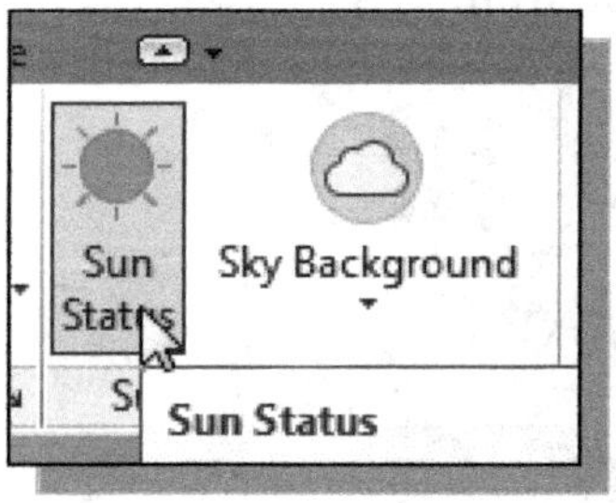

18. Click on the **Sun Status** icon to toggle *OFF* the lighting effects of the sun.

➢ Note that the **Sky Background** can also be turned *OFF* in the toolbar area as shown.

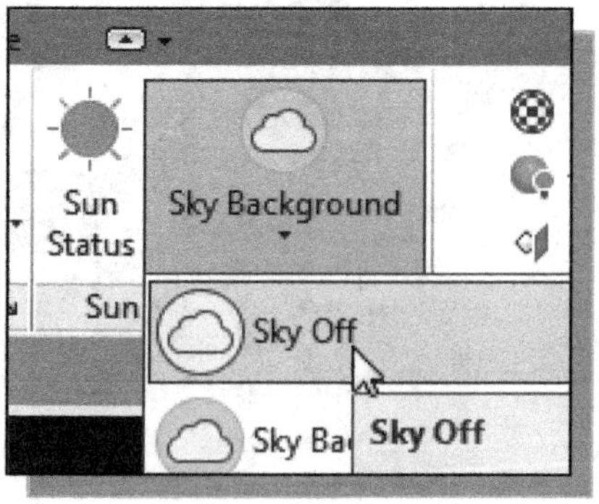

Create a Point Light

A point light radiates light in all directions from its location. A point light does not target an object. Use point lights for general lighting effects. To use the individual lights for more realistic rendering, the *Default Lighting* mode needs to be switched *OFF*.

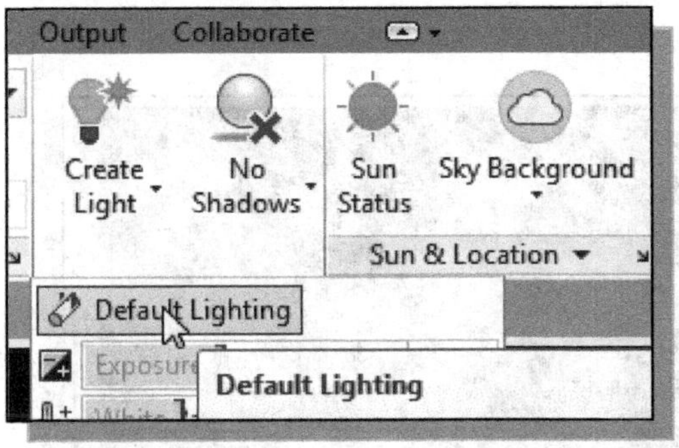

1. In the *Lights* toolbar, click on the **Default Lighting** icon to turn it *OFF*. Note that the *Light glyph display* mode is still switched *ON* when the *Default Lighting* is turned *OFF*.

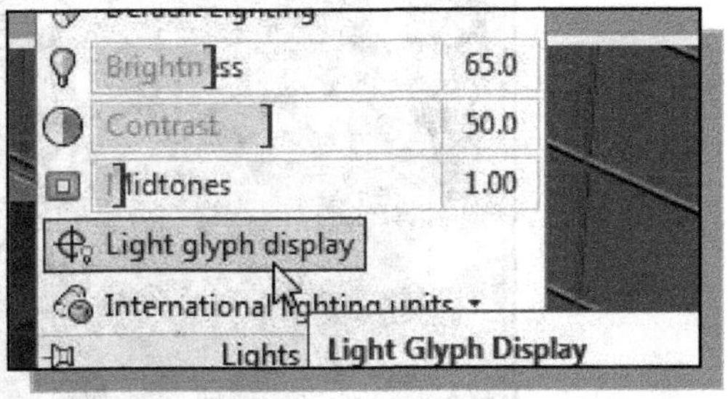

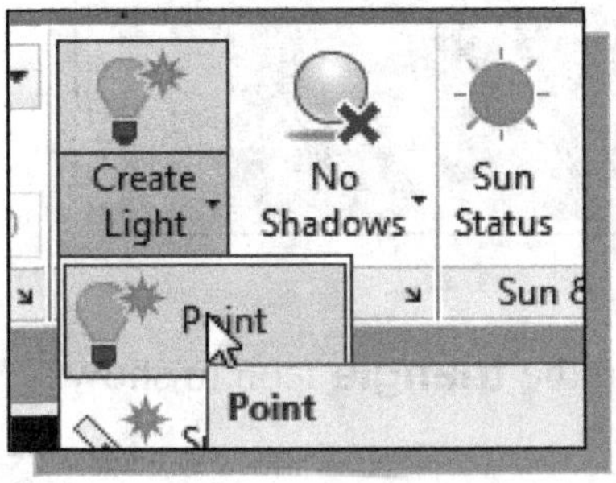

2. In the *Lights* toolbar, click on the **Create Point Light** icon to activate the command.

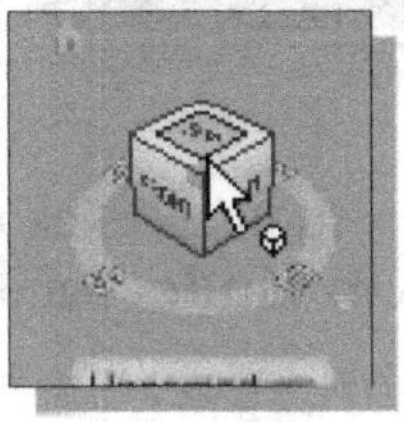

3. Set the display option to **Top** view by clicking on the top face of the ViewCube as shown.

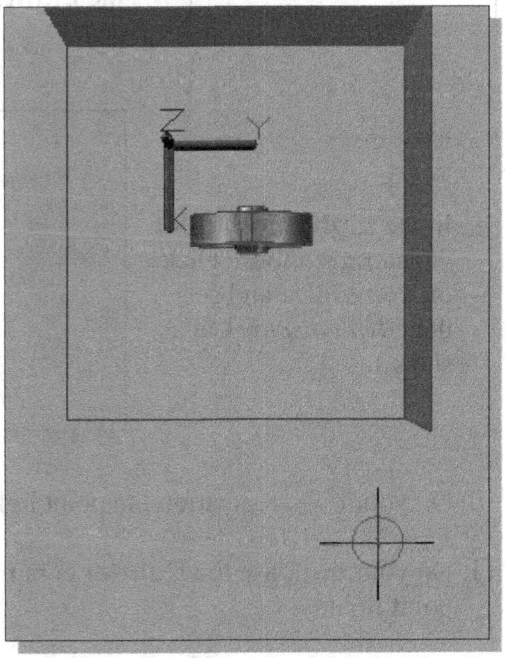

4. Place the point light in front of the *Pulley* design and near the right side wall as shown.

5. In the option list, select **eXit** to create the point light.

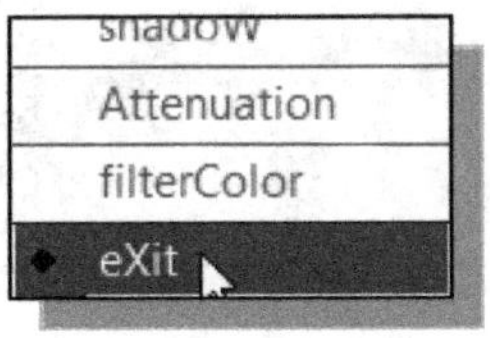

6. On your own, reset the display to **SE Isometric**.

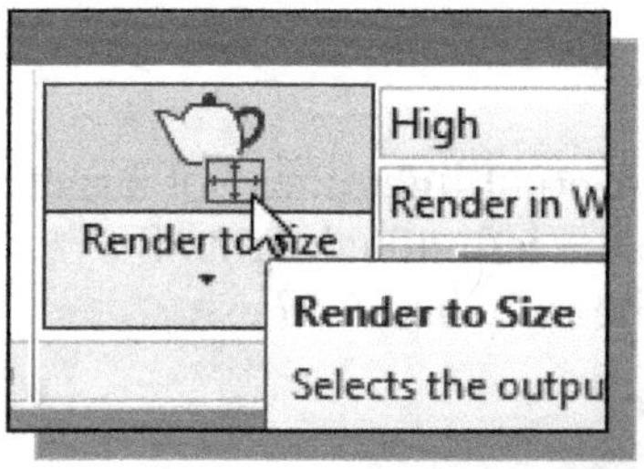

7. In the *Render* toolbar, click on the **Render** icon to start the **Render** command.

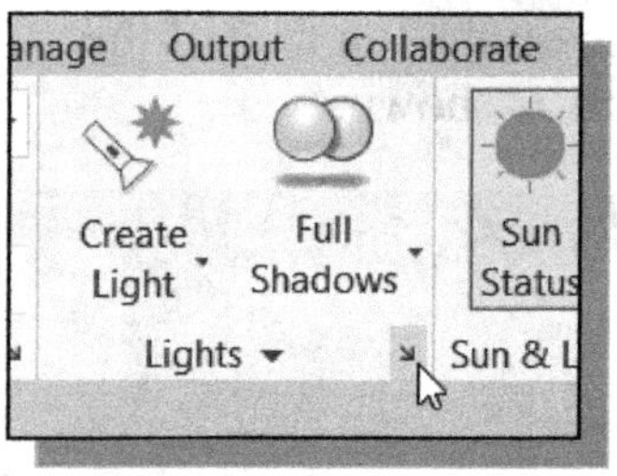

8. In the *Lights* toolbar, click on the **triangle** icon to show the **Lights in Model** panel.

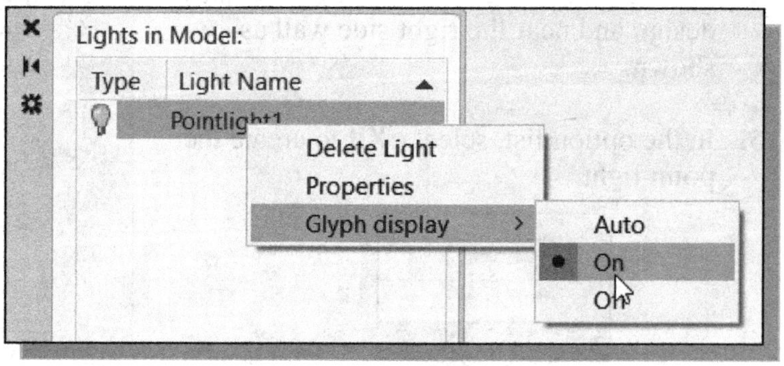

9. In the **Lights in Model** panel, right-mouse click on *Pointlight1* and set the *Glyph display* **On** as shown.

10. On your own, reposition the point light higher by using the grip editing options.

11. On your own, use the **Render** command to examine the effects of repositioning the point light.

Changing the Applied Materials

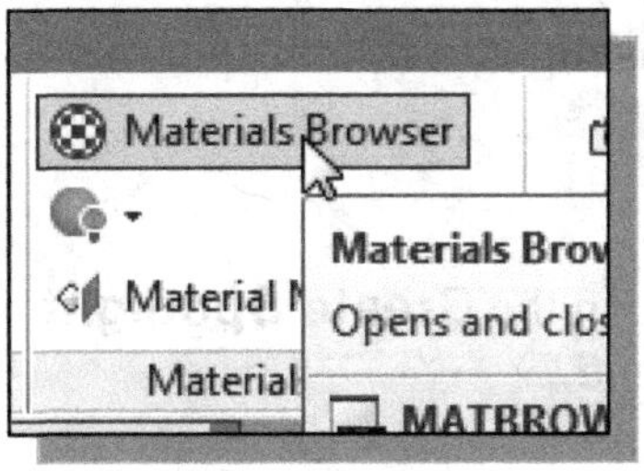

1. Select the **Materials Browser** icon in the *Materials* toolbar to open the AutoCAD *Materials Browser*.

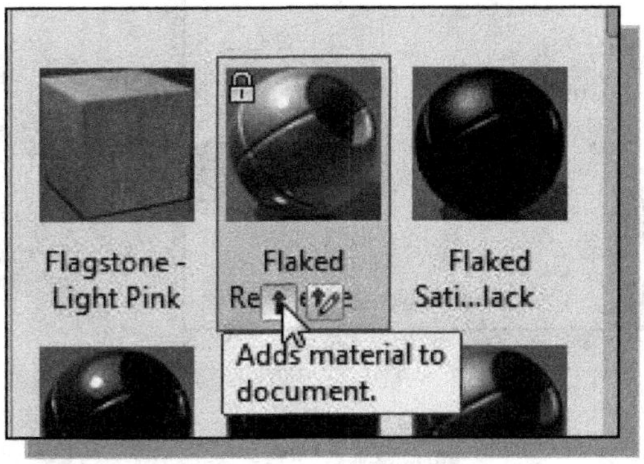

2. Add the **Flaked Reflective – Beige** material to the *Document Materials* list as shown.

3. Drag and drop the **Flaked Reflective** material on top of the ***Pulley*** design as the new material.

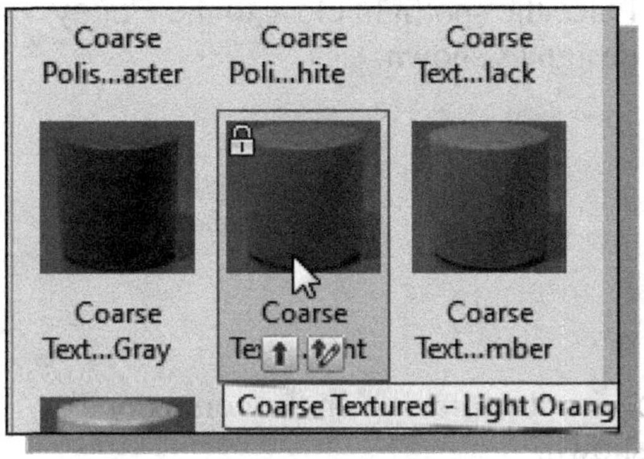

4. Add the **Coarse Textured – Light Orange** material to the *Document Materials* list as shown.

5. Drag and drop the **Coarse Textured** material on top of the **walls** as the new material.

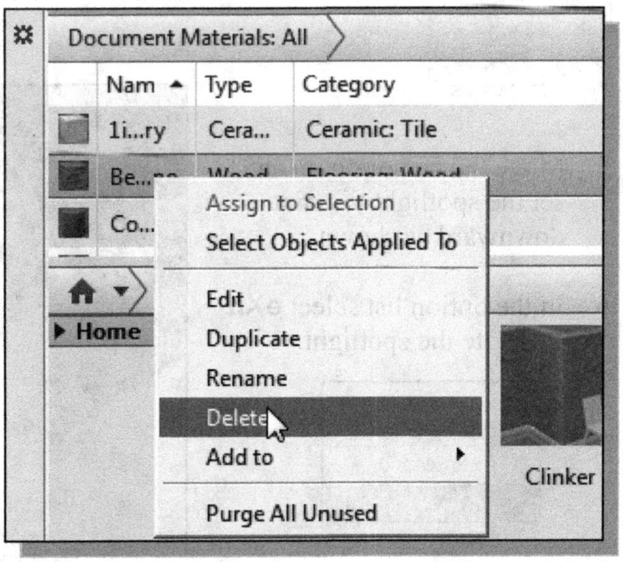

6. Any material listed in the *Document Materials* list can also be removed by using the option list as shown.

7. On your own, use the **Render** command to examine the effects of the newly applied materials.

Create a Spotlight

A spotlight distribution casts a focused beam of light like a flashlight, a follow spot in a theater, or a headlight.

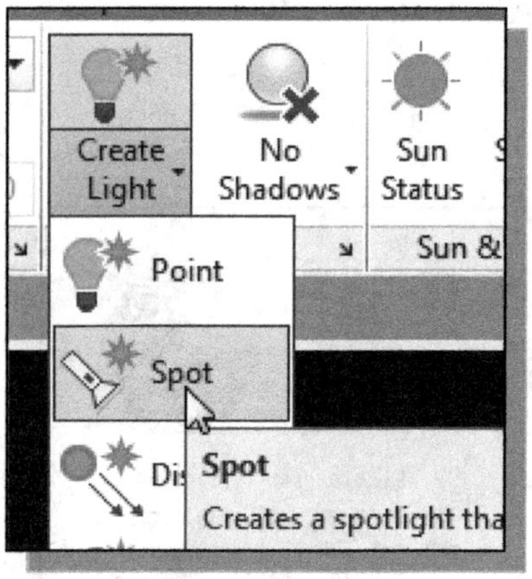

1. In the *Lights* toolbar, click on the **Create Spotlight** icon to activate the command.

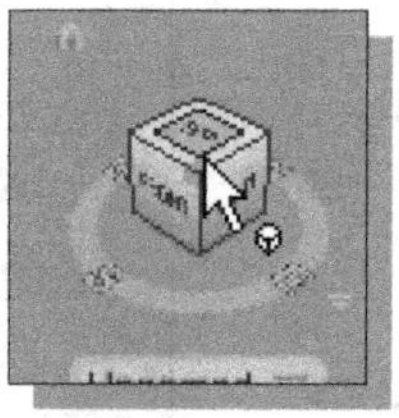

2. Set the display option to **Top** view by clicking on the top face of the ViewCube as shown.

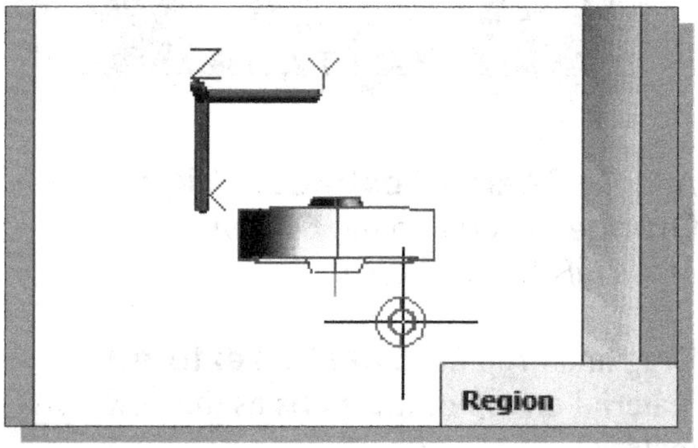

3. Place the spotlight close to the *Pulley* design as shown.

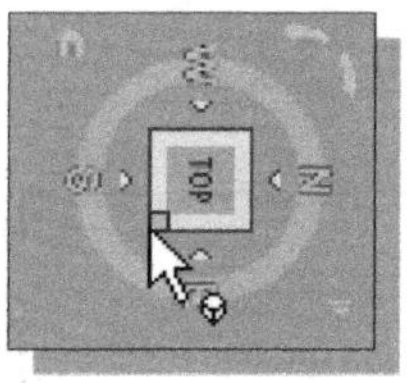

4. Switch to the **SE Isometric** view by clicking on the corresponding corner of the ViewCube as shown.

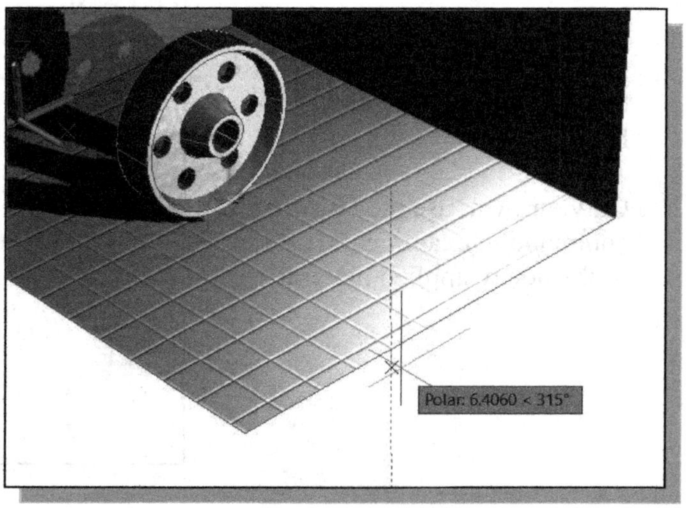

5. Move the cursor down and set the spotlight to point downward as shown.

6. In the option list select **eXit** to create the spotlight.

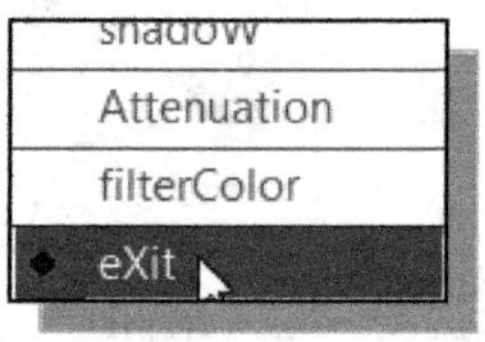

7. In the **Lights in Model** panel, right-mouse click on *spotlight2* and set the *Glyph display* **On**.

8. On your own, experiment with the **grip-editing tools** and adjust the spotlight so that it is above the *Pulley* design. (Hint: Click at the center of the triad to reposition the spotlight.)

- The intensity of the lights can be set through the **Properties** option. (Right click in the *Lights in Model* panel.)

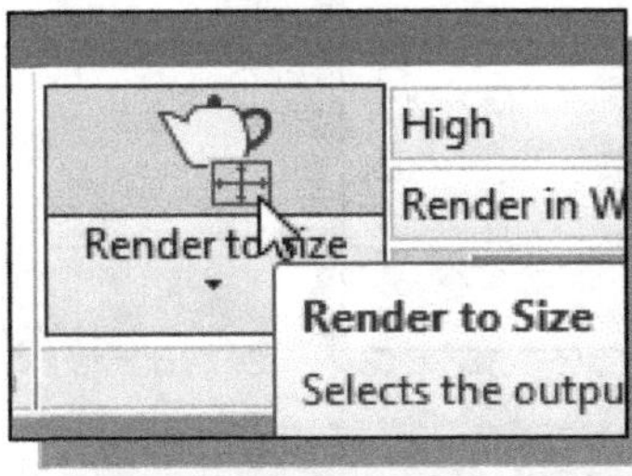

9. On your own, set the *Render* resolution to **Medium**.

10. In the *Render* toolbar, click on the **Render** icon to start the **Render** command.

- Note that the rendering requires many more calculations as the settings, such as additional materials and lights, become more complex.

Removing a Light

Lights can be removed just as easily as they can be added to the scene.

1. Click on the **point light** icon to pre-select it in the graphics area.

2. Hit the **[Delete]** key once to remove the selected point light.

3. On your own, use the **Render** command and examine the effects without the point light.

Create a Distant Light

A *distant light* emits uniform parallel light rays in one direction only. A *From* point and a *To* point are required to define the direction of the light. The intensity of a distant light does not diminish over distance; it is as bright at each face it strikes as it is at the source. Distant lights are useful for lighting objects or for lighting a backdrop uniformly. The lighting of the *Sun & Sky Background* option is an example of the effects of a *distant light*.

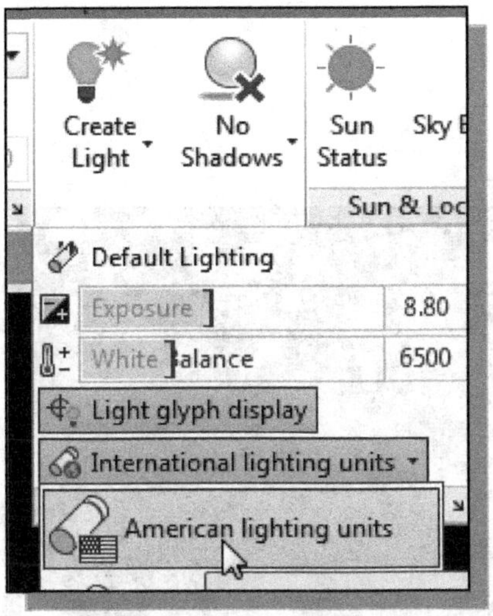

1. In the *Lights* toolbar, switch to using the ***American lighting*** simulation mode.

- The *American Lighting* simulation can be used to give the scene a more realistic appearance. Individual lights can be added and properties adjusted. The user can create **point lights**, **spotlights**, and **distant lights** to achieve the desired effects. The effects of changes are visible in the viewport in real time.

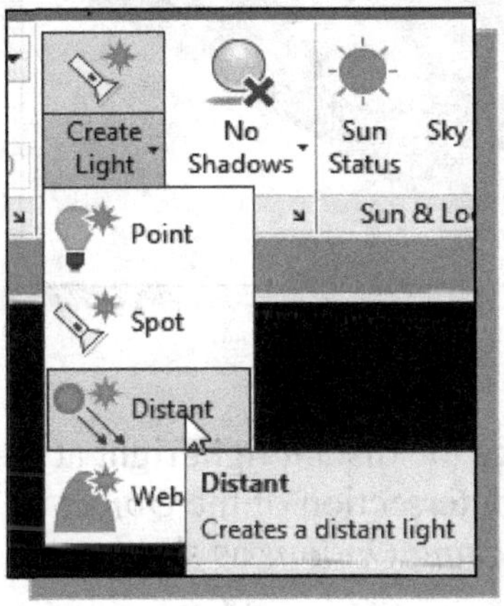

2. In the *Lights* toolbar, click on the **Distant Light** icon to activate the command.

3. Click **Allow** to add the additional distance light to the current system.

4. Set the display option to **SE Isometric** view by clicking on the corresponding corner of the ViewCube as shown.

5. In the *Status Bar* area, switch ***ON*** the *Object Snap* and *Object Snap Tracking* modes as shown.

- Note that *distant lights* are not represented by glyphs in the drawing because they do not have a discrete position and affect the entire scene. We will use the *Object Snap* options to position the distant light.

6. Move the cursor to the upper right corner of the right vertical wall to activate the *Object Snap Tracking* option.

7. Also move the cursor to the front corner of the floor to activate the *Object Snap Tracking* option.

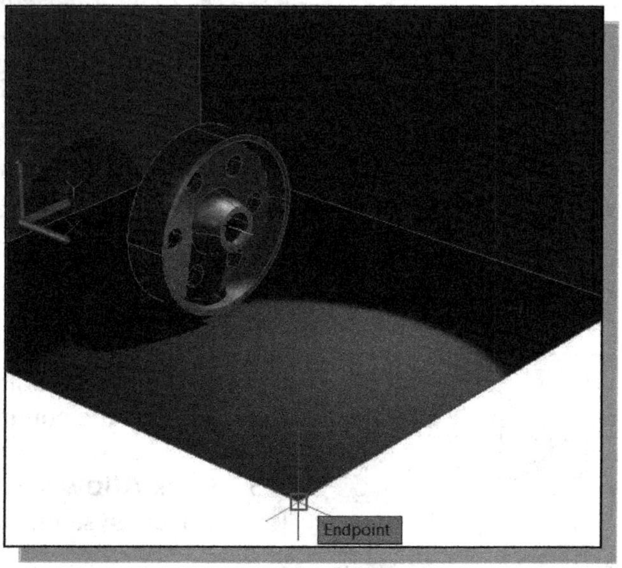

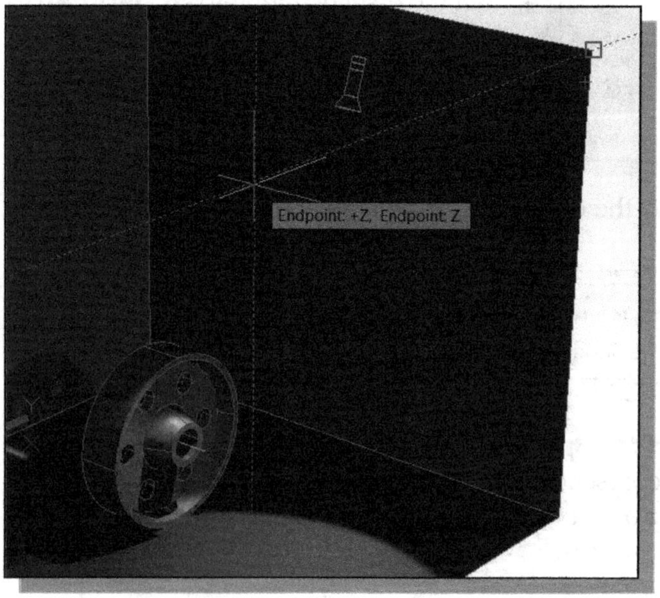

8. Place the distant light right at the intersection of the *Object Tracking Options* as shown.

- A *From* point and a *To* point are required to define the direction of the light. We have identified the *From* point.

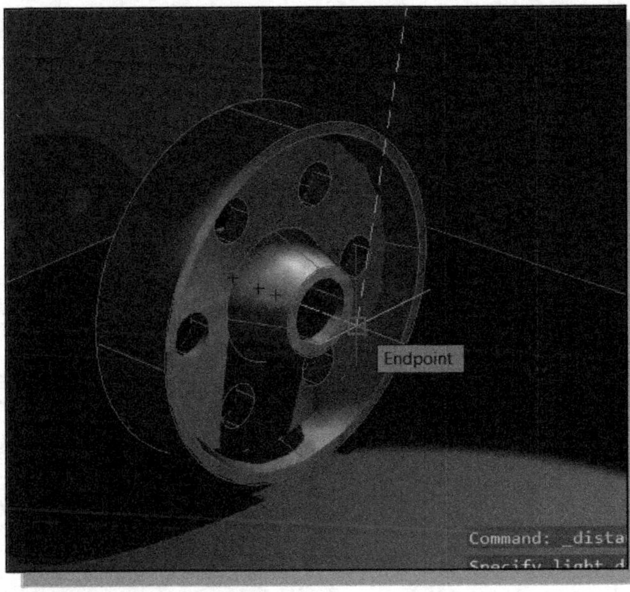

9. Snap to the right endpoint of the centerline, or the center point of the *Pulley* design, as shown.

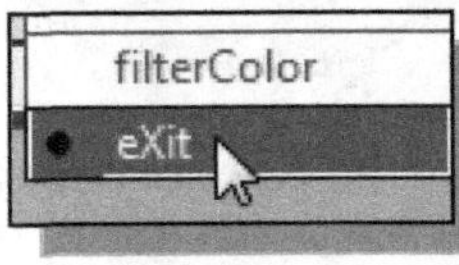

10. Click once with the **right-mouse-button** to bring up the option list and select **Exit** to create the distant light.

11. On your own, use the **Render** command and examine the effects with the added distant light.

Create New Materials

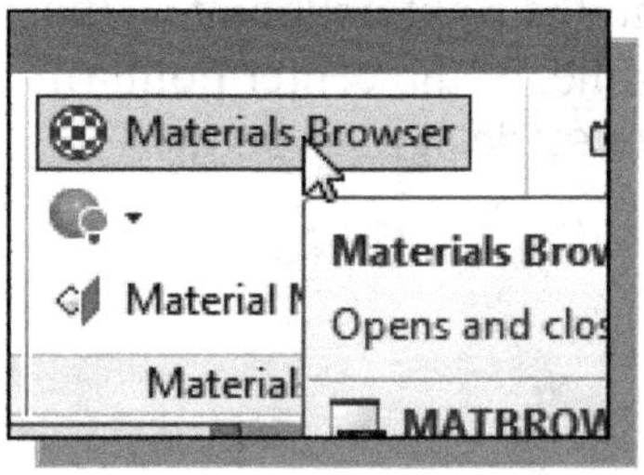

1. Select the **Materials Browser** icon in the *Materials* toolbar to open the AutoCAD *Materials Browser*.

2. Click on the **Create Material** icon at the bottom of the *Materials Browser* dialog box as shown.

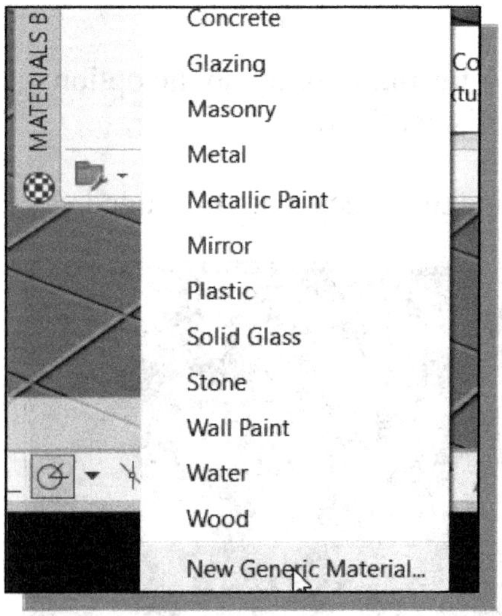

3. Select **New Generic Material** as the category for the new material.

4. Enter **Solid Red** as the name of the new material.

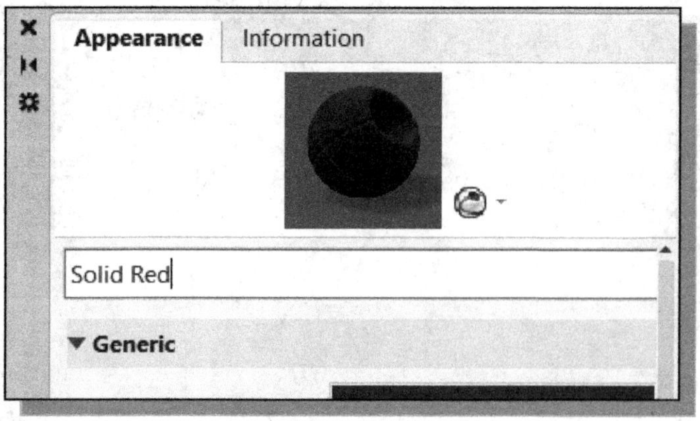

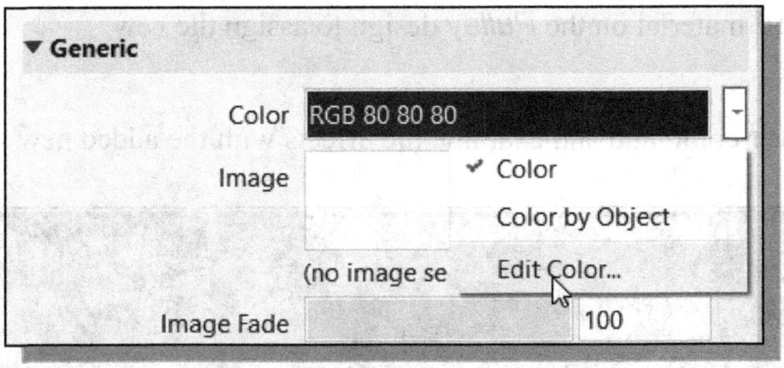

5. Click on the **down arrow** next to the *Color* box to display the option list.

6. Select **Edit Color** in the list as shown.

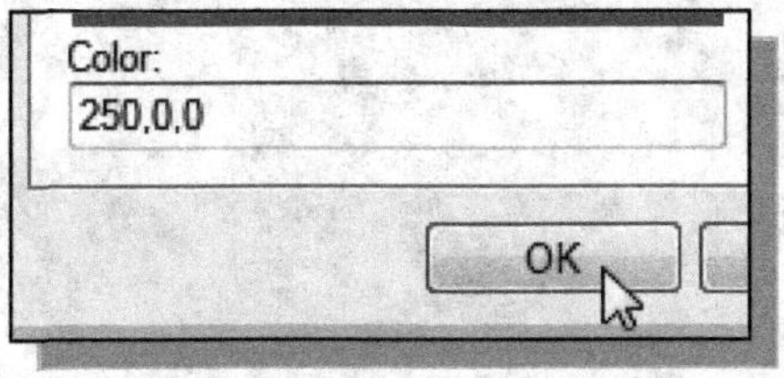

7. Set the *Color* to **250,0,0** for the RGB elements as shown.

8. Click **OK** to accept the settings.

9. Click on the check box next to the ***Reflectivity*** option and set the *Direct* and *Oblique Reflectivity* values to **30** as shown. Note that *0* means *no reflections* and *100* means *maximum reflections*.

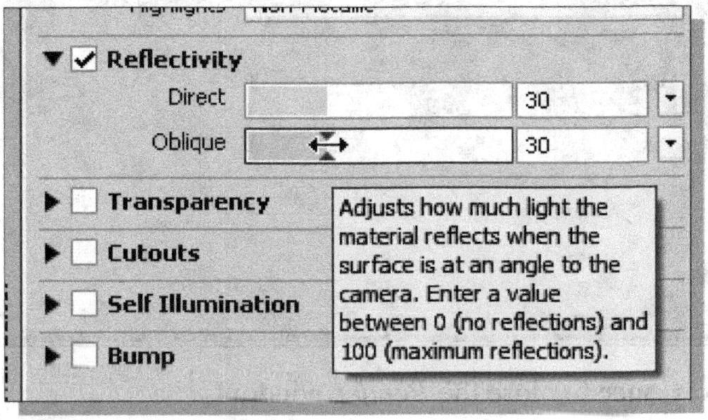

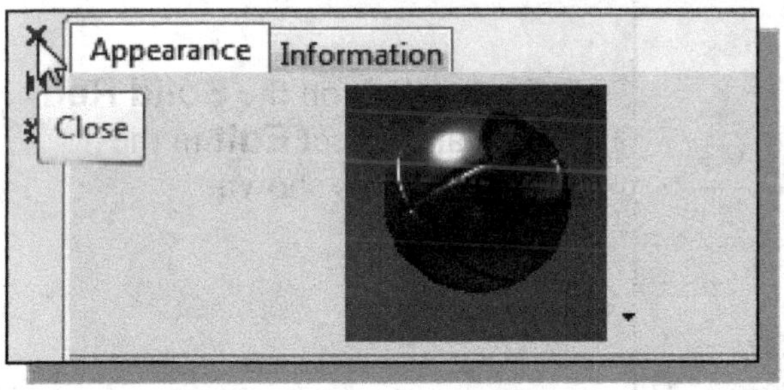

10. Click **Close** to accept the settings and exit the *Material Editor*.

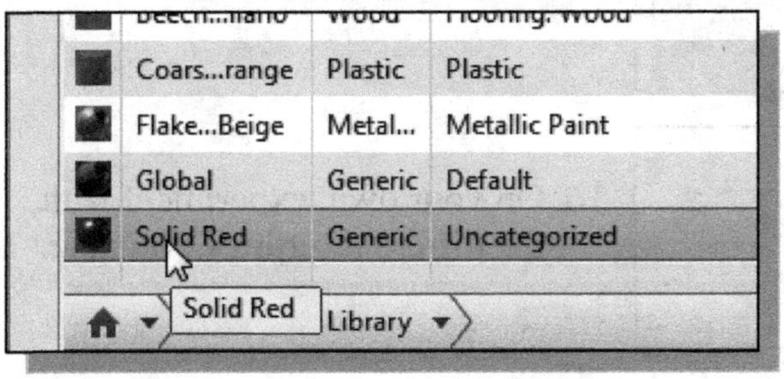

11. Note the newly created material is listed in the *Document Materials* list as shown.

12. Drag and drop the **Solid Red** material on the *Pulley* design to assign the new material.

13. On your own, use the **Render** command and examine the effects with the added new material.

14. Hit the **[Esc]** key once to close the *Render* window.

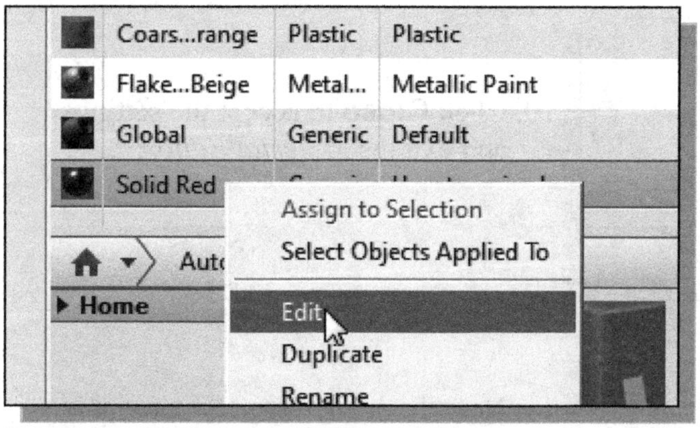

15. **Right-click** on the **Solid Red** icon and select **Edit** in the option list as shown.

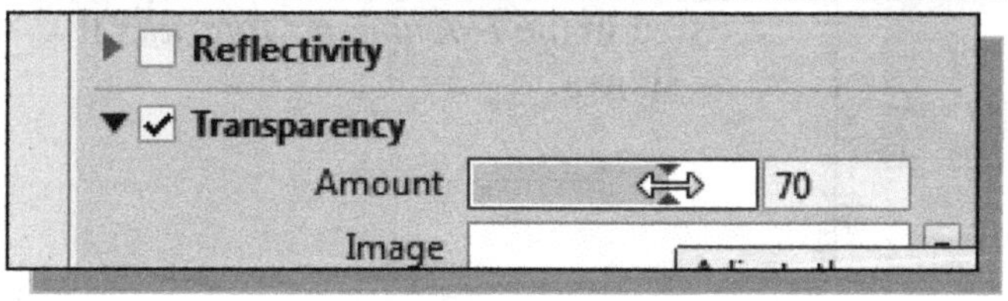

16. On your own, experiment with the different settings available.

Save the Rendered Images

- The rendered images can be saved and reused.

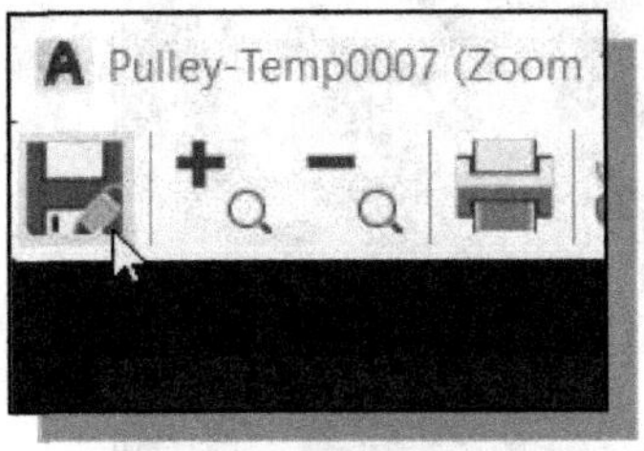

1. Choose **Save** in the *Render Window* toolbar.

2. In the *Render Output File* dialog box, choose the desired output image format, such as **BMP**, **JPEG**.

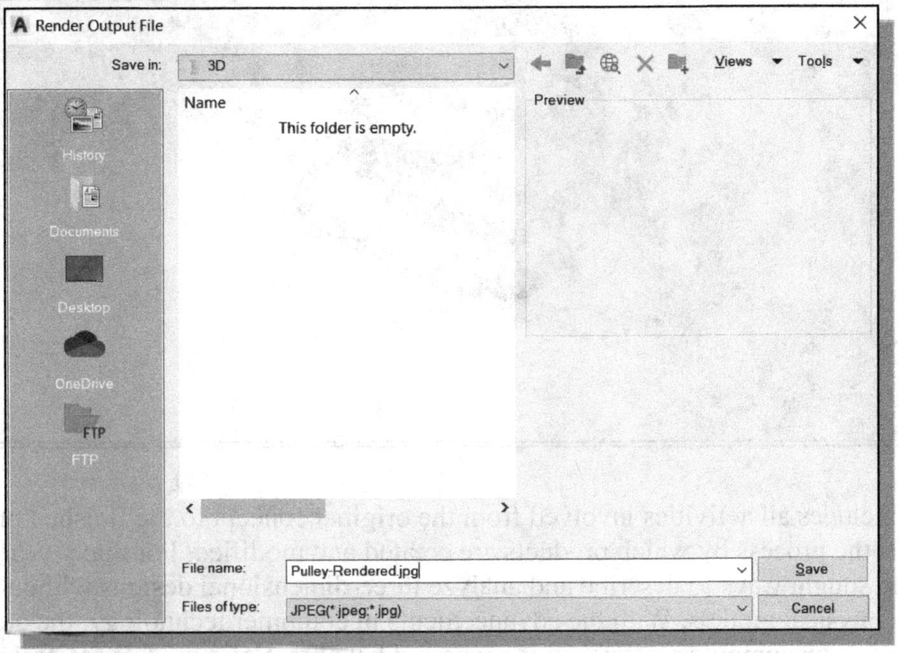

3. Enter a file name in the *File name* box as shown.

4. Click **Save** to save the image.

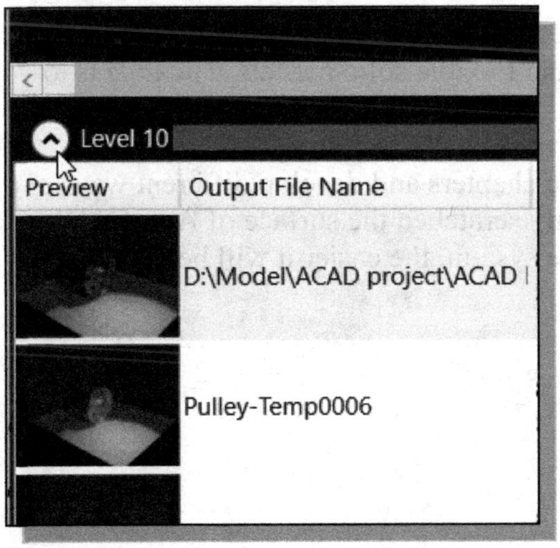

5. Near the bottom of the render image window, click on the down arrow to expand and display the rendered image list. Note that previously rendered images can also be recalled, saved and/or removed.

Conclusion

Design includes all activities involved from the original concept to the finished product. Design is the process by which products are created and modified. For many years designers sought ways to describe and analyze three-dimensional designs without building physical models. With the advancements in computer technology, the creation of solid models on computers offers a wide range of benefits. Solid models are easier to interpret and can be easily altered. Solid models can also be analyzed using finite element analysis software, and simulations of real-life loads can be applied to the models, and the results can be graphically displayed.

Throughout this text various modeling techniques have been presented. Mastering these techniques will enable you to create intelligent and flexible solid models. The goal is to make use of the tools provided by AutoCAD and to successfully create solid models of the design. In many instances, only a single approach to the modeling tasks was presented; you are encouraged to repeat all of the chapters and develop different ways of thinking in accomplishing the tasks. We have only scratched the surface of AutoCAD's functionality. The more time you spend using the system, the easier it will be to perform design and modeling tasks with AutoCAD.

Review Questions:

1. Describe the general procedure to create a photorealistic rendering in AutoCAD.

2. What are the different lighting simulation modes available in AutoCAD?

3. Which lighting simulation mode produces the most realistic rendering?

4. What are the three different types of lights we can create in AutoCAD? Provide a brief description for each type of light.

5. How do we create and alter a material in AutoCAD?

6. Identify the following commands:

(a)

(b)

(c)

(d)

Exercises:

1. Render the birdhouse created in Chapter 11 using the *Sun & Sky Background* option.

2. Render the *Guide-Block* design created in Chapter 6 using the *Spotlight* and *Distant light* options. (Hint: Adjust the intensity of the lights to create different effects.)

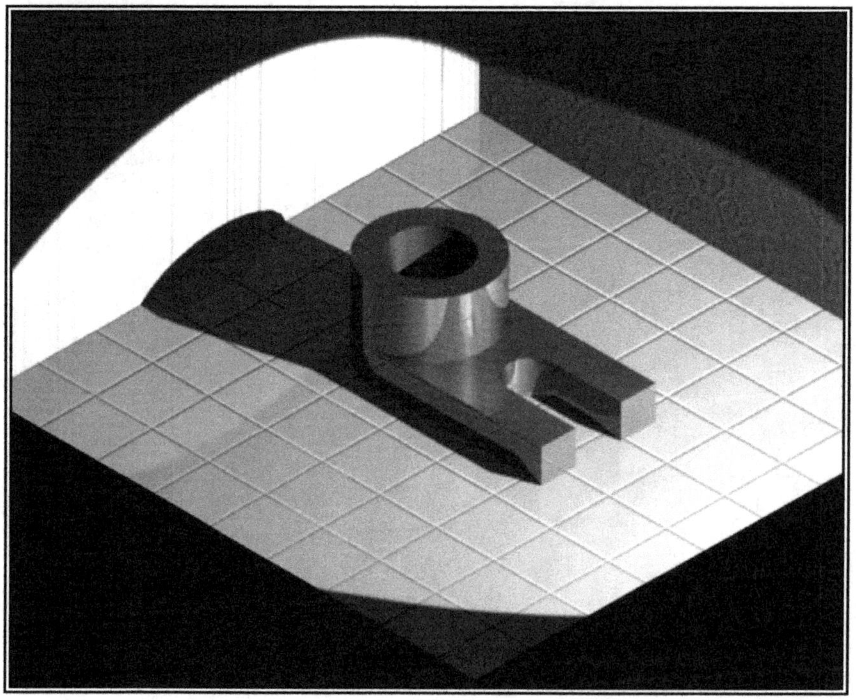

INDEX

A
Arcball, 2-16
Array, 3D, 8-15
Auxiliary View, 9-10

B
Binary Tree, 6-4
Block, solids, 6-7
Boolean Intersect, 6-3
Boolean Operations, 6-3
Boundary Representation (B-rep), 7-2
Box, Solid, 6-7
Box Method, 2-2
Break, 4-21
Buttons, Mouse, Intro-12

C
CAD, Intro-2
CAE, Intro-2
Canceling commands, Intro-12
Cartesian Coordinate System, 1-16
CIRCLE command, 2-19
Close dialog box, 1-19
Close window, 3-4
Combine Parts, 8-14
Command prompt, Intro-8, Intro-10
Command line area, Intro-9
Computer Geometric Modeling, Intro-2
Conceptual design, 11-2
Conceptual Visual Style, 4-8
Control Vertices, 5-22, 5-28
Constructive solid geometry, 6-2
Coordinate systems, 1-16
Coordinates, 1-9
Copy Faces, 10-8
Copy Object, 2-20, 3-6, 3-10, 3-22
Copy & Paste, 9-17
Create Drawings, Intro-7
Create Material, 12-26
CSG, 6-3
Current UCS, 3-20
Cursor Coordinates Display, Intro-10
Customization icon, Intro-10
Cylinder, Solid, 6-9

D
Distant Light, 12-23
Draft Angle, 10-10
Drafting Settings, 1-7, 3-8
Draw toolbar, 1-9
Drawing Layout, 9-4
Drawing Limits, 1-6
Drawing Views, Scale, 9-26
Dynamic UCS, 10-24, 11-7
DVIEW, 9-16

E
Edge, hidden, 4-16
Endpoint, snap, 1-13
Erase, 1-15
Esc, Intro-12
EXIT, Intro-14
Explode, 2-17
Extract faces, 10-8
Extend, 3-23
Extrude, 5-5, 7-2, 7-15
Extrude, Draft Angle, 10-10

F
Face, 3D, 4-2, 4-10, 4-14
FILLET, 10-6
Fillet, 3D, 10-16, 10-17
Folder, create new, Intro-14
Format, pull-down, 1-5
Four Viewports, 3-14
Free Orbit, 2-16
From, Snap, 2-11
Front view, 3-23

G
Global space, 1-16
Graphics window, Intro-8, Intro-9
GRID Interval setup, 1-7
GRIP, editing, 3-23, 4-17, 10-23

H
Help, Intro-13
Help Line, Intro-8, Intro-13
Hide, 1-20
Hidden, 2D, 3D, 4-8, 4-13

I
Imprint, 11-21
Inquiry, 7-17
INTERSECT, 3-9
Invisible Edge, 4-16
Isometric Views, 1-17, 9-27

J
JOIN, 6-3

L
Layers Control toolbar, Intro-11
Layer, New, 1-21
Layer Properties Manager, 1-21
Layout, 9-7
Layout tab, 9-4
Lighting Simulation, 12-8
Limits, 1-6
LINE command, 2-9
Line, Close, 7-9
Local Coordinate System (LCS), 1-16

M
Mass Properties, 7-17
Materials, 12-9
Meshes, 4-2, 4-5
Midpoint, Snap, 1-11
Mirror, 3-15, 7-14
Mirror 3D, 8-13
Model Space, 9-4
Model tab, 9-11
Modeling toolbar, 6-7
Modify toolbar, 1-10
Mouse Buttons, Intro-12
Move, 6-17
Move UCS, 1-23
Multiview drawing, 9-2, 9-9

N
Named view, 3-20
Network Surface, 5-29
New UCS, 3-18
New UCS, Face, 7-18
NURBS, 5-2, 5-21

O
Object Properties toolbar, 1-23, 3-12, 3-17, 4-19, 7-8
Object Snap, 1-11, 3-8
Object Snap settings, 3-8
Object Snap toolbar, 2-10
OFFSET, 1-10
On-Line Help, Intro-13
One Viewport, 3-17
Open a Drawing, 4-4, 4-18
Orbit, Free, 2-16

P
Page Setup, 9-4
Paper Space, 9-4
Photometric, 12-8
Plan view, 3-20
Planar Surface, 5-13
Polar Angle settings, 3-8
Polar Tracking, 3-8
Polyline, 1-9
Point light, 12-17
Profile, 5-5, 5-8
Press/Pull, 11-8
Primitive Solids, 6-3
Properties, 1-19
Pull-down menus, Intro-8

Q
Quadrant, Snap to, 2-21
Quick Select, 3-15
Quit, Intro-14

R
Realistic Visual Style, 4-8
RECTANGLE command, 1-25
RECTANGULAR Array, 10-19
Reference area setup, 1-6

Region, 4-2, 7-10
Region, Subtract, 8-8
Render, 12-2
Repeat, 2-9
Revolve, 7-2, 8-12
Revolved Feature, 8-2
Revolved Surfaces, 4-3, 4-20
ROTATE, 7-6
Rotate Faces, 6-16
Rotate a View, 9-22
Rotate, 3D, 7-12
Rotate UCS, 1-27
Rounds, 3D, 10-16
Ruled Surfaces, 4-3, 4-20, 4-24

S

SAVE AS, 1-15
Scale Drawing Views, 9-26
Screen Layout, Intro-8
SE Isometric, 1-17
Section View, 9-23
Selection window, 1-18
Settings, 3-8
Shade toolbar, 4-8
Shaded Solids, 6-14
Shape before size, 11-3
SHELL, 10-18
Show Startup dialog box, 2-4
Single Line Help, Intro-8
Snap from, 1-13
Snap Interval Setup, 1-7
Snap to Endpoint, 1-13
Snap to Midpoint, 1-11, 2-10
Snap to Quadrant, 2-21
Solid Editing, 10-8
Solid Modelers, Intro-4
Solid, 2D, 4-2
Spline, 5-22
Spotlight, 12-20
Standard Views, 9-7
Start From Scratch, 2-5
Startup options, 2-4
Startup window, 2-5
Status Toolbar, Intro-10
SteeringWheels, 6-18
Stretch, 3-24
Subtract, 6-3, 6-12
Sun & Sky Background, 12-11
Surface Modelers, Intro-4
Surface Modeling commands, 4-20
Surfaces toolbars, 4-5
SW Isometric view, 3-24
Symmetrical Features, 8-2

T

Tabulated Surfaces, 4-3, 4-20, 4-23
Taper Angle, 10-10
Thickness, 1-2, 1-19
Thickness option, Rectangle, 1-25
3 Point, UCS, 3-18, 4-5
3D Face, 4-10
3D Hidden, 1-20
3D Modeling, Intro-3
3D Rounds and Fillets, 10-16
3D view, 1-17
3D Wireframe, 2-2~2-4, 2-17, 4-8
Thin Shell, 10-18
Title Block, 9-6
Tools, pull-down, 1-7
Top view, 3-14
Trim, 1-14
Trim Surface, 5-14
2½D solid modeling approach, 1-19
2D Extrusion method, 2-2
2D Drafting & Annotation, 1-4
2D Wireframe, 1-29

U

Undo, 1-14
Union, 6-10
Union surface, 5-19
Units Setup, 1-5
UCS, 1-2, 3-7, 4-5
UCS, 3 point, 3-18
UCS icon, 3-19
UCS II, 3-7, 5-3
UCS Toolbar, 3-7
User Coordinate System (UCS), 1-2
User Coordinate System, 1-16

V

View, Hidden 3D, 1-20

View, named, 3-20
View, 3D Views, 2-7
View toolbar, 2-16
ViewCube, 4-12
Viewports, 3-14
Viewport Scale, 9-17
Visual Styles, 1-29, 4-8
Visualize, 12-7

W

Wireframe, 2D, 4-8
Wireframe, 3D, 2-2~2-4, 2-17, 4-8
Wireframe Modeler, Intro-3
Wizard, quick setup, 2-5
World Coordinate System, 1-18
World space, 1-16
World UCS, 4-9

X

X-Axis Rotate UCS, 1-27
XY-Plane, 2-7

Y

YZ-Plane, 1-16

Z

Zoom All, 1-7, 3-6
ZX-Plane, 1-16

9781630578275